THE GOLDBECKS' GUIDE TO GOOD FOOD

THE GOLDBECKS' GUIDE TO GOOD FOOD

by

Nikki and David Goldbeck

THE ALL-NEW VERSION OF THE PIONEERING
SUPERMARKET HANDBOOK—
YOUR COMPLETE SHOPPING GUIDE TO THE BEST,
MOST HEALTHFUL FOODS AVAILABLE
IN SUPERMARKETS, NATURAL FOOD STORES,
AND BY MAIL

NAL BOOKS

NEW AMERICAN LIBRARY

NEW YORK AND SCARBOROUGH, ONTARIO

NAL BOOKS TRADEMARK REG. U.S. PAT. OFF. AND FOREIGN COUNTRIES
REGISTERED TRADEMARK—MARCA REGISTRADA
HECHO EN HARRISONBURG, VA., U.S.A.

SIGNET, SIGNET CLASSIC, MENTOR, ONYX, PLUME, MERIDIAN
and NAL BOOKS are published *in the United States* by NAL PENGUIN INC.,
1633 Broadway, New York, New York 10019, *in Canada*
by The New American Library of Canada Limited, 81 Mack Avenue,
Scarborough, Ontario M1L 1M8

Library of Congress Cataloging-in-Publication Data

Goldbeck, Nikki.
  The Goldbecks' guide to good food.

  "The all-new version of the pioneering Supermarket handbook—
your complete shopping guide to the best, most healthful foods
available in supermarkets, natural food stores, and by mail"
  Includes index.
  1. Marketing (Home economics) 2. Cookery.
I. Goldbeck, David. II. Goldbeck, Nikki. Supermarket
handbook. III. Title. IV. Title: Guide to good food.
TX356.G646 1987   641.3   87-15203
ISBN 0-453-00566-7

First Printing, October, 1987

1 2 3 4 5 6 7 8 9

PRINTED IN THE UNITED STATES OF AMERICA

Rededicated to the preservation of the family farm.

ACKNOWLEDGMENTS

Our thanks to friends and family who put up with our antisocial behavior during the writing of this book. We also express our appreciation to the following people for lending us their help: Tom Harding, Organic Food Production Association of North America; Sandra Marquardt, National Coalition Against the Misuse of Pesticides; William Shurtleff, The Soyfoods Center; Judy Fishetti, librarian, Woodstock, New York, and Irene Pink, Veronica Johnson, and Molly Allen for their concerned, thoughtful, and professional editing.

Special thanks to Ruth Desmond, Federation of Homemakers, and Beatrice Trum Hunter for inspiration.

Contents

Introduction

A revolution is taking place in America's kitchens and marketplaces. As a consequence, our food supply is getting better all the time, and although it is still laden with problems, there is a greater selection of whole and minimally processed foods than shoppers have seen in decades. Significantly, it is the consumer who is largely responsible for these advances by making informed choices in the market.

This is the conclusion we reached as we retraced our steps through the United States fifteen years after the publication of *The Supermarket Handbook* in order to research this *Guide to Good Food*. We traveled the country with clipboards and tape recorders in hand and, as before, we filled our shopping carts with the finest foods North America has to offer in order to obtain for consumers the information they are entitled to have about the food they buy.

It was the purpose of *The Supermarket Handbook* to demonstrate how supermarket foods might be used to build a healthful diet. *The Goldbecks' Guide to Good Food* follows in that tradition and, as is documented throughout this book and in "The State of the Plate," which follows, it is even easier to succeed in supermarkets today. *The Supermarket Handbook*, first published in 1973, did not list brand names of products from natural food stores because at that time there were only a limited number of these outlets, and furthermore, many people were not ready for their offerings. But now there are more than 8,300 natural food stores (as compared to 1,200 in 1968), plus an astounding 2,200 supermarkets with natural food sections.

In the chapters that follow, we will acquaint you with the best choices you can make to bring flavorful, nutritious, and wholesome foods into your home whether you shop in the supermarket, natural food store, produce market, specialty shop, or via mail. It will come as no surprise that shoppers are in need of assistance in the supermarket, but the success of natural foods is not without its problems, as questionable ingredients can appear in these products too.

Our purpose is to make marketing as convenient as possible for consumers since, as one observer put it, "America is the only place you can get an ulcer trying to have a healthy diet." When reading this book, keep in mind that changes in food selection and habits needn't come all at once. You can

1

use the information in this book to make gradual adjustments in your diet as they fit your life-style. Or, you may want to clean out your pantry and start anew.

The Supermarket Handbook was written originally because we felt we were on a "fabricated food merry-go-round"—that is, foods are first highly refined and then manufacturers try to compensate by "fortifying" them with nutrients and fiber. Or, one food additive or pesticide is banned only to be replaced with yet another.* We were fed up with this situation and realized we had to take more responsibility for our well-being, rather than relying on the food industry and government agencies, who were not, in our view, living up to their obligation to the public.

Our *Guide to Good Food*, like its predecessor, is based on the premise that even if the safety of individual additives or pesticides could be established, it is impossible to calculate what happens when these chemicals are mixed with *other* additives and pesticides, or for that matter alcohol, drugs, etc., in the body. Additionally, where safety of a substance is not a major concern, we think consumers should be aware that in almost all cases food additives mask the use of inferior ingredients. There is no need to color food that has its own vibrant hue or to thicken sauces with starch or gums if they are rich in traditional ingredients; artificial flavoring and flavor enhancers aren't needed to make real food appealing, but are almost mandatory in "technological" foods. Similarly, an ounce of process cheese may have the equivalent of 5 ounces of milk, as the Kraft Company has advertised, but natural cheddar cheese has 8 to 10 ounces. (In the process version the incorporation of water with the assistance of chemical emulsifiers accounts for the difference.) It is also questionable whether chemically preserved foods are still nutritionally viable or only retain the *appearance* of freshness.

As a result of these concerns we have come to the conclusion that the best way to have a "worry-free" and nutritionally superior diet is to consider all additive-dependent foods, as well as those that have been diminished through refinement, unacceptable. Although ingredient labeling has improved, it is still often either deficient or overly complicated, making it difficult at times to judge the nature of packaged foods. (One professional food publication, after summarizing a number of new and confusing label regulations, editorialized: "All readers will be given a test. If anyone passes, it means they didn't understand the question.") Therefore, as in the previous editions of *The Supermarket Handbook,* our *Guide to Good Food* lists by name Exemplary Brands that meet our test of wholeness:

Foods that are free of chemical additives and left in the whole, unprocessed state or processed as little as possible to render them suitable for eating.

---

*For example, in *The Supermarket Handbook* (1973) we noted that action was being taken to ban the food coloring Red #2. We predicted at that time that it would be replaced with another of "undetermined safety" (mostly to assure an uninterrupted supply of bright red maraschino cherries for fruit cocktail). Not surprisingly, its replacement, Red #4, was also banned; at this writing the safety of Red #40, Red #4's replacement, is a serious concern, and it, too, may be

Even we were impressed by the volume of new Exemplary Brands—necessitating a double column format at the end of each chapter. Nonetheless there are times when our rule of wholeness may have to be bent a bit, for although we have found something suitable in every food category, an Exemplary Brand may not be available in your part of the country. To assist you in making a reasonably good purchase, a "Glossary of Food Additives" has been included in the Appendix. Here you will discover which additives you may want to make allowances for if your choices are limited, and which ones should always be left on the shelf.

Due to the continuing threat to health and the environment from pesticide usage, our *Guide to Good Food* also includes, for the first time, listings of foods grown organically, that is, on naturally enriched soil and without the use of hazardous chemicals. The formation of the Organic Foods Production Association of North America (OFPANA) to develop standards and certification is a welcome step in building confidence in these pure foods. Organic food is no longer a fringe movement. There are strong indications that in ten years, 20 percent of the food market here and in Europe will fall into this category.

Most of all, *The Goldbecks' Guide to Good Food* is a book about healthful foods. While the recommendations will help you select products in the markets, we have not stopped there. Nutrition, quality, handling, and storage are all part of the picture presented in each chapter.

We have not included recipes in this edition, but to assist you in using your wholefood purchases to best advantage, we hope you will take a look at our *American Wholefoods Cuisine* (NAL/Plume), which actually is a companion to this *Guide to Good Food*. There you will find more than 1,300 recipes from our kitchen, ranging from short-order to gourmet, all based on the foods recommended in this volume, plus more than 300 pages on general food preparation. Note, however, that you needn't cook to garner the benefits of wholefoods, as there are now more prepared foods of wholefoods quality to choose from. In addition, many healthful meals are simply "assemblages" or require only minimal preparation.

HOW TO USE THIS BOOK

Before you begin traveling with us through the food aisles in Part II: In the Market, we offer below a key that summarizes the standards used in selecting our Exemplary Brands. Following that is an essay on our modern food system which we call "The State of the Plate."

In Part I: The Informed Shopper, we present "The Story of Food Additives, Pesticides, and Packaging" so that you can learn some of the details as

---

outlawed. (We wonder what number will be next.) Similarly, the aborted attempt to ban saccharin resulted in the introduction of yet another sugar substitute with its own set of problems, and the restrictions on the fumigant EDB have given impetus to the introduction of problematic food irradiation.

to how chemicals get into our foods in the first place and who watches over the food supply to protect us from possible health hazards and unscrupulous practices. "A Primer on Food Labels" comes next to help you understand the fine points of food labeling and judge products you find on your own. Since this book is intended to help you select the best food available no matter where you shop, "To Market, To Market," the last chapter in Part I, surveys the various places where wholefoods are likely to be found.

In Part II we take you aisle by aisle, letting you know what to look for and how to evaluate what you find. At the end of each food chapter we provide a "General Rule of Purchase," a basic shopping guideline for each food category, plus a unique listing of "Exemplary Brands"—products gleaned from America's markets that meet our wholefoods guidelines.

In the Appendix, in addition to the "Glossary of Food Additives," there is "A Guide to Government Agencies" and "A Guide to Private Organizations Working in the Areas of Food and Agriculture," both of which offer places to register your concerns, gather more information on food issues, and, if you wish, participate in policy making.

THE EXEMPLARY BRANDS

In researching and preparing the Exemplary Brands we naturally had to set certain standards. Our main consideration for each food item was "Is it as unadulterated or unprocessed as possible?" We reject out of hand all products that to our knowledge contain any chemical additives and hydrogenated oils. With few exceptions, highly processed ingredients such as refined sweeteners, refined grains, and vegetable gums are also unacceptable. What remain are what we call "wholefoods"—foods that have undergone only enough processing to render them tasty without destroying their inherent value; foods that do not depend on highly processed ingredients in their manufacture, and are free of artificial flavoring, artificial coloring, chemical preservatives, and other synthetic additions.

In general, we found the products listed as exemplary by visiting supermarkets and natural food stores in different parts of the country. As a follow-up, we sent query letters to more than 1,000 companies. We would like to thank those who responded. The fact that many manufacturers did not respond confirms once again how indifferent many food companies are to genuine consumer interests.

It is likely that some brands in your area may be unknown to us; therefore, the fact that a brand is not listed does not necessarily mean it does not offer a perfectly sound choice. Here we counsel you to read the label, keeping in mind the guidelines in the General Rules of Purchase for that particular food. If the list of ingredients does not violate any of our warnings, by all means buy the product. Or, if your market doesn't carry an Exemplary Brand that you are interested in, ask them to order it. Most stores will stock any item if they know they have a ready buyer in you and your friends.

Those of you who have been using *The Supermarket Handbook* to guide your food purchases may be dismayed not to see some previously recommended foods in this new volume. Their absence may be due to one of the following reasons:

- A change in product formulation.
- More stringent guidelines on our part as the result of new information about certain ingredients.
- More available high-caliber choices in the category in question, making products with some previously accepted drawbacks such as refined flour or refined sweeteners no longer exemplary.

In reading the list of Exemplary Brands note too that within a manufacturer's line not all varieties may be acceptable. We are also sure that some products may be included which might not have been had we more information. In some cases this is the result of our own human limitations, but in larger part is due to the secrecy of industry and the policies of our government.

Even after you have your shopping down to a system, so that you know at a glance what you will and will not buy, go back to checking the labels periodically. This way you'll know when anything new has been added—either to the product or to the available choices.

KEY TO THE EXEMPLARY BRANDS

The following is a key to the numbers that appear after some of the listings in the Exemplary Brands. We have added this new feature in order to highlight foods we consider to be superior because they were organically grown or contain some ingredients from organic sources. Also noted, to provide leeway to the consumer, are foods that are additive-free but somewhat diminished by the inclusion of refined grains or refined sweeteners.

[1]*Organic.* Refers to products whose predominant ingredients are organically grown. In the case of meat, poultry, and byproducts it indicates animals raised without the routine use of drugs.

[2]*Some organic ingredients.* While some of the components are organically grown, others are not.

[3]*Contains refined sweeteners.* Some foods are sweet by definition (pastries, ice cream, sweet relishes, etc.). When refined sugars are the only drawback to this kind of product and few naturally sweetened alternatives are available, they may be tolerated. We point this out, however, for those who may not want to make this concession. On the other hand, where more acceptable choices can easily be made (i.e., unsweetened fruit spreads, sparkling juices, honey-sweetened yogurt), we do not make such allowances.

[4]*Contains refined grains.* When some refined grain is used in conjunction with what is primarily a wholefood, it may be a good transition food or accepted for lack of better choices.

JOIN US

The Goldbecks' Guide to Good Food is a living, growing volume and we welcome your advice to keep it that way. Have you discovered or do you produce a noteworthy item in your area that we've neglected to mention? Has something new been added to the picture that should be included in these pages? Have we erred in any of our recommendations?

If you have any information you feel would be helpful to your fellow shoppers we would be happy to receive it, check it out, and include it in future editions of this book. Make sure you include full particulars concerning your recommendation: brand name, product type, ingredient list, price, and address of manufacturer. Or, you can just send us the label.

Our mailing address is Goldbeck, P.O. Box 87, Dept. GGF, Woodstock, NY 12498. We cannot acknowledge letters unless a stamped, self-addressed envelope is enclosed.

The State of the Plate

*I wondered miserably why refrigeration
had spoiled so much while it kept
things from spoiling.*

—M.F.K. Fisher

We regret that this *Guide to Good Food* is needed at all. We used to say that *The Supermarket Handbook* was on "self-destruct" since it seemed in the late 1970s that complete labeling of food was finally going to be a reality. While it is true that there is much more information on today's food packages than ever before, there are still huge gaps in ingredient labeling. In addition, as food processing techniques have become increasingly complex, and dependence on agricultural poisons has escalated, it is time for all of us to lend greater support to the food manufacturers and growers who use alternative approaches. We must also consider the impact of our food and agricultural techniques on the world's biosystems.

What is heartening, however, is that the message long advocated by the often maligned natural food advocates has finally gotten across—*food and health are related!* Even conservative health professionals can no longer deny the role food plays in keeping us fit. After generations of resistance, scientific and medical authorities have at last admitted that there is a link between the quality and amount of food we eat and the incidence of cancer, heart disease, adult-onset diabetes, and obesity, as well as the health of the newborn. Much of the progress that has occurred is the direct result of attitudes fostered by the 1977 landmark report of Senator George McGovern's Select Committee on Nutrition and Human Needs, which paved the way for what is known today as the Dietary Goals for the United States (see page 152). The story of how these Dietary Goals were watered down through politics and special-interest pressures is another nutrition scandal, but even in their present form these guidelines still stand as a powerful tool for reorienting our dietary direction.

The signs of change are everywhere, not just in the markets, but in restaurants and health clubs and in the media messages that we are receiving daily. We used to joke that the only time the word *nutrition* was mentioned in advertisements was for either pet food or lawn food, but today nutrition sells. The interest in human nourishment, however, has also created new problems for the consumer: The processed food industry has rendered the word "natural" meaningless, through misuse and takes advantage of our concern about fiber, cholesterol, fat, salt, sugar, calcium, and such by offering us highly contrived solutions.

7

What is most exciting for us is the increase in the availability of wholefoods in North America today. Of special interest is the growth in popularity of many of the products featured in the original *Supermarket Handbook,* for their success proves how powerful our cash-register ballots can be.

When we pointed out that within the supermarket there was a collection of wholefoods available to consumers, we had no idea how our point of view would come to be accepted. Today, judging from our research, more and more shoppers know there is a vast difference between butter and margarine, natural and process cheeses, pure oils and hydrogenated ones, whole grain cereal and hardly-any-grain cereal, real fruit juices and watered-down drinks, 100 percent nut butters and sweetened emulsified ones, etc. Little did we know when we demonstrated on the "Phil Donahue Show" how consumers could mix juice with carbonated water as an alternate to soda pop, that seltzer, practically unknown in 1976, would grow in sales, in at least one major metropolitan market, to the point where it was the single fastest moving item from warehouses.

Similarly, tuna canned in water, which represented 40 percent of the market in 1979, now accounts for 70 percent; tofu production in 1983 was double that of 1978; brown rice crackers, unheard of outside natural food stores in 1976, are available everywhere. One major producer of naturally raised beef reports that in 1979 there was virtually no interest in his product, but by 1986 he was selling 25,000 animals and taking them into the supermarket. Purchases of unseasoned frozen vegetables soared by 343 percent between 1980 and 1984, and during this period unsalted canned vegetables and fruits packed in unsweetened juice came into their own. Herbal tea sales doubled between 1982 and 1987. Variety bread sales (whole, cracked wheat, and multigrain) have grown by 151 percent since 1972. Today, one-third of potato chips are unsalted. In addition, according to the USDA, from 1982 to 1985 Americans reduced their consumption of bacon by 21 percent, hot dogs, eggs, and beef by 16 percent, fresh pork by 14 percent, refined sugar and sugary foods by 29 percent, salty foods by 21 percent, butter by 5 percent, and other fats and oils by 11 percent. During the same time span not only was fruit and vegetable consumption up 25 percent, but Americans also enlivened their market baskets with the likes of jicama, Jerusalem artichoke, cactus leaves, and seaweed.

The natural food industry, too, has made enormous strides in developing products to appeal to the American palate. Today the shelves of natural food stores abound with familiar-looking cereals, breads, sauces, snacks, beverages, desserts, prepared foods, entrées, and more, all made to wholefoods standards and many packaged like typical mass-market fare.

Natural food stores, which for generations have had to contend with both government harassment and public scorn, are understandably concerned about the new supermarket competition that wholefoods success has brought. However, to us there is no comparison between these markets, for the joy of going to a natural food store is not having to read every label. We believe that as long as natural food stores maintain high standards, they will prosper.

While consumers are faring better in terms of choices and availability, the fight for purity in America's food supply is far from over. In 1976, Americans consumed, on average, 5 pounds of additives, including pesticides; in 1986, it was closer to 10 pounds—almost half an ounce a day! In 1984, the *FDA Consumer*, a government publication, reported that pesticides in foods were "Public Worry No. 1." This concern is well founded. With more than 55,000 man-made agricultural compounds, our monitoring system is virtually useless. While DDT and even EDB may seem like history, we are still living with their consequences and adding new hazards every day, from Alar to Zeranol.

On the bright side, consumers can look to improvements in the quality of a number of foods as a direct result of public concern and pressure and some responsive companies. Methylene chloride, a solvent used to decaffeinate coffee, is classified as a carcinogen but the Food and Drug Administration (FDA) has not prohibited its use. Nevertheless many coffee processors voluntarily turned to less suspect techniques when consumers voiced their concern and showed a preference for chemical-free decaffeinated coffee in the market. The action led by Safeway and taken up by many major supermarket chains in 1986 to refuse apples treated with the toxic chemical Alar is another example of the power the consumer has assumed, as is the announcement by the Heinz Company that it will no longer use any produce in its baby foods that has been sprayed with pesticides under review by the Environmental Protection Agency (EPA).

In a related victory the U.S. Senate passed legislation in 1986 that would require the EPA to speed up retesting of pesticides already on the market. It is hoped this new law will reduce the projected time for retesting the 600 active ingredients in pesticide products from twenty-five years to nine years.

In addition, an awareness of the relationship between fat and salt and cardiovascular disease is growing. Public health officials have noted in several studies a decline in deaths related to heart disease and credit this to changes in diet and to exercise.

While food industry executives figure out how they can cash in on granola or reengineer foods through biotechnology, Robert Rodale, William Shurtleff, the Lundberg brothers, and others work to develop and popularize foods like amaranth, tempeh, and organic strains of rice that will keep all humankind healthy, not just a few fat.

Still there is much that those who control the American food system should be ashamed of:

■ The coopting of "natural": While for decades the processed food industry has been saying that there is no advantage to natural foods, today they stick the term on almost anything if it will help sales. Significantly, a number of companies have been forced by the Better Business Bureau to discontinue improper "natural" references in advertising.

■ Partial hydrogenation of oils is highly suspect because it creates a form of fat unknown in nature and simultaneously destroys vital components in the oil that have health-promoting effects (e.g., vitamin E, phytosterols).

Nonetheless, this process is becoming more widespread because it offers technological convenience to food processors.

■ Fructose, touted as a "natural sweetener" and fruit derivative, is actually more processed than cane sugar and in most cases has never been near fruit.

■ In 1987, saccharin, considered a co-carcinogen even by the conservative Food and Drug Administration, celebrates the tenth anniversary of its exemption by Congress from the Delaney Clause, the law established to protect us against just such substances. The U.S. government actually allows saccharin-containing food intended for human consumption to be sold with the warning: "Use of this product may be hazardous to your health"!

■ Rather than trying to minimize chemical proliferation, the government is establishing "safe thresholds" for cancer-causing agents. Not content with undercutting the Delaney Clause through loose legal interpretations (following), the food industry-supported Hatch Amendment, which died in committee, would have reconfirmed that we are all human guinea pigs. This bill sought to change the law to permit additives that pose a "small" health risk, even cancer, and would have allowed the gradual withdrawal of harmful additives rather than their outright banning.

■ The FDA, whose mandate it is to protect the public, has for the first time applied the *de minimus* legal principle to our food laws. This ancient legal rule permits courts to dismiss suits over "trifles" in order to save them from addressing suits over pennies. The rule is now being applied to permit the government to dismiss something that is no trifle: a little risk of cancer.

■ The regulatory agencies have not paid adequate attention to residues of aflatoxin, a carcinogenic mold, in food. The Environmental Protection Agency has established allowances that are much too liberal and has done almost nothing to encourage (or mandate) better growing, storing, and manufacturing techniques which could greatly reduce this serious problem.

■ Bacterial contamination of food, especially poultry, is believed to be responsible to a large extent for nearly 40,000 confirmed cases of salmonella poisoning a year in the United States (and according to officials, the actual figure could possibly be as high as 6 million since many cases go unreported or unconfirmed). This figure represents a 50 percent increase in the last ten years. The situation is so critical that one USDA senior inspector and the National Academy of Sciences have recommended that warning labels be put on poultry. But the government has taken few steps to remedy the problem, which is linked to several industry practices including the routine use of antibiotics in animal feed and poor poultry handling techniques.

■ The European Common Market recommended rejecting meat from 400 American meat-processing plants because of what they claim to be insufficient inspection standards. Many U.S. officials believe this is merely a political/economic ploy. However, there may be more to this than meets the eye: Ray Lett, President Reagan's choice to oversee the USDA inspection program, considers meat inspection a "luxury."

■ The FDA, the agency responsible for the safety of most foods other than meat and poultry, has undergone such severe budget cuts that it has been forced to curtail enforcement and reduce its manpower. If things continue in this direction, industry observers at the Community Nutrition Institute believe "the effect would be essentially to remove the federal government as an active presence in regulating food safety."

■ The nuclear energy industry has fought for approval of the irradiation of many foods despite serious concerns about the effect on the food itself as well as on the environment. As was the case with processed foods and pesticides, the far-reaching health and social consequences of an irradiated food supply are being sidestepped.

■ Although glass is unquestionably the least controversial packaging material in terms of health, during the past decade U.S. production of plastic bottles has grown five times faster than the output of glass containers. Plastic is also beginning to replace metal cans, and even containers that do not appear to be made of plastic, like retort pouches and aseptic paper packages, have a plastic component. Many of the known toxicants in plastic are still tolerated by the government; an FDA official has admitted that the agency "work(s) from the assumption that something from the plastic will always leach into the food." Not to be ignored is the fact that this plastic never biodegrades and is difficult to recycle, making it a primary environmental pollutant.

■ Since processed food is based on each manufacturer's individual and often secret formula, labels are needed to "explain" these foods to consumers. Today, nutrition labeling is only required on products that make some specific dietary claim. The food industry has successfully blocked nutrition labeling of all processed foods on the basis of costs, particularly those involved in the analysis of the product. This, however, is not the consumer's problem. Food is our lifeline, and when it comes in its simple whole form it is easy to predict its value. If someone chooses to alter it, they should also be obligated to demonstrate where the food now fits into the scheme of things. David suggested years ago at FDA hearings that nutrition labeling be required only on processed foods. This would provide a financial incentive to produce simple wholefoods and place nutrition labeling where it is really needed.

■ Despite the proliferation of artificial sweeteners and "lite" foods, more than one quarter of American adults are overweight, and as a group Americans are heavier than they have been at any time in the past. According to one recent study the proportion of children who are overweight has increased 50 percent in the last 20 years.

■ Unsubstantiated recommendations about individual nutrients have brought an onslaught of new "fortified" foods. To help ward off osteoporosis, a bone disease mostly affecting menopausal women, calcium enrichment is in vogue. There is no real evidence that this is a useful or even safe practice. Likewise, fiber enrichment is being promoted as a panacea despite widespread disagreement about its effects and, according to FDA commissioner Dr. Frank Young, "no basis" for the National Cancer Institute's recommendation that Americans consume 20 to 30 grams of fiber per day.

Obviously, we cannot expect America's diet and food supply to remain as it was a century ago, for it must keep up with contemporary life-styles. The question is whether we choose to solve the call for fewer calories, less fat, adequate fiber, vitamins and minerals, and cheaper protein through the clever use of traditional foods or the commercial use of dubious ingredients and processes. Today you can increase the fiber content of your diet by as much as 400 percent by purchasing a bread that includes wood pulp (cellulose), or you can benefit from the conventional fiber found in whole grain products, dried beans, fresh produce, etc. Similarly, you can reduce your fat and cholesterol intake by using fabricated egg products, or you can take advantage of the cuisines that use inherently low-fat/low-cholesterol foods such as soyfoods or bean/grain combinations so that real eggs become much less of a problem.

Our agricultural system, which may be technologically the most advanced in the world, not only produces tasteless, poison-encased food but it is now in the process of developing what can only be called "Frankenstein foods" through biotechnology. (Among other things, this new science, also known as gene splicing, will involve the release into the environment of genetically altered substances not known in nature and the development of pesticide-resistant crops so that *more* pesticides can be used.) If the results of this research have as much impact as the byproducts of the agri-chemical revolution, some of which are listed below, we are in for a frightening future.

■ Due to runoff from agricultural and industrial pollution, America has virtually lost freshwater fish as a food source. A 1974 study revealed that 80 percent of domestic fish contained pesticide residues and 65 percent had multiple contamination. Now in many areas of the country officials actually suggest that people eat no more than one fish a week from inland waters and that children and pregnant and lactating women avoid them entirely. The effect of this pollution on the spawning grounds of ocean fish is still unknown.

■ The Amazon forest is being leveled at the rate of 5,000 to 10,000 acres a day, largely to provide grazing for cattle in order to keep up with the demand that has been created for meat. No recognition is given to the fact that the Amazon basin provides 40 percent of the world's oxygen. Today, purchasing pure water seems almost normal. Will we one day feel that way about *buying oxygen?*

■ The destruction of the American farm continues. Although it is almost undisputed that the small farm offers the most efficient form of food production, government policy supports industrial farms that can barely produce a calorie of food for each calorie of fuel invested (as contrasted to family farming which produces much more than a calorie). Significant, too, is the loss of the "greenbelt" that farms traditionally provided as a balance to the cities, surrounding them with open spaces, fresh air, alternate occupations, and fresh food.

■ While agriculturalists are proud of how many people agribusiness techniques feed, we wonder if the 2,000 people killed and those maimed by the leakage from the fertilizer plant in Bhopal, India, are factored into their equation. A 1985 study commissioned by the EPA revealed that in the previous five years 135 people had died and 1,500 were injured in the almost 7,000 toxic chemical leaks that occurred in the United States.

What to do? Our happy solution, as presented in this book, begins at your own table. Remember, our cash-register ballots have already affected many of the items stocked on the nation's food shelves. It is most important that we continue to support *genuine* wholefoods and organic products and soundly reject any pretenders. You can also make a deep impression on food companies by sending them a label from one of their wholefoods competitors and letting them know you would buy their product if it met the competition's standards.

Putting pressure on government helps too. Write to your state and national representatives and federal agencies and tell them your concerns. ("A Guide to Government Agencies" in the Appendix will help you to direct your letters appropriately.)

As we said at the outset, there have been some remarkable changes in America's food-buying habits in the past fifteen years, with more products available and more markets featuring them. But with the attempt to pervert the notion of pure or "natural" by food conglomerates, and with the advent of irradiation, biotechnology, and the ability to engineer "foods" that provide no nutrients, today's food processing may someday seem benign. In fact, FDA's Dr. Sandford Miller has called some of these prospects "frightening."

Unless consumers communicate in the marketplace that they want *wholefoods,* our traditional food supply and all that goes with it could be headed for extinction.

Part I

THE INFORMED SHOPPER

Chapter 1

The Story of
Food Additives, Pesticides,
and Packaging

The human food supply was essentially the same up until the 1900s. Before that time most prepared food was made at home, or when store-bought, was produced locally in a fashion similar to home-made food—what was called "kitchen quality." Around the turn of the century, and accelerating with the world wars, a totally new type of food appeared that is known today as processed food. These products were dependent on advances in technology and the development of chemical food additives.

Some of this processing is quite welcome. Gutting and plucking poultry, churning cream into butter and ice cream, preparing bread, pasta, basic condiments like catsup, mustard, soy sauce, and similar time-consuming projects are all jobs that people are happy to put in someone else's hands. But much of the processing done today to provide this convenience is really quite unnecessary. Had synthetic and refined ingredients not been invented, people would still eat, but it is doubtful that the giant food conglomerates would exist.

Given the fact that we have allowed an industrial food supply to develop, each of us must now decide which food ingredients and processes we find suitable.

FOOD MOVES OFF THE FARM

Food, once simple fare, has been transformed into a complex network of chemicals. Take a look at a typical American-style breakfast consisting, for example, of a fruit drink, eggs, potatoes, toast, and coffee. Without added coloring, flavoring, sweeteners, and acidifers, the fruit drink is nothing more than plain water. The chicken that laid the egg was routinely given antibiotics and her feed laced with pigments that promote yolks with a deep yellow color. To keep the potatoes from sprouting during storage, a "sprout inhibitor" may have been used, and if they were purchased precut and frozen, a "whitener" was added to keep oxygen from turning them brown. The flour

17

may have been bleached to its white hue and the bread that is made from it formulated with dough conditioners to ensure that each loaf is identical; the bread is probably fortified with synthesized vitamins, and added preservatives help maintain an appearance of freshness. The margarine on the bread depends on a sophisticated technology to hydrogenate the oil it is built on; emulsifiers are responsible for its texture, and it has been colored pale yellow. If decaffeinated coffee is served, a solvent may have been used to extract the caffeine. The coffee could be lightened with a nondairy creamer that relies on texturizers, stabilizers, and flavoring agents to give it an identity, and sweetened with an entirely synthetic substance. The irony is that to clean up, a dishwashing soap that contains real lemon juice is available!

The list of techniques and additives available to the food industry is almost limitless. As foods become more convenient and contrived, our bodies come in contact with compounds humans have never before encountered. The average additive consumption per person, including pesticides, is about 9 to 10 pounds a year—double the amount consumed just ten years ago. Given the abundance of chemicals in our food that were not there just a generation ago, it is no wonder that so many people are concerned. Are these substances bad for us? Do they serve the consumer? Or do they just make money for the food industry?

We cannot deny that the American food system provides affordable food in variety and quantities unimagined by our predecessors, but unfortunately it seems that the real purpose of food has been put on a back burner. Product acceptability, rather than human health and nutrition, appears to be the predominant focus of food technology. What sets food additives apart from traditional ingredients is that they are almost universally of more use to the manufacturer than to the consumer. That is, while food ingredients provide nutritional value, food additives offer mainly sensory value (color, flavor, texture, and shelf-life).

Many people say they would prefer to do without most additives, even if it means a little inconvenience, higher prices, and a less diverse food supply. Food manufacturers say that consumer expectations and the desire for foods to be perpetually on the market at the lowest prices, without seasonal or geographical limitations, make food additives essential.

THE GOVERNMENT ACTS
A Lesson from History

"The object of all unprincipled modern manufacturers seems to be the sparing of their time and labour as much as possible, and to increase the quantity of the articles they produce without regard to their quality. The ingenuity and perseverance of self-interest is proof against prohibitions and contrivances to elude the vigilance of the most active government."

Frederick Accum, *A Treatise on Adulteration of Food and Culinary Poisons, Etc.*, London (1820)

In the early 1900s there were concerns that the U.S. food supply was both substandard and dangerously adulterated and so the government decided that there was a need for laws to protect the public health. As the above excerpt illustrates, food adulteration was nothing new, but in the past it had been a local problem. With the advent of large food processors, however, it became a matter of national and later international concern.

The 1906 Pure Food and Drug Act, and the more comprehensive Food, Drug and Cosmetic Act of 1938, gave the government the authority to regulate chemicals and additives and remove poisonous substances from the market. The Food and Drug Administration (FDA) was established to enforce these laws. The magnitude of the job was so great, and the situation so serious, however, that by 1949 a special congressional committee was set up to investigate the use of chemicals in food. As a result, the law was fortified in 1954 by the Pesticide Chemicals Act and updated in 1958 with the Food Additives Amendment, and again in 1960 with the Color Additives Amendment. The intent of this legislation was to ensure the safety of food chemicals when properly used. At the same time, the burden of proof of safety was transferred from the government onto industry.

These laws, codified in Title 21 of the Code of Federal Regulations, cover various aspects of food production including additives, cleanliness standards, ingredient standards, standards of fill, packaging, and labeling. The laws were originally intended to apply to manufacturers' practices, not the consumer need for information. Although this has changed somewhat today, it helps to explain why there is so much missing from the labels of the food we buy.

Food Standards

One act of the law was to establish Standards of Identity (or recipes) for certain basic food staples (listed below). These are essentially definitions of

---

FOODS GOVERNED BY A STANDARD OF IDENTITY

milk and cream of all varieties, including yogurt
cheeses
frozen desserts
bakery products
wheat and corn flours and related products, including rice
macaroni and noodle products
canned fruit
canned (and bottled) fruit juices
fruit butter, jelly, and preserves
frozen cherry pie
canned vegetables, including tomato concentrates and catsup

vegetable juices
frozen vegetables
eggs and egg products
canned oysters, salmon, shrimp and tuna, and frozen breaded shrimp
cocoa products, including chocolate
nuts and peanut products
soda
margarine
sweeteners (dextrose, glucose, and lactose) and table syrups
salad dressing, mayonnaise, and flavoring extracts

---

food content and quality. The standards tell manufacturers which ingredients are permissible in these foods and in what amounts. If a manufacturer follows these rules, the common name for the product (for example, white bread, process cheese) can be applied. Originally many ingredients were exempt from labeling as long as the standard was adhered to. This is still the case, but to a much lesser degree as the FDA is gradually changing standards to require more ingredient labeling.

Nonstandardized Foods

Those products which do not have a specific standard are called "nonstandarized" and can be made to the manufacturer's specifications. They must list complete ingredients on the label, although additional laws do create exceptions to this general rule.

Agencies in Authority

Not all food laws are within the jurisdiction of the FDA. The U.S. Department of Agriculture (USDA) is responsible for overseeing certain animal products and the Bureau of Alcohol, Tobacco, and Firearms regulates alcoholic beverages. Other relevant restrictions on food are scattered throughout a variety of other government offices (see "A Guide to Government Agencies" in the Appendix).

WHAT ARE ADDITIVES?

A food additive is legally defined as any substance, other than the basic foodstuffs, that becomes a component of a food or otherwise affects its characteristics. Additives in food are not a new phenomenon. Humans have been tinkering with foods for thousands of years, using salt, herbs, spices, and smoke to add to their appeal and to preserve them. But today the resources we have for altering our food supply are not so limited. The National Academy of Sciences has identified some 8,600 food additives, excluding the many compounds that find their way into the food supply via pesticides, drugs fed to animals, water pollutants, and chemicals that migrate from packaging materials.

Intentional Additives

An intentional additive is added by the processor to serve a specific function. According to the Code of Federal Regulations, even a material used in packaging—for instance a preservative—may be considered an additive if it migrates into the food and serves some purpose there. For the most part, intentional additives appear on the label of all foods, but there are exceptions as you will see when you get to the individual food chapters.

Incidental Additives

An incidental additive serves no function in a food, and is not added directly but enters via another ingredient in which it did have a specific function. (For example, the antioxidant in oil added to bread.) Certain "processing aids," which are added to a food during production but are likely to be removed before the food is packaged, or which are converted during processing to another substance that is normally found in foods, or those present in the finished food in such small amounts that they no longer have any functional effect, are also considered incidental additives (for example, the hydrogen peroxide used to stabilize milk prior to cheese-making). The same is true for certain elements that migrate to food from equipment or packaging.

Consumers have very little control over the ingestion of incidental additives since these additives are not revealed on food labels. It is important to be aware of their existence, however, because they do add to our daily intake of chemicals.

Pesticides, by the way, are not considered additives, although their presence in foods has certainly been established and they do enter our bodies to add to what is referred to as the "toxic load."

How an Additive Gets Approved

In order to introduce a new chemical into the food supply, certain requirements must be fulfilled. Most important from the public standpoint, the petitioner must provide evidence of its safety obtained from animal feeding studies.

The role of the FDA in this process is limited to safety. It does not determine if an additive is needed, only if under the intended conditions of use it will "do no harm."

How an Additive Gets Removed

When the FDA suspects that an approved additive is not safe, it takes steps to remove it from the market. But just as introducing a new additive is a costly and time-consuming process, so is banning one.

In order to disallow an additive, there must be "an orderly review" of all scientific data in support of this action. In the meantime, while debate over the additive's safety is in progress, the FDA cannot prohibit its use.

The GRAS List

When the Food Additives Amendment was passed in 1958, there were already many additives with a long history of use to be considered. To assist industry, the FDA compiled a list of those that could be "generally recognized as safe" (GRAS) on the basis of past experience. Since 1958, new substances have been classified as GRAS based on scientific data.

GRAS substances are not legally considered food additives. They do not have to be registered with the FDA, as additives do, before they can be used by a food processor. Because of this, there are no records as to how much of any GRAS substance is consumed annually. In addition, if the safety of a GRAS substance is questioned, it is up to the government, not the manufacturer, to provide relevant scientific data.

Both saccharin and cyclamates were at one time GRAS chemicals, as were bromated vegetable oil, NDGA, glycine, and a number of coal tar dyes. The banning of cyclamates from the American table actually initiated a review of the GRAS list. Eventually each GRAS substance will be (1) reaffirmed as GRAS; (2) placed on a new GRAS list with restrictions as to use; (3) converted to general food additive status; or (4) if judged unsafe, banned. In the last review published in 1980, of the 415 GRAS substances being evaluated, 305 had been deemed safe, 5 given restrictions, 19 needed further study, and the remainder were in various stages of review.

Prior-Sanctioned Substances

Another legal distinction created by the 1958 amendment is that of "prior-sanctioned substances"; these had already received some form of official permission before this date and thus were given "squatter's rights." Although they are not subject to the same scrutiny as new food additives, permission to use a prior-sanctioned substance can be, and has been, rescinded if evidence is introduced that shows it to be harmful. Here again, the burden of proof lies with the government.

PESTICIDES: THE PRICE OF LARGE-SCALE FARMING

For centuries, food has been grown on land that was replenished in a number of logical and simple ways. Waste material from plants and animals was added back to the soil to fertilize it, crops or fields were rotated to allow the soil to rejuvenate, and cover crops called "green manure" were planted periodically because of their ability to naturally enrich the soil. Since the sixth century B.C., farms have operated in this manner, becoming virtually self-sustaining "closed systems."

Around the turn of the twentieth century, methods were developed to artificially return to the soil its three key constituents—nitrogen, phosphorus, and potash—using petrochemical-based, factory-made products (similar to the enriching of bread with select synthetic nutrients). This made possible the shift from family farms of a few hundred acres to large-scale industrial farms of tens of thousands of acres. Along with these chemical fertilizers, special high-yield seeds have been developed which, unfortunately, are often less resistant to insects and plant disease. To compensate, industry has responded with pesticides to kill bugs, herbicides to destroy weeds, fungicides to eradicate bacteria—"cides" of all kinds to kill anything that moves.

The law does not consider these pesticides additives, but no matter how you classify them, they are an inseparable part of the food we eat. Pesticides, by definition, are chemicals toxic to pests, be they weeds, microorganisms, insects, or vermin. Unfortunately, many poisons that destroy these undesirable pests are so potent that they also endanger humans, causing cancer, birth defects, nerve damage, genetic mutation, and other debilitating or lethal effects.

These agrichemicals can enter the food chain as a result of direct application to crops, or indirectly through flesh, eggs, or dairy products of animals that consume pesticides in their feed. They may also enter the food chain due to long-term, low-level contamination of the environment. In fact, DDT, which was banned in the early 1970s, is still the most commonly found pesticide in foods.

Agricultural pests are certainly not a recent nuisance, but our capacity to irradicate them en masse with pesticides facilitated the growth of large-scale farming as practiced today. It is now almost impossible for this type of farming to exist independent of these poisons. More than 500 million pounds of pesticides and herbicides were used in the United States in 1982. During the last thirty years it has been estimated that pesticide use has increased tenfold. These statistics are especially significant in light of widespread agreement that since World War II, when the pesticide onslaught began, loss of crops to insects has doubled.

One reason the farmer is losing the bug war is that broad-spectrum pesticides are simultaneously killing off natural predators that formerly helped keep pests in check. There are now also hundreds of harmful insect species that have developed resistance to popular insecticides, just as some weeds are evolving that resist herbicides. In order to keep up with the pests, farmers are on a treadmill, having to increase dosages and change pesticides. Unfortunately, our ability to produce these chemicals has outpaced our means of testing them or detecting them in food.

Real Fears

A major problem facing policymakers and the public is how to determine a balance between the damage pests do and the health and environmental problems and unknown risks that eliminating them with chemicals presents.

A National Academy of Sciences study concluded that 64 percent of pesticides have not even been minimally tested for toxic effects. A 1982 House agriculture subcommittee report estimated that between 79 and 84 percent of all pesticides sold in this country had not been sufficiently tested for carcinogenic effects, between 90 and 93 percent had not been adequately tested for genetic mutations, 60 to 70 percent had not been assessed for their capacity to cause birth defects, and 29 to 47 percent had not been screened to determine if they have adverse effects on reproduction. There is very little information on the potential long-term chronic effects of exposure to pesticides, or how individual sensitivity levels might affect us.

Many pesticides used in the past have been removed from our agriculture system, including chlordane and heptachlor which, until the mid-1970s, were the two most widely used pesticides in the world. DDT, 2,4,5–T, Silvex, aldrin, dieldrin, DBCP, and EDB are examples of other once popular poisons that are now banned in the United States. (For a complete list, see "Suspended and Canceled Pesticides" in the Appendix.)

Moreover, a number of chemicals that are currently in use are either suspected or known to cause cancer. Despite the absence of any proof that there can be a safe level of exposure to carcinogens, tolerance levels have been established for many of these chemicals. One deterrent to banning these chemicals is that the current law requires the Environmental Protection Agency to pay an indemnity to the manufacturers of pesticides canceled by the agency to compensate for leftover stock. The indemnification cost for the pesticide dinoseb alone is estimated at $60 to $120 million. This could rapidly exhaust the agency's entire budget which is about $60 million annually.

We must also contend with the fact that the law governing pesticides is full of loopholes. For example, it does not require studies of "inert ingredients" that do not actually kill pests themselves but are used to hold or deliver the active ingredients in pesticides. A review in 1984 of dicofol, an insecticide approved in 1957 and still in use, revealed that 15 percent of it was actually DDT, which its manufacturer classified as "inert."

Another problem is that no tests are available to determine the presence of certain chemical residues in food, and even some of the chemicals that have tolerance levels which require monitoring cannot be accommodated. An FDA spokesman revealed to the Government Accounting Office that "even with unlimited resources, it would be impossible to provide ongoing surveillance over the full expanse of potential pesticide/commodity combinations." The type of multi-residue testing generally used to detect chemicals covers only about 90 of the almost 600 chemicals that are currently registered for domestic use on food.

Even those that are considered safe at current tolerance levels are present in what may be more significant amounts than the government assumes. A 1983 study conducted by the Natural Resources Defense Council (a private foundation) on ten types of fresh produce sold in San Francisco markets showed 44 percent of the seventy-one samples contained residues of nineteen different chemicals and 42 percent of these had residues of more than one pesticide. This latter figure is especially notable since the EPA does not usually consider the effects of combinations of chemicals when setting its residue limits. In comparison, the State of California pesticide residue monitoring program detected pesticides in only 7 to 20 percent of its samples of the same crop varieties during its 1979 to 1982 monitoring. In 1986 a report by the General Accounting Office criticizing the FDA monitoring system lent support to the Natural Resources Defense Council findings.

We should also mention that no consideration is given to the fact that children weigh less than adults and therefore are more vulnerable to the effects of these chemicals, as are those who may be ill or have a weakened immune system. Furthermore, pesticide residues are not limited to raw crops and the processed foods that contain them, but also show up in meat, eggs, dairy products, fish, and even drinking water.

Processing of foods can help to reduce some residues, but another important fact that has been ignored in setting limits is that some remaining pesticides become more dangerous after cooking or from the metabolic transformations that occur during digestion.

There is also the risk that some lower animal and plant species may not be as tolerant of poisons as humans, and while we may survive them, our resources, including these potential food sources, as well as our air and water supply may not. Unless these, too, are protected, our life support systems remain in jeopardy.

The Food Factor

Individual pesticide intake may be higher than predicted because in establishing tolerance levels a so-called food factor is used as a crude estimate of the amount of a particular food that the average person eats yearly. For many, this "average" projection is quite low. For example, one could easily consume a half pound of avocado, blueberries, peas, or eggplant in a single meal. Many other predicted patterns of food consumption are equally as unrealistic as you will undoubtedly notice when you look at the following list showing the Environmental Protection Agency estimates for various common staples. (The EPA is said to be updating these figures.)

ARE ADDITIVES AND PESTICIDES SAFE?

It is virtually impossible to guarantee safety for any chemical additive or pesticide. Tests can only be conducted to determine the presence of known hazards. If none are found, then it is assumed to be safe. For legal purposes, this means "there is a reasonable certainty in the minds of competent scientists that the substance is not harmful under the intended conditions of use." Today there is a growing awareness that the science of toxicology on which our food regulation system is based is too costly, too slow, and too inaccurate to make such determinations. The head of the Environmental

EPA "FOOD FACTORS"

Food	Estimated Amount Consumed per Person per Year (pounds)	Food	Estimated Amount Consumed per Person per Year (pounds)
Almonds	0.5	Maple syrup	0.5
Apples	39.4	Meat, red	168.2
Apricots	1.8	Millet	0.5
Artichokes	0.5	Milk, fresh	307.4
Asparagus	2.2	Mushrooms	0.5
Avocados	0.5	Nectarines	0.5
Bananas	22.0	Oats	5.6
Barley	0.5	Okra	1.1
Beans, dry	4.8	Olives	1.0
Beans, snap	15.3	Onions	12.9
Beets	2.7	Oranges	33.7
Blackberries	0.5	Papayas	0.5
Blueberries	0.5	Peaches	14.0
Butter	6.4	Peanuts	0.8
Broccoli	1.6	Peanut butter	4.8
Brussels sprouts	0.5	Pears	4.0
Cabbage	11.5	Peas	10.8
Cantaloupe	8.1	Pecans	0.5
Carrots	7.5	Peppers	1.9
Cauliflower	1.1	Pineapple	4.6
Celery	4.5	Plums	1.4
Cheese	17.5	Pork	51.4
Cherries	1.6	Potatoes	84.4
Chicken	40.0	Prunes	0.6
Coffee	11.6	Raisins	0.6
Corn, sweet	22.3	Raspberries	0.5
Corn, grain	15.6	Rice	8.6
Cream	2.1	Romaine	0.5
Cucumbers	11.3	Rye	0.5
Dates	0.5	Sesame seeds	0.5
Eggplant	0.5	Soybeans	
Eggs	43.1	(as shortening)	14.3
Figs	0.5	Spinach	0.8
Filberts	0.5	Strawberries	2.9
Fish and shellfish	16.9	Sugar	56.6
Grapefruit	15.4	Sweet potatoes	6.2
Grapes	7.0	Tea	1.1
Honey	1.0	Tomatoes	44.7
Ice cream	42.6	Turkey	5.1
Lemons	2.7	Walnuts	0.5
Lentils	0.6	Watermelon	22.3
Lettuce	20.4	Wheat	161.3

Protection Agency's Laboratory Data Integrity Section has said, "There are no answers in toxicology, only opinions."

Testing for Safety

Modern ethics no longer permit "a poison squad" of humans, as was used in the early days of the FDA, to establish the safety of food additives. So, our testing is done on animals, using two or more species and often spanning several generations. During this time, researchers look for the additive's potential to cause genetic or birth defects, cancer, and other chronic ailments. Only recently have scientists also begun to consider behavioral changes that can be induced by certain food chemicals.

The use of animal testing has often been criticized. The pro-additive faction is quick to question the validity of such tests, pointing out that mice are not people, and anyway, no normal person consumes the volume of a single chemical administered in these tests. This, they conclude, makes the results of animal studies irrelevant to the human species.

Indeed, the limitations of animal testing (and there are many) need to be considered, but in their support it has been found that epidemiological studies and other short-term tests done on bacteria, plants, and insects seem to corroborate animal testing. Moreover, although pessimists insist that "everything causes cancer," if a substance cannot produce cancer, no dose, no matter how large, will cause cancer in animals.

Researchers defend the large doses used in the testing by saying that they may help compensate for the many different carcinogens the average person is exposed to, for while these testing procedures expose the animal to only one chemical at a time, people are faced with both the cumulative and combined effects of various toxins.

Legal Limits

If scientific evidence indicates that an additive is safe, the FDA establishes guidelines for its use. After determining the maximum amount that can be used without producing any undesirable effects on the test animals, a hundredfold margin of safety is imposed. This means that a food processor may use no more than 1/100th of this "no effect" level in any single food product.

In addition to the limits placed on these "safe" additives, if a food cannot be made without the use of an otherwise dangerous substance, special rules can be applied to permit its use and simultaneously impose limits in order to protect the public. These limits are known as "tolerance levels"; they are set by the FDA after public hearings and are based somewhat on the extent to which they cannot be avoided in food production, in conjunction with other possible avenues of exposure (as via air or water). Nitrites are one example of what is considered an unavoidable but toxic additive for which a tolerance level has been established. Tolerance levels are also in effect for certain pesticides and molds which are considered harmful to people but currently integral to some foods. The FDA has, in certain circumstances, ignored the law regarding tolerance levels in favor of "action levels." They differ in that the public does not participate in the determination process and considerations other than health are involved. That is, business concerns, state government viewpoints, and political pressures all play a role in setting action levels. The FDA favors action levels, which tend to be more lenient and less cumbersome for the agency to determine than tolerance levels. In 1987 the U.S. Court of Appeals ruled action levels illegal, protecting the public's right to "notice and comment."

Who Does the Testing?

The manufacturer of an additive or pesticide is responsible for running safety studies. Most manufacturers hire testing firms to do this for them. The government then assesses the data. Unfortunately, shoddy record-keeping and falsifying information are not unheard of. A nationwide review of seventy major testing firms in 1979 revealed twenty-five to be seriously deficient in one or more areas of critical research. In fact, the principals of one of the largest testing companies, Industrial Bio Test Laboratories, were convicted of fradulent actions and, as a result, a substantial number of products on the market today—many of them pesticides, some food additives—have not been adequately tested. Even the National Toxicology Program, the government agency set up in 1978 specifically to upgrade testing, has found its contract laboratories to be guilty of sloppy work. In 1984, the National Research Council reported that "on the great majority of the substances, data considered to be essential for conducting a health-hazard assessment are lacking." Of the samples they screened, only an estimated 10 percent of pesticides and 5 percent of food additives had sufficient backing.

This is a frightening predicament for, as Senator Edward Kennedy succinctly put it, "If the integrity of that data is questioned, then the whole regulatory process is questioned. If the data are proven false, then the regulatory decisions may be tragically wrong."

Who's Keeping Tabs?

The Food and Drug Administration is the principal agency charged with monitoring foods for chemical residues, assisted by the U.S. Department of Agriculture, which polices the specific animal products under its jurisdiction. Generally the presence of contaminated food (above tolerance levels) is only recognized by some telltale incident, since sampling of foods, due to budget constraints, only covers a small portion of food production and is quite sporadic. Alarms only begin to sound when people show visible signs of poisoning, as they did in 1979 when one of the earliest scandals involving PCB-contaminated eggs came to light, or in 1985 when watermelons tainted with the chemical aldicarb (brand name Temix) showed up in the supermarket. Even after hazardous levels of chemicals are known to be present it can be a lengthy process to trace the source of contamination and recall the product. In every situation where this has occurred, a good deal of the food had already been consumed before the product was taken off the market.

In order to keep watch over additives in the diet in general, the FDA also conducts what is called a "Total Diet Study." In a laboratory in Kansas City, scientists analyze over 200 popular American foods yearly, looking for substances that shouldn't be there, such as high levels of pesticides, industrial chemicals, and such. Simultaneously, they measure for certain essential minerals. While chemical residues are routinely found, the FDA asserts that they are almost always within "acceptable" limits.

The Circle of Poison

Even when chemicals are banned in this country we are not free of their threat. A "circle of poison" exists when the United States exports agricultural chemicals that cannot be used domestically to recipients who often are not aware these chemicals are prohibited in the United States, and then imports the foods the chemicals are used on. A study released by the General Accounting Office in 1986 revealed that only 1 percent of imported food is checked for illegal pesticide residues. Despite this small sampling, between 1979 and 1985 the FDA found illegal residues in 6 percent of the imports it tested—double the rate for domestic food. The study also found that the FDA seldom takes corrective action, rarely imposes fines, and has failed to develop a comprehensive program to monitor the safety of imported food.

Among the foreign foods commonly imported into the United States, bananas, cocoa, sugar, tea, coffee, tomatoes, olives, rice, soybeans and corn have at times been treated with pesticides that we do not allow in this country because they are known to cause cancer, birth defects, and gene mutations. It is estimated that the United States imports about 600 different food commodities from over 150 countries. There are hundred of pesticides and therefore hundreds of tests that would have to be conducted to identify all the chemical residues in these products.

A LOOK AT THE ISSUES

As the field of nutrition science has grown, our perception of what is safe has undergone significant modification. When the first pure food act was enacted in 1906, the major issue was acute toxicity leading to immediate illness or death. In the last few decades, chronic diseases have become the focal point of public attention. The wholesomeness of the total food supply, not just individual components, has become a subject of widespread interest.

The Delaney Clause: The Clause That Represses

A pivotal clause in the Food Additives Amendment known as the Delaney Clause specifies that "No additive shall be deemed safe if it is found to induce cancer when ingested by man or animal. . . ." This was an expression by Congress about the degree of risk regarding cancer to which the public should be exposed; as far as Congress was concerned, not even a remote chance was acceptable.

This single paragraph is one of the most controversial issues facing Congress. Its opponents state that modern technology allows detection of substances in such minute amounts—amounts that were formerly imperceptible—that the costs of determining safety under the Delaney Clause are unreasonable. (If the Hatch Amendment had passed, the law would have been weakened by allowing additives that are known to cause cancer in humans and animals and judging them individually on a risk-benefit basis. It would also have allowed the gradual phasing out of outlawed chemicals, rather than their immediate banning.)

Supporters of the existing law reply that since we do not know how cancer starts, how can we permit even limited amounts of suspicious additives. "Is the trigger just a single molecule of a carcinogen?" wondered nutrition authority Dr. Jean Mayer when defending the Delaney Clause.

Furthermore, what science or the law cannot tell us is what the cumulative effect of a chemical might be, since some are stored in the body unchanged and may build up to a toxic level. In the case of cancer, for example, it is hypothesized that the disease may be induced by minuscule amounts of a substance over a long period of time. We must also weigh the potential effects in a diversified population that includes infants, pregnant women, the sick, and the elderly. It is not the healthiest person, but the most susceptible, that the law should take into account.

Complex Combinations

All the testing and restrictions placed on additives are based on using them one at a time. During the tests, animals are given adequate food and water and live in a controlled, relatively comfortable environment. Unfortunately, most of us are not so insulated in our lives. Each day we breathe air and drink water that has been polluted by automobiles, industry, and the byproducts of our technological life-style. We may smoke, drink, and take medications that add to the load our bodies must handle. We may be faced with minor and major stresses at home, at work, at school, or just during ordinary social interactions. On top of this, we do not consume just one food additive at a time, but perhaps dozens in a single sitting.

Tests for safety do not consider the combined effects of these various factors. However, this does not diminish their impact. It is easy to see why this kind of testing is not done though, for with so many permutations and combinations, it is virtually impossible.

Natural Poisons Versus Added Dangers

Two arguments are often raised in defense of additives. The first is that many foods that have been part of the human diet for generations contain compounds that are inherently toxic. For example, potatoes, lima beans, cabbage, and spinach all contain certain chemical components that have been deemed hazardous. The fallacy of this reasoning is that generally these toxins occur in such small amounts that under normal circumstances no danger arises; moreover, they are often counteracted by antitoxins that are also present in these foods that minimize their effect. In any event, why add more toxins to those that occur naturally in the foods we eat?

The second defense of food additives claims that the body has defense mechanisms capable of dealing with the small amount of poisons in our food. This is a reasonable concept and probably explains why many of the naturally occurring toxins in food were apparently harmless to our ancestors. However, this concept does not hold up entirely since the liver, the principal organ involved in detoxifying the body, does have its limits. The capacity of the liver is affected by how much it must deal with at any one time, and while it is coping with these toxins, how much damage it incurs. Until the liver completes its job, a process that can take several hours or days, the toxins can still damage other organs.

Another relevant fact is that many chemicals, and most particularly pesticide residues, are not so easily eliminated. Instead, they are stored by the body in fat tissues where they tend to accumulate.

There is no question that the human body can cope with a certain amount of invasion, or toxic load, also termed the "total body burden." But as with everything else, the amount of abuse that can be tolerated varies from person to person. When resources are overtaxed and wear out, illness becomes inevitable.

Excess Minerals from Additives

Many additives are composed of minerals that are also nutrients. While this can be beneficial, it can also add up to excesses that are suspected of producing adverse effects on the body (see "A Glossary of Food Additives" in the Appendix).

WRAPPING IT UP:
PROBLEMS WITH PACKAGING

The primary function of packaging is to control the interaction between food and the environment in order to protect the quality and lifespan of the food for as long as possible. This is of no small importance to the food industry, for without a protective barrier of some kind most of the mass-market products sold today would not be possible.

The package can also fulfill certain consumer needs. When paperboard cartons first appeared as a replacement for milk bottles these innovative containers were so attractive to consumers they virtually eliminated the glass alternative. Convenience of this kind is still important to people and as life-styles change, manufacturers are paying close attention to how they can accommodate perceived consumer habits. For example, as family together-ness declines and people look to foods that are easy to prepare in single portions, large units give way to individually wrapped items. In addition, companies are looking to provide containers that offer a means of storage, a cooking vessel (for use in microwave ovens), and a disposable serving dish all in one. A receptacle that is lightweight, easy to carry, and unbreakable is another asset many consumers look for.

In all of this, two important criteria from a health standpoint are often ignored. One is the inseparable relationship between the package and the contents. The movement or migration of packaging materials to food is regulated by the Code of Federal Regulations in a manner similar to food additives, but by no means does this assure the absence of nonfood ingredi-ents in our food supply. As a matter of fact, it gives widespread permission for this to occur.

Another matter of great concern is the impact all this has on the environ-ment. Better than 600 pounds of packaging are produced per person each year to wrap our food purchases. The trend toward smaller enclosures and the use of more nonbiodegradable plastics means increased garbage and pollution in the future.

A Review of Traditional Packaging Materials

No packaging, it seems, is perfect. While glass is the safest in terms of chemical migration, it is heavy and breakable.

In individual tests done on canned foods, research has shown that tin and iron show up in the contents. This is considerably increased when foods are placed in the refrigerator in opened cans. The problem can be minimized by applying an enamel or lacquer coating to the inside of the can to prevent corrosion.

Lead used to solder cans is another issue that has received widespread publicity. The toxic effects of this metal have long been recognized. Lead can cause anemia and it can damage the kidneys and the central nervous system in children, and the peripheral nervous system in adults. Public awareness about the potential dangers has put pressure on the food industry to produce seamless two-piece cans or cans with electrically welded side seams which do not require lead solder, and by the end of the twentieth century, if not sooner, lead-soldered cans will probably be extinct.

The switch from steel to aluminum cans that has been embraced by the beer and soft drink sector introduces a new concern. Aluminum is another toxic metal and we have found very little data on its transfer from container to contents.

While paper seems to be an innocuous material, to present an honest picture we must inform you that several of the chemicals used in the production of paper packaging are regulated because of known hazards they can impose on health. Included in this category are polychlorinated biphenyls (PCBs), several defoaming agents which contain a formaldehyde compound, and "slimicides" used to control slime on the paper surface. Furthermore, there are a multitude of other processing adjuncts which are used in or on the paper, on coating materials, and in the glues and adhesives used to construct packages. The list of possible packaging additives in the Code of Federal Regulations is so extensive you begin to wonder how many of these could possibly have been tested during the short time packaged foods have been sold in their current volume.

Plastics

Of all packaging materials currently in use, plastics present the most concern in terms of human exposure to carcinogens. Whether rigid or soft, they contain "loose" chemicals that can leach into foods. Foods with a high fat content appear to be most susceptible and the application of heat, as in boil- and bake-in bags, also seems to initiate higher levels of chemical migration. According to an official at the FDA, the agency "works from the assumption that something from the plastic will always leach into the food."

Certainly the history of plastic packaging materials has not been very reassuring. One of the earliest hazards which came to light in the 1970s was the presence of carcinogenic vinyl chloride polymers (like PVC) in many varieties of plastic from pliable film wraps, to semirigid and rigid bottles, blister packs, cap liners, and even tubing used in the transport of some foods. While restrictions have been placed on its use, vinyl chloride still remains in some, but not all, plastic wraps (including Saran and Reynold's Plastic Wrap), plastic containers used for cooking oils, and plasticized coatings for cans and paperboard. It is also still part of the barrier layer of many plastic laminates, but there it is generally separated from the food itself by another plastic which forms the actual food contact surface. Moreover, the FDA has proposed rules that would open the way for wider use of PVC in packaging food and beverages in the future.

After thirty years of use in plastic bottles, studies also revealed substantial migration of the suspected carcinogen acrylonitrile into beverages. It was banned for use in soft drink containers after considerable stalling, but retained with limits for use in many other plastic packages. Now new formulations are reinstating acrylonitrile in beverage containers.

Another common plastic component, which goes by the initials DEHP and is actually a plasticizer used to make PVC more flexible, has also been linked to cancer, but as of 1987 no action has been taken to prohibit it.

DEHP is commonly found in plastic wraps used for meat, cheese, fruits, and vegetables, as well as in bottle caps and food container liners.

A host of other chemicals, many that are prohibited as direct additives in food products, are employed in plastics. Most food processors who use these containers are probably not even aware of their presence.

Aseptic Packaging

Probably the most successful new package in the food industry today is the aseptic container, which has taken shape as the "soft box" now being used primarily for beverages. Often referred to as "Brik Pak," the trade name of the most popular model, these paperboard cartons are made of layers of paper, aluminum foil, and an inner coating of polyethylene plastic next to the product. A sterilizing agent, usually hydrogen peroxide, is used to flush each box. Japanese studies have implicated hydrogen peroxide in duodenal cancer, but most authorities now say the solution is removed by evaporation and the minute levels that remain are "well within established guidelines."

At the Second National Conference for Food Protection in 1984, sponsored by the American Public Health Association together with several professional associations, the experts had the following comments concerning aseptic processing:

- "Aseptic packaging involves high-temperature, short-time (HTST) sterilization of food. Under these conditions, new reactions can occur between food components *that may not have occurred under other heating conditions*." [emphasis ours]

- One question of particular importance was how this heat would affect the complex interaction between carbohydrates and proteins, a phenomenon that occurs with heat and is known as the "Maillard reaction." Extensive studies have shown that Maillard reactions lead to "a decrease in nutritive value of food, particularly of the protein" as well as "the possible formation of mutagens and other toxic compounds." It was their advice that new methods of applying heat to food, including HTST used for aseptic processing, should be carefully monitored for both a decline in nutritional value and any toxic effects.

Further issues relating directly to the packaging materials include:

- Migration of compounds in the protective films and adhesives.
- Degradation of film components with subsequent migration or volatization.
- Interaction of packaging compounds with food components to form new compounds.
- Changes in package compounds due to ionizing radiation or oven or microwave heating which may be applied in the future.
- Hazardous compounds from packaging extracts caused by microbes or enzymes in the contents.

Recycling

More than 50 billion pounds of garbage are produced yearly in this country and only a small percentage is recycled because there are few cost-effective systems in place.

At least some packaging materials eventually break down and return to the earth. This is not without its drawbacks, though, because residues of chemicals applied to some of the biodegradable papers, for example, pollute the ground, and burning of other substances can produce dangerous toxic emissions. But more serious are those wastes that continue to accumulate on this planet. According to the Environmental Action Foundation, discarded beverage containers represent 30 to 60 percent of American garbage build-up. They are "the most hazardous, most costly, and least biodegradable portion . . . An aluminum can takes five hundred years to biodegrade, a glass bottle one million years, and a plastic container will NEVER biodegrade naturally." Another organization, the Worldwatch Institute, has some equally fascinating figures. They claim that "throwing away any aluminum beverage container wastes as much energy as pouring out a can half-filled with gasoline."

The move toward plastics in packaging is most disturbing. While glass and metal cans are at least recycled in many places, there is little use for plastic discards. A pilot project at Rutgers University is working to develop technology to deal with plastic, experimenting with products ranging from filler for ski jackets to car bumpers.

CONSUMERS' CHOICE

As you can see, the consumer who puts absolute faith in our system of testing, monitoring, and regulating food manufacture and safety is living an illusion. As the commercial use of food additives, agricultural chemicals, and complex systems of technology and packaging expand yearly, the concerned individual must decide where his or her personal limits lie. One thing we can state for sure is that your body has no requirement for chemical additives. It is also virtually assured that you cannot avoid them totally. Therefore, those who wish to control their ingestion of food additives should take the following steps.

Become Informed

Reading food labels can help you avoid certain additives. Those that are required to be there, by law, are discussed in Chapter 2, "A Primer on Food Labels." Many others, however, are hidden from view, especially those that are present in other additives. Therefore, the fewer direct additives you consume, the less likelihood there is of receiving more indirectly. While an additive-free label does not guarantee purity, the presence of some chemicals almost always suggests more.

Choose Foods Appropriately to Minimize Additives

Once you are acquainted with the functions of various additives and their drawbacks you can decide which, if any, offer advantages to you personally. In addition to the references to certain additives scattered throughout the book, a brief guide to some of the most common additives can be found in the Appendix. If convenience, storage-time, and/or cosmetic appeal have a high priority in your life, you may find yourself tolerating some exceptions to our recommendations. On the other hand, while you may decide that you can't afford moldy bread and are therefore willing to accept calcium propionate added as a preservative, you can certainly exist quite comfortably without pink cereal and so may easily forgo artificially colored breakfast food. Keep in mind, however, that even seemingly harmless food additives usually give the manufacturer an excuse to use less care or less real food in formulating a product.

Eating Lower on the Food Chain to Minimize Pesticides

Because animals eat thousands of pounds of feed in their lifetime and accumulate some of the chemicals in this feed in their fat tissues, animal products—in particular, flesh and rendered fat—can add dramatically to your own chemical intake. One way to avoid this is to give preference to foods lower on the food chain such as beans, grains, nuts, seeds, fruit, and vegetables.

Pay Attention to Packaging

Purchasing food in bulk represents the best way to reduce contamination from packaging materials and is also most protective of the environment. (We are concerned, though, about the cleanliness and freshness of unpackaged foods; see Chapter 3.)

Glass is the preferred method of packaging food. Colored glass will help offset the degradation of nutrients by light. Although glass does not biodegrade rapidly, it can and should be reused or recycled whenever possible.

Lacquers and enamel-lined cans minimize the chances of metal migrating into foods. Lead solder has not yet been removed from all cans, but you can usually identify soldered cans by a short indentation or gully at the seam, sometimes surrounded by what looks like a dull gray stripe. Welded cans, which are lead-free, have no gully and there is a uniform smooth black line along the joint. Seamless cans, which are also lead-free, usually have a rounded edge at the bottom (and of course, no seam).

CANS AT A GLANCE

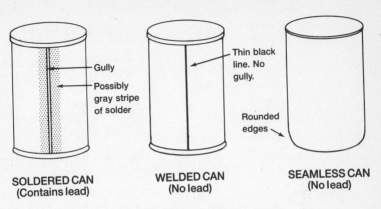

SOLDERED CAN
(Contains lead)

WELDED CAN
(No lead)

SEAMLESS CAN
(No lead)

SOLDERED AND LEAD-FREE CANS

Most metals are more reactive in the presence of oxygen so we also recommend that foods (or beverages) not be stored in open metal containers.

Due to all the substances that potentially come in contact with food from paper packaging, when we shop we try to keep in mind that the simpler the package (i.e., plain bags), the less manipulation it has been through.

Greatest attention should be paid to avoid packaging that puts food in direct contact with plastics (including all-plastic containers, plastic-lined containers, plastic film, retort pouches, and Brik-Paks). Not all of these materials are equally suspect; however, there is no easy way to distinguish one plastic product from another in packaging. Moreover, none of this plastic is biodegradable and there are still few recycling uses. When plastic is the only option, consider transferring the food to glass, cellophane, paper bags, and other inert alternatives after the package is opened.

Express Your Opinion

If the government and the food industry never hear from you, they have every reason to assume you are satisfied. Congressional representatives are in Washington to express the attitudes of their constituents; when food issues are being discussed, let them know how you feel. And let the appropriate agencies know too; you would be surprised to find how much influence your letters concerning specific issues have. Appropriate agencies and their addresses are listed in "A Guide to Federal Government Agencies" in the Appendix.

Chapter 2

A Primer on Food Labels

Title 21 of the Code of Federal Regulations contains the guidelines for what goes into standardized food products (listed on page 19 of Chapter 1), and also outlines the details that must be given on all food labels. Labeling is crucial because the formulas for manufactured foods are so complex it is almost impossible to determine what is being offered unless it is printed on the package.

HOW TO READ A FOOD LABEL

You will find the following information on the "principal display panel" (the part of the label most likely to be displayed), or on the "information panel" (directly to the right of the principal display panel). Every requirement must be satisfied in English, even on imported products.

1. The name of the product.

2. The variety, style, and packing medium in conjunction with the name. For instance, "sliced" beets, or peaches "packed in heavy syrup."

3. Where appropriate (as explained later), the word *imitation* followed by the name of the food being simulated.

4. For some foods, the percentage(s) of a characterizing ingredient(s), or information concerning the inclusion or exclusion of a specific ingredient(s), or the need to add an ingredient(s). For example, a beverage that appears to include juice, but actually does not, would have to state on the label that it contains no juice. A boxed mix used in the preparation of a stew to which you are expected to add the meat must state this.

5. The net quantity. This is the total amount, liquid included, in the container, expressed by weight, measure, numerical count, or some combination of these. If the food is a liquid, then fluid measure will be provided as fluid ounce, pint, quart, gallon, or some unit of these. If the food is solid, semisolid, or a mixture of solids and liquid, weight will be expressed in pounds or ounces. Some conscientious manufacturers also list "fill weight," which is the solid content before liquid is added. Dry measure such as bushel, peck, dry quart, or dry pint can be used for items customarily sold in this way, such as certain fresh fruits and vegetables.

6. The name and address of the manufacturer, packer, or distributor. The street address can be left out if it is listed in the phone directory. If the

How to Read a Food Label

PRINCIPAL DISPLAY PANEL   INFORMATION PANEL

manufacturer's name is not given, the connection of the person whose name does appear on the label must be described, as in "Distributed by," "Packed for," or some similar phrasing. If you have any questions, comments, or complaints about the product, this is where you are supposed to address your communications. (As we found out in researching our *Guide to Good Food*, however, this abbreviated address is usually not sufficient for letters to reach their destination.)

7. For all nonstandardized foods (those not described specifically by the Code of Federal Regulations), a list of ingredients in descending order of predominance by weight. That is, what there is the most of comes first, and the least of last.

Standardized foods need only list ingredients (also in descending order) if required by their specific standard of identity. These regulations are covered more explicitly within the individual food chapters.

8. For the most part, ingredients are listed by their specific name, except that:

■ "Spices" and "flavorings" may be declared in these general terms. (While the names of the individual seasoning ingredients may be essential to people with food allergies, as well as to those with taste preferences, industry contends that to give this information they would have to divulge trade secrets.)

■ The presence of coloring must generally be acknowledged, at least with the word "coloring." When an artificial coloring is used, it must bear the "artificial" qualifier. Only FD & C yellow #5 must be mentioned specifically. In the case of butter, ice cream, and certain cheeses, however, the law has been constructed so that even the FDA cannot mandate the declaration of added coloring (except yellow #5) on the label.

■ When used as an ingredient in another food product, a standardized food need only declare those ingredients required to be divulged by its own standard. (For example, a product which uses a colored cheese would not have to list the presence of color on the package.)

■ Dairy products need not specify if they are fresh, concentrated, reconstituted, or dried.

■ Butter oil and dehydrated butterfat may be declared as "butterfat."

■ Whether the egg component is fresh, frozen, or dried, it may be listed as "egg," "egg yolk," or "egg white."

■ Rather than specifying the enzymes used to culture a dairy product, the word "cultured" is sufficient.

9. The source of all fat incorporated into a product must be declared. This may be preceded by a collective reference, such as "vegetable shortening" or "blend of vegetable oils," as long as the common name of each fat follows. If any fat or oil is partially or completely hydrogenated, this too must be indicated.

If fat does not compose a predominant portion of the product, some flexibility is allowed so that the processor can use what is most available. In this case, the list of fats may be preceded by "contains one or more of the following," or the words "or" or "and/or" may be inserted into the list. This may result in the listing of ingredients that are not actually present, and while it is to the economic advantage of the manufacturer, it may narrow the choice of products for people who wish to avoid certain fats. (Manufacturers argue that printing different labels is expensive, which may be true. It seems to us that where alternate ingredients may be utilized, a single label which lists the possibilities and is then punched appropriately—the way a train ticket is—would satisfy everyone.)

10. Any chemical added to prevent or retard deterioration must reveal its function, such as "preservative," "to retard spoilage," "a mold inhibitor," etc. By way of explanation, the generic "leavening," "yeast nutrients," "dough conditioners," and "firming agents" may precede the list of ingredients used in this manner.

11. As with color, only the collective noun "flavor" need appear. Since there are about 1,700 permitted flavor ingredients, and the average number used in a single processed food is 40 (with as many as 125 in some), the

government feels it would be "impractical" to identify them on the label. However, there are some clues to help you determine the general direction the manufacturer has taken in flavoring the product:

■ "Natural flavor" refers to a spice, herb, fruit, vegetable, edible yeast, meat, fish, poultry, egg, or dairy product or some form of fermentation, distillate, isolate, extract, or concentrate of these items. If the source of flavoring is otherwise derived, it must be modified by the word "artificial."

■ If the flavor is a distinguishing component, a complex format for disclosing the characterizing flavors is required. Accordingly, if the flavor is natural, no qualifiers are needed, as in Blueberry Muffins. However, if the flavor is usually imparted by a food (like blueberries) but the manufacturer chooses to use a natural flavoring instead, the word "flavored" must be inserted in the name, as in "Blueberry-Flavored Muffins." The term "natural" may precede "blueberry" if the manufacturer desires, as in "Natural Blueberry-Flavored Muffins."

■ If any artificial flavor is used, the name must be accompanied by the words "artificial" or "artificially flavored." Using our initial example, this would give us "Artificially Flavored Blueberry Muffins" or "Blueberry Muffins with Artificial Flavor" (see label illustration, page 39).

12. When a product is labeled "smoked," the food may be processed with the actual smoke generated from burning hardwood, hardwood sawdust, or corn cob, or it may be exposed to liquid smoke that has been vaporized. If any other source of smoke flavoring is applied, it must be called "artificial."

Bulk Labeling

All these regulations may be circumvented if a food is not sold in packaged form. However, by law, if the food is received by the seller in bulk, the bulk display container or a placard nearby is supposed to reveal the same information.

Labeling Exemptions

"Incidental additives," as described in Chapter 1, need not be declared on the label. This gives manufacturers a way of hiding ingredients that are there in "insignificant" amounts or amounts they do not consider "functional." As a result, colorings, flavorings, and preservatives present in an ingredient, fumigants applied during storage, defoaming and clarifying agents used in production, anticaking agents and iodide in the salt, and much, much more are not revealed.

"Fanciful" Foods

In the past, any food not produced in a typical or traditional manner, or according to the Standard of Identity where one existed, had to be labeled "imitation." Many consumers perceive of foods labeled "imitation" as inferior and expect them to have artificial ingredients and additives. To avoid stigmatizing such foods, a descriptive name or a fanciful title may now be used, provided the item in question is "nutritionally equal to or better" than the original, and the new name is not misleading.

This concept of nutritional equivalence means that a specific list of nutrients are similarly present. Calories and fat, however, may differ from the original. Thus, rather than calling mayonnaise with less than the required amount of fat "imitation mayonnaise," it may be designated "reduced calorie mayonnaise." Similarly, a cheese which has had its fat content altered but is considered to resemble mozzarella in all other respects, may be called "pizza mate" rather than "imitation mozzarella." The law does not state that the nutrients in question must come from food, and thus fortification with synthetic nutrients is often used to help a product achieve this status.

The concept of nutritional equivalency has been justifiably criticized, for these judgments are based on limited scientific knowledge, use a very narrow group of nutrients as a criteria for nutritional worth, and ignore other unmeasured or as yet unknown factors that may represent great differences between a traditional food and one fabricated in its image.

Imitation Foods

If a food resembles another but does not measure up nutritionally, as explained above, it must be branded "imitation."

Irradiation

As discussed in Chapter 23 and mentioned in several of the specific food chapters, certain raw commodities have at this writing been approved for irradiation. When this is done it must be indicated to the consumer with the words "treated with radiation" or "treated with irradiation" and this symbol:

LOGO FOR IRRADIATED FOOD

Furthermore, the FDA is encouraging manufacturers to state the purpose and type of irradiation, for example "treated with X-rays [or gamma radiation or electron beams] to control spoilage [or extend shelf life or inhibit maturation]."

Since irradiation is such a new approach to food handling, the government has decided that this labeling format will be reviewed again after a trial period of use, so at this point the ultimate future of irradiation labeling remains uncertain. In any case, when an irradiated food is used in another product (for instance, the flour in baked goods, the fruit or vegetables in a frozen or canned product, the seasoning in a prepared food), it is unlikely this will ever show up on the label.

ELECTIVE INFORMATION

Some information that is offered voluntarily is still subject to federal regulation. Moreover, sometimes putting some facts on the label makes others mandatory.

Number of Servings

The number of servings contained in a package is voluntary in most cases. When this is communicated, the label must specify the quantity of each serving in terms of weight, measure, or numerical count. When nutrition labeling is present, serving information becomes mandatory.

Geographical Nomenclature

Reference to a country or other specific locale on the label must refer to the actual place of origin, except when a geographical term is part of the accepted product name, as in "Vienna sausage"; or, where the term identifies a particular style of product, as in "Canadian style bacon"; or, where the place is so fanciful or arbitrary that no confusion could exist, as in "Moon cheese."

On the other hand, the FDA does not require that imported foods show their place of origin. One reason consumers might want such details, however, is to help determine the possible presence of food chemicals permitted abroad that are restricted here.

Food Grading

The U.S. Department of Agriculture's system of food grading was designed as a tool for marketing at the wholesale level. It is voluntary and exists only for certain commodities. Today these grade names are being used increasingly at the retail level and appear as a confusing plethora of numbers, letters, and adjectives on the label.

Currently there is no uniformity to grading and USDA Grade AA, Grade A, No. 1, Prime, Extra Fancy, or Fancy may all represent top grade depending on where they appear. It is just as possible, though, that U.S. No. 1 will represent the lowest grade in the line. In any event, this is more a beauty contest than an actual statement of quality, grade usually being determined solely by appearance.

Quality Control

Unlike grading, inspection seals are useful to the consumer and reflect food safety. A USDA logo on the label is permitted only for products whose overall quality control program is approved by the agency. If the claim corresponds to a partial control program under USDA approval, the nature of the program must be shown—e.g., "Fat Content Controlled—USDA Approved." Quality control programs designed outside the USDA, according to a firm's own system, must indicate who is monitoring the system—e.g., "Quality Assured by Sam's Packing Company."

Nutrition Labeling

Nutrition labeling can be done voluntarily; it becomes mandatory, however, in three instances:

1. When a processor makes any nutritional or dietary claims on the label or in advertising (other than sodium-related or a simple percent of butterfat). Foods labeled "rich in calcium" or promoted as "high fiber" are typical examples.
2. When a food is fortified with a nutrient.
3. Infant, baby, and junior-type foods promoted for children under four.

Nutrition labeling is actually of greatest value to the consumer of processed foods, rather than to those who purchase wholefoods, and it can help pinpoint the subtle differences between similar items. Those concerned with monitoring certain nutrients, be it fat, carbohydrate, cholesterol, sodium, or the like, can also find assistance through nutrition labeling.

A LOOK AT A NUTRITION LABEL

When a label contains nutrition information, it must adhere to a set format (see illustration page 45). It begins with serving (or portion) size, followed by servings per container, and then for each serving, the calories, protein, carbohydrate, and fat in grams, the sodium in milligrams, plus the percentage of the U.S. Recommended Dietary Allowances (U.S. RDAs) for protein, vitamin A, vitamin C (ascorbic acid), thiamin (vitamin B_1), riboflavin (vitamin B_2), niacin, calcium, and iron. (The U.S. RDA is based on a set of reference figures that are deemed sufficient to keep adults in good health when consumed on a daily basis.)

Optional information includes the potassium content in milligrams, and the percent U.S. RDA for vitamin D, vitamin E, vitamin B_6, folic acid (folacin), vitamin B_{12}, phosphorus, iodine, magnesium, zinc, copper, biotin, and pantothenic acid. Any references to fatty acid composition (saturated, unsaturated) and cholesterol must comply with the layout described on page 46.

When a product is meant to be further prepared at home (as a cake mix) or eaten in conjunction with another food (as ready-to-eat cereal), a second set of figures can be presented to show the nutrient content after such preparation (according to package directions).

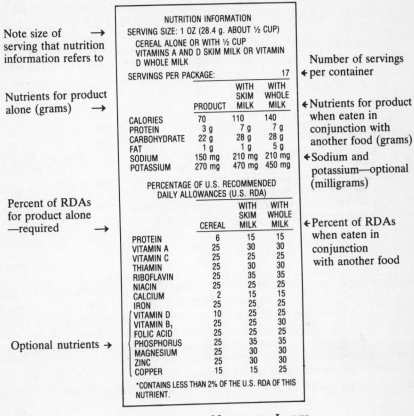

Note size of →
serving that nutrition
information refers to

Nutrients for product
alone (grams) →

Percent of RDAs
for product alone
—required →

Optional nutrients →

Number of servings
← per container

← Nutrients for product
when eaten in
conjunction with
another food (grams)

← Sodium and
potassium—optional
(milligrams)

← Percent of RDAs
when eaten in
conjunction
with another food

NUTRITION INFORMATION
SERVING SIZE: 1 OZ (28.4 g. ABOUT ½ CUP)
CEREAL ALONE OR WITH ½ CUP
VITAMINS A AND D SKIM MILK OR VITAMIN
D WHOLE MILK

SERVINGS PER PACKAGE: 17

	PRODUCT	WITH SKIM MILK	WITH WHOLE MILK
CALORIES	70	110	140
PROTEIN	3 g	7 g	7 g
CARBOHYDRATE	22 g	28 g	28 g
FAT	1 g	1 g	5 g
SODIUM	150 mg	210 mg	210 mg
POTASSIUM	270 mg	470 mg	450 mg

PERCENTAGE OF U.S. RECOMMENDED
DAILY ALLOWANCES (U.S. RDA)

	CEREAL	WITH SKIM MILK	WITH WHOLE MILK
PROTEIN	6	15	15
VITAMIN A	25	30	30
VITAMIN C	25	25	25
THIAMIN	25	30	30
RIBOFLAVIN	25	35	35
NIACIN	25	25	25
CALCIUM	2	15	15
IRON	25	25	25
VITAMIN D	10	25	25
VITAMIN B$_1$	25	25	30
FOLIC ACID	25	25	25
PHOSPHORUS	25	35	35
MAGNESIUM	25	30	30
ZINC	25	30	30
COPPER	15	15	25

*CONTAINS LESS THAN 2% OF THE U.S. RDA OF THIS
NUTRIENT.

How to Read a Nutrition Label

THE DRAWBACKS TO NUTRITION LABELING

While the data on a nutrition label is taken quite literally by most label readers, in actuality the values offered are only an approximation since the precise level of many nutrients is affected by species, growing conditions, handling, storage, and preparation. That is to say, "every apple is different."

Unfortunately, it is easy to get the impression from nutrition labeling that a refined product is comparable to a wholefood since only certain select nutrients are considered. The reality is that the wholefood may contribute important trace minerals and fiber that are not enumerated in nutrition labeling. In fact, the current format gives fake foods a competitive edge over real foods if they contain large amounts of added fortification.

Sodium Disclosures

Any reference made to salt or sodium on the label mandates quantitive sodium labeling, but unlike other nutritional claims does not need to be accompanied by complete nutrition labeling.

There is also a precise meaning to the terms that manufacturers may use when making a sodium claim:

- "Low sodium" contains 140 milligrams of sodium or less per serving.
- "Very low sodium" contains 35 milligrams of sodium or less per serving.
- "Sodium-" *or* "salt-free" contains less than 5 milligrams of sodium per serving.
- "Unsalted" or "no salt added" means processed without the salt normally added to such products. This does not necessarily mean sodium-free since other sodium-based compounds may be added.
- "Reduced sodium" contains 75 percent less sodium than in a regular version of the same product or a competitor's product.

Fat Facts

A food label may voluntarily include specific information on fatty acid composition only if it contains more than 10 percent fat and not less than 2 grams of fat per average serving. Any food making a statement about polyunsaturated and saturated fats must provide complete nutrition labeling, plus "percent of calories from fat," and, to the nearest gram per serving, the amount of fatty acids in each of these categories.

The nutrition information below is taken from the label of a safflower oil that makes the claim "High in Polyunsaturates." The paragraph marked

---

Nutrition Information per Portion

portion size ....1 tbsp (14 g)	% of calories from fat 100
portions per bottle 64	polyunsaturated, g* 11
calories 120	saturated, g* 1
protein, g 6	cholesterol, mg* 0
carbohydrate, g 0	sodium, mg 0
fat, g 14	potassium 0

*Information on fat and cholesterol is provided for individuals who on the advice of physicians are modifying their intake of fat and cholesterol.

NUTRITION LABEL FOR A PRODUCT
MAKING A SPECIFIC REFERENCE TO FAT COMPOSITION

by the asterisk is also required by law when claims about fat or cholesterol are made.

If there is any statement regarding cholesterol (this is voluntary), complete nutrition labeling must accompany it. Cholesterol content will be given per serving and per 100 grams of food.

These are the *proposed* guidelines for manufacturers when making cholesterol claims:

- "Cholesterol free" contains less than 2 milligrams of cholesterol per serving.
- "Low cholesterol" contains less than 20 milligrams per serving.
- "Cholesterol reduced" products are reformulated or processed to reduce cholesterol by at least 75 percent. (This statement must compare the new product with the old, for example "cholesterol reduced from 120 milligrams to 30 milligrams per serving.")

Products with significantly less cholesterol than before, but not 75 percent less, can still make comparative claims on the label, such as "This cake contains 35 percent less cholesterol than our regular cake; cholesterol lowered from 70 milligrams to 45 milligrams per serving."

Be aware that many fats and oils that do not contain any cholesterol may still increase cholesterol in the body, particularly saturated oils like palm and coconut. The USDA rules in regard to red meat and poultry products require that in order to bear a percent fat-free statement—e.g., "95 percent fat free"—a complementary statement of fat content must be included—e.g., "5 percent fat." This is to avoid consumer confusion which might lead some to interpret "95 percent fat free" to mean 95 percent of the fat has been removed. (Other "low fat" claims are discussed in Chapter 17.)

Foods for Weight Control

Foods labeled "low calorie" must contain a maximum of 40 calories per serving *and* 0.4 calories per gram. Foods that are naturally low in calories are not allowed to call themselves "low calorie," for this might suggest that they are lower in calories than other foods in the same class. For example, since all mushrooms are low in calories, the label "low calorie mushrooms" would be misleading. A mushroom label could, however, read "mushrooms, a low calorie food," without violating the law.

A "reduced calorie" food must be at least one third lower in calories than a similar food in which the calories have not been reduced *and* it must not be nutritionally inferior to the unmodified version (based on the same criteria used for imitation foods).

If the term "diet" or "dietetic" appears with no further qualification, it meets the standards of low calorie or reduced calorie products. Be sure to read the label carefully for other explanations, however, such as "for diabetics," or "for low sodium" or "modified fat" diets.

"Sugar free" indicates no nutritive carbohydrate sweetener has been added, including sucrose, malt, fructose, honey, molasses, maple syrup, concentrated fruit juice, etc. "No sugar added," however, is not federally regulated and usually refers only to the absence of refined sucrose. If a food is labeled "sugar free" or "sugarless" but is neither low calorie nor reduced calorie, the label is supposed to make this clear, perhaps with a statement such as "not a reduced calorie food," or "intended to reduce tooth decay."

The words "light" and "lite" are uncontrolled (as of 1987) in all but meat and poultry products. (Legislation has been proposed which may change this in the future.) While some companies use them to describe low calorie foods, they are just as likely to coincide with reductions in salt, sugar, breading, alcohol or fat, an increase in water, or simply to refer to the color or texture of the food.

FOOD FORTIFICATION

Foods whose labels show added nutrients are classified as "fortified." When fortification restores nutrients lost in processing and is in accordance with certain specifications, such foods are called "enriched," even when the original, unrefined product may have had a higher overall nutrient profile (see Chapter 5).

Fortification may be employed to address an identified public health need, such as adding iodine to salt to prevent goiter or vitamin D to milk to prevent rickets. Or, it may be used to bolster processed foods.

Where fortification occurs, you will not find out what "incidental additives" are included along with the nutrients in the form of carriers and preservatives.

Food Is More Than a List of Nutrients

There is concern that consumer reliance on fortification, which is usually reserved for a few select nutrients, could lead to otherwise deficient diets since fortification can obscure the total nutritional value of foods and often seduces consumers away from less processed natural foods. It is generally accepted that in addition to a prescribed amount of protein, fat, carbohydrate, and some isolated vitamins and minerals, other "accessory substances" within food (such as enzymes) are needed to keep people healthy. This issue of the "unknown" has been raised repeatedly. As early as 1907, Sir Frederick Gowland Hopkins (who was to receive a Nobel prize in 1929) found that rats failed to grow on a diet of artificial milk, but adding a small amount of cow's milk to their ration caused them to thrive. More recently, noted biochemist Dr. Roger Williams has observed that animals breed more successfully when they consume fresh vegetables as opposed to nutritional supplements. The reason—food is more than a simple list of nutrients.

In addition to giving the public a vastly oversimplified viewpoint of the components of food, fortification can lead to nutritional imbalances due to the interactive effects of certain nutrients. That is, an increased intake of one nutrient through fortification can bring about an increased need for another. If the second nutrient is not included in fortified foods and is not readily available naturally in other foods in significant quantity to meet these elevated demands, unhealthy imbalances can occur. Finally, the person who routinely consumes fortified foods may be getting an excessive amount of many vitamins and minerals. This has been recognized as a problem with fat-soluble nutrients and scientists now suspect that even water-soluble nutrients in excess are not benign.

FOOD DATING CODES

Even the notorious Jack Benny couldn't conceal his true age as effectively as many prepared foods do. Food dating is not regulated by the federal government; however, some states and localities have their own requirements for certain products (e.g., milk). Traditionally, most dates on food packages have been written in code for use by industry. Many companies do voluntarily offer dating information to the consumer, however.

Open Dating

When the date is provided for consumers, it can mean one of four different things.

Pack date is the day the product was manufactured, processed, or packaged. It tells how old the product is. A pack date is usually found on packaged foods with a long shelf-life.

Pull or **sell date** is the last day the product should be sold, assuming it has been handled properly. It allows time for home consumption, but how much time is not revealed. Cold cuts, dairy products, and bakery goods most commonly use pull or sell date.

Expiration date is the last day the food should be eaten. Infant formula and yeast are examples of foods that carry expiration dates.

Freshness date or **use-before date** is the time in which the product remains at highest quality. Sometimes foods are sold at a reduced price for a few days after this.

Blind Dates

While there is no single format used in commercial manufacturing codes, there is almost always a hidden indication of date of processing or packaging.

The numbers can be as straightforward as 62685 representing June 26, 1985, but it is just as likely that the first number indicates the year, so that 5355 could be interpreted as the 355th day of 1985 (or December 20, 1985). Or, the first two digits could mean the week of manufacture and the last the year. For example, 016 is deciphered as the first week of 1986, or January

1–7, 1986. Unfortunately, other numbers may be inserted in the code to represent the product, shift, plant, hour, etc.

If you really want to know about a particular product, check with the store manager or write to the manufacturer.

AMBIGUOUS LANGUAGE

Some of the descriptions on the label that are totally unregulated may hold quite different meanings for the manufacturer and the consumer. Until certain terms are clarified, a wise shopper should look behind these statements in order to steer clear of unscrupulous merchandisers.

Natural

A 1984 government survey found that 63 percent of those polled believed "natural" foods were more nutritious and 47 percent were willing to pay a 10 percent premium for these foods. If some uniform meaning were ascribed to the word "natural," these attitudes might be justified. As it stands, though, "natural" has not been given an official government definition, except for meat.

Indeed, "natural" cheeses contain artificial coloring and preservatives; "natural" ice creams are not only loaded with sugar but may include such untraditional ingredients as vegetable gum and mono- and diglycerides; "natural" breads are often made of refined white flour and are fortified with synthetic nutrients; some "natural" cereals are more highly sweetened than processed varieties; foods that are "naturally flavored" may also contain artificial flavoring, preservatives, thickeners, and colorants. Even margarine, a totally fabricated product, has been described as "natural" by some manufacturers.

Some "natural food" companies also include white flour, hydrogenated shortening, hydrolyzed vegetable protein, soy protein isolates, vegetable gums, and refined sweeteners in their products.

In all fairness to the consumer, a "natural product" should have all ingredients fully identified, including minor ingredients within ingredients. In addition, the condition of each ingredient should be described: whether it has been bleached, dehydrated or dried, hydrogenated, defatted (using a solvent), rolled, ground, etc. Processing should be limited to what could be done in a typical, well-equipped home kitchen.

NATURAL MEAT

The USDA does restrict use of the term "natural" for meat and poultry to those that "do not contain any artificial flavor or flavoring, coloring ingredient or chemical preservative, or any other artificial or synthetic ingredient, and the product and its ingredients are not more than minimally processed." If the meat or poultry product contains all natural ingredients, but they are not normal constituents of the product in question—e.g., beet powder used to color gravy—the statement "all natural ingredients" must be used in lieu of "all natural." Even this is not totally reliable, because sugar, large amounts of salt, hydrogenated fats, textured vegetable protein, and similarly highly processed ingredients do appear in some products the USDA allows the manufacturer to call "natural."

Organic

"Organic" is no less troubling than "natural." Technically, "organic" means "chemical compounds containing carbon." Many agricultural chemicals are carbon-based and could meet this definition. However, the term as popularized by J.I. Rodale is intended to mean something else.

Most authorities agree that "organically grown" food means food that has been raised without pesticides, synthetic fertilizers, or other related chemicals, in soil that is nourished only with the addition of live matter and mineral fertilizers. While the federal government places no such limits on the term "organic," some state governments do. As of 1986, California, Oregon, Maine, Washington, Minnesota, Massachussetts, Nebraska, and Montana had established "organic" laws.

"Organically processed" food, in addition to being organically grown, should not be treated with any artificial or synthetic additives in its preparation.

When "organic" is applied to animal-derived foods it means that the feed and water were free of pesticides and chemical contaminants, that there has been no routine use of growth stimulants, hormones, or other drugs, and that the latter were used only as required for treatment of an illness and then within a restricted time from slaughter or milking. The USDA does not permit the word "organic" on meat and poultry labels, but foods meeting these specifications may be labeled "naturally grown."

Organic farm organizations, processors, and distributors have joined together in a number of trade organizations. These groups run certification programs which include annual farm visits, sworn affidavits, and detailed questionnaires as to growing, harvesting, and storage practices. These are some of the logos of certified organic products:

ORGANIC CERTIFICATION

Some farmers adhere to organic principles and techniques called "biodynamics." Products grown or raised in this manner can be certified by the Demeter Association and will bear this logo:

BIODYNAMIC CERTIFICATION

Other reliable proof may be a notarized statement, backed up possibly by the retailers' own investigation of the distributor and/or grower. Furthermore, the store should have documentation posted.

Food Frivolity, or Is It Fraud

Many of the descriptive adjectives on labels contribute to confusion rather than consumer education. For example:

■ A brief reference to certain ingredients, additives, or nutrients some place other than the complete ingredient list often leads consumers to make other assumptions about a product. For example, "with honey" or "yogurt-coated" is used to make a product seem wholesome, even when these foods may only be minor constituents in products otherwise compromised by undesirable ingredients. Similarly, "no preservatives," "no salt," "no cholesterol," "no sugar," "no calories," "no artificial coloring or flavoring" are all negative references, not statements of what a food offers. They are designed to give you the idea that the entire contents are "natural," or that *this particular brand* has no preservatives, cholesterol, etc., and the competitor does, even though they may really only be proclaiming the absence of things that were never there in the first place. ("Contains no cholesterol" on a jar of vegetable oil might create the impression that other vegetable oils contain cholesterol, but in truth all nonanimal foods are cholesterol free. A pasta that informs "no color added" on the label does not mention that all pasta, by law, is free of coloring.)

■ Sometimes the product name itself is deceptive. You would expect "Honey Wheat English Muffins" to contain prominent amounts of both honey and whole wheat. In the leading national brand, however, the honey is joined by corn syrup and the whole wheat is present in lesser amounts than refined flour. And who would expect the primary ingredient in "Lemon and Pepper Seasoning" to be salt?

■ "Real," "pure," and "100%" are words that may stimulate false security. How pure is "pure juice" to which sweetening has been added, or "pure vegetable shortening" which is hydrogenated, colored, and preserved? Similarly, "100% corn oil" may refer to the absence of other oils, but not to a lack of processing or preservatives.

■ You may also begin to wonder about the term "fresh" when it is applied to vacuum-packed salad with a two-month shelf-life, aseptically boxed milk, and similar items whose life span has been stretched scientifically beyond normal limits.

■ When the label or advertisement tells you "Brand X tastes *like* fresh peanut butter," don't assume that it includes any peanut butter (or whatever else it tastes "like").

■ Many foods are described as "golden," "rich," "whipped," or some other taste-tempting adjective. The manufacturer is counting on you to assume that it's golden because they use eggs, or rich because they use butter, or that the whip comes from cream.

■ Watch out for foods that are "buttery," "chocolatey," "fruity," or any other "y." According to the dictionary, the suffix *y* is used to indicate "somewhat like, suggesting." This means the flavor may be somewhat like butter, but the food need not actually contain any butter.

■ Cream is spelled CREAM, not CREME, if it's the real thing. "Creme" is usually made from corn syrup, gelatin, hydrogenated shortening, milk derivatives, mono- and diglycerides, artificial flavoring, and such. This "creme" has no less fat than "cream" does.

■As explained previously, the word "flavor" placed after a specific flavor source means that the flavor, not the source, was added. Thus, "cherry flavor" tells you the product has the flavor of cherries (synthetic or real), not that it contains cherries.

Chapter 3

To Market, To Market

The best way for you to receive the most from your food dollar is to learn how to "market." We use this term in the traditional sense of taking advantage of the best source for each food.

Not so long ago it was customary to patronize the local butcher, baker, greengrocer, and grocery store. Then the supermarket came along and these specialty shops nearly became extinct. Within a single generation, though, customers had a sense that something was missing. Slowly, natural food stores, fish markets, cheese shops, and such began to resurface; some all-purpose supermarkets, feeling the pressure, turned to mini-markets within the larger unit. Consequently, today the strategy of individualized "marketing" has been revived and smart consumers utilize the natural food store, supermarket, specialty shops, coop, farmers' market, and even mail-order sources to get what they want.

NATURAL FOOD STORES

The natural food store has been the conscience of America's food supply. Without the concern of the people who established these alternative markets, real food would probably only be a memory today.

The most important aspect of the natural food store is quality. Unless the store sells only wholefoods, it is no different than any other grocery store. We say this because there are those within the industry who think it is all right to carry marginal products (incorporating refined flours, sugar, caffeine, and hydrogenated oils), as long as the ingredients are labeled. We disagree. If people want to worry about ingredients they can shop at a supermarket; when we go to the natural food store, the joy is not having to scrutinize labels.

Another wonderful aspect of natural food stores is that they are generally small businesses which can give personal attention. This feature enables them to respond to requests for specialized items.

The Organic Option

If you are interested in buying organically grown foods, the natural food store presents the best chance of finding them. The food staples that are most available with an organic option are grains and grain-based products, including flour, pasta, hot and cold cereals, and mixes and baked goods which incorporate organic grains. Organic beans, nuts, and dried fruits are also possible, but are not as widely available. A few companies produce nut butters from organically grown nuts and organic tofu is quite common. There are also several lines of prepared wholefoods that utilize at least some organic ingredients in the recipe.

"Natural" meat raised without drugs, and organic produce are also available in many natural food stores. (See page 51 for information on organic certification.)

Pricing

Popular items at the natural food store are becoming competitive price-wise, but you may pay a premium in some cases for what are still, essentially, specialty foods of the highest order. This is particularly true if they are certified organic. The price of natural foods reflects several factors: First, they generally come from small family operations. Second, they rarely benefit from government subsidies. Third, the distribution system is smaller, which increases prices.

However, the true cost of America's "cheap food policy" as reflected at the supermarket is not only what you pay at the store but is revealed in the expense of health care, environmental clean-up, loss of topsoil, the disappearance of family farms, and the erosion of rural life.

DIRECT FARMER-TO-CONSUMER MARKETING

One of the best ways for consumers to get high-quality foodstuffs *and* support local food producers is to make use of the many direct outlets.

Farmers' Markets

Probably the oldest form of direct marketing still in operation are farmers' markets. Here the consumer can get fresh, sometimes organic produce at good prices and the farmer has the opportunity to earn more money by not having to share the profits with the middlemen.

You can find the location of farmers' markets in your area from the state government or from the county cooperative extension office, found in the phone directory under "[county name] cooperative extension."

Greenmarkets

Greenmarkets are the city's answer to farmers' markets. With this wonderful innovation, run by several city and state governments, a site is designated and rural growers truck in their produce on specified days. Check with your local government for locations.

You Pick It

Pick-your-own farms provide the opportunity to get some exercise while you stock up on inexpensive, seasonal food. The local cooperative extension office should be able to supply a list of farms that make this option available.

WHOLESALE

Anybody can purchase food wholesale and, in fact, this is what you are really doing when you belong to a coop. To buy from the source or a wholesale distributor you usually must order in case lots and sometimes meet a minimum dollar requirement.

Central Produce Markets

Most large cities have central markets for produce, meat, and fish where wholesalers and retailers do their buying. You'll have to arrive early in the morning and compete with commercial buyers, but in return you will get the freshest food at the best prices. To succeed at these markets it is a good idea to cultivate one or two accommodating suppliers. Trying to bargain with a different seller each time you go may not result in the best buys; steady customers are generally awarded preferential treatment.

Food Coops

There were an estimated 6,000 to 7,000 food coops in the United States in 1985. All you need to start a food coop is a few people who want to buy together and share the work (and the savings). For information on how to set up a food coop, contact the National Cooperative Business Association, P.O. Box 8293, Dept. GGF, Ann Arbor, Michigan 48107, or *Cooperative Grocer* magazine, 5 Cameron Ave., Dept. GGF, Cambridge, Massachusetts 02140.

SUPERMARKETS

The supermarket, which first appeared in the late 1930s, changed the way Americans eat, because it changed the way we shop. Consumers switched from loyalty to a retailer to brand loyalty, and mass merchandising created a demand for unnecessary and previously unimagined foods. For some people the number of choices in the supermarket is downright dizzying. Significantly, most of the 20,000 items stacked on the shelves are merely variations of 200 or so basic ingredients. There is no question that you could ignore 95 percent of what is displayed and still enjoy a commendable diet.

Nevertheless, if you shop conscientiously, you can survive fairly well in most supermarkets today. You can find many exemplary natural cheeses, yogurt, whole grain crackers and cereals, juices, bottled water and seltzer, dried beans, grains, flour, seasonings, natural peanut butter, oil, and more. A good strategy may be to supplement these foods with selections from other sources.

BULK FOODS

One of the big surprises in retailing has been the success of bulk foods within supermarkets, as well as the success of stores that deal exclusively in bulk food. In a sense, it is a reversion to the "cracker barrel" selling approach supermarkets were designed to put an end to.

Although the prices of bulk foods should be lower, to reflect less packaging and lower advertising costs, this is not always so.

Consumers should be concerned both with the labeling of bulk foods and with sanitation. According to the FDA, all bulk containers should have complete ingredient labeling. We advise against buying any item in bulk, other than fresh produce, dried beans, grains, nuts, herbs and spices, and other single-ingredient products, unless they are fully labeled.

Shop only where foods are protected from contamination, both while on display and during customer self-service. According to FDA guidelines, all containers must be off the floor and covered; in self-service situations they must close automatically. Manual dispensing utensils such as tongs and scoops should be tethered or there should be a "holster" to house them. A supply of bags, cups, etc., must be on hand, as well as a marking pen. We are sorry to report that many stores we have visited seem to be as lax about these sanitary precautions as they are about labeling.

The FDA stresses, and we agree, that the consumer's responsibility is equal to the store's in maintaining cleanliness. So keep children away from the bins and keep your hands out. If samples may be tasted, make sure you pick them up with a utensil.

Do not be deceived into thinking that just because food is sold in bulk it is healthier or better quality. It can be better or worse, but unless it's properly identified, don't be fooled by the "old-time" look.

SPECIALTY STORES

Cheese shops, bakeries, fish stores, meat markets, and similar single-category food stores are good places to find fresh products, but keep in mind their offerings may not necessarily be superior in terms of ingredients.

"GOURMET" FOODS

What generally distinguishes "gourmet" foods is the fact that they are uncommon (and thus costly). Often they are imported or locally made. None of this precludes processing or food additives or mandates that they be nourishing.

Many people, however, associate gourmet food with natural, whole, or even organic food. While in some cases they may be the same, it is just as likely that they are not. With the proliferation of gourmet food shops and similarly geared areas in supermarkets and natural food stores, the wholefoods consumer may want to look closely at what is being presented. Sometimes that's not easy since many imported packaged foods, in violation of the law, do not have complete ingredient labeling or addresses. In addition, state law may not require locally prepared or packaged goods to be labeled.

Most disturbing is the fact that with imported foods you actually stand a chance that inside the fancy package there are residues of pesticides that have been banned in the United States, but are used abroad (see "The Circle of Poison," page 29).

CONVENIENCE STORES

In a pinch you might find nuts, dried fruit, dairy products, and juice in a convenience store. These small "gas 'n' go" type markets only stock a limited selection of mostly big brand-name processed foods, but do often stay open after the supermarkets close. Note, however, a study done in the Boston area in 1983 by the *Griffin Report,* a food marketing trade magazine, reported these stores to be 46 percent more expensive than supermarkets. (They are often inexpensive places to buy gas, though.)

FOOD BY MAIL

For some people the greatest deterrent to eating well is not the cooking or clean-up, but the shopping. This is quite understandable given the distance you sometimes have to travel to find good food, or the time it takes to wend your way through the aisles to find it amid the undesirable offerings and then stand in line to pay.

It is possible to enjoy an exemplary diet and never leave home. The following companies sell high-quality organic food by mail. All have a catalog or price list available, often accompanied by an in-depth discussion of each item. (This is very valuable since when you buy by mail you do not have the opportunity to read the label and ferret out products with unwanted ingredients.) Prices tend to be competitive with comparable foods sold at the store, although the added shipping can mean ultimately higher costs. Note that we are not talking about the mail-order companies that market expensive so-called gourmet food gifts; however, sending a present from one of the companies listed here is a wonderful way to introduce friends and family to the possibilities of real food.

General Foods

These companies carry a complete line of organic and wholefoods staples, as well as prepared items which may include cheese, meat, baked goods, and more.

Deer Valley Farm, Dept. GGF
R.D. 1
Guilford, NY 13780

Jaffe Bros.
P.O. Box 636, Dept. GGF
Valley Center, CA 92082

Little Bear Trading Co.
226 E. Second Street, Dept. GGF
Winona, MN 55987

Shiloh Farms
P.O. Box 97, Dept. GGF
Sulphur Springs, AR 72768

Walnut Acres
Dept. GGF
Penns Creek, PA 17862

Produce

Organic fruits and vegetables via UPS.

Colvada Date Company
P.O. Box 908, Dept. GGF
51-392 Highway 86
Coachella, CA 92236

Smile Herb
P.O. Box 989, Dept. GGF
4908 Berwin Road
College Park, MD 20740

Organic fruits and vegetables via UPS. *(continued)*

Timber Crest Farms
4791 Dry Creek Road, Dept. GGF
Heraldsburg, CA 95448

Meat

Naturally raised meat and wild game.

Butterfield Buffalo Ranch
Route 3, Dept. GGF
Belat, KS 67420

Carrington Ward Ranch
7320 Country Road 53, Dept. GGF
Center, CO 81125

Czimer Foods
Route 7, Box 285, Dept. GGF
Lockport, IL 60441

Great Western Buffalo Trading
   Company
1807 Highway 41 South, Dept. GGF
Twin Bridges, MT 59754

Menuchah Farms Smoke House
Route 212, Dept. GGF
Salem, NY 12865

Natural Beef Farms
4399-A Henninger Court, Dept. GGF
Chantilly, VA 22021

Pine Ridge Farms
P.O. Box 98, Dept. GGF
Subiaco, AR 72865

Summerfield Farm
Route 1, Box 43, Dept. GGF
Boyce, VA 22620

Teel Mountain Farm
Dept. GGF
Standardsville, VA 22973

Wilderness Gourmet
P.O. Box 3257, Dept. GGF
Ann Arbor, MI 48106

Cheese

Cheese made from chemical-free animals.

Eiler's Cheese Market
R. 2, Dept. GGF
De Pere, WI 54115

Hawthorne Valley Farm
Box 225 A, R.D. 2, Dept. GGF
Ghent, NY 12075

Bread

Superb breads made only from organic flours.

Baldwin Hill Bakery
Baldwin Hill Road, Dept. GGF
Phillipston, MA 01331

Bread Alone
Route 28, Dept. GGF
Boiceville, NY 12412

Grain

Hand-picked rice grown by native American Indians.

Northern Lake Wild Rice Company
P.O. Box 28, Dept. GGF
Cass Lake, MN 56633

Part II

IN
THE
MARKET

Chapter 4

The Grain Silo

One fortunate consequence of the popular interest in improving personal nutrition, and hence physical well-being, is a renewed interest in the use of grains. Grains, of course, constitute the essential ingredient in flour, hot and ready-to-eat cereals, pasta, crackers, breadstuffs, cookies, cakes, and pastries. What might be less apparent is that grains are also a primary source of nourishment for the animals that provide us with meat, eggs, and dairy products.

THE GOOD NEWS ABOUT WHOLE GRAINS

The key words that came to the nutritional forefront in the 1980s all apply to whole grains: high fiber, complex carbohydrates, low fat, low sodium. By now, most people have heard of dietary fiber, a noncaloric carbohydrate in foods that appears to be endowed with many health-giving properties. This fiber is available in several forms, among them bran. The bran in whole grains is acclaimed primarily for its ability to promote speedy transit of food wastes through the bowel. The bran in oats has been praised for its cholesterol-lowering capability, and wheat bran, too, may mitigate the effects of dietary fats. In addition, the fiber in whole grains helps maintain even blood sugar levels.

Although grains are often not appreciated for the nourishment they provide, whole grains offer an economical source of protein that can be maximized by serving them with beans, or small amounts of animal protein in the form of meat, cheese, milk, or eggs. They also contain significant quantities of B vitamins, vitamin E, magnesium, copper, zinc, and other trace minerals.

Those who are weight conscious should be aware that many popular weight-control books have created the false impression that carbohydrates are fattening. The fact is, on an equal weight basis carbohydrates and proteins have the same number of calories, while fat has more than twice this amount. Since grains are almost pure carbohydrate, they actually furnish fewer calories than an equal weight of the meat, dairy products, eggs, and other fatty animal foods we regard as protein sources. Moreover, when unrefined carbohydrates are eaten, their fibrous nature creates a feeling of fullness, encouraging us to stop eating sooner.

WHOLE GRAIN OPTIONS

Rice

Most people who eat white bread are aware of the existence of whole wheat breads and know that these breads are more healthful, but many do not know that the same parallel exists with rice. For rice to be edible, only the indigestible hull that surrounds it need be removed. This rice is called "brown" or "natural" rice.

Despite its name, once brown rice is cooked, the color is only slightly different from that of "white" rice, and is actually a much more appealing creamy hue. The difference lies in the nutritional value and in the taste. The bran and germ that remain contain the highest quality protein, along with fiber, calcium, phosphorus, iron, vitamin E, and most of the B vitamins. Moreover, brown rice has a nutty flavor; the only taste white rice has comes from added seasonings or gravy. The method of cooking for brown rice is identical to that for white rice, except that brown rice requires 45 to 50 minutes to cook.

Changing from white to brown rice is one of the simplest and most satisfying improvements you can make in your diet. For convenience, we always cook up a large quantity at one time so that we have enough to serve at several different meals during the week.

VARIETIES OF BROWN RICE

Brown rice is available in long-, medium-, and short-grain varieties. The size has no significant bearing on nutrition, only on the consistency after cooking. The longer the grains the more separate and fluffy they will be; shorter grains cook up tender and moist and tend to cling together (ideal for croquettes, puddings, and similar dishes).

Basmati rice is a variety of long-grain rice that is prized for its alluring aroma and nutlike taste. It is popular with Indian cooks, but is suitable to other cuisines as well. Although the typical refined basmati rice is no more nutritious than other forms of milled white rice, a brown basmati rice has been introduced recently and its taste is superb.

Pecan rice and *texmati rice,* hybrids of basmati, are available in the natural whole-grain form and have a nutty flavor similar to wild rice.

Wehani is another specialty whole-grain rice bred in California from basmati seeds. It has a lighter texture than regular brown rice and is similar to cracked wheat when cooked.

Sweet brown rice is a short, sticky variety with a naturally sweet flavor that is prized for desserts and traditional Oriental pastries.

Instant brown rice is made quick-cooking by partially cooking the grain and then freeze-drying, puffing, rolling, or microwaving it to speed the absorption of water later on. There are several brands of quick-cooking brown rice which, according to industry figures, retain all the wholesomeness and cook up in a mere 10 to 15 minutes. Although we find the texture suffers somewhat in the processing and are concerned about possible microwaving, if time is important, instant brown rice is fast.

WHITE RICE—AND WHAT IT LACKS

This is the rice we are offered most often in this country, although those who value real food for both taste and nourishment wouldn't touch it with a ten-foot chopstick. Debranning and polishing rice removes almost all of the important nutrients. To compensate, its surface may be coated with vitamins and minerals; this rice is described as "enriched," but it is still no match for brown rice. With some brands this enrichment may even end up down the drain, since washing the grain before cooking can remove the added nutrients. This warning is supposed to be included on the label, but if you don't read the directions you may miss it.

Glucose and talc may be added to white rice to improve its appearance. This is known as coated rice; its popularity in Latin and Oriental markets is somewhat disturbing since talc can be contaminated with cancer-causing asbestos.

CONVERTED RICE

In converted or parboiled rice, some of the vitamins and minerals are forced into the central starchy endosperm before the bran and germ are removed. Although this process does conserve some of the nutrients, it ignores the important fiber. Converted rice is usually enriched with B vitamins, and may have BHT added as a preservative. This will appear on the label.

PRESEASONED RICE

There is nothing wrong with the concept of preseasoned rice mixes or pilafs; however, many brands, including some of the whole-grain varieties, contain such questionable ingredients as sugar, MSG, hydrolyzed vegetable protein, cornstarch, caramel color, hydrogenated oils, and, almost always, salt. Moreover, they are expensive.

It is a simple task to enhance the flavor of rice by adding your own seasonings, although with the natural richness of brown rice this jazzing up isn't even necessary. For the benefit of those willing to pay for the convenience of having someone else do the job, however, we have listed several seasoned rice blends in the Exemplary Brands that can fit into the wholefoods kitchen.

RICE CAKES

Rice cakes, discussed in greater detail in Chapter 8, are a phenomenally successful food innovation. Made of puffed brown rice pressed into crackers, they provide a way to bring this grain to the table without cooking. They are an excellent "underlayment" for stews, cooked vegetables, and similar dishes that you would normally serve over rice.

MOCHI

One of the most intriguing forms of rice that has entered the American food scene recently is mochi (pronounced moe-chee). A Japanese food that is centuries old, mochi is made by pounding steamed sweet brown rice to form a compact slab. When baked for just 10 minutes (easily done in a toaster oven), it puffs up into an eccentrically shaped "muffin" with a crisp crust and chewy interior. This product is particularly good for those who are allergic to wheat or corn.

To find mochi, you will have to visit a natural food store. Domestically made varieties are stored in the refrigerator, while most imported ones do not require refrigeration. Mochi is available plain (nothing more than sweet brown rice) or delicately seasoned with herbs or spices.

Most of the companies packaging mochi provide handling and cooking instructions on the wrapper. It is easy to prepare and fun to eat. We like to stuff cooked mochi with nut butter, fruit preserves, cheese, or a bean spread.

Wheat

Wheat is perhaps the most familiar grain in the American diet since most of our prepared cereals and baked goods depend on it. However, few people know wheat in its unprocessed state: wheat berries and cracked wheat.

WHEAT BERRIES

Wheat berries, the original form of the grain before it is ground into flour, are available in natural food markets and from most of the nonspecialized mail-order sources listed in "Food by Mail," on page 59. They have a deliciously chewy consistency when cooked and can be served like rice as a side dish, used as the foundation for a hearty main dish casserole, or you can toast the wheat berries in a dry skillet for a crunchy snack. They also produce a tasty, subtly sweet sprout.

CRACKED WHEAT AND BULGUR

Cracked wheat is made by crushing the toasted whole wheat berry; to make bulgur the wheat is parboiled before crushing. These forms of wheat are cherished by hurried cooks since they can be eaten without cooking (requiring merely a brief soaking) or can be cooked in just 15 to 20 minutes. There is not much difference in taste and use, and the two are often marketed interchangeably. They are fairly common in supermarkets, natural food stores, and many ethnic groceries.

SEMOLINA

Also marketed under the name *couscous,* semolina is derived from a specific variety of wheat known as durum. Although durum wheat has more protein than other common strains of wheat, semolina contains neither the vital bran nor the germ, making it a refined grain, which we do not endorse.

WHEAT GERM

Wheat germ is the growth center for the wheat kernel, containing its storehouse of protein, fat, vitamins, and minerals. This qualifies it as the best part of the grain. While we prefer to see wheat consumed intact as nature intended, in itself wheat germ is a useful booster for other foods. Adding it to grain-based dishes or sprinkling it on breakfast cereal will enhance both the quality and quantity of protein in these foods. In addition, since most of the nutrients used to artificially enrich refined grains and prepared cereals are naturally present in the germ, a liberal sprinkling can replace commercial fortification.

You will usually find wheat germ in the same section of the store as cereal. Vacuum packaging is preferred to keep it fresh. Toasted varieties are more popular than raw wheat germ; they offer only slightly less food value and have a taste and texture that is generally preferred. Avoid those that are presweetened; the addition of "Sugar 'n Honey" means proportionately less protein, vitamins, and minerals, and it adds 1 tablespoon of sugar per cup.

Defatted wheat germ is only a part of a part of the whole grain. It is used frequently by the food industry as it is less likely to spoil. In your own kitchen just keep in mind that wheat germ is perishable; to prevent rancidity, keep it in the refrigerator once the seal on the package is broken.

BRAN

Bran became publicized during the last decade when there was speculation that lack of fiber in our diet was a contributing factor to constipation, hemorrhoids, and bowel cancer. This still unproven theory is currently being capitalized on by many food processors.

Despite the popularity of miller's or wheat bran (and increasingly oat, corn, and rice bran), bran in itself is only part of the "whole" and not a balanced food. Since no food in its natural state consists entirely of "roughage," it comes as no surprise that as valuable as bran may be in enhancing the digestion of food and regulating the body's blood chemistry, it may also have some adverse effects. High concentrations of bran, for example, may interfere with the absorption of certain minerals. There has also been some concern that bran may be an irritant to the gastrointestinal tract. Thus, bran is probably best considered as a supplement in a diet devoid of whole grains.

WHEAT MEAT

The Orient is the source of a novel wheat product known as *gluten* that is an interesting substitute for meat. You may have had this food in Chinese cuisine without realizing it, as it is a common basis for many vegetarian "meats."

Gluten is actually the principal protein in wheat and can be isolated by holding a ball of dough under water and kneading it until the starch is washed away. The opaque, rubbery mass that is left is then dried or used fresh.

The form called *fu* is dried gluten; when it is rehydrated it has the delicate texture of fish fillets, but no taste of its own. Fresh gluten is also bland in its pure state, but it is always highly seasoned and cooked before it is packaged and sold commercially as *wheat meat, seitan, wheat roasts,* and *cutlets.*

Although similar to meat in form and use, and described as almost pure protein, by itself gluten is not a high-quality protein. In order to give it dietary worth, a gluten product should be coupled with some animal protein, or with beans and nuts, or beans and another grain. Wheat meat accompanied by tofu on rice or served with a milk-based gravy (animal or soy) are two examples of good gluten combinations.

Gluten products are easily found in stores selling packaged Oriental foods and are becoming increasingly available in natural food stores. They can be identified by the terms *gluten* or *wheat protein* on the label. Be sure to read the ingredients if the gluten has been transformed into a "meat substitute," for many of these products contain undesirable flavor enhancers like MSG and hydrolyzed vegetable protein, artificial color, and artificial flavor.

Buckwheat

Buckwheat will grow almost anywhere, making it a popular grain from Manchuria to Minnesota. In addition to possessing an uncommon earthy flavor, it boasts a higher protein content than most grains. Some people may recognize it by its alternate name, *kasha.* It can be found in most supermarkets and natural food stores, and is most commonly available in the roasted form, either whole or in coarse, medium, or fine grind.

Rye

People probably drink more rye (in the form of distilled alcohol) than they eat. If they do know it in some other form, it is probably as rye bread, which generally has only a fraction of rye flour mixed with an abundance of refined wheat. In addition to rye flour and rye flakes (see Chapter 10), there are rye berries; just as with wheat berries, rye berries can be boiled or pan-toasted for your eating enjoyment.

Barley

Barley is lower in fiber than other grains, but it is the easiest to digest, which accounts for the age-old English remedy of barley water for stomach ailments. The hull is almost always removed through the abrasive action of pearling machines. *Scotch* or *pot* barley is obtained after the third pearling, while *pearl* barley is more highly processed, undergoing two or three more passes through the machine.

Wild Rice

Technically wild rice is a grass, not a grain. It is native to the Great Lakes region of North America and for years was hand-cultivated exclusively in its natural habitat by the Chippewa Indians. Now it is being commercially planted and mechanically harvested, but this does not seem to have reduced its price, which is quite dear. In fact, in some ways the traditionally cultivated grain is more economical, for it swells to four times its volume and cooks in half the time required for the "modern" variety, which only triples in size.

In addition to being offered on its own, wild rice is often packaged in combination with white or brown rice. This may be less of a bargain than it appears when you consider that most brands contain only 14 to 18 percent wild rice.

In determining whether wild rice is worth its price, bear in mind that, along with its alluring nutlike flavor, it is rich in iron and has better protein value and more B vitamins than other grains. Wild rice is also virtually free of fat and is well tolerated by those with other sensitivities to grain.

Before you make your purchase you might also want to weigh the benefits of buying the hand-picked product. The Indians still grow their wild rice as their ancestors did, without pesticides or chemical fertilizers. (Indian-grown rice is available at stores or by mail from Northern Lake Wild Rice Company, P.O. Box 28, Dept. GGF, Cass Lake, MN 56633.) Other Minnesota growers are not so conscientious and do use chemicals. Commercial producers in California claim they do not use pesticides, but they grow their wild rice on land previously used to cultivate white rice, which means it may contain chemical residues from the past. Canadian wild rice is also raised without pesticides and while it makes no "organic" claims, it is most likely to be chemical-free since it comes from sparsely populated regions of northern Canada.

Millet

Among its virtues, millet boasts the highest quality protein and the greatest tolerance for adverse growing conditions of any of the common grains. Although archaeological data trace its use to before 4000 B.C., it is hardly known in this country and you will probably only find it in natural food outlets. The tiny seed can be simmered like all other grains and is enhanced by gentle pan-toasting first. Millet is another grain that is well tolerated by those with grain allergies.

Maize (Corn)

Maize is probably America's most important contribution to the world's diet, but unfortunately the common practice of milling the grain into grits and meal, removing the hull and germ, accounts for a dramatic reduction in most of its nutrients. Although refined corn grits are a popular staple in the South, they hardly measure up to any of the other grains we have presented in this chapter.

The use of cornmeal as a baking ingredient is discussed in Chapter 5.

Other Grains: Oats, Amaranth, Triticale, Quinoa

To learn more about oats, turn to Chapter 10.

If you are curious about some of the newer grains that are being touted for their higher protein value like triticale (a wheat-rye hybrid) and amaranth (a mainstay of the Aztec and Inca diets prior to 1500 that is now staging a comeback), turn to Chapter 5.

If you have not yet heard of quinoa (pronounced keen-wa), it is because it has only recently been introduced to North America, although South Americans have been cultivating it for centuries. This "supergrain" is said to offer close to twice the protein of most other grains and cooks in just 15 to 20 minutes into a delicate dish with a distinct, almost squashlike flavor. Although we find it similar to grits, in reality it is very different from anything we have eaten before, another factor that makes quinoa so intriguing. Quinoa tends to be expensive; since the seeds mature at an uneven pace and must be harvested by hand, even with optimum conditions production costs will remain high. However, the returns in terms of nutrition (in addition to its protein, quinoa is rich in fiber and offers more fat, iron, calcium, and phosphorus than other grains), yield (its promoters claim that during cooking quinoa expands to five times its volume), and unusual flavor account for the growing market for this food.

SELECTING GRAINS

When shopping for grains, you can ensure quality by inspecting before you buy. If you are buying from an open bin, look for a high percentage of unbroken grains with only a few loose hulls. There should be a minimum of immature green-tinged grains and no stones, dirt, or other nongrain debris.

You can further verify the quality of your purchase when you cook it. Most of the grains should sink when covered with water. If you see more than a fraction floating on the top, buy another brand or find another bulk source next time.

Choosing Organic Grains

In an earlier age, when small farmers grew crops for local markets and almost immediate consumption, there was less need to protect grains from insects, mold, rot, and other field and storage infestation. Now that most grain is grown on huge farms, stockpiled for as long as two to three years, and shipped across continents, these problems have taken on gigantic economic and social proportions.

In early 1984, intensive media coverage of grain contamination with ethylene dibromide (EDB) alerted Americans to the potential hazards of current practices in grain production. Even though EDB and several other similarly toxic grain fumigants are now banned, many people recognize that chemical contamination continues and welcome the opportunity to buy chemical-free grains. A few respected companies offer this option through natural food stores, and their products are occasionally available in supermarkets too.

PROPER STORAGE

Most grains are extremely stable before they are milled into flour, and if kept cool and dry in an airtight container out of direct sunlight, they will last for years. (We found living proof of this several years ago when we visited the Cairo museum in Egypt and saw samples of grains thousands of years old that had been placed in the pyramids.) Brown rice is the single exception, for it possesses an enzyme that can produce rancidity and a characteristic sour odor. To preserve its goodness, keep brown rice in an airtight container in a cool place—which means the refrigerator in warm weather—and try to use it within three to six months. However, the quick-cooking variety does not need special handling as the responsible enzyme has been deactivated.

Considering the number of insects that thrive on grains and the number of chances they are given to crawl in and lay their eggs, you should not be surprised if you occasionally encounter a few of these pests in your storage container. Although the thought of eating them may not be very appetizing, these bugs are actually harmless. If you wish to use the grain immediately, put it in a pot of water and scoop out the bugs when they float to the top. (If you want your grains to be as clean as possible, you should rinse them before cooking anyway.) If the damage is not too extensive and you wish to save the grain, you can simply sift the bugs out through a strainer; to kill any unhatched eggs, stick the grain in the freezer for three days, then return it to a clean storage container.

RECOMMENDATIONS

General Rule of Purchase: Buy whole, unseasoned grains including brown rice, wheat berries, cracked wheat, buckwheat groats, rye, barley, wild rice, millet, and quinoa. Whenever possible, take advantage of organic sources. The grain itself should be the only ingredient in the package, unless you prefer to pay for someone else to add the seasoning.

Preseasoned grains will list all the ingredients on the label. The whole grain, herbs, spices, salt (practically unavoidable), and perhaps some dehydrated vegetables are the only ingredients you should accept.

Exemplary Brands

Brown Rice

Alma's Brown Rice
Arrowhead Mills Brown Rice,[1] Brown Basmati Rice, Quick Brown Rice
Cheristar Brown Rice
Chico-San Natural Brown Rice, 10-Minute Brown Rice, Organic Brown Rice[1]
Comet Natural Long Grain Brown Rice
Coop Brown Rice
Eden Brown Rice[1]
El Molino Brown Rice
Evans Long Grain Brown Rice
Giant Food Long Grain Brown Rice
Gibbs Brown and Wild Rice
Golden Grain Brown Rice
Golden Harvest Brown Rice, Quick Cooking Brown Rice
Hinode California Brown Rice
Kokuho Rose Brown Rice
Konriko Brand Original Brown Rice, 1912 Style Bran Rice, Wild Pecan Rice
Little Bear Brown Rice[1]
Lundberg Organically Grown Brown Rice,[1] Premium Brown Rice, Sweet Brown Rice, Wehani, Tasty Flakes, Country Wild Mix, Short and Sweet, Sweet Wehani, Jubilee

Mahatma Natural Long Grain Brown Rice
Pacific Brown Rice
Pathmark Natural Long Grain Brown Rice
Riceland Natural Brown Rice
Riviana Quick Cooking Brown Rice
River Brand Natural Long Grain Brown Rice
S&W Brown Rice, Quick Cooking Natural Long Grain Brown Rice
Southern Brown Rice, Long Grain Basmati Brown Rice, Organic Short Grain Brown Rice[1]
Springfield Brown Rice
Stone Buhr Brown Rice
Texamati Brown Rice
Texas Rose Brown Rice
Townhouse Long Grain Brown Rice
Tree of Life Brown Rice
Tsurumai California Brown Rice
Uncle Ben's Select Brown Rice
Waldbaum's Natural Long Grain Brown Rice

Mochi

Eden Mochi
Grainaissance Mochi
Kendall Food Company Organic Mochi[1]

Mitoku Mochi
The Bridge Mochi

Wheat

Alma's Cracked Wheat
Arrowhead Mills Whole Grain Wheat, Cracked Wheat, Bulgur
Eden Wheat Berries,[1] Durum Wheat,[1] Bulgur
Ener-G Bulgur Wheat
Golden Harvest Whole Wheat Berries, Bulgur Cracked Wheat

Kursteaz ala Cracked Wheat Bulgur
Little Bear Wheat Berries,[1] Durum Wheat,[1] Cracked Wheat[1]
Natural Way Mills Wheat Berries,[1] Cracked Wheat[1]
Old World Bulgar
Sovex Bulgur Wheat

Gluten

Lima Seitan[1]
Mitoku Seitan

Upcountry Seitan[2]
Whole Wheat Zenryu-Fu

Buckwheat

Arrowhead Mills Buckwheat Groats
Eden Buckwheat,[1] Kasha
Little Bear Buckwheat[1]

Moore's Buckwheat
Pocono Brand Roasted Buckwheat Groats
Wolffs' Kasha

Rye

Arrowhead Mills Whole Grain Rye[1]
Eden Rye Berries[1]

Little Bear Rye Berries[1]
Natural Way Mills Rye Berries,[1] Rye Grits[1]

Barley

Arrowhead Mills Pearled Barley,[1] Hulled Barley[1]
Eden Barley[1]

Little Bear Hulled Barley[1]
Natural Way Mills Barley[1]

Wild Rice

Canoe Brand Wild Rice
Chippwas Nett Lakes Natural Wild Rice
Fantastic Foods Wild Rice
Gibbs Wild Rice
Gourmet House Extra Fancy Wild Rice
Mac Gregor's Wild Rice

Mille Lacs Wild Rice
S&W Autumn Harvest 100% Wild Rice
Sauvageau 100% Pure Minnesota Wild Rice
Shiloh Farms Wild Rice
Voyageur Wild Rice, Giant Canadian Wild Rice

Other Grains

Ancient Harvest Quinoa
Arrowhead Mills Millet,[1] Quinoa
Eden Millet[1]
Little Bear Millet[1]

Natural Way Mills Millet,[1] Amaranth,[1] Whole Corn[1]
The Mother Grain Quinoa

Preseasoned Grains

Ener-G Old World Wheat Pilaf Bulgur
Fantastic Foods Spanish Brown Rice, Brown Rice with Miso

Hain Natural 3-Grain Italian Style Side Dish
Lundberg Pilaf Dinner
Norganic Wheat Pilaf

[1]Organic
[2]Some organic ingredients

Chapter 5

Sifting Out the Flour

Since flour is only one processing step away from the grain, it should come as no surprise that just as we emphasize whole grains, we also rely on the whole grain flours that are made from them. For many years, people rejected products made with whole grain flour, finding them too dense and strongly flavored, but recent improvements in these flours, as well as better recipes, have brightened the prospects for baked goods with integrity. We have found in our own kitchen that there is a real potential for homemade whole grain breads, muffins, crackers, pancakes, Danish, brownies, cookies, cakes, and pastries, if you choose the flour and the recipe wisely.

THE STORY OF FLOUR

Once upon a time, wheat was truly worthy of its status as the foundation of "the staff of life." The flour milled from this grain was made by crushing the entire kernel—bran, germ, and endosperm—between two stones, leaving all the native nutrients intact. This flour was known as *graham* or *whole wheat*.

In the 1880s, when modern technology replaced the millstones with steel rollers, the bran and germ were automatically separated out, making it easy to sell each part individually. The portion that we call *white flour* is composed entirely of the starchy endosperm and is devoid of bran's fiber and the germ's vital nutrients.

When it is first milled, white flour is creamy in color. When it is left a few months to age, the flour whitens naturally and becomes easier to handle. This is known as *unbleached flour*.

Since storing flour while it ages involves time and money, producers are often eager to speed up this process. At one time, agene gas was used for this purpose; it was banned after the discovery that it caused fits in dogs. Today, seven different methods of chemical bleaching and aging are still available to the flour industry in order to whiten its product and at the same time sterilize it so it does not support insect life. At least one of the chemicals, chlorine, becomes incorporated into the flour. Chemically treated flour carries the term "bleached" immediately before or after the name on the package. Note that when bleached flour is used as an ingredient in another food, it is supposed to be specified.

76

In addition to bleaching agents, several dough conditioners may be used to improve the handling quality. The presence of any conditioning agents must be specifically declared. The use of malted barley and ascorbic acid is not really objectionable for this purpose; however, the use of bromates is, and bromated flour can easily be avoided by reading the label.

The milling industry is well aware of the abuse it has inflicted on white flour. To "compensate," a standard of enrichment has been established. In order to bear the term "enriched," of the twenty-two nutrients removed at the mill, three B vitamins, and iron must be added; the addition of calcium is optional. At present, thirty-five states require that white flour and any products dependent on this flour be enriched.

MINERALS LOST IN MILLING WHEAT TO WHITE FLOUR

Element	Percent Loss
Calcium*	60
Chromium	40
Cobalt	88
Copper	69
Iron*	75
Manganese	86
Magnesium	78
Molybdenum	48
Phosphorus	75
Potassium	73
Selenium	16

*These are the only minerals used in enrichment. When they are added, their levels greatly exceed the normal mineral content of the whole grain.

As this table illustrates, considering what is lost, the term enriched is actually applied rather loosely. Moreover, one of the most valuable constituents, fiber, is almost negligible in the end product.

BUYING THE BEST FLOUR

Wheat Flour

In the product defined by the federal government as *whole wheat,* the proportion of natural wheat constituents—that is, the bran, germ, and endosperm—must be unaltered. Since high-speed steel milling separates these components, whole wheat flour milled in this manner is actually "reconstituted." Some contend that there is no difference between this whole wheat and the stone-ground variety in which the original bran and germ are retained; others feel that the germ is "smeared" in the high-tech process and that this makes the flour more susceptible to rancidity. While traditional stone grinding may have a slight edge, the current methods of stone grinding are likely to be quite different from the slow, careful process that took place down by the old mill stream. For example, where formerly the stones would rub the grain gently to break it down, today wheels of carborundum grind the grain so quickly that high temperatures result, which may damage the flour.

Whole wheat flour may be treated with conditioning agents and when this occurs, it must be stated on the label. While bleaching is also permitted, we have never encountered chemically bleached whole wheat flour in our travels.

Although there are reputed to be about 30,000 strains of wheat, only a few are of concern to the consumer. With the exception of durum wheat, which must be specified, the label designations that follow are purely voluntary. They may be applied to both the refined and the whole grain forms. Keep in mind that the word "wheat" must be accompanied by the term "whole" if the bran and germ are included. On labels, refined white flour is sometimes called "wheat flour," giving people the mistaken impression they are getting whole wheat flour—or at least something "more healthful" than white.

The product labeled **bread flour** is derived from a variety of wheat that is high in gluten, which allows the bread to expand and hold its shape, producing a light, well-risen loaf. The variety marketed as **pastry flour** is made from a soft wheat that is lower in protein and higher in carbohydrate, and generally favored for producing tender cakes and pastries. **All-purpose flour** is a blend of these wheats.

Durum flour is ground from a high-protein, hard wheat and is generally reserved for pasta. Unless the label specifies whole durum flour or whole durum wheat (rather than durum flour or semolina), the bran and germ will be missing.

There are two other forms in which wheat flour is marketed. Both are refined and do not receive our recommendation. **Instantized, instant-blending,** or **quick-mixing** flour is an extremely fine grind of refined soft wheat that has been processed to dissolve quickly in liquids for fine sauce making. **Self-rising** flour is prepared by adding sodium-based leavening salts and salt to the refined white (and generally bleached and/or enriched) flour.

Cornmeal

Although we tend to view corn as a vegetable, it is really a grain whose true name is maize. It is popular practice to refine corn into alcohol, sweeteners, and oil, but far less common to simply grind it and make use of the whole grain.

Like all other grains, corn is composed of an outer hull, an embryo or germ, and a starchy endosperm. It is this starchy portion that predominates in most cornmeal and cornstarch. The germ, once the oil is extracted for corn oil, is relegated to animal feed. This is unfortunate, because the protein and mineral content of the germ could better be used to nourish people.

Labeling on cornmeal is controlled by law. *Yellow* or *white cornmeal* must contain both the germ and the fibrous bran. *Bolted yellow* or *bolted white cornmeal* will have most of the fiber—but not the germ—sifted out. The word "degerminated" signals that both of these valuable constituents have been removed.

Any of these three products may be enriched, which is also stated on the label. Three B vitamins and iron will be added; it is up to the manufacturer to decide if vitamin D and calcium will also be included.

Self-rising cornmeal, popular in the South, is prepared by adding salt and a sodium-based leavening agent to cornmeal, thereby greatly elevating the sodium content. Most self-rising cornmeal is based on the refined grain.

Corn flour is produced from cleaned, bolted cornmeal, ground small enough to pass through a fine sieve. While some of the germ may be lost in this process, corn flour is nutritionally superior to degerminated meal.

Corn is quite low in protein content, and a good deal of scientific effort has been expended to improve this. The result is a new *high-lysine cornmeal* with better protein value and a crunchier texture than other cornmeals on the market.

Blue corn is another novel variety. Far from being a new genetic strain, however, this corn was a staple of the native American Indian diet long before any yellow strains were cultivated. Blue corn is also higher in protein and is characterized as sweeter, making it ideal for baked goods. Lavender corn bread and purple pancakes may be a shock at first sight, but since your taste buds are color blind, you should have no trouble making the adjustment.

Soy Flour

Soy may be a bean, but like grain, it is also processed into flour, providing high-protein meal. This flour is rarely used alone. Combined in a ratio of about 1:12 with other flours, it can enhance the food value and actually improve the texture and keeping quality of baked goods without altering their taste.

Soy flour is available in **full-fat** and **defatted** form. The defatted variety is exposed to chemical solvents and moreover lacks the nutritional balance of the whole bean flour. Thus, full-fat or whole soy flour, despite its slightly beany taste, is a more desirable choice. You may also find this flour described as **soya**. Technically, soya signifies that the beans were lightly toasted prior to grinding, which some feel enhances the flavor.

Rye, Buckwheat, Barley, Rice, Oats, Millet

All of these grains can be finely ground for use in baked goods, pancakes, and other traditional flour products. In selecting these flours, you will want to get the whole grain form when a choice exists. Dark rye and buckwheat flours have a much higher nutrient level than the medium and light varieties.

Since these flours lack the gluten found in wheat, any breads, cakes, and muffins made exclusively from them tend to be compact, with a dense, crumbly texture. To "lighten" them, you may combine these flours with whole wheat in a ratio of about 40 percent wheat to 60 percent specialty grain.

Triticale

Triticale is a new strain of grain made by crossing wheat and rye to produce a better protein content and a greater yield. It is available toasted and flattened into flakes and finely ground into flour. Triticale has excellent baking qualities, but it is low in gluten, so for a more traditional leavened product, using two-thirds triticale to one-third wheat may be preferred. While still not as readily available as other flours, triticale can be found in many natural food stores.

Amaranth

Amaranth flour may also be new to you, but this grain was apparently grown for at least 8,000 years in Central and South America before it almost disappeared in the early 1500s. There is good reason for the renewed interest in amaranth. This tasty grain is higher in protein than most other grains, has more fiber than wheat and rice, and is resistant to drought and most pests. Unfortunately, harvesting is labor-intensive and this is reflected in its price and scarcity. You are most likely to find this flour in natural food stores and through mail order outlets. Health Valley Foods, whose products are distributed nationally, is one pioneer in its commercial use.

In your own kitchen you can enjoy amaranth by using it in your favorite recipes to replace up to half the flour specified.

Gluten Flour

Gluten flour is made by washing off the starch from wheat and isolating the protein. Although this protein is not notable from a nutritional standpoint, it contains strong, expandable fibers that enable bread to rise high and maintain volume. For this reason, some people add 5 to 10 percent gluten flour when baking with low-gluten flours like rye, buckwheat, barley, oat, millet, triticale, or amaranth to enhance the texture.

SELECTING AND STORING WHOLE GRAIN FLOURS

Intact, a kernel of grain is well protected from moisture and air, but once the protective covering is broken by grinding, the resulting flour is vulnerable to spoilage. The best rule is to buy only as much flour as you can use within three to six months. Given the opportunity, we prefer to buy flours that have been stored in a cool environment since this helps slow down nutritional deterioration and protects the fat from developing a bitter flavor. (The refrigerator is one storage option; however, a special cool room to hold flours, grains, nuts, etc., is the sign of a superior store.)

Some experts feel that airtight packaging seals in moisture and has a mold-promoting effect on flour. On the other hand, excessive moisture loss speeds the aging process and a package that "breathes" in the dry environment of a store may suffer. This is a point in favor of bulk bins. When buying in bulk, however, the cleanliness of the store, care in sanitizing the bins, and a hygienic means for customers to serve themselves are essential.

To preserve the quality of flours at home, store them in a cool spot. If you do not have such a space, or when the weather is warm, keep them in a moisture proof container in the refrigerator or freezer. Because of its high fat content, soy flour should always be refrigerated.

CHOOSING THICKENING AGENTS

Cornstarch, potato starch, and *arrowroot* are starchy plant extracts that have many of the same uses as flour. Their ability to absorb liquids makes them highly desirable as thickeners. Although they are refined, they are chemical-free and you may prefer them to flour for making delicate white sauces, gravies, and puddings.

Do not, however, look too favorably upon manufactured soups and spaghetti sauces that rely on these thickeners. When they are used in this manner, they are apt to mask a high liquid content and a dearth of nutritious food ingredients. Moreover, *modified food starch,* which is popular with food processors, is not so innocent. In creating this highly unnatural product, thickening starches may be treated with a combination of acids and/or bleaching agents to change their basic nature to stand up under extreme heat, severe mechanical agitation, and an acidic environment. This produces a starch practical for commercially homogenized sauces and gravies, soups, salad dressings, baby food, pie fillings, and other foods that undergo considerable handling. We automatically reject any product that contains modified starch.

THE RIGHT MIX

No prepared food can be better than the ingredients that comprise it. Thus, you might guess how we feel about buying pancake, biscuit, muffin, cornbread, and cake mixes that depend on refined grains and refined sweeteners, and are further compromised by the addition of artificial colors, flavors, preservatives, hydrogenated shortening, vegetable gums, and similar nontraditional ingredients.

Most people who buy mixes are surprised when they see how easy it is to prepare some of these same foods "from scratch," especially less complex items like biscuits and pancakes where the product is only three premixed ingredients (flour, salt, and leavening) to which you still have to add egg, oil, liquid, and possibly sweetening. Nonetheless, sometimes it "feels" easier to use a mix.

There are a few mixes on the market that use ingredients a cook can be proud of; there are also a few less laudable ones containing some processed ingredients in conjunction with wholefoods which are at least additive-free. In the Recommendations that follow, we distinguish between the Exemplary Brands and those that are Acceptable with Reservation because they contain either refined flour or sugars. Mixes containing hydrogenated fats, preservatives, artificial color, or similarly unsuitable ingredients are never a good buy.

RECOMMENDATIONS

FLOUR

General Rule of Purchase: Purchase organically grown flours whenever available. Select whole wheat flour that has not been bleached, or treated with bromate, or phosphate conditioners. Avoid white flour (also called wheat flour), but if you must use it, choose the unbleached rather than the bleached variety.

The word *cornmeal* alone on the label means the bran and germ are still there, making this the preferred purchase; bolted cornmeal contains the germ but lacks the fiber; degerminated cornmeal is the counterpart of white flour and even when enriched is not an exemplary buy.

Don't forget to vary your diet with a selection of whole grain flours: wheat, cornmeal, rye, buckwheat, soy, oat, barley, brown rice, millet, triticale, and amaranth.

*Exemplary Brands*_____

Whole Wheat Flour

Arrowhead Mills Whole Wheat,[1] Whole Wheat Pastry,[1] Whole Durum Wheat[1]
Coop Whole Wheat
Cresota Whole Wheat
Eden Whole Wheat,[1] Whole Wheat Pastry,[1] Durum[1]
Elam's Whole Wheat, Whole Wheat Pastry
Fisher Whole Wheat, Graham
Fred Meyer Graham
Giant Foods Stone Ground Whole Wheat Graham

Gold Medal Whole Wheat
Golden Harvest Whole Wheat, Whole Wheat Pastry, Graham
Harrington's Hodgson Mills Whole Wheat Graham
Hecker's Whole Wheat
Jewel Evans Stone Ground Whole Wheat
King Arthur Stone Ground Whole Wheat
Krusteaz Whole Wheat
Little Bear Whole Wheat,[1] Whole Wheat Pastry,[1] Graham[1]

Whole Wheat Flour (continued)

Martha White Whole Wheat
Moore's Graham
Mrs. Wright's Whole Wheat
Natural Way Mills Whole Wheat,[1] Whole Wheat Pastry,[1] Whole Durum Wheat[1]

Pillsbury Whole Wheat
Pioneer Stone Ground Whole Wheat
Rogers Whole Wheat
Schmidt Whole Wheat
Stone Buhr Graham

Cornmeal

Arrowhead Mills Cornmeal,[1] Blue Cornmeal,[1] Hi-Lysine Cornmeal[1]
Beattie's Stone Ground
Blue Corn Connection[1]
Cross Brand Old Virginia Style Stone Ground
Eden[1]
Fred Meyer
Golden Harvest Stone Ground Yellow
Harrington's Hodgson Mills Yellow, White

Jewel Evans Stone Ground
Little Bear Cornmeal,[1] Corn Flour[1]
Lima Pimiento[1]
Lima Polenta[1]
Natural Way Mills[1]
Old Time
Prairie Sun Hi-Lysine
Shiloh Farms Corn Flour[1]
Stone Buhr
21st Century Foods Masa[1]

Soy Flour

Arrowhead Mills
Eden[1]
Fearn Natural Soya Powder

Fred Meyer
Golden Harvest
Stone Buhr

Rye Flour

Arrowhead Mills
Eden[1]
Fisher
Fred Meyer
Golden Harvest
Harrington's Hodgson Mills

Krusteaz
Little Bear[1]
Natural Way Mills[1]
Pillsbury
Rogers
Stone Buhr

Buckwheat Flour

Arrowhead Mills
Eden[1]
Elam's
Fred Meyer

Golden Harvest
Moore's
Natural Way Mills[1]

Other Flours

Arrowhead Mills Amaranth,[1] Brown Rice,[1] Oat, Millet, Barley, Triticale, Ezekiel
Eden Brown Rice,[1] Quinoa
Elam's Brown Rice
Ener-G Brown Rice
Fred Meyer Barley, Brown Rice, Oat, Triticale

Golden Harvest Barley, Oat, Brown Rice
Little Bear Brown Rice,[1] Barley,[1] Millet,[1] Multi-Grain[1]
Moore's Millet, Brown Rice, Barley, Oat
Natural Way Mills Amaranth[1]
Old Mill Triticale
Shiloh Farms Barley,[1] Oat,[1] Brown Rice[1]

MIXES

General Rule of Purchase: All ingredients are on the label. Look for mixes made only from whole grains, dry milk, leavening, and salt. Accept with reservation mixes that also include some refined flour and sweetening.

Avoid mixes wholly dependent on refined flours or that contain any partially hydrogenated fats, artificial coloring, preservatives, or other similar ingredients.

Mixes that are formulated specifically for bread, corn bread, and muffins can be found in Chapter 7. Cake mixes are listed in Chapter 33.

Exemplary Brands

Arrowhead Mills Griddle Lite, Buckwheat, Triticale Pancake Mixes

Blue Corn Connection Pancake and Waffle Mix[1]

Country Life Natural Foods Waffle and Pancake Mix[2]

Fearn Low Sodium 7-Grain, Whole Wheat, Buckwheat, 7-Grain Buttermilk Pancake Mixes; Whole Wheat,[2] Brown Rice Baking Mixes

Fred Meyer 10-Grain Pancake and Waffle Mix

Hain Whole Wheat Baking Mix

Harrington's Hodgson Mills Buckwheat Pancake Mix

Health Valley 7 Sprouted Grains Pancake Mixes

Moore's Flour Mill 10-Grain Pancake and Waffle Mix

Nature's Choice Buckwheat, 7-Grain Pancake Mixes[2]

Rich Earth Pancake Mix

Ross' Blue Heaven Pancake and Waffle Mix[1]

Savannah Buttermilk Flapjack Mix[1]

Acceptable with Reservation

Arrowhead Mills Multigrain Pancake Mix[4]

Aunt Jemima Buckwheat, Whole Wheat Pancake and Waffle Mixes[3,4]

Bouchard Family Farm Buckwheat Pancake Mix[4]

Clifton Mill Whole Wheat, Buckwheat, Cornmeal Pancake Mixes[3]

Fearn Soy-O Pancake and Waffle Mix[4]

Harrington's Hodgson Mills Stone Ground Whole Wheat Buttermilk Pancake Mix[4]

Jewel Evans Original Non Complete Pancake Mix[3,4]

Mille-Lacs Wild Rice Pancake Mix[4]

Moore's Flour Mill Cornmeal and Whole Wheat,[4] Whole Wheat and Soya,[3,4] Buckwheat[3,4] Pancake and Waffle Mixes

Post Rock Amaranth Pancake Mix[3,4]

THICKENERS

General Rule of Purchase: All brands of cornstarch, potato starch, and arrowroot are the same. Avoid processed foods that contain modified food starch.

[1]Organic
[2]Some organic ingredients
[3]Contains refined sweeteners
[4]Contains refined grains

Chapter 6

Pasta: Making the Best of It

Take the grain, grind it into flour, knead it with water and/or egg, cut it into fanciful shapes, and presto—pasta. When made from refined grains it is largely a high-carbohydrate product; when whole grains are employed, the fiber, protein, mineral, and vitamin content are praiseworthy. Either way, most children and adults love the stuff, and if it is selected wisely and used to its full potential, it deserves this adoration.

THE POWER OF PASTA

Pasta's attributes are numerous. It is certainly convenient; the dried variety can travel from pantry to table via a pot of boiling water in just about 10 minutes. It is extremely versatile and lends itself to almost any topping from simple oil and garlic or grated cheese to elaborate fish, meat, vegetable, or cream sauces. And, as everyone knows, pasta is economical.

Until recently, pasta was regarded as fattening, but since complex carbohydrates have come into favor, and athletes have begun to tout "carbohydrate loading" for peak performance, its reputation has improved. Unadorned, pasta is not a major source of calories, with just over 200 per average serving (2 ounces dry weight).

As with other wheat products, traditional pastas do not stand on their own as a source of protein. This can be overcome, as some manufacturers have done, by combining the wheat with soy or other bean flours, corn, rice, amaranth, or sesame meal, or by serving the pasta with a complementary food containing beans or animal protein, as people have been doing for centuries.

While you might suspect that incorporating eggs in noodles would give them a higher protein value than macaroni products (which are egg-free), this is not the case because noodles are usually made from a softer wheat with less protein, whereas most macaroni is prepared from the higher-protein durum wheat.

Although pasta is publicized as a source of B vitamins, cooking destroys some of its inherent B vitamins as well as those added to the enriched product. Moreover, since the B vitamin riboflavin is sensitive to light, attractive counter displays of pasta in glass jars or plastic bins quickly

85

detract from the food value of the product; within two days, more than 50 percent of the riboflavin may be lost.

Fat and cholesterol are negligible in macaroni products and appear in modest amounts in egg noodles. While both macaroni and egg noodles are also low in sodium, this is negated if they are cooked with salt as the package instructs. Fortunately, the addition of salt to the water is purely a matter of taste and eliminating it will not affect the finished dish.

FRESH PASTA

Not too long ago the only way one could have fresh pasta was to make it at home. This is no longer so. Freshly made varieties can be found in the refrigerator and freezer cases of specialty shops throughout the nation, while some supermarkets carry fresh pasta in their gourmet and deli departments.

Fresh pastas are generally made with some variety of refined high-gluten flour, with or without the addition of eggs. Some have a fresh, canned, or dried vegetable component added for color and flavor appeal. Note that because fresh pasta is often manufactured and sold locally, what appears on the label may be governed by individual state requirements and unless the pasta is transported across state lines, ingredient labeling may be lacking.

It is hard to find mass-marketed fresh pasta made exclusively with whole grain flour.

"FEDERAL PASTA": THE OFFICIAL REQUIREMENTS

When most people think of pasta they usually have the dried type in mind. Despite advertising that pits one brand of pasta against another and employs such slogans as "Premium pasta—made with special care," the federal Standards of Identity assure that within a given category most brands are very much alike.

There are two government classifications for dried pasta: macaroni products and noodles.

■ Macaroni products include pasta composed primarily of flour and water—spaghetti, vermicelli, macaroni, shells, ziti, rigatoni, lasagna, and other familiar Italian-style pastas.

■ Noodles include egg-enriched items such as noodles and egg barley.

Macaroni Products

The name "macaroni product" is reserved for the dried dough made from wheat and water. Spaghetti, macaroni, or vermicelli are alternate designations, governed by certain size requirements. Any macaroni product can also contain a choice of optional ingredients including egg white (fresh, frozen, or dried), disodium phosphate (added to decrease cooking time), gluten (wheat protein added for texture), glyceryl monostearate, and specified seasonings, including salt. The label need not mention the presence of the egg white, salt, or gluten. This mostly affects people with particular food sensitivities; however, dried egg whites may pose additional health concerns for everyone (see page 172). Often the manufacturer will volunteer that the pasta is made from durum flour or semolina. As you may recall from Chapter 5, durum flour (unless modified by the word "whole") has had the bran and some or all of the germ removed; semolina is more coarsely ground, but similarly refined. Because a creamy color is preferred in pasta, this flour is never bleached.

ENRICHED MACARONI

Most American-made macaroni products are enriched, which means that the B vitamins niacin, riboflavin, and thiamin plus iron are added in designated amounts; vitamin D and calcium are optional. These nutrients may be supplied by synthesized supplements or preferably by nutritional yeast or partially defatted wheat germ; such distinctions on the label are voluntary.

FORTIFIED MACARONI

One way to make enriched macaroni better is to fortify it with protein. The label will indicate this and will also specify the source of this protein, which may be soy, sesame meal, amaranth, whey, or nonfat dry milk, all of which complement the wheat product nicely. A fanciful name may be used as well, as is the case with Superoni, a widely available fortified spaghetti.

VEGETABLE MACARONI

Vegetable macaroni products need include only 3 percent tomato, artichoke, beet, carrot, parsley, or spinach from either the fresh, canned, or dried vegetable or a puree or paste. The small amount of vegetable used provides little flavor or nutrition, but adds aesthetically in terms of appearance. No egg white or disodium phosphate is permitted, and the macaroni may or may not be enriched, as indicated on the label.

WHOLE WHEAT MACARONI

When a macaroni product is made with whole wheat flour, this is included in the name, that is, "whole wheat macaroni product" or "whole wheat spaghetti, macaroni, vermicelli." This pasta will not contain egg white, added gluten, or disodium phosphate. Many of the whole wheat pastas on the market are made with organically grown wheat and several are enhanced with wheat germ and other grains.

NOODLES

The main difference between noodles and macaroni products is the inclusion of the egg yolk. Most noodles make use of dried egg powder rather than fresh eggs. In addition, disodium phosphate may not be used in noodles.

MISLEADING LABELING

■ Many brands of pasta state on the label "no artificial color added." This appears to be a case of petty deception, since the government Standard of Identity prohibits artificial color (and preservatives) in both macaroni products and noodles.

■ Pasta that boasts "no salt added" is telling you something since salt may be present without being listed in the ingredients. Just because no salt is added, however, does not mean the product is sodium-free, since macaroni products may contain significant levels of sodium if the additive disodium phosphate is used.

■ Fortified macaroni is sometimes promoted as "high-protein," creating the impression it is a good stand-in for meat. On a dry-weight basis its protein content may look impressive, but when you compare normal serving sizes, other protein foods usually have more to offer. Of course, if you add a protein-rich topping the picture can be brighter.

MACARONI MEETS THE MICROWAVE

Drying is the trickiest part of pasta manufacture and may take as long as thirty-six hours using conventional methods. To save time, many commercial operations are turning to microwave drying.

Because we believe adequate studies have not been done to determine the effects of microwave cooking, we are somewhat suspicious of this technique. It is impossible to know for certain when microwave drying has been employed; however, it is said to have a slight puffing effect which reduces the home cooking time. Therefore, any pasta that is promoted as "quick cooking" or "light and fluffy" is likely to be a microwave graduate.

VARIATIONS ON A BASIC THEME

Pasta products have been fashioned in more than 600 different shapes and sizes, but all are molded from the same basic doughs. This does not necessarily mean they all taste the same, though, for length and thickness alter the "mouth feel" and the way the pasta holds the sauce. In the case of whole wheat pasta, this may be especially important; while some varieties are very much like refined pasta in taste and texture, others are far more assertive and initial acceptance may hinge on the form they take. For those not accustomed to the robust flavor and the chewier texture of whole wheat pastas, thinner and smaller varieties like noodles, elbow macaroni, spirals, and shells may be a good starting place.

Imported Pasta

Imported Italian pasta is the biggest competition for American pasta makers. In order to bear the name spaghetti, macaroni, etc., all imported pastas must conform to the American federal recipe. The major distinguishing factor is that most American products (other than the whole grain) are enriched, while most imports are not. Other differences are subtle. Italian pastas are yellower, for example, due to a greater concentration of natural pigment in Mediterranean durum wheat. They may also differ slightly in the texture, since some Italian companies still roll the pasta out before it is shaped, while most U.S. companies use an extrusion system.

"Light" Pasta

"Light" pasta, marketed as "calorie-reduced enriched spaghetti," is made from typical macaroni ingredients. In comparing the "light" variety with the regular spaghetti made by the same manufacturer, we discovered that the reduced-calorie pasta is merely formulated to absorb more water; thus, less dry weight goes further. If you do not follow the instructions to cook less initially, you will miss out on this savings. You should also be aware that the disodium phosphate used to assist in this process adds noticeably to the sodium content.

Substitute Macaroni Products

Pasta products that call themselves "substitute" do so not because they are inferior but because they deviate from the federal standard. One way in which they may differ is by replacing some of the wheat flour with flour made from the vegetable called the Jerusalem artichoke. This creates a pasta with a slightly lower carbohydrate content, but unless whole durum wheat flour is used with the Jerusalem artichoke flour, you will be buying a refined product.

Corn Pasta

For those who want a break from wheat, there are several varieties of corn pasta on the market. Although they are made of ground whole corn, the protein, vitamin, and mineral contents are not a match for wheat-based pasta. And while all pastas are best "al dente," corn pasta in particular requires careful timing to keep it from becoming soft and pasty.

Oriental Noodles

It is believed that some form of pasta was eaten in Asia long before the Italians invented macaroni. Only recently have people in the Western Hemisphere begun to use some of these Oriental noodles.

Soba noodles, a Japanese specialty, are made from 40 to 100 percent buckwheat flour. Long, narrow noodles that are about as thick as they are wide, they are excellent in soups as well as in sauces. **Somen** are equally thin but somewhat flatter, and are made of wheat flour which may be whole, a combination of whole and sifted whole wheat flour, or totally refined. **Udon** contain the same ingredients but are thicker and chewier. Another intriguing import is the **jinenjo noodle,** which combines the starch of a wild Japanese mountain potato with wheat and buckwheat.

Prepared Pasta Entrées

To learn more about prepared canned and frozen pasta entrées, turn to Chapter 28.

RECOMMENDATIONS

FRESH PASTA

General Rule of Purchase: Federal laws do not necessarily apply to locally made products and thus fresh pasta may not have ingredient labeling. Fresh pasta is made with flour, water, sometimes eggs, and select seasonings. Look for those made with whole grain flours and fresh eggs. Refined flours, which are more commonly employed, are not recommended, but if such a product is selected and the ingredients are specified, choose only those made with unbleached flour. The addition of a vegetable component is acceptable, but does not make pasta any more commendable.

*Exemplary Brands*_____

Bread & Circus Whole Wheat, Spinach   Nasoya Fresh Pasta[1]
Linguinis, Fettucinis[1,4]

MACARONI PRODUCTS

General Rule of Purchase: All ingredients are not necessarily on the label. Look for *whole grain macaroni products,* and especially those containing organic flours; anything added, other than salt, is on the label.

In *macaroni products* made with refined flour, look for those specifying durum wheat or semolina, although listing the type of wheat is voluntary. Egg white, gluten, and salt may be unavoidable because they do not have to be listed. You can (and should) avoid disodium phosphate and glycerol monostearate, as they must be labeled.

While products made with refined flour are never exemplary, an *enriched macaroni product* that gets its added nutrients from nutritional yeast and wheat germ is preferred to a synthetically fortified variety. Supplying this information on the label is voluntary.

Enriched wheat macaroni products fortified with protein will reveal the source of the added protein. Such products contain about 7 percent more protein than traditional pastas but are otherwise identical.

Combination *wheat and soy macaroni products* are only 3.5 percent higher in protein than plain pasta, and are not enriched. Although they do not contain egg white or disodium phosphate, they may have salt and gluten hidden from view.

Vegetable macaroni is identical to its plain, enriched, or whole wheat counterparts except that it contains 3 percent or more of a vegetable ingredient and no egg white or disodium phosphate. Once again, the addition of salt and, in all but the whole wheat variety, gluten may not be revealed.

*Exemplary Brands*_____

De Boles Natural Gourmet Whole Wheat Pastas[1]
De Cecco Whole Wheat Pastas
Del Verde Whole Wheat Macaronis
Eden Whole Wheat Pastas,[1] Artichoke Spaghetti,[2] Sesame Rice Spirals,[2] Spinach Pastas,[2] Tomato Fettucine,[2] Vegetable Pastas,[2] Buckwheat Elbows,[2] Quinoa Flats[2]
Erewhon Whole Wheat Pastas,[1] Vegetable Elbows,[2] Artichoke Spaghetti,[2] Sesame Rice Spirals,[2] Spinach Flats[2]
Fisher's 100% Whole Wheat Macaroni
Gabriele Whole Wheat Spaghetti, Artichoke Whole Wheat Spaghetti, Whole Wheat Elbow Macaroni with Mixed Vegetable Powder

Golden Harvest Pastas[1]
Harrington's Hodgson Mills Whole Wheat Lasagna, Whole Wheat Spaghetti
Health Valley Amaranth Wheat Pasta,[2] Whole Wheat Pasta with Wheat Germ,[2] Whole Wheat Spinach Pasta with Wheat Germ,[2] Whole Wheat Pasta with Wheat Germ and Four Vegetables[2]
Healthway 100% Stone Ground Whole Wheat Cut Spaghetti, Sesame Elbows[4]
In-Ag Dark Lupini Pasta
Johnson's Whole Wheat Pastas, Spinach Ribbons, Sesame Rich Spirals
Lima Spaghetti,[1] Horns[2]
Nature's Cuisine 100% Stone Ground Whole Wheat Spaghetti, Elbows
Old Stone Mill Sesame Elbows[4]

Exemplary Brands (continued)

Pure and Simple Whole Wheat Pastas,[1] Spaghetti with Spinach[2]
Roman Meal Natural Foods Multigrain Pastas[4]
Viva Pasta Ribbons[2,4]

Westbrae Natural Whole Wheat Pastas,[1] Sesame Rice Spirals,[2] Spinach Pastas,[2] Veggie Bows,[2] Soy Spaghetti[2]

NOODLES

General Rule of Purchase: All ingredients are not on the label. Look for whole wheat flour (organic preferred). When noodles are enriched or contain a vegetable component or have added soy, this will precede the name. Whole eggs or yolks alone are always found in noodles; if specified, fresh eggs (rather than frozen or dried) are preferred. Avoid glycerol monostearate. (Salt and gluten may be added, but omitted from the ingredient list.)

Exemplary Brands

Deluca's Home Style Enriched Whole Wheat Noodles
Eden Whole Wheat Noodles
Harrington's Hodgson Mills Whole Wheat Noodles, Whole Wheat Spinach Noodles

Pennsylvania Dutch Whole Wheat Noodles
Westbrae Natural Egg Noodles[2]

CORN PASTA

General Rule of Purchase: All ingredients are on the label. Most are made with whole grains. Organic preferred.

Exemplary Brands

De Boles
Golden Harvest

Westbrae

ORIENTAL NOODLES

General Rule of Purchase: All ingredients are on the label. Look for brands made from the whole grain alone or combined with sifted wheat. Organic preferred.

Exemplary Brands

Chico-San Organic Soba Noodles,[1] Organic Udon Noodles,[1] Genuine Soba Noodles, Genuine Mugwort Soba Noodles
Eden Sobas, Kuzu Kiri, Udon
Erewhon Japanese Pasta[4]

Premier Japan Soba, Udon
Soba Shop Buckwheat, Without Salt, Ito,[4] Jinenjo Sobas,[4] Whole Wheat Somen; Whole Wheat, Traditional,[4] Genmai Udons[4]

Exemplary Brands (continued)

Soken Jinenjo Noodles, Soba

Westbrae 100% Buckwheat, 80% Buck-
wheat,[4] 40% Buckwheat,[4] Jinenjo Sobas;[4]
Whole Wheat, Brown Rice Genmai
Udons,[4] Whole Wheat Somen; Kuzu Kiri

[1]Organic
[2]Some organic ingredients
[4]Contains refined grains

Chapter 7

Your Daily Bread

The word *bread* is richly endowed with meaning. When you are asked to "break bread" with someone, it is an invitation to dine. The Lord's Prayer uses "bread" as a symbol of all food. We are asked to "cast our bread upon the waters" if we want an abundant life, and contemporary jargon equates bread with money.

Ironically, much of today's bread would not even fulfill the spirit of these expressions, much less the substance. While bread can be a valuable source of vitamins, minerals, fiber, and supplementary protein, it can also furnish highly processed artificial ingredients as well as unnecessary salt, fat, and sugars.

This is not to suggest there are no good options, for the American bread aisle has become a dynamic place. With the emphasis on fiber and natural foods, bread bakers have begun to reverse what was recently seen as a downward sales spiral. We see familiar sliced breads sandwiched between crusty French and Italian loaves, round pita pockets, chewy bagels, fatty croissants, rolls, biscuits, muffins, chapatis, tortillas, and all manner of specialty breads baked with sprouted grains, vegetable components, nuts, seeds, fruit, and to our consternation, even wood pulp. More selections can be found in the frozen food case and at the delicatessan display.

Many of these breads sport seductive names which we call to your attention because often they are not what they seem. "Nature's Own," "Nature's Triumph," "Earth Grains," "Farm Bread," "American Heritage," "Home Pride," "Country Grain," and "Old Country" are just a few. (*Bakery* magazine reports that about a dozen breads include "Country" on the label.) By playing up their use of honey, cracked wheat, multigrains, sprouted wheat, stone-ground wheat, bran, wheat berry, butter, sourdough, granola, yogurt, natural wheat, golden wheat, and such, they aim to create the image of honest, homey bread. Frequently, this is an incomplete picture.

Given all these choices and hype, it takes a dedicated shopper to find a bread that meets the wholefoods criterion. Happily, changes in the law since *The Supermarket Handbook* was written now require that all ingredients be declared on the label, so an informed purchase is possible. Moreover, supermarket fare has broadened in many regions, and natural food stores continue as reliable sources of wholesome bread, prepared by what appears to be a growing number of independent bakeries.

BREAD "LINES"

Now that complex carbohydrates have received the stamp of approval, the industry is eager to let consumers know how good wheat is for them. In one public relations campaign, the Wheat Industry Council designed a symbol with the logo "Wheat, Good for Life," and urges bakers to use it in ads, displays, and point-of-sales material, as well as on labels. Since this logo is not restricted to products using unrefined wheat, it may appear on baked goods that are devoid of many of the nutrients that do, indeed, make wheat "good for life."

In a series of commercials, Wonder Bread, which used to "help build healthy bodies 12 ways," claimed "nutrition that whole wheat can't beat." When this was criticized as a blatant overstatement, it was altered to: "Whole Wheat does have more fiber and some nutrients, but Wonder has as much thiamin, niacin, and iron . . . after all, the government set the standards." But as illustrated in the comparison on page 96, the government standards for enrichment still leave refined grains in an inferior position.

Aware that consumers today are upset by the use of the chemical additives, the strategy of many bread companies has been to do away with preservatives and use that as a selling point. Nevertheless, many breads promoted as "no preservatives added," "100 percent natural", etc., still include large amounts of refined white flour, hydrogenated shortening, and dough conditioners as well.

Placing bread on special display racks and in the deli and dairy sections, together with the introduction of on-site bakeries, has also made some breads seem more wholesome than they may actually be.

The Poverty of Enrichment

Most people like bread and enjoy eating it, but do so with the belief that it is fattening and has little food value. While it is true that no single food can provide a nourishing diet, many of the important but less publicized vitamins and minerals have been traditionally supplied by whole grain foods and these nutrients are not restored by the enrichment of white bread. The presence of these native nutrients is a more valid reason for selecting a bread than the addition of the protein, thiamin, niacin, riboflavin, calcium, and iron which manufacturers prefer to stress, but which are generally better supplied by other foods.

The Fuss About Fiber

Recognition of the benefits of fiber, or roughage, has brought about another significant development in the bakery. For decades, bakers and nutritionists put little stock in the value of fiber; only "health faddists"

THE HIDDEN VALUE OF WHOLE WHEAT (VERSUS WHITE) BREAD*

Bread 1 ounce	Calories	Fiber[1] grams	Magnesium mgs.	Copper mgs.	Zinc mgs.	Vit.B_6 mgs.	Pantothenic Acid mgs.	Folacin mcgs.
Whole Wheat	70	1.6	27	0.10	0.48	0.05	0.21	16
White	76	0.4	6	0.04	0.18	0.01	0.12	10

*Source: *Provisional Table on the Nutritient Content of Bakery Foods and Related Items,* USDA, 1981.

[1]As yet there is no standard procedure for analyzing fiber, and different laboratories often obtain different values. Mean values for fiber from many published sources were used to obtain these figures.

believed it had health-promoting qualities. However, as soon as promising medical reports became common consumer knowledge, fiber began to sell bread.

What is fascinating about this is that the bakery industry, which has been selling us the soft, squeezable stuff, made no attempt to improve it by producing a good-quality, inexpensive whole grain loaf. To our great disappointment, they chose another route instead: white bread in an even more processed state. "High-fiber breads" (also promoted as "diet breads" because they contain fewer calories) may contain as much as 400 percent more fiber than whole wheat bread; this fiber is gained by adding inexpensive nonfood sources such as powdered cellulose, which is more commonly recognized by the name wood pulp.

The marketing of such bread raises many questions. How many consumers are aware that there is a derivative of wood in their bread? Is wood suitable for human consumption? Just because fiber is important, do we need 400 percent more than that which occurs naturally in grain? And again we ask, why not simply promote a mass-marketed, reasonably priced, whole grain bread? We know it is possible, for we have seen soft whole wheat bread that can make a peanut butter and jelly sandwich that would please any generation.

Bread and the Dieter

Most "diet" breads achieve their reduced-calorie status in one of two ways: Their manufacturers add pure fiber, as described above, or they cut a thinner slice. While streamlining the size of the slice may help you cut out some bread calories, to maintain your desirable weight on a long-term basis you need foods that are a concentrated source of nutrients, not empty calories blown up by wood and hot air.

Unrefined carbohydrates supply natural fiber which absorbs moisture during digestion and creates a feeling of fullness. Whole grains also offer a satisfying taste, instead of blandness. This is the kind of bread weight-conscious people should be eating. As you can see from the preceding comparison, whole grain breads are no higher in calories than white breads.

THE STANDARD LOAF

Federal standards of identity for bread were originally written to guarantee what was considered a minimum of wholesomeness. The law prevented anyone from using highly popular names such as "white bread" or "whole wheat bread" unless certain specifications were met. When these standards were fulfilled, the product was exempt from complete ingredient labeling. Today, although standardized breads still exist, the labeling exception does not, and thus the consumer is able to freely compare products.

Those breads that are governed by the federal regulations include white bread, whole wheat bread, enriched bread, egg bread, milk bread, and raisin bread.

Nonstandardized or specialty breads cannot use the above names and are free to use any formulation they like, but as with standardized breads they must list all ingredients on the label. Common examples of specialty breads include rye, pumpernickel, corn, wheat, cracked wheat, sprouted breads, English muffins, pita bread, and more.

Common Commercial Bread Ingredients

In theory, bread is a simple food made from flour, water, and yeast. In practice, however, the recipe for bread has become quite complex, for in addition to the typical ingredients you might use in a homemade loaf, bakers may also add yeast nutrients, dough conditioners, dough strengtheners, and "other ingredients that do not change the basic identity or adversely affect the physical and nutritional characteristics of the food."

Since many of the terms that are listed on the label do not refer to ingredients found in your kitchen cupboard, they may be meaningless to you. Following is an explanation of what they are and how to evaluate them when choosing a bread.

Flour or Wheat Flour: Flour or wheat flour is the same as white flour. It has been refined to eliminate the vital bran and the germ and is probably bleached. It has little to recommend it in the way of nutrition (see Chapter 5).

Unbleached Flour: This too is a refined white flour and, contrary to what people have been led to believe, is certainly not untainted by chemicals; it has merely escaped the final bleaching process. When the choice is between bleached and unbleached flour, we suggest you choose the latter, but our preference is to reject both.

Enriched Flour: This means that of the twenty-two nutrients known to be removed during the milling of white flour, three of the B vitamins are replaced, along with iron salts and possibly calcium. (Four out of twenty-two—some enrichment!) A number of states require this enrichment in all refined breadstuffs sold in-state.

Whole Wheat Flour: In order for bread to be called "whole wheat," "graham," or "entire wheat" bread, 100 percent whole wheat flour must be used. This flour may be bleached, although it's uncommon, and it may be treated with potassium bromate (bromated). Such treatment will be disclosed on the label.

Shortening: Fat makes bread tender and helps keep it fresh. French breads, Italian breads, pita breads, and other breadstuffs with little or no shortening do not keep as well as breads with a substantial amount of added fat. The term *shortening* on a label includes animal or vegetable fat. Some bakers use butter or liquid oils. Others employ partially hydrogenated oils or perhaps margarine, with all the additives inherent in these products. Thus, "all-vegetable shortening" is not necessarily a selling point to the informed consumer who has read Chapters 20 and 21.

We are sorry to report that several breads which were formerly recommended in *The Supermarket Handbook* and which many consumers have come to view as superior supermarket brands no longer qualify as Exemplary Brands due to their reliance on partially hydrogenated oil.

Water: Since about 40 percent of bread dough is made up of water, even small variations in the composition of the water can make a substantial difference in the quality of the finished product. When you bake bread at home you are generally not concerned with uniformity; if on one occasion your bread rises more than on another, or has a softer crumb, or slices a little better, you won't give it much thought as long as you enjoy the taste. If you were a baking conglomerate, however, and were licensing your formula all over the country, you would want each loaf to be the same.

Thus, "conditioning" the water with chemical salts may play a part in the formula of the factory baker. These water conditioners are usually referred to on the label as "yeast nutrients" or "dough conditioners," because they serve these functions as well.

Dough Conditioners: Several different agents are commonly used in bread making to strengthen the dough structure, soften and whiten the crumb, improve volume with less yeast and shorter risings, and make the bread easier to slice. The use of conditioners also makes dough easier to process and more tolerant of harsh mechanical handling and machine "abuse."

What is especially disturbing about these additives is that normally the fermentation that takes place while bread is rising helps make certain minerals more available to the body. The use of dough conditioners is said to reduce this important fermentation time by as much as 75 percent. (Sprouting has a similar effect, and the sprouting of grains and overnight fermentation of dough that is standard procedure in many primitive cultures and in breads baked according to macrobiotic principles gives it increased nutritional value.)

In the early days of commercial baking, sugars, malted barley, and later malted wheat acted as dough conditioners. Dextrin, a starch derivative, and dextrose, a sugar, are still used for this purpose by some bakers. Others prefer to use enzyme preparations. More offensive are the harsh oxidizing agents such as bisulfites and calcium peroxide. Some popular chemical dough conditioners like mono- and diglycerides may even be used in so-called natural breads since they are derived from fats. The fact is, none of these fat derivatives exist in nature in the refined form in which they are utilized commercially.

Yeast Nutrients: Yeast nutrients promote yeast activity, allowing the baker to produce a larger loaf from fewer ingredients. They may take the form of traditional foods like malt or milk sugar, but may just as easily be the same chemical salts used to condition the water.

Sweetening: Sweeteners in the form of sugar, corn syrup, fructose, dextrose, honey, and molasses are used to feed the yeast, flavor the bread, and enhance browning. Although no sweetening really adds to bread's food value, honey and molasses are at least less refined and actually better for the bread, too, since both increase its moisture retention and produce a loaf that stays fresher longer without any chemical assistance.

Emulsifiers: Another extensive group of additives can soften the bread and extend its shelf-life. Common commercial emulsifiers are hydroxylated lecithin, mono- and diglycerides, and most recently, sucrose fatty acid esters. When these substances are added, the amount of natural and traditional emulsifiers like milk and eggs, which add to the nutritional value (and the manufacturer's cost), can be reduced or eliminated.

Preservatives: Most bakers contend that the preservatives they add are for the convenience of the consumer, enabling the product to be kept for several days after purchase without mold formation. In truth, they are really for the convenience of the manufacturer, making it possible to market baked goods far from the factory. Although preservatives have become practically synonymous with adulteration in many people's minds, the most common substances used for this purpose are far more benign than some of the other ingredients in breads.

In yeast-leavened products, sodium and calcium propionates are still the most widely used antimicrobials. In baked goods leavened with baking soda or baking powder, sorbates and a family of chemicals known as methyl and propyl parabens may be used as well.

Certain food ingredients such as salt, sugar, vinegar, and spices are also preservatives. Recently, manufacturers have been using raisin juice, which has a high acid content and inhibits mold growth. Another fairly new approach is the introduction of acid-producing bacteria which, like vinegar and raisin juice, create an environment that is not favorable to certain microorganisms. All these tactics allow a "no preservatives added" tag line and do not interfere with product integrity.

While "no preservatives added" is considered a selling point at this time, we again emphasize that any breads considered natural on this basis alone may contain far more questionable ingredients. In fact, bread may suffer its worst setback yet as a result of this quest to be preservative-free. The reason is irradiation, a process approved for wheat. Although irradiation is being promoted in glowing terms, this technique is actually fraught with uncertainties. We hope both you and the baking industry take the time to become informed about the hazards of an irradiated food supply before this bread becomes a reality. (For more information see Chapter 23.)

Coloring: Artificial coloring is not commonly found in bread, but some manufacturers do use caramel color to impart the darker hue that people generally associate with whole grains. This is a misleading tactic and, in addition, makes use of a colorant that many criticize as unsafe.

Unreal Bread at Unreal Prices

When we give workshops we are frequently asked why wholefoods tend to be more costly than their refined counterparts. In a preconference speech prior to the 1985 Bakers' Expo, the president of Quality Bakers of America offered a clue as far as bread is concerned. A one-pound loaf of white bread at the time averaged 55.3 cents nationwide; a one-pound loaf of whole wheat bread averaged 86.3 cents.

"Nobody in this room can tell me that there is a 31-cent difference in cost," he said. "The 31-cent difference between white and whole wheat signifies a spreading of cost to carry our low or no-margin white bread." So, you see, you are forced to pay a premium for a better product in order to subsidize an inferior bread that is priced to sell; perhaps the baking industry is aware that if white bread weren't cheap, it would have no reason for being at all.

SELECTING SPECIALTY BREADS

Now that you are more comfortable with some of the common terms on a bread label you should have no trouble spotting a high-quality whole wheat loaf. The selection of specialty breads can be a bit confusing, though, due to the lack of federal standards coupled with some vague areas in their labeling.

Rye Bread

As a result of the federal rules, rye bread can legally have as little as 3.1 percent rye flour. Most often, sandwich or deli-style ryes are made with 20 to 40 percent light or medium rye flour. Unfortunately, the consumer has no way to know for sure because ingredient labeling does not call for such detailing. Since ingredients appear in the order of predominance, you do receive a clue, however, depending on which is listed first, rye or wheat flour.

There are a few brands of 100 percent rye bread which you can identify immediately by the absence of other grains on the label. They are often made without fat and have a dense crumb and compact size; lacking the gluten found in wheat, which enables the dough to expand and entrap air, this bread will not rise to any great extent. All-rye breads are frequently presented as square, thinly sliced loaves. Several exemplary choices are imported from Germany; a hermetically sealed package may be used to keep them fresh for several months before opening, but once the seal has been broken, refrigeration is recommended. Sometimes these dense, square breads are called pumpernickel.

Pumpernickel

More often, what is marketed as pumpernickel is a blend of white flour with dark rye flour and perhaps coarse rye meal. The characteristic dark color may be accentuated with molasses, coffee, carob or, even less desirably, caramel color. The presence of more rye and the coarse meal accounts for the higher fiber and mineral content of this bread as compared to deli-type ryes.

Multi-Grain Breads

There is a growing trend in commercial bread-making toward the incorporation of other cereal grains, including oats, corn, rye, cracked wheat, rice, millet, triticale, and barley (some of which may be sprouted), as well as soy and flaxseed. Many of these combination breads use the evocative "health" and "country style" names mentioned in the beginning of this chapter.

Some of these breads are quite commendable. Others contain some refined flour and sugar. (We have rated these as "Acceptable with Reservation.") Unfortunately, most of these breads include several refined sweeteners (corn syrup, fructose, and sugar), partially hydrogenated oils, bromated flour, yeast nutrients, dough conditioners, emulsifiers, and caramel color. Here it is easy to be fooled by clever product names and claims of "all natural," "no preservatives," and "no artificial coloring," or the highlighting of a few select ingredients on the label such as "made with whole grains and honey."

When you read the list of ingredients in these breads, remember that they are presented in descending order by weight. If yeast and salt appear before sunflower seeds, wheat germ, rye meal, oat flakes, barley grits, bran, etc., as they do in several "health" breads, how much of these healthful ingredients could actually be present?

One of the novel combination breads worth mentioning goes under the name Ezekiel, inspired by the biblical story of the prophet Ezekiel who was reported to have fasted for 390 days on water and bread made from wheat, barley, millet, beans, and lentils, all of which are included in the formula of breads using this name.

Other new exemplary products offer enhanced protein by combining whole wheat flour with amaranth and soy flours.

Sourdough Breads

Traditional sourdough bread is produced by using a fermented starter to leaven a simple wheat- or wheat and rye-based dough, creating a distinct sour flavor favored by some. Unfortunately, the popularity of the sourdough flavor has been the impetus for commercial bakers to use synthesized acids that mimic this taste.

Still, there are a few high-quality sourdough breads, generally manufactured in small local bakeries, that are fat- and sugar-free and take advantage of whole grains and the traditionally long fermentation. The famed sourdough bread of San Francisco, however, is essentially a white bread whose only advantage is a lower fat content when compared with sandwich breads (making it similiar to most Italian and French loaves marketed throughout the country).

Sprouted Breads

The use of sprouted grains as a partial component of bread has been a promotional point for many "health"-oriented breads. As we have noted previously in the discussion of dough conditioners, the sprouted grains can produce a more nutritious loaf; however, when they are used in small quantities, simply so the bread can be called "sprouted," the addition profits the baker more than the consumer.

At the other end of the spectrum are some wholesome breads made entirely of sprouted grains. Sometimes referred to as "flourless" bread, the resulting loaf is dense and chewy, almost like cake, with a moist interior, a hard crust, and a sweet, nutlike flavor. Some varieties are made from wheat or rye alone; others include various grains, spices, dried fruit, and nuts. Many, but not all, are free of flour, fat, yeast, salt, and sweetening.

"Super" Bread (or Sliceable Vitamins)

"Enriched special-formula breads," as they are legally known, are being test-marketed at this writing. They differ from standard enriched white bread because they are highly fortified with specific nutrients as recommended by the National Academy of Sciences Food and Nutrition Board.

We continue to be amazed by the concept of using food as a carrier for nutritional supplements, whether it is bread or ready-to-eat breakfast cereal. This practice ignores some vital nutrients and raises the likelihood that people will wind up with multiple doses of a few select nutrients obtained from super-enriched foods that provide 100 percent of the daily requirement *and* one-a-day vitamins in tablet form, creating not only a false sense of security but also possible potentially harmful imbalances.

Bagels

This ethnic bread, once confined almost exclusively to metropolitan areas in the Northeast, is now popular coast to coast. The basic bagel formula is fairly straightforward—high-gluten wheat flour, water, yeast, salt, oil, and sometimes malt. This may be varied with onion, caraway seed, sesame seed, poppy seed, raisins, sugar, and a small proportion of whole wheat or rye flours. Some exemplary bagels, found primarily in natural food stores, dispense with the refined flour altogether and base their recipe on whole wheat and perhaps some rye.

Now that bagels have risen from a fresh bakery item to a shelf staple, we have seen the introduction of preservatives to the traditional recipe. If you wish to avoid them, be sure to read the list of ingredients.

Pita

Pita, the round bread that forms a pocket when cut crosswise (and therefore is sometimes referred to as *pocket bread*), is another ethnic bakery product that is becoming more common in whole wheat form. When made with whole wheat flour, water, yeast, salt, sometimes vinegar (used in warm weather as a mold inhibitor), and no fat or sweetening, this can be a very commendable and versatile breadstuff. But not all brands are so pristine. Just because they are whole wheat doesn't mean they are free of unnecessary sweeteners and additives. One whole wheat brand that is marketed frozen has the most contrived recipe of all.

English Muffins

Nothing is more American than the English muffin! The recent introduction of a "honey wheat" version would be a promising development were it not that most honey wheat muffins still have more white flour than whole wheat flour, and contain corn syrup in addition to honey, as well as partially hydrogenated oil and mono- and diglycerides.

There are, however, a few exemplary whole grain English muffins marketed through health-oriented stores across the country.

Croissants

It is curious that a culture that so emphatically denounces butter and saturated fats in one breath should so eagerly embrace a breadstuff dripping with both, but there is no question that the French import, the croissant, has taken a strong hold in the U.S. market. The typical croissant derives more than half its approximately 200 calories from fat. (In most breads, fat accounts for less than 10 percent of the calories.) Even "wheat 'n honey" croissants cannot make up for this excessiveness.

For those who can afford this extravagance, there are a few brands of 100 percent whole wheat croissants. And if you are going to indulge in any type of croissant, at least get the authentic product. The famous French food authority Escoffier is probably gagging in his grave at the thought of croissants made with margarine.

Tortillas

The popularity of Mexican food has increased the availability of corn and wheat tortillas. They are especially useful for those sensitive to yeast. (Corn tortillas are unleavened; wheat tortillas are generally leavened with baking powder, although occasionally yeast is used.) The cornmeal tortilla is also welcomed by anyone who needs to avoid wheat, and as an additional plus, it is salt and fat-free.

The tortilla made with corn, water, and lime (calcium hydroxide) can be found in virtually every grocery store in America, sometimes with a propionate preservative added, almost as often without. Natural food stores offer an even better product made with organically grown corn.

A TRADITIONAL FOOD TALE

The lime in corn tortillas serves a very important purpose and its presence is an interesting lesson in how ancient rituals should influence modern practices. Here is the story:

Before modern milling came along, the Indians boiled their corn in a mixture of ashes and water prior to pounding it into a paste. Once the millstone was invented, this process was abandoned. Soon after, corn-dependent cultures began to exhibit a host of disease symptoms. It was later discovered that the alkaline ash freed the B vitamin niacin, which had kept the Indians from getting the deficiency disease we now call pellagra. Today, the boiling of corn in lime provides the same service.

In choosing a wheat tortilla, look for a whole wheat formula that is free of hydrogenated shortening. While less easily found than corn and refined wheat tortillas, they do exist.

Note that tortillas are usually kept in the refrigerator case with the dairy products, or in the freezer.

Chapatis

Whole wheat chapatis, an unleavened bread developed in India and made from a simple dough of flour, water, oil, and salt, are also available in limited supply. They are generally found in natural food stores and may be made with organically grown grain. Because they are unleavened, chapatis are ideal for anyone who must avoid yeast.

Salt-Free Breads

The typical one-ounce slice of commercial bread contains 110 to 150 milligrams of sodium; many natural food store offerings have reduced this to 80 to 100 milligrams, and whole wheat pita may contain as little as 30 to 50 milligrams (or 100 milligrams per 2 to 3 ounces of bread). Salt-free products are made to satisfy special dietary needs. In the market they are often kept in the freezer because the reduction in sodium makes the bread more susceptible to spoilage. Some breads add potassium chloride to compensate for the lack of flavor. While minimal amounts of potassium chloride are probably harmless, widespread use of this salt substitute may not be benign (see Chapter 38).

Anyone concerned about sodium should be aware that cornmeal tortillas are usually unsalted.

Yeast-Free Breads

Baked goods leavened with baking powder or baking soda are known as quick breads. Muffins, biscuits, steamed canned brown bread, Southern-style corn bread, and tea breads all come under this heading. In selecting these products, use the same standards you would for seeking out whole grain sandwich breads—no hydrogenated shortenings, refined sweeteners, preservatives (sorbates are common), artificial coloring, flavoring, and such. If specified, aluminum-free baking powder is preferred. Remember, tortillas, chapatis, and some sprouted breads offer additional yeast-free choices.

"ALL BAKING DONE ON THE PREMISES"

How many times have you been attracted by this invitation? No matter how much sophistication we (your authors) acquire about food industry practices, we still want to believe that products baked in the store are akin to those we might bake at home. We are not alone; surveys indicate that consumers feel that fresh-prepared foods at bakery/deli counters are nutritious and preservative-free. In contrast, they believe commercially prepared bakery foods contain preservatives and are not natural.

It takes only a quick glance through any of the bakery trade publications to show that this is wishful thinking. Many stores that offer homemade breads and muffins rely on mixes or frozen unbaked doughs that are as contrived as the standard shelf offerings, and sometimes more so. What is even more distasteful is that because they are sold on-site they may not be required to show a list of ingredients.

Don't let a homey name or fresh bakery smell lure you. If the ingredients are not listed, assume they are not worth knowing.

THE NEIGHBORHOOD BAKER

The 1950s were considered the golden age for retail bakeries. There was at least one to be found in every village, more in larger towns, and it seemed like there was one on almost every block in the cities. Not so today, where shopping malls, supermarkets, convenience stores, and fast food franchises exist in abundance. Even where local bakeries still do operate, it is up to the individuals who run them to determine how pure their baked goods will be. They too may succumb to the shortcuts offered by chemicals, enzymes, and the extracted components of food.

THE NEW COMMUNITY BAKERS

While the conventional bakery is disappearing, wholefoods bakeries are rising up throughout the country, turning out products that merit the good reputation bread has enjoyed worldwide for centuries. These enterprises are a valuable resource in the communities they serve and may sell directly to the consumer or market through retail food stores. A few have even built up a considerable mail-order trade.

Our list of Exemplary Brands includes the breadstuffs made by the community bakers we have encountered during our in-store research, even though their products are sold only within a limited radius. If you are lucky enough to have access to locally made wholefoods baked goods, be sure to take full advantage; if there is no such baker in your area, see if you can't encourage one. This is an ideal venture for the entrepreneur and many models exist to help one become established. As you can see from "Food by Mail" in Chapter 3, it is even possible to get good bread delivered to your door.

MIXES: HOME BAKED,
BUT NOT HOMEMADE

As with all foods, the criteria for selecting bread should be based on the presence of ingredients common to your pantry. Can you imagine not being able to bake because you are out of BHA, sodium stearoyl lactylate, or phosphoric acid? If you can't get these ingredients directly, why ingest them through someone else's recipe?

If you wish to bake bread at home from a mix or frozen dough, you must be discriminating. One typical rye bread mix, which ironically is marketed as having "no artificial colors, flavors, or preservatives," contains:

wheat flour (bleached), malted barley flour, rye flour, salt, skim milk, dried malt syrup, sugar, partially hydrogenated soy oil, spice, sodium stearoyl lactylate (dough conditioner), yeast, phosphoric acid, lactic acid, mono- and diglycerides (emulsifier), acetic acid, propionic acid, onion powder, potassium bromate

If you wish to use a mix for bread or muffins, the ingredients should be as simple as a homemade recipe. That is, whole grain flours, dry milk powder, leavening, salt, and perhaps some nutritional yeast, herbs, or spices. (By the way, most pancake mixes and all-purpose baking mixes listed in Chapter 5 can be used to fashion biscuits and muffins as well.)

KEEPING BREAD

Whether you have purchased your bread at the store or baked your own, you'll want to preserve the freshness as long as you can. Those of you who are convinced food needs to have added preservatives will be surprised to find that a loaf of bread can easily be kept for a week without them if it is prepared with fresh, high-quality ingredients in the first place.

Crisp-crusted breads should be stored in a paper bag or other device that lets some air circulate for the first day or two; otherwise the crust will soften. After this period, it should be placed, like all other breads, in nonporous material such as foil or reusable plastic bags to prevent drying out. If the package recommends refrigerator storage, by all means follow this advice. Storing bread in the refrigerator does dry it a bit but will prevent the growth of mold; it is a must in warm weather. Bread destined for the toaster can be stored in this manner as well.

We like to keep a variety of whole grain breads on hand at all times to complement the menu. The freezer is a great aid here, particularly for storing mail-order purchases or brands that are not regularly available. Bread can successfully be frozen for six months or longer if closely wrapped in an airtight package. When a few slices are needed, remove them from your "freezer breadbox" and let them stand at room temperature. In less than half an hour, your bread will be restored to its original texture. Of course, any frozen bread can be toasted or warmed in the oven (or toaster oven) immediately.

Packaged breads often carry a pull date (or last day of sale), which you should routinely check before you buy. If you plan to freeze your purchase, you may want to consult with the store to find out if they receive their baked goods fresh or frozen. We have seen breads on the shelf or in the refrigerator which we know, from the distributor, are sent out frozen. While refreezing is not harmful, multiple thawings will diminish eating quality.

BREAD CRUMBS

With few exceptions, the prepared bread crumbs, coatings, and stuffing mixes on the market are made from refined breadstuffs and contain other undesirable ingredients. Thus, the best way to obtain high-quality bread crumbs and bread cubes is to use the good bread you buy. Simply put bread slices out on a plate at room temperature for several hours until they become hard and no moisture is left in them. You can grate them immediately in the blender, processor, or with a hand grater, or store them whole in an airtight container. Dry, hard bread will not grow mold, and each time you have an extra slice you can add it to your bread-crumb jar.

RECOMMENDATIONS

BREAD

General Rule of Purchase: All ingredients are on the label. Look for breads made with whole grains, nonhydrogenated oils or butter, fresh dairy products, and honey or molasses, if sweetened. Of special interest are those breads made with organic ingredients.

Consult the list of ingredients to avoid white (also known as wheat) flour, partially hydrogenated shortening, dough conditioners, mono- and diglycerides, caramel coloring, as well as artificial coloring, and preservatives. Try to avoid yeast nutrients for they are a sign of a lesser quality bread.

Unless you are acquainted with the baker or the baker's practices, avoid items sold in in-store bakeries or loose in display cases that do not reveal their contents. The use of some white flour or refined sweetener diminishes the product to "Acceptable with Reservation" status.

Exemplary Brands

Whole Wheat Breadstuffs

Abiqua Farm Whole Grain Wood Oven Bread

Aladdin Whole Wheat Pita

Alvarado Street Bakery Whole Wheat Bread; Hot Dog and Hamburger Buns[2]

Baldwin Hill Sesame Wheat, Salt Free Whole Wheat, Raisin Breads; Whole Wheat Bread Crumbs[1]

Baltic Bakery Stone Ground Whole Wheat Bread

Berkshire Mountain Bakery Sourdough Sesame Bread[1]

Big Deal Bakery Bran, Carrot, Banana Muffins; Banana Bread

Black Forest 100% Stone Ground Cashew Date Bread

Bread Alone Miche Bread[1]

Bubble Pouch Poppy Seed, Sesame Seed, Onion, Herbal, Raisin Cinnamon, Cashew Orange Breads[2]

Cedar Lane Chapati (Salted, Unsalted), Tannour Bread; All Purpose Breading Meal

Crumbs Bakery Whole Wheat, Herb, Molasses Date Breads

Food For Life Bran for Life Bread and English Muffins; Carrot, Banana, Bran, Corn, Date, Raisin Spice Muffins; Honey Wheat Berry, Indian Chia with Sprouted Whole Wheat, Jerusalem Artichoke, Sprouted Alfalfa, Low Sodium Whole Wheat, 100% Stone Ground Organic Whole Wheat[1] Breads; Sprouted Wheat Burger Buns

Garden of Eatin' Bible Bagels,[1] Chapatis,[1] Bible Bread (Regular, No-Salt,[1] Thin, Thin Bread,[1] Sourdough Slims[1])

Grain-Bin Stone Ground 100% Whole Wheat, Raisin Walnut, 3-Seed Breads

Hawaiian Bagel Whole Wheat Bagels, Pita

Health Farms Whole Wheat Pocket Bread

Innisfree Bakery Whole Wheat, Sprouted Wheat, Sunflower Sesame, Cinnamon Raisin, Vermont Sweetbread with Maple Syrup Breads;[2] Honey Raisin Bran Muffins[2]

Joseph's Middle Eastern Whole Wheat Pita

Justice Bakery Sprouted Whole Wheat Bread

Kaplan's Bakery Poppy Seed Rolls, Lavash

Kroger Deli Bakery 100% Wheat Pocket Bread

Legume Blueberry, Raisin Bran Tofuffins

Life Line Cinnamon Raisin Bread

Lifestyle Whole Wheat Croissants

Little Bear Bagels[2]

Living Lightly Organic Pockets[1]

Main Stay Sprouted Wheat, Sourdough, Molasses Raisin, Whole Wheat, Salt Free Whole Wheat, Date Nut Breads; Cracked Wheat Rolls

Matthew's Whole Wheat, Cinnamon Raisin, Pita Breads; Whole Wheat English, Cinnamon Raisin English Muffins; Salad Rolls

Middle East Bakery Pita Bread

Mrs. Gooch's Natural Whole Grain Muffins

Nassraway Whole Wheat Pita

Natural and Kosher Whole Wheat Pita[1]

Natural Food Mill Bakery Carrot, Bran, Apple Bran, Banana Muffins

Natural Foods Milk Creek Sprouted Wheat, Sweet Free 100% Whole Grain, Cinnamon Raisin Breads; Sprouted Wheat Sandwich Buns

Nature's Cupboard Whole Wheat, Whole Wheat with Raisins and Cinnamon, 4-Seed Breads

Nature's Garden Bakery Diet Bran Muffins[2]

Old Country Whole Wheat Pita

Old World Pocket Bread

Poncé Wheat, Sesame Breads;[1] Brioche[2]

Pritikin Stone Ground Whole Wheat, Apple Cinnamon, Onion Dill Breads

Shiloh Farms Whole Wheat Pita With Salt; No Salt Added, Whole Wheat Hot Dog and Hamburger Buns; Whole Wheat, Whole Wheat No Salt Added, Whole Wheat Raisin, Whole Wheat Sunflower, Bran Breads

Simple Treat Herb Bakery Herb and Onion Bread

Spruce Tree Whole Wheat Bread

Staff of Life Natural Foods Bakery Whole Wheat, Sesame Wheat, Carrot Poppy, Sourdough Whole Wheat French, Unleavened Tibetan Breads; Sesame Burger Buns

Sunbelt Country Bran Bread

Sunrise Crunchy Kokua, Salt Free Kokua, Whole Wheat Sourdough, Cinnamon Raisin Breads; Bran Muffins; Whole Wheat Buns, Cinnamon Raisin Rolls

Survival Premium Whole Wheat, Standard Loaf Stone Ground 100% Wheat Breads; Date Bran Muffins

The Bakery Home Style Wheat Bread[1]

The Better Bagel Bagels[2]

The Good Bread Bakery Cracked Wheat, Whole Wheat Breads[1]

Whole Wheat Breadstuffs (continued)

The Muffin Man Whole Wheat, Sunflower, Raisin Breads;[2] Muffins[2]

The Renaissance Bakery Whole Wheat, Raisin Breads[1]

Toufayan 100% Whole Wheat Pita, Salt Free Pitettes

Tree of Life Pocket Bread,[1] Burger Buns[1]

Uprisings Bakery Basic Whole Wheat, Whole Wheat Onion, Sourdough, Raisin, Honey Bran Breads;[1] Raisin Bran, Banana Muffins[2]

Whole World Bakery 100% Whole Wheat Rolls, Hamburger Buns

Whole Wheat Natural Bakery Whole Wheat, Sprouted Wheat Breads; Hot Dog, Hamburger Rolls

Women's Community Bakery Honey Whole Wheat, Salt Free Honey Whole Wheat Breads[1]; Whole Wheat Rolls;[2] Breakfast Bran, Spicy Apple Muffins[2]

Your Black Muslim Bakery Natural Parker House Rolls; Natural Wheat Raisin, Honey Wheat Breads

Mixed Grain Breadstuffs

Alvarado Street Bakery Whole Wheat Oatmeal, Whole Wheat Bran with Millet Breads[2]

Baba's Oat, Sunny Millet, Whole Wheat Breads

Baldwin Hill Rye Bread[1]

Berkshire Mountain Bakery Sourdough Rice Bread[1]

Big Island Bakery Stone Ground Multi-Grain Bread[1]

Boulangerie Natural Whole Grain Rolls

Bread Alone Mixed Grain, Norwegian Farm, Finnish Sour Rye, Pumpernickel Raisin Breads[1]

Crumbs Bakery Cracked Wheat Bread

Food For Life Soya Protein, Sprouted Rye, Oatmeal Pecan Breads

Fred Meyer Nutrition Center 9 Grain Bread

Garden of Eatin' Pumpernickel Bagels,[1] Swedish Rye Pocket Bread[1]

Grain-Bin Sesame Crunch, 9-Grain Breads

Guisto's Vita-Grain Rolls

Health Valley Amaranth Bread

Highland View Whole Wheat, Golden Grains 8 Grain Breads

Justice Bakery Flaxseed Oat, Sour Onion Rye, Sunflower Millet Breads

Katy's Whole Wheat, Salt Free Whole Wheat Breads, Rolls, Buns

Main Stay Oatmeal, Triticale Rye, Pumpernickel Breads

Nasoya Foods Corn Cakes[2]

Natural Food Mill Bakery 7-Grain Sprouted Wheat Honey English Muffins, Boulangerie Whole Grain Rolls, New World Multigrain, Triticale Breads

Natural Foods Milk Creek Bakery 4x5 Multi Grain Bread

Nature's Cupboard Yogurt Oatmeal, 10-Grain Breads

Poncé Barley Bread[1]

Pritikin Rye Bread, English Muffins

Ruhrtaler Whole Wheat Bread

Run Runner's Country Cottage 8 Grain and Honey Bread, Rolls

Shiloh Farms Sprouted Seven Grain with Salt, No Salt Added, Sprouted Five Grain with Salt, No Salt Added Breads

Simple Treat Herb Bakery Swedish Rye Bread

Solstice Bakery Sprouted Wheat Berry Bread[2]

Spruce Tree Sesame Soy Protein, Sourdough Rye, Onion Rye, Pumpernickel, Rice Breads

Staff of Life Natural Foods Bakery 10 Grain, Salt Free 10 Grain, Sprouted Grain, Vegetable Herb, Sourdough Rye, Oatmeal Molasses, Harmony, Seed, Pumpernickel Breads; Onion Rye Rolls

Sunbelt 7 Grain High Protein Bread

Sunrise Multigrain, High Protein, Pumpernickel Breads

Survival Sliced Sandwich Buns, Sesame Surviva Bread

The Bakery Sesame Millet Crunch, Home Style 9, Grain Breads;[2] 7-Grain Sourdough Whole Wheat Bread, Rolls[2]

The Good Bread Bakery Sunflower Barley, Sourdough, Cornmeal Millet, Oatmeal Raisin Breads[1]

The Muffin Man Corn and Molasses, Rye, Seven Grain Breads[2]

To-Fitness 6+2 Bread

Uprisings Bakery Oat Sunflower Bread[2]

Whole World Natural Bakery Peasant Bread

Women's Community Bakery Warm Morning Cinnamon Granola, Oatmeal Raisin, 8 Grain Breads[2]

Sprouted Breads

Alvarado Street Bakery Sprouted Wheat, Sprouted Barley Breads[1]

Food For Life Whole Grain, Bran Plus, Cinnamon Raisin 7-Grain, Ezekiel 4:9, 7-Grain, Whole Wheat, Organic 7-Grain,[1] Sprouted Wheat Breads

Garden of Eatin' Flourless Sprout Breads[1]

Katy's Sprouted Wheat, Sprouted 8 Grain Breads

Lifestream Flourless Essene Breads[2]

Oasis Flourless Sprouted Breads

Solstice Bakery Sprouted Wheat,[1] Wheat with Dates and Nuts,[2] Rye[1] Breads

Supersprouts Sprouted Seed, Rye, Wheat with Raisin or Dates Breads; Sprouted Rye Rolls with Onions

Survival Honey Sprouted Wheat, Standard Loaf, Double Bran, Raisin Breads

Wheat-Free Breadstuffs

Bread For Life 100% Rye Bread

Dimflmeier 100% Plus Rye, Sourdough Rye Breads

Food For Life Apple Oatmeal Spice Muffins

Lotus Bakery Sourdough Rye, Onion Rye Breads[1]

Mystic Lake Dairy Brown Rice Bread

Natural Food Mill Wheat Free Muffins

Nature's Garden Bakery Bavarian Sourdough Rye,[2] Macrobiotic Whole Wheat,[2] Wheat Free Millet Breads

Old Germany Pumpernickel

Pema Pumpernickel

Poncé Rye Bread[1]

Richter Schwarzbrot Rye Bread

Ruhrtaler Pumpernickel

Staff of Life Natural Foods Bakery Wheatless Pumpernickel, Rye

21st Century Masa Corn Tarts[2]

Tortillas

Best Buy Corn Tortillas

Bien Padre Corn Tortillas

Casa Sanchez Corn Tortillas

Cedar Lane Corn Tortillas[1]

El Charrito Corn Tortillas

El Galindo Corn, Whole Wheat Flour Tortillas

El Muchacho Corn Tortillas

El Progresso Corn Tortillas

El Ranchito Corn Tortillas

El Toro Corn Tortillas

Fontova Corn Tortillas

Garden of Eatin' Corn, Whole Wheat Flour Tortillas[1]

Gardenia Brand Corn, Stone Ground Whole Wheat Tortillas

Health Valley Organically Grown Tortillas[1]

La Estrella Corn Tortillas

La Fronteriza Corn Tortillas

La Tortilla Factory Corn Tortillas

Le Toro Corn Tortillas

Mar-kes Corn Tortillas

Moctec Corn Tortillas

Natural and Kosher Corn, Whole Wheat Flour Tortillas[1]

One Kilo Brand Corn Tortillas

Pinata Corn Tortillas

Reser's Corn Tortillas

Senor Reser's Corn Tortillas

Senor Suarez Corn Tortillas

Stella's Stone Ground Corn Tortillas

Taco Shak Corn, Stone Ground Organic Corn[1] Tortillas

The Taco Maker Corn Tortillas

Acceptable with Reservation

These may contain some white flour, or sugar, but in general use other high-quality ingredients and may be the only choice in some circumstances.

Abiqua Farm Lite Rye, Hunter's Hearty Rye, Edleweis Light Rye Breads;[4] Whole Grain Rolls[4]

B&M New England Brown Bread[3]

Baldwin Hill Sourdough French Bread[1,4]

Baltic Bakery Pumpernickel, Latvian Rye, Lithuanian Rye Breads[3,4]

Bread Alone Swiss Peasant Bread[1,4]

Breads For Life Seven Grain, Sprouted Rye, Sprouted Wheat Breads[4]

Columbia Union College Sprouted Wheat, Oatmeal Breads[4]

Crumbs Bakery Sourdough Rye, Italian Breads[4]

Dimflmeier Holzofen, Pumpernickel, Raisin Pumpernickel, Black Forest Breads[4]

Food For Life Gluten, Millet, Soya Carob, Soya Sunflower Breads[4]

Guisto Millet Soya,[3,4] Vita-Grain High Protein and Soya,[4] Sourdough Rye[2,4] Breads

Howie's Baltimore Bagels[4]

Katy's Soy Protein, Rye Breads[4]

Mainstay Herb Dinner Rolls[4]

Natural Foods Milk Creek Bakery Just Plain Sandwich Buns,[4] Honey Wheat, Creole French Breads[4]

Nature's Garden Bakery Sourdough Gluten Rolls[1,4]

Rudolph's Linseed Rye Bread[4]

The Bakery Dill Rye, Home Style Country Light Breads[2,4]

Tree of Life Wheat Berry Bread[2,4]

Your Black Muslim Bakery Natural Wheat Egg Bread[4]

BAKING MIXES

General Rule of Purchase: All ingredients are on the label. Select those fashioned from whole grain flour, dry milk powder, leavening, and common seasonings. Whey is often used and should not disqualify a mix. Some refined flour, sugar, and dextrose diminish a product to "Acceptable with Reservation" status. Avoid stearoyl lactylate, bromates, mono- and diglycerides, preservatives, artificial color and flavoring, and similar nontraditional ingredients.

Arrowhead Mills Bran Muffin, Whole Wheat Bread Mixes

Fearn Natural Bran Muffin Mix

Moore's Flour Mill Cornmeal, Raisin Bran, Spice Apple Bran, Date Nut Bran Muffin Mixes

Nature's Choice Pumpernickel, Zucchini Quick Bread Mixes[2]

New World Multi-Grain Bread Mix

Willamette Valley Mills 100% Whole Wheat Biscuit Mix

Arrowhead Mills Multigrain Bread, Biscuit, Corn Bread Mixes[4]

Fearn Natural Corn Bread Mix[4]

[1]Organic
[2]Some organic ingredients
[3]Contains refined sweeteners
[4]Contains refined grains

Chapter 8

Sorting Out the Crackers

The Scandinavians have a name for crackers that really tells you what they are: "flat breads." If you use crackers for everyday eating, as you would bread, you'll find that you can greatly expand the choice of bread-stuffs acceptable to your inner ecology. Since crackers are available made from rye, corn, oats, and rice—an assortment of grains often overlooked in our wheat-oriented country—they offer an excellent opportunity to broaden the diet. We always keep a large selection on hand to complement meals and for snacking.

You may have to look around the supermarket to find what you are after. A portion of one shelf is generally set aside specifically for crackers, but they may also be intermingled with the cookies or displayed on the small shelves above the meat counter or freezer case. Further selections can often be found in the diet or natural food section.

CRACKING THE LABEL

Everything that goes into the dough is stated on the label, so be sure to read the list of ingredients before making your purchase. Look for brands that use the finest natural ingredients, which means whole grains, vegetable oils, honey, and seeds. Some crackers may be as simple as whole grain flour and water; others are leavened, shortened, and lightly sweetened. Many contain salt, but there are also a number of salt-free choices.

Watch out for: white flour, wheat flour (another way of saying white flour), enrichment, sugar, dextrose, corn syrup, partially hydrogenated shortening, margarine, artificial or caramel color, artificial flavor, yeast nutrients, dough conditioners, sodium propionate, BHT, BHA, or other preservatives. If you find any of these ingredients on the label, you may want to ban the cracker from your shopping cart.

Crackers keep indefinitely if stored in a dry environment—a factor that adds to their appeal. In fact, the original American cracker—hardtack or pilot's biscuit—was invented to sustain sailors during long sea voyages. Therefore, the addition of preservatives to today's crackers seems unnecessary.

Crackers do not have to contain any fat, but when they do, select those made with vegetable oils like soybean, corn, safflower, and peanut, which furnish important unsaturated fatty acids. Olive oil is also fine, but it is rarely used in baked goods. Highly saturated fats like coconut and palm oils and butter are less desirable. Lard is a saturated fat that is likely to contain chemical preservatives even though that may not be reflected on the label. Partially hydrogenated oils and margarine are not acceptable.

We want to emphasize that phrases like "nothing artificial" and "all natural ingredients" do not necessarily translate to wholefoods, and that even "natural stone-milled grains" are often stripped of the bran and germ. A cracker that offers "corn, wheat, and rice" may well be made with refined versions of these grains, "a century-old recipe" may have depended on white flour and sugar, and "no artificial colors or flavors and no preservatives" doesn't guarantee that there is nothing else objectionable in the package. All of these ploys are popular with cracker makers.

Whole Wheat Crackers

We have found that the word *wheat,* either in the product name or in the list of ingredients, often tricks consumers. Remember, wheat only indicates the type of grain. *Whole* wheat is your guarantee that the wheat is still intact, not "a blend of hearty wheat," "stoned wheat," or any other misleading modifiers.

"Whole wheat goodness," a favorite advertising slogan, is often attached to crackers that are, in actuality, partially refined. Sometimes this refinement is quite extensive, evidenced when white flour, wheat flour, or just flour is the first ingredient, with whole wheat following several paces behind. The dark color of pumpernickel crackers can also be misconstrued, for that deep brown often comes from the addition of caramel color or molasses, and does not reflect the whole grain as many shoppers suppose.

WHOLE WHEAT MATZOH

The very first cracker came about accidentally when the Jews fled Egypt before their bread had a chance to rise. This unleavened bread, called matzoh, is still being manufactured today, and several whole wheat brands exist with the added virtues of being salt-, yeast-, and fat-free.

WHOLE WHEAT BREAD STICKS AND PRETZELS

Several bread sticks which are made from 100 percent whole wheat are on the market, as are whole wheat pretzels. Both salted and unsalted versions abound. They need not be relegated to snacking. Serve them with a slice of cheese, smear them with peanut butter or your favorite spread, and dunk them in dips. You may find people who are resistant to whole wheat accept these bread sticks and pretzels with pleasure.

CRACKERS FOR FIBER FANS

If you stick with whole grains, you will probably have adequate roughage in your diet. However, if you want more, high-fiber crackers are available. These flat breads contain wheat bran, which is generally their foremost ingredient and is responsible for their unusual texture, reminiscent of compressed shredded wheat.

Rye Crackers

Crackers that are made totally or predominantly from rye flour range from paper-thin to thick and airy. These crackers are often described as crispbreads. Many are fat-free, some contain no salt, and others no yeast. In some the rye is combined with whole wheat, oats, and barley.

Rye contains a form of carbohydrate that has a high water-binding capacity; it absorbs moisture and swells when it reaches the stomach, creating a feeling of fullness. For this reason, and because rye is also digested more slowly, rye crackers are useful for curbing the appetite.

Rice Cakes and Crackers

Rice cakes, regarded as a macrobiotic eccentricity just a few years ago, are now sold in every supermarket and natural food outlet. They are nothing more than puffed brown rice compacted into chewy rounds about 3½ inches in diameter; in texture they might remind you of Styrofoam. Despite the variety—rice alone or in combination with millet, sesame, or buckwheat, lightly salted or unsalted—all taste pretty much the same. While we wouldn't exactly rate rice cakes as exciting, a light toasting considerably improves their crispness so that the sensation is similar to eating popcorn. Spread with a nut or fruit butter they are an appealing snack. You can also use them in place of rice as the grain base of a meal. Because they are free of wheat, fat, yeast, and are available salt-free as well, rice cakes are suitable for almost everyone's diet.

Rice snaps are another innovation in all-rice crackers. These tiny, thin, crispy rounds, available plain or seasoned, are also wheat-, yeast-, and fat-free and make an excellent snack cracker and dip chip. Beware: Do not confuse the fine wholefoods version with their less wholesome counterparts made from rice not described as brown or whole grain.

Oat Cakes

Your chances of finding crackers made entirely of oats are more limited, but there are a few imported oat cakes around. Unfortunately, most seem to include some refined sweetening, but they do offer a welcome change for those trying to get away from wheat and yeast.

Tacos and Tostados

When corn tortillas are deep fried, they are transformed into tostados; when bent into U shapes they become taco shells. Typically, they are an amalgamation of corn flour (with the germ, minus the bran) and oil. Unfortunately, the quality of the oils may not be the highest; although those made with coconut or palm oil are acceptable, any made with partially hydrogenated oil should be avoided. There is no need to settle for a brand made with salt. Most natural food stores offer tortillas and tacos of highest quality, made with polyunsaturated oils and other organic corn. There is even the choice of blue corn varieties.

You will find the addition of lime (or calcium hydroxide) is universal. As we explained in the previous chapter, this is not an objectionable additive, but simply a technique that improves the nutritional quality of the corn.

With Salt or Without

You would expect crackers that taste salty or have visible grains of salt polka-dotting the surface to contain a considerable amount of sodium. Not surprisingly, Saltines outrank all competitors, with 440 milligrams per ounce. The typical commercial cracker is more likely to fall within the range of 200 to 300 milligrams per ounce.

Wholefoods crackers apparently garner good taste from their ingredients because most of the brands we have recommended don't appear to depend on salt for flavor. With few exceptions, when salt is added, the sodium content is just above 100 milligrams per ounce. Several companies provide unsalted twins to these products, which contain a mere 3 milligrams of sodium per ounce.

CARE AND HANDLING

Crackers have excellent keeping qualities and will stay fresh as long as you keep them in a dry, airtight environment. They go limp when exposed to moisture. If this happens, they can be rejuvenated in a 300°F. oven in about five minutes or toasted briefly at the lowest setting in a toaster oven. Once they cool, they will be crisp again.

CRACKER CRUMBS

Crackers can replace bread in almost every situation. One job they perform admirably is often overlooked and that is as crumbs. Commercial cracker crumbs are as undesirable as most crackers, but this needn't faze you. Homemade cracker crumbs can be prepared quickly and easily by grinding whole grain crackers in the blender or food processor. If you have neither of these devices, simply place the crackers in a sturdy plastic bag and go over them several times with a heavy rolling pin.

RECOMMENDATIONS

General Rule of Purchase: All ingredients are on the label. Look for crackers made with whole grains. Avoid those whose label reveals white flour, wheat flour, sugar, dextrose, corn syrup, partially hydrogenated oils, margarine, artificial color and flavor, yeast nutrients, dough conditioners, and preservatives.

Exemplary Brands

Whole Wheat Crackers

Ak-Mak Cracker, New Country Style Armenian Cracker Bread
Barbara's Breadsticks
Borden's Krisp and Natural Whole Wheat Crackerbread
Croustipain Craquelins Whole Wheat Snack Bread
Floridor Zweiback[4]
Frattorie & Pandea Whole Wheat Bread Sticks
Goodman's 100% Whole Wheat Matzoh
HUG Dar.Vida Swiss Whole Wheat Cracker
Health Valley Cheese Wheels, Stoned Wheat Crackers
Hol.Grain Whole Wheat Lite Snack Thins
Horowitz and Margareten 100% Whole Wheat Matzoh
Kitov Whole Wheat Sesame Bread Sticks
Lima Whole Wheat Toasts,[1] Limakrok[1]
Manischewitz Whole Wheat Matzoh
Nature's Cupboard Stone Ground Wheat and Sesame Cracker[4]
Old San Francisco Style Whole Wheat Sesame Bread Sticks
Streit's 100% Whole Wheat Matzoh
Whole Wheat Cracker H

Mixed Grain Crackers

Barbara's Lightbread
Eden Brown Rice Crackers
Floridor Crisp Breads
Gourmet Thins Scandinavian Crispbreads
Health Valley Wheat and Sweet Rye, 7 Grain and 7 Vegetable Crackers
Ideal Flatbreads
Jaus 4 Grain Crispbread
Lima Biscuits[1,3]
Lazzaroni Germovita a la Segala,[3] a la Cereali Misti[3]
Risopan Crispbread

Rye Crackers

Farm Verified Organic Rye Crispbread[1]
Finn Crisp Rye Bread Wafers
Fjord Crispbread
Kavli Norwegian Crispbread
Kings Bread Crisp Bread
Master Old Country Hardtack, Low Sodium Crackers
Ralston Purina Natural Rye Crisp
Siljans Knackebrod
The Original Rytak Knackebrod Crispbread
Wasa Crispbread Sport, Hearty Rye, Lite Rye, Golden Rye[4]

Rice Crackers

Abe's Rice Cakes
Arden Rice Cakes
Chico-San Rice Cakes
Edward and Son Baked Brown Rice Snaps
Feather River Rice Cakes
Golden Harvest Rice Cakes
Hain Rice Cakes
Harvest Moon Crackers
Hol.Grain Brown Rice Lite Snack Thins
Konriko Brand Original Brown Rice Cakes

Lundberg Rice Cakes, Organic Brown Rice Cakes[1]
Pacific Rice Products Crispy Cakes
Premier Japan Brown Rice Crackers
Quaker Rice Cakes
Skinny Haven Unsalted Rice Cakes
Spiral Brand Rice Cakes
The Emperor's New Wafers
Westbrae Brown Rice Wafers, Rice Cakes

Corn Crackers

Arga Taco Shells
Diago Taco Shells
El Rio Taco Shells
Food Club Mexican Style Taco Shells
Gardenia Taco, Tostados Shells
Gebhardt Taco, Tostados Shells
La Cocina Taco Shells

Mission Taco Shells
Ortega Taco Shells
Reser's Taco Shells
S&W Ole Real Stone Ground Taco Shells
Thrifty Maid Taco Shells

Oat Crackers

Paterson's Oatcakes

Walker's Highland Oatcakes[3]

High-Fiber Crackers

Bran o Crisp

Fantastic Foods Fiber Crisp

Cracker Crumbs

Horowitz and Margareten Whole Wheat Matzoh Meal

[1]Organic
[3]Contains refined sweeteners
[4]Contains refined grains

Chapter 9

Filling the Cereal Bowl:
Cold Cereals

Throughout its history, ready-to-eat breakfast cereal has been promoted for its health benefits. C. W. Post, creator of Grape Nuts, originally included a pamphlet detailing his views on nutrition with each box of his product. And what American doesn't know that Wheaties is touted as the "breakfast of champions"? Health claims, free samples, and coupons were such successful marketing approaches for ready-to-eat cereal that the unglamorous grain became permanently married to elaborate packaging and advertising. But the fact is, up until recently ready-to-eat cereal was the classic example of what has gone wrong with our food supply.

For generations, people who recognized the important relationship between food and health have tried to alert us to the diminished value of processed cereals, as well as the abundance of sugar and other undesirable ingredients that most of them contain. No match for the power of corporate public relations and advertising, they were seldom listened to, and often laughed at, but fortunately their perseverance has not been in vain. An increasing awareness among Americans that the big four cereal makers may have been short-changing our health for their profits has resulted in some improvement at the supermarket level. To its credit and our benefit, the natural food industry has always provided whole grain, unsugared, unadulterated breakfast cereals. Now their lines have expanded into remarkably familiar forms—flakes, O's, and even crispies.

CEREALS IN CRISIS

How much value can you really expect to get from a product whose very nature depends on the steaming, pressurization, drying, shredding, flaking, toasting, and what-have-you of once-healthful grains? We say "once" because after so much handling, the original nutrition can't help but be diminished.

119

A "Sparkle" of Sugar

Kids have long been the primary audience for cereal manufacturers. To appeal to their imagination and keen senses, a few simple grains are turned into a seemingly endless parade of shapes, sizes, colors, and flavors. Familiar cereals suddenly become "new" by adding fruit or chocolate flavoring (natural or artificial); indeed, they are masked to taste like anything but grain. Or, they may be reshaped into miniature glazed doughnuts or chocolate chip cookies, or speckled with marshmallow stars. With the aid of chemical dyes, they come in most of the colors of the rainbow, sometimes all in one box. Smurfs, Gremlins, Strawberry Shortcake, Cabbage Patch Kids, GI Joe, and Mr. T are no longer fictional characters but something to eat. By comparison, Tony the Tiger looks tame. It's been a long time since kids could be seduced by the mere promise of a "snap, crackle and pop."

Most consumers know that too much sugar is not good, but how can we protect ourselves from slick marketing consultants like the one who conceived of renaming Sugar Smacks, Honey Smacks, although the cereal still contains 57 percent added sweeteners, and only about 7 percent of this sweet taste even comes from honey; the rest is sugar and corn syrup. When Cheerios was repackaged with sugar, honey, and brown sugar syrup and alluringly called Honey-Nut Cheerios, who would guess that 36 percent of the calories would come from added sweeteners (the equivalent of 2.5 teaspoons of sugar per 1-ounce serving).

Following a great deal of negative publicity about sweetened cereals in 1977, the Kellogg Company took out several large ads in newspapers throughout the country. Their purpose was to justify the use of sugar in cereals by implying that they would not be eaten without it. Referring to their Sugar Frosted Flakes, the company reassured us that they add "25 percent of the U.S. RDA of 7 essential vitamins and 10 percent of the U.S. RDA of vitamin D and iron." To attract the kids, the ad declared, they add a "sparkle of sugar frosting."

In a follow-up ad, we learned what they meant by a "sparkle." According to the company's own figures, in a 1-ounce serving of Sugar Frosted Flakes there are 11 grams of sugar (or just shy of 1 tablespoon); a little math reveals that the "sparkle" accounts for 40 percent of the contents.

If you think that replacing sugar with the sugar substitute aspartame (Nutrasweet) is a viable solution, read Chapter 31 before you make your purchase. Perhaps the biggest paradox here is that one reported side effect of aspartame is that it increases the desire for sweets, rather than satisfying it.

Now some might argue that if the cereal company doesn't add the sugar it will be added at the table anyway. This may be so, but unsweetened cereals at least provide an opportunity to control (and ideally reduce) the amount of sugar you use. Moreover, if you compare the cost of Kellogg's Corn Flakes with its presweetened counterpart, Frosted Flakes, you will discover you are paying a 50 percent markup to have someone do the sugaring for you.

Red, White, and Blue Cereals

Ready-to-eat breakfast cereal may be an American creation but that doesn't mean it has to look like the flag. Despite the fact that as a group artificial food colorings have been banned more than any other type of additive, they are very common in children's cereals. They should head the list of ingredients to avoid.

Sodium in Cereal

Now that nutrition labeling on some cereal boxes is more complete, you can get a better idea of how much sodium some of the ready-to-eat cereals are adding to our daily diets. Many of the simpler cereals are free of salt, but as the list of ingredients expands, salt is almost invariably present. Although several cereals contain only 100 milligrams of sodium, in most of the ready-to-eat cereals the sodium content ranges from about 200 to 300 milligrams per 1-ounce serving. While this is just a fraction of the 1,100 to 3,300 milligrams that the National Research Council considers "safe and adequate" for an adult, it may be an unsuspected source for those who are trying to modify their sodium intake and is, in fact, higher than the levels found in a comparable weight of many "salty" snacks (see table on page 499). Granola-type cereals and whole grain brands that are salt-free contain less than 15 milligrams of sodium per ounce.

"No Preservatives Added"?

Time does not march on for many of today's cereals which, if you check, have a shelf-life of a year or more. BHA and BHT are the most commonly used cereal preservatives; they may be added directly to the grain, or to the packaging. While the latter seems like an improvement, some of the chemical still migrates to the cereal. Moreover, you will not always be informed of the presence of preservatives in packaging since a certain amount can be used in the production of the container; until this limit is exceeded, the preservatives BHA and BHT are considered incidental to the cereal and thus need not appear on the label.

Our in-store research has revealed that many cereals previously treated with preservatives no longer appear to be. Unfortunately, the technique of hiding preservatives in the packaging may be the reason. The only consolation, if this is the case, is that these chemicals are at least present in a lower concentration than before.

Cereals as Supplements

Most ready-to-eat cereals have at least seven vitamins plus iron added, to a level of 25 percent of the U.S. Recommended Daily Allowance per serving. A few processed cereals are supplemented with as much as 100 percent of the U.S. RDA for some select nutrients in a single serving. Since there are at least fifty substances known to be needed in the diet and probably many more that have not yet been discovered, it is important to recognize that even when the "scoreboard" on the side of the box claims 100 percent of the U.S. RDA for all the nutrients listed, this is a far cry from 100 percent of your total daily nutritional needs. Furthermore, many factors influence how the body absorbs nutrients, including the presence of other nutrients. One of the most important unanswered questions surrounding fortification of foods is how well the added supplements are utilized. And, can a high level of one nutrient possibly inhibit the body's ability to absorb others? (Studies have shown, for example, that iron and folate supplements block zinc absorption, while an overload of zinc depletes the body of copper.)

THE (COMPLETE) TOTAL STORY

Some cereals are so highly fortified that they cannot be called a breakfast cereal, but must be called a "supplement cereal." This helps explain why Total looks so good in its advertising. Watch out for ads that compare the "vitamin nutrition" of highly fortified cereals to less fortified or unfortified brands.

Fiber: Myth or Miracle?

Cereals geared toward the "adult market" assume that the over-twenty set can be wooed by promises of less sugar and more fiber. Judging by the impressive sales of the current high-fiber offerings, which range from 100 percent bran for the committed to 40 percent for those less certain, they may be right.

Ironically, many researchers believe that in high concentrations, bran, or cereal fiber, may rob our bodies of the very nutrients fortified cereals use as their selling point. Too much of this fiber, it appears, may "kidnap" such essential nutrients as copper, zinc, phosphorus, magnesium, iron, and calcium as it wends its way through the digestive tract. (We just can't seem to get it through our heads that there can be "too much of a good thing.")

Most high-fiber cereals provide some indication of fiber content. Personally, we are wary of any product that contains much more than 4 grams of fiber per ounce, or 14 percent fiber by weight, which is about double the natural proportion in whole grains.

Madison Avenue Granola

In many minds, natural cereals and granola are synonymous. The granola concept was popularized in the 1960s in counterculture kitchens. It was a hearty blend of grains (usually oats with optional wheat germ, rye flakes, soy grits, millet), nuts, seeds, and dried fruit, coated lightly with unsaturated oil and sweetening, and oven-roasted.

Unfortunately, when "granola" as interpreted by Madison Avenue hit the supermarket shelves, in many cases all that was left of the original cereal was the name. Only the oats and a smattering of nuts and dried fruit remain. The high-quality oils are often replaced with coconut or partially hydrogenated oils. The traditional honey, maple syrup, and molasses sweeteners have been supplemented with brown sugar and corn syrup, so that now many mass-market granolas range from 22 to 31 percent sugar.

SUITABLE CEREALS

We hope you haven't given up in despair by now, because actually the list of chemical-free, sugar-free, whole grain ready-to-eat cereals has grown in the last few years. In addition to the granola-types (and indeed, there are some good ones), some of America's original cereals like puffed grains, rice crispies, and corn flakes have gotten a new lease on life.

Good Granolas

When oats are coupled with other grains, soy flour, and a variety of nuts and seeds, *and* unsaturated oils are employed, *and* the sweetening is within reason, a satisfying, nourishing breakfast can be had. The granola-type cereals we have included in the Exemplary Brands all meet this criteria. Keep in mind, however, that these cereals are dense, and since a 1-ounce serving may measure only ¼ cup, the calories they provide can add up rapidly.

Muesli-type cereals are untoasted versions of granola and thus should meet the same standards.

Puffed Whole Grains

Most of the unsweetened puffed cereals on the market were relatively unadulterated to begin with, but relied on refined grains. Now whole grain puffed wheat, rice, corn, and millet are available. The cereal called Kashi actually incorporates seven puffed grains, plus sesame seeds for enhanced protein.

While some brands still give the sensation of eating encapsulated air, Health Valley "Lites," according to the manufacturer, uses a patented high-speed steam technique that puffs the whole grain in a mere thirty seconds rather than the traditional eight minutes, and so offers something to bite into.

Brown Rice Crispies

Crispy brown rice provides a whole grain offering that actually retains its crunch long after the milk is added. This is one of our favorites and can be purchased with sea salt and without, plain or lightly sweetened with brown rice syrup.

Real Flakes

When it comes to flakes, whole grain wheat, corn, and oats with no sugar are offered by several companies. Most have malt added which imparts its own sweetness. Some further "enhance" the taste with salt and unsweetened fruit juice. Depending on how you view synthetic vitamin fortification, your choice might be influenced by its presence in some brands. We regret that Kellogg discontinued two original Nutri-Grain varieties, barley and rye, because they offered a chance to get some alternative grains onto the wheat-oriented American table. The later addition of a brown rice-corn blend, however, indicates the success of the line.

Add raisins to whole wheat flakes and you transform the cereal into raisin bran in the eyes of cereal companies. Raisin bran is available unsweetened, although not from any of the major cereal makers.

Cheery-O's

If O's are more your style, here, too, you now have more to choose from. All are made with oat flour, some with added brown rice flour, some with wheat germ, and others wheat-free. The best of them will not have added sugars or salt. Nor will they be fortified. One company offers them flavored with fruit juice and colored with natural food colors for "kid appeal."

Sprouted Cereals

Sprouted cereals are another recent innovation on the cereal shelf. During the sprouting process some of the cereal starch is naturally converted to maltose, which lends a touch of sweetness. The grains are then dried and packaged with nuts or fruit for a crunchy cereal with a nutty taste. Remember, the more different grains in the box, the broader the nutrient base will be.

MAKING NUTRITIONAL ASSESSMENTS

Once you have ferreted out the cereals with desirable ingredients, nutrition labeling can assist you in making a nutritionally sound choice. A 1-ounce serving of most ready-to-eat cereals averages about 100 calories; the slight deviations above and below this are really not very significant. What does matter, though, is the size of the serving you are likely to eat, since 1 ounce can vary from as little as ¼ cup for granola-type cereals to 2 heaping cups for some of the puffed varieties.

Most cereals are low in fat, containing only 1 gram or less per ounce. The granola types are the exception, and between the added oils and the nuts, they are apt to contain from 3 to 5 grams of fat per ounce, which is still not excessive if you stick to small servings.

Protein is not a selling point for ready-to-eat cereals. About 2 to 3 grams per ounce (without milk) are all you will get from a typical 1-ounce serving, and even the "high-protein" kind will contain, at most, 6 grams. In terms of your daily needs, this is not very impressive. (As a general reference, 35 grams suffices for a 50-pound child, 40 grams for a 110-pound person, and 58 grams for a 160-pound adult.)

What should influence your purchase is the ratio of protein to carbohydrate. It should be roughly the same as the ratio which occurs naturally in the whole grain. Thus, for all wheat-based cereals the goal is at least 1 gram of protein for every 8 grams of carbohydrate; for oats it should be closer to 1 to 4 or 5; for corn a ratio of 1 to 10 is about the best you can do in ready-to-eat cereal, and for rice a realistic figure is only 1 to 12. The lower the ratio the better, and the addition of wheat germ, nuts, amaranth, soy flour, and other protein fortifiers can improve it. On the other hand, a reliance on refined grains and the introduction of sugars will offset the balance and this is what you want to avoid. The following table of Select Cereal Values will allow you to judge some commercial offerings. The figures for protein and carbohydrates on the package will help you to rate those not in our listing.

You may also want to take sodium levels into account, and keep in mind that 1 teaspoon of sugar (sucrose) weighs 4 grams.

SELECT CEREAL VALUES*

Cereal 1 ounce	Grain	Protein grams	Carbohydrates grams	Ratio	Sucrose grams	Sodium mgs.
Arrowhead Mills:						
Nature O's	mixed	5	20	1:4	1	14
Puffed Corn	corn	6	22	1:3.7	0	3
Puffed Rice	rice	2	24	1:12	0	3
Puffed Wheat	wheat	4	22	1:5.5	0	3

SELECT CEREAL VALUES* (continued)

Cereal 1 ounce	Grain	Protein grams	Carbohydrates grams	Ratio	Sucrose grams	Sodium mgs.
Maple-Nut Granola	mixed	4	17	1:4	NA	12
Barbara's						
Corn Flakes	corn	2	24	1:12	NA	310
Brown Rice Crisps	rice	2	26	1:13	NA	300
Erewhon:						
Crispy Brown Rice	rice	2	24	1:12	NA	185
General Mills:						
Kix	corn	2	24	1:12	2	310
Trix	corn	1	25	1:12	12	170
Cheerios	oats	4	20	1:5	1	290
Honey-Nut Cheerios	oats	3	23	1:8	10	250
Wheaties	wheat	3	23	1:8	3	370
Lucky Charms	oats	2	24	1:12	11	185
S'mores Crunch	corn, wheat	1	24	1:24	11	220
Good Shepherd:						
Traditional	oats, wheat	4	17	1:4	NA	0
Grainfields:						
Wheat Flakes	wheat	3	20	1:7	NA	<10
Corn Flakes	corn	2	24	1:12	NA	<10
Health Valley:						
Brown Rice Lites	rice	2	24	1:12	0	0
Golden Wheat Lites	wheat	4	22	1:5.5	0	0
Golden Corn Lites	corn	6	22	1:3.7	0	3
Oat Bran Flakes	oats	3	22	1:7	NA	10
Raisin Bran	wheat	3	24	1:8	NA	1
Granola	mixed	4	20	1:5	NA	10
Kellogg's:						
Nutri-Grain Corn	corn	2	24	1:12	2	185
Corn Flakes	corn	2	25	1:12	2	280
Frosted Flakes	corn	1	26	1:26	11	200
Rice Krispies	rice	2	25	1:12	3	280
Frosted Krispies	rice	1	25	1:25	10	210
Special K	wheat	6	20	1:3	2	230
Nutri-Grain, Whole Wheat	wheat	2	24	1:12	NA	195
Raisin Bran	wheat	3	31	1:10	12	210
Froot Loops	mixed	2	25	1:12	13	125
Kolln:						
Crispy Oats	oats, rice	4	22	1:5.5	NA	2
Kretschmer:						
Granola	oats	3	19	1:6	NA	10
Nabisco:						
Shredded Wheat	wheat	2	19	1:9	0	<10
Team	mixed	2	24	1:12	5	NA

SELECT CEREAL VALUES* *(continued)*

Cereal 1 ounce	Grain	Protein grams	Carbohydrates grams	Ratio	Sucrose grams	Sodium mgs.
New Morning:						
Oatios	oats, rice	4	20	1:5	NA	0
Fruit-e-O's	mixed	2	24	1:12	NA	0
Post:						
Grape Nuts	wheat	3	23	1:8	NA	190
Fruity Pebbles	rice	1	25	1:12	12	150
Quaker:						
Corn Bran	corn	2	24	1:12	6	300
Cap'n Crunch	corn, oats	1	24	1:24	12	220
Natural	oats, wheat	3	18	1:6	5	10
Ralston:						
Rice Chex	rice	1	25	1:25	2	280
Wheat Chex	wheat	3	23	1:7	2	200
Cookie Crisp	mixed	1	25	1:25	13	190
Skinners:						
Raisin Bran	wheat	3	21	1:7	NA	60

*Source: Manufacturer's data.
   Recomended protein-carbohydrate ratio: wheat 1:8; oats 1:5 or lower; corn 1:10 or lower; rice 1:12.
   Mixed = three or more grains including wheat, oats, rice, corn, rye, amaranth, triticale.
   NA = no figures available.
   < = less than.

GETTING THE MOST OUT OF CEREAL

In order to take full advantage of ready-to-eat cereal, you should mate it with a food that helps complete its protein. The traditional addition of milk fulfills this purpose. Wheat germ also enhances its protein value. So, too, do beans and nuts, which means the soybean-based beverages now widely available in the natural food market, and nut milks based on tahini, almonds, peanuts, etc., can all do justice to the cereal bowl.

RECOMMENDATIONS

General Rule of Purchase: All ingredients are on the label, and even for cereals in bulk bins this information should be available. Look for ready-to-eat cereals made from whole oats, wheat, rye, millet, corn, and rice that are fortified naturally with wheat germ, nutritional yeast, nuts, seeds, flaxseed, and dried fruit. Accept honey, molasses, maple syrup, brown rice syrup, or fruit juice sweeteners only when used judiciously. Avoid refined sweeteners, artificial color and flavor, and BHT/BHA preservatives. All but the granola varieties should be fat-free.

Read the nutrition information when it is available to determine how much sodium and added sugar you will get from the cereal. Do not be taken in by brands that claim to be "natural" or preservative-free and then include large quantities of sweeteners and partially hydrogenated oils. And remember, ingredients are listed in descending order by weight. When it comes to sweeteners, several scattered about the list may divert your attention from the actual total amount.

Exemplary Brands

Granola and Muesli Types

Alpen (No Sugar Or Salt Added)
Alpenzell Swiss Muesli
Arrowhead Mills Granola, Crunch
Barbara's Fruit Juice Sweetened Granola
Better Way Granola
Bioforce Breakfast Muesli[2]
Coop Honey Granolas
Country Life Natural Foods Apple Natural Swiss Style Cereal, Cashew Date Delight
Eden Granolas
Erewhon Granolas
Familia No Sugar Added
Golden Harves 7 Grain Honey, Premier Raisin Bran Granolas
Good Shepherd Cereals
Grainland Coconut Almond Crunch, Golden Cashew Raisin, Fruit n' Nut Cereals

Grinola
Health Valley Real Granolas, Real Natural Cereals, Healthy Crunch, Orangeolas, Swiss Breakfast Cereals
K&L Protein Cereal
Lassen Dietetic Almond Crunch, Honey Crunch
Lima Muesli[2]
New Morning Maple Nut Muesli
Sovex Honey Almond Granola
Staff of Life Granola
Uprisings Bakery Granolas
Vita Crunch 7-Grain Granola
Westbrae Granolas
Women's Community Bakery Date Crunch, Granula, Cinnamon Apple Granolas[2]

Puffed Cereals

Alps Natural Nutrition Brown Rice Cereal
Arrowhead Mills Puffed Wheat, Millet, Rice, Corn
El Molino Puffed Wheat, Rice, Corn
Golden Harvest Toasted Puffed Rice, Wheat, Corn
Health Valley Golden Corn, Wheat, Brown Rice Lites

Kashi Puffed Seven Whole Grains and Sesame
Pure and Simple Puffed Wheat, Corn, Rice, Millet
Stone Buhr Plain, Honey Coated Puffed Rice, Corn, Wheat

Crispy Rice

Barbara's Brown Rice Crisps
Erewhon Regular, Unsalted Crispy Brown Rice Cereals
Grainfields Toasted Crispy Brown Rice
Lundberg Sweet Brown Rice Crunchies
New Morning Crispy Brown Rice with Amaranth

Perky's Crispy Brown Rice, Apple & Cinnamon Crispy Brown Rice, Carob Flavored Crispy Brown Rice, Raisin Sweetened Nutty Rice
Stowe Mills Crispy Brown Rice

O's

Arrowhead Mills Nature O's
Barbara's Toasted O's
Golden Harvest Toasted Oat Cereal

New Morning Oatios, Wheat Free Oatios,
  Fruit-E-O's
Stowe Mills Old Fashioned Golden Oats

Wheat Flakes

Arrowhead Mills Bran Flakes
Back to Nature Granola Flakes
Barbara's Raisin Bran
Erewhon Raisin Bran, Fruit 'n Wheat,
  Wheat Flakes
Golden Harvest Whole Grain Wheat Flakes
Grainfields Whole Wheat Flakes, Raisin
  Bran

Health Valley Stoned Wheat Flakes, Rai-
  sin Bran
Kellogg's Nutri-Grain Whole Wheat, Whole
  Wheat with Raisins
New Morning Super Raisin Bran
Uncle Sam Cereal
Zwicky Whole Wheat Kollath Flakes

Corn Flakes

Arrowhead Mills Corn Flakes
Barbara's Corn Flakes
Grainfields Corn Flakes

Kellogg's Nutri-Grain Corn
New Morning Corn Flakes

Sprouted Cereals

Back to Nature Banana Crisp, Apple Cinnamon Crisp, Raisin Bran Crunch, Honey
  Bran Crunch

Health Valley Sprouts[2]

Other Cereals

Arrowhead Mills Grainstay
Golden Harvest Cereal
Health Valley Wheat Germ Cereal, Oat
  Bran Flakes, Amaranth Flakes
Kellogg's Nutri-Grain Brown Rice with Al-
  monds and Raisins
King Natural King Krunch

Krolln Oat Bran Crunch, Fruit 'n Oat Bran
  Crunch, Crispy Oats
Loma Linda Ruskets
New Morning Super Bran
New World Raisin Bran, Multi Grain Cereal
Post Grape Nuts, Raisin Grape Nuts
Sun Meadow Fruit Grains

[2]Some organic ingredients

Chapter 10

Filling the Cereal Bowl:
Hot Cereals

Although cold cereals are somewhat more attractive than hot cereals from the cook's standpoint, cooked cereal is a breakfast with real staying power, especially appealing on cold, damp days. Unrefined grains, which is what good hot cereals are made from, are a valuable source of B vitamins, iron, zinc, phosphorus, other trace minerals, and fiber. In combination with milk, either animal, nut, or soy, they offer high-quality protein.

Almost the only change that has taken place after centuries of eating gruel and porridge has been to reduce the cooking time of some cereals by grinding or partially precooking the grain. Less desirable brands become "quick-cooking" by the addition of enzymes or disodium phosphate.

If you select whole grain cereals, there is no need for them to be "enriched." Fortunately, hot cereals do not lend themselves to being shaped into this year's cartoon character and there doesn't seem to be a market for blue oatmeal. So, for the time being, these cereals are safe on that score. Preservatives are not common, but BHT and BHA do show up on a label occasionally. And although refined sweeteners and artificial flavors are by no means as popular here as in ready-to-eat cereals, some of the fruit- and spice-enhanced products are diminished by these factors.

HOT CHOICES

Oatmeal

Unlike other grains, when oats are milled only the inedible hull is discarded. The bran and germ remain in the edible portion. The hulled whole grain, known as the groat, is the basis for all the oat cereals on the market. The terms "Irish" and "Scotch" can be used to describe any of these oat forms.

Steel-cut oats are produced by simply slicing the groats. They require soaking and thirty to forty-five minutes cooking, but the extra attention is well worth it, for they produce a smooth, creamy porridge with unequaled flavor. These oats are not widely available in stores, but can be purchased from several mail-order sources.

130

Rolled or *old-fashioned oats* are made by slicing the groats, steaming them to soften some of the starch, then rolling them into flakes and drying them. This increases the surface area so that they cook up in a mere five minutes for a fine cereal.

Quick oats are produced in a similar manner, but the groats are cut more finely and rolled until they are quite thin. Quick oats do not seem to be appreciably different in terms of nutrition than longer-cooking varieties, but they do not have the quality that gives oatmeal its true taste appeal.

Even *instant oats* can be acceptable, although their texture leaves a lot to be desired. We also object to those brands that derive much of their value from fortification with unnatural amounts of B vitamins, calcium, and iron. In others, the presence of added salt is deplorable, and all of the preflavored varieties are sweetened and frequently artificially flavored as well.

Oat bran has been credited as an effective means of lowering blood cholesterol and reducing insulin dependence in diabetics. It is available on its own as a hot cereal. In a diet low in fiber perhaps this can be recommended, but as discussed under "Bran," in Chapter 4, it is not a wholefood in itself, and it would make more sense nutritionally to get oat bran in conjunction with the rest of the groat.

Wheat Cereal

Several hot wheat cereals are on the market. Some are rolled like oats, others are coarsely or finely ground to speed cooking, and occasionally they are toasted to bring out the nutty wheat taste. All are nutritionally comparable if the bran and germ are left intact and nothing else is added.

Unfortunately, some companies take an otherwise fine cereal and add BHA or BHT to the packaging material. While we prefer this to the addition of preservatives directly to the grain, there is probably some migration of the chemical and actually no real reason for it to be there in the first place.

Some wheat cereals mix in other grains, while some are fortified with soy which improves the protein quality. A few wheat cereals are made from the "heart" of the wheat, plus wheat germ and bran—this is a way of saying all the parts are there, but together they may not necessarily equal the whole. While this is better than eating the refined grain (as in Cream of Wheat), we believe the balance nature intended between the bran, germ, and endosperm is probably the best one.

Farina is the only cereal that has a federal Standard of Identity. Accordingly, farina refers to wheat which has had the bran removed; it may or may not contain the germ. This will not be declared on the label unless the manufacturer chooses to do so; if it isn't mentioned, assume the germ isn't there. If the label says "enriched," the farina will contain the B vitamins thiamin, niacin, and riboflavin, as well as iron in amounts far exceeding the natural whole wheat; it may have vitamin D and calcium added as well. We do not recommend the use of hot cereal as a vitamin supplement, especially when the B vitamins are added with no regard to their natural ratio and with no compensation for folacin, pantothenic acid, and B_6, which are normally found in whole wheat.

Cream of Rice

Standard supermarket hot creamy rice cereal is manufactured from white rice, and whether it is "enriched" or not, our sentiments about it are the same—negative.

Brown rice cream, or what may simply be described as quick-cooking brown rice cereal, is available in natural food outlets. Kokoh is the name of a baby cereal made from finely ground brown rice plus sweet rice, oats, and sesame seeds. This is a highly digestible cereal with a much better nutritional profile than the cereals generally promoted for infants. Adults seem to like it too.

Another interesting brown rice cereal on the market is a Japanese import packaged in boil-in bags and described as a "porridge." It contains brown rice, barley, whole wheat, plum extract, carrot, burdock, and kombu (a seaweed), and is a savory breakfast dish.

Rye Cereal

Rye flakes and cream of rye cereals are less readily available than other hot breakfast cereals but can be found in some supermarkets, natural food stores, and mail-order outlets. Rye cereal is similar to oatmeal but is a bit chewier and has a more distinctive taste. Rye is said to have an exceptional moisture-retaining capacity which some people contend produces a longer-lasting feeling of satiety than other cereals. Thus, it is often a favorite of those who are watching their weight.

Corn Products

The selection of cornmeal as a grain is covered in Chapter 5.

Cornmeal cooks up to a smooth, creamy porridge; it requires four parts water, unlike the usual ratio of two parts water to one part grain for most hot cereals. If you stir in some raisins and drizzle some molasses on top with the milk, the cereal will taste like Indian pudding, one of our favorite desserts.

Corn grits, whether they are regular or quick-cooking, yellow or white, enriched or not, are devoid of fiber and germ, and one of the least nutritious cereals on the market.

Mixed Grains

There are several choices of hot mixed-grain cereals, some fortified with soy and wheat germ for added protein, and several especially hearty ones with sunflower seeds, flaxseeds, and dried fruit. Avoid those that are sweetened, as well as the occasional brand with added fat.

A few cereals have nonfat dry milk added to them. While it may seem this would enhance the protein value, there is some question as to how stable the protein in the milk is over time, especially in the presence of the carbohydrates that are so abundant in cereals. Thus, if you wish to fortify your cereal in this manner, it is probably wiser to add dry milk to the cereal when you cook it.

Other grains like brown rice, kasha, millet, barley, and cracked wheat can also be served for breakfast (see Chapter 4). If you have any cooked grains left from a previous meal, try them with hot milk and honey in the morning. Or, for a savory touch, serve them with either ground sesame seeds or soy sauce.

RECOMMENDATIONS

General Rule of Purchase: All ingredients are on the label. Choose cereals made with whole grains. Those with added soy or wheat germ will have a higher protein value. Avoid those treated with enzymes or disodium phosphate to make them "quick-cooking" and those with salt, refined sugars, and preservatives (BHT/BHA).

Oats, whether steel-cut, rolled, or old-fashioned, or quick cooking are all worth buying. Instant oats should be avoided if they contain salt or are enriched or presweetened.

Choose *whole wheat* cereal, whether rolled or otherwise. Although still acceptable, reconstituted wheat, in which the "heart" of the wheat is combined with wheat germ and bran, is a less natural form. Avoid farina unless described as containing the germ on the label.

Brown rice and *rye cereals*, as well as *unbolted cornmeal*, are a fine basis for a hot cereal. Additional grains suitable for hot breakfast cereals are included in Chapter 4.

Mixed grains, especially those enhanced with soy, wheat germ, nuts, and seeds complete the picture (and the protein).

*Exemplary Brands*_____

Oats

A&P Hot Quick Oats
American Prairie Porridge Oats,[1] Quick Oats[1]
Arrowhead Mills Steel Cut Oats, Instant Oatmeal, Oat Groats
Buckeye Old Fashioned Rolled Oats
Crystal Wedding Oats

Eden Rolled Oats
Elam's Steel Cut Oats, Scotch Style Oats, Stone Ground Oatmeal
Food Club Quick Oats
Fred Meyer Steel Cut Oats, Oat Groats
Giant Foods Quick Oats
H-O Quick Oats

Oats (continued)

Harvest Quick Oats
John McCann's Irish Oatmeal (Regular, Quick-Cooking)
Kroger Quick Oats
Little Bear Rolled Oats[1]
Lima Oat Flakes[1]
Minute 3 Brand Old Fashioned Oats, Quick Oats, Raisin Oats
Moore's Flour Mill Oatmeal

Publix Quick Oats
Quaker Old Fashioned Oats, Quick Oats
Safeway Quick Oats
Shur-Fine Quick Oats
Stone Buhr Old Fashioned Oat Flakes, Scotch Oats, Quick Cooking Rolled Oats
Tree of Life Rolled Oats, Steel Cut Oats
Triangle Cream Flakes Rolled Oats

Wheat

Arrowhead Mills Cracked Wheat Cereal[1]
Back to Nature Red Bird Germade, High Protein Farina, High Fiber Farina
Elam's Cracked Wheat Cereal
Krusteaz Zoom
Lima Wheat Flakes[1]
Fred Meyer Whole Wheat Farina

Moore's Flour Mill Whole Wheat Farina
Mother's Rolled Whole Wheat
Natural Way Mills Special Wheat Cereal[1]
Stone Buhr Manna Golden Cereal, Old Fashioned Wheat Flakes
Wheatena

Rye

Cream of Rye

Lima Rye Flakes[1]

Rice

American Prairie 5-Grain Cereal[1], Creamy Rye & Rice[1]
Arrowhead Mills Rice and Shine
Eden Rice Cream[1]
Erewhon Brown Rice Cream

Lima Rice Flakes[1]
Lundberg Creamy Rice Cereal[1]
Pacific Rice Quick 'N Creamy Hot Brown Rice Cereal

Mixed Grains

Arrowhead Mills Bear Mush, 7-Grain Cereal, 4-Grain Cereal with Flaxseed
Eden Kokoh,[2] Seven Grain Cereal[2]
Elam's Complete Cereal
Erewhon Barley Plus
Fred Meyer Wheatless Cereal, 4 Grain Cereal
Health Valley Hearts O' Bran
Jewel Evans 10 Grain Cereal
Kashi
Little Bear Koko Rice, Breakfast, Multi-Grain Cereals[1]
Lima Breakfast Flakes,[2] Kokoh

Monarch's Red River Cereal
Moore's Flour Mill Apple Cinnamon and Grains
Mother's Quick Cooking Barley
Orowheat Old Fashioned Recipe with Oats, Wheatberry and Barley Cereal, Hot Cereal 7-Grain Recipe with Wheat, Oats and Rye
Premier Japan Quick Brown Rice Porridge
Roman Meal 5-Minute Cereal, 5-Minute Cereal with Oats
Stone Buhr Hot Apple Granola, 7-Grain Cereal

[1]Organic
[2]Some organic ingredients

Chapter 11

Spilling the Beans

The biggest food bargain we know of is commonly packaged in a plastic bag or cardboard box with a see-through window. This gem will cost you anywhere from 39 cents to about a dollar a pound, enough for eight to ten servings. Each one of those servings will be abundant in protein, iron, thiamin, and riboflavin. What we're talking about is dried beans—also known as legumes or pulses. This prince of the food world provides a rich, tasty source of nourishment for millions of people daily in South America, Europe, Asia, and the Middle East.

In this country, however, beans are often viewed as poor people's food. This should not be the case, for they are the basis of some of the most interesting, satisfying, and effortless meals served anywhere.

Every supermarket devotes a section to dried beans and they are one of the most popular bulk items in natural food stores, where they are sometimes but not always organic in origin. A well-stocked market is likely to include more than a dozen varieties. This large selection is actually surprising in view of the fact that so many people in this country are still unaware of the many possibilities dried beans offer. We are disappointed to find that dried soybeans, one of the most nutritious vegetable foods known, are still rarely found in supermarkets, although they are a common item in natural food outlets.

THE BEAUTY OF BEANS

Protein content and low cost are only two of the noteworthy qualities of dried beans. Perhaps one of their biggest selling points is that unlike animal forms of protein, beans are low in fat. Soybeans and peanuts are the exceptions here, but the fat that they contain is largely unsaturated and, like all other beans, they are cholesterol-free. Soybeans are also rich in lecithin, integral to the proper utilization of dietary fats. In fact, soy is the source of most of the commercial lecithin used in food manufacture. Moreover, in several research projects, beans have been shown to reduce the low-density lipoproteins (LDL's) in blood cholesterol and the triglycerides that are most frequently associated with an increased risk of heart attack.

What beans are high in is complex carbohydrates; in fact, their fiber content is reputed to be second only to bran. This is a multifold benefit because the particular fiber in beans, in addition to possibly moderating fatty substances in the blood, helps regulate blood sugar and bowel function; it can even affect body weight by promoting a sensation of fullness, thus counteracting feelings of hunger.

Getting the Most Out of Beans

Beans are a primary source of protein in much of the world. Like other plant proteins, though, they perform better if they are served with complementary foods, like grains and certain nuts and seeds. When these foods are combined, they make an ideal nutritional match, each supplying what the other lacks. This natural combination is reflected in many traditional specialties—Spanish rice and beans, Mexican frijoles with tortillas (or bean tacos), Middle Eastern falafel (chick-pea-fritters) with tahini (sesame seed sauce), Hoppin' John (black-eyed peas and rice) from our own Southern heritage, and the common coupling of bean dishes with pasta on Italian menus.

It is known that iron absorption is enhanced by vitamin C. Thus, one way to maximize the iron potential in beans is to serve them with vitamin C-rich fruits and vegetables like citrus fruit, broccoli, bell peppers, tomatoes, cabbage, or any dark leafy greens.

BUYING FOR VARIETY

Here are some of the most popular varieties:

AZUKI (OR ADUKI) Possibly the least familiar of the beans except in Japanese or macrobiotic circles, this small reddish bean is reputed to be the easiest to digest.

BLACK BEANS (OR BLACK TURTLE BEANS) Small oval-shaped black beans, made famous in black bean soup.

BLACK-EYED PEAS (OR COW PEAS) Small, oval-shaped beans which are creamy white with a small black spot on one side. Popular in Southern and soul food cookery.

BROAD BEANS (OR FAVA BEANS) Dating back to early Greek and Roman civilizations, these hardy kidney-shaped beans are still favored in Greece, Egypt, and southern Italy. Their tough leathery skins require prolonged cooking to soften, which may account for their lack of popularity in the United States.

CANNELLINI BEANS (OR WHITE KIDNEY BEANS) A favorite of Italian cooks.

GARBANZO BEANS (OR CHICK-PEAS) These round golden beans have a characteristic nutlike flavor. They are among the most popular beans.

GREAT NORTHERN BEANS A large white bean favored in stews and home-baked beans.

KIDNEY BEANS Kidney beans are deep red and, not surprisingly, shaped like kidneys. They appear most often in Mexican dishes, especially chili, tacos, and refried beans.

LENTILS One of the oldest cultivated foods, lentils come in a range of colors including brown, green, and red-orange. Lentils cook in only thirty to forty-five minutes and do not need presoaking. They are used most often in soups and curries.

LIMA BEANS These are broad and flat, and come in small and large sizes. Because they contain measurable amounts of a cyanide-producing compound, they should be boiled in an open pot before they are eaten so that the noxious gas can escape with the steam. In the West, we cultivate low-cyanogen varieties; however the beans from Java and Burma may have twenty to thirty times more of this compound, making it advisable to buy domestic limas. Lima beans make an excellent vegetable accompaniment, as well as a rich soup, and are a popular ingredient in casseroles.

MUNG BEANS Primarily known in the form of sprouts, these small olive-green beans can be cooked and eaten like all other beans.

NAVY BEANS This general name is applied to all small white beans, great northern beans, and pea beans.

PEA BEANS Small, oval, and white, they hold their shape particularly well, even when cooked until very tender. Favored in baked beans and soups.

PEANUTS While generally treated like a nut in the culinary sense, botanically the peanut is a bean, albeit one with a high oil content. The Southern practice of boiling peanuts in the shell for "goobers" is one example of their gustatory potential.

PINTO BEANS A relative of the kidney bean, only beige-colored and speckled. Can be used interchangeably with pink or red kidney beans in any recipe.

PINK BEANS Members of the kidney bean family, these are more delicate in flavor, but used similarly.

SOYBEANS The soybean is the most virtuous of all the beans. It is the only food in the vegetable kingdom that, by itself, is a well-balanced protein. An acre planted in soybeans can produce 33 percent more protein than any other crop and twenty times more than if the land were used for raising beef. Although there are cookbooks devoted to the soybean, these beans can be used just as you would any other and require no special handling other than a longer cooking time. They have a pronounced beany flavor.

In response to the growing interest in soybeans, some farmers have begun to recultivate more traditional varieties, among them a yellow "vegetable" soybean and a black soybean, both of which are reputed to be especially nutritious and tasty.

SPLIT PEAS Available in green and yellow (the yellow ones have a less pronounced flavor), split peas have had the skin removed by mechanical processing. They are especially convenient to use, as they cook in a relatively short time and do not require soaking. Thus, they can be prepared in the pot along with rice or other grains for protein-rich dishes. They are, of course, best known for their use in split pea soup.

WHOLE PEAS Dry peas, made from mature fresh green peas, may be served in many ways. One of the nicest is just plain boiled and seasoned with butter. Unlike split peas, they must be soaked before cooking. When they are sprouted, they approximate fresh peas in taste.

WINGED BEANS (OR DAMBALA) If you haven't heard of this bean you're not alone, for the dambala is still primarily confined to the tropical zone. Given its virtues, though, it is a good bet it will show up in our markets soon. Nicknamed "the supermarket on a stalk," almost every part of the plant is edible including the leaves, the flower, and the asparagus-like tendrils. The winged bean plant forms a small tuber underground that has a delicate, nutty flavor and a high protein content. If this weren't enough, even the stalk can be used for animal fodder.

BUYING FOR QUALITY

Although peas, lentils, and many beans are officially inspected before or after processing, retail packages seldom show the federal or state grade. You can, however, do your own grading, since most dried legumes are available either loose or in see-through packages. Consider these factors when examining them:

Color: Dried beans should have a bright, uniform color. Fading is an indication of long storage, which means the beans won't be fresh, will take longer to cook, and will be less tasty. Cloudiness on the surface could indicate mold.

Size: Select beans of uniform size. Small beans cook faster than large ones, so a variety of sizes will result in uneven cooking; by the time the larger beans are tender, the small ones will be mush.

Defects: Cracked coating, foreign material, many discolorations, and perforations in the package itself are all signs of possible damage, decay, and a low-quality product. Buy beans free of any visible defects.

Additives: As with all foods, organically grown beans are preferred. For the most part, all dry beans are otherwise similar. There is a rare exception to this general rule, illustrated by one product we have run into only in southern markets so far: that is, "flavored" dry beans to which hydrolyzed vegetable protein, salt, caramel color, sugar, partially hydrogenated oils, modified starch, artificial and natural flavors, and an anticaking agent have been added. Needless to say, we would not consider this an acceptable purchase.

STORAGE

Store dried beans at room temperature, enclosed in the package they came in, or if bought in bulk (or once the package is opened), in a covered container. They will keep almost indefinitely as long as they are in a dry environment; however, the older they get, the more cooking they will need. It is therefore unwise to mix an old batch of stored beans with a newly purchased one.

Cooked beans can be stored in the refrigerator for at least one week, or in an airtight container in the freezer up to six months.

BEANS AND BLOATING

"Bean gas," or flatulence as it is more technically labeled, is what keeps some people from enjoying beans. Although sometimes you just can't overcome it, there are certain tactics that have been successful for many people.

One common cause of gassiness is the complex sugars in beans, which are difficult for the body to break down and so pass largely undigested into the larger intestine. There, resident bacteria cause them to ferment, forming carbon dioxide and hydrogen gases. Because these offending sugars are water-soluble, they can be reduced by discarding the soaking water before cooking, and for those who are particularly susceptible, replacing the water halfway through cooking as well. This does have the drawback of reducing the B vitamins and the protein somewhat, but the sacrifice is small compared to the remaining nutritional return from the beans.

Incomplete cooking of the beans is another common cause of poor digestibility. If the starch is not adequately softened, the digestive system will have trouble handling it.

Those who have avoided beans for this reason may be reassured to learn that frequent bean eaters suffer less distress.

OTHER WAYS TO BUY BEANS

Canned Beans

Our discussion has so far focused on beans in the dried form. Beans are also available in cans, cooked and ready to be seasoned in your kitchen. The price you pay for this convenience is high, about double that of the dried beans, but an even bigger disadvantage is the universal addition of salt, the frequent inclusion of EDTA (an antioxidant to preserve color in the beans), and the occasional presence of refined sweeteners in the form of sugar and corn syrup. Fortunately all ingredients are on the label.

Note that the use of these ingredients varies not only from brand to brand, but within a single manufacturer's line. Both navy beans and great northern beans are frequently canned without EDTA; the situation for other varieties is unpredictable. Since all the canned beans included in the Exemplary Brands contain salt unless otherwise noted, be sure to make adjustments when following a recipe.

Prepared Beans

For those who really need convenience, there are preseasoned canned bean products and dry bean mixes that can serve you well. To find out more about them, turn to Chapter 28.

Bean Sprouts

By now, most people have probably seen bean sprouts in the market. These are the product of a germinating seed, the most popular commercial choices being mung beans (seen in Oriental dishes), alfalfa (alone or with radish seeds) and possibly clover. The selection and handling of fresh sprouts is discussed in Chapter 24.

You can also make your own sprouts. While special sprouting seed mixtures are available, practically any whole bean (and grain or seed as well), unless chemically treated, can be turned into sprouts. This can be done indoors year-round, requires no elaborate equipment, and guarantees the freshest sprouts possible for salads, snacking, or cooked vegetable dishes. The easiest seeds to sprout are alfalfa, lentils, mung beans, soybeans, chick-peas, radish seeds, and dried whole peas. When fresh peas are out of season, sprouted whole peas are especially nice as an ingredient in prepared dishes. Whole grains like amaranth, triticale, rye, and wheat berries also make tasty sprouts. (Directions for sprouting can be found in our cookbook *American Wholefoods Cuisine,* as well as in many other naturally oriented books.)

Once beans are sprouted, the carbohydrates and consequently the calories are reduced, the vitamin B content increases, vitamin C which is absent in the dried bean is generated, and if sprouts are exposed briefly to sunlight, chlorophyl and vitamin A appear as well. There are those who praise sprouts as the only truly "live" food.

RECOMMENDATIONS

DRIED BEANS

General Rule of Purchase: While not widely available, a few companies offer some organically grown varieties. We list only these below because most brands of nonorganic beans are pretty much alike. Watch that you don't accidentally pick up an artificially flavored, preseasoned product.

Exemplary Brands

Arrowhead Mills Mung,[1] Pinto[1]   Little Bears[1]
Eden[1]

CANNED BEANS

General Rule of Purchase: Choose canned beans only when you can't cook your own. The label lists all the ingredients. Avoid nonessentials like sugar, corn syrup, and the preservative disodium EDTA. Salt will be practically unavoidable. Note that ingredients vary with the bean as well as with the brand.

Exemplary Brands

Acme Great Northern
Alpha Beta Great Northern
Ashley's of Texas Garbanzo
Avondale Great Northern
Bi-Lo Great Northern
Bush's Best Great Northern, Navy, Mixed
Cedar Creek Boiled Peanuts
Coop Garbanzos
Eden Pinto,[1] Great Northern[1]
El Jibarito Pigeon Peas
Food Club Great Northern, Navy

Gebhardt Pinto
Georgia Gold Green Peanuts in Brine
Giant Food Black-Eyed Peas
Goya Small White, White Kidney, Black, Small Red, Pink Whole Peas, Pea Beans, Field Peas with Snaps
Greer Great Northern, Navy
Hain Soy
Hanover Great Northern
Janet Lee Great Northern
La Preferida Black

Exemplary Brands (continued)

Loma Linda Green Soy
Lord Chesterfield Boiled Peanuts
My-Te-Fine Small Red
Pastene White Kidney, Kidney, Cannellini, Roman, Cranberry
Pathmark Pink, Small White, White Cannellini
Progresso Fava, Roman, Black, Lupini
Redgate Navy
Richfood Great Northern, Navy

Rienzi Red Kidney
Roddenberry's Peanut Patch Green Boiled Peanuts
Staff Great Northern
Superfine Red Kidney
Thrifty Maid Great Northern, Navy, Butter Beans, Green Boiled Peanuts
Town House Great Northern, Navy
Western Family Great Northern

[1]Organic

Chapter 12

Soyfoods:
World Class Protein

Despite the fact that the soybean is this country's number-one cash crop, despite the fact that the United States is the largest exporter of soybeans, and despite the fact that this extremely versatile, nutritious, and easy-to-grow plant is touted as the world's most important legume, on the domestic front it is used mostly for animal feed and for its oil, which is the principal ingredient in most margarines and shortenings. But the times are changing. Informed consumers looking for good-quality protein, free from cholesterol and low in saturated fat, now see the value in consuming soybeans directly in soybean-based foods, rather than indirectly through the hogs, cows, and chickens that fed on them.

With Americans' increased exposure to Asian cultures, they have had a chance to experience and enjoy the benefits of the culinary refinement of soy-based foods. For better and for worse, new food technologies also have created more uses for soybeans in the expanding area of prepared foods, from soy sauce to soy "ice cream." America has become a major participant in the soyfoods revolution. Where barely a decade ago tofu production in this country was confined to Oriental communities, soy "dairies" specializing in tofu, tempeh, miso, and related "deli" items are now springing up coast to coast. Even many large food conglomerates have turned to textured soy protein production.

The list of foods on page 144 produced from the soybean illustrates the bean's vast potential. Beside each item is the chapter in this book where you can find further information.

TOFU

In the Orient, tofu is poetically referred to as "the meat of the fields." It is also called *bean curd*, and this high protein food is the precipitate made from mixing soybeans and water with a mineral coagulant in a process similar to cheese making. As such, it contains all the virtues of the bean itself and, because it consists largely of water, it is low in calories as well. We are pleased to report that this nourishing, reasonably priced, minimally processed food is no longer confined to Oriental and natural

A SUMMARY OF SOY FOODS

Soyfood	Description	Chapter Location
Tofu	A curd made by precipitating the protein in liquefied soy milk using a mineral coagulant	12. Soyfoods
Soy Milk	A liquid extracted from soybean mash	15. Milk and Its Many Forms
Soy Oil	Fat extracted from the bean using a complex system of refining	20. Looking for Oil
Tempeh	A mold-fermented soy patty	12. Soyfoods
Soy Sauce	A fermented-soybean seasoning sauce	38. Seasonings
Miso	A fermented-soybean paste resembling thick soy sauce	38. Seasonings
Natto	A bacteria-fermented soybean	37. Condiments
Soy Grits	The coarsely ground residue of defatted soybeans (oil extracted)	12. Soyfoods
Soy Flour	A finely ground version of soy grits or, if full-fat, made from the dehulled bean with the oil intact	5. Sifting Out the Flour
Soy Protein Concentrate/Isolate	Various refined and highly processed soy protein extracts	12. Soyfoods
Soy Ice Cream	A frozen dessert made from one or more soy-derived products	34. Frozen Desserts
Soy Nuts	Roasted split soybeans	30. Snacks
Soysage, Soy Patties, etc.	Meatlike foods produced from a variety of soy-based products	28. Prepared Foods

food markets, but can be found in the produce section of almost every American supermarket.

For those who have not yet had a chance to try tofu, it has a rather soft texture and neutral flavor that is usually enhanced by serving it in a mixed vegetable dish or with a sauce. It serves well as a substitute for cheese or meat in many traditional recipes and is so versatile it can appear in any course of the meal from soup to dessert.

Buying Tofu

Although all tofu is similar, it is not quite the same. Your selection is best made on the basis of intended use and personal preference.

There are small but perhaps significant differences in tofu ingredients. Packaged tofu will display a complete list of ingredients; bulk offerings are often undescribed.

The soybeans may be organically grown. This is more common in brands made in local soy dairies than it is in those offered by Oriental markets.

The coagulent employed may be bittern or natural nigari (derived from seawater), pure magnesium chloride, which is extracted from liquid nigari, calcium chloride (a chemically synthesized salt), or calcium sulfate, also known as gypsum. All are acceptable. Nigari is the most traditional, and tofu afficionados feel it produces the best-tasting product. There is, however, a small nutritional advantage to using calcium-based coagulants because they impart this important mineral to the tofu. One additional possibility is lactone or glucono delta-lactone, which is derived from cornstarch and often used to make the silken variety of tofu; it is usually coupled with monoglycerides, defoaming agents which are not essential to the tofu-making process and which we try to avoid.

Selecting Tofu

The best tofu is freshly made and brought to the market in buckets that are delivered frequently in the manner of fresh bread. To keep its quality, the chilled waterbath it is displayed in should be changed every day or two. This tofu should be purchased (and consumed) within one to three weeks of manufacture. Learning the delivery schedule of the tofu-maker is one way to ensure the freshest tofu. Frequent handling by customers can rapidly diminish the quality. A sour odor, slippery surface, and unpleasant strong flavor are all signs of age. Blocks of tofu with pieces missing have probably been overhandled.

TOFU IN ITS MANY FORMS

Firm: Pressed so there is less moisture and a relatively higher concentration of nutrients. Located in the refrigerator.

Regular: Softer and more delicate in texture. Located in the refrigerator.

Soft: Slightly sweeter with a higher water content. Favored for desserts. Located in the refrigerator.

Silken: Also sweeter with a custard-like texture. Usually packaged in shelf-stable aseptic boxes.

Smoked: Usually precooked in a soy sauce-based seasoning, then smoked to achieve a browned surface, pleasant flavor, and firm, cheeselike texture. Located in the refrigerator or drygoods shelf.

Dried: A freeze-dried product that is stored at room temperature and reconstituted with boiling water. Has a chewy texture (akin to frozen tofu) and is especially useful for traveling, emergency measures, camping, etc.

Tofu Pouches (or *age*—pronounced "ah-gay"—or *aburage*): Deep-fried cubes of tofu that are hollow inside. Located in the refrigerator or freezer.

The trend today is toward vacuum packing of fresh tofu, which preserves it for three to five weeks with refrigeration. Some companies are pasteurizing the tofu as well to extend this time period and allow for nationwide distribution. Be sure to check the expiration date on the wrapper. While the packaged product is fresh in the technical sense—neither sour nor spoiled—it does lack the clean, crisp flavor of a tofu that is just a day or two old. This, we suppose, is a compromise that comes with mass availability, but we still prefer tofu sold in bulk when we are sure of its freshness and cleanliness.

Tofu also comes canned in water and salt, sometimes labeled "tow-fu." In addition, the silken variety may be aseptically packaged and subject to ultrahigh temperature sterilization; like similarly packed milk and juice, this product has a room-temperature shelf-life of three to six months. What is not so attractive is that the carton is sterilized with hydrogen peroxide (not revealed on the label as it is a "processing aid"), and monoglycerides are added as a defoaming agent (revealed on the label).

Keeping Tofu

Tofu is highly perishable, so keep it cold. When bought in bulk or removed from its sealed package, it is best stored in a covered container, submerged in water which should be changed daily. Use as soon as possible or within one to three weeks of manufacture. Use unopened packages before the pull date.

Fresh tofu is odorless and has a smooth, but not slick surface. If either of these characteristics change, that is if the tofu develops an unpleasant smell or a slippery texture, it is probably spoiling. Tofu that has passed perfection can be refreshed by simmering it in water for ten minutes; it should then be used promptly.

Frozen Tofu

Many people are not aware that tofu can be frozen. Freezing has many advantages, not the least of which is having tofu on hand for virtually instantaneous use. In addition, freezing changes the texture from a soft, delicate curd to a chewy, spongelike consistency that is similar to chicken or veal and often more acceptable to the Western palate.

Tofu can be frozen for later use directly in the package, but we find it more convenient to slice it into 2-ounce portions, pat it dry, and enclose it in clear wrap, foil, or freezer paper before storing. To defrost it, simply unwrap the frozen tofu, place it in a bowl, and cover with boiling water; in about five minutes, when the water has cooled down and the tofu is pliable, squeeze it between your palms to release the water (just like a sponge), and it's ready for use.

For *American Wholefoods Cuisine* we developed a number of frozen tofu recipes ranging from Tofu "Chicken" Salad to Tofu à la King, which can help you to appreciate this age-old concept borrowed from the tofu masters.

Prepared Tofu Products

The popularity of tofu has brought about several ready-to-eat tofu products. Tofu may be sold dipped in a soy sauce marinade and baked or broiled, transformed into a burger, or prepared as a "no-egg" or cottage cheese-like salad, spread, or dip. The label on these foods reveals all. They are a good introduction to tofu for the uninitiated, and also provide an alternative for those with little time for cooking. Exemplary products are listed in Chapter 28.

TEMPEH

Tempeh is a dense, compact patty made by culturing cooked cracked soybeans with a mold. (If tofu can be likened to cheese, then tempeh is akin to blue cheese.) It is a newcomer to the American food scene, but in Indonesia, its home, it has been savored for centuries. Since its introduction to the U.S. marketplace in the late 1970s, tempeh has been quickly gaining well-deserved favor and is the fastest-growing segment of the soyfoods industry.

Tempeh is somewhat unappealing to look at in the uncooked state; the beans are held together with white mold and the surface may be freckled with gray or black spots that are merely an indication of the natural fermentation. Nevertheless, the firm texture, mild, mushroomy taste, and impressive nutritional content make it easy to overlook first impressions. In fact, fermentation of the soybean during tempeh manufacture improves the protein and increases the B vitamin content, including the production of vitamin B_{12}, which rarely occurs in the plant kingdom. Moreover, despite the high fiber content, the iron and zinc tempeh contains are easily assimilated by the body. Like other soy products, tempeh is cholesterol-free and low in sodium.

Buying Tempeh

You are most likely to find this valuable food in the refrigerator or freezer at a natural food store. It most often appears as a flat, rectangular block sealed in a tight-fitting polyethylene wrapper, although it may be formed into a cylinder, pyramid, or individual cakes.

The ingredients in all unseasoned soy tempehs are similar: soybeans, Rhizopus oligosporus (which is the active culturing agent), and in some varieties, cider vinegar. Several manufacturers offer tempeh made from soy plus assorted grains as well as totally grain-based versions.

Many tempeh makers also offer their product in a "burger" version in single-serving packages, preseasoned and precooked by broiling or frying (although they do need to be reheated). You will find a reference to these and other ready-to-eat tempeh-based items in Chapter 28.

Keeping Tempeh

Tempeh has a long shelf-life of three weeks under refrigeration, longer if vacuum packed, and months at 0°F., making it easy to have some on hand at all times. Most packages are stamped with a recommended last day of sale. It can spoil, however, and spoilage may be a little difficult to spot. Fuzzy white patches in a concentrated area, unusual coloration (that is, pink, orange, or green, rather than the usual black or gray spotting), and an unmistakable ammonia-like odor are all signs that it is past its prime.

USING MORE SOY

If you are eager to incorporate the soyfoods we have been discussing into your meals but feel you could use more guidance, the Soyfoods Center is a good resource. If you send a business-size stamped self-addressed envelope to the Soyfoods Center, P.O. Box 234, Dept GGF, Lafayette, CA 94549, you can receive their catalog of books and other related products that will turn you into a soy expert.

MILDLY MODIFIED SOY

Soy flour and *soy grits* represent the crudest forms of processed soy protein. They are made by steam cleaning, dehulling, and grinding the bean. *Defatted flour* and *grits* result from extraction of the oil using a petroleum-derived solvent, hexane, which is said to totally dissipate. These products are about 55 to 65 percent protein by weight and still retain most of the original plant components.

The terms *soy granules, textured soy*, and *soy protein* have no clear meaning. Based on our discussions with manufacturers who list them on the label, they are most often a ground form of the bean or an extruded form of the flour.

HIGH-TECH SOY

Not all soy products are commendable. Rather, *soy concentrates* and *soy isolates* which are used as fillers, meat extenders, and to create "meat substitutes," are products of technological alchemy. They have had most of the native nutrients processed out, creating a refined protein that has no natural counterpart. In many ways it is as unbalanced as sugar (refined carbohydrate) and bran (isolated fiber).

Soy concentrates, which average about 70 percent protein, are produced by acid removal of the carbohydrate from defatted soy flakes. Although the remaining concentrated protein may be marketed as a coarse powder, it is more frequently "textured" into flakes, crumbles, or chunks. Bland in taste and neutral in color (although it is often further compounded with caramel coloring for increased marketability), soy concentrate may be used institutionally to extend meat recipes and commercially to create chicken, veal or beef patties, or perhaps the restructured pork ribs sold at a local fast-food restaurant. (Presently, these products can contain up to 50 percent soy concentrate and still be called meat.)

Soy isolates are even more highly processed. They are almost pure protein, the result of a multistep process using harsh alkalizers, acids, and sulfiting agents. Soy isolates are a common component of many new-generation soy products from milk-free infant formula to "breakfast links" to soy ice cream. The ultimate in highly processed, refined ingredients, they do not come close to representing a wholefood.

One other concern with soy isolates is the loss of protein quality and the formation of a protein component known as lysinoalanine (LAL) that can interfere with the body's ability to metabolize phosphorus, zinc, and vitamins E, K, D, and B_{12}. Although supplements are added to infant formulas in an effort to compensate, the use of soy protein isolates in other products is not monitored for potential nutritional imbalances. As a result of the spray-drying step, soy protein isolates are also frequently contaminated with nitrites at levels approaching those in many cured meats.

TEXTURED SOY PROTEIN PRODUCTS

Another common processed soy product, *textured vegetable protein* or TVP, is particularly popular with food manufacturers for its ability to take on colors, flavors, and shapes. It is often used to make meat look-alikes or analogs. The source of soy protein used to make TVP may be as innocent as soy flour or as contrived as soy isolate. When soy isolate is used to create a meat analog, it is fed under pressure into a machine that actually spins it into fibers similar to those used in rayon and nylon production. Indeed, the manufacture of this "spun" soy protein was inspired by a chemical process employed during World War II in an attempt to make synthetic wool. The resulting "threads" of protein are devoid of taste and odor. By adding flavors, spices, coloring agents, binders, and other supplementary ingredients, then cutting, cooking, and shaping, a final product that mimics meat emerges.

TVP-based products may be promoted as possessing no animal fat or cholesterol but a considerable amount of partially hydrogenated fat is often added. Moreover, in addition to the questionable synthetic flavorings and colorings in most of these items, the amount of sodium generally used, both in the obvious form of salt and the hidden guise of hydrolyzed vegetable protein, places them among the highest sodium-containing processed foods, providing about 600 milligrams of sodium per serving. Finally, from a purely ecological standpoint, the procedure for making many forms of TVP is energy-intensive, in direct contradiction to the premise that food should produce energy, not consume it.

To present the other side of the picture, this processing of the bean is still more energy- and land-efficient than meat production and the end product requires no refrigeration. Thus, TVP may play an important role in hunger relief efforts where protein fortification and storage capabilities are a priority. For the vegetarian who craves foods that can match the taste and texture of meat without incorporating any of the animal, there are a few manufacturers who use the textured protein as the basis for otherwise uncompromised products (see Chapter 28).

RECOMMENDATIONS

General Rule of Purchase: All soy-based products, including tofu, tempeh, and prepared foods made with soy flour, soy protein concentrates and isolates, and textured vegetables protein will list all ingredients on the label.

Tofu made with organically raised beans is preferred. Nigari, magnesium chloride, calcium sulfate, calcium chloride, or glucono delta-lactone are all acceptable ingredients, but avoid tofu made with glucono delta-lactone if it also contains monoglycerides. Tofu made with calcium is richer in this mineral.

Tempeh made with organic soybeans is preferred. Sometimes other beans or grains are combined with the soy. Rhizopus oligosporus is the traditional culturing agent and the addition of cider vinegar is fine.

Avoid soy products containing soy concentrates and isolates.

Exemplary Brands

Tofu

Aloha
Azumaya Tofu, Fried Soybean Puffs
Banyun
Blue Ridge Soyfoods[1]
Brightsong[1]
Bud Inc.[1]
Calco[1]
Cathay
Cleveland Tofu Company[1]
Dae Han[1]
Eden Dried
Frieda of California

Furama
Garden of Eatin' Honorable[1]
Green Cow[1]
Hawaii
Health Valley[1]
Hinode French Fried Pouches
Hinoichu Tofu, French Fried Pouches
Island Spring[1]
KA.ME Tow-Fu
Kinai Tofu, Abura Age
Living Lightly[1]
Marjon

Tofu (continued)

Nasoya Foods[1]
Nature's Spring[1]
New Day[1]
New Leaf[1]
Nutri Gourmet
Roland Tow-Fu
San Diego Soy Dairy[1]
San Pan Inn Tow-Fu
Soy Power[1]
Soya
Soyplant[1]
Spring Creek Soy Dairy[1]

Stowe Mills Pasteurized[1]
Sun Luck
Sunwest Natural Foods
Swan Gardens[1]
The Soy Shop[1]
Tofu Shop[1]
Tomsum Pasteurized
Tree of Life[1]
Twin Dragon
Yaupon[1]
Zena Naturals

Tempeh

Appropriate Foods
Farm Foods Tempeh Starter
Kingdom Foods Soybean,[1] Brown Rice and Soy[2]
Lightlife Soy,[1] Soy and Three Grain[2]
Nasoya Foods[1]
New Leaf[1]
Pacific Foods[1]
Soy Power[1]

Soyfoods Unlimited Soy,[1] Soy and Brown Rice,[2] Soy and 5 Grain[2]
Soyplant Premium Soyfoods[1]
Tempeh Works[1]
Turtle Island Soy Dairy Soy,[1] 5 Grain[2]
21st Century Foods Soy,[1] Soy-Millet,[1] Sesame Wheat[2]
White Wave Soy,[1] 5 Grain[2]
Yaupon[1]

[1]Organic
[2]Some organic ingredients

Dining in the Wholefoods Style

The search for the optimal diet appears to be never-ending and is likely to remain so since, as noted nutritionist Roger Williams has said:

"Nutrition is an important part of life and life cannot be reduced to a rule of thumb. . . . The best we can do is muddle through using the best knowledge we have."

Just as our faces and physiques are different, so too are our nutritional needs.

DIETARY GUIDELINES FOR THE UNITED STATES

Rather than following a rigid meal plan, we favor dietary "goals" as exemplified by the U.S. Dietary Guidelines below. This allows people room to adapt good nutrition principles to personal needs, taste preferences, income, lifestyle, etc.

- Eat a variety of foods.
- Maintain a desirable weight.
- Avoid too much fat, saturated fat, and cholesterol.
- Eat foods with adequate starch and fiber.
- Avoid too much sugar.
- Avoid too much sodium.
- If you drink alcoholic beverages, do so in moderation.

GOLDBECKS' DIETARY GUIDELINES

Despite Roger Williams's admonition, we do have a loose axiom we like to follow: *Eat each day as if you were dining in a different foreign country.*

This is a sure way to get true variety and exemplifies what we call the wholefoods philosophy, which is based on certain facts of human nature. As Reay Tannahill explains in her book *Food in History*:

"What most people eat today is the product of thousands of years of dietary choice, the outcome, in effect, of an almost Darwinian process of natural selection. The foods which have survived in different regions of the world have become those best fitted not only to cultivation conditions, but to the specific requirements of the inhabitants."

Dr. Ross Hume Hall, noted Canadian biochemist, offers this important information:

"Our digestive and metabolic processes were genetically fixed to the dietary patterns of at least 50,000 years ago when human beings, as we know ourselves today, first appeared."

THE WHOLEFOODS PHILOSOPHY

These observations and others have led us to the following logical and practical conclusions about our diet. We should:

- Rely on historically selected foods taken in proportions close to that of our ancestors. This means less animal and more vegetable protein and minimizing processed, fabricated, and fragmented foods.
- Reduce our intake of food components which do not exist in nature and to which our bodies are unaccustomed.
- Vary food selection to maximize the chance of receiving unknown nutrients and natural detoxifiers, as well as the known nutrients.
- Eat foods as close to nature (whole) as possible, as it is well established that this is when they are richest in nourishment and flavor.

VARIETY THROUGH PROTEIN

One of the easiest ways to increase the variety in your diet is to reduce your meat consumption, as this food tends to crowd out others. Throughout this *Guide to Good Food* we refer to the various foods which offer protein alternatives to animal products. In general, nonanimal proteins, including beans, grains, nuts, and seeds, are inexpensive, cholesterol-free, low in saturated fats and often in overall fat as well, and highly versatile.

The best way to get the most value from vegetable proteins is to combine them in a meal with each other, or with small amounts of animal proteins. In this manner they will furnish all the essential amino acids the body needs to build protein. Macaroni and cheese, rice and beans, and peanut butter sandwiches are classic examples of food combinations which make ideal protein. For more information, see *American Wholefoods Cuisine* (NAL Books/Plume).

The four boxes below list the foods rich in protein. To turn nonanimal protein foods into high-quality protein it is best to combine them with one of the foods pointed to. (This is known as protein complementation.) Note that there are no arrows pointing out from the animal foods because they can stand alone.

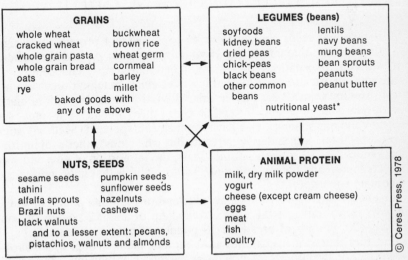

GRAINS

whole wheat	buckwheat
cracked wheat	brown rice
whole grain pasta	wheat germ
whole grain bread	cornmeal
oats	barley
rye	millet

baked goods with any of the above

LEGUMES (beans)

soyfoods	lentils
kidney beans	navy beans
dried peas	mung beans
chick-peas	bean sprouts
black beans	peanuts
other common	peanut butter
beans	

nutritional yeast*

NUTS, SEEDS

sesame seeds	pumpkin seeds
tahini	sunflower seeds
alfalfa sprouts	hazelnuts
Brazil nuts	cashews
black walnuts	

and to a lesser extent: pecans, pistachios, walnuts and almonds

ANIMAL PROTEIN

milk, dry milk powder
yogurt
cheese (except cream cheese)
eggs
meat
fish
poultry

© Ceres Press, 1978

*Nutritional yeast has an amino acid pattern similar to legumes and thus can be combined with the same foods to enhance their protein value.

Chapter 13

Let's Get Nuts (and Seeds)

Remember the old-fashioned description of a real gourmet meal, one that's complete from "soup to nuts"? Well, if you dine at our house, some days what you might get is a complete meal of soup *and* nuts. Maybe that doesn't sound like much, but those nuts have a lot to offer. They can provide the basis of a wonderful array of dishes from burgers to pie crusts, one indication that nuts are not meant just for snacking.

A nut is defined as a dry fruit or seed with a hard, separable shell and an edible interior kernel. Included in this definition are not only the commonly recognized nuts, but chestnuts and coconuts and the edible seeds like sunflower, pumpkin, and sesame. Because coconuts differ dramatically from other nuts in terms of nutrition and are marketed like fresh produce, they will be dealt with separately in Chapter 25. Peanuts are treated here like nuts, although botanically speaking they belong to the same family as dry beans, split peas, and lentils.

THE NUTRITION IN A NUTSHELL

Most nuts and seeds contain from 15 to 25 percent protein (by weight) and offer varying amounts of the B vitamins, vitamin A, and the minerals iron, calcium, phosphorus, potassium, magnesium, zinc, and copper. Almonds and filberts are particularly high in calcium, pumpkin seeds are high in iron, sunflower seeds are high in thiamin, and peanuts are high in niacin.

Most nuts average about 50 to 60 percent fat (by weight), but some, such as pecans and macadamias, may have as much as 70 percent. Seeds are somewhat lower in fat, just under 50 percent. But while most other protein foods (meat, cheese, eggs) contain saturated fats, the fat portion of nuts and seeds is largely mono- and polyunsaturated. Another plus is that nuts and seeds do not contain cholesterol.

The energy provided by nuts may be friend or foe. One pound of shelled almonds, for example, is the caloric equivalent of about 2 pounds of boneless beef, 2.5 pounds of bread, or 10 pounds of potatoes. A single cup of peanuts furnishes as many calories as about nine medium apples, 3½ cups of brown rice, or twenty-eight average-size carrots. Consequently, for most of us, nuts are best used in small portions to enhance other ingredients in a dish both nutritionally and aesthetically.

154

A NUTRITIONAL COMPARISON OF NUTS AND SEEDS*

Food 1 pound, shelled	Calories	Protein grams	Fat grams	Carbohydrate grams	Calcium mgs.	Iron mgs.	Sodium mgs.	Potassium mgs.	Vitamin A IU	Thiamin mgs.	Riboflavin mgs.	Niacin mgs.
Almonds												
raw	2713	84.4	245.9	88.5	1061	21.3	18	3506	0	1.09	4.17	15.9
roasted in oil, salted	2844	84.4	261.7	88.5	1066	21.3	898	3506	0	.23	4.17	15.9
Brazil nuts	2967	64.9	303.5	49.4	844	15.4	5	3243	trace	4.35	0.54	7.3
Cashews												
roasted in oil	2545	78.0	207.3	132.9	172	17.2	68	2105	450	1.95	1.13	8.2
Chestnuts	880	13.2	6.8	191.1	122	7.7	27	2059	NA	1.00	1.00	2.7
Filberts (Hazelnuts)	2876	57.2	283.0	75.8	948	15.4	9	3193	NA	2.09	NA	4.1
Peanuts												
roasted in shell	2654	119.4	222.0	93.9	329	10.1	23	3195	NA	1.46	0.60	78.0
roasted in oil, salted	2654	117.9	225.9	85.3	336	9.5	1896	3057	NA	1.45	0.59	78.0
Pecans	3116	41.7	323.0	66.2	331	10.9	trace	2735	590	3.90	0.59	4.1
Pignolias	2496	140.8	214.4	52.8	NA	NA	NA	NA	NA	2.88	NA	NA
Piñon	2880	59.2	275.2	98.8	48	24.0	NA	NA	160	5.76	1.12	20.8
Pistachios	2694	87.5	243.6	86.2	594	33.1	NA	4409	1040	3.04	NA	6.4
Pumpkin seeds	2508	131.5	211.8	68.0	231	50.8	NA	NA	320	1.09	0.86	10.9
Sesame seeds	2645	82.7	242.7	80.0	500	10.9	NA	NA	NA	0.82	0.61	24.5
Sunflower seeds	2540	108.9	214.6	90.3	544	32.2	136	4173	230	8.89	1.04	24.5
Walnuts												
Black	2849	93.0	269.0	67.1	trace	27.2	14	2087	1360	1.00	0.50	3.2
English or Persian	2953	67.1	290.3	71.7	449	14.1	9	2041	140	1.50	0.59	4.1

NA = no figures available
*Source: *Nutritive Value of American Foods in Common Units*, Agriculture Handbook No. 456, USDA, November, 1975.

Getting the Most Out of Nuts

The amino acids in which nuts and seeds are the weakest are easily supplied by dairy products, beans, or wheat germ. Coupling nuts with soy flour or wheat germ in patties, loaves, and baked goods creates an ideal protein. This principle is observed in several of the mixes described in Chapter 28.

In order to be of use, any food must be well digested. For this reason, it is particularly important to chew nuts and seeds thoroughly. (This offers the additional benefit of massaging the gums. Also, according to some oral health practitioners, eating nuts, and peanuts in particular, after a sweet may adjust the chemical balance in the mouth and help reduce the incidence of tooth decay.)

NUTS IN THE SHELL

One of the major advantages of nuts and seeds is that they do not have to be prepared for eating, except perhaps for some shelling. The shell is a natural container for the nutmeat and the best there is for maintaining freshness and preserving the nutritional value. Moreover, when you do your own nut cracking, casual overindulgence is unlikely.

The shell is also a shield of protection against chemical invasion. Although the shells of nuts may be treated with lye and gas to soften and loosen them, and although they may be bleached and possibly dyed and waxed, this mistreatment doesn't penetrate to the edible portion. Since you will discard the shell, you needn't be too concerned about this processing. Pistachios are the one exception. Their natural shell is cream colored; if the choice is between dyed red nuts or no nuts at all, choose the latter.

Most nuts in the shell are not roasted. Peanuts, however, usually are, and while roasting does not significantly affect their food value, they may also be impregnated with salt, which is a concern for many people. All this should be stated on the label if they are packaged. For variety, you may want to try unroasted peanuts. They are quite different in taste, more like peas than nuts.

Pistachios are always roasted in the partially opened shell and are generally presalted, although unsalted varieties are available. Both raw and roasted unhulled pumpkin and sunflower seeds are acceptable, particularly if they are left unsalted.

Selecting Unshelled Nuts and Seeds

Nuts and seeds sold in the shell should be your first choice. Although cosmetizing of the shells makes it difficult to judge quality, look for specimens that are free from splits, cracks, holes, and surface mold. Most nuts when fresh are firmly held in their shell; kernels that rattle may be shriveled by age or spoilage.

Ripening takes place in the fall; thus, the crop that comes to market at this time of year is likely to be the current harvest. From late spring to summer, nuts in the shell are taken from storage.

SHELLED NUTS AND SEEDS

Nuts and seeds sold out of the shell may be raw or roasted, whole or in pieces. The shelled version is especially handy if you need to use a large quantity of nuts or seeds for cooking.

Elaborate machinery is used for cleaning, grading, bleaching, cracking, and packing most shelled nuts and seeds. For some varieties processing remains, at least in part, more primitive. Practically all cashew processing takes place in India and each kernel is removed by hand. Pine nuts are also shelled by hand, which helps account for their steep price.

Some nuts are blanched to remove the skin covering the nutmeat. For almonds, this blanching is traditionally done in a hot water bath, but in a newer "improved" method the kernels pass through a hot chemical solution first to loosen the skins. The uneven contours of the walnut make the removal of its outer membrane more difficult, so walnuts are first immersed in a lye solution, then rinsed.

It is hard to imagine that this blanching does not cause some nutritional deterioration, but we have not been able to find much comparative data except in terms of fiber, which is noticeably reduced. There is no reason, other than appearance, that the skin must go, and it probably does in part protect the delicate interior from deterioration by air and light.

The sesame seed, being so tiny, is difficult to hull. Although the hull is edible, it contains a substance that binds the calcium in the seed so tightly that it cannot be absorbed by the body. This same compound may also irritate the gastrointestinal tract and precipitate kidney stones. In the amounts that most people consume, it is unlikely these negative effects will be encountered, but if you wish to take advantage of the calcium and choose the hulled sesame seed, the trade-off will be the loss of small amounts of iron and thiamin, almost all the potassium, and possibly some of the oil and protein. The technique most often employed to remove the hull is dependent on lye. An entirely mechanical method which we prefer is used by some companies that distribute to the natural food market. Any differentiation made on the packaging is strictly voluntary.

Quality Control

Once they are out of their protective shells, nuts and seeds are more likely to deteriorate. Rancidity is a primary problem because of the high oil content. Warm temperatures, humidity, and sunlight all accelerate the process. Logically, you should aim for the opposite conditions in storage and make sure these conditions prevail where you purchase the nuts and seeds as well.

Consider, too, that the more exposed the surfaces are, the easier it is for the oil the nuts contain to spoil. Thus, whole nuts have a longer lifespan than halves, pieces, slivers, and, at the bottom of the line, nut meals. For this reason, ground meals should be kept in the refrigerator, and other nuts and seeds in a cool place.

Nuts and seeds are also very susceptible to infestation by insects, especially in warm climates. This may be deterred by cold storage or, less commendably, by fumigation. Practically all imported shelled nuts will have been fumigated. Unfortunately, there is no way the consumer can know which of these methods was chosen for domestic varieties, except to buy from an organic source.

Mold is another potential serious problem; aflatoxin, a known carcinogen, is the mold the government checks for in monitoring nuts. Peanuts are the most susceptible; small amounts of aflatoxin in peanuts are considered unavoidable. Currently the government allows higher levels in peanut products than in any other foodstuff. With cooperation from industry these levels could be reduced significantly; it is mainly cost that has stood in the way, but new inexpensive tests recently developed may change this situation. Trusting the grower is one way to protect yourself if you are concerned. We personally have confidence in both Walnut Acres (a mail-order source) and Arrowhead Mills (supplier to many natural food stores).

Defective kernels are more susceptible to mold and this should be considered when you make your purchase. Look for clean, plump kernels of fairly uniform size and color. However, color can be misleading since it may be enhanced by chemical "whitewashing." Graying or blackening of the surface are definite signs of decay. Avoid nuts that are shriveled and, if sampling is possible, be aware that fresh nuts are crunchy; if they seem limp or rubbery, they are on the decline. If they burn the back of your throat when you swallow them, they are rancid.

Roasted Nuts and Seeds

The most serious adulteration of nuts and seeds is found in the "roasted" variety. It would be more accurate to call roasted nuts "French fried," because they are actually immersed in a bath of hot oil. The oil may be partially hydrogenated or treated with preservatives to inhibit oxidation, and although it permeates the kernel, the additives in the fat are considered "incidental" and may not show up on the final product label.

To compound this misuse, roasted nuts are usually heavily salted; this is what you are munching when you dig into the "cocktail nuts." For this reason, shelled roasted nuts and seeds are never considered an exemplary buy.

Dry-Roasted Nuts and Seeds

Dry roasting, which is done in large ovens by dry, hot air, is acceptable if nothing else is added. Unsalted dry-roasted peanuts are the most common item in this category. Unsalted dry-roasted cashews, sunflower seeds, or mixed nuts (peanuts, almonds, cashews, filberts, pecans) exist, but are not available everywhere.

Whenever dry-roasted nuts and seeds are seasoned, their quality declines; not only do salt and other spices enter the scene, but invariably vegetable gums, modified starch, dextrin, corn syrup, hydrolyzed plant protein, and MSG are added as well.

Many people have the mistaken idea that dry roasting reduces the calories in nuts and seeds. This is not so, for their inherent high fat content is not altered. What dry roasting does offer is an option for less salt and less deterioration from high-temperature frying in oil of questionable content.

"Lite" Peanuts

If fewer calories are what you're after, low-fat peanuts are the answer. Fat reduction is achieved by pressing the nuts to remove some of their native oil, then roasting them in oil (usually unsaturated sunflower or safflower oil). They may be left unsalted or sprinkled with sea salt.

Low-fat peanuts are lighter in weight as well as lower in calories; based on equal volume, they contain half the calories of regular roasted peanuts.

SOY NUTS

Although not really a nut at all, when soybeans are deep-fried they are referred to as soy nuts and used in snacking or cooking. While we are still not in favor of this French-frying system, soy nuts are much lower in fat than nuts and comparatively low in calories. Use soy nuts judiciously to enhance the protein in nut mixtures, nut or grain burgers, and grain- or vegetable-based entrees. Be sure to purchase the unsalted variety.

NOT NUTS

The poet Joyce Kilmer wrote that "only God can make a tree," but this has not impressed the food industry, which now manufactures "nuts." "Wheat nuts," with a texture, color, and flavor that mimics nuts, have come into favor with food processors. They may be marketed as a snack item, or used in candy, bakery products, frozen desserts, cereals, and other prepared foods. While they are often promoted as a nutritious replacement for nuts, the following typical formula may lead you to question this:

Hydrogenated soybean oil *[the first ingredient!]*, wheat germ, sugar, sodium caseinate, soy protein, salt, natural and artificial flavor, artificial color, FD&C yellow No. 5.

A SPECIAL WORD ON CHESTNUTS

The only nut which must be cooked in some manner after you buy it is the chestnut. Chestnuts are more starchy than other nuts, with little fat and protein, and fewer vitamins and minerals. However, they are delicious if you select them with care.

Chestnuts are in season from late fall through the beginning of winter. Their shells should be a deep reddish brown, smooth and silky to the touch. If they feel dry or brittle, they are old. They should be stored at room temperature.

When fresh chestnuts are not available, you may be able to find canned boiled chestnuts, usually imported from France and packed in water, in some specialty departments. Be sure to get the unsweetened kind. These delicacies can be used to dress up a vegetable or grain dish.

A STORAGE GUIDE FOR NUTS AND SEEDS

To remain fresh and crunchy, nuts and seeds must be protected from heat, air, and moisture. If still in the shell they can be kept out in a bowl, but are best consumed within a month. If you want to keep them for as long as a year, store them in a covered container.

Shelled nuts and seeds should be put out in bowls only for immediate snacking. Otherwise, they should be stored in well-sealed containers. If they are to be used within two to three months, they can be kept at cool room temperature, but if stored on an open shelf, they should be out of the sun's direct rays. Nuts and seeds kept in the refrigerator maintain quality for as long as a year, and in the freezer keep even longer.

NUT AND SEED BUTTERS

When nuts and seeds are ground to a paste they are referred to as "butters." Peanut butter is the most well-known example. While over the years food processors have compromised this North American mainstay by diluting the peanuts with added oil, sugar, salt and additives, in the last few years this trend has begun to reverse.

We have been especially amused by the ads for one popular commercial supermarket peanut butter proclaiming only "half the sugar" of other "leading national brands." This is quite a breakthrough for an industry that made its fortune by taking a simple food like ground nuts and sweetening it into junk food status. Until a few years ago, unadulterated nut butters could be found only in natural food stores; today the unsweetened version is on the shelf in almost every supermarket.

While peanut butter is still the most widely available nut butter, the popularity of almond butter is spreading. Other specialty butters include cashew, sunflower, roasted sesame, macadamia nut, and even filbert (for hazelnut).

Peanut Butter Standards

The government has set standards only for peanut butter. Accordingly, the product is composed of a minimum of 90 percent roasted peanuts and no more than 10 percent seasoning and stabilizing ingredients. Salt and any nutritive sweeteners may be added; most popular brands of peanut butter contain from 150 to 200 milligrams of sodium in a 2-tablespoon serving, while "lightly salted" are closer to 120 milligrams. Unsalted peanut butter contains less than 10 milligrams.

To keep the butter from separating, a stabilizer in the form of hydrogenated oil coupled with mono- and diglycerides may be added. This saves you the "trouble" of having to stir in the oil that naturally rises to the surface of nut and seed butters.

If the peanut skins are left on, the label must say "prepared from unblanched peanuts (skins left on)." Blanching also removes the tiny "heart" at the base of the kernel. Some manufacturers claim unblanched peanut butter is more nutritious; some consumers say it has a bitter taste.

Artificial sweeteners, chemical preservatives, and coloring are prohibited. Everything that is added will be on the label except that, unlike most other foods, the specific type of added oil need not be given.

Selecting Peanut Butter

In an attempt to compete in the growing market for natural peanut butter, some companies have eliminated the salt and/or added sugars, but still retain the hydrogenated fat. Those that have gone "all natural" often call themselves "old-fashioned" and contain no sugars or hydrogenated fat, but frequently keep the salt. Thus, depending on your particular concerns, you will need to carefully scrutinize the label. We prefer to eliminate all three and get a peanut butter with ground nuts only.

There are disadvantages to buying store-ground peanut butter. Oxygen in the package is a major factor in reducing stability. A half-filled container of freshly ground peanut butter may therefore be more vulnerable to spoilage than an airtight jar of a commercial brand, especially if the peanuts were not stored with care to begin with. If your peanut butter is ground on the premises, choose a well-filled container and store it in the refrigerator, as you should all nut butters once the seal on the container is opened.

Selecting Other Nut and Seed Butters

The preceding rules of selection apply to other nut and seed butters, and, likewise, all ingredients will be on the label. Note that while almond butter may be diminished by the addition of hydrogenated oils and mono- and diglycerides, other nut and seed butters can only have salt added.

One of the most seductive nut butters is made with macadamias. Because it is higher in fat and lower in protein than all other nut butters, we counsel you to be sparing if you can. Try to think of it as a dessert treat, not a nourishing sandwich filling.

SOLVING A STICKY PROBLEM

If anyone in your household complains about the layer of oil that rises to the top of the jar, store it upside down initially. In this way it can be stirred gently to recombine the oil without splattering. Once it is amalgamated, refrigeration will keep it that way. If you are a calorie or fat counter, you may even want to pour off some of the oil. Admittedly, this makes the butter really stick to the roof of your mouth. Mixing in a little water or, better still, yogurt when spreading time comes will help alleviate any dryness.

Tahini

Tahini is a spread made from ground sesame seeds and is alternatively known as sesame butter. This puree is a common ingredient in Middle Eastern cuisine, forming the basis of the garlic-laden sauce served over falafel, as well as the sweet confection known as halvah. Especially rich in calcium, tahini is an excellent addition to the diet. All brands are free of additives and even an organic option is offered.

STORING TAHINI

Although tahini is free of preservatives, one major manufacturer says it needs no refrigeration. Nonetheless, we keep ours in the refrigerator and in this way are spared the task of stirring the oil back in each time.

RECOMMENDATIONS

NUTS AND SEEDS

General Rule of Purchase: Unshelled, unsalted nuts and seeds are top choice. While cosmetically treated shells are common, the ones you really should avoid are the dyed red pistachios.

Select only shelled nuts and seeds that are raw or those that are dry roasted and unsalted, preferably with the skins still on (unblanched).

Avoid preseasoned dry-roasted nuts as all contain sweeteners, vegetable stabilizers, and flavor enhancers as well as salt. Avoid roasted nuts as they are really deep fried and usually highly salted.

Prepacked nuts and seeds in vacuum-packed cans, jars, and see-through bags are acceptable provided they contain no preservatives (antioxidants).

Exemplary Brands

Nuts

Adams All American Unsalted Dry Roasted Cashews, Peanuts, Mixed Nuts
Aster Fresh Dry Roasted Virginia Peanuts in the Shell
Azar Almonds, Walnuts, Black Walnuts, Pecans, Nut Topping
Balanced Foods Raw Almond Meal
Bell Brand Pecans, Almonds
Blue Bell Almonds, Walnuts, Pecans
Blue Diamond Whole Natural Almonds
Bordon's Peanuts in the Shell
Bowl O Nuts Nuts in the Shell
Casey's Unsalted Dry Roasted Peanuts
Chippers Unsalted Dry Roasted Peanuts
Clement Faugier Whole Chestnuts in Water
Colony Walnuts, Pecans, Unsalted Dry Roasted Peanuts
Conserverie de Kerlebert Whole Chestnuts
Crescent Recipe Almonds, Walnuts, Pecans, Filberts, Brazil Nuts
Diamond Pecans, Brail Nuts, Hazelnuts, Walnuts in the Shell
Diamond of California Shelled Walnuts
Earthly Delights Unsalted Natural Pistachios in the Shell, Almonds
Ever Fresh Peanuts in the Shell
Evons Walnuts, Black Walnuts, Pecans
Fisher Unsalted Dry Roasted Peanuts
Flanigan Farms Dry Roasted Peanuts, Pignolias, Unsalted Macadamia Nuts, Almonds, Raw Cashews, Pecans, Walnuts, Natural Pistachios Dry Roasted in the Shell

Food for You Cashews, Almonds, Mixed Nuts
Funsten Pecans, Walnuts, Black Walnuts
Gary's Peanuts in the Shell
Gold Crest Unsalted Dry Roasted Peanuts
Grand Union Unsalted Dry Roasted Cashews, Mixed Nuts
HFS Brand Raw Almonds
Hoody's Unsalted Dry Roasted Peanuts, Raw Spanish Peanuts, Peanuts in the Shell, Walnuts, Brazil Nuts, Filberts
Houston's Unsalted Peanuts in the Shell
Jimbo's Jumbo Raw, Roasted Unsalted Peanuts in the Shell
Kountry Fresh Unsalted Dry Roasted Peanuts
Laura Scudder Walnuts, Pecans, Almonds, Goobers, Natural Pistachios in the Shell
Leavitt's Americana Unsalted Dry Roasted Peanuts, Cashews, Mixed Nuts
Martinelli's Fresh Roasted Peanuts in the Shell
Mr. Jolly's Almonds in the Shell
Parker's Pride Unsalted Dry Roasted Soynuts
Pathmark Shelled, Unshelled Walnuts
Planters Pecans, Almonds, Walnuts, Nut Topping, Unsalted Dry Roasted Peanuts, Cashews, Mixed Nuts
Pride O the Farm Raw Cashews
Sach's Dry Roasted Peanuts in the Shell
Sun Giant Uncolored Pistachios
Sun Valley Almond Meal

Nuts (continued)

Three Star Natural Foods Raw Cashews, Almonds, Pignolias, Pecans, Brazil Nuts, Filberts, Macadamia Nuts, Mixed Nuts

Tree of Life Raw Almond Meal
Waldbaum's Unsalted Dry Roasted Cashews, Mixed Nuts

NOTE: Almost every supermarket has a house brand of unsalted, dry roasted peanuts.

Seeds

Balanced Foods Raw Pumpkin, Raw Sunflower Meals
Crescent Recipe Sunflower Seeds
David's No Salt Sunflower Seeds in the Shell
Earthly Delights Roasted Unsalted Sunflower Seeds in the Shell
Fisher Unsalted Sunflower Seeds
Flanigan Farms Pumpkin Seeds, Sunflower Seeds
Giant Foods Unsalted Dry Roasted Sunflower Seeds

HFS Pumpkin, Sunflower Seeds
Hoody's Raw Shelled Sunflower Seeds
Oroko Hulled Sunflower Seeds
Planters Unsalted Dry Roasted Sunflower Seeds
Stone Buhr Unshelled Sunflower Seeds
Sunshine Valley Sunflower, Pumpkin, Sesame Seed Meals
Three Star Natural Foods Raw Shelled Sunflower Seeds, Pepitas
Tree of Life Raw Sesame, Pumpkin, Sunflower Seed Meals

NUT AND SEED BUTTERS

General Rule of Purchase: All ingredients are on the label. The best nut and seed butters contain nothing but the ground nut or seed. "Natural" or "old-fashioned" peanut butter may contain salt. Avoid brands with added sugar, dextrose, hydrogenated oil and mono- and diglycerides.

Exemplary Brands

Peanut Butter

Adam's Natural Old Fashioned
All American Deli Style Old Fashioned
Arrowhead Mills[1]
Bazzini Old Fashioned, Raw
Bee Nut Butter
Carriage House Old Fashioned Natural
Collegedale Old Fashioned
Collegemaid
Country Pure Brand Old Fashioned
Crazy Richard's All Natural
Deaf Smith[1]
East Wind
Eden
Erewhon
Hazel Old Fashioned
Health Valley
Healthway
Hollywood Natural
Holsum Old Fashioned
Knudsen Natural

Krema Old Fashioned
Laura Scudder's Old Fashioned
Maranatha
Market Street
NEOPC
Nature's Harvest Old Fashioned
New Life Natural Old Fashioned
Old Stone Mill Natural
Old Thyme 100% Natural
Pal's Old Fashioned Style
Polaner Natural
Shedd's Old Fashioned
Smucker's Natural
Spanky's
Sunny Jim's Pure Old Fashioned
The Natural Food Store Gourmet
Tree of Life
Westbrae
Woodstock Old Fashioned

NOTE: Many supermarkets have a house brand of natural or old-fashioned peanut butter.

Almond Butter

Bazzini Raw
East Wind
Erewhon
Gourmet Butters & Spreads California
Hain Raw, Toasted

Krema
Roaster Fresh California
Season's
Spanky's
Westbrae Toasted

Tahini

Alyamani
Arrowhead Mills[1]
East Wind
Erewhon
Hain
Joyva
Krinos
Lima
Maranatha

NEOPC
Near East
Norganic
Protein-Aide
Pure and Simple Bread Spread
Sahadi
Tarazi
Westbrae
Ziyad

Other Nut and Seed Butters

Bazzini Raw Cashew
East Wind Raw Cashew
Erewhon Cashew, Sunflower, Sesame
Hain Raw Sunflower, Raw Cashew, Toasted Cashew
Krema Cashew
Kuro Goma Unique Japanese Sesame Spread
Maranatha Roasted Filbert, Roasted Cashew, Cashew-Peanut-Date, Toasted Sesame

Market Street Cashew
Once Again Nut Butter Collective Hazelnut
Protein-Aide Sesame-Peanut
Regal Hawaiian Delight Macadamia Nut
Tropical Dream Macadamia Nut
Westbrae Toasted Sesame, Raw Cashew, Roasted Cashew, Cashew-Date-Peanut
Woodstock Cashew

[1]Organic

Chapter 14

The Eggs in Your Basket

When it comes to nutrition, eggs are high on the list of esteemed foods. It is the egg, not milk, that should have been popularized as nature's most nearly perfect food, for with the exception of vitamin C, the egg is a balanced source of all the important vitamins and minerals; in addition, each large egg boasts six grams of high-quality protein.

The egg yolk also contains cholesterol, which is used by the body to make cell membranes and hormones. During the last few years cholesterol has been implicated as a contributory but not necessarily primary factor in heart disease. In the controversy surrounding this issue, there has been, until recently, general consensus that high levels of blood cholesterol are a warning sign of potential heart disease and that lowering blood cholesterol can reduce the risk. Studies released in 1987, however, dispute this relationship. Moreover, there is a lack of agreement as to what specific measures will most effectively alter cholesterol levels and many authorities say that only those with high blood cholesterol should restrict their diet, while others say that everyone would do well to moderate their cholesterol intake.

Even though one large egg yolk does furnish close to the daily cholesterol recommendation in the most strict diets, it also supplies an abundance of lecithin which can help counteract fatty deposits in the arteries. The point is not to eliminate eggs from the menu, but rather to try to avoid using them indiscriminately. The egg should be regarded as a nutrition powerhouse. As such, it can be used in place of meat and other fatty foods to enhance meals based on beans, whole grains, and fresh produce. When this kind of traditional diet is maintained, the balancing mechanism in the body should be able to accommodate the modest use of eggs.

Whether you choose to adhere to the more stringent suggestion of some medical advisers that you eat no more than four egg yolks per week (the whites are cholesterol-free), or go on being a "two-egg-a-day (wo)man," the following information will help you to choose your eggs wisely.

SELECTING EGGS

Because of the technological methods used in large-scale egg production, ideally the eggs you choose should come from free-running hens raised on a drug-free diet. You are most likely to find these at the natural food store, although many small farms and farm stands carry them too. However, this option is not always available, in which case you should expect your eggs to contain some chemical residues. For example, because laying hens are so closely quartered in modern egg-producing operations, antibiotics are routinely fed to them to help avert epidemics. A form of chemical control is also used to eliminate the hordes of flies swarming around the hen house.

Grade and Freshness

Eggs are graded by size and quality. Requirements differ from state to state. Size is determined by a prescribed weight range for a dozen eggs, while quality grades are set by appearance. Many of the state standards parallel USDA grades.

When an egg carton bears the USDA shield, it means that sample batches have been checked by a full-time federal inspector in the packing plant. This ensures that the eggs have been handled in accordance with certain government criteria for cleanliness. All egg producers with flocks over 3,000 must adhere to these standards.

The three possible grades—U.S. Grade AA (or Fancy Fresh Quality), U.S. Grade A, and U.S. Grade B—are based on freshness and quality at the time of packing. Because Grade AA eggs have only a ten-day expiration date, they are less likely to be found in large markets. Grade A eggs have a thirty-day shelf-life and are more commonly available. Keep in mind that grading merely informs you of how the egg started out and, depending on how it has been handled in the interim, may not necessarily be an indication of freshness at the time of purchase.

Similarly, the expiration date, which is mandatory only in some states, is determined from the day of packing, not the day the egg was laid. Luckily, most eggs are boxed soon after and are generally fairly fresh when they reach the market.

Make sure you buy eggs from a refrigerated case, as temperature is a key factor in deterioration. An egg at room temperature loses more quality in one day than it will if held one week under refrigeration. Plan to consume eggs no later than a week from the last day of recommended sale.

It is said that younger hens lay better quality but smaller eggs. If you are looking for the best, perhaps medium to large eggs are a better choice than extra large or jumbo.

Cracked Eggs

Sometimes cartons of lightly cracked eggs are offered for sale. Because they may contain bacteria which have seeped through the cracks and penetrated the internal membrane, you are taking a big chance when you use cracked eggs unless they are well cooked—either hard boiled or used in baked goods. Never use leaking eggs.

Color Is Only Shell Deep

Despite the fact that one regional egg council boasts that "Brown eggs are local eggs and local eggs are fresh," the only real difference between brown and white eggs is the breed of the laying hen. Color has no bearing on flavor or quality, and certainly not on freshness.

DOING YOUR OWN EGG GRADING

Unlike nutshells, which are long-term storage containers for nuts and protect their freshness, eggshells are porous. The porous shell allows the egg to "breathe," and the consequent loss of carbon dioxide, which begins as soon as the egg leaves the hen, causes the egg's composition and flavor to change.

When you break a really fresh egg, the area it covers is small. The yolk remains round and upstanding and the thick, cloudy white stands plentiful and firm around it. Surrounding this thick white will be a smaller area of thin white albumen. As the egg ages, the white begins to spread and the yolk begins to flatten. The amount of thick white becomes smaller and smaller until finally the yolk is flat, breaks easily, and is surrounded by a large, thin, clear white area. This is the sign of an old, low-quality egg.

You can detect aging in a hard-cooked egg when the yolk is far off center and the air pocket is large, evidenced by a large dent in the white.

The color of the yolk is not a reliable sign of quality. In the past, a deep yellow yolk was one indication that the hen had fed outdoors on vitamin A-rich vegetation. Today, this no longer holds true since the FDA permits four feed additives that increase the yellow color of the yolk.

Stale Eggs Float

As an egg ages, it also loses moisture and the inner air pocket grows larger. A fresh egg, still in the shell, will sink when put into a 10 percent salt solution (2 tablespoons salt to 1 cup of water). A moderately fresh egg will remain suspended in the solution in an upright position. A stale egg will float to the top.

STORAGE: PUT ALL YOUR EGGS IN ONE (COVERED) BASKET

Keep your eggs in the refrigerator and try to use them as soon as possible. If you don't use eggs frequently, buy only a half dozen at a time.

RAW EGGS

Grade AA	Grade A	Grade B	Grade C

Round yolk; firm compact white	Slightly more spread-out white	More spread-out white; somewhat flattened yolk	Very spread-out white; very flattened, easily broken yolk

HARD-COOKED EGGS

Grade AA	Grade A	Grade B	Grade C
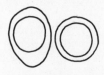			
Well-centered yolk	Slightly off-center yolk	Off-center yolk	Off-center irregular yolk

FRIED EGGS

Grade AA	Grade A	Grade B	Grade C

Firm white; firm round yolk	Somewhat spread-out white	Spread-out white; slightly flattened yolk	Very spread-out white; very flattened yolk

Fresh eggs will have firm, upstanding yolks and whites; as they age, the yolks and whites flatten and spread.

Do not wash eggs before storage. When the egg is laid, the shell is surrounded by a thin covering (or bloom) that acts as a seal and prevents bacteria from penetrating. Washing removes this natural protection and facilitates the entry of germs. For this reason, the commercial washing of eggs is prohibited in other countries. The U.S. egg industry, however, believes eggs should be washed prior to marketing to destroy surface bacteria. This is doubly unfortunate since the chemicals used in the washing solution may penetrate the shell.

Buy unwashed eggs if you have the chance. Purchases made at or close to the farm are more likely to be of this variety. Expect some of them to be slightly soiled. Although eggs should not be washed before storage, it is good practice to do so just prior to cracking them in order to get rid of any bacteria picked up from other foods or as the result of handling.

In no case does the shell offer total protection. The tiny holes which allow moisture to escape also permit outside odors and flavors to be absorbed. Keeping eggs in a covered box will cut down this invasion and prolong their life. Therefore you may want to invest in a covered egg container (available in housewares and camping supply stores) or keep them in the original carton rather than relying on an open refrigerator rack. Eggs should be stored point down. The rounded end of the shell is stronger and has less chance of breaking. Also, the internal structure is such that when eggs are stored point up the yolk is more likely to pull free from the white and migrate off-center.

Out of the shell, eggs can be stored for two or three days in a covered container in the refrigerator (with a small loss of quality and nutrients). Extra egg whites can be stored in a tightly covered container in the refrigerator for a week. For longer storage (up to six months), place the container in the freezer. Yolks are best kept under a covering of cold water in a closed container. They can be held in the refrigerator only two to three days, and freezing is not recommended because of their high fat content.

THE CARE AND HANDLING OF HARD-BOILED EGGS

Hard-boiled eggs aren't as tough as everyone thinks. If they're not handled with care they can be a source of serious food poisoning. The culprit is a rather common practice—cooling the eggs in their cooking water. When eggs are cooked in the shell, their external barrier breaks down and leaves them more susceptible to bacterial invasion. To keep them safe they should be cooled quickly in a cold water bath and refrigerated at once.

If you are lucky enough to be able to buy really fresh eggs, wait at least four days before you attempt to hard-cook them. Eggs that are any fresher than this will be impossible to peel. One of the great mysteries of life is how to peel hard-boiled eggs easily. If the eggs are to be used promptly, we offer the following advice from two professors at the University of Georgia:

After the eggs are cooked, drain them and drop them immediately into ice water, as cold as possible. Let them stand for one or two minutes, no longer. When ready to peel the eggs, return them to a kettle of boiling water for 10 to 20 seconds. The contracting and expansion should cause them to peel easily.

UNSCRAMBLING EGGS

If you happen to mix hard-boiled eggs with uncooked eggs, do not worry—there is an easy way to tell them apart. Hard-boiled eggs will spin rapidly on their side, while raw eggs will not.

PROCESSED EGG PRODUCTS

Preboiled Eggs

You might encounter preboiled eggs in the shell in the form of pickled eggs. At their most innocent, these are nothing more than eggs in vinegar seasoned with salt and natural flavorings. Some manufacturers add preservatives as well, which you will notice on the label. The major drawback to pickled eggs is their high sodium content.

The consumer who buys premade egg salad at the deli counter or prepared foods garnished with egg, or selects chopped egg bits from the salad bar, should be aware that these items are often made from hard-cooked egg products supplied for industrial use. They may be "fresh-cooked hard-boiled eggs" coated and sealed to remain fresh as long as ninety days without refrigeration, or a hard-boiled "egg cylinder," a continuous roll of whites and perfectly centered yolks. Some may contain preservatives. Unfortunately, you have no way of knowing what kind of eggs have been used, but we are always suspicious when we find perfect egg slices garnishing salads and sandwiches.

Liquid Eggs

Several years ago, premixed eggs and premade omelets were quite common in the freezer case at the supermarket. In researching this *Guide to Good Food*, we did not encounter one such product and are pleased not to have to waste many words on these unnecessary items. It is still likely, though, that you will encounter them indirectly, since several liquid egg products are available to the food processor. Premixed, presweetened yolks are commonly used in baked goods, ice cream, and egg nog. Presalted yolks go into salad dressings and mayonnaise. Whites treated with a whipping agent are used in certain cakes, meringues, and candy. For health purposes, liquid egg products are always pasteurized to free them of salmonella micro-organisms. Unfortunately, this also destroys some of the native vitamins and enzymes.

Dried Eggs

Other processed egg products include dried whole eggs, dried egg yolks, and dried egg whites. Since you are most likely to buy dried eggs as a component of another food, the presence of any additives used in preparing the eggs becomes "incidental" and may not show up on the label. In addition, the technology of drying creates an undesirable by-product in the egg, known as lysinoalanine (LAL), that may adversely affect the body by interfering with its use of certain vitamins and minerals.

SUPPORTING FRESH EGGS IN PROCESSED FOODS

The law allows the term *egg* to be used in the ingredient list of all foods without qualification, so you may not be able to detect the presence of liquid pasteurized eggs or dried eggs. Dried eggs are commonly added to commercial breads, cakes, cookies, pasta, salad dressing, ice cream, and in fact to all conceivable egg-containing foods. If you wouldn't use these eggs in your home, why bring them in in this disguised form?

The manufacturer who chooses to add the word *fresh* is letting you know that unprocessed egg was used. You may want to support those who have tried to maintain integrity in this way by seeking out such products and by demanding more informative labeling in general.

EGG SUBSTITUTES

Rather than taking the time to educate people regarding the appropriate use of the egg, the food industry has opted for artificially constructed "substitutes." There are several products marketed as egg replacers. Those available in liquid form are essentially egg whites combined with vegetable oil and thickeners, and made to appear more attractive with synthetic nutrients and coloring agents. The most popular of the liquid egg substitutes sells for about three times the price of a dozen eggs. The dried version combines the powdered white with proteins manufactured from milk or soy, along with preservatives, texturizers, and, once again, colorants. None of these meet with our approval.

As an alternative, some health practitioners suggest that people who are cholesterol-conscious buy real eggs and use only the whites. This is certainly a better buy monetarily than the contrived egg substitutes. However, it is advice we take exception to since the white has less food value than the yolk. We suggest that if you do choose to use only the white, you at least upgrade the nutritional value of the final product by adding soy flour or nonfat dry milk, two protein-rich items that are free of both cholesterol and chemical ingredients.

Those who wish to abstain from using any part of the egg are offered the commercial option of totally starch-based egg replacers made from tapioca, potato starch, calcium carbonate, and a cellulose-based filler. While this may do the work of the egg in cooking situations, it does not provide the nutrition.

RECOMMENDATIONS

FRESH EGGS

General Rule of Purchase: Look for an outlet that offers eggs from free-running or uncaged hens, preferably raised without drugs and on chemical-free feed. Buy from a refrigerated case and pay attention to the last day of recommended sale if it is given. Choose U.S. Grade A or better, or your state equivalent.

Exemplary Brands

Nest Eggs[1]

[1]Organic

Chapter 15

Milk and Its Many Forms

Is milk rally nature's most perfect food, as is often claimed by the dairy industry? Certainly many health advocates would dispute this notion, pointing out that humans are the only animals that consume the milk of another species. Although the basic components of all milks are similar (water, protein, lactose, fatty acids, vitamins, and minerals), the fact that the proportions vary so much from one species to the next does lead one to suspect that the specificity of different milks is for good reason.

The human is also the only animal that continues to drink milk well beyond infancy, even though the lactase enzyme needed to properly digest milk wanes as we grow older. And while the amount of milk and milk products consumed by Americans may be good for business, the high fat content in milk does not appear to be good for health.

A FRESH LOOK AT MILK

Despite these criticisms, milk is in many ways a highly nutritious food. It is an excellent source of protein, calcium, phosphorus, and the B vitamin riboflavin. Whole milk is a natural source of vitamin A. Reduced-fat milks have A added, and most of the milk sold in the United States is fortified with vitamin D as well.

Whole Milk

Standards for the composition of whole milk vary slightly from state to state, but 3.25 percent milk fat and 8.25 percent milk solids (based on total weight) are the minimum requirements to meet the "whole milk" specification. It is this fat content, as well as the 33 milligrams of cholesterol per cup, that has done the most to damage milk's reputation.

Reduced-Fat Milk

Low-fat milk may contain from 0.5 percent to 2 percent milk fat. The law requires the phrase "X percent milk fat" to accompany the name on the

174

label so it is clear how much fat remains. If a virtually fat-free product is desired, *skim milk* is available.

Protein fortified in the name indicates that nonfat milk solids have been added to reduced-fat milk. This is done to increase the viscosity of the product, which some people find enhances its palatability. Emulsifiers and stabiliziers may be added along with these extra milk solids and this will be indicated on the label.

Protein, minerals, and B vitamins remain intact when fat is removed from milk, but fat-soluble vitamins are lost. To compensate, vitamin A is always added and the addition of vitamin D is optional. Although supplementation with these vitamins is on the label, the carriers used to get them into the milk are not. Milk fat also contains vitamins E and K, which are not replaced; although there are no "recommended daily allowances" established for these vitamins, they are vital to health. Moreover, some fat (but not too much) maximizes calcium absorption so that the full benefit of this mineral may not be obtained from milk devoid of its fat component.

Even with the fat reduced, low-fat milks are not entirely cholesterol-free (which is fine, since we do need some cholesterol). The 2-percent-fat variety contains 18 milligrams of cholesterol per cup, 1-percent-fat milk contains 10 milligrams of cholesterol per cup, and skim milk measures in with just 4 milligrams per cup.

R-RATED MILK

Despite our national preoccupation with blood cholesterol levels and heart disease, no responsible medical authority recommends using low-fat milk in the diet of children under two. The concentration of protein, sodium, and other mineral components overworks their kidneys, and it appears that infants fed skim milk may not receive enough fat to promote adequate growth and good health.

Pasteurization versus Raw Milk

The debate between raw milk advocates and opponents has been a particularly heated one over the years. Almost all the milk available in this country is mass-distributed and since so much milk is produced daily, pasteurization or ultrapasteurization is deemed necessary to destroy potentially harmful bacteria and give milk a longer shelf-life. Pasteurization is no panacea—many dairy-related cases of food poisoning are from pasteurized milk—not raw.

The heat of pasteurization (and ultrapasteurization, which is a variation on pasteurization using much higher temperatures but for a shorter period of time) does affect the composition of milk, however. Thiamin, one of the B vitamins, is reduced after this heat treatment, and the native enzymes and any natural vitamin C are completely destroyed. Admittedly, these are not nutrients in short supply in the average diet. Of greater interest is the claim that an enzyme known as xanthine oxidase (XO), which some health researchers say precipitates atherosclerosis or hardening of the arteries, is enhanced through pasteurization (and ultra pasteurization).

Yet another argument in favor of raw milk concerns B-lactoglobulen, a frequent allergin. Heat heightens its effect, so those sensitive to B-lactoglobulen may be able to handle raw milk but react adversely to pasteurized milk. (Conversely, persons sensitive to another allergen, lactalbumin, are able to tolerate boiled milk.)

Despite a federal court ruling in 1987 banning raw milk and raw milk products from interstate sale, it can still be sold within states. As of 1987, the following states allowed the sale of raw milk, with many (as noted) limiting this to direct farmer-to-consumer sales:

When buying commercial raw milk make sure it is "certified." This means the dairy has been state-inspected and meets rigid sanitary regulations.

STATES PERMITTING LOCAL SALE OF RAW MILK

Arizona	New Hampshire
Arkansas (at the farm only)	New Jersey
California	New Mexico (at the farm only)
Connecticut	New York
Georgia	North Dakota
Idaho	Oklahoma (at the farm only)
Illinois (at the farm only)	Oregon
Iowa (at the farm only)	Pennsylvania (at the farm only)
Kansas (at the farm only)	South Carolina (at the farm only)
Massachusetts	Texas (at the farm only)
Michigan (at the farm only)	Utah
Minnesota (at the farm only)	Vermont
Missouri (at the farm only)	Washington
Montana	Wyoming
Nebraska (at the farm only)	

Homogenization

Homogenization is the process by which the fat globules in milk are reduced in size (and increased in number) so that the fat particles are evenly distributed throughout the liquid. Not that long ago, unhomogenized milk was widely available and it was one of life's pleasures to skim the cream that rose to the top. Homogenized milk, however, has more body and a creamier flavor, and this kind of uniformity and "convenience" are what the dairy industry strives for in its products.

The effect of homogenization on health is another concern. It has been proposed by Dr. Kurt Oster, a cardiologist and author of the book *The XO*

Factor, that the xanthine oxidase (XO) enzyme referred to on page 176 also becomes biologically more active following homogenization. His research, which supports the theory that this leads the way to atherosclerosis, merits serious consideration since, unlike pasteurization, there are no health or safety reasons to justify homogenization.

Low-Sodium Milk

One does not generally think of milk as a salty food, but a quart, whether whole, low-fat, or skim, averages close to 500 milligrams of sodium. This figure increases in "protein fortified" varieties. Those who consume a quart of milk a day take in about one sixth of the daily recommended limit of sodium (which is 3.3 grams). It is possible to purchase low-sodium milk in some areas. In this product the sodium content is reduced to only 24 milligrams per quart.

Buttermilk

True buttermilk is the liquid left over after butter is churned. Such traditional buttermilk is a fine, wholesome food. It is also practically nonexistent on a commercial scale.

Today, most buttermilk is produced by inoculating milk with microbes which mimic the old-fashioned buttermilk flavor. Usually, fluid skim milk is employed, although cultured buttermilk may alternatively be made with concentrated milk, nonfat dry milk, or whole milk (often called "Bulgarian style"). All ingredients will be indicated on the label. It may have added "butter flakes" or "butter granules" (which may be artificially colored), salt, and stabilizers such as gelatin and vegetable gums, all of which you may want to avoid. The addition of milk solids or other milk protein derivatives and sodium citrate can all increase the sodium content.

Often, reclaimed stale milk is used and when this is the case, buttermilk undergoes a lot more processing. Unfortunately, there is no definitive way to determine this from the label, but since salt can mask "off" flavors, it is more likely that unsalted cultured buttermilk begins with a fresh milk sample. That gives you two reasons to avoid the salted variety.

Goat's Milk

Fresh goat's milk is not widely encountered in the supermarket, but it can be found in natural food stores around the country. It may be raw, pasteurized, or ultrapasteurized. Due to the nature of the fat, it is not subject to homogenization.

For those sensitive to the protein components in cow's milk, goat's milk seems to offer a viable alternative, as the incidence of intolerance is low when compared with cow's milk.

The cholesterol content of goat's milk is 28 grams per cup, which is slightly lower than whole cow's milk, but the overall fat content is slightly higher. This fat, however, contains more of the essential unsaturated fats than cow's milk fat does.

Since goats are less troubled than cows by mastitis (an inflammation of the teats that requires antibiotic treatment), contamination of the milk with antibiotics has not been seen.

MILK INTOLERANCE

For decades the milk industry has bombarded us with the message "You never outgrow your need for milk." If you care about accuracy, the slogan should really be "you never outgrow your need for the *nutrients in* milk." While milk is certainly a convenient and familiar way to get many essential nutrients, there are other equally good sources. This is important to know since many people do outgrow the ability to digest milk properly and become lactose-intolerant.

Lactose is the sugar in milk that gives it sweetness. For many people who lack a sufficient amount of the enzyme needed to digest milk sugar, its effects are not so sweet, resulting in bloating, gas, cramps, and/or diarrhea. The problem is most common in ethnic groups whose ancestors drank little milk, primarily Orientals, blacks, American Indians, Jews, and those of Mediterranean extraction, although it can afflict anyone and often doesn't become significant enough to notice until about age thirty-five. Those groups who have trouble with milk generally hail from sunny climes where there was little dairying. The problem of lactose intolerance is yet another piece of evidence to support our wholefoods philosophy that we should stick as close as possible to the diet of our ancestors (see "Variety on the Table," page 152)

Reduced-Lactose Milks

In response to the increased awareness of milk intolerances, several new milk products have been introduced which increase the options for those who have difficulty digesting milk. One wonders, however, if this does not defeat nature's plan to limit the consumption of milk.

One way to improve the digestibility of milk is culturing it with a specific lactose-digesting bacteria, creating a product called **sweet acidophilus milk**. Low-fat milk is most commonly chosen as the basis for this cultured product, although federal standards allow the use of whole or skim milk as well. The name must include this information—i.e., "cultured milk" for the whole milk variety, "cultured low-fat milk," or "cultured skim or nonfat milk." The addition of vitamins A and D is voluntary and most manufacturers utilize the option, as indicated on the label. Other permissible ingredients are milk solids and several milk protein derivatives like whey, lactalbumin, and caseinates; these may be spelled out or simply lumped together under the term "protein fortified" on the ingredient list. Ultrapasteurization may be applied, but right now it is not common. If this treatment is used, it must be indicated on the label.

Lactose-reduced milk is produced by the direct addition of the lactase enzyme to the beverage. Most milk treated in this manner is ultrapasteurized.

CONTAMINATED MILK

The presence of chemical residues from the pesticides sprayed on feed crops and the antibiotics routinely fed to cows is not unique to milk, but the effects cannot be ignored. Scientists have found that the deadly salmonella bacteria in milk which have been traced to several outbreaks of food poisoning in the past few years are more virulent as a result of the resistance they have built up to antibiotics. In addition, contamination of milk with illegal pesticides has been reported in several states. The Food and Drug Administration also admits that it does not have sufficient data to ensure that the level of the carcinogenic mold aflatoxin permitted in feed results in safe milk.

HOW FRESH IS THE MILK?

From all visible signs, milk appears to be a fresh, wholesome food, but if you saw it through a microscope you would find thousands of bacteria and related microorganisms swimming around in it. If milk is not kept cold at all times, these bacteria will multiply; even at the standard refrigerator temperature of 40°F. they can double within about a day and a half. While this is not necessarily harmful to you in terms of health, it leads to an unpleasant-tasting product and more rapid spoilage.

The date on the container is one of the most important ways to ensure quality, yet this dating is quite variable. In New York City, for example, the last day of sale is a mere four days after pasteurization. In most other places in New York, New Jersey, and Pennsylvania, this is extended to nine days. In other parts of the country, it can be weeks. This range in dating is generally reflected in the milk; where laws are more stringent, milk tastes better and measures lower in bacteria tests.

Buying the Best (and Keeping It That Way)

Right now, the last day of sale is generally all the consumer has to go on. If the date of pasteurization becomes available on the container, your chances of obtaining fresh milk will improve; ten days seems to be a reasonable outer limit. In any case, select the freshest container according to date and use the milk up in as short a time as possible. It may interest you to know that low-fat milk and skim milk are even more vulnerable to spoilage than whole milk.

Attention to some other details will also help get the freshest milk into your glass:

■ Make the dairy case the last stop in the market (or next to last if you plan to buy frozen foods). When you get home, unpack these perishables first and put them right away.

■ Optimal milk storage temperature is 40°F. Unfortunately, this rule may be violated by the store when transferring milk during delivery and in stocking the shelf. Moreover, temperatures in display cases are frequently higher than they should be. If you are following recommended storage and use procedures and find your milk spoils or sours, return it to your grocer.

■ In open display cases, cold air is concentrated at the lower portions. If milk is stacked in the cases, the containers at the top may not meet temperature standards.

■ Milk does not perish all at once, but gradually. Every minute out of the refrigerator shortens its life, so keep the container out just long enough to pour what you need.

■ Light is also destructive to milk. This is another reason milk shouldn't be kept out too long.

■ If you've poured more milk than you can use, don't pour the extra back into the container or mix it with other stored milk. Store it separately in a jar.

Packaging

Milk is rarely sold in glass bottles as it once exclusively was; today, it is most commonly found in paperboard cartons and plasticized containers. Which of these preserves milk's quality best is a subject of intense industry debate.

According to the paperboard packaging industry, milk packaged in plastic and exposed to the unshielded fluorescent lights common in supermarkets and dairy cases loses a significant amount of its riboflavin and vitamin A. Paper cartons, they say, block out 98 percent of this harmful light, guarding milk's nutrition and protecting it against light-induced "off" flavors.

FDA sampling of milk has revealed, in fact, that it frequently does not meet the nutrient claims on the label. However, rather than implicating any packaging in particular, the agency suspects exposure to light, elevated temperatures, and poor stock rotation in general are the leading causes.

NON-REFRIGERATED MILKS

Dried Milk

Removing the liquid portion of milk makes it a long-lived, shelf-stable powder. Three forms of dried milk—whole, low-fat, and nonfat—are available. The first of these contains the lactose, milk proteins, milk fat, and minerals in the same proportions found in fluid whole milk. In addition, it may contain vitamins A and D (and carriers), emulsifiers, stabilizers, anticaking agents, and antioxidants. All of the additives, with the exception of the carriers for the added nutrients, are required to appear on the label.

The standards for low-fat dried milk are the same, except that the fat content is reduced and supplementation with vitamin A is mandatory.

Nonfat dry milk, which has virtually all the fat removed, is by far the most common form of dried milk. This powder can be a very useful cooking ingredient but shouldn't be used exclusively to replace fluid milk, as it is not a wholefood. Like liquid skim milk, nonfat dry milk is missing the fat-soluble vitamins A, D, E, and K. Government regulations allow for synthetic replacement of A and D and the label will tell you if this has been done. No other additives are permitted. Due to the absence of fat and the concentration of milk solids and minerals, nonfat dry milk should not be used extensively in feeding children under two. As with fresh nonfat milk, it does not meet their nutritional needs and puts stress on their kidneys.

It has been postulated that one effect of the heat of drying (as well as sterilizing for canning and UHT) is to reduce the availability of calcium and perhaps even cause the resulting product to promote tooth decay. In addition, the method of drying can diminish the quality of the protein. Spray-drying is a low-heat process which apparently does not significantly change the nutritional makeup; all nonfat dry milk currently packaged for the consumer uses this technique. Hot roller or drum-drying subjects the milk to more extreme temperatures, reducing the protein quality and destroying B vitamins; milk dried by this method is commonly used in commercial baked goods, candies, and some processed meats.

Some companies have tried to overcome the public's resistance to dried milk by introducing flavors to the powder. The sweetener they add, whether sugar or aspartame, and the imitation flavoring make this a less, rather than more desirable product.

An additive-free powdered whole goat's milk is now on the market, but is enormously expensive. Folic acid, a B vitamin, is frequently added.

QUALITY

Always buy dried milk that has the U.S. Extra Grade mark in a shield. This means the milk comes from a government-inspected plant and is your safeguard against harmful bacteria.

STORAGE

The idea behind dried milk is to create a product with a long shelf-life. This does not mean it lasts forever. Once the package is opened, air and moisture can enter and promote bacterial growth. To avoid this, the opened package of dried milk powder should be stored in an airtight container in a cool place.

Improper storage can also damage the protein in dried milk. Stored above 70°F., it can lose half its potency in six months. With refrigeration the same product will keep for one year; held at 0° F. it will remain fresh more than two years.

Reconstituted dried milk should be handled the same way as fresh fluid milk.

Dried Buttermilk

Buttermilk adds a unique taste and texture to certain recipes. In many households, however, there is the question of what to do with the rest of the quart after the buttermilk biscuits or pancakes have been made. Dried buttermilk comes to the rescue. This product is ideal for cooking as it is shelf-stable and can be doled out as needed.

It appears that all dried buttermilks are not alike. Most are a powdered version of the common cultured beverage. Sacco powdered buttermilk, on the other hand, is made from the real churned buttermilk that is a by-product of butter making, plus milk proteins in the form of whey and sodium caseinate. The reconstituted Sacco product is not recommended for drinking, however, as the flavor does not match what consumers have come to expect from commercial buttermilk.

To maintain quality, store like any dried milk in a cool, dry place.

Canned Milk

In the 1970s it was discovered that the lead content of the average 13-ounce can of evaporated milk was close to the daily permissible level from all sources for children aged one to three and that this milk, which is often used in homemade infant formula, greatly exceeded the safe upper limit for infants under a year. Consequently, it was suggested that the canned-milk producers abandon the use of lead-soldered cans, a step taken several years earlier by infant-formula manufacturers. Despite industry resistance, consumer reaction to the issue was strong enough to finally induce action. The switch from soldered to welded cans has now been accomplished and the lead is gone.

EVAPORATED MILK

Evaporated milk is produced by the partial removal of liquid from fresh whole milk that has been pasteurized, homogenized, and vitamin D-fortified.

'he milk is then sealed in cans and heat-sterilized so no refrigeration is
ecessary, but as the heat treatment is more intense than with other dairy
roducts and damages some of the amino acids, this milk is less useful as a
ooster for the protein in cereals, grains, and potatoes.

A variety of chemical stabilizers may be added to evaporated milk, but
he current regulations require they be listed on the label. There you will
lmost always find disodium phosphate and carrageenan, so you may be
aking a chance of bringing home unwanted additives if you make this
urchase.

Evaporated skim milk is less readily available. Although the same addi-
ives are permitted, they do not seem currently to be included in any of the
rands we have seen. Evaporated skim milk must be fortified with vitamins
A and D.

Canned evaporated goat's milk is also available. As is the case with
evaporated cow's milk, carrageenan and disodium phosphate are common
additives. The B vitamin folic acid, or folacin, is usually added to this form
of processed goat's milk too.

SWEETENED CONDENSED MILK

Sweetened condensed milk is evaporated milk (which in this case is
unfortified and chemical-free) plus 40 percent or more added sweetener in
the form of sucrose, dextrose, corn syrup, or some other nutritive carbohydrate sweetener. Additional lactose may be added to stabilize the milk and
prevent crystallization. If you plan on adding refined sugar to whatever you
are using the sweetened condensed milk for, you might as well keep the
product on your shopping list, but if you turn to Chapter 31, you'll find out
why we've crossed it off ours.

IMITATION MILK

Whether it is called "imitation milk," "substitute milk," or possibly even
"melloream," this product is a fabricated composite of dairy derivatives,
sweetening, fat, and various "functional additives" that thicken, stabilize,
emuslify, enrich, and flavor the mix. Although it is promoted as "cholesterol-
free," it is actually high in saturated fat because coconut oil or other
partially hydrogenated oils are included in the formula. The sodium content
is comparable to that of real milk and the vitamins and minerals that are
present are only there through the hand of man. In some imitation products
the amount of protein is not even half that of cow's milk. Enough said.

UHT Milk

Ultrahigh temperature (UHT) milk combines short-term exposure to
extremely high heat with a new packaging technique in order to give the
beverage a three-month room-temperature shelf-life. This procedure has

been used throughout the world for some time, but has only been permitted in the United States since 1981, when the special aseptic packaging required received FDA approval. This nonrigid carton, commonly known as Brik Pak, was originally held up by Japanese tests that suggested the hydrogen peroxide used as a sterilizing agent caused cancer in rats, but the FDA found these studies inconclusive and granted its approval. Once again industry triumphs and the public becomes the testing ground.

Pasteurized, homogenized milk is already a big step away from true fresh (raw) milk. If UHT products are allowed to become the standards for "fresh," we may deceive our taste buds, but at a possible cost to our bodies. Note that the heat of this processing reduces the quality of the protein slightly and limits its ability to enhance the protein in grain. It may also have a negative effect on the calcium.

Once the UHT package is opened, the milk must be kept in the refrigerator and used within a week or so, just as with fresh milk.

NONDAIRY MILKS

Soy Milk

Soy milk, in nonrigid cartons and soft pouches, has been a runaway success in natural food stores. It is neither a dairy product nor really milk in the traditional sense of being secreted by the mammary gland of an animal; it is a soybean extract obtained by grinding soybeans to a flourlike consistency, cooking the "flour" in water to destroy any nutrient-inhibiting enzymes, and pressing out the nutritious liquid. Today, vacuum drying and a series of heat applications are used to overcome the "beany" taste that once limited soy milk's appeal.

NUTRITIVE QUALITIES

While not quite the nutritional equivalent of animal milk, soy milk's flavor and texture make it interchangeable in terms of use. The advantage of soy milk is that it lacks cholesterol and lactose. Although it is close to whole milk in overall fat content, the fat is largely unsaturated. Mineral values vary widely from brand to brand. Soy milk may contain thirty times more iron than cow's milk, and retains the lecithin and vitamin E found naturally in the bean. Soy milk's major limitations are that it lacks vitamins A and D and has a low calcium value, from 18 percent to 40 percent that of cow's milk; however, it does offer slightly more protein.

SELECTING SOY MILK

Soy milk is primarily a natural food store item. Some brands are produced from organically grown soybeans as indicated in the list of Exemplary Brands.

Soy milks are distributed in flexible foil-like aseptic packages and aseptic boxes that can be kept at room temperature. Most are marked with a last day of recommended use. Once opened, the milk is as perishable as the animal product and requires cold storage.

Soy milk is available plain and in a variety of flavors including vanilla, chocolate, carob, carob mint, coconut, and cranberry, and malted versions of some of these. Several companies add oil to give the milk more body. Some of the flavored varieties are lightly sweetened with honey, malted barley, or maple syrup, while those marketed as "malted" are really more akin to a milkshake in terms of sweetness. All these ingredients will be indicated on the label; you may also encounter lecithin and kombu (a seaweed), harmless ingredients used to enhance the flavor and consistency, as well as carrageenan and vegetable gums, which we prefer to avoid. Unfortunately, at this time if you wish to use this product you cannot avoid the somewhat controversial aseptic packaging.

Perhaps the biggest drawback to soy milk is the cost. Even if you arrange for a case price with your local natural food source, which is practical since soy milk has good keeping qualities, it will cost substantially more than cow's milk. One reason for the high price is that the soybeans used in the manufacture of this primarily Japanese-produced product come from the United States and are subsequently shipped back to us accompanied by an increase of more than 60 percent water. As the market for soy milk continues to grow, however, we can look forward to larger packages, more domestic processing, and frequent "specials," which should make it more affordable.

Nut and Grain Milks

There are also prepared nut- or grain-based beverages to take the place of cow's milk. Although these products are in very limited distribution, they can be found in some natural food stores. Essentially they consist of either a blend of almonds and water or a dilution of cultured rice known as *amazake*. An unrefined sweetener may be added. Although these alternative beverages can be used whenever milk would be appropriate, they are not the nutritional equivalent of milk, containing far less protein, calcium, and vitamins A and D.

CREAM AND IN BETWEEN

Cream and half-and-half differ from each other only in the percent of fat they contain. To manufacture either one, the fatty portion is separated from the milk, as it is for all milk products, and butterfat is then added back to meet specific requirements. Half-and-half weighs in at 10.5 to 18 percent fat; light, "coffee," or "table" cream has 18 to 30 percent fat; light whipping cream has 30 to 36 percent fat, and heavy (whipping) cream a whopping 36 percent fat or more. Except for their taste and high vitamin A levels these products do not have much to recommend them.

Ultrapasteurization

In order to extend the shelf-life, any of these products may be subject to the high-heat process known as ultrapasteurization. This will be specified on the label, and when the process is used, it is likely that mono- and diglycerides (emulsifiers), and calcium carrageenan, sodium alginate, sodium citrate, disodium phosphate, or other stabilizing salts will also be used, adding more sodium to the diet unnecessarily.

Interestingly, there may be no way to differentiate the containers of ultrapasteurized products except by the required labeling, which makes it very difficult to notice the difference at a glance. Nonetheless, when our local supermarket tried to replace regular half-and-half with a similar ultrapasteurized variety, there was an uproar which brought the original back.

Note that ultrapasteurization reduces cream's whipping properties, which leads right into the next subject: imitation cream and nondairy whipped toppings.

"Creamers"

Imitation "creamer" is a synthetic substance made in the image of cream. It is often served by restaurants in tiny sealed plastic cups that many people mistake for the real thing.

The description of this product as nondairy does not mean it is fat-free. This realization is a disappointment to the many people who use cream substitutes and coffee whiteners because they are concerned about the high saturated fat content of real cream. The truth is that the coconut oil and palm oil used as the base for imitation creamers are more highly saturated than butterfat (although they do not contain cholesterol). In addition, creamers contain chemical stabilizers and emulsifiers (including several sodium-based salts), corn syrup (as much as 50 percent of the product), anticaking agents, acidity regulators, and artificial coloring and flavoring.

When you compare liquid nondairy creamer to half-and-half you discover that it has just about the same number of calories, twice the sodium, and two and a half times the carbohydrates (in the form of refined sweetening) of its dairy model.

THE NATURAL COFFEE LIGHTENER

Those looking for something that will mellow their coffee or tea without any additives should consider nonfat milk powder—the sugar-free, fat-free, chemical-free, shelf-stable, low-cost alternative.

Whipped "Cream"?

Another concocted dairy substitute which bears only a visual resemblance to the real thing is frozen, premade whipped topping. Originally, all of these whipped toppings—a rather unappetizing blend of water, hydrogenated coconut and palm kernel oil, sugar, corn syrup, sodium caseinate, dextrose, natural and artificial flavors, polysorbate 60, sorbitan monostearate, xanthan gum, guar gum, and artificial coloring—were dairy-free. In order to appeal to a population more interested in "real" foods, manufacturers now produce a new generation of whipped toppings with 30 to 54 percent "real dairy ingredients." In the more modest ones, skim milk is the only ingredient in addition to those listed above. A richer version uses cream and the preservative BHT.

Nothing can alter the true nature of these products, which is closer to sweet whipped margarine than to whipped cream. In addition, their calorie and fat content is one and a half times that of pressurized canned whipped cream.

If all this makes you decide to move on to canned whipped cream, just check the ingredients before you make that your choice. You will find that while it does contain real cream, it unfortunately also features sugar, corn syrup, mono- and diglycerides, artificial flavor, carrageenan, and a nitrous oxide propellant.

REAL WHIPPED CREAM

If you want this classic topping, your best bet is to buy heavy cream and whip it yourself. Admittedly, fresh whipped cream is higher in calories and fat than its imitators, but this is only due to the fact that less air has been incorporated into it. So, unless you find air satisfies your appetite, you should be able to make fresh whipped cream go twice as far as ready-whipped and frozen substitutes. This will just about even out the calorie and fat figures.

SOUR CREAM

As with buttermilk, today's sour cream is not much like the kind our grandmothers might have made. Originally, sour cream was nothing more than heavy sweet cream that had been set to sour in the warmth at the back of a stove. This sour cream was often thin and varied from mildly tart to quite acid.

The sour cream you buy today has licked the problem of inconsistency. A series of exposures to extreme heat and pressure, and the addition of rennet and unspecified "safe and suitable" ingredients (so described in its federal

Standard of Identity) to prevent the liquid from separating out, create a uniformly thick, taste-controlled product. Given the fact that cream doesn't have much nutritional value to begin with, sour cream, after the multiple heat treatments used for its transformation, does not offer much except vitamin A, fat, and calories, plus an admittedly luscious flavor and smooth, delicate texture.

All ingredients are on the label, and if you live in the eastern part of the country you will at least have the choice of several brands free of unnecessary gelatin, starch, and vegetable gums which make the sour cream unpleasantly stiff. In other parts of the country you may not have this option unless consumers begin to demand it.

CRÈME FRAICHE

Crème fraiche is a thick, tantalizingly piquant cream with as much as 40 percent butterfat. It is a popular French specialty that has no American counterpart. Except for the rare specialty store that carries it (or Devonshire cream, which is the English version), the closest commercial product we have encountered is the thick layer of fat that rises to the top of unhomogenized yogurt.

YOGURT

Plain, unflavored yogurt may well be the most versatile food in your kitchen. It can replace mayonnaise and sour cream; unlike these high-fat items, yogurt offers protein, calcium, and B vitamins instead of excess calories.

Yogurt is produced by the interaction of milk with specific bacteria that convert some of the lactose into lactic acid and curdle the milk, creating a thick, tart, custard-like product. All the nutritional benefits of milk are carried over. Some studies indicate that the protein in yogurt is actually more digestible, increasing its nutritive value. Although a good deal of the milk sugar is still present, many people who are lactose-intolerant are able to tolerate yogurt. Other unique properties attributed to yogurt include its possible antibiotic activity and cholesterol-reducing capability.

The original marketing strategy for yogurt, in the 1950s, was to promote it as a diet food aimed at the female market. Sales during this time were so low that most supermarkets didn't even bother to stock it. Although yogurt was once the butt of many health food jokes, today its average annual consumption is better than three pounds per person and it is one of the most actively moving dairy items, with new varieties introduced at an almost frenzied rate.

Is It Really Yogurt?

Many of the products trying to cash in on the new yogurt culture are so contrived that their "yogurt" component is of little value. One thing we can tell you for sure is that the term "natural," as it appears on the label, is meaningless.

The early inhabitants of the Mediterranean region and Eastern Europe, where yogurt has been popular for hundreds of years, would be amazed at some of the products that are being sold under that name today. As a result one must pay attention to be assured of making a good choice. In essence, yogurt need not be anything more than milk and yogurt cultures. Unfortunately, there are other considerations.

First there is the question of whether the yogurt contains live, active bacteria. If it doesn't, it will not supply many of the anticipated benefits. To give you an idea of how little this matters to some manufacturers, some yogurt is subjected to heat after production to extend the shelf-life. This not only destroys the microorganisms that cause yogurt to spoil, but its favorable bacteria as well. Fortunately, any company that uses this approach must indicate it on the label with the phrase "heat treated after culturing."

Second is the quality of the milk used. Sheep's milk, which is the basis for the most prized Bulgarian yogurts, has the optimal makeup to produce a rich, creamy product with a mild flavor and uniform texture. Cow's milk and goat's milk do not perform as well, so to overcome any wateriness, milk solids, cream, and thickening agents are commonly added. The milk solids add to the nutritional content; the cream adds possible unwanted fat and calories; agar, pectin, and gelatin, derived from seaweed, fruit, or animal bones, give the yogurt a jellied texture. Most objectionable are modified food starch, guar gum, locust bean gum, carob bean gum, carrageenan, and similar highly refined thickeners added to give a pudding-like consistency and cover up a possible lack of quality.

Selecting Yogurt

In some areas of the country, it is almost impossible to find a brand that is nothing but milk and milk solids plus added yogurt culture. Even with the offerings at the natural food store you may have to opt for a yogurt that contains agar, pectin, or gelatin until better products are demanded; any other ingredients certainly lessen the desirability.

Whether you choose whole-milk, low-fat, or nonfat yogurt will depend on what it is you're looking for. Predictably, the higher the fat content, the greater the number of calories, but some people contend that in choosing whole-milk yogurt you also get a much better-tasting product. The milk will be pasteurized or ultrapasteurized before culturing (this is not necessarily specified on the label). It will usually be homogenized as well, although there are a few brands made from unhomogenized milk which develop a rich layer of "cream" on top that can be skimmed off and used like crème fraiche or butter as a spread.

Flavored Yogurt

In any flavored yogurt you can expect to get an extra 50 to 150 calories, largely from the added sweetening. While this may not seem like very much, it translates to 2 or more tablespoons of sugar in a single cup of yogurt. Along with the sweetening you will also get assorted flavorings and colorings, some from natural sources like beets, grapes, annatto seeds, and turmeric, some from a chemist's beaker. Some companies also add salt to their flavored yogurt.

As if choosing from a variety of flavors (which were found in a blind taste test to be virtually indistinguishable) weren't enough, you must also decide if you want the flavor blended throughout, as in the so-called Swiss- and French-style yogurts, or if you prefer to mix in the fruit at the bottom. Perhaps you like the chewy texture of nuts, dried fruit and cereal offered by some companies. Or maybe you'd rather drink it down "Sippin' " style. And then there's the new "custard style" with a creamier texture thanks to the unprecedented addition of egg yolks!

The federal Standard of Identity does not allow preservatives to be added to yogurt. We have, however, seen sorbic acid and potassium sorbate on the ingredient list of some flavored yogurt containers. Any brand containing preservatives is adulterated and in violation of the law.

YOGURT WITH REAL TASTE

You are always best off buying the simplest unflavored yogurt you can find and adapting it to your tastebuds by adding fresh or dried fruits, unsweetened fruit purees, an unrefined sweetener or a jam sweetened with unrefined sweetener, or better still, fresh vegetables (e.g., diced cucumber and tomato with garlic) and herbs (mint, dill). Finish off your creation with a topping of nuts and wheat germ. If this makes your children feel different from their friends, you may want to follow the example of a friend of ours who reuses commercial containers, filling them with her own yogurt concoctions.

If you still insist on buying a flavored yogurt, fruit as opposed to preserves, and honey or maple syrup rather than sugar, fructose, or corn syrup, are the better choices.

Soy Yogurt

Those who must avoid milk will be interested in nondairy soy yogurt. A new arrival in natural food stores, this yogurt is made from soy milk and bacterial cultures. Gelatin is added to some brands to maintain the typical yogurt consistency. There is no need, however, for the quality to be com-

COMPARATIVE NUTRIENTS IN MILK IN ITS MANY FORMS*

Product 8 ounces	Calories	Protein grams	Carbo-hydrates grams	Fat grams	Chole-sterol mgs.	Sodium mgs.	Calcium % US RDA
Cow's milk products							
Whole Milk	150	8	11.4	8.2	33	120	29
2% low-fat milk	121	8.1	11.7	4.7	18	122	30
1% low-fat milk	102	8	11.7	2.6	10	123	30
Skim milk	86	8.3	11.9	0.4	4	126	30
Buttermilk	99	8.1	11.7	2.2	9	125-257	29
Half & half	315	7.2	10.4	27.8	89	98	25
Light cream	469	6.5	8.8	46.3	159	95	23
Heavy cream	821	4.9	6.6	88	326	89	15
Whipped cream, pressurized	154	1.9	7.5	13.3	46	88	6
Sour cream	493	7.3	9.8	48.2	102	123	27
Yogurt, plain low-fat	144	11.9	16	3.5	14	159	41
Yogurt, fruit low-fat	239	11	42.2	3.2	12	147	38
Goat's milk	168	8.7	10.9	10.1	28	122	33
Human milk	161	2.5	17.0	10.8	34	42	8
Soy products							
Soy beverage (Eden Original)	160	9.4	13.2	8.5	0	113	6
Soygurt (Cream of the Bean, flavored)	255	6.7	45.2	5.3	0	20	7
Substitutes							
Imitation milk	150	4.3	15.0	8.3	trace	191	8
Coffee whitener	336	2.4	27.3	23.8	0	190	2
Nondairy dessert topping	239	0.9	17.3	19.0	0	19	†

† = less than 2 percent
*Source: *Composition of Foods, Dairy and Egg Products*, Agriculture Handbook No. 8-1, USDA, 1976, and manufacturers' data.

promised by the addition of high fructose corn syrup, isolated soy protein, salt, and several thickening agents, as has been done in at least one brand we have encountered.

KEFIR

Kefir is a cultured milk drink with the consistency of buttermilk and a flavor reminiscent of yogurt. Like both, it is made by culturing milk, generally whole milk, with various bacteria. It is then usually flavored with fruit and sweetened with honey or fructose. It may also have vegetable color added. All the ingredients will be listed on the label.

Most of the kefir on the market is sold in natural food stores. It can be habit forming so take note that along with the friendly bacteria comes what may be a less welcome dose of fat, sweetening, and calories. It is probably best considered as an alternative to a milkshake.

INDUSTRIAL DAIRY DERIVATIVES

A number of dairy derivatives are finding their way into the food supply and you may wish to know more about them in order to make appropriate food choices. In general, products using these ingredients do not make it into our shopping cart, for although derived from a natural source, these isolated components of milk are a far cry from being a whole, balanced food.

Dairy derivatives fall into two categories: *whey* and *caseinates*. They may appear on the label as whey, modified whey, sweet dairy whey, and sodium or calcium caseinate. Their manufacture provides the dairy industry with a welcome outlet for its surplus milk, and because they are relatively inexpensive, food processors are using them more and more to replace dried milk (which offers much more balanced nourishment) in product formulation. Dairy derivatives are frequently found in dairy products, imitation dairy products, frozen desserts, protein-fortified drinks, baked goods, candy, and other snack items.

RECOMMENDATIONS

FRESH MILK

General Rule of Purchase: There is little difference between brands of *pasteurized, homogenized cow's milk*, with most being fortified with vitamin D and, if fat has been reduced, vitamin A as well. Avoid ultrapasteurized milk.

Sweet acidophilus milk lists the ingredients on the label. All brands appear to be the same. *Lactose-reduced milks* are all ultrapasteurized and therefore less desirable.

Look for unsalted *buttermilk*. Avoid buttermilk containing colored butter flakes, guar gum, gelatin, and carrageenan, all of which will be disclosed on the label.

Raw milk should only be purchased from a certified dairy, indicated on the label, or if obtained directly from the farm it should be guaranteed safe by a certificate of inspection.

Goat's milk should be certified if raw, or pasteurized. Avoid ultrapasteurized products.

*Exemplary Brands*_____

pasteurized, homogenized cow's milk—all brands, similar
sweet acidophilus milk—all brands similar
Brentland Farm Goat Milk
Brookside Dairy Farms Goat Milk
Crest Mor Brand Raw Certified Goat Milk
Friendship Low Fat Buttermilk
Green Gold Valley Raw Goat Milk
Handy Handle Raw Milk
Irish Hills Goat Milk
Jersey Dairy Grade A Raw Milk
Knudsen Real Churned Buttermilk
Maranata Hills Raw Goat Milk

Millers Grade A Raw Milk, Raw Buttermilk
Mrs. Brown's Cultured Buttermilk
Prink Hill Goat Milk
Red Gate Farms Raw Goat Milk
Redwood Hill Farm Raw, Pasteurized Goat Milks
Singing Winds Raw, Pasteurized Goat Milks
Steuve's Natural Raw Certified Milk, Raw Buttermilk
Tall Talk Raw Goat Milk
Valley Hill Farm Raw Milk
Zone Goat Milk

DRIED MILK

General Rule of Purchase: Choose U.S. Extra Grade. Avoid *whole milk* and *low-fat* varieties if they contain emulsifiers, stabilizers, anticaking agents, and preservatives. With the exception of the carriers for the added vitamins, all ingredients will appear on the label.

Nonfat dry milk contains only vitamin enrichment. Most brands are the same.

Choose either *dried buttermilk* made from the liquid cultured product or a variety produced from real churned buttermilk. In the latter case, milk protein derivatives like whey and sodium caseinate may be unavoidable.

*Exemplary Brands*_____

Darigold Powdered Cultured Buttermilk
Ener-G Cultured Buttermilk
Meyenberg Powdered Goat Milk

Miracle Brand Powdered Goat Milk
Sacco Cultured Buttermilk Powder

CANNED MILK

General Rule of Purchase: All ingredients are on the label. *Evaporated skim milk* appears to be additive-free. The whole milk version, whether cow's or goat's, is more likely to contain unwanted additives such as carrageenan and disodium phosphate.

Sweetened condensed milk is not recommended due to its high sugar content.

NONDAIRY MILK

General Rule of Purchase: Soy milk is a completely labeled food which may be no more than soybeans and water, or may also be sweetened and flavored. In the latter case, there is an ample choice of brands that employ honey, malted barley, or maple syrup and natural flavorings. Other acceptable ingredients include oil (not hydrogenated), lecithin, and kombu. Avoid products that contain vegetable gums, salt, and sodium or potassium bicarbonate. The only unavoidable drawback is the aseptic packaging.

Nut and *grain milks* made from almonds or cultured rice (known as amazake) are of additional interest when a nondairy product is desired. All those now on the market are additive-free.

CREAM/HALF AND HALF

General Rule of Purchase: Purchase the fresh product, pasteurized or certified raw. Sterilized or ultrapasteurized varieties are Acceptable with Reservation provided they do not have additives like sodium citrate, disodium phosphate, sodium alginate, mono- and diglycerides, and carrageenan. All ingredients will appear on the label.

Reject imitation cream and coffee whiteners.

SOUR CREAM

General Rule of Purchase: Look for sour cream made with cream, culture, rennet, and possibly nonfat milk solids. In some parts of the country, gelatin is unavoidable. Avoid those made with locust bean gum, carrageenan, tapioca, or mono- and diglycerides. All ingredients will be on the label.

*Exemplary Brands*_____

Acme Sour Cream
Axelrod Sour Cream
Breakstone's Sour Cream
Cabot Vermont Sour Cream
Crowley Sour Cream
Daisy Brand Sour Cream
Finast Sour Cream
Food Club Sour Cream
Heluva Good Sour Cream
Hood Sour Cream
Hughes Sour Cream
Knudsen Hampshire Sour Cream
Lucerne Sour Cream

Nancy's Sour Cream
National Sour Cream
Natural and Kosher Sour Cream
Old Mill Sour Cream
Pathmark Sour Cream
Penn Maid Sour Cream, Sour Half and Half
Sealtest Sour Cream
Staff All Natural Sour Cream
Sundance Sour Cream
Valley Gold Sour Cream
Waldbaum's Sour Cream

YOGURT

General Rule of Purchase: All ingredients are on the label. Select *plain, unflavored yogurt.* If possible, avoid those thickened with gelatin, agar, pectin, or tapioca, and reject brands with modified starch and gums. You may want to try a brand made with unhomogenized milk. If you wish to avoid cow's milk, it is possible to find yogurt made from goat's milk or soy milk.

When buying *flavored yogurts,* look for those with fruit, unrefined sweeteners, natural flavors, vegetable coloring, perhaps agar, pectin, or tapioca to keep the fruit mixture from separating, and nothing more. Avoid brands with modified food starch, sodium citrate, vegetable gums, corn syrup, artificial color and flavor, citric acid, and tartaric acid, as well as sorbic acid and potassium sorbate, which, if present, are added illegally. Also avoid yogurts which have been heat processed after the milk has been cultured, indicated by the words "heat-treated after culturing" following the name.

*Exemplary Brands*_____

Acme All Natural Plain Lowfat Yogurt
Axelrod Easy Dieter Low Fat, Whole Milk Yogurts
Breyer's Plain Yogurt
Brown Cow Plain, Flavored Yogurts
Columbo Plain Whole Milk, Natural Light Yogurts
Cream of the Bean Plain, Flavored Soy Yogurts[2]
Dannon Plain, Non-Fat Yogurts
Dutch Plain Yogurt
Erivan Acidophilus Yogurt
Giant Food Plain Yogurt

Hedgebrook Farm Plain, Flavored Yogurts
Honey Hill Farms Plain, Fruited Yogurts
Irish Hills Dairy Sipping Yogurt
Jewel Plain Yogurt
Kroger Plain Yogurt
La Yogurt Plain Yogurt
Lacto Natural Plain Yogurt
Mystic Lake Dairy Goat Milk Yogurt
Nancy's Lowfat Plain, Honey Yogurts
Natural and Kosher Bulgarian Style Plain, Fruit Yogurts
Pathmark Plain Yogurt
Pavel's Yogurt

Exemplary Brands (continued)_____

Penn Maid Plain Nonfat Yogurt
Prink Hill Goat Milk Yogurt
Staff Plain Yogurt
Stonyfield Farm Plain, Fruit, Garden Salad
   Yogurts

Sundance Plain Yogurt
Waldbaum's Lowfat Plain Yogurt
Yogo Non Dairy Soy Yogurt
Yoplait Plain Yogurt

KEFIR

General Rule of Purchase: All ingredients are on the label. Most brands are sweetened with honey, maple syrup, or fructose. Sometimes harmless vegetable coloring is added.

Exemplary Brands_____

Alta Dena Plain Kefir
East Coast Maple, Pina Colada Kefir
Mathis Strawberry, Peach, Red Raspberry
   Kefirs

Nancy's Strawberry, Raspberry, Blueberry
   Kefirs

Chapter 16

Cheese:
Why the Mouse Roared

The declining interest in red meat and whole milk consumption that has been attributed to health concerns about saturated fat, cholesterol, and sodium does not seem to have extended to cheese even though it contains all three in significant amounts. While all varieties of cheese have enjoyed a steady growth in popularity, we are pleased to report that interest in natural cheeses has outpaced the fabricated process and imitation products.

Many supermarkets have several cheese sections. The usual selection of domestic cheese is still housed in the dairy case, but now there may be a second gourmet display with prewrapped imported items of random weight. In addition, cheese may also be sold in the deli department. The types of cheese in these three areas may not be all that dissimilar, but they are merchandised and packaged differently to appeal to separate audiences.

Natural food stores, too, have increased their line of cheese. Many of their offerings are imported or have special characteristics that reflect prominent health concerns: e.g., low sodium, reduced-cholesterol, no coloring, no rennet, alternative milk origins (raw milk, goat's milk). Soy cheese has become another option. Ironically, double and triple "crème" high-fat imported cheeses have also been quite popular in this market.

The expanding array of natural cheeses has made it much easier for the shopper to avoid what are known as "process" cheeses. These are industrial creations which use technology to fashion cheeselike substances out of milk, dairy by-products, water, salt, and lots of chemical additives.

THE NUTRITIVE VALUE OF CHEESE

Cheese is a concentrated source of most of the nutrients found in milk and is similarly valuable for increasing the quality of vegetable proteins (see "Variety on the Table," page 152). Although the protein in cheese is still considerable, about 20 percent of the original milk protein is lost to the whey, the liquid that is drained off in the cheese-making process. On the other hand, the whey contains much of the original milk sugar (lactose), so that people with a lactose intolerance often find cheese, especially the drier, harder varieties, more digestible than other dairy products.

197

Ripening of the cheese also brings about a change in the protein structure. Many extensively ripened cheeses have been found to have a high level of compounds known as amines, especially near the surface. These amines may trigger headaches in sensitive individuals. This is why soft unripened cheeses like cottage cheese can often be tolerated by migraine sufferers when ripened cheeses, such as Swiss, cannot.

Other milk nutrients that are available in cheese include calcium (except for cottage cheese, cream cheese, Brie, and Camembert, which have a relatively low calcium content), phosphorus, vitamin A, and much of the riboflavin and thiamin. In the ripening stage, the level of certain B vitamins has even been shown to increase. As a result, the rind of certain cheeses like Brie, Camembert, Limburger, and Gruyère may be quite nutritious.

Fat Fundamentals

The fat content in most cheeses is proportionately high, accounting for as much as 70 to 90 percent of the calories. About half of this fat is saturated.

The actual amount of fat averages about 6.5 to 9 grams per ounce (28 grams) of cheese. Surprisingly, some varieties that are thought of as rich because of their creamy texture and flavor are in the lower realms, while others that seem rather dry and crumbly and give the impression of being lower in fat are actually in the upper echelons. This is due largely to the moisture content of the cheese and is a phenomenon that often makes it difficult for consumers to estimate the fat content of many cheeses they encounter, even when they find some clues on the label.

On some cheeses the percent of fat by weight is listed. (Note that this is not the same as percent of calories contributed by fat.) The figure may be shown as "28 g fett in 100 g ost," which appears, for example, on a wheel of Jarlsberg and translates to 28 grams fat in 100 grams of cheese. This is relatively clear and indicates that 28 percent of the content is fat. Or, the label may read "50 percent matière grasse," as on some Brie, which in English means 50 percent fat. From this you might assume that the Brie has almost twice the fat content of the Jarlsberg. However, this is not the case. The confusion is caused by the fact that fat content is sometimes based on dry matter (designated as IDM or "In Dry Matter" by the cheese industry), not the total weight of the cheese. Unfortunately, this detail is not revealed on the label. In the case of the Brie, the designation "50 percent matière grasse" really means 50 percent of the dry weight is composed of fat. With a moisture content between 45 and 50 percent, overall fat is only 25 to 27 percent, or slightly less than the Jarlsberg.

The fact that a cheese is made from part skim milk is no guarantee that it is lower in fat. A high proportion of dry weight to moisture might still add up to a concentrated fat content in the finished product. In addition, while some of the fat may have been removed before the milk is processed into cheese, cream may have been added as a separate ingredient.

To add to the confusion, cheeses that are marketed as "low cholesterol" are often mistakenly believed to be low in fat. An ounce of cheese generally furnishes 20 to 30 milligrams of cholesterol. When a manufacturer wishes to alter this, a cholesterol-free vegetable oil may be substituted for the natural butterfat. However, this cheese will still probably derive more than 70 percent of its calories from fat.

Because one can hardly be expected to decipher this information at the store, the end of this chapter features a table of Cheese Nutrients for some of the more popular varieties on the market. Here we list calories, protein, fat, cholesterol, and sodium, currently the areas of greatest concern to most people. As you will see, they can vary considerably.

The Salt Content

If you are anxious about sodium, bear in mind that cheese is traditionally made with salt and can contain anywhere from 100 to 300 milligrams per ounce (a typical pre-cut slice of packaged cheese). In some varieties, particularly process cheeses, the amounts are higher. People who want to avoid sodium can select low-sodium cheeses which range from less than 10 milligrams to 55 milligrams of sodium per ounce. Not all reduced-sodium cheeses are this low, however; there is at least one pasteurized process cheese that calls itself low-sodium yet contains 200 milligrams of sodium per ounce. (Note that standard Gruyères and many brands of mozzarella contain just half this amount.)

Because salt-free cheeses can be unappealingly bland, some manufacturers add potassium chloride. Since the safety of increased potassium and chloride intake is no more assured than high sodium consumption, this does not seem to be a wise practice.

You should also note that low-sodium cheeses are more perishable than salted versions.

Calorie Content

As a rough guide, 1 ounce of cheese furnishes about 100 calories. Because of their higher water content, process cheeses tend to have somewhat fewer calories than the natural cheeses they are fashioned after. If you are trying to cut calories, your best bets are cottage, pot, farmer, and ricotta cheeses, all of which are relatively low in fat and high in moisture content, and contain from 25 to 50 calories per ounce.

NATURAL CHEESE MAKING

As we have indicated, cheese falls into two separate and distinct categories—"natural" and "process." Natural cheeses are the product of a highly developed method that is centuries-old. Process cheeses are created by technology developed only a few decades ago, designed to make natural cheese go farther through artificial means.

Natural cheese is made by separating the milk solids (the curd) from the liquid portion (the whey), a process which is facilitated by the action of rennet (an enzyme that coagulates milk) and bacteria. The characteristic flavor and body are produced by varying the milk source (cow, goat, sheep), by the addition of salt and other seasonings, by the use of specific bacteria and molds, by manipulating the mixture, and by changing the time, temperature, and ripening climate. The result is hundreds of different tastes, textures, and varieties of cheese.

Most of the rennet used commercially is a natural enzyme obtained from the stomachs of calves that have been butchered for veal. Plant enzymes can also be used to make rennetless cheeses, but they are less efficient. The added bacteria are the same microbes that bring about normal souring of milk.

CHOOSING NATURAL CHEESES

With rare exceptions, natural cheeses are the cheeses to buy. The composition of many of these cheeses is regulated by a government Standard of Identity. Since certain untraditional steps are permitted, including the addition of acidifying and neutralizing agents, bleaching of the milk or coloring with vegetable matter or synthetic agents, and the use of mold inhibitors (preservatives), all natural cheeses are not exactly what we would consider "natural."

In the next few pages we will take a look at some of the standardized varieties, as well as some other popular cheeses that enjoy widespread distribution but are not specifically regulated by a Standard of Identity in order to help you make an informed choice. In many instances, imported cheeses are less likely to contain some of the undesirable additives, for in Europe cheese is a treasured food and the controls over its processing are more in line with traditional methods.

Common Ingredients and Labeling

The labeling of cheese ingredients is somewhat vague. Bacteria used to initiate the cheese-making process may be referred to as "cheese cultures." The enzymes used to separate the curds and whey, whether animal, plant, or microbial (yeast) in origin, may be identified either as "rennet" or "rennin," or more often with the general term "enzymes." Preservatives like sodium benzoate may be hidden in some of these enzyme preparations and there is no way of telling since the manufacturer is not required to reveal this on the cheese label.

For most varieties, calcium chloride, which is harmless, can be added to the milk to assist coagulation. It does not have to appear on the label.

Another hidden practice employed in the production of some cheeses is the use of hydrogen peroxide to sterilize the milk. This method can reduce the quality of the protein. Moreover, since rennet does not work in the presence of hydrogen peroxide, if it has not dissipated by the time cheese production begins, the hydrogen peroxide may have to be neutralized by the addition of yet another enzyme. None of this is ever indicated on the label.

Cheese is one of only three foods (the others are butter and ice cream) that, due to the powerful dairy lobby, may be colored without any indication on the label. (The law does require, however, that FD & C yellow #5, which a significant number of people react adversely to, be specifically labeled in all foods.) Sometimes this information is presented voluntarily, and often harmless vegetable extracts are the source. To add to the confusion, the Standard of Identity for a few cheeses prohibits the use of coloring agents entirely.

Bleaching of the milk with benzoyl peroxide may be used to color the cheese. It is now required that this be stated on the label. The vitamin A value of bleached milk has to be restored with supplements and this will not be listed on the label.

Preservatives, mold inhibitors, and antimycotics, all chemicals that inhibit the growth of yeast and molds, may be used to coat the surface of some bulk forms of cheese, or they may be incorporated into the plastic cheese coating. Sorbate preservatives are permitted in consumer-size packages as well. The direct addition of these additives to the cheese must appear on the label, but when they are used in the packaging material, they may not always be revealed since below a certain level they are not deemed to be "functional" additives.

Raw Milk Cheese

Since the 1940s, the use of pasteurized milk for cheese-making has been the general rule in this country. (For the most part, the milk is not homogenized, except in the production of certain soft cheeses.) The main effect of pasteurization, other than to destroy potentially harmful bacteria, is on flavor; cheese made with pasteurized milk tends to be less full bodied and blander.

When raw milk is used, U.S. law requires the cheese to be aged for at least sixty days to render harmless any bacteria that may be present. This ruling dates back to a time when cattle diseases transferable to humans were prevalent and unsanitary manufacturing conditions were common. Today, such diseases are rare and most cheese factories are thoroughly sanitized, but the FDA believes that the rule should still be enforced for the protection of public health. Europeans do not have the same fears and consequently many more cheeses produced abroad are made from unpasteurized milk. To be imported into this country legally, however, they must meet the same criteria as domestic varieties.

Since certain fresh cheeses cannot be held for the requisite period of time and still retain the same eating quality, the flavor of feta, mozzarella, Brie, Camembert, and similar cheeses on foreign shores often seems to be superior. In recent years, some of these cheeses have been sneaking across our borders. In addition, some states permit unaged raw cheeses to be made and sold within their jurisdiction.

Raw milk cheeses may be found in any store that sells cheese, and often is not even proclaimed on the label. Most imported Swiss, for example, is made with unpasteurized milk. While companies that choose to market raw milk cheeses and promote them as such usually cater to consumers who look for purity of ingredients, the use of raw milk does not guarantee the absence of coloring, preservatives or other chemical additives.

Unripened Natural Cheese

An unripened cheese is one that is not aged. It is made to be eaten soon after manufacture.

SOFT UNRIPENED CHEESE

Soft unripened cheeses have a high moisture content and are highly perishable.

Cottage Cheese: There are three varieties of cottage cheese: dry curd, low fat, and regular. The basic curd is made from skim milk. Salt is added at the manufacturer's discretion. The label of brands that employ acid coagulants rather than the more conventional enzymes will say "directly set" or "curd set by acidification."

A creaming agent or dressing provides the milk fat required to meet the federal Standard of Identity. It may be cream, milk, or "substances derived from milk" and "any safe and suitable ingredients." This leaves the manufacturer with a wide-open field. The more contrived formulas conveniently mask the dressing, which can make up as much as 45 percent of the product, by giving it the appearance of curds using thickeners like carrageenan, locust bean, xanthan and guar gums, mono- and diglycerides, and polysorbate 80. A sweetener may also be added; dextrose seems to be the most popular choice.

The simplest of cottage cheeses is called *dry curd cottage cheese.* It contains less than 0.5 percent milk fat and no dressing. *Low-fat cottage cheese* and plain *cottage cheese* are prepared by mixing dry curd cottage cheese with dressing to raise the fat level. To qualify as low-fat the milk-fat content must be between 0.5 and 2 percent by weight and the label must reveal exactly where it lies within this range. The product simply called *cottage cheese* has at least 4 percent by weight milk fat, as also specified on the label. Waistline watchers should note that cottage cheeses promoted specifically for dieters are equal in calories to all other 1 percent fat brands and are more likely to contain additives.

Although all the ingredients in cottage cheese are shown on the package, the law does not require the listing to be very specific. For example, the milk used may be shown as "skim" with no indication as to whether it was fresh or reconstituted; the adjective "cultured" before "milk" may indicate the use of lactic acid-producing bacteria, and "enzymes" can mean rennet or any other milk-clotting enzymes. "Kosher enzymes" indicates a nonanimal source. The use of calcium chloride to aid coagulation is not required on the label.

When the words "all natural" appear on the container, the product must be viewed with skepticism since many companies consider the vegetable gums used in the creaming agent natural, despite the fact that they are a highly processed ingredient and not natural to cheese. Also, when "natural flavor" is included in the ingredient list, it is probably a laboratory creation as described in "Imitation Cheese," page 211. Since a well-made, additive-free cottage cheese should have a crisp, clean taste with no outside help at all, the addition of anything to accentuate the taste may be a coverup for poor quality. It is especially absurd to see natural flavor touted in a brand that is chock full of thickening agents.

Sorbate preservatives are another item to watch for on the label. Cottage cheese has a fairly long shelf-life without the use of preservatives.

There are no rules regarding the amount of salt that can be used. The values in the table of Cheese Nutrients, on page 217, are only averages and do not reflect all brands. Without sodium labeling it is really impossible for the consumer to make an informed choice since products range from no salt added in a few select products to 200 to 500 milligrams of sodium per half cup in most popular brands. However, since salt is a preservative, you should be aware that salt-free cottage cheese may not keep quite as long as the salted variety.

Cream Cheese: Cow's cream and possibly fresh, dry or concentrated milk (some liquid removed) plus water are the basis of this soft spreadable cheese, which, according to federal standards, contains no less than a hefty 33 percent milk fat. Neufchâtel cheese is practically identical but has a slightly lower fat content. Unlike most other cheeses, cream cheese and Neufchâtel do not contribute much in the way of protein or calcium.

In addition to bacteria and milk-clotting enzymes, cream cheese may include gelatin, alginates, or more commonly, vegetable gums added to thicken it and impart a rubbery texture. Their presence is indicated on the label and, once again, although they may be derived from natural sources rather than chemical substances, they are not natural to dairy products, nor are they unrefined or wholefoods. If you can, avoid them.

Fortunately, cream cheese made without gum is available; it may be more crumbly, but it is just as tasty. You can improve the texture and food value by mashing or whipping it with yogurt.

Farmer Cheese: Farmer cheese is much like dry curd cottage cheese that has been pressed into block form. Unfortunately potassium sorbate preservative may be added; look for it on the label so you can avoid these brands.

Pot Cheese: This is similar to dry curd cottage cheese: it is made without salt and is free of undesirable additives.

Ricotta Cheese: Ricotta resembles cotttage cheese, but has a finer, lighter texture and a pleasing cooked-milk flavor. It is excellent for baking and it is the traditional filling for stuffed pasta.

Ricotta means "recooked" and refers to the fact that it is traditionally made from the coagulable material in the whey that is left over after other cheeses are manufactured. Since the whey retains much of the milk sugar, ricotta has a slightly sweet flavor. Those sensitive to lactose may find it a difficult cheese to digest.

In the United States, whole or skim milk is almost always used to make ricotta in addition to and often in greater amounts than the whey; it is labeled *whole* or *part skim milk ricotta,* depending on which is used. The coagulant may be referred to only as a "starter" on the label; vinegar is the most common choice. Some manufacturers ensure cohesiveness by adding gelatin. Although gelatin may be an innocuous addition, it imparts a rubberiness not characteristic of high-quality ricotta. For this reason, we do not include ricottas containing gelatin in our Exemplary Brands; however, in some places consumers have few other options. Most brands of ricotta are salted, but a salt-free product is in limited distribution.

FIRM UNRIPENED CHEESE

Firm unripened cheeses contain less moisture than the soft, making them less perishable.

Feta: Feta is Greek in origin and, when made there, it is generally of unpasteurized sheep's milk or, less commonly, goat's milk. The feta manufactured in this country is more likely to be made from pasteurized cow's milk. After the cheese is formed it is packed in barrels in a saltwater brine and left to pickle. No preservatives are needed, as any microbial action is arrested by the brining solution.

If you find feta too salty for your taste, you can rinse it in cold water. While it lasts longer if stored in the refrigerator in a saltwater bath, if you keep it in plain unsalted water it will lose some of its saltiness.

Mozzarella: Mozzarella is the cheese popularized by pizza. It is made from pasteurized milk, either whole or skim.

The moisture content of this cheese is between 52 and 60 percent. In *whole milk mozzarella* the fat makes up not less than 45 percent of the remaining solid mass. For the *part skim* varieties, the milk fat content is between 30 and 45 percent of the solid portion. *Low-moisture* mozzarella, often described as "string cheese," may be made from homogenized milk. Its moisture content is between 45 and 52 percent and while the percent of fat parallels its full moisture counterpart, the actual amount is slightly higher due to the reduced moisture level.

Coloring may be added to mask or neutralize any yellowing of the curd, and preservatives may be added as well. Only the preservatives have to be shown on the label.

Ricotta Salata: This dry ricotta is a delicate, slightly crumbly slicing cheese that is made by draining and pressing the curds of soft ricotta to reduce the moisture content. It is quite salty but has a relatively low fat content.

Ripened Natural Cheese

A ripened cheese is one that is aged under conditions favorable to the growth of certain molds or bacteria which are responsible for the characteristic taste and texture. The longer a cheese ages, the more pungent it becomes; if you eat part of a ripened cheese soon after it is purchased and have another piece sometime in the future, the flavor may be quite different. Cold storage slows the ripening process.

SOFT RIPENED CHEESE

Included in this group are Brie, Camembert, and Limburger. These cheeses are prized for their rich, buttery texture and are best eaten at room temperature. All are free of coloring and preservatives.

Brie: Brie is no longer an exclusively French product and, as with so many foods, its popularity has been its downfall. At room temperature a well-made Brie softens as it ripens and becomes a delicate ivory color throughout. In judging a whole cheese, look for a soft, cushiony white or pinkish rind. If wrapped, the rind should not stick to the paper, nor should it be sunken. The thin edible rind should barely contain the cheese, and a high-quality Brie will start to "run" when cut. Its flavor may vary from mild to strong but should have a subtle earthiness about it with a hint of mushroom. Any cheese showing uncharacteristic surface mold or smelling like ammonia should be avoided.

If Brie is not fully ripe, it can be held a few days at cool room temperature. If cut too soon its interior will be marred by a hard chalky line. Once it has been cut it will not ripen further; however, its flavor will continue to develop. Once ripe, the cheese can be refrigerated, but this will cause slight toughening.

The best Brie is made from unpasteurized milk or *lait cru.* Many of the factory-made Bries are bland and characterless. French imports labeled Brie de Meaux Fermier and Brie de Melon are farm-made and considered the best.

Camembert: Like Brie, Camembert is ripened by the action of molds, bacteria, and probably yeasts as well on its surface, creating the edible white rind that encases it. The buying and handling guidelines are the same as for

Brie. Slight differences in the curing process determine individual flavor characteristics.

Limburger: Limburger and Limburger-type cheeses, like Liederkranz, Schloss, and Old Heidelberg, have a zesty flavor and an even more pronounced smell. They are usually well wrapped to prevent their odor from escaping, but if possible try to detect and avoid any that have an ammonia overtone, which is an indication that they are past their prime.

Store Limburger and its relatives in the refrigerator, well covered to keep the smell from penetrating other foods.

SEMISOFT AND HARD RIPENED CHEESE

Semisoft ripened cheeses, such as Muenster, Monterey Jack, and brick, contain from 25 to 30 percent fat unless otherwise specified in their Standard of Identity. They start out quite mellow, but some develop a fuller flavor with age.

In general, hard ripened cheeses, such as cheddar, colby, and Swiss, contain a minimum of 30 percent fat unless individual standards specify otherwise.

Most semisoft and hard ripened cheeses can have coloring added, and whether it is revealed on the label or not varies with the standards that govern them. Where no specific standards apply, general regulations prevail and color need not be disclosed. Sorbic acid, potassium sorbate, and sodium sorbate preservatives may be added to consumer size packages of slices and chunk cuts of these cheeses; this will always be indicated on the label. Even without preservatives, these cheeses keep well when properly handled.

Brick: Brick cheese is a semisoft cheese related to Limburger. It is usually quite mellow, but it may have a deceivingly pungent odor. Coloring may be added without mention on the label.

Cheddar: Cheddar is classified as a hard cheese and is available either white or orange, in varieties of mild, medium, sharp, and extra-sharp. The milk used to make cheddar may be sterilized with hydrogen peroxide prior to culturing, but this is not mentioned on the label. It is possible to find "farmhouse" cheese or other high-quality varieties made from unpasteurized milk, which are far superior to the characterless mass-produced cheddar found in conventional dairy cases.

When color is added it may not necessarily be stated, but it is fairly easy to spot by the exaggerated yellow-orange color in some offerings.

Colby: Colby is similar to cheddar but is milder in flavor, less salty, and usually has a slightly higher moisture content and thus a softer body. It may have coloring added without any indication on the label. Smoke flavoring may also be added, but this must be revealed.

Washed Curd Cheese: Washed curd cheese is similar to cheddar and ranges from semisoft to almost firm. It gets its name from the practice of washing the curds with water before they are salted. This increases the moisture, makes the texture somewhat open and softer, and decreases the lactose content. Like cheddar, washed curd cheese may be made from milk treated with hydrogen peroxide, and it may have color as a hidden additive.

Edam: Edam may have as little as 22 percent fat, making it somewhat lower in fat than other cheeses in this group. Imported varieties are likely to be free of artificial color; domestic ones may not be. The label is of little help here. The surface of the cheese is usually protected by red paraffin, which is also considered an identifying symbol.

Fontina: Fontina has a delicate, nutty flavor and varies from semisoft to hard depending on the length of curing. In Italy it is made from sheep's milk, but American and Danish versions use cow's milk. There is no specific Standard of Identity for fontina; thus, it conforms to the general requirements for this category and may have color added without being listed on the label.

Gouda: Gouda is almost identical to Edam in terms of mellow flavor, handling, and labeling requirements. The only difference between the two is that the milk fat level of Gouda is higher. Like Edam it too may be covered by a protective layer of paraffin.

Gruyère: Swiss-type cheeses like Gruyère are characterized by the addition of bacteria which create pockets of air that expand and form holes in the curds as the cheese solidifies. These holes are usually small in Gruyère and the cheese has a creamier texture and slightly piquant flavor that tends to be saltier than ordinary Swiss. No coloring or bleached milk can be used. The milk is usually unpasteurized and the cheese must be aged at least ninety days. In judging quality, select a cheese that has a little moisture in the holes and watch out for cracks just beneath the rind, splits in the flesh, and an overall greasy appearance on the surface.

Havarti: This Danish-made cheese comes in a moderate (24 percent) fat and a high (35 percent) fat form. It is a creamy, mild, slicing cheese perforated with numerous small holes. Although havarti is seldom colored, if coloring is added it will be indicated on the label.

Kashkaval and Kasseri: Both Kashkaval and Kasseri are firm cheeses, similar in texture to cheddar, produced in Greece from sheep's milk. They make fine cooking cheeses and are often fried for a Greek specialty called saganaki. The major limitation is their saltiness, especially Kashkaval. These cheeses follow the general rules for firm ripened cheese, but are not likely to be colored.

Monterey or Monterey Jack: Monterey Jack is a mild white cheese similar in taste to Muenster, but slightly drier. It has become quite popular for Mexican style cooking. The Standard of Identity requires the milk to be pasteurized. Coloring is not allowed.

Hot Pepper Cheese is frequently made by adding bits of pickled jalapeno and red pepper and their juices to Monterey Jack. The peppers are likely to be pickled in a brine of vinegar, oil, spices, and salt.

Muenster: American Muenster has a flavor that is consistently mellow in contrast to European Muenster, which can be quite "complex" in taste. Muenster may be colored without any indication on the label. The coloring is frequently on the surface, and generally carotene, a natural vegetable extract, is responsible for its orange hue.

Port du Salut: First made by monks in the mid 1800s, this cheese is also known as *monk's cheese, Trappist cheese,* in Canada as oka, and in the United States as either *Port-Salut* or *Saint Paulin.* It is a mild cheese with a flavor reminiscent of a mellow, buttery Gouda. Despite its delicate flavor, it has a faint but pungent odor similar to Limburger, so that it may appear to be stronger than it actually is. Having no specific Standard of Identity, it conforms to the general guidelines for semisoft and hard ripened cheese.

Provolone: Provolone cheese has a smooth but stringy texture, a light color, and a mellow but well-salted taste. It comes in several shapes, but usually the slices are round.

The milk used to make provolone may be bleached. If it is not bleached, blue or green coloring may be added to neutralize any natural yellowing in the curd. While the bleaching should be indicated on the label, added coloring need not be.

Provolone may be smoked or may have a liquid wood smoke condensate added for flavor. If the later tactic is employed, "added smoke flavor" must appear on the label immediately after the name. If it is not smoked the words "not smoked" must be included with the name. If there is no reference at all to smoke, the cheese is considered to have been traditionally smoked over wood. (See page 211 for more on problems associated with smoked cheese.)

Swiss (or Emmenthaler): The cheese we commonly call Swiss in this country is known as Emmenthaler in Europe. The milk used to prepare this cheese may be raw or pasteurized, with no indication of which on the label. It may also be bleached to give it a pale yellow color, but the label must tell you if the milk has been so treated. If it is not bleached, color may have been added, and on domestic Swiss cheese there is no sure way of telling since this needn't be revealed. However, Swiss law prohibits the use of coloring agents, so you can be sure that imported Swiss or Emmenthaler has not been artificially colored.

HARD DRY, OR GRATING CHEESE

Hard dry cheeses tend to be sharp flavored (they are aged at least six months) and are used mostly for grating. Because of their low moisture content, these cheeses keep for many weeks without much change in flavor and without the risk of mold growth. Despite this, the Standard of Identity permits the addition of sorbate preservatives. This is more common in domestic than imported brands and, as with all cheeses, it is revealed on the label. Artificial color may also be added, but does not have to be included on the label.

Parmesan (or Reggiano): Parmesan cheese is often made from unpasteurized milk, which may be bleached. If so, "bleached with benzoyl peroxide" will be stated on the label. When the milk is bleached, no coloring may be added; otherwise color may be added without your knowing it.

Romano: The fat content of Romano is slightly lower than that of other grating cheeses and the milk may be cow's (Vaccino), sheep's (Pecorino), goat's (Caprino), or a combination of these. This will be indicated on the label. Once again, the milk may be bleached (stated on the label), or blue or green coloring matter may be added (not stated). Watch for the use of preservatives (listed on the label).

Sap Sago: This dry grating cheese is made entirely from skim milk and is virtually fat-free. It has a pale green color, assisted by the addition of dried clover, and is formed in the shape of a truncated cone. Sap sago has a sharp, pungent, and very salty flavor. No preservatives are employed.

Pregrated Cheese: Pregrated cheeses made from one or a combination of cheeses are likely to contain a mold inhibitor, an anticaking agent, and flavoring, either natural or artificial. All this must appear on the label.

Although we have provided the names of a few additive-free pregrated cheeses in our Exemplary Brands, freshly grated cheese is much livelier in taste, has a better texture, and does not contain unwanted ingredients. Moreover, you will not have to deal with the complexities of determining how much of which cheeses are present in the container, as follows:

If only one cheese is used, the name will be "grated (variety) cheese." If more than one cheese is used, and each is at a level of at least 25 percent of the final weight, the name will be "grated (variety) and (variety) cheese," listed in order of predominance by weight. If any of the cheeses included make up only 10 percent of the total, the term "with other grated cheeses" will be tacked on to the name. If none of these situations applies, the name will be simply "grated cheese" and a breakdown of the contents will be given in the ingredient list. The term "American cheese" used here denotes cheddar, colby, or washed curd, not the pasteurized process variety called American.

MOLD-RIPENED CHEESE

Mold-ripened cheeses are characterized by a tangy flavor and blue veins that run through them produced by the mold that grows in the interior during the curing period. All are semisoft and may be pasty or crumbly in consistency. Choose those with a whitish rather than a gray or tan background and avoid pieces that are dark or dry toward the outer edges.

Blue (Bleu): The spelling "bleu" is an indication of the French imported version; "blue" is domestic. Despite its rich taste, blue cheese is no more fatty than other cheeses. Blue or green coloring may be added to neutralize any yellowing (not labeled) or the milk may be bleached (labeled). The cheese may have preservatives (labeled).

Gorgonzola: Gorgonzola, an Italian form of blue cheese, may be made from goat's or cow's milk, or a mixture of the two. Regulations governing coloring, bleaching, and preserving are the same as for blue. Gorgonzola is unique among the blue-veined cheeses in that it melts nicely and can be used very successfully in cooking.

Roquefort: This form of blue-veined cheese is made from sheep's milk and is free of all unwanted additives, making it the preferred choice among the standardized mold-ripened varieties. It tends to be salty and crumbly.

Stilton: This is the English form of blue-veined cheese. It has a firm, buttery texture, a higher fat content, and is milder than either Gorgonzola or Roquefort. There is no U.S. Standard of Identity for this cheese.

Chèvre

Chèvre is French for "goat," and when applied to cheese this term connotes all cheeses made with goat's milk. Once you become familiar with it, the flavor can never be mistaken for anything else.

Although a few years ago goat cheese was hardly known in this country, its incorporation into nouvelle and California-style cuisines has turned it into an American infatuation. In France it is eaten mainly as a dessert cheese. Here we use goat cheese in all manner of cooked dishes, from pasta to goat cheese soufflé.

The best chèvre is made locally and is barely a few days old. In a few areas of this country, small-scale goat cheese making has started to flourish. Most of the goat cheese imports are factory made.

Young rindless goat cheeses are moist and creamy, and spread easily. As they age and moisture evaporates, the texture becomes firmer, then crumbly, and finally hard and dry. As the moisture decreases, the flavor intensifies, the saltiness becomes quite pronounced, and finally only a few hardy devotees find the cheese palatable.

Montrachet is the most widely available French goat cheese in America. Formed into a log, it may be snowy white or coated with black ash. When still fresh it is quite mild, offering an excellent introduction to the goat cheese family. Other rindless cheeses in this category include the log-shaped *St. Christophe,* the pyramid-shaped *Valençay* and *Pouligny,* and the tapered cylinders of *Chabi* and *Chabichou.*

Some forms of goat cheese are inoculated with bacteria in order to form a soft natural rind. These cheeses ripen more like Camembert, taking on a smooth buttery consistency at their peak, becoming rank and ammoniated past this stage. Typical examples include *Bucheron, Lezay Buch, Carre d'Alzou, Capricorne,* and *Tomme de Chèvre. Crottin de Chavignol* represents a form of chèvre generally marketed in a fairly advanced stage, although the samples imported here are often still too young to satisfy the cheese afficionado's expectations.

Smoked Cheeses

Direct smoking and the application of condensed smoke from hardwood sawdust may be used to impart flavor to cheese. The possible production of compounds in the smoking process that have been inconclusively implicated in connection with cancer complicates the picture here. Because there is a lack of reliable data to exonerate smoked cheeses, we suggest minimizing your selection of them. With the exception of some provolone, the label will indicate when a cheese has been "smoked."

IMITATION AND SUBSTITUTE CHEESES

If, for any reason, a cheese does not conform to the Standard of Identity, it cannot use any of the names described up to this point. If the product is nutritionally comparable to a regulated cheese it may be identified as a "cheese substitute," or by a fanciful name. For example, if vegetable oil is used to replace the natural milk fat in mozzarella, the product may be called "Pizza Mate." Similarly, if skim milk is used to reduce the fat content of cheddar, the resulting cheese may be called "Taco-Mate" or perhaps "ched-style." Only if it is nutritionally inferior, based on a limited number of designated nutrients, must the word *imitation* appear.

One common misconception about imitation and substitute cheeses is that they do not contain dairy ingredients. We wish to stress that they all include some form of cheese, as well as other milk derivatives (like casein) and therefore cannot be used by anyone who must avoid milk products.

Imitation and substitute cheeses do not have to contain objectionable ingredients, but many seem to, perhaps to cover an inferior flavor and texture.

Cheese flavors, both natural and artificial, are frequently added to imitation and substitute cheeses. "Natural flavors" are created by adding enzymes to cheese pastes. The fact that they are "natural" may not be a vast improvement over the artificial flavors prepared in a test tube, since these flavors may have added color and are frequently extended with dried corn syrup, malto dextrin, sodium caseinate, MSG, disodium guanylate and inosinate, hydrolyzed plant protein, powdered cellulose, and hydrogenated soy or cottonseed oil. The resulting natural cheese flavor is capable of intensifying the taste of young cheese ten to twenty times that of ripened cheese. What this means is that flavor can be maintained by using less cheese or by decreasing the ripening phase, a time- and money-saving step for the process food industry. "Natural cheese flavor" is also used in the production of processed cheeses, cheese-flavored crackers and snacks, cheese sauces, dressings, dips, seasoning blends, premade omelets, and casseroles.

Soy Cheese

Cheese based on soy milk has recently added a new category of cheese products to the market. In terms of calories, protein, and overall fat content soy cheese competes quite favorably with animal cheeses (see Soya Kaas in the table of Cheese Nutrients, page 217). It is both lactose- and cholesterol-free and the sodium content is about average for cheese. Note, however, that soy cheese is held together with vegetable gums and will contain either the milk derivative calcium caseinate (in which case it is not dairy free) or isolated soy protein.

PROCESS CHEESE

Those cheeses that are not made directly from milk, but are processed from cheese and cheese products are known as "process" and "cold pack" cheeses and must be so labeled. Their supposed advantage over natural cheese is that they melt and spread easily, making them more "convenient." During processing, they are heated to halt ripening and to keep the flavor and texture constant. An assortment of emulsifiers and stabilizers may be added to guarantee consistency. In taste, however, these cheeses never approach the richness of natural cheese and their texture is dull. A large part of the price goes toward the purchase of chemicals and water. The addition of salt, on top of that present in the original cheeses that serve as their foundation, makes most of these processed products extremely high in sodium.

In 1985, when promoting their process American cheese, America's biggest cheese maker explained that they put "5 full ounces of milk into every slice," in contrast to some manufacturers who put in only 2 ounces. What their TV ads neglected to say, but what a close examination of their print ad revealed, was that the cheese they used as a comparison was actually imitation cheese slices. Had they compared their product to natural cheddar, it would have been a different story: a comparable portion of natural cheddar contains 8 to 10 ounces of milk!

One might expect that the substitution of chemicals and water for milk would result in lower prices. To our surprise, when we looked in our local supermarket we found pasteurized process cheese products and several brands of natural cheddar were within the same price range.

Thanks to changes in the law, you no longer have to read the fine print to determine the type of cheese that is being offered. In the recent past, it was the practice of some manufacturers to subordinate the words "pasteurized," "blended," "process," "food," and "spread," (all terms that reveal a processed variety) and give undue prominence to the word "cheese." Now all the words forming the name must be given equal status. Revisions in the law also make it easier to find out what's in these products.

One thing you do not learn from reading the list of ingredients, however, is the quality of the raw materials used to make process and cold-pack cheeses. "Green," or low-cost young cheese is often incorporated into these products and the excess salt used helps to overcome the lack of a developed taste.

Pasteurized Process Cheese

The cheese described on the label as "pasteurized process" is made by grinding and blending one or more natural cheeses (excluding cream cheese, Neufchâtel, cottage cheese, and a few other select varieties). The cheeses are heated and mixed with water, an emulsifier (which may be any combination of thirteen different chemicals), optional milk fat, acids, artificial coloring, and flavoring ingredients, including salt, in an effort to create a smooth, and in the words of the federal government, "homogenous, *plastic* mass" (emphasis ours).

As with natural cheeses, the use of coloring agents need not be mentioned

---

ADDITIVES COMMONLY USED IN PROCESS CHEESE

The following is a list of common additives; notice how many of these contain sodium and how many contain phosphorus (indicated by the word phosphate), which in excess can interfere with calcium absorption.

Monosodium phosphate
Disodium phosphate
Dipotassium phosphate
Trisodium phosphate
Sodium metaphosphate (sodium hexametaphosphate)
Sodium acid pyrophosphate
Tetra sodium pyrophosphate
Sodium aluminum phosphate
Sodium citrate
Potassium citrate
Calcium citrate
Sodium tartrate
Sodium potassium tartrate

on the label. All other ingredients will be spelled out, including the permissible preservatives sorbic acid, potassium sorbate, sodium sorbate, sodium propionate, and calcium propionate (more sodium-based additives).

Some of the more popular forms of pasteurized process cheese are American cheese, pasteurized process Swiss, and sweet munchee.

Pasteurized Blended Cheese

The product labeled "pasteurized blended cheese" is similar to pasteurized process cheese except that Neufchâtel or cream cheese may be added and emulsifiers or acidifying agents may not be. This makes it more acceptable, but it is unfortunately less available. With the exception of coloring, all ingredients must be on the label.

Pasteurized Process Cheese Food

This product is similar to pasteurized process cheese except that it contains less cheese and has an additional dairy ingredient (milk, cream, whey, milk fat, albumin, or a dry form of these) instead. Emulsifying salts are not mandatory, but generally they are included. The final product may have a lower fat content than pasteurized process cheese.

The only advantage of process cheese food over process cheese is that all the ingredients, including any added color, must appear on the label.

Pasteurized Process Cheese Spread

A pasteurized process cheese spread is produced in the same manner as a pasteurized process cheese food but has an even higher moisture content and therefore contains even less cheese.

Pasteurized process cheese spread is often packaged in jars or loaves and may be flecked with pimientos, fruits, vegetables, or meat.

When Velveeta is advertised as "made from natural cheeses," the manufacturer is choosing to ignore the fact that the label of this pasteurized process cheese spread also shows it contains water, whey, whey protein concentrate, skim milk, sodium citrate, milk fat, salt, sodium phosphate, sorbic acid, annatto, and oleoresin paprika.

Instead of emulsifiers, a category of additives known as stabilizers are permissible in process cheese spreads in order to prevent separation. The possibilities include carob bean gum, gum karaya, gum tragacanth, guar gum, gelatin, sodium carboxymethylcellulose (cellulose gum), carrageenan, oat gum, algin (sodium alginate), propylene glycol alginate, and xanthan gum. Moreover, a sweetener in the form of sugar, dextrose, corn syrup, glucose, malt derivatives, or hydrolyzed lactose may be included. All ingredients are listed on the label.

Cold Pack or Club Cheese

The difference between this category and the pasteurized process cheeses described above is the absence of heat in the processing. Products labeled *cold pack* or *club cheese* will not contain any emulsifiers but may have acidifiers, water, salt, coloring, seasonings, and preservatives. Everything but the coloring will be declared on the label.

If it is a *cold pack cheese food*, cheese plus the same dairy ingredients allowed in pasteurized process cheese food will be present. In addition, sweeteners and guar or xanthan gum stabilizers may be used. All ingredients, including the color, will be listed for the consumer.

"NATURAL" COLD PACK CHEESE?

While most of the cheese products described in this section contain chemical additives and are oversalted, and occasionally even sweetened, it is possible to produce a product that meets all the legal requirements of a cold pack cheese and still qualifies as an additive-free food. This has been accomplished by several companies whose cold pack cheese spreads contain a blend of cheddar or Swiss cheese, whey solids (not exactly a wholefood but at least free of synthetics), water, cream, annatto (vegetable) color, and seasoning ingredients. Some examples are included in the Exemplary Brands.

STORING CHEESE

All unripened cheeses (cottage, ricotta, cream, farmer, pot, feta, mozzarella, ricotta salata) are perishable and must be stored in the refrigerator. When you shop, check the pull date on the label when it is provided by the manufacturer and try to use the product within a week of this date.

For long-term storage, all other cheeses should also be kept in the refrigerator, but if cheese moves quickly in your house you can follow the European custom and keep a special cheese drawer or box in a cool part of the kitchen or dining area. Room temperature brings out the full flavor of cheese, but be aware that unrefrigerated cheese will become stronger sooner.

The rind or wax coating on cheese protects the unexposed surfaces, but once cheese is cut, its shelf-life is reduced. The usual method for keeping the cut surface of cheese from drying out is to cover it with a tight plastic wrapper. Since several of the flexible film wrappers are made with chemicals that can migrate into foods, especially those with a high fat content, we prefer to use plastic bags or foil. An alternate method, which eliminates the need for a wrapper, is to butter the exposed edges, which keeps the cheese moist and preserves the consistency. Smelly cheeses should be tightly covered so that their odor doesn't penetrate other foods.

While it is not generally recommended, cheese can be frozen in pieces of no more than 8 to 10 ounces. To restore it to eating quality, thaw it slowly preferably in the refrigerator. Cheese can be grated directly from the frozen state, and blue-veined cheeses can even be sliced for crumbling into salads or cooking without defrosting.

Natural cheese will not sour or turn rancid, but it will become stronger with age until it reaches a point where it is hard to enjoy the flavor or the odor. In its last days it can be used in dishes that call for melting. Mold on the outside of cheese is not harmful but should be cut or scraped off. It is a sign that the cheese has passed its prime and should be used in the near future. Moreover, if the mold appears to have penetrated the interior, it is best to discard the cheese.

TAINTED CHEESE

From time to time accounts appear in the news about cheeses that have become contaminated with bacteria and are blamed for serious illness and even deaths. When this occurs, it is not the result of faulty handling of the cheese itself, but rather due to the presence of bacteria in the original milk. This may happen at the farm or it may be caused by improper sanitation at the cheese plant. Such outbreaks are beyond the consumer's control and are not confined to cheese, or to any other natural food for that matter. In such cases, the consumer is dependent on the integrity of the manufacturer and on the FDA and state health agencies for speedy action and recall so that the situation does not escalate. It is interesting to note in light of the negative publicity regarding raw milk that virtually all these contaminations involve products made with *pasteurized* milk.

CHEESE CHECKPOINTS

Here is a quick summary of what to look for on the cheese label before you buy:

- If the cheese is natural, the name either appears alone, such as "Cheddar Cheese," or is preceded by the word "natural."
- If the cheese is otherwise processed, the words "pasteurized process," "pasteurized blended," "pasteurized process cheese food," "pasteurized process cheese spread," "cold pack" cheeses, or "club" cheese will appear with the name.
- Added preservatives.
- Coloring, although it is not always listed.
- Salt, although it is not always indicated.
- Bleaching of the milk with benzoyl peroxide.
- The type of milk used. If not stated, the milk is cow's milk. If sheep or goat's milk is used, this will be specified.

- Most domestic cheese is made with pasteurized milk. If raw, it is cured for a specified period of time to ensure its safety. The label need not give any of these details. Only pasteurized milk or aged cheese may be legally imported.
- The degree of curing, a key to flavor, which is sometimes indicated by the terms "mild" or "mellow," "aged," or "sharp."
- Nutritional information. Products that make any nutritional claims must now substantiate them with figures; others may voluntarily disclose such information. This can be useful in making comparisons.
- A clue to the fat content may appear on the bulk packages of many imported cheeses. Remember, this figure may be relative to solid matter only (IDM) and is thus influenced by the overall moisture content of the cheese.

CHEESE NUTRIENTS*

Cheese 1 ounce	Calories	Protein grams	Fat grams	Saturated fat grams	Chole-sterol mg.	Sodium mg.
Natural Cheeses						
Alpine Lace[1]	90	NA	NA	NA	20	35
Blue	100	6.1	8.2	5.3	21	396
Brick	105	6.6	8.4	5.3	27	159
Brie	95	5.9	7.9	NA	28	178
Camembert	85	5.6	6.9	4.3	20	239
Cheddar	114	7.1	9.4	6.0	30	176–240
Low-sodium cheddar	114	7.1	9.4	6.0	30	6
Colby	112	6.7	9.1	5.7	27	171
Cottage, 4% fat	29	3.5	1.3	0.8	4	114
Cottage, 2% fat	25	3.9	0.5	0.3	2	115
Cottage, dry curd, unsalted	24	4.9	0.1	NA	2	9
Cream cheese	99	2.1	9.1	6.2	31	84
Edam	101	7.1	7.9	5.0	25	274
Feta	75	4.0	6.0	4.2	25	316
Fontina	110	7.3	8.8	5.4	33	NA
Gouda	101	7.1	7.8	5.0	32	232
Gruyère	117	8.5	9.2	5.4	31	95
Havarti (45%)[2]	91	6.7	7.0	4.3	21	200
Havarti (60%)[2]	118	5.4	10.6	6.5	31	200
Limburger	93	5.7	7.7	4.8	26	227
Monterey Jack	106	6.9	8.6	NA	NA	152
Mozzarella, whole milk	80	5.5	6.1	3.7	22	106
Mozzarella, whole milk, low moisture	90	6.1	7.0	4.4	25	118
Mozzarella, part skim	72	6.9	4.5	2.9	16	132
Mozzarella, part skim, low moisture	79	7.8	4.9	3.1	15	150
Muenster	104	6.6	8.5	5.4	27	178
Dorman's Low-Sodium Muenster[1]	110	6.0	8.0	NA	NA	95

CHEESE NUTRIENTS* (continued)

Cheese 1 ounce	Calories	Protein grams	Fat grams	Saturated fat grams	Cholesterol mg.	Sodium mg.
Neufchâtel	74	2.8	6.6	4.2	22	113
New Holland[3]	90	7.0	8	NA	NA	100
Parmesan	111	10.1	7.3	4.7	19	454
Parmesan, grated	129	11.8	8.5	5.4	22	528
Port du Salut	100	6.7	8.0	4.7	35	151
Provolone	100	7.2	7.6	4.8	20	248
Ricotta, whole milk	49	3.2	3.7	2.4	14	24–52
Ricotta, part skim	39	3.2	2.2	1.4	9	35
Polly-O, no salt[1]	50	3.5	4.0	NA	NA	10
Romano	110	9.0	7.6	NA	29	340
Roquefort	105	6.1	8.7	5.5	26	513
Samsoe[2]	102	7.6	7.8	4.7	24	200
Swiss	107	8.1	7.8	5.0	26	74
Dorman's No Salt Added Swiss[1]	110	8.0	8.0	NA	NA	8
Tilsit	96	6.9	7.4	4.8	29	213
Substitute Cheese						
Fisher Shredded Taco Mate[1]	90	6.0	7.0	2.0	10	NA
Heidi Ann Natural Lite Ched Style[1]	83	9.0	5.0	NA	14	68
Soya Kaas[1]	78	6.7	5.6	NA	0	168
Pasteurized Process Cheese						
American Cheese	106	6.3	8.9	5.6	27	406
American Cheese Food	93	5.6	7.0	4.4	18	337
American Cheese Spread	82	4.7	6.0	3.8	16	381
Velveeta, Loaf[1]	80	5.0	6.0	NA	NA	430
Borden's Lite Line[1]	50	7.0	2.0	NA	10	410
Weight Watchers Reduced Sodium, 60% Less Fat[1]	50	7.0	2.0	NA	NA	200
Swiss Cheese	95	7.0	7.1	4.6	24	388
Swiss Cheese Food	92	6.2	6.9	NA	23	440
Cold Pack Cheese						
Wispride[1]	90	5.0	7.0	NA	NA	205

*Source: *Composition of Foods, Dairy and Egg Products,* Agriculture Handbook No. 8-1, USDA, (1976) unless otherwise noted.
[1]Manufacturer's figures.
[2]Danish Cheese Board figures.
[3]This cheese is considered reduced fat and salt.

RECOMMENDATIONS

NATURAL CHEESE

General Rule of Purchase: Choose natural cheeses. Avoid those containing a preservative or mold inhibitor (indicated on the label) and those made with bleached milk (also on the label). When color is added it may not necessarily be noted although some brands offer this information voluntarily.

The following cheese varieties are not subject to coloring:

Feta	Limburger	Jarlsberg
Ricotta salata	Liederkranz	Kashkaval
Brie	Gruyère	Kasseri
Camembert	Havarti	Monterey Jack
Imported Emmenthaler	All blue cheeses	All goat's cheese

Because there are so many brands and such inadequate labeling, it is best to read the description of each variety within the chapter.

Note: The following list is only of brands that are unique by virtue of being low in sodium, made with raw milk, if pregrated do not contain additives, etc. There are many other acceptable choices that you can ferret out on your own.

Exemplary Brands

4 C Grated 100% Pecorino Romano, Parmesan
Calabro Pregrated Romano, Parmesan
Chehalis Natural Raw Goat Milk Cheeses
Colonna Grated Parmesan
Coop Regular and Low Sodium Raw Milk Cheeses
Dorman's Lo-Chol Imitation Semi-Soft Cheese, Natural Low Sodium Muenster, No Salt Added Gouda Type, No Salt Added Swiss
Erewhon Raw Milk Cheeses
Featherweight Low Sodium Cheeses
Good Health No Salt, Low Sodium, Low Sodium/Low Fat Cheeses
Green Bank Farm Regular, Low Sodium Raw Milk Cheeses
Health Valley Regular, No Salt Raw Milk Cheeses
Heidi Ann Natural Reduced Fat, Low Sodium Cheeses
Jason Grated Parmesan
Joan of Arc Chevrigotte
Kraft Grated Romano, Parmesan
Morningland Dairy Regular, No Salt Raw Milk Cheeses

Natural and Kosher Regular, Low Sodium Raw Milk Cheeses
Natural Farms Regular, Low Sodium Raw Milk Cheeses
NEOPC Regular, Low Sodium, No Salt Raw Milk Cheeses
New England Country Dairy Raw Milk Cheeses
New Holland Reduced Fat and Salt Cheeses
North Farm Raw Milk Cheeses
Pathmark Grated Parmesan, Italian style Hard Grating Cheeses
Progresso Grated Romano, Parmesan
Rosewood Farms Raw Milk Cheeses
Sharon Valley Farms Raw Cheeses
Singing Winds Raw Milk Goat Cheese
Sonoma Farms Raw Milk Cheeses
Steuve's Natural Regular, Low Sodium Raw Milk Cheeses
Tillamook Low Sodium Cheddar
Tree of Life Raw Milk Cheeses
Waldbaum's Imported Parmesan, Parmesan and Romano

COTTAGE CHEESE

General Rule of Purchase: *Dry curd cottage cheese* is always fat- and additive-free.

For both *low-fat* and *regular cottage cheese*, look for brands that contain only milk, cheese cultures, enzymes, cream, and possibly salt. Avoid those in which the creaming mixture includes several undesirable ingredients such as carrageenan, locust bean gum, xantham gum, guar gum, mono- and diglycerides, polysorbate 80, and dextrose; all are revealed on the label. Listing of the milk fat content is also mandatory.

Exemplary Brands

Alpenrose 2%, 4% Cottage Cheeses
Alta Dena Dry Curd, Low Fat Cottage Cheeses; Kefir Cheese
Berkeley Farms Regular, Low Fat Cottage Cheeses
Breakstone's All Natural Dry Curd, 2%, 4% Cottage Cheeses
Carnation Small Curd Dry Curd Cottage Cheese
Darigold Dry Curd Cottage Cheese
Dean Foods Dry Curd Cottage Cheese
Edgemar Low Sodium, Low Fat Cottage Cheese
Foremost So.Lo, 4%, with Chives Cottage Cheeses
Friendship Dry Curd, Pot Style, 4% Cottage Cheeses; Hoop Cheese; Regular, No Salt Added Farmer Cheeses

Hughes Farmer Style, Low Fat Cottage Cheeses
Knudsen's Low Fat, 4% Cottage Cheeses
Lucerne Dry Curd Cottage Cheese
Michigan Old Fashioned Cottage Cheese
Nancy's Cultured Rennetless Cottage Cheese
Nordica Cottage Cheese
Pathmark 4% Cottage Cheese
Ralph's Low Fat, 2%, 4% Cottage Cheeses
Richfood 4% Cottage Cheese
Skaggs Alpha Beta 2%, 4% Cottage Cheeses
Steuve's Natural Raw Cottage Cheese
Sundance Cottage Cheese
Tuttle Diet Aid Low Fat, Regular, Chive Cottage Cheeses

RICOTTA

General Rule of Purchase: All ingredients appear on the label. Look for those with only cultured milk, starter (or vinegar), and perhaps salt. Thickening agents such as gelatin are unnecessary, but in some areas there is no other choice.

Exemplary Brands

Acme All Natural Whole Milk Ricotta
Breakstone's Whole Milk Ricotta
Calabro Part Skim, Whole Milk, No Salt Added 100% Skim Milk Ricottas
Fierro Part Skim, Whole Milk Ricottas
Finast Part Skim, Whole Milk Ricottas
Food Club Part Skim Ricotta
Giant Food Part Skim, Whole Milk Ricottas
Grand Union Part Skim, Whole Milk Ricottas
Lamagna Ricotta
Maggio Whole Milk Ricotta

Micelis Part Skim, Whole Milk Ricottas
Natural and Kosher Part Skim Ricotta
Pathmark Part Skim, Whole Milk, Whole Milk No Salt Added Ricottas
Polly-O Part Skim, Whole Milk, Part Skim No Salt Ricottas
Sargento Part Skim Ricotta
Sorrento Part Skim, Whole Milk Ricottas
Stella Ricotta
Waldbaum's Whole Milk Ricotta

CREAM CHEESE

General Rule of Purchase: Cream cheese made from cultured milk, cream, and salt only is preferred. We list only the brands that do not contain gum thickeners.

*Exemplary Brands*_____

Gina Marie Old Fashioned

Fleur.de.Lait Old Fashioned

COLD PACK CHEESE

General Rule of Purchase: Cold pack cheese is usually additive-laden, but a few unchemicalized varieties are available. Look for those containing only natural cheese(s), whey solids, water, cream, annatto (vegetable color), and seasonings.

*Exemplary Brands*_____

Good Health Low Fat Cold Pack Vegetable Spread
Merkt's Cold Pack Cheese Food
North Farm Cheddar Cold Packed Cheese Food

Ostrom Farm of Wisconsin Cold Pack Cheese Food

Chapter 17

Meeting the Challenge of Meat

Is meat a natural food? This may seem like a silly question, but so many nonfood substances are ingested by and injected into our livestock that it's hard to say how much is real animal and how much is chemical creation.

Throughout the ages, long before "modern meat," many people rejected meat eating for both health and spiritual reasons. Although we ourselves do not eat meat, we aren't saying everyone else should follow suit. There's no question, though, that on average, Americans should consume less (and better quality) meat. In most of the world, meat has traditionally been considered a luxury; only in the Western nations, and more recently those other countries trying to emulate the Western diet, is it assumed to be a necessity. Interestingly, Americans now seem to be recognizing that meat has been overemphasized in the diet, and recent polls indicate a surprising 52 percent of those surveyed believe "that no one needs to eat meat more than once or twice a week."

We do not view our meatless diet as a deprivation, but as an opportunity to make use of the many cuisines that are not meat-dependent, a point of view we developed in our cookbook, *American Wholefoods Cuisine*.

TOWARD HEALTHFUL DIETS

The latest reports indicate that American consumers continue to turn their backs on red meat, primarily for reasons of health. An awareness of physical well-being, as well as of the dangers of too much fat and cholesterol, seems to have prevailed over efforts by both government and trade associations to convince the public that "nothing satisfies like beef." A vice-president of Oscar Mayer Foods notes that if this shift away from meat represents a trend, "consumer spending for meat would fall to zero by the year 2000."

The Place of Meat in the Diet

Most people regard meat as an important source of protein. This attribute of meat cannot be denied. One ounce of beef, veal, pork, or lamb furnishes about 6 to 7 grams of protein. The daily recommended protein intake for adults is approximately 54 grams for men and 45 grams for women; the figures for children are less, depending on age and weight. Thus, if you were to fulfill your entire protein need for the day with meat (no dairy, grains, beans, nuts, or seeds at all), you would only need to eat at most 9 ounces. Most meat eaters take in this amount at a single meal and consume other protein-providing foods throughout the day. This is a matter of concern, for, as you are about to see, this protein is accompained by a great deal of fat, cholesterol, chemical residues, and bacteria, as well as being expensive.

What's the Beef?

There are conflicting opinions among anthropologists and nutritionists about the role meat played in the prehistoric diet. If, as we explained in Dining in the Wholefoods Style (page 152), the diet of our ancestors is a good model of our own diets and if people have been eating meat for more than 40,000 years, as some claim, why the current concern? To find the answer, it is interesting to compare the nutritional makeup of the diets of prehistoric societies *presumed* to be meat eaters with the diet mix today.

In an article entitled "Paleolithic Nutrition" in the *New England Journal of Medicine* (January 31, 1985), the authors conjecture that although our current intake of animal protein seems to approximate that of the first "biologically modern" men and women, the overall nutritional makeup of our diet is dramatically different as a result of the composition of meat today and of the other foods eaten in conjunction with it. Here are some of the reasons:

■ Free-living animals are composed of about 3.9 percent fat. In contrast, animals raised for meat consumption are now 25 to 30 percent fat.

■ The fat in wild game is estimated to contain over five times more polyunsaturated fat per gram than that in domesticated livestock. Among them is one of the omega-3 fatty acids currently being studied for its apparent protective action against heart disease and other health problems often associated with aging (see Chapter 19). Modern meat contains virtually none of this nutrient.

■ The ratio of polyunsaturated to saturated fat in the Paleolithic diet was believed to be 1.5 to 1. Modern U.S. diets not only contain twice as much total fat, but have a reversed ratio of polyunsaturated to saturated fat of about 0.5 to 1.

■ The cholesterol levels of wild and domesticated animals are apparently quite similar. Paleolithic people may well have consumed just under 600 milligrams of cholesterol daily (to the dismay of current policy makers who recommend only 300 milligrams of cholesterol).

■ The Paleolithic diet is believed to have provided a fraction of the sodium content of the typical American diet.

■ The intake of wild vegetables is believed to have provided our ancient ancestors with an abundance of calcium, vitamin C, and most other vitamins and minerals. The fiber content of their diet was more than double the current U.S. average and approached that common in rural Africa today, where most of the studies supporting a high-fiber diet originated.

Chemical Residues in Meat

The original motivation for eliminating meat from our own diet came from increased awareness of the nature of meat production in this country. It is not widely appreciated, but cattle can do something quite remarkable—consume vegetation that is otherwise useless to man and convert it into protein. But in the Western world a preference for tender strains of beef have brought about a dependence on alfalfa, corn, soybeans, and other cultivated crops, along with "feed-lot" techniques in which animals are housed in confined areas and induced to consume contrived diets based on these energy-expensive grains plus nutrient supplements, hormones, and other drugs. With these methods, the meat producer achieves the greatest weight gain with the least amount of actual feedstuffs in the shortest period of time. (Concern over these raising and feeding practices is more widespread than one might imagine. An article in *Mother Jones* revealed that the Ronald Reagan family had its beef specially raised by a cattleman who used no drugs in order to produce what is called "natural beef.")

HAZARDOUS HORMONES

In the 1970s a synthetic hormone known as DES, which had been used in animal feed since 1954 to increase weight gain, was found to cause cancer in humans. It took nearly ten years for a ban on all uses of DES in animals to go into effect. Thus, for thirty years people unwittingly consumed this hazardous drug.

Despite the removal of DES, several other growth stimulants are still available to meat producers. (Once again the "chemical merry-go-round" continues; one chemical is banned only to be replaced with another dubious substance.) One of the most widely used of these drugs is believed by some medical investigators to be responsible for abnormal sexual development in children, a problem that has been seen repeatedly in Puerto Rico.

It has also been pointed out that since most of the growth stimulants are similar to female hormones, weight gain in the animal is fat rather than protein-rich muscle—mimicking the natural structure of the female animal.

One bright note is the decision by the European Common market to ban the use of implanted hormones in any meat produced or imported by member countries. This could have a ripple effect in the United States because it will curtail our ability to export to these nations.

ANTIBIOTICS ON THE DINNER TABLE

Antibiotics, described as the "wonder drugs" of modern medicine, have certainly more than lived up to their reputation as far as the meat industry is concerned. Used initially to help check the spread of infectious diseases in penned animals, another side effect soon became obvious—regular doses of these drugs accelerated the animals' growth.

A lengthy government report has spelled out many concerns regarding the routine use of such medicated feed. One is that low levels of antibiotics in feed could lead to the development of antibiotic-resistant bacteria and, through genetic coding, this resistance could be transferred to other bacteria, animals, and humans. Warnings about the dangers this could pose were ignored until, in 1983, eighteen people in the Minneapolis area were stricken with severe gastrointestinal ailments attributed to a resistant strain of salmonella bacteria in hamburger meat from steers routinely fed a form of tetracyline. And in 1987, the Centers for Disease Control, after studying a similar case of food poisoning in California, reported that there is a conclusive link between food poisoning and antibiotic drugs used in feed. Worried that continued use of medicated feed "may erode public confidence in our product," the National Cattleman's Association finally recommended that routine use of tetracycline be halted. We have no idea how well this recommendation is being followed.

Unfortunately, even if the antibiotics used to treat people are ultimately prohibited in animal feed, meat may still be tainted with similar medications reserved for animal use. Moreover, the illegal use of veterinary drugs, which has been well documented, presents an additional threat to public health.

PERSISTENT PESTICIDES

Most animal exposure to pesticides is indirect and unintentional, the result of their being used to grow feed crops, to control weeds on grazing land, to keep insects from destroying stored grain, and to keep animal dwellings pest-free. The reason that meat products pose a concern on this front is that pesticides and related chemicals tend to accumulate in fatty tissues and so we get a double dose—from the agricultural products we eat and from the buildup in the animals we consume. (A typical steer consumes a ton of grain and 300 to 400 pounds of other high-protein feed just at the feed lot.)

For many of these pesticides and other environmental contaminants a maximum residue allowance in animal flesh (and milk and eggs) has been set by the Environmental Protection Agency. This is not a safe or no-risk level, but rather one at which "residues are expected to occur" but which has been determined to pose "an acceptable risk" or to be "unavoidable." The extent of this problem is demonstrated by the government contention that any action to prevent the sale of meat exhibiting residues of DDT and dieldrin (both identified as carcinogens) would disqualify most domestic products.

DRUG ABUSE AND DETECTION

According to a 1986 estimate by the Office of Technology Assessment, virtually all chickens, 90 percent of veal calves and pigs, and 60 percent of beef cattle raised for food are routinely fed medicated feed. Between 1973 and 1984, the National Residue Program, which monitors animal products for drugs and chemicals, detected at least one major residue problem in every animal species slaughtered under federal inspection. To compound this, a 1986 congressional committee report claims that many livestock producers do not abide by the withdrawal regulations for approved drugs and that 90 percent of the 20,000 to 30,000 animal drugs currently in use have never been FDA approved. This information is well documented. The committee also charged that the FDA did not revoke the approvals of nearly a dozen animal drugs after finding them to be potential carcinogens.

An additional concern is how well these residues are monitored. Only a minute sampling of animals is inspected, in the range of one out of every 11,000 livestock animals and one out of every 575,000 birds, and the U.S. Department of Agriculture's testing program looks for less than a third of the possible contaminants. Even within this small group, residues in excess of the legal limits are not uncommon. Of the 143 drugs and pesticides that have been at issue, 42 are suspected of causing cancer, 24 of causing birth defects or endangering the fetus, 12 of causing mutations or having an adverse effect on reproduction, and 11 are reputed to cause other toxic effects.

Even when violations are picked up, the time factor usually makes it impossible to track down and remove the contaminated meat from the market before it is sold.

Carcinogens in the Feed

Another potentially dangerous situation occurs when mold-contaminated grains are included in the animal's diet. Health officials in Great Britain say they are "appalled" at the amount of the cancer-causing mold aflatoxin that is tolerated in livestock feed in the United States. According to the EPA, aflatoxin is "at least 1,000 times more potent" than the pesticide EDB, which caused such a scandal and was finally banned in 1984.

MEAT-BORNE ILLNESS

Drug resistant bacteria, chemical residues, and carcinogenic molds are not the only ways meat can make you sick. Poor sanitation is said to cause approximately 200,000 recorded cases of food poisoning and an estimated 1.3 million cases of "flu" annually, and these figures are rising.

Concern about this has initiated a government monitoring system. While meat appears to be less problematic than poultry, in the first half of 1984, disease-causing organisms were found in 22 percent of the samples of cooked beef inspected.

The Meat Inspection Act sets certain standards for government inspection of meat processing facilities, but periodic reviews have revealed an alarming number of violations that go uncorrected. This problem seems to be escalating as processors develop techniques that allow them to slaughter and dissect more carcasses a day than inspectors can monitor.

A government-supported review of the situation concluded that the nation's meat and poultry inspection program has "no comprehensive statement of criteria, no systematic accumulation of data, and no complete technical analysis of the hazards or benefits to human health." Inspection procedures were deemed inadequate to deal with either chemical or bacterial risks. Apparently officials in Washington are not concerned. Budget cuts are repeatedly proposed that would force the agencies responsible for overseeing meat and poultry inspection to cut back so drastically that there will not be enough inspectors to staff even the existing meat and poultry processing facilities. A report to the USDA by the European Community issued in 1986 shows greater concern abroad; their review of U.S. meat plants found that if they were located in Common Market countries all would probably not be able to sell beef or pork because they do not comply with minimum facility and sanitary requirements for slaughtering and processing meat.

THE FAR-REACHING EFFECTS OF A MEAT-BASED DIET

Those who criticize meat consumption do not do so only for personal reasons. America's meat-eating habits also have economic, environmental, and humanitarian repercussions.

Human Costs

It is only because we have a surplus of vegetable protein in this country that we can afford to use animals as food. In 1947 an international conference was held at the United Nations to discuss world shortages of food and grains. All nations were urged "to economize [on] the use of grain and to limit the feeding of grain to livestock." Four decades later, America is consuming close to record high levels of grain-fed meat and it is estimated that more than half the grain produced by American farmers is fed to livestock. It is said that a steer in a feed lot in this country consumes more grain in three weeks than a person in India eats in a year. A retired official at the U.S. Department of Agriculture estimated that the soybeans alone fed to animals for a year would satisfy the protein requirements of 200 million people. Even more startling are statistics on world food consumption. According to resource geographer Georg Borgstrom, the "developed" world, with 28 percent of the earth's population, consumes two-thirds of the world's grain and three-fourths of its fish (a good part of which, like the grain, ends up as cattle feed).

Ecological Costs

Our external equilibrium as well as our personal health suffers from our demand for meat. Animal production strains our natural resources as a result of overgrazing, energy-intensive, soil-eroding farming techniques employed to raise animal feed, and the pollution of water from accumulated animal wastes that seep into the soil around feed lots.

Because other countries now emulate our diet, our domestic practices are felt worldwide. One of the most dramatic effects is the destruction of the Amazon basin where deforestation, largely for cattle ranching and agriculture, is leading to a decrease in the world's oxygen supply, 40 percent of which is produced in that area. Ironically, an overwhelming proportion of South American beef is not consumed there but is exported to the United States, where most of it ends up in fast-food chains.

SELECTING FRESH MEAT

Here are some guidelines to help you locate the best buy for your health. As you will see, the possibility of obtaining natural meat, similar to other organic food, is much more feasible today than it was a few years ago.

In general, avoid buying meat that is frozen (or that is labeled to indicate that it has been frozen and defrosted). Meat that is frozen is likely to have gone through partial defrosting and refreezing, and is therefore subject to more deterioration and a higher bacterial count than fresh cuts of meat. If you want frozen meat, buy a fresh piece and freeze it at home; since it cannot be stored indefinitely, at least this way you are sure its life isn't being overextended.

Beef

Beef is the most readily available, most popular, and probably the most tainted of all meat products. A steer takes longer to raise than other meat-producing animals and so the cattle rancher feels a particular urgency to get beef to market as quickly and efficiently as possible. In the natural order of things, the animal experiences eighteen months of calfhood (when its meat is still veal) and seven months of adolescence when it is neither delicate enough to sell as veal nor tasty enough to call beef; it becomes genuine beef after it has passed the age of two. ("Baby beef," the brainstorm of some PR person, is slaughtered well before its prime and is the least likely to be recognized as beef in a blind taste test.) Full flavor does not develop until the animal is three, and it is said to keep improving until the age of six, when a decline sets in.

Years ago, steers were kept three years before slaughter, but today cattle are generally sent to market before this time. To compensate for lack of flavor, tenderness has been the selling point. This is determined primarily by internal fat (or marbling). Pumping the animal with hormones and antibiotics makes possible a rapid weight gain, largely from fat. If the fat were reduced, you would wind up with meat that was not just tasteless but tough as well—not a very tempting prospect.

GETTING A BUM STEER

Bulls, or uncastrated males, are the preferred source of red meat in Europe, yet the most unlikely to appear on the American table. This is because bulls are more fiesty and difficult to manage than steers and, with 38 percent less fat on their carcass, bulls do not meet the top USDA grades and so command lower prices. Their appeal is even further reduced by the fact that bull meat is not only a bit tougher, it is also darker, giving the impression it is not fresh. Thus, although consumers say they want leaner beef and the industry says it is eager to cut back on its costs (bulls grow faster on less feed and do not need female hormones to fatten them up), bull raising has not been pursued in the United States to any extent.

"LITE" BEEF

As is typical of agribusiness, rather than raising bulls, new (and expensive) breeds are being cultivated to a "lite" standard. "Lite" beef, recently recognized by the USDA, must have 25 percent less fat than the established standard for that grade. Thus, a steak labeled "Good" that is also Lite has 25 percent less fat than a Good steak that's not Lite, and this holds true for cuts that are Choice and Prime as well. Thus, beef with the least fat becomes Lite Good, then Good, then Lite Choice, Choice, Lite Prime, and finally the fattiest, Prime.

An additional label on meat that has been developed by a private organization bears the letters N.E.F. (for Nutritional Effects Foundation). A status of N.E.F.1 indicates a fat content of no more than 3.5 percent; N.E.F.2 indicates no more than 6 percent fat.

Note that a reduced fat content does not necessarily mean a reduced cholesterol content in the meat.

NATURAL BEEF

Meat that has been raised without the assistance of growth stimulants, hormones, steroids, antibiotics, or any other drugs is often referred to as "natural." (The government prohibits the use of the word "organic" here.) In some instances the animals are also fed an organic diet, as is the case with

Coleman Natural Beef which the company says is raised on unsprayed grasses and in the virgin plains of Colorado.

Unfortunately, current USDA guidelines only require that to be called "natural," meat products be "minimally processed" and free of artificial coloring, flavoring, and preservatives. One further stipulation, that any meat described as "natural" on the label must carry a statement as to how it qualifies, can help you determine if it is also drug-free. Read these statements closely because "natural" claims are being made for meat that meets organic standards (i.e., no drugs *ever*) as well as for meat that is "free of *residual* hormones and antibiotics," which means the cattle was exposed to these drugs at one time.

The N.E.F. label referred to above can also help you distinguish meat that is less laden with drugs. According to its program standards, any meat that has been subjected to drugs the FDA is considering banning cannot be N.E.F. approved, even if this ban has not yet been implemented by the government.

Of these "natural" meats, beef is the most readily available, although natural beef still comprises only a fraction of a percent of the total beef sold in this country. It is most likely to be found in the few natural food markets that carry meat, at more progressive supermarkets such as Grand Union in the East, through buying cooperatives, directly from the farm, or possibly even by mail (see "Food by Mail," on page 59 of Chapter 3).

Veal

From a nutritional standpoint, veal, although costly, is the best buy. Because it is the leanest of all meat, with very little waste, it is easy to determine how much you are getting for your money. However, from a humanitarian viewpoint and insofar as the use of antibiotics in meat is concerned, white or milk-fed veal rates quite poorly.

NATURAL VEAL

One Chicago-based nonprofit organization called the Food Animal Concerns Trust (FACT) has brought to the market a chemical-free veal raised humanely without the typical cruel confinement. This product, sold under the brand name Rambling Rose, is available to restaurants and select retail markets; it is ruddy in color and said to have a mild, meaty flavor instead of being white-fleshed and bland like conventional anemic veal.

Lamb

Lamb has never been especially popular in the United States, perhaps because of its well-defined flavor. You'll find, however, if you don't overcook lamb it has a pleasing, delicate flavor, not the gamey taste many people find objectionable.

In terms of nutrition, lamb has less internal fat (marbling) than beef and its fat is a little less saturated. Although loin and rib chops are more expensive, which people often interpret as a sign of better quality, leg of lamb at half the price is more desirable, being only about half as fatty.

Of all the foreign meat imported into the United States, New Zealand Spring Lamb is the most noteworthy. The most significant thing about it is that, according to the New Zealand Lamb Information Center, "in New Zealand all sex hormones and tenderizers are banned, and animal tranquilizers are not in use." So, if the store you shop in carries it and has a well-maintained freezer, frozen "Genuine Spring Lamb from New Zealand" may be a good choice.

Pork

Pork's high fat content makes it a questionable buy. Even though the pork industry claims today's pork is 50 percent leaner, it is still 18 to 25 percent fat. One reason for its leaner profile may stem from the fact that pigs are being slaughtered at an earlier age (seven months), when the water content of their flesh is still high. As a result, you buy water at the price of meat and get less flavor in the deal.

The attractive pink color of pork is not an indication of freshness, as it is with beef. This color is induced by a tranquilizer injection into the animal before slaughter. (If the industry has its way, pork may be as much as 70 percent leaner in the future due to a synthetic hormone, PST, which may be approved in 1988. Although PST advocates claim the hormone disappears almost immediately after injection, long-term effects of eating pork treated with PST are still unknown.)

DISEASE-FREE PORK

Trichinae, a parasite that affects pork and causes trichinosis in humans, is probably the primary nemesis of the pork industry. Fear of trichinosis makes consumers distrust pork, overcook it, and then complain about its taste.

The Centers for Disease Control estimates that there are 150,000 to 300,000 new cases of trichinosis in this country yearly, several of them fatal. Although some people have the idea that federal inspectors check for trichinae, the law does not require they do so and, until recently, there were no speedy or economical means of detection. But now, all of a sudden, the public has several defenses against this parasite. The most reassuring one is a new test that quickly picks up the larvae in meat. Good hog raising practices can thus be certified by this simple test, which is cheap and poses no threat to meat plant employees or the consumer.

Another new approach is the one industry is championing. Pork is the first animal product slated for irradiation and if this approach is followed, all specimens, whether contaminated or not, may be subject to radiation. Retail food packages will have to indicate that this treatment has been used.

Several consumer groups are opposed to pork irradiation on the grounds that it may endanger workers, the environment, and the health of consumers. To add to the general concerns about irradiation, there is a particular problem with pork: because of its high fat content it is especially susceptible to radiation damage, producing potentially carcinogenic by-products. Irradiated pork is also nutritionally inferior to nonirradiated pork, sustaining a loss of more than 50 percent of the B vitamin thiamin.

Proper cooking is yet another option for dealing with trichinosis. For years it has been recommended that pork be cooked to an internal temperature of 170°F., but now this has been reduced to 160°F. A special warning has been issued against preparing pork in a microwave oven, however; in microwave-cooked pork the trichinosis parasite may survive even at 170°F., particularly in large boned pieces. The meat may look well done, but the microwave's uneven cooking can hinder actual destruction of the parasite. This is disturbing since consumers often rely on a visual assessment in cooking pork, assuming that gray flesh is safe and a pink color indicates more cooking is needed. With microwave cooking, however, this is not a true gauge.

Ground Meat

It is not surprising that chopped meat is frequently cited as a cause of food poisoning. Bacteria may be present in the frozen trimmings that make up one component of the product, and much of the equipment used to grind meat has difficult-to-reach spots that escape sanitizing and thus harbor bacteria. Furthermore, grinding facilitates bacterial growth by increasing the surfaces exposed to air.

Ground meat generally starts to loose its bright color six to eight hours after processing. The dulling that occurs is partially the result of bacterial growth. Two techniques may be employed by butchers to salvage meat after it has lost its "bloom." One is "reworking" the meat by sending it through the grinder again. This may enhance its appearance, but it does not help reduce bacteria. "Seeding" freshly ground meat with discolored meat is also standard policy for many retailers. This practice only serves to contaminate the fresh meat with bacteria.

Somewhere behind the sterile meat showcase with its plastic-wrapped packages, you can usually find a butcher. If you intend to eat chopped meat, your best bet is to cultivate the butcher's friendship. Even supermarkets will grind meat to order. This is your only guarantee that the ground meat you buy is not derived from old, undesirable, or fatty parts, and that the luscious red color is really an indication of freshness. Another alternative is to purchase a hand grinder and grind your own.

Hamburger or *chopped meat* may contain pork, lamb, and veal trimmings, diaphragm, and esophagus. Federal regulations limit fat content to 30 percent (often identified as 70 percent lean). Note that since meat ground on

he store premises is not subject to federal regulations, it may have an even
higher fat content unless the label states otherwise.

In terms of yield, the more expensive leaner grinds like sirloin, and the
cheaper fatty grinds from chuck or unidentified "ground beef" generally
cook down similarly, the former losing water and the latter some of the fat.
Consequently, the added expense of "lean" choices is not always justified.
In a 3-ounce portion of cooked ground beef the caloric savings between the
leanest beef at 15 percent fat prior to cooking, and common ground beef
(which averages 24 percent fat before cooking) is only about 10 calories, and
the fattier choice has just 3 grams less protein. Note that leaner grinds do
not fry up well and so are more suited to dishes that do not call for
prebrowning of the meat and in which a dense, firm product is desirable.

Some consumers try to reduce the fat and stretch food dollars by buying a
soy-beef blend. As explained in Chapter 12, the isolated soy protein which
may be incorporated into these blends is a highly processed ingredient and,
while perhaps less tainted than the beef, may have the disadvantageous
effect of binding some of the minerals (like iron) for which meat is prized in
the first place. Therefore, you are probably better off adding your own
extender such as whole grain bread crumbs, cooked brown rice, soy grits,
wheat germ, or ground oats.

Organ Meats

Meat is given the prime position it occupies in menu planning because it is
rich in protein, B vitamins, and minerals, particularly iron. The best source
of these nutrients in meat is found in what are termed "variety meats," or
organ meats. These include liver, kidneys, tongue, brains, and heart, usually
from steers, calves, and (in the case of hearts and livers) from chickens.

One possible drawback to these organ meats, however, is their high
cholesterol content. While 3.5 ounces of beef contain about 90 milligrams of
cholesterol, an equal portion of beef liver contains 440 milligrams and in beef
kidneys it reaches 770 milligrams. In addition, if you wish to eat these animal
parts, and especially the liver and kidneys, it is worth finding an organic
supplier since these organs, which are detoxifiers in animals just as they are
in humans, are the repository for undesirable chemicals. (On a mass-market
scale, no source of organic organs is known to us.)

Do not buy organ meats that have been frozen and defrosted. Retailers
often save these parts in the freezer until they accumulate enough to sell and
then defrost them so they appear fresh at first glance (although any ethical
butcher will put out a sign stating "frozen, defrosted"). Variety meats are
more perishable than other cuts and by buying them in this manner you risk
faulty freezing and improper defrosting, which can lead to extensive bacterial growth. Of course, as with all other meat, never refreeze organ meats.

New Ranching Ventures

In this country, meat eating is centered around beef, pork, and lamb, in addition to poultry, but this is not so in other parts of the world where yak, camel, goat, and dog are common fare. While these "delicacies" have not yet been accepted here, some enterprising ranchers have come up with what they feel to be more marketable meatstuffs.

RABBIT

Rabbit meat is said to be sweet and tender, lower in fat and cholesterol, and higher in protein than other meats on the market. Rabbits are small, adapt to most climates, and convert feed efficiently into meat. They are also notorious reproducers. Frozen rabbit can occasionally be found in the market. That it has not found a wider audience may reflect an ongoing affection for the Easter bunny.

DEER (VENISON)

Wild game has been hunted for the table throughout all of recorded history and some people feel that morally and nutritionally this is the only meat really fit to eat. Indeed, wild venison does have a unique link to another era, but this may soon fade if deer farming catches on. Although it is already a thriving business in West Germany, New Zealand, and Great Britain, raising deer for food is a new industry in North America. It is too early to tell if this cultivated venison will compare favorably with the meat of the wild deer, with its lean muscle and distinctive flavor. At present, farm-raised deer are allowed to roam within a fenced-in area that keeps out predators, and natural vegetation still accounts for much of their diet. Once they have exhausted their grazing area, though, perhaps the deer will follow the path of the pig and steer and become just another factory animal.

BUFFALO

Buffalo (or more accurately bison) is another alternative for those looking for more acceptable meat. Free of growth-stimulating drugs, considerably lower in fat than even "lite" beef, and 50 percent lower in cholesterol than beef, buffalo has become the meat of choice for a growing minority of meat eaters. Although only available in a few specialized shops, buffalo meat can be mail-ordered (see "Foods by Mail" on page 59 of Chapter 3). For more information, contact The National Buffalo Association, 10 Main Street, Dept. GGF, Fort Pierre, S.D. 57532.

Kosher Meat

The Jewish religion imposes certain restrictions on meat in order to make it acceptable to some practitioners. The general term for meat that satisfies these restrictions is *kosher*. Although many people have the impression that kosher meat is raised in a unique manner, in fact, the animals are the same. The features that distinguish kosher meat from nonkosher meat have to do with the method of slaughtering and the treatment thereafter.

The koshering process generally employs a technique of salting to extract the blood from the animal. As a result the meat may contain two to three and one half times more sodium than its unkoshered counterpart. Soaking kosher veal or beef in water for an hour can remove excess sodium; however, this tactic seems ineffective for chicken.

MEAT GRADING

It is difficult to let your eye be the guide to buying meat since special lights and layers of wrapping often make it hard to get an unembellished view. When you have the chance to actually see the meat, remember that fresh meat is bright in color. The older the meat, the duller the flesh, and in the case of beef, the darker too, unless it's from a bull. The texture should be velvety, not coarse; the fat portions should be white, not yellow.

There are also three different categories of government-regulated meat-judging in this country.

Cleanliness

The sanitation inspection is the most important. This has been discussed earlier in the chapter and if the past is any indication of the present and future, our system of federal and state inspection is unfortunately not always much of a guarantee of cleanliness or safety. However, in a properly assessed carcass the round USDA inspection stamp (below) does have some value.

Quality Grade

Meat is also rated for quality according to a government grading system, a voluntary service purchased by the slaughterhouse. Quality grade is based solely on appearance and is noted by a shield with the letters USDA.

Higher-grade carcasses are more uniform in size, with a good intermingling of fat with lean and a thick, firm fat covering. This meat is expected to be juicy and tender. Lower grades have more protein, vitamins and mineral value. Current USDA grading practices have been criticized as being inaccurate as well as varying from one part of the country to another, but for what it's worth, they include Prime, Choice, and Good for all graded animals, with an additional five gradations for beef (Standard, Commercial, Utility, Cutter, and Canner), two for veal (Standard and Utility) and one for lamb (Utility). No quality grades exist for pork.

Prime meats rarely go to the retail market, usually ending up in restaurants; many stores offer only Choice. If lower grades are available where you shop, there are reasons for buying them. First of all, these cuts are less fatty, and although this may suggest a less tender piece of meat, if cooked using a long, slow method like braising, the results can be delicious as well as a boon to your health. Another reason to choose a lower grade is that these animals have spent less time on the feed lot and so their intake of chemically treated feed is somewhat reduced.

The terms "prime," "choice," and "good" can be used only on meat that has been graded by government inspectors. Often, though, stores buy ungraded meat and do their own grading based on their own standards. Their grade stickers, which may look like the official seal without the letters USDA, are only relevant in making comparisons to similar items in that store, and descriptions such as "select," "fancy," "finest deluxe," "supreme," and such are subjective in nature.

Yield Grade

The final government grading system is called a yield grade. An animal with a low yield grade usually provides leaner cuts. Unfortunately, yield grades appear on whole carcasses, not on the precut packages on display in the meat cooler, so they are unlikely to be available to assist your selection.

PACKAGING

While we're at the meat counter we'd like to put in a word about packaging. This is an important consideration for your health and the health of the environment.

About 90 percent of beef now comes to the store precut, sealed in vacuum bags, and packed in boxes, the work of the butcher having been done at the processing plant. "Boxed" veal, lamb, and pork are also appearing in increasing quantities. Prepackaging of meat in this manner is gaining popularity with meat processors because it enables them to put their name on products and develop a consumer interest in brand-name meat. The evolution from whole chickens to brand-named parts (see Chapter 18) has been credited with increasing chicken sales and now the meat industry hopes that recognizable brands and more convenience packaging will do the same for its lagging sales. But just as commercial chickens are all comparable whether they carry a company logo or not, most branded meat is raised in the same manner as the anonymous offerings.

While the meat industry claims that vacuum-packed meat undergoes less handling at the retail end and is thus more hygienic, some bacteria prosper in this sealed environment. Samples of vacuum-packed pork and lamb have been found to contain *Campylobacter jejuni* organisms, a bacteria that health experts believe causes an estimated 2 million outbreaks of food poisoning a year.

Certainly this method of marketing meat requires a redefinition of the term "fresh" since vacuum-packed meat can be kept several weeks longer than meat cut on the premises. In some cases it has up to a thirty-day shelf-life.

If the meat you are contemplating is more traditionally packaged, check to see if the tray it is resting on is plastic. Most plastic is a nondegradable material that remains in the environment forever. You and your butcher have a choice. Compressed paper containers, although not recommended for long-term storage, are made from recycled paper, and when they are tossed into the garbage, break down and return to the land. Some markets prefer nonplastic see-through trays that burn cleanly and decompose completely. Of course, if you patronize a meat market or other outlet that displays fresh meat unpackaged in a refrigerated case, you will not have to concern yourself with this.

Warning: Never purchase meat in a closed container that is damaged in any way.

PROCESSED MEAT

Ever since the early days of food processing and the era of the "muck-rakers" such as Upton Sinclair, author of *The Jungle*, aspersions have been cast on processed meats. There have been scandals about unhygienic conditions and jokes that "everything but the squeak" goes into these products. Today the processing plants may be cleaner, but processed meats are still the source of some repellent ingredients. Fortunately for the consumer, everything is on the label.

The term "processed meat" encompasses all meat that is changed from its original fresh state to another form, usually by curing, smoking, comminuting (reducing to small particles by mechanical means), seasoning, or cooking. All varieties of sausage (which includes frankfurters), ham, bacon, luncheon meats, corned beef, jerky, head cheese, and scrapple fall under this heading. These products may be sold canned, refrigerated, or frozen. The original reason for this processing was preservation, but the resulting flavor, texture, economy, and convenience account for most of their audience today.

The majority of processed meats are pork-based, but some beef products as well as other meat trimmings and organs find their way into many formulations, as do a variety of binders and extenders, flavoring agents, preservatives, water, and salt. A casing around this amalgamation helps define its form. Sheep, pig, or cow tissues are used to make the casings that are edible. Artificial casings made from cellulose or cotton particles help establish the shape of skinless franks and some sliced processed meats; these are removed before the meats are packaged and sold.

A Look Inside the Wrapper

Processed meats have gained a bad reputation because of their high fat, high sodium, chemically laden composition. Where product Standards of Identity exist, 30 to 50 percent of the weight may consist of fat. With as much as 50 to 80 percent of the calories derived from this fat, and with, for most, more than 300 milligrams of sodium in just 1 ounce, their effect on the diet can be devastating. For instance, two hot dogs without any "fixings" furnish just about the bottom end (1,100 milligrams) of the recommended daily total of sodium; the average smoked sausage, weighing 2.5 ounces, contains 1,120 milligrams of sodium.

In terms of protein, they are no match for other protein foods. Averaging 3 to 5 grams per ounce, they offer only 50 to 60 percent as much of this nutrient as a comparable portion of unprocessed meat, fish, poultry, eggs, cheese, or beans. Thus, based on price they may seem economical, but in terms of nutritional return they are hardly a bargain.

The Cancer Connection

One important concern about processed meats centers around the additives used to preserve them, particularly sodium and potassium nitrate and nitrite. Of all food additives, these preservatives have remained the most controversial and the least controllable. There is widespread agreement that these additives produce nitrosamines which cause cancer, mutations, and other toxic effects, yet they have remained in processed meats largely because the meat industry claims it has not been able to find a suitable replacement that will guarantee safety in a mass-produced, nationally distributed product.

Interestingly, small-scale local manufacturers have been quite successful in eliminating the use of these agents, and a process developed for mass production by the University of Wisconsin using sugar and lactic acid has proven adequate. The USDA has not given its permission to use this no-nitrite formula, however, because they say the color of bacon would be less acceptable to consumers. Some observers believe that once the industry finds an artificial color and flavor that mimic the pink hue and cured meat flavor that the public identifies with processed meats, the prohibition of nitrites will be far more likely to occur.

In the meantime, experimentation with the so-called Wisconsin Process, as well as with sodium ascorbate, potassium sorbate, vitamin E, and other means of bacterial inhibition in conjunction with fewer nitrites has shown the problem can be reduced although it has not eliminated nitrites completely. On the other hand, a rising incidence of illegal residues of nitrosamines in bacon has been reported by Cornell University researchers, with some samples registering eleven times more than the USDA allows. In bacon fat, the nitrosamine levels were almost twice as high as in the bacon itself.

Many people simply refuse to believe that our government would permit any real harm to come to us and prefer to think the dangers of nitrosamines are exaggerated. Would that they were right! Here is a statement from the director of the carcinogen program at the Cancer Research Center in Maryland:

> Nitrosamines are among the most potent carcinogens we know. They are most effective in eliciting tumors when given by mouth in many small doses over a long period, rather than as a large single dose.

This is exactly how people ingest them! We urge you, when sodium or potassium nitrate or nitrite is revealed on the label, "don't bring home the bacon." Moreover, do not cook in bacon fat, which can have as much as four times the nitrosamines as the meat itself, and try to stay away from the vapors of nitrite-containing meats when they are cooking; some nitrosamines are volatile and can be inhaled.

Even in the absence of nitrites, related carcinogens are likely to appear in smoked processed meats as a result of the interaction between certain meat proteins and some of the natural components of smoke. Smoked meats like kielbasa, mettwurst, smoked country-style pork sausage, cappicola, chorizos cervelat, salami, pepperoni, Berliner, bologna, bacon, and hot dogs, frank furters, or wieners may all be troublesome.

Mechanically Separated Meat (MSM)

Otto Von Bismarck, chancellor of Germany in the 1870s, is reputed to have said, "No man should see how laws or sausages are made." The timelessness of this statement is proved by a new ingredient currently in use—mechanically separated meat (MSM).

To produce MSM, muscle tissue and the bone to which it is attached are ground and then sieved to remove any large bone fragments; finely ground bone, marrow, cartilage, and connective tissue are retained. When MSM is used, the USDA only requires the words "mechanically separated (species)" to appear in the list of ingredients. But those worried about the residues of lead, cadmium, fluoride, and other contaminants in bone, as well as increased calcium, cholesterol (some say by as much as 50 percent), and nucleic acid (a substance that gout sufferers must watch), think the public has a right to be better informed. They suggest that the phrase "contains——% powdered bone" should appear next to the product name, a more truthful statement since only a portion of MSM is meat. Industry has fought this, claiming the "negative implications" of such a statement will turn people off their products. At present, MSM is limited to no more than 20 percent of the product in processed meats.

Warning: MSM is prohibited in baby foods because its fluoride levels can be excessive. Inexplicably there isn't a warning on adult products that contain MSM indicating that they are unsuitable for babies.

Selecting Processed Meat

Nitrite-free and unsmoked processed meats do exist; a few may be found in the supermarket and additional choices are likely to be available in meat markets, gourmet shops, and natural food stores. Some specific brand names appear in the Recommendations, but since many nitrite-free products are made and marketed locally, an investigation on your own may turn up others in your locale.

Here's what to look for on the label (or what to ask the butcher about):

■ *Fresh sausage products* are neither cured nor smoked and thus are the most likely to be nitrite-free. This category includes "fresh sausage," "Italian sausage" (not "cured" or "smoked"), "country-style sausage," "uncured sausage," "breakfast sausage" (which is usually beef rather than pork), "bockwurst," and "bratwurst." It may come in links, patties, or rolls, fresh or frozen. When the ingredient list includes only pork and/or beef, salt, honey, and spices, these products are acceptable. Sugar, corn syrup, dextrose, sodium erythorbate, and binders such as whey and sodium caseinate make them less so. Other added chemicals such as MSG, BHT, BHA, and propyl gallate disqualify them altogether.

■ *Cured processed meats* that are nitrite-free will say "uncured" or "no nitrates or nitrites added" on the label. The ones you are most likely to find, often in the freezer, are uncured bacon and hot dogs, although uncured bologna, knockurst, salami, certain types of sausage, Berliner, mettwurst, and kielbasa are all possible as well. The absence of nitrites results in a light brown, rather than pink color, and the flavor may not be exactly what you're used to. Note that these products are smoked and thus may still pose a risk. Other undesirable additives include phosphate-based compounds, MSG, hydrolyzed vegetable protein, sugar, corn syrup, dextrose, sorbitol, and the preservatives BHT, BHA, and propyl gallate.

■ If you find a *nitrite-free ham* (one that is "uncured" or simply "salt cured," as the great hams of the world once were), you may want to check the label for added water, as four types of ham have been distinguished by the USDA, as follows:

Fresh Ham with No Water Added.

Ham with Natural Juices, which the law requires to be 18.5 percent by weight protein.

Ham with Water Added, with 10 percent water and 17 percent protein by weight.

Ham and Water, which can contain any amount of water as long as the producer indicates how much on the label.

As much as two-thirds of the ham marketed in the United States falls into this last, unpredictable group.

Note that *Honey Cured* ham may contain up to 50 percent sweeteners other than honey in the curing solution.

■ *Smoked meat* is unfortunately not always easy to distinguish. According to the U.S. Department of Agriculture, certain processed meats that "by virtue of experience" the consumer expects to be smoked need not allude to this process on the label. Thus, some people do not even suspect that frankfurters, bacon, bologna, kielbasa, and the other processed meats whose characteristic flavoring is dependent on smoking have been treated in this manner. If the manufacturer wishes to, however, those that have been exposed to smoke from burning hardwoods or natural liquid smoke vapors may be labeled either "naturally smoked" or "smoked." When liquid smoke is used, but not in vaporized form, the label is required to state "smoke flavored" or "smoke flavor added." When artificial smoke flavoring is used the package must use these words specifically. If you are concerned about the tars and other possibly harmful by-products generated during smoking, you may find smoke "flavor" preferable.

■ *Scrapple* is a specialty product that is not cured or smoked. A blend of minced pork meat and by-products (skin and organ meats), pork fat, starch (cornmeal and/or flour), salt, and spices, this processed meat is a favorite in the South. Several brands maintain an additive-free status, which includes the absence of MSG and any sweetening. Once again, the product comes refrigerated and frozen. You may also find hogshead cheese that is similarly acceptable.

■ *Lite, light, lean* or *low-fat,* and *extra lean* have finally been defined in relation to meat and poultry products. "Lite" or "light" as well as "lower fat" and "leaner" may now describe an item that has either no more than 10 percent fat or contains at least 25 percent less fat than the majority of representative products in the same category. If "light" is used to mean less salt, sodium, breading or calories, the specific way in which it is lighter must be explained.

"Lean" and "low-fat" meats contain no more than 10 percent fat, while "extra lean" varieties have a maximum of 5 percent fat. These welcome rulings should put an end to the deceptive claims in this area that have seduced consumers in the past.

■ *Reduced-sodium* products must contain 75 percent less sodium than traditional counterparts. *Less sodium* comparisons are permitted only if a 25 percent reduction is achieved.

Remember, salt and fat are present in all processed meats in amounts higher than recommended by health authorities, so be sure to integrate these foods wisely into your overall diet.

PREPARED MEAT DISHES

When it comes to prepared packaged meat items, including soups, stews, breaded and pre-formed cutlets, frozen and canned meat entrées, and the individual portions of precooked, unfrozen, "microwave and eat" meat that are being pushed as new convenience products, all ingredients are on the label. Be sure to read it carefully to weed out products with nitrites and nitrates, MSG, hydrolyzed plant protein, textured vegetable protein, sugar, salt and other undesirables. While you're reading the label, look for another common ingredient that may not be so objectionable but gives rise to a certain deception (which the food industry calls "labeling flexibility"). The listing of "meat stock," "beef broth," and such may be a way of concealing both water and salt. A leading supplier of concentrated stock to the industry advises manufacturers that their product "enables the processor to replace the word 'water' on the label with 'beef stock' by adding 135 parts water to one part beef stock." Furthermore, "a product incorporating beef stock with salt added can be identified on the label as 'beef stock' or 'beef broth.' "

CONSUMER RESPONSIBILITY

Food safety and inspection are only partially government and industry jobs. Consumers must also do their part to ensure that meat does not become a source of food poisoning.

Storage

Uncooked meat spoils quickly. It must be stored in the coldest section of the refrigerator and then not for more than a few days. If you plan on using the meat within two days of purchase, it can be refrigerated in the original (transparent) wrapper. If you buy meat in market paper, rewrap it before storing. If you plan to keep the meat longer than two days, remove excess moisture and wrap it loosely so that air can circulate. This will discourage bacterial growth.

The following chart will help you determine how long your purchase will keep. If you will not be using the meat promptly, it is best to freeze it as soon after purchase as possible; as meat ages, both flavor and food value begin to deteriorate. Do not wash meat before freezing, but do wipe the surface with a clean cloth to remove any surface bacteria, and make sure it's

COLD STORAGE OF MEAT

Product	Refrigerator (days at 40°F.)	Freezer (months at 0°F.)
Fresh Meat		
Roasts (beef)	3 to 5	6 to 12
Roasts (lamb)	3 to 5	6 to 9
Roasts (pork, veal)	3 to 5	4 to 8
Steaks (beef)	3 to 5	6 to 12
Chops (lamb)	3 to 5	6 to 9
Chops (pork)	1 to 2	3 to 4
Hamburger and stew meat	1 to 2	3 to 4
Sausage (pork)	1 to 2	1 to 2
Deer	3 to 5	6 to 12
Rabbit	1 to 2	12
Cooked Meat		
Cooked meat and meat dishes	3 to 4	2 to 3
Gravy and broth	1 to 2	2 to 3
Processed Meat		
Bacon	7	1
Frankfurters, unopened	14	
Frankfurters, opened	7	1 to 2
Ham (whole)	7	1 to 2
Ham (half)	3 to 5	1 to 2
Ham (slices)	3 to 4	1 to 2
Luncheon meats, unopened	14	
Luncheon meats, opened	3 to 5	1 to 2
Sausage (smoked)	7	1 to 2
Sausage (dry, semi-dry)	14 to 21	1 to 2

dry before you wrap it; the idea is to keep out all air and moisture. Package it so that it is air- and moisture-tight and label the package with the cut and date of freezing. The combination of high fat content and seasonings accelerates rancidity, so cured meats do not freeze very well. For the same reason, it is better not to season raw chopped meat before you freeze it.

Defrosting Meat

It is not necessary to thaw meat before cooking. Steaks, hamburgers, and other cuts that will be broiled without a sauce have a fresh flavor if they are cooked directly from the frozen state. Thaw meat, when necessary, in the refrigerator. Never soak frozen meat in hot water to thaw it; you'll be creating a haven for microorganisms. Do not refreeze meat.

THE DANGER OF CROSS-CONTAMINATION

As trivial as it sounds, please be very careful in the kitchen when you handle all animal products. Sanitation is important. Various forms of food poisoning, from mild, hardly traceable, but definitely uncomfortable varieties to the severe deadly kind are widespread. According to the U.S. Department of Agriculture, meat is the most common catalyst.

Immediately discard any paper that has been in contact with raw meat and be sure to thoroughly wash the work area, particularly cutting boards, utensils which have touched the meat, and your hands before you begin preparing other food. It is also important that raw meat seepage (blood, water) does not come in contact with foods that are eaten raw.

Cooking

The proper cooking of meat is of vital importance, for it is this exposure to heat that kills harmful bacteria. For this reason, don't encourage the eating of blood-red or raw meat, even though it may be very tempting to nibble during preparation.

The protein in meat is extremely heat-sensitive. Very high temperatures reduce protein quality and also denature it in ways that turn meat tough and dry. Longer cooking at lower temperatures will give juicy, tender results, with a uniform color, less shrinkage, and the least nutritional loss. In general, braising, pressure cooking, oven roasting, and broiling beneath the heat source are the most satisfactory methods.

Invest a few dollars in a meat thermometer. It takes the guesswork out of meat cookery. "Minutes per pound" is only a rough guide and will vary with true oven temperature (which often does not match what the dial is set at), thickness of the cut, bones, and fat content. The meat thermometer will let you check the temperature in the center of the meat. Make sure it isn't touching a bone.

LEAST DESIRABLE METHODS OF COOKING MEAT

Charcoal Broiling: Cooking meat directly over heat imparts a savory charred flavor but may add something else less palatable—carcinogens. When meat, especially fatty cuts, are cooked *over* coals, and to a lesser extent on gas or electric grills, some of the constituents in the meat are transformed into undesirable compounds. To minimize this risk, if you must grill meat, try to use an approach where the fat cannot drip on the heat source and the smoke does not come in direct contact with the meat (for example, placing the meat in a pan over the coals, or wrapping it in foil). Using a low temperature and selecting lean cuts will also reduce carcinogens.

Pan Frying: The pan frying of hamburgers also has been shown to form compounds that may trigger cancer. The potential seems to increase as meat goes from rare to well-done, so that pan frying of chopped meat (especially to the well-done stage or beyond) and the use of an electric hamburger cooker are deemed less desirable than oven methods or broiling with the heat coming from above.

Microwaving: While microwave cooking is quick, it isn't always even, especially in foods with bone mass, dense fat, and variable moisture content. As a result, when large cuts are cooked in a microwave oven some spots overcook while others remain at just the right temperature to turn them into a bacterial breeding ground. Another criticism of microwave cooking of meat is the lack of research as to the possible creation of unnatural fat forms and the effect this has on health. Finally, meat cooked in a microwave oven does not have the same appearance as conventionally cooked meat. You can get around this by using a microwave browning spray which paints food with salted water colored with burnt sugar (caramel), but this hardly seems like a way to enhance its appeal.

Keep Meat Hot or Cold

Do not leave cooked meat at room temperature or even on a warming tray for more than two hours, and only purchase cooked meat at a store if it is displayed there in a cooler. As we have stated before, bacteria thrive in a warm environment and leaving meat out on a buffet table is an invitation to trouble.

A good rule is to keep meat at a temperature either *above 140°F.* or *below 40°F.* If you plan to store cooked meat for a future meal get it into the refrigerator or freezer as soon after cooking as possible.

ANY PROBLEMS OR COMPLAINTS?

If you still aren't sure about how to handle meat or understand the label, or if you find an unwholesome product or unsanitary meat case when you are shopping, you can go directly to the U.S. Department of Agriculture by calling their toll-free Meat and Poultry Hotline. The phone number is 800-535-4555, or if you are in Washington, D.C., 447-3333 (accessible by TDD). There is someone there to help you Monday through Friday from 10 A.M. to 4 P.M. Eastern Standard Time. At other times a machine will take a message.

RECOMMENDATIONS

Note: Products labeled "lite" or "light" have at least 25 percent less fat than conventional versions. "Lean" and "low-fat" mean the fat content is no more than 10 percent; "extra lean" has a 5 percent fat ceiling. Those bearing the term "reduced sodium" have at least 25 percent less sodium.

FRESH MEAT

General Rule of Purchase: Look for *natural* meat and make sure that it is described on the label as coming from animals raised drug-free. Avoid any irradiated meat. Meat graded "Good" has less fat than "Prime" or "Choice."

The meat you buy should be as fresh as possible, so check the date on the package. Meat packed in compressed paper or butcher's paper is preferred over meat packed in plastic.

Ground meat is best ground to order. Avoid products prepared with processed soy extenders.

Exemplary Brands

The following are drug-free, natural products:

Coleman Natural Beef, Ground Beef, Liver, Lamb, Veal, Pork, Rabbit[1]
Maverick Natural Beef
Natural Light Beef

Oregon Home Grown Beef, Pork[1]
Rambling Rose Free Range Veal[1]
Shiloh Farms Ground Beef, Beef Patties[1]

PROCESSED MEAT

General Rule of Purchase: All ingredients appear on the label; however, those that are smoked may not state this on the package unless "smoke flavoring" is the source. Look for processed meats that forgo chemical additives. *Fresh sausage* is the most available choice, being both uncured and unsmoked. Common names include "fresh sausage," "Italian sausage," "country-style sausage," "uncured sausage," "breakfast sausage," "bockwurst," and "bratwurst"; these may appear as links, patties, or rolls, fresh or frozen. *Scrapple* is another often acceptable processed meat item.

Typically cured meat products that forgo the nitrites will be designated "uncured" or "no nitrates or nitrite added."

Exemplary Brands

Because of the paucity of choices, we have included products containing refined sweetening or grain (noted in their listing), but no other noxious ingredients such as MSG, nitrate and nitrite preservatives, propyl gallate, BHT/BHA, sorbitol, or phosphate compounds. Keep an eye out for new and local brands of processed meats that meet these standards.

Bella Donna Fresh Italian Sweet and Hot Sausage
Bi-Lo Pork Sausage
Briggs Old South Scrapple[4]
Carmella's Sweet Italian Sausage[3]
Coleman Natural Sausage, Bratwurst, Wieners, Franks, Lunch Meat[1]
Colony Foods Nitrite Free Wieners, Knockwurst, Bologna, Salami, Breakfast Sausage
Cooke's Plantation Brand Mild Pork Sausage Patties[3], Little Links[3]
Edward's Fresh Pork Sausage[3]
Esskay Pork Sausage
Food Lion Pork Sausage[3]
Green Hill Countrystyle Scrapple
Gwaltney Williamsburg Brand Mild Country, Hot Pork Sausages,[3] Old Fashioned Salt Cured Bacon
Habbersett Country Scrapple[4]
Hatfield Scrapple
Health Valley Sliced Breakfast Beef, Sliced Smoked Pork Belly, Uncured Cooked Sausages

Jamestown Brand Pork Sausage[3]
Jesse Jones Country Sausage[3]
Jones Country Scrapple,[4] Breakfast Sausage, Light Breakfast Links,[4] Minute Breakfast Links, Sausage Patties, Little Pork Sausages
Kirby and Holloway Country Style Scrapple[3,4]
Krauss Farm Country Brand Breakfast Sausage Links, Roll
Laurent's Hogshead Cheese
Meese's Hot Country Sausage[3]
Olde Towne Pork Sausage[3]
Rapa Scrapple[4]
Richfood Mild Country, Pork Sausages[3]
Samuel Sandler Kosher Nitrite Free Hotdogs
Savoie's Fully Cooked Dressing Mix
Shiloh Farms Uncured Hot Dogs, Brown 'n Serve Links, Sandwich Loaves[1]
Strode's Country Scrapple[4]
Tobin's Bockwurst
Usingers Famous Bratwurst[3]
Wild Winds Hot Dogs

[1]Organic
[3]Contains refined sweeteners
[4]Contains refined grains

Chapter 18

Making the Best of Birds

There are many common misconceptions about the nature of poultry production in this country. Even though America stopped raising birds on farms more than twenty years ago, most people do not realize that poultry today is more a product of invention, than of nature. This change is not without a price in terms of both quality and cleanliness.

A BIRD'S EYE VIEW
OF THE POULTRY INDUSTRY

From conception to consumption, most chickens and turkeys lead a life dependent on mechanization. The exception is a small minority of free-running birds raised in a farm-like setting without chemical enhancement.

Poultry by Prescription

Rather than repeat what has been said elsewhere, we suggest you look back at the section on "Chemical Residues in Meat," on page 224 of the previous chapter, for it applies equally to birds. While many consumers may take comfort in the less fatty makeup of poultry, its chemical profile is not so innocent.

One chemical residue that affects chickens, but not other animals, is a larvacide fed to them to prevent flies from hatching in their manure. Residues of a potentially hazardous by-product of this drug have appeared in chicken meat.

The dangers of our chemically centered agriculture and animal husbandry are not imaginary. One year, as many as eight million chickens exhibiting excessively high levels of the cancer-causing pesticide dieldrin had to be destroyed. In this case, consumers were lucky; the discovery was made before the birds hit the stores.

You might be further dismayed to learn that a government study has noted that when a problem does arise, the contaminated animal can be identified and removed from the market only in cases where the carcass is coded, frozen, and stored for a lengthy period, such as is usually done with turkeys. Even so, things don't always turn out as planned. In one notewor-

hy case, when the USDA found illegal residues of a cancer-causing drug in
urkeys during a routine inspection, thousands of birds were impounded but
a mixup occurred and by the time it was noticed, the contaminated birds had
been shipped out and processed into turkey rolls. The government decided
to let the matter slide to avoid any embarrassment to the USDA or the drug
residue program.

When you consider that since 1979 the rate at which chickens are processed has increased more than fourfold, it seems miraculous that inspectors
pick up any defects at all.

Inspection

The Poultry Products Inspection Act provides for mandatory federal
inspection of poultry processing plants to prevent the sale of products that
"are unwholesome, adulterated or otherwise unfit for human consumption."
Unfortunately, poultry inspection appears to be even more lacking than
meat inspection, described in the previous chapter.

Not only have sanitation practices in poultry plants been singled out as
shoddy, but the poultry industry has been particularly resistant to improving
these conditions, as sanitation and inspection slow down production.

Poultry-Borne Illness

The change from small-scale farming to industrial production has introduced widespread bacterial contamination of poultry. This problem is so
serious that in 1986 the administrator of the Food Safety and Inspection
Service (FSIS) characterized poultry as a "health hazard," and during a 1987
Congressional hearing a veteran government meat and poultry inspector
declared that labels on beef, pork, and poultry should read: "Eat at Your
Own Risk."

According to the Centers for Disease Control, bacterial contamination of
food is responsible for 6 million cases of food poisoning and 4,000 to 5,000
deaths annually. Poultry is considered to be the worst offender, with an
estimated 25 to 40 percent of chickens housing salmonella and more than 85
percent of chicken and turkey products registering *Campylobacter jejuni*
bacteria. (*C. jejuni* infection in humans is also a leading cause of the nerve
disorder known as Guillian-Barre syndrome.)

This frightening situation has several causes: increased bacterial resistance
due to the antibiotics routinely administered to birds; an inadequate inspection system and lack of USDA microbial standards; and no effective means
of controlling the spread of bacteria, given the huge number of birds that
are processed daily.

For example, although most people think of a bath as a form of sanitation, despite the addition of antimicrobials (which are absorbed into the
flesh along with the water), nearly half of the tank water used in poultry
processing to bathe and chill the birds after slaughter contains salmonella

bacteria. This has been documented repeatedly in processing plants through out the country. The most recent report by the FSIS in 1986 found that in 24 out of the 29 plants surveyed, the chill water was contaminated with salmo nella, as well as *Escherichia coli* bacteria.

On top of the immediate illness caused by these poultry-borne microorga nisms, there is another extremely important issue—their possible long-term effects on human health. Studies on chronic inflammatory diseases, such as arthritis and heart disease, show that they can be precipitated by contami nated foods. This suggests that the public health danger from food poisoning is also a threat in terms of more lasting, debilitating disease. Furthermore, once the chronic illness occurs, its predisposition may be passed on to future generations because the bacteria that are responsible appear to modify the human genetic code.

Contrary to what many consumers believe, the meat and poultry sold at the market are not inspected for salmonella or campylobacter.

Grading

Although there is a government grading system for poultry, carried out on a voluntary basis, it is really not very meaningful to the comparison shopper since most retail poultry is Grade A anyhow. This grade merely means it is meaty, has a well-developed fat layer (even if these qualities are chemically induced), and has no surface defects. Grade B and C birds are usually sent to the processing plant to be turned into soup, canned or frozen dinners, poultry franks, etc.

THE CONTRIVED CHICKEN

Chicken production starts with genetic breeding geared to producing big-breasted, meaty birds. Life itself begins in a mass-hatchery where climate-controlled incubators are programmed to unleash thousands of chicks at a time. The chicks are then stacked on trays and bused to contract farms where enormous coops, housing perhaps 30,000 birds in each, become their homes for the next seven weeks until slaughter. Only those birds bred to be "stuffers" are allowed to hang around for almost three more weeks to achieve their heftier girth. This is quite a contrast to the 1950s, when it took fourteen to sixteen weeks to raise a chicken with enough meat to market.

Not Exactly Chicken Feed

With only three-quarters of a square foot to move in, exercise is not an option. But the birds have no real need to move about because everything in the coop is delivered. A scientific blend of feed is provided through a

THE VARIETIES OF POULTRY

The name assigned to each type of bird helps the buyer determine species, age, and in turn what can be expected from the purchase. Older birds are generally more flavorful, yet may be less tender and more suited to stewing than roasting. The oldest birds may be rather "gamey" in taste.

Rock Cornish Game Hen or Cornish Game Hen: A young immature Cornish chicken or progeny of a Cornish chicken and any other breed usually five to six weeks old, with a ready-to-cook weight of not more than 2 pounds.

Rock Cornish Fryer, Roaster, or Hen: The progeny of a cross between a Cornish and a Rock chicken. No weight specifications.

Broiler or Fryer Chicken: A young chicken, usually under thirteen weeks old, of either sex.

Roaster or Roasting Chicken: A young chicken, usually twelve to twenty weeks old, of either sex.

Capon: A surgically unsexed male chicken, usually under eight months old.

Hen, Fowl, Baking, or Stewing Chicken: A mature female chicken, usually older than ten months, with meat less tender than that of a roaster.

Cock or Rooster: A mature male chicken with toughened and darkened meat.

Fryer-Roaster Turkey: A young immature turkey, under sixteen weeks old, of either sex.

Young Turkey: A bird that is under eight months of age.

Yearling: A fully matured turkey, but usually less than fifteen months old.

Mature or Old Turkey (Hen or Tom): This bird is usually older than fifteen months, with toughened flesh.

Broiler or Fryer Duckling: A young duck, usually under eight weeks old.

Roaster Duckling: A young duck, usually under sixteen weeks old.

Mature or Old Duck: A duck that is usually older than six months, with toughened flesh.

Young Goose: A tender-meated bird.

Mature or Old Goose: A bird with a toughened flesh.

Young Guinea: A tender-meated bird.

Mature or Old Guinea: A bird with a toughened flesh and a hardened breastbone.

Squab: An immature pigeon that has extra-tender meat.

Pigeon: A mature pigeon with toughened flesh.

chute and the light may be left on close to twenty-four hours a day so the birds can eat continuously.

In addition to their opportunity to eat constantly, chickens today convert feed into meat with greater efficiency. In the 1950s, almost twice as much feed was consumed to produce a pound of meat than is needed thirty years later. This shift has been accomplished mainly through the use of growth stimulants, including routinely administered antibiotics in the manner used for livestock. The possible repercussions of this practice, presented in the section on "Antibiotics in Meat," on page 225 of the previous chapter, are equally applicable to birds.

In addition to corn and medication, poultry feed may also include a dye extracted from marigold petals. This deceptive practice gives the birds the golden hue some people mistakenly identify with grain-fed poultry.

Selecting Chickens

BRAND-NAME BROILERS

Each year the number of independent chicken farmers seems to drop, a surprising contrast to the growth in popularity of the bird. In the mid-1970s, there were about 200 producers; by the mid-1980s, the number was down to 120, with the 60 biggest companies selling 85 percent of the birds and the top 5 of these accounting for 39 percent of sales.

In each part of the country a brand-name chicken now dominates the market. Whether it's labeled Holly Farms, Tyson, Con Agra, Gold Kist, Foster Farms, Country Farms, or Perdue, the bird is handled pretty much as described above.

LOWER-FAT CHICKENS

The current fad is toward fat reduction in the chicken industry. USDA regulations allow a "lower fat" description on any poultry product that contains 10 percent or less total fat or 25 percent less fat than the majority of similar products on the market.

In chicken, fat is reduced in part by removing the leaf fat (the fat that surrounds the posterior cavity of the bird) and the contents of the body cavity (the neck, stomach and heart). Interestingly, while this results in a lower total fat content, it does not alter the fat content of the flesh (which ranges from 3 percent fat in white meat to 6 percent fat in dark meat for the average bird). Removing the skin and any visible globules of fat at home, however, will produce a reduction in the fat content of the flesh.

Another approach chicken processors use to reduce fat is to administer a high protein diet. As one producer explains it, to take body fat off a chicken it is fed "basically the same thing you would eat: food that is low in calories but high in protein." Perhaps this is beneficial to personal health, but this practice is quite disturbing in terms of world ecology. Using high-protein feed consisting of "fish, soybeans, alfalfa, yellow corn, and even ground-up cookies" to feed animals is an affront to all the hungry people in the world and wasteful of resources.

You can expect to pay a 10 percent markup for lower-fat chicken. If you want to save both money and fat, consider trimming the chicken yourself as described above and give preference to light meat which contains about 3 grams less fat than dark meat (at a savings of about 27 calories) per 3½-ounce serving.

FREE-RUNNING, NATURAL BIRDS

It may sound corny, but a scientifically run university study has shown that happy birds are healthier birds. Chickens that get to roam and peck outdoors are bound to be less stressed than industrial chickens confined indoors to a cubicle. Although free-running chickens do not always lead a chemical-free life, they are a step above corporate chickens.

If you wish to take advantage of the nutritional assets of chicken without having to worry about antibiotics and other questionable feed additives in your diet, seek out a source of organically raised birds. Not only are these birds brought up drug-free, but the water bath used on them after slaughter is supposedly neither chlorinated nor fluoridated.

Local farms often sell natural (i.e., organic) chickens, and natural food stores may carry them as well. You will find these birds—even if frozen—are superior in every way to the celebrity chickens at the supermarket, despite the fact they don't get their names on TV. As with meat be sure to verify the farmer's definition of natural.

CHICKEN CHECKPOINTS

Although much of their physical appearance is scientifically induced, what is visible is still the only means you have of judging birds. For tender meat, choose chickens that are plump and show no surface skin defects. Yellow, grain-fed chickens were at one time the most flavorful, but skin color is meaningless as it can be manipulated with dyes as explained earlier. You could be offered a lavender chicken and it would have no more meaning in terms of quality than the common white to golden yellow.

READY-TO-EAT CHICKEN

Many stores sell ready-to-eat chicken. Unless it is hot off the broiler, do not buy it. Even then, you should be cautious. You have no way of knowing how fresh the bird was before it was cooked, how careful the cook was, or how the bird was handled after cooking. We've already expressed concern about bacterial food poisoning due to poultry consumption. Statistics indicate that purchasing prepared birds from a delicatessen doubles your chances of getting sick.

LET'S TALK TURKEY

Like the modern chicken, turkey is now bred for convenience, not flavor. Immediately after they're hatched, baby turkeys are transferred to breeder stoves that simulate a mother's warmth, and when they are big enough for the barn they are given a cubicle that is 2½ to 4 feet to dwell in. While once it took thirty weeks to raise a 20-pound bird, feed efficiency, with the aid of drugs, has cut this time almost in half.

If you are over sixty you may remember the gamey tang of old-fashioned turkey. But the 20-pound bird is too big for most families and apartment-sized ovens do not readily accommodate the characteristically high breast-bone. The short stocky bird now in favor bears little resemblance to the turkey the Pilgrims hunted.

Somehow, in reducing turkey's size and flattening its breast, the taste has suffered too. The only flavor you are likely to get from the birds on today's market comes from the basting oil the manufacturer injects.

Naturally Raised Turkeys: Something to Be Thankful For

The one time you are apt to get a bird that resembles old tom turkey is around Thanksgiving and Christmas, when relatively small-scale turkey farming flourishes in some parts of the country. (Where only twenty years ago, 20,000 turkeys was an impressive flock, today growing a million birds on a single turkey farm is no big deal.) Many butcher shops and natural food stores scout around for such birds for holiday offerings, taking advance orders so they can meet the demand.

In addition the natural food store may be the source of turkey raised naturally on a drug-free diet. Take this opportunity to see what traditional feasting is all about.

Self-Basting Turkeys Are Turkeys

Once their life has ended, things may even get worse for turkeys. Unlike other birds, they are often injected with a basting solution and when you add this to the weight gained in the chill bath, as much as 10 percent of your purchase may be extraneous liquid.

Self-basting turkeys are quite prevalent in the market. These unfortunate birds are injected with broth, water, and/or oil-based solutions. The fat is never butter, as one well-known brand name might lead you to believe; most commonly it is (saturated) coconut oil and/or partially hydrogenated soybean oil. For flavor, salt, sugar, hydrolyzed vegetable protein, and artificial flavoring are added. Sodium-based phosphates are also used to bind its moisture and make the bird seem "juicy." Coloring, polysorbate 80, and mono- and diglycerides "enhance" consistency and appearance.

DUCK, GOOSE, AND OTHER GAME BIRDS

Some specialty meat markets offer ducks, geese, Cornish game hens, guinea hens, and pigeons fresh (that is, "never frozen"), but in general they are marketed frozen at the supermarket. All brands are pretty much the same.

REMODELING THE BIRD

Not very long ago, poultry came in just one form—the whole bird. In the late 1960s, prepackaged chicken parts became fashionable, and legs (with or without thighs), breasts (with or without wings), or mixed packages allowed consumers to choose the pieces they prefererd. Then separately marketed turkey drumsticks and rolled boneless chicken and turkey breasts made their appearance.

Since very few people favored the necks and backs of these birds, a new outlet for several billion spare parts had to be invented. That's how poultry franks, poultry rolls, chicken burgers, chicken loaf, chicken bologna, turkey ham, turkey salami, poultry nuggets, and such came to be.

Mechanically Separated Poultry (MSP)

Most of the poultry used in processed poultry products, including canned, minced, and deviled chicken, pot pies, chow mein, croquettes, ground poultry, and the novelty products listed above, comes either from laying hens past their prime or from the parts that are not in great demand. To obtain the most meat possible, the carcass itself is ground, becoming MSP, the poultry counterpart to mechanically separated meat (MSM), described on page 240. MSP contains high levels of calcium (a health problem for some people), fluoride, and contaminants that are deposited in bone matter. In addition, MSP has about twice the cholesterol of regular poultry. Unlike MSM, MSP need not be listed on the label and even appears in baby food.

Ground Poultry

Ground chicken and turkey, packaged in plastic casing and looking very much like a sausage roll, are often found in the freezer case. It is only about 15 percent fat, considerably less than the 30 percent maximum the USDA imposes on ground beef, and can be used in a similar manner. Although the only ingredient on the label is "chicken" or "turkey," it is actually mechanically separated poultry which means ground bone is present as well.

Rolled Poultry Roasts

Another popular form of the bird is the so-called rolled roast: a processed product in which loose pieces of boned meat are pressed together and rolled into a solid, ready-to-roast shape. Although a few products are no more than flesh, skin, and salt, most have such uncustomary ingredients as sodium phosphates, brown sugar, and sodium erythorbate. Sodium levels, at

400 milligrams per ounce, give this meat more than seventeen times the sodium of unprocessed light poultry meat.

If it is "hickory smoked," it may also contain sodium nitrite. Where there is some sort of gravy added, it may contribute even more unwanted ingredients to this list.

Poultry Rolls

Chicken and turkey rolls and packages of these sliced products are prepared from meat (MSP most often), skin, and broth that have been reformed into a solid mass with the aid of several of the following: modified food starch, nonfat dry milk, egg albumin, gelatin, sugar, dextrose, sodium phosphates. Some brands are more offensive than others in terms of additives, but the origin of the meat is nothing to crow about in any of them, nor is the sodium content, which for 3 ounces of chicken roll is around 445 milligrams and for the same quantity of turkey roll may be 500 milligrams.

Cured Poultry Products

Poultry franks and cold cuts, what the industry describes as "pegboard" items, are cured in a manner similar to traditional hot dogs, bologna, ham, salami, and the other processed meat products they are meant to mimic. The same carcinogenic nitrites impart flavor, color, and protection against botulism (see page 239 in Chapter 17).

These processed, cured products can be quite fatty; poultry franks contain as much as 20 percent fat, which adds up to about 70 percent of their calories. Poultry bologna may contain up to 30 percent fat. They are also generally quite salty; poultry franks average 500 to 650 milligrams of sodium each (for just over 1.6 ounces), turkey bologna contains from 675 to 800 milligrams per 3 ounces, and chicken bologna tends to run even higher, ranging from just under 900 to just over 1,000 milligrams in a 3-ounce portion.

As with processed meats, processed poultry products that are smoked aren't always marked as such. If some reference to smoking is made, however, it parallels the guidelines for smoked meat. Thus, "naturally smoked" is reserved for poultry products that derive their flavor from direct cooking over hardwood, mesquite, corn cobs, etc; "smoked" can describe both the above process or the use of liquid smoke vapors. Any other manner of imparting a smoked quality must be indicated beside the name and in the list of ingredients with a statement such as "smoke flavoring added" or "artificial smoke flavoring added," whichever is applicable. As with meat, if you are concerned about the potential hazards of "natural" smoking, you may find "smoke flavoring" is an asset.

To find nitrite-free products, look in the cooler or freezer at the natural food store. Turkey breakfast links, turkey Italian sausage, chicken and turkey bologna, and chicken and turkey franks—described as uncured to indicate the absence of chemical curing agents—may all show up there. These "natural" products are also usually free of refined cereals and sweeteners, MSG, and mechanically separated poultry. Remember, however, they may still be smoked.

The Labeling of Poultry Products

In describing the poultry portion of any poultry-containing food, a certain format must be followed. When the word *meat* is used in conjunction with the type of bird (i.e., "chicken meat," "turkey meat") the flesh, minus the skin and fat, is implied. If the light and dark meat are not present in their natural proportion, a qualifying statement, as described below, must be provided.

THE PROPORTION OF LIGHT AND DARK MEAT IN POULTRY PRODUCTS

Label Terminology	Percent Light Meat	Percent Dark Meat
Poultry meat	50–60	50–35
Light or white meat	100	0
Dark meat	51–65	49–35
Light and dark meat	35–49	65–51
Mostly white meat	66 or more	34 or less
Mostly dark meat	34 or less	66 or more

When the name of the bird alone (i.e., "chicken," "turkey") appears, it means that other edible parts such as skin and fat are present, but not in excess of their natural proportions. In the case of turkey, this means that skin can make up 15 percent of the raw or 20 percent of the cooked weight. For chicken, the allowance is 20 percent of the raw and 25 percent of the cooked weight. When skin and fat are above the normal ratio, their presence must appear in the ingredient list.

The value of this labeling to the consumer is that when the term "chicken meat" appears alone, you can expect a leaner product than you get with "chicken." When "chicken meat" is joined by "chicken fat" or "chicken skin," you get more of these constituents than you do from chicken alone. None of this precludes the presence of bone, which can comprise up to 1 percent of the weight. These same principles apply to products based on other birds.

POULTRY ORGAN MEATS

In the discussion of "Organ Meats" on page 233 of the previous chapter, we explained how the liver and kidneys reflect drug misuse in animals. In poultry, too, these organs are likely to contain chemical residues unless the birds are organically raised.

CONSUMER RESPONSIBILITY

As we have already stated, poultry is believed to be the primary cause of food poisoning in this country. The consumer can cut down on this problem by handling the bird carefully at home.

Storage

When you get fresh poultry home, loosen any tight wrapping and remove the giblets and liver from the cavity. Place the loosely covered bird in the coldest part of your refrigerator. The raw bird can be kept for only one or two days as it spoils even more quickly than meat. For longer storage, it should be frozen. The following guidelines may be helpful.

COLD STORAGE OF POULTRY

Product	Refrigerator (days at 40°F.)	Freezer (months at 0°F.)
Fresh Poultry		
Chicken and turkey (whole)	1 to 2	12
Chicken pieces	1 to 2	9
Turkey pieces	1 to 2	6
Duck and goose (whole)	1 to 2	6
Giblets	1 to 2	3 to 4
Cooked Poultry		
Covered with broth, gravy	1 to 2	6
Pieces not in broth or gravy	3 to 4	1
Cooked poultry dishes	3 to 4	4 to 6
Fried chicken	3 to 4	4

Defrosting the Bird

Frozen poultry can be cooked from the frozen state or thawed first. If you are adding other ingredients or stuffing the bird, thawing will be necessary to prevent excess water from seeping inside or into the sauce. Bacteria will thrive unless thawing is done properly. Refrigerator thawing is the preferred way. Turkeys over 18 pounds may take up to three days to thaw, and a 20-pound bird will need an additional day.

If time is short, frozen poultry can be defrosted out of the refrigerator by placing it, in its watertight wrapper, in a cold water bath. Change the water often to hasten the process. With this method, small birds will take about one hour to thaw, a 12- to-16-pound specimen six to eight hours, and a 20-pound turkey up to 12 hours.

Poultry can also be thawed at room temperature, but this is only suggested for birds small enough to defrost fully in a couple of hours. It should be left out only until just pliable.

Stuffing

As for prestuffed birds, why not stuff your own? Stuffing is often the favorite part of a poultry dinner, and when you make it yourself you have an opportunity to be creative and add some extra nutrients to your meal (as opposed to the refined starch stuffing the manufacturer puts in).

Actually, the simplest and safest way to cook homemade stuffing is outside the bird. Unstuffed birds cook in less time and take less work, since you do not have to bother getting the stuffing into or out of the bird. (Stuffing cooked outside the bird can also be enjoyed by non meat-eaters.)

If you want to stuff the bird, do not insert the dressing until you are ready to put it in the oven. Be sure to pack the mixture loosely inside. Stuffing swells and bacteria multiply rapidly in this cozy environment; when the stuffing is tightly packed, the heat cannot circulate properly to destroy bacteria. Allow an extra fifteen minutes cooking time per pound for stuffed poultry. Immediately after cooking, separate the stuffing and the bird. Never refrigerate the leftover stuffing inside the bird.

Take Care to Prevent Food Poisoning

Although bacteria are usually killed by the heat of cooking, a raw infected bird can spread bacteria to other foods and kitchen surfaces.

■ To avoid cross contamination, never allow foods that will be eaten raw to come in contact with raw poultry flesh, uncooked poultry juices, or anything that has touched them. Wash your hands and the work surface immediately before and after touching raw poultry, and clean all equipment (cutting board, knives, shears, etc.) after you've finished with it.

■ Do not partially cook a bird one day and finish the job the next. This practice only gives bacteria additional opportunity to grow. Cook the bird completely at one time.

■ Cook poultry thoroughly. When the flesh is poked with a fork the meat juices should be clear, not pink.

■ Do not rely on microwave cooking for poultry. Laboratory testing of microwave versus conventional oven cooking of chicken indicates significant levels of bacteria in about 90 percent of microwaved samples, and salmonella in particular in more than 50 percent when manufacturer's cooking directions were followed. It was therefore suggested in an article in the *Journal of the American Dietetic Association* "that entirely new cooking techniques and criteria need to be developed for use in microwave cooking."

■ Remember, if you stuff the bird do not pack it tightly and be sure to remove any remaining stuffing from the cavity before you store it.

■ As with meat, don't leave cooked poultry or stuffing containing poultry by-products at room temperature for more than two hours. To minimize chances of food poisoning either keep it hot (above 140°F.) or cold (below 40°F.).

ANY PROBLEMS OR COMPLAINTS?

If you have any questions or complaints about poultry, whether they concern labeling, buying, storing, preparation, or unwholesome products or store conditions, you can reach the U.S. Department of Agriculture toll-free by calling their Meat and Poultry Hotline. The phone number is 800-535-4555, or in Washington, D.C., 447-3333 (accessible by TDD) Monday to Friday from 10 A.M. to 4 P.M. Eastern Standard Time.

RECOMMENDATIONS

FRESH POULTRY

General Rule of Purchase: Buy fresh "natural" birds (adhering to organic standards) whenever possible. Farm-raised, free-running birds, which may not be certified chemical-free, are your next choice. Despite the fancy brand names some may bear, most other fresh and frozen chicken, turkey, duck, goose, and Cornish game hens are all about the same.

When buying turkey, be sure to read the label carefully so you can avoid a bird that is "basted," "marinated," or has ingredients added "for flavor" such as water, broth, coconut oil, partially hydrogenated soybean oil, salt, sugar, hydrolyzed vegetable protein, artificial flavor, annatto color, polysorbate 80, mono- and diglycerides, and sodium phosphates. Sometimes, but not always, their absence is indicated by the words "natural" or "minimally processed."

Precooked birds should be avoided unless they are hot off the rotisserie and you plan to eat or refrigerate them immediately.

*Exemplary Brands*_____

Shelton's Turkeys,[1] Fryers[1]   Shiloh Farms Chickens,[1] Turkeys[1]

PROCESSED POULTRY

General Rule of Purchase: Best choices are canned chunks of poultry meat with or without added salt. We hesitate to recommend plain, unsalted, ground chicken and turkey because they are likely to be made from mechanically separated poultry (not indicated on the label). Avoid other processed poultry items unless their integrity is not compromised with high levels of added salt and fat, sugar, dextrose, corn syrup, modified starch, refined grains, MSG, hydrolyzed vegetable protein, nitrites, sodium phosphates, and similar nonfoods, all of which are revealed on the label.

Look for additive-free poultry franks, poultry sausage, and even frozen poultry entrées made from naturally raised birds, honey, unrefined grains, and real herbs and spices at the natural food store. These items are most often found in the freezer.

Exemplary Brands

Colony Foods Nitrite Free Chicken, Turkey Wieners
Featherweight Unsalted Boned Chicken with Broth
Health Is Wealth Uncured Chicken Franks
Health Valley Salted, No Salt Added Chunk Chicken; Uncured Cooked Poultry Bologna
Hormel Chunk Breast of Chicken

Shelton's Cooked Uncured Turkey Franks,[2] Corn Dogs,[2] Turkey Sausages,[2] Turkey Jerky,[2] Chick-a-dee's, Breaded Fried Chicken,[2] Chicken and Turkey Pies,[2] Frozen Chicken and Turkey Entrées[2]
Shiloh Farms Chicken, Turkey Pies[2]
Sun Harbor 100% Natural Chicken Mixin's
Swanson Canned Chicken
Valley Fresh Canned Chunk Chicken

[1]Organic
[2]Some organic ingredients

Chapter 19

A Fishing Trip

Fresh fish has never been more popular in the United States than it is today. People have suddenly begun to recognize how versatile a food it is and are willing to venture beyond fish sticks and canned tuna. But it is really the awareness that fish is a low-calorie, low-fat, high-protein food that has won it an audience whose culinary habits are influenced by matters of health.

There is an environmental crisis, however, lurking below the calm waters of America's rivers, that has made inland fish virtually off limits as a safe source of food. Warnings have been issued throughout the entire country to reduce or forgo consumption of many freshwater species because they contain dangerous levels of pollutants. These disclosures are all the more upsetting in light of recent discoveries about the potential health benefits of eating fish. One wonders what additional evidence America needs to admit its industrial system is damaging life on earth.

Fortunately, there are still plenty of ocean fish to choose from. Consumers have also discovered better choices when it comes to processed fish, and in turn manufacturers are responding. The most remarkable shift has been in canned tuna, where the percentage of the product packed in water nearly doubled between 1979 and 1984. Significant, too, is the growth of reduced-sodium and even no-salt options.

FISH FOR HEALTH

Having entered the twentieth century well fortified with antibiotics, drugs, and an intricate system of medical testing and intervention, Western medicine has tended to resist the idea that nutrition is a real factor in the rise of modern illnesses. In the 1960s, some small concession was made to the idea that consumption of fats and cholesterol could affect heart disease. By 1980, the medical community had gone a step further, acknowledging a link between diet and some forms of cancer as well.

Although it's been an upstream battle all the way, new information about fish may finally be changing attitudes about nutrition and health for a long time to come.

The Well-Known Nutritional Benefits of Fish

As most dieters already know, fish is an excellent source of low-calorie protein. A 3-ounce portion of broiled fish provides about half the adult U.S. Recommended Daily Allowance (RDA) for this nutrient, with just about 150 calories; this protein is easier to digest than that in other forms of meat.

Fish fat is rich in vitamins A and D, which are vital for healthy skin, bones, teeth, and eyes. The meaty portions of fish supply the B vitamins, which also promote the well-being of the skin and the nervous system.

Fish, especially ocean varieties, pick up important minerals from the waters they inhabit. Most are good sources of potassium and phosphorus; saltwater fish provide iodine and selenium; shellfish are among the richest sources of zinc. Fish that are canned with the bone in, like mackerel, salmon, and sardines, contribute significant amounts of calcium.

An Update on Fats and Fish Oils

Physicians have been advising patients to eat fish for several years, emphasizing the leaner types and recommending restraint when it comes to shellfish, which contain higher levels of cholesterol. Ironically, nutritionists are now starting to offer just the opposite advice. What brought about this change in attitude concerning selection was the recent discovery that two of the fatty acids in fish, grouped together under the heading "omega-3's," may possess some unique properties.

Studies indicate that the omega-3's in fish oils may protect against heart disease by reducing blood cholesterol (especially the suspicious low-density lipoproteins) and triglyceride levels. They also seem to inhibit the tendency of blood cells to form the artery-blocking clots that can cause strokes, as well as the fatty placque on arterial walls that leads to hardening of the arteries and high blood pressure.

FISH IS BRAINFOOD

Modern science now offers support to the popular notion of fish as brain food. The same omega-3's that appear to benefit the heart are also found in high concentration in the brain and the retina of the eye. This is believed to be especially significant for infants, since studies reveal that nursing mothers can increase the level of omega-3's in their milk by consuming a diet rich in fish oils. Prepared infant formulas, on the other hand, contain virtually none of these fatty acids.

FISH AS HEALTH FOOD

There is also evidence that these omega-3's can enhance our health in other ways, easing a number of complaints, including headaches, premenstrual discomforts, asthma, and such inflammatory ailments as arthritis.

STAY YOUNG WITH FISH

Some scientists even suggest that fish may protect us against the effects of time. As people age, protein is deposited in various parts of the body, including the heart, kidneys, and other organs, eventually wearing down all the systems. In laboratory studies, mice given a fish oil concentrate exhibited less of this protein deposition than other mice receiving corn oil.

FISH VERSUS FISH OILS

Studies that point to the role of fish oils as therapeutic agents are not conclusive evidence that isolated omega-3's can counteract specific ailments. The usefulness of these studies lies in the discovery that fish oils are very complex and that therefore it may be important to consume fish in their natural form. These findings should not be taken out of context and used as a means of promoting concentrated fish oil supplements. They can, in fact, be dangerous since excess amounts of omega-3 fatty acids could result in bleeding problems and may increase the need for vitamin E. These supplements also furnish significant amounts of cholesterol. Moreover, since chemical contaminants are deposited in fat, concentrates of fish oils may also be concentrates of PCB's and other chemical toxins.

In general, the fattier the fish, the more omega-3's it has to offer. However, because of the pollution of inland waters you should stay away from fatty freshwater fish and give greater emphasis to ocean species. A list of fatty fish appears on page 269.

OMEGA-3'S AND NON-FISH EATERS

Those who do not eat fish will be pleased to learn that omega-3's can be obtained from the following foods, which incidentally are also cholesterol-free: butternuts, walnuts and walnut oil, wheat germ oil, soybean oil and lecithin, soy foods, seaweed, and several leafy greens lead by purslane (a popular vegetable in Mediterranean countries).

DANGERS OF THE DEEP

Increasing your intake of fish may have health benefits, but you should be aware that there are some hazards in fish eating as well. Right now, less than one-third of all fish consumed in this country are inspected for safety and wholesomeness. Until we have legislation requiring mandatory inspection of fish products (as exists for meat and poultry) there will be no way to guarantee the absence of harmful microorganisms and chemical residues.

Chemical Waters Make Chemical Fish

The chemical contamination of fish has become an issue of national concern. Studies made as early as 1974 revealed that about 80 percent of inland fish samples exhibited chemical residues. Dangerous pesticides, PCB's, and methylmercury have found their way into lakes, rivers, deltas, and ocean banks through agricultural runoff, winds, and industrial dumping of wastes. So have a variety of toxic metals such as cadmium, lead, selenium, and arsenic.

Some states have actually been forced to close some of their fishing waters or place limits on the amount of fish taken. Several state health departments have recommended that pregnant and nursing women and young children refrain from eating fish from certain lakes and rivers. The Environmental Protection Agency suggests that people consume fish taken from any of the five Great Lakes no more than once a week.

This problem is shared all over the country, with chemical waters and cancerous fish showing up from the Niagara River in New York to the Santa Ana in California, the Puget Sound in Washington, and the Florida Keys. While excellent advances have been made in cleaning up many bodies of water, the residues of decades of abuse still contaminate sediments at the bottom of rivers and lakes. It could take several hundred years for some of the existing problems to be totally eradicated—and this estimate assumes that no more chemicals enter the waters in the meantime.

If you are a fish eater, all this should enrage you, for you have been virtually denied the enjoyment of an entire species—inland fish. Even if you are not inconvenienced by this particular situation you should be angry, for here is incontrovertible proof of how disregard for the environment can affect us for decades, if not centuries. Perhaps we can prohibit the commercial sale of fish from polluted waters, but how will we survive if pollution of this kind spreads to our entire food supply?

Sushi Lovers Take Note

In countries where raw fish eating is popular and roe (or caviar) is a staple as well as a delicacy, a variety of parasitic and bacterial diseases are common. As sushi and marinated raw fish (in the popular Latin American dish ceviche, for example) gain a broader audience, the risk of eating raw or insufficiently cooked seafood becomes a real concern in the United States. The fish most likely to be infected include pike, salmon, perch, Rockfish (Pacific red snapper), Atlantic cod, American plaice, tuna, mackerel, herring, turbot, and all shellfish.

FISH FARMING (AQUACULTURE)

Aquaculture refers to the raising of aquatic animals and plants in a controlled environment. As traditional fish species become increasingly less available due to overfishing and pollution of their environment, the appeal of fish farming grows. Although some people promote this as a way to help eradicate world hunger, in reality the aquaculture being practiced in the United States is centered on high-priced "luxury" species, with salmon, trout, catfish, abalone, sturgeon, shrimp, clams, mussels, lobster, and oysters comprising the bulk of the harvest. As a matter of fact, 40 percent of oysters and virtually all the trout and catfish eaten in the United States right now are bred on fish farms.

Treading in Uncertain Waters

In many ways, aquaculture today parallels the poultry raising of a few decades ago, and commercial fishermen probably have good reason to fear that, like the independent chicken farmer, they will be pushed out of business by the corporate fish farmer. Campbell's, Con Agra, AMFAC, Ralston Purina, General Mills, Weyerhauser, and other giant corporations are all participants in the aquacultural revolution alongside little-known fledgling entrepreneurs.

It is not only the threat of big business that has fishermen and environmentalists leery, though. Despite a few model projects demonstrating that aquaculture can provide both an energy-efficient and inexpensive source of protein, most commercial operations have spawned more problems than they are likely to solve.

Lack of federal and state controls everywhere but Alaska leaves the entire system of fish farming unregulated. Government guidelines are scattered among several agencies, data on drugs and chemical additives are scant, and there is no system of inspection such as exists for meat and poultry, as negligent as these may be. Before fish farming is embraced on any large scale, we would hope to see the issues of product safety, environmental impact, economic repercussions, and effect on energy resources addressed. One outgrowth of fish farming that has just been identified exemplifies the problems inherent in this revolutionary enterprise. Apparently the paint routinely used to coat the salmon tanks contains a toxin that may contaminate the fish. Cooking the fish will not rectify this.

It is hoped that the short-term benefits of increased supplies will not be at the long-term cost of extinction of both commercial fishermen and free-swimming fish.

How Are Farm Fish Grown?

Normally fish do not compete with people for their nourishment. They feed off algae, larvae, and insects to ensure a well-rounded diet. Penned fish, on the other hand, are raised on man-made diets that include soybean meal, corn, fish meal (with added preservatives), wheat, and sorghum. As a result, they grow twice as fast as fish grow naturally. Farmed fish are vaccinated against disease, and for further insurance pesticides may be added to the water to kill off certain disease-causing parasites. Prophylactic drugs are also routinely administered to prevent infection.

Other unnatural acts that are used to improve their growth and taste include sterilizing the fish so that their energy is spent getting bigger, not reproducing, and giving them hormones to induce sex changes.

Interestingly, several reports claim farm-grown fish have higher levels of cholesterol and triglycerides (fats), while the omega-3 fatty acids appear to be significantly reduced.

Labeling

There are no laws governing the labeling of farm-raised fish, but many proud producers volunteer this information on packages of their home-grown catfish, salmon, trout, and such. "Farm raised" or "farm grown," as well as any reference to "grain fed," indicate the fish has been cultivated.

In addition to domestically raised species, "farm fresh" salmon imported from Canada and Norway, plus tilapia, sometimes described as St. Peter's fish and originating in Israel or Latin America, are sold in the American marketplace.

BUYING FRESH FISH

If you intend to get the benefits of fish, which seafoods make the best catch?

Fish Habits and Habitats

Although future developments may change the truth of this statement, fresh ocean fish presently seem to be the most untainted food available in the nonorganic marketplace. Note, however, that those that come into warm inland waters to spawn, like striped bass, bluefish, and salmon, may pick up contaminants. Also, the larger predatory fish like tuna and sword-fish have a greater tendency to accumulate chemical pollutants from the little sea creatures they feed upon. In all cases, the smaller fish within a particular species are apt to have less chemical accumulation than the larger, older ones.

As with ocean fish, freshwater species that prey on other fish, such as lake trout and salmon, have higher toxic levels. The same is true for bottom feeders like catfish when matched against top feeders like bass and brook trout.

In the table on Fatty Versus Lean Fish, we have separated freshwater and saltwater species so that you can minimize contaminants.

Fatty Versus Lean Fish

The list on page 269 classifies fish according to fat content; those with less than about 5 percent fat are considered lean. In terms of toxicants, lean fish are preferable. To capitalize on the presence of beneficial omega-3 fatty acids, however, the situation is reversed. While all fish contain some omega-3's, the amount decreases as the fat content decreases (and so do the calories). As a rough guide, to get the same amount of omega-3's that are found in ½ to 1½ pounds of fatty fish, you must eat 2 to 3 pounds of lean fish.

Selecting Fish for Freshness

No fish can match the quality of truly fresh fish, if you assign to *fresh* the meaning "just caught." Thanks to modern air freight, it is now possible for fish to arrive anywhere in the country within a short time. But no thanks to modern science, it may have been transported to shore in an ice bath infused with chemicals to maintain its freshness. Other preservative measures that may be used on fish include spraying with chlorine to inhibit bacterial growth, and dipping fillets in a weak polyphosphate or sodium phosphate solution "in order to seal in the juices." It is impossible to say how widespread these practices are since few fish purveyors seem to be aware of them or are willing to admit it. Only in California is the label required to reveal the use of phosphate dips.

In rating fish and fish products, consumer publications like *Consumer Reports* and industry magazines like *National Fishermen* have often had uncomplimentary things to say, the latter going so far as to report that "much of the fish sold in chainstores is not edible." This poor quality, however, is not attributed to the initial processor so much as to unsound retail practices. Common faults include the display of fish on open counters unprotected from flies, airborne microorganisms, and customer handling; warm spotlights that inadvertently heat the fish; and the intermingling of cooked and raw products.

At the market fresh fish should be in an enclosed case, preferably un-wrapped, and kept on ice or at 33°F. It should not be subjected to excessive heat from overhead lights or the sun.

Smell and appearance are still the only indication of quality in fish.

FATTY FISH

Ocean Varieties
Anchovies
Bluefish (spawn in fresh water)
Butterfish
Dogfish
Eel
Halibut, Greenland
Herring
Mackerel
Mullet
Pompano
Rainbow Trout (spawn in fresh water))
Redfish
Sable
Salmon (spawn in fresh water)
Sardines
Shad (spawn in fresh water)
Smelt
Sturgeon
Tuna
Whitefish

Freshwater Varieties
Brook Trout
Carp
Catfish
Chub
Eel
Lake Salmon
Lake Trout
Lake Whitefish

LEAN FISH

Ocean Varieties
Bonito
Cod
Flounder
Grouper
Haddock
Hake
Halibut, Pacific
Ling
Monkfish
Ocean Perch
Pollack
Porgie
Rockfish
Red Snapper
Scrod (a name applied to several types
   of lean fish)
Sea Bass
Sea Trout (spawn in fresh water)
Shark
Skate
Sole
Striped Bass (spawn in fresh water)
Swordfish
Tilefish
Turbot
Weakfish
Whiting (kingfish, silver hake)

Freshwater Varieties
Pike
Pickerel
Smelt
Yellow Perch
Yellow Bass
White Bass

Because of its delicate structure, fish spoils readily. A fresh fish never smells or tastes "fishy." Nor should it have an ammonia-like smell, except for a few esoteric varieties from the shark and skate families. It may, however, have a mild fresh aroma like sea water or seaweed.

If you buy a whole fish, or have an opportunity to see it whole make sure the eyes are clear and bulging, the gills intact and bright red, and the scales tight, bright, and shiny. The freshest fillets are a uniform light color and should actually be translucent. Fresh fish flesh is firm, compact, and springy; when you press it lightly with your finger, no indentation remains. If the flesh appears opaque, flakes apart when touched, or is yellowed along the cut surface, deterioration has begun.

Do not buy fish that was originally frozen and thawed prior to sale. Once defrosted, fish deteriorates rapidly.

The Food and Drug Administration has expressed some concern over vacuum-packed fish since botulism-causing bacteria spores which thrive in anaerobic conditions may produce toxins before the fish smells bad enough for consumers to recognize it is unacceptable. As a matter of fact, experts advise not buying any prewrapped fish.

Frozen "Fresh" Fish

Freezing masks all the visual signs for assessing freshness and makes it impossible to determine how old the fish really is. Moreover, frozen fish is never as tasty as its fresh counterpart. Freezing breaks down the delicate flesh and when it thaws it is mushy and rather tasteless. In addition to the loss of flavor, when you buy fish prefrozen you can't be sure how the fish was handled between the packer (assuming it was at its peak of freshness then) and the store.

If you do buy frozen fish, try to avoid added phosphates. Note, however, they may not always be listed on the label. Also make sure the fish is solidly frozen and that there is no frost on the package or tears in the wrapper. Have the store pack it in a freezer bag, and if it becomes soft on the way home, do not refreeze it, but simply change your menu to include fish that day.

Cuts of Fish

Fish is sold in the forms described below, all of them ready to cook and eat. As a buying guide, plan on ¾ to 1 pound per serving if you buy a whole fish, ½ pound per serving if you buy pan-dressed fish, and ⅓ pound per serving of fillets, steaks, or fish sticks.

Whole Fish: The fish may be just as it comes from the water, or it may be "drawn" (meaning the entrails have been removed).

Pan-Dressed: The fish has been scaled and freed from all viscera and blood, and the head, tail, and fins are usually removed.

Fillets: The meaty sides of the fish are cut lengthwise away from the backbone. The skin, with the scales removed, may be left on one side.

Steaks: Slices are cut crosswise from the whole fish with skin and scales removed. These come from larger fish, weighing over 4 pounds.

Fish Sticks: (Not to be confused with prepared frozen fish sticks.) Pieces are cut from fillets or steaks into fingers 1 inch wide and 3 inches long.

CONSUMER RESPONSIBILITY

As with meat and poultry, your responsibility doesn't end at the market when you buy fish. After careful selection, proper storage and preparation are the deciding factors in your family's attitude toward seafood.

Storage

As soon as you get fresh fish home, place it in its original wrapper or transferred to a covered dish in the coldest part of your refrigerator. Plan to use it the same day.

If there is a change in the menu and you won't be using the fish immediately, freeze it. Wrap it in moistureproof paper, as you would meat, and if you have several steaks or fillets, separate them with pieces of freezer paper. Fish can be kept solidly frozen at 0°F for one to two months.

Thawing Fish

There is usually no need to defrost fish before cooking unless you plan to bread it or stuff it. Just add ten minutes or so to the cooking time. If you must thaw it, place the wrapped package on the refrigerator shelf for three to four hours. Thawing at room temperature is risky; if fish stands for any length of time once it's defrosted, it will begin to decay. Cook the fish as soon as it's thawed. And remember, never expect frozen fish to be as juicy or delicate as fresh.

Cooking Fish

To destroy any harmful organisms in fish it should be thoroughly cooked. The test of doneness is still cooking until it flakes when probed with a fork. In actual practice, all parts of the fish should reach 145°F. for at least 5 minutes. In the oven this translates to 13 minutes per inch of thickness at 450°F., rather than the old rule of 10 minutes.

SHELLFISH

There are two principal classifications of shellfish: *mollusks* (the soft-bodied, hard-shelled creatures of the sea such as clams, mussels, oysters, scallops, squid, snails, and slugs) and *crustaceans* (the firmer fleshed, horny-shelled, limbed creatures such as lobsters, shrimp, prawns, and crab). Most of these are prized as delicacies by their fans and criticized by health authorities who claim they are high in cholesterol and crawling with pathogens.

Cholesterol in Shellfish

Shellfish have been associated en masse with cholesterol and are often eliminated from diets aimed at controlling heart disease. To present a fairer picture, these seafoods should be viewed individually, for some, like clams, scallops, oysters, and mussels are really quite low in cholesterol. Even the shrimp, lobster, and crab that are shunned by cholesterol counters are on par with poultry and many meats. This, of course, assumes you eat these foods without the melted butter that so often adorns them.

More important, though, these shellfish are much lower in fat than land animals, and the fats they do contain are rich in the omega-3's we discussed earlier in the chapter, which are thought to reduce blood cholesterol levels.

Contamination in Shellfish

The singing legend of Sweet Molly Malone was a childhood favorite in Nikki's home. It is the tale of a young fishmonger who wandered the streets of Dublin selling cockles and mussels. "She died of a fever, and no one could save her," the song goes, but few people who sing this line (as well as the victim herself) probably are aware of the origins of her illness. It is not hard to guess—it was her contaminated shellfish.

Certain shellfish, primarily mollusks, are notorious for their capacity to survive in sewage-polluted waters. Whatever contaminants are in the water are sure to get inside their shells, and usually at higher concentrations; the level of harmful bacteria in their meat can be three to twenty times that of the water they dwell in. Perhaps this is some form of revenge against their human predators, for the organisms that cause cholera, hepatitis, gastroenteritis, and a host of other diseases in humans accumulate in these marine animals with no apparent ill effect to them.

One of the most toxic organisms that infect shellfish are dinoflagellates, creatures that are so tiny they cannot be seen until they "bloom" in such large numbers that they color the water, creating "red tides." Actually, red tides may be caused by other organisms as well, but when dinoflagellates are involved, anyone eating the shellfish can contract paralytic shellfish poisoning (PSP)—an illness that begins within thirty minutes of ingestion and progresses from tingling of the lips, gums, tongue, and face to muscular weakening, paralysis, and sometimes fatal respiratory failure. Unfortunately, shellfish can be toxic without the red tide becoming visible. Luckily, scientific equipment can detect low levels of the toxin-producers in water, which is why shellfish should only be taken from approved areas.

Selecting Safe Shellfish

Oysters, clams, and mussels taken from state-certified waters provide some assurance of an untainted product. In order to be shipped interstate, all packaged fresh or frozen oysters, clams, and mussels must be tagged. Dockside buyers, shippers, shuckers, and repackers must keep records so that any outbreak of food poisoning can be traced back to the source. This record-keeping chain sometimes works as intended, but often fails because diggers tags fall off and lots are often mixed to fill customers' orders. Professional diggers and shippers are now making an effort to develop safety measures of their own to protect their image. Buying from an established retail outlet will help guarantee that the seafood has come from safe waters; roadside sellers may not be so selective.

Interestingly, shellfish from "mildly polluted" waters can be harvested and treated to remove pollutants. As you may have guessed, there is no way to know that this has been done.

CLAMS, OYSTERS, AND MUSSELS

There seems to be some wisdom to the admonition about eating clams and oysters only in months with an R in them, which means the colder months. When waters are cold, levels of bacteria tend to fall. Also, cold water diminishes the appetites of many mollusks and so they accumulate fewer pathogens.

Clams, oysters, and mussels should be alive when purchased, which means the shells will be firmly sealed or will shut immediately when touched. They will open easily once they are cooked. If it is necessary to keep them for a few hours before cooking, store them in the coldest part of the refrigerator on a bed of ice or cover with a damp cloth and place them in a leakproof dish that allows air to flow.

Raw clams and oysters may be your idea of a seductive meal, but it can turn out to be a sickening one. Most illnesses associated with shellfish come from eating the food raw. Even if it is certified as clean this only means it is free from coliform bacteria, but not other disease-causing organisms. At the least these shellfish should be steamed for six minutes. The taste of steamed shellfish is close to raw if you can learn to like your clams and oysters on the rubbery side. Note, however, that even this is not a guarantee of safety since only very high heat will destroy the hepatitis A virus and no amount of cooking will completely deactivate the toxins that cause paralytic shellfish poisoning.

SCALLOPS

Scallops are already removed from the shell when they reach the store. Bay scallops, a rare (not available in the summer) and expensive delicacy, are small and pinkish. The sea scallop, a larger, meaty, white version, is found in markets year-round. Fresh scallops should have no odor. Frozen scallops are more common than fresh.

LOBSTER AND CRAB

Lobsters and crabs may have an exotic reputation, but these scavengers have the unappealing habit of feeding off the waste of other underwater creatures.

Lobsters and crabs should be alive when you buy them and cooked within the next few hours. When you get lobsters or crabs home place them on top of ice that is covered with several layers of heavy paper. The object is to keep them alive right up to preparation. With crustaceans, you can't escape having to do your own butchering. Lobsters and hardshell crabs will die shortly after you plunge them into the boiling cooking water. Soft shell crabs should be killed by piercing them with a sharp knife between the eyes just prior to preparation.

SHRIMP

Shrimp are the most frequently chosen shellfish; according to an estimate in *Forbes* magazine, by the end of the '80s the annual *American* consumption of shrimp could equal the entire current world supply.

In *The Supermarket Handbook* we stressed a strong preference for fresh, as opposed to frozen, shrimp. We were later informed by a reader in the fish business that shrimp is always frozen before you get it. If it appears fresh in its shell, she explained, it has been defrosted by the purveyor. The same is true of "fresh" shrimp that is peeled and deveined. According to the National Fisheries Institute, this is indeed the situation unless you are fortunate enough to live along the coast.

To prevent shrimp from developing "black spot," a discoloration that occurs naturally as they lose their freshness, they are often sprayed with sulfites shortly after harvest. This is routine on shrimp boats that stay out for more than a day, and accounts for about 60 percent of the domestic haul. The FDA permits sulfite residues on shrimp up to 100 ppm (parts per million). Since sulfite residues in excess of 10 ppm must now be declared on all foods, you will at least be apprised of this practice. Of course, if you buy loose shrimp at the market where it has not had a label affixed to it, this information may not be apparent.

SQUID

Squid are rather odd multiarmed creatures that belong to a high order of mollusks, along with cuttlefish and octopus. They sometimes go by their Italian name, calamari. If you are lucky, the job of cleaning the squid will have been done by the seller. If not, you will have to cut out the backbone and reach in to remove the ink sack inside. (This is a bag of fluid which squid spray when danger is near.) If the ink sack is intact, you may want to squeeze some of this black liquid into a dish to use, as Italian chefs do, to add color and flavor to a rice (risotto) or pasta dish.

In buying fresh, cleaned squid, look for firm specimens with a translucent, milky-white flesh and a fresh, sweet smell. The best squid have their purplish skin intact, but these are hard to find.

PREPARED FRESH FISH

Many stores offer precooked fish dishes ready to take home and eat. These come in a variety of forms including stuffed baked fish, fish pancakes, fish balls, breaded fillets and sticks, and more. Unless they are eaten immediately, which means just after cooking, the risk of ingesting harmful bacteria is high. Cooked fish items that are not displayed in a refrigerator case should never be bought (or sold). Unfrozen cooked fish that is offered for sale more than one day after preparation is not edible.

This advice carries over to precooked shellfish and all seafood salads. These items have a refrigerator shelf-life of just a few days and cannot be frozen. It is also important that if these foods are displayed in a case alongside raw fish, they have no physical contact with each other; the transfer of bacteria from the raw to the cooked product can make you ill.

PROCESSED FISH
AND SHELLFISH PRODUCTS

By using fish trimmings and presently under-utilized species, the processing of fresh fish into canned and frozen fish products can make inexpensive protein more available. Unfortunately, most often when fish is fashioned into fish spreads, cakes, croquettes, balls, loaves, breaded or battered sticks and fillets, casseroles, and such, it is compromised by some unwanted additives, refined ingredients, and a good deal of salt.

Processed Frozen Fish Products

Fresh fish, even saltwater varieties, are naturally low in sodium, but once they are processed the reverse is true. For example, while fresh broiled cod contains 110 milligrams of sodium per 3.5 ounces, most breaded or battered frozen cod fillets hit the 800-milligram mark; those packaged in sauce average 400 milligrams.

The addition of phosphate compounds to help retain moisture and texture in frozen fish products is also objectionable since the American diet is generally overloaded with phosphorus. This may have an adverse effect on calcium absorption, which can later be reflected in the integrity of our bones.

Ironically, items that are fried, by far the most popular variety, add the kind of fat to the diet that most fish eaters want to avoid.

Most of the bad news is on the label for you to read. Generally you will be overpaying for enriched wheat (white) flour, water, modified cornstarch, sugar, dextrose, salt, partially hydrogenated oil, whey, malt, egg solids, leavening, MSG, natural and artificial flavor, spice, dough conditioners, sodium aluminosilicate, methylcellulose, TBHQ (preservative), calcium propionate (preservative), sodium tripolyphosphate (to retain moisture), and caramel color; many of these ingredients even appear in products marketed as "natural."

In addition to what appears on the label, you will also have to contend with what does not. In making fish sticks, fish cakes, and similar deboned minced fish products, the trimmings from fillets are often used. To amass the amount needed, this deboned flesh may be frozen for later use. When this occurs the fish is subject to thawing and refreezing. This facilitates bacterial growth, results in some loss of protein quality and, most important, accelerates rancidity in the fish, which is harmful to both your health and your eating enjoyment. Even "fillets" are often twice frozen, for much of the fish used in American processing plants originates on foreign shores. In this case, the fresh-caught fish is first cleaned, sectioned, and frozen in large blocks, and then later power-sawed into portions, breaded or sauced, partially cooked, and refrozen. By the time it gets to the store it is a long way—and a long time—from the sea.

The coating on breaded fish generally accounts for 30 to 40 percent of the weight of the product, and can go as high as 60 percent. Even "light" breaded fish gets at least 20 percent of its weight from the breading component. When a batter coating is used, it is likely to account for 54 to 68 percent of the final weight. When frozen in sauce, fish accounts for only 52 to 67 percent of the contents.

The situation for shrimp is equally as bad. The recipe for this product is based on a government standard which allows the processor to include only 50 percent shrimp in the package—they might just as well call it "Shrimped Bread." Even the "Lightly Breaded" variety is only 65 percent shrimp.

As a result of all this manipulation, what is supposed to be a high-protein, low-fat, low-calorie food often has its protein reduced by a third, its calories increased 75 percent, and its fat content tripled as shown in the following comparison:

FRESH COOKED VERSUS PROCESSED FISH

Fish 3.5 ounces	Calories	Protein grams	Fat grams	Sodium mgs.
Fresh broiled cod	170	28.5	5	110
Gorton's Batter Fried Fish Fillets	275	8.4	17	805

Smoked Fish

The smoking of fish is costly in several different ways. First, there is the price, which can easily range from $15 to $50 a pound for such delicacies as smoked salmon or sable. Then, there is the problem smoked foods pose in the diet. Carcinogenic nitrosamines have been detected in smoked fish. This hazard is compounded when the fish is cured with nitrites, as smoked salmon (lox) frequently is. Because smoked fish are more often an unlabeled "deli" purchase than a packaged product, you may not be aware of the chemicals that are added. Smoked fish also tends to be high in sodium.

Simulated Seafood

The name *surimi* might not be familiar, but if you think you've gotten a bargain at the fish store because the inexpensive seafood salad you purchased had such big chunks of crab meat, chances are you've tasted it. Surimi is a processed fish product that dates back to twelfth-century Japan when fishermen discovered that by steaming or broiling a seasoned fish paste it could be kept longer than the fresh fish. Surely these ancient "food technologists" never imagined this simple invention would later be flavored, colored, and shaped to look like crab, shrimp, lobster, scallops, or other seafood.

Surimi is made from white-fleshed fish like cod or pollack which is mechanically deboned and washed to a clear, odorless pulp. Next sugar, salt, potassium sorbate, MSG, and starch may be added. Then the entire mixture is formed into blocks and frozen. Later, this surimi paste can be flavored, colored, textured, and shaped by extrusion, fiber spinning, weaving, heat injection molding, or a similar technology depending on what fake product it will be used for.

As you might suspect, the severe washing, dilution with starches and water, and high-technology shaping result in a product that is nutritionally inferior to both the original fish it is made from and the one it mimics. It is also a good deal saltier.

If you are looking for crab legs in the fresh fish case, be sure to read the label carefully or you may end up with "Imitation Crab Meat Seafood Sticks," a blend of "pacific pollack, wheat flour, potato starch, salt, crab extract, and artificial color." If you purchase a packaged surimi product, it will probably go by some fanciful name like "Sea Tails," "Sea Stix," "King Krab," or something similarly suggestive but nonspecific. It may go on to explain the product as "a unique seafood blend of white fish and king crab." As revealed in smaller print in the list of ingredients, this "unique blend" also contains egg white, potato starch, sugar, sorbitol, natural and artificial flavor, cornstarch, egg yolk, artificial color, sodium pyrophosphate, and salt (to the tune of 720 milligrams of sodium per 4-ounce serving). If you shop at the deli counter, you may get surimi in your seafood salad and be none the wiser; there is no requirement in most states that you be informed, and unless you are sensitive enough to notice that its dense, gelatin-like consistency is too uniform and too smooth to be true, even eating won't tell you.

Because surimi itself has no color, taste or odor, it is likely to appear in the future in other forms. The Japanese have been making surimi hot dogs in the image of American ball park franks for years.

Canned Fish

The heat of canning is destructive to protein, vitamins, and minerals, but in terms of additives, canned fish fare better than other processed fish products. One problem unique to canned seafoods, however, is the formation of mineral crystals (called struvites) in the fish after processing. These glassy-looking crystals are not harmful, but they do detract from the appearance. To prevent their formation, pyrophosphates, compounded with sodium, may find their way into the can. This shows up on the label and we do not recommend products that employ this additive.

Fish oil may be desirable in the diet, but the addition of more fat from the vegetable oils canned fish are frequently packed in may not be so welcome. We do not reject canned fish products because of this, but you may find it is preferable to select items packed in water, broth, or a similar low-fat medium.

While salt is a common additive in canned fish products, some progressive companies have begun to offer salt-free alternatives or have cut back on this ingredient by as much as 50 to 60 percent. Usually this is promoted on the label.

The can itself is probably the worst part of this product. A report in *Science* magazine on the extent of lead in our environment cites lead-soldered cans as one vehicle of exposure. Comparing fresh tuna to tuna packed in unsoldered cans, the investigators found a 20-fold increase in lead; with lead-soldered cans there was a 4,000-fold increase! (For information on lead-free cans, see page 36.)

ANCHOVIES

Anchovies are tiny fish of the herring family that are salted or pickled and acked in oil. They are very salty, but used with a light hand, anchovies can dd zip to salads, homemade pizza, sauces, and egg dishes. The best brands re those imported from Spain and Portugal that feature the flat or rolled illets in a bath of salt and olive oil.

HERRING

The most common way you'll find herring in this country is salted, ickled, or smoked, dressed with a sauce, and packed in a jar. As you can ee from their labels, pickled herring in sour cream almost always has a enzoate and/or sorbate preservative, as do some of the vinegar- or wine-reserved items. A few brands of "Lunch Herring," "Party Snacks," and ther forms of herring in wine sauce do come chemical-free, but they usually contain sugar. When these products are sold unpacked, delicatessen-style, he ingredients are usually identical to the jarred product although they lack a label to inform you.

Herring also comes in a can, where it may be referred to as "fish steaks" or kippers (which are smoked herring fillets). These canned herring products are packed in soybean or sild oil and again can be quite salty.

SALMON

The federal Standard of Identity allows canned salmon to be packed in one of several forms.

Plain salmon consists of steaks from which some skin and the large backbone may be removed; however, small portions of the bone remain and melt into the flesh during the heat processing. This elevates the calcium content, making 3 ounces of canned salmon just about on a par with an 8-ounce glass of milk. (This varies somewhat with the variety, with sockeye the highest in calcium, followed closely by coho and chum, then pink, and finally chinook, with about 60 percent of sockeye's calcium value.)

Skinless and boneless salmon, declared as such on the label, is free of skin and bones and thus has a lower mineral value. *Minced salmon* and *salmon tips* or *tidbits* refer to products made from these smaller fragments.

Most of the popular brands of canned salmon contain salt, contributing from 772 milligrams of sodium for a 7¾-ounce can of coho to a high of 1,148 milligrams for an equal portion of sockeye. The unsalted product contains 90 to 140 milligrams of sodium. An occasional brand will be packed in salmon oil, and a new test-market product comes chunk style, like tuna, packed in water.

The species of salmon used appears as part of the name on the label. The visible differences in color and sensory quality of the flesh are also reflected in their nutritional composition. The deeper colored salmons are highest in fat content and therefore contain more omega-3 fatty acids and calories.

They are also the most expensive varieties. In terms of use, all types are interchangeable.

Chinook or *king* is the by far the richest in oil (even though its color ranges from deep salmon to almost white). Its canned flesh breaks into lovely large chunks. *Sockeye, blueback*, or *red salmon* is deeply colored firm textured, and breaks into medium-size pieces. It ranks behind chinook in fat. *Coho* is lighter than sockeye, but still has a rich salmon color. Its flesh also breaks up into nice size flakes. *Pink salmon* has a paler colored flesh and correspondingly less oil. *Chum* is the palest, least oily, and least expensive

SARDINES

Sardines do not refer to any specific species, but rather to fish that are very small. *Natural sardines* come packed in salted or unsalted brine with nothing else added; in oil (olive, soybean, or sild oil), which sometimes has added seasonings; in tomato sauce (which may contain cellulose gum); and in mustard sauce.

The presence of bone in canned sardines accounts for the fact that there is as much calcium in a typical 3¾-ounce can of the fish as there is in 10 ounces of milk. Unless the sardines are unsalted, however, this is accompanied by more than 500 milligrams of sodium.

Chunk light sardines, another form of sardine on the market, is prepared from the little-known pilchard fish found mainly in Peru. Packed "tuna style" in water and salt, this item is more economically priced than tuna, which it is said to resemble. Since pilchard, unlike tuna, does not swim with dolphins (see "The Tuna Dilemma," page 281), this product does not raise moral conflicts for those who draw specific lines about which animals to consume and which warrant protection.

SHRIMP

Canned shrimp is permitted by its Standard of Identity to contain water, salt, lemon juice, acids, sweetening, flavoring, sodium bisulfite, and calcium disodium EDTA. All ingredients are required to appear on the label. The presence of sweetening, sulfites, and EDTA seems to be unwarranted since several companies appear to offer a product with only shrimp, water, and salt.

TUNA

One of canned tuna's biggest selling points is that it doesn't taste "fishy" and it comes packaged free of scales and fins so that it doesn't seem so much like fish. Recently, there has been a big change in how tuna is packaged. In 1979, about 60 percent of canned tuna came bathed in oil. Today, more than two-thirds of tuna sales are for the water-packed variety. The savings is about 135 calories per one half can (6.5-ounce size). (By draining the oil from an oil-packed can you can pour off 60 calories.) The move to water-pack tuna has unfortunately dealt a major blow to the U.S. tuna industry, which traditionally has used oil; most water-packed tuna comes from Thailand, Japan, Taiwan, and the Philippines.

THE TUNA DILEMMA

Dolphins frequently swim with the yellow fin variety of tuna, the prize light meat catch, and thus become innocent victims of tuna fishing. This has created a moral dilemma for many. The Marine Mammal Protection Act, passed in 1972, has helped to curtail the slaughter of dolphins, but regulates only American fleets. Since some countries have more lax attitudes than others concerning the hunting of marine mammals, a bill has been proposed in Congress to require the labeling of country of origin on products so that consumers who might want to select their canned fish based on moral issues can do so.

While American fishermen are forced by the law to be more selective, it seems only white albacore tuna is caught dolphin-free. The Friends of Animals recommends boycotting all tuna (and salmon) to put pressure on industry to ban the use of nets in favor of "long-lining," which protects the dolphins. Increased consumption of tuna, by the way, is not only endangering the dolphins; it is also accelerating the extinction of two tuna species, the yellow fin and the blue fish.

To further complicate selection, white tuna, especially in the solid-pack form, is the most likely to contain pyrophosphates to inhibit crystal formation. Other objectionable things to watch for in the list of ingredients for all forms of tuna (solid, chunk, flake, or grated) are partially hydrogenated oils, MSG, hydrolyzed protein, and smoking of the fish prior to packing. Also watch out for tuna with xanthan gum added, as this product is being test-marketed.

LOW-SODIUM TUNA

The American tuna industry has gone after the low-sodium shopper, offering the product in oil or water with 50 to 60 percent less salt. (Regular tuna averages 850 to 1,000 milligrams of sodium in a 6½-ounce can.) An even rarer find is tuna to which no salt at all is added (for a sodium value of about 100 milligrams or less per 6½ ounces). In addition to not preserving the freshly caught tuna in a saltwater brine, processors have had to be more selective in choosing the fish, since some tuna species have a naturally higher sodium content. Lower sodium tuna are all light-meat species. This presents a problem for those who are both health conscious and humanitarian, since, as we mentioned, most light tuna varieties including bluefin, yellow fin, and skijack school with dolphins. Only the white albacore reportedly does not.

For the privilege of buying a reduced-sodium tuna, the manufacturer will assess you 40 cents or more a can. If this offends you or you cannot find a low-sodium product that otherwise meets your standards, you will be happy to learn that simply draining either oil- or water-packed tuna will reduce sodium by 15 percent and, according to researchers at Duke University Medical Center, a three-minute rinse under the faucet will wash 80 percent of the sodium off the regular water-packed product. The only nutritional disadvantage we have seen documented is the loss of nearly half the calcium (of which tuna a not a good source anyway). However, it is probable that other water-soluble nutrients, like the B vitamins that are prevalent in tuna, could also be diminished by this washing.

MOCK TUNA

If you wish to protect dolphins, in addition to pilchard, try bonito, a relative of tuna and similarly packaged in oil, vegetable broth, and salt. Be sure to consult the label for undesirable seasoning ingredients such as hydrolyzed protein and MSG.

OTHER CANNED FISH PRODUCTS

A variety of other canned fish products appear somewhat sporadically on the market. These include:

■ Clams with or without their shells, in water and/or clam juice, salt, and sometimes citric acid. A specialty product of smoked baby clams in oil is also available, as are similarly packed smoked mussels.

■ Fish flakes consisting of cod, haddock, hake, and salt.

■ Salted rainbow trout fillets packed in water.

■ Crab meat in water, salt, and citric or ascorbic acid, which are almost always added to preserve color and are not especially objectionable. Less attractive is the use of aluminum sulfate and EDTA.

■ Octopus and cuttlefish (close relatives of squid) in its own ink, plus oil, salt, and seasonings.

■ Smoked frog legs in oil and salt.

■ Jack mackerel in water and salt, or fillets of mackerel in oil and salt.

■ Caviar (fish roe), which generally is not canned, but jarred. Be sure to read the label here as some caviar, whether red (salmon), black (sturgeon), or golden (whitefish), have added coloring. Other additives to watch for on the label include gum thickeners and sodium benzoate as preservative.

■ Canned fish balls consisting of haddock and/or cod prepared with potato starch, salt, spices, and perhaps milk.

RECOMMENDATIONS

FRESH FISH

General Rule of Purchase: Look for fresh, unfrozen fish, preferably salt-water varieties (see listing on page 269).

Farmed fish can sometimes be identified by the words "grain fed," "farm raised," and "farm grown" on the label. Although they may have fewer environmental pollutants, you may want to avoid them if you are concerned with the routine use of hormones, medicated food, etc., in raising them.

Frozen fish is less attractive, but at least it can be additive-free. Avoid brands that contain phosphates in the list of ingredients. Choose only those that are solidly frozen, without frost or package defects.

SHELLFISH

General Rule of Purchase: Look for lobster, crab, clams, oysters, and mussels that are alive on purchase. Buy only from reputable sellers, particularly when it comes to oysters, clams, and mussels; tagged offerings provide some assurance of hygiene.

Shrimp have at one time been frozen, unless you are buying them along the coast. You may want to avoid shrimp (and lobster) that have been bathed in sulfites; new regulations require that this be indicated to the consumer.

Scallops are usually frozen, but fresh are available.

PREPARED FRESH FISH AND SHELLFISH

General Rule of Purchase: Avoid precooked fish or seafood unless you know it is freshly made or was chilled immediately after preparation. Do not buy any product that is more than one day old.

PROCESSED FROZEN FISH AND SHELLFISH

General Rule of Purchase: Avoid frozen fish and shellfish products unless the label reads like a wholefoods recipe. All ingredients are on the label.

Even in products that declare themselves "100% natural, no additives, no preservatives," you may want to avoid refined flour, sugar, dextrose, cornstarch, oils, salt. In the more contrived products you will also want to watch for dough conditioners, phosphates, MSG, partially hydrogenated oil, sodium aluminosilicate, methylcellulose, and preservatives like calcium propionate and TBHQ.

SMOKED FISH

General Rule of Purchase: Smoked fish does not always reveal ingredients since it is often sold from a fish or deli case rather than in packaged form. Assume that smoked fish contains nitrates or nitrites unless you are otherwise informed. (Remember, smoking itself is a controversial process you may wish to avoid.)

CANNED FISH

General Rule of Purchase: When buying canned fish, give preference to those packed in water and with reduced sodium. All ingredients are given on the label. Check to avoid phosphates, gums, benzoate preservatives, sulfites, disodium EDTA, MSG, hydrolyzed protein, and partially hydrogenated oils.

Exemplary Brands

Anchovies:
Those packed in olive oil are preferred.

Most brands are similar.

Bonito:
Avoid those with MSG and hydrolyzed protein. All brands contain salt.

Coop Chunk Light Bonito
Eatwell Bonito Chunks

Clams:
Should contain only water and/or clam juice, salt, and sometimes citric acid.

All brands are similar.

Crab:
Acceptable brands contain salt, water, and sometimes citric or ascorbic acid. Avoid those with EDTA or aluminum sulfate.

Geisha Snow Crabmeat
S & W Fancy Dungeness Crab
Wakefield Snow Crabmeat, Snow Crabmeat with Shrimp

Fish Roe:
Avoid those with added coloring, gums, and preservatives.

Romanoff Red Salmon, Golden Whitefish Caviars

Herring:
Avoid sorbate preservatives, always found in Herring in Cream Sauce, sometimes in other styles as well. The following brands are chemical-free, but do contain sugar.

Dak Marina Lunch Herring,[3] Herring and Dill,[3] Marinated Herring Fillets,[3] Herring in Sherry[3]
Ma Cohen's Lunch Herring,[3] Party Snacks[3]
Montrose Herring in Wine Sauce[3]
Nathan's Herring Tasti Tidbits,[3] Old Fashioned Herring[3]
Noon Hour Imported Fillets of Herring in Wine Sauce[3]

Jack Mackerel:
Should contain salt and water only.

All brands are similar.

Oysters:

All brands are similar; contain salt and water only.

Salmon:

All brands are similar except those that are prepared without salt or the occasional brand with added salmon oil.

The following have no salt:
Featherweight Salmon
Nutradiet Red Sockeye, Fancy Blueback Salmons

Sardines:

A variety of packing mediums may be used, and except for the occasional presence of cellulose gum in those packed in tomato sauce, all appear to be additive-free.
Unsalted sardines are available as follows:
King Oscar Sardines in Water—No Salt Added
Lillie Skinless and Boneless Sardines in Water—No Salt

Roland Skinless and Boneless; Portuguese Sardines—in Water-Low Sodium
Season Sardines in Norwegian Sild Sardine Oil—No Salt Added, Sardines in Water—No Salt Added, Sardines in Soy Oil—No Salt Added

Shrimp:

Avoid sweetening, sulfites, and EDTA. An acceptable brand contains only salt, water, and sometimes citric acid.

Duet Tiny Shrimp
Marvelous Deveined Shrimp, Regular Pack Shrimp
S & W Deveined Small Size Whole Shrimp
Treasure Bay Shrimp

Tuna:

Avoid partially hydrogenated oils, phosphate compounds, MSG, hydrolyzed protein, and xanthan gum.
3 Diamond Chunk Light Tuna in Water
A&P Chunk Light Tuna in Oil, in Water
Acme Chunk Light Tuna in Oil, in Water
Albertson's Chunk Light Tuna in Oil, in Water
Alpha Beta Chunk Light Tuna in Oil
Blue Bay Chunk Light Tuna in Oil, in Water
Bonnie Hubbard Chunk Light Tuna in Water
Chicken of the Sea 50% Less Salt Chunk Light Tuna in Oil, Chunk Light Tuna in Water
Coop Chunk Light Tuna in Water—Regular and Unsalted; Light Tuna Packed in Vegetable Oil
Cottage Grated Light Tuna
Deep Sea Chunk Light Tuna in Water—Seasalted and Unsalted
Double Q Chunk Light Tuna in Oil, in Water
Econobuy Chunk Light Tuna in Water
Empress Chunk Light Tuna in Water

Featherweight Light Tuna Chunks—Water Pack, No Salt
Flav-O-Rite Chunk Light Tuna in Oil, in Water
Food Club Chunk Style Light Tuna in Oil
Foodworld Chunk Light Tuna in Oil, in Water
Frazier Farms Chunk Light Tuna in Water
Geisha Chunk Light Tuna in Water
Genova Tonno
Giant Chunk Light Tuna in Oil, in Water
Golden Harvest Chunk Light Tuna in Water—No Salt
Grand Union Chunk White Tuna in Oil
Halfhill's Chunk Light Tuna in Water
Health Valley Best of Seafood Fancy Albacore Solid White Tuna in Water—Unsalted, Chunk Light Tuna in Water
Jewel Chunk Light Tuna in Oil, in Water
King Tuna Light Meat Chunk Style in Water
Kroger Chunk Light Tuna in Oil, in Water
Lady Lee Chunk Light Tuna in Oil, in Water
Mega Chunk Light Tuna in Water
My-Te-Fine Chunk Light Tuna in Oil, Water Pack

Tuna (continued):

National Chunk Light Tuna in Oil, in Water
Ocean Crest Chunk Light Tuna in Water
Our Pride Chunk Light Tuna
Pacific Crest Chunk Light Tuna in Water
Parade Chunk Light Tuna in Oil, in Water
Pathmark Chunk Light Tuna in Oil, in Water
Piggly Wiggly Chunk Light Tuna in Oil, in Water
Ralph's Chunk Light Tuna in Water

Richfood Chunk Light Tuna in Oil, in Water
S & W Fancy Solid White Albacore Tuna
Scotch Buy Chunk Light Tuna in Water
Staff Chunk Light Tuna in Oil, in Water
Star Kist Chunk Light Tuna in Oil, in Spring Water, Select Tuna in Oil, in Spring Water
Von's Chunk Light Tuna in Water
Waldbaum's Chunk Light Tuna in Water
Western Family Chunk Light Tuna in Oil

Other Fish Products

Beach Cliff Fish Steaks
Beaver Fish Flakes
Clear Springs Rainbow Trout
Crown Prince Chunk Light Sardines Tuna Style
Danny Boy Chunk Style Pilchard in Water
Geisha Good and Chunky Chunk Pacific Sardines in Water

Goya Cuttle Fish in Its Ink; Octopus in Olive Oil, in Garlic Sauce
Iceland Waters Fish Balls
KAME Smoked Hind Frog Legs
La Monica Scungilli
Napoleon Fish Balls in Fish Bouillon
Orlando Calamari
Zesterlands Fish Balls in Their Own Juice

[3]Contains refined sweeteners

Chapter 20

Looking for Oil

Our Paleolithic ancestors were migrant hunter-gatherers whose intake of fat was indirect, consumed in meat and seeds. With the domestication of animals and the rise of agriculture came ways to obtain fats and oils as separate entities. The rendering of fat from meat, the pressing of oil from seeds or fruit (olive and palm), and the concentration of fats from milk for butter represented a new level of culinary potential. Gradually, as technology and the Industrial Revolution infiltrated the food-processing industry, new techniques were discovered for producing concentrated fats with a long shelf-life and great commercial versatility.

In the last seventy years the average per capita consumption of fats has risen 30 percent, an increase brought about by changes in meat and dairy consumption, as well as by the direct ingestion of processed fats in the form of margarine, lard, butter, vegetable oils, and the like. In this same period, the consumption of chemically modified fats—that is, products such as margarine and plasticized shortening that employ hydrogenated oils—has tripled. These figures represent a major alteration in the makeup of the American diet, and one that all health authorities believe we should be concerned about.

NUTRITIONAL FACTS ABOUT FAT

Surveys indicate that on an average the typical American diet derives 35 to 40 percent of its calories from fat, although these figures often go as high as 45 or even 50 percent. In a 2800-calorie diet, this comes out to 110 to 155 grams of fat daily (1 gram of fat furnishes 9 calories). While it is not known what the optimal amount of fat in the diet is, 15 to 25 grams a day is believed to satisfy human needs.

In spite of its negative associations, fat does play an important role in human nutrition. In addition to providing energy, fat prolongs digestion, contributing to a feeling of fullness, adds palatability to foods, acts as a carrier for the fat-soluble vitamins A, D, E, and K, and furnishes essential fatty acids like linoleic and linolenic acids and possibly the omega-3's that are necessary for life and growth. Other components of fat such as lecithin, cholesterol, phytosterols, chlorophyll, and a host of other fatty acids also play important roles, but much less emphasis has been put on this.

Saturated Versus Unsaturated Fats

For years the public has been bombarded by the message that polyunsaturated oils (most vegetable oils) are healthy alternatives to animal fats. More recently, the monounsaturates like those in olive and peanut oils have been praised. No wonder so many people are confused.

Saturated, monounsaturated, and polyunsaturated are technical terms used to classify fats according to their structure. These designations relate to the number of hydrogen atoms in the fat and the bonds or available openings ("sites") that exist between the hydrogen and the carbon atoms in the fat. In a saturated fat the carbon sites are all filled up. Animal fats are largely saturated and this causes them to be solid at room temperature.

In a monounsaturated fat, only one site is open for hydrogen atoms. In a polyunsaturated fat, more that one site is open. Monounsaturated and polyunsaturated fats are both referred to as unsaturated and are liquid at room temperature.

These different forms of fat have various implications for health, but most of the studies that have been done are not definitive and thus the subject produces considerable controversy. At present, saturated fats are believed to harm the circulatory system, while unsaturated fats are thought to have little ill effect in terms of heart disease, and possibly some benefits. Unfortunately, this is not the end of the story since some scientists are concerned that the nature of polyunsaturated fats makes them highly reactive which could cause them to oxidize and form carcinogenic compounds.

Before we go any further we wish to stress that most of the information on fat and health is inconclusive and that is why we recommend you be moderate in your use of fat in all three of these naturally occurring forms.

Concentrated Fat as Food

Fats do not exist in an isolated form naturally and thus the concentrated fats we use—butter, lard, and oil—must be extracted from the wholefoods to which they are bound. Butter is produced from cream by agitation, or churning, which causes the fat to come together in clumps. Lard is rendered from animal tissues with the use of heat. Vegetable oils are separated from the seed, nut, or fruit pulp by pressing or with chemical solvents. The principal edible vegetable oil seeds are soy, corn, peanut, cottonseed, sunflower, coconut, palm kernel, and to a lesser extent safflower, sesame, and rapeseed. Olive and palm oils are derived from the fruit pulp itself. These vegetable oils will be the focal point of the remainder of this chapter. Butter and lard will be discussed in the following chapter.

OIL PROCESSING

When we consume a wholefood, for example peanuts, we receive not only the fat it contains, but many complementary nutrients. But over time people learned to segregate the oil portion and use this concentrated fat to enhance other foods, much as they did with sugar. Although sugar is often used as a symbol of our perverted food system, fat is an equal culprit and, in fact, it may be even more seductive. Research has disclosed that despite our well-known national sweet tooth, most subjects fed a mixture of sugar and cream rejected it as too sweet at a level of just 10 percent sugar. But when the fat was raised to 50 percent or more, the product was still judged to be tasty. This may account for the vast use of fats by the processed food industry.

Extracted oils spoil easily. This limits their commercial use, so to accommodate the needs of large-scale producers and the manufacturers of processed foods they generally undergo significant alteration before and after extraction. This manipulation begins at the source. Rather than relying on traditional varieties of oil-bearing plants, breeders have developed new strains that are high in more stable, but less healthful fatty acids.

Although the specifics of manufacture vary somewhat with the oil, the basic steps can be summarized for them all: extraction, refining, bleaching, and deodorizing. During this processing, valuable nutrients are lost and many chemical agents are involved.

Hydrogenation

The oil that is produced after all this handling is likely to be highly reactive and unstable. To counteract this, processing begets more processing and the polyunsaturated oil may be converted to a more stable (and more saturated fat) by hydrogenation. In the process, fatty compounds are created that are biochemically unique (that is, man-made), making hydrogenated oils the least natural fats available. Ominously, scientists still lack a complete understanding of the effects of this technology on the body. (For further information see "Hydrogenation," pages 297 of the next chapter.)

With all the emphasis that has been placed on polyunsaturated fats, it is surprising to learn how much oil is subject to this artificial saturation. If you read labels, you will realize that the food industry relies heavily on this technology, evidenced by the terms *hydrogenated* or *partially hydrogenated* preceding the specific oil in the list of ingredients for many foods. The production of margarine and solid vegetable shortenings would be impossible without it.

UNREFINED OILS

Those oils that have not been subject to any of these treatments following extraction are termed "crude" or "unrefined" oils. They are likely to have a cloudy sediment and carry the distinctive flavor of the nut, seed, or bean of origin. They are considered suitable for salad dressings, stir frying, sautéeing, and baking, but do not take well to the high temperatures of deep frying. Unrefined oil does not need to be refrigerated, except in very warm weather or if it will not be used for several months. Cold will cause the oil to become cloudy and partially solidified. This is not harmful and it will revert to its liquid state when it returns to room temperature.

Almost every oil has an unrefined version available in natural food stores. **Olive oil**, however, is the most universally available choice. Recently, olive oil has gained favor owing to reports that monounsaturated fats, which comprise more than 70 percent of this oil, may be effective in reducing blood cholesterol.

The best quality olive oil is termed *extra virgin*. *Virgin* is from lesser grade olives and may result from a second pressing, but in any event these oils are left unrefined and have a distinctive olive flavor and green hue. Subsequent pressing yields oils of harsher flavor labeled simply *pure olive oil*. This product may be refined using a chemical solvent or hot water process.

REFINED OILS

Refined oils are bland, odorless, colorless, and also the most commonly available.

Cold Pressed Oil

Many oils are labeled "cold pressed," giving the impression that the oil is extracted in the absence of heat and is somehow more nutritious. Actually, some heat is used in the extraction of nearly all vegetable oils. The real distinction is in the word "pressed," used to signify that the oil has been produced by the expellor method rather than by using chemical solvents. Natural food stores offer this type of oil.

The fact that the oil has been pressed does not exclude the use of other undesirable processes. At least the label will inform you when emulsifiers, preservatives, and antifoaming agents have been added.

Solvent-Extracted Oils

Those oils extracted using chemical solvents dominate the supermarket shelf. They have undergone the most handling and retain the least amount of native nutrients. They are also likely to be further diminished by anticlouding agents, preservatives, and possibly even partial hydrogenation. Any such treatment should appear on the label and makes such oils unacceptable from our point of view.

PROTECTING YOUR OIL

It is unhealthy to consume fats that are even slightly rancid. The best protection for oils is to keep them cool, out of direct sunlight, and provide them with a suitable antioxidant. The food industry relies heavily on chemical additives, which appear on the label as BHT, BHA, propyl gallate, and citric acid or isopropyl citrate.

We prefer to avoid these chemicals and take a more natural approach, which is to add vitamin E, a natural antioxidant, to all the oils we buy. Interestingly, this essential nutrient is required by the body to properly metabolize unsaturated fats and so we meet the needs of the oil and our bodies by adding 200 units of E per pint of oil as soon as it is opened and repeating this every few weeks until the oil is consumed. (Before it is opened the sealed container provides adequate protection.) Vitamin E can be purchased in liquid form in dropper bottles, or you can squeeze the contents of vitamin E capsules into the oil.

We also preserve oils by keeping those high in polyunsaturates refrigerated, and by buying in small enough quantity so that they do not sit around for months. We leave only a little oil out for day-to-day use stored in an opaque container.

SELECTING SALAD
AND COOKING OILS

What oil to cook with and what to use in salad dressings are among the most common questions we are asked. Because oils differ so in their fatty acid composition, the best approach is to select several. By varying the oil you use, you will provide yourself with monounsaturates, polyunsaturates, and other fat components without having to worry about what the latest studies have turned up.

The following table shows the relative proportion of saturated, monounsaturated, and polyunsaturated fats in the most popular oils. This pattern holds whether they are unrefined, cold pressed, or solvent-extracted. Note, however, that if the oil has been hydrogenated to any degree, these figures are no longer valid.

In any case, keep in mind that oils are generally not needed in the diet to satisfy any nutritional requirement. The body can easily get all the fats it needs in wholefoods. The primary use of these oils is aesthetic; use them sparingly, as you would a seasoning or condiment, instead of regarding them as a principal food ingredient.

TYPICAL FATTY ACID COMPOSITION OF THE PRINCIPAL VEGETABLE OILS*

Oil	% saturated	% monounsaturated	% polyunsaturated
Coconut	87	6	2
Corn	13	24	59
Cottonseed	26	18	52
Grapeseed	10	16	70
Olive	13	74	8
Palm	49	37	9
Palm kernel	81	11	2
Peanut	17	46	32
Safflower	9	12	75
Safflower, high oleic	6	75	14
Sesame	14	40	42
Soybean	14	23	58
Sunflower	10	20	66
Walnut	9	22	63

*Source: *Composition of Foods, Fat and Oils*, Agriculture Handbook No. 8-4, 1979.

Fear of Frying

Extreme temperatures can cause fats to break down and form unhealthful compounds. Thus, fats that withstand high temperatures best should be given priority for deep fat frying. The oils traditionally considered most suitable include peanut, soy, sesame, and corn oil, all of which can be heated to above 400°F. before they start to smoke and create harmful by-products. While some people add safflower oil to the list, in our opinion it is less appropriate. Although it may not smoke readily, its extremely high proportion of polyunsaturated fats makes it quite susceptible to other forms of heat degradation.

The addition of emulsifiers (mono- and diglycerides and polysorbates) lowers the smoking point of oils and reduces their suitability for frying. Another chemical to avoid is methyl silicone, added to some oils to keep foaming to a minimum during frying. All these additives appear on the label.

Of course, the best way to avoid the hazards of frying is to minimize your intake of fried foods, especially those foods where you have no information about the fat used or how it has been handled.

Sautéing and Baking

For other cooking applications, where the oil itself does not reach such high temperatures, the choice is greater. If flavor does not interfere, unrefined oils are preferable. Many cultures traditionally use olive oil which lends a specific flavor to some classic dishes.

In baking, where the strong taste of an oil may not be welcome, a refined corn, safflower, sunflower, or even soy oil will suffice. Cold-pressed varieties are best for they have the least chemical residue.

Cold Service

For salad dressing and similar uncooked uses, oils can be chosen for how they complement the flavor of a particular dish. Olive, sesame, corn, and peanut are more assertive, while safflower, sunflower, and walnut are better with more delicate flavors.

"LIGHT" OILS AND OTHER GREASY PRACTICES

All vegetable oils furnish an equal number of calories, about 120 per tablespoon. Many manufacturers claim "no cholesterol" on the label of their products, but since vegetable oils do not contain cholesterol to begin with, this is a meaningless sales tactic.

When you see a vegetable oil that is described as "light," you might wonder in what way this is so. For once the term is being used in its traditional sense, for this oil is not lighter in the sense of "dietetic," it is lighter in color or flavor! This lightness is of no particular advantage to the consumer; in fact, it usually indicates a high level of filtering, bleaching, and deodorizing. Of course, the manufacturer wants you to think that "lighter" refers to something more desirable, like fewer calories or a lower fat content.

PESTICIDES IN OIL

The knowledge that most agricultural products are routinely sprayed with chemicals in the field causes some concern about the pesticide residues in any of the oils extracted from them. Monitoring has revealed pesticides in samples of both crude and processed oils.

For a while, cottonseed oil was especially criticized since cotton is not traditionally raised as a food crop. We have been informed, however, that cotton raised for oil is grown mostly in Iowa, Nebraska, and the Dakotas, not in the South. The shorter growing season there prevents maturation of the fiber-producing cotton boll which is the prime target of persistent pests. Thus, dependence on insecticides in growing cotton in those areas is no greater than for any other oil-bearing crops.

PACKAGING

Clear plastic containers are becoming increasingly popular for packaging oil. Some of the compounds used in the manufacture of these containers may migrate into the oil. For that reason, we recommend glass bottles or tins. If you have no other choice, it is probably a good idea to transfer the oil to a glass or stainless steel container after you open it since contact with oxygen accelerates the chemical transfer.

A NEW PROBLEM:
RAPESEED OR CANOLA OIL

Rapeseed oil, derived from the rape plant, contains a specific fatty acid known as erucic acid which has quite a disagreeable nature; high levels of erucic acid have caused heart lesions and cardiac defects in test animals. Until now, this oil has been prohibited in the United States.

In Canada, where rapeseed oil is permissible, plants with a low erucic acid level have been raised and the oil from this plant has recently gained U.S. FDA approval. This concerns many consumer advocates, who feel there is no need to include this oil in a food category already burdened with potential problems. Low erucic acid rapeseed (LEAR) oil may also go by the name *canola*.

FAT SUBSTITUTES

Nonstick Cooking

An assortment of nonstick cooking sprays is available to assist the cook who wants to cut back on fats. Their main attraction is that they deliver a small, controlled amount of fat into the pan. If you can manage to be quick about it, you will use only about 7 calories worth of spray to cover a 10-inch skillet, but this spray-on coating will cost about four times what you would pay for plain bottled oil.

At best, nonstick sprays are no more than oil diluted with grain alcohol and lecithin plus an unnamed propellant to get them out of the can. More often the oil is hydrogenated. In some brands this is compounded with nonspecific "vegetable oil derivatives" (which are actually some form of mono- and diglycerides) and preservatives. Many of these ingredients may be considered "natural" by the food industry, but since they are mostly derived from already refined oils they are a far cry from wholefoods.

You may therefore want to reject this product in favor of a quick wipe of oil around the pan, using a paper towel. All you need is a very thin coating and this will be a cost-effective way to keep calories and fat to a minimum.

Fake Fat

Problems with weight control and diet are giving processors an open field to develop nonfood foods. The idea behind these "Frankenstein foods" is to make substances that you can eat, but that your body does not utilize. The fact that something passes through the digestive system without being absorbed, however, is no guarantee it is safe. In fact, it can possibly irritate the stomach or intestinal lining, or it can kidnap nutrients and thus reduce the value of other foods.

The first of the artificial fats is known as sucrose polyester (SPE). Avoid it and other similar imposters that will start to replace fat in products in the future. Luckily, this will always show up in the list of ingredients.

RECOMMENDATIONS

General Rule of Purchase: Look for the least processed oils labeled crude, unrefined, or in the case of olive oil, extra virgin or virgin. Avoid those with additives such as isopropyl citrate, BHT, BHA, propyl gallate, polysorbate 80, oxystearin, and methyl silicone. Most important, avoid any hydrogenation. All of this is supposed to be stated on the label.

Note: Our Exemplary Brands include only oils packaged in glass or tins to avoid the possibility of chemicals from plastic bottles leaching into the oil.

Exemplary Brands

Unrefined Oils

Olive Oil: Choose extra virgin or virgin; all brands similar.
Arrowhead Mills Soybean, Safflower, Sesame, Corn Germ, Peanut, Sunflower, Wheat Germ
Eden Corn, Safflower, Sesame
Erewhon Safflower, Sesame, Corn

Protein Aide Extra Virgin Sesame
Spectrum Organic Olive,[1] Corn, Safflower, High High Oleic Safflower, High Oleic Sunflower
Zorba Safflower, Sunflower, Corn, Organic Olive[1]

Refined Oils

An American Delicacy Sunflower, Peanut
Belle Maison Grapeseed
Caruso Corn
Cento Blended
Golden Harvest Corn, Sesame, Peanut
Hain Cold Pressed Sesame, Safflower, Peanut, Corn, Walnut, Avocado, Soy, Cottonseed, Almond, Apricot, Wheat Germ, Garlic 'n Oil, All Blend

Health Valley Sesame, Safflower, Corn, Peanut, Sunflower, Soy, Best Blend
Hollywood Safflower, Peanut
Huile de Pepins de Raisin
Maître Jacque Grapeseed
Pope Blended
Rougie Walnut
Spectrum Sesame, Safflower, High Oleic Safflower, Soy

[1]Organic

Chapter 21

Butter Versus Margarine and Other Solid Shortenings

The U.S. government Standard of Identity, or recipe, for margarine defines it as a "food in plastic form." Although this is just a description of its consistency, margarine may well resemble this synthetic more than it does any traditional food.

The substitution of margarine for butter is a common practice in many households; three times as much margarine as butter is consumed in America and margarine occupies five times more space than butter on the typical supermarket shelf.

Originally, margarine became popular because it was less expensive than butter, but economy is rarely the motivating force behind its use now. Today, the fat used in margarine is its real selling point. But since the total amount of fat in butter and margarine is the same—80 percent—its appeal must lie elsewhere. Indeed, it is the "vegetable oil" derivation of margarine and the "no cholesterol" advertising that has convinced people of its benefits.

Although it cannot be ignored that butter is a source of cholesterol, the relationship of dietary cholesterol to blood cholesterol levels is probably the most widely disputed area in the diet-health paradigm (see page 166, Chapter 14). It also cannot be ignored that margarine is a source of considerable amounts of undesirable hydrogenated oil. So, while those concerned with heart disease may consider margarine to be the miracle food of the century, we seriously question this belief.

HYDROGENATION: FATTY ACIDS MOLDED BY TECHNOLOGY

As mentioned in the previous chapter, the use of partially hydrogenated vegetable fats in the form of margarine, oil, and shortening, has brought about a major change in fat consumption in the United States during the twentieth century. What's more, the incidence of cancer of the colon and breast, both of which have been related to dietary fat, correlate closely with our national intake of partially hydrogenated fat.

We believe that the current dietary advice to reduce overall fat and to give preference to vegetable fat dodges the issue of greatest import: How does the alteration of fatty acids during hydrogenation affect our national health? We are particularly interested in this from the standpoint of which foods become the target of dietary criticism or promotion. There are many who hold that eggs, dairy products, and meat, all of which are replete with essential nutrients, are the repository of evil fats and cholesterol. Meanwhile, foods lacking nutritional integrity like doughnuts, chips, and similar fried snacks, as well as table spreads, commercial shortenings, and hydrogenated salad oils, have been able to hold their own; as massive promotions inform us, they are made using "all vegetable shortening." Perhaps the time has come to consider the meaning of this statement.

The fact that the creation of partially hydrogenated fats reduces the availability of the essential fatty acids required for optimal well-being, and that the newly created fatty acids may have a harmful effect of their own, is apparently immaterial to the food processor. You on the other hand may be concerned to learn that these new forms of fat are suspected of interfering with fat metabolism, disrupting normal heart functions, enhancing fatty deposits in the arteries, inhibiting the production and utilization of substances in the body which influence the immune system, and reducing the body's ability to rid itself of carcinogens, drugs, and other toxins.

MARGARINE

Fat makes up 80 percent of the content of margarine whether it is in the stick, soft tub, or liquid form. This fat may come from rendered animal fats, but is more likely to be vegetable in origin. In accordance with the Standard of Identity, these fats "may have been subjected to an accepted process of physio-chemical modification," a fancy allusion to the treatment known as hydrogenation.

Margarine and Hydrogenated Oil: An Inseparable Relationship

The ability to hydrogenate oil is essential to the production of all margarine. Its importance to the manufacturer is, first, to reduce certain polyunsaturated fatty acids which, although essential to the body, are susceptible to rancidity and, second, to keep the oil from reverting to its natural liquid state. Without this technology, liquid oils could not be transformed into a spread.

During the partial hydrogenation that takes place in margarine production, some of the unsaturated fatty acids in the oil become saturated; other fatty acids take on a new configuration that does not exist in nature. A peculiar trait of these new fatty acids is that they have a wide "plastic range" which allows them to stay soft and spreadable under cold storage and retain this quality without liquefying when left at room temperature.

How Hydrogenated Is It?

We often see ads that imply margarine and related spreads made from "100 percent safflower" or "100 percent corn oil" are somehow superior. There is never any acknowledgment that much of the oil used in the product has been hydrogenated and consequently there may only be from 14 to 44 percent polyunsaturated fatty acids left. Therefore, from our point of view, the type of oil these spreads are made from is virtually irrelevant once it is hydrogenated.

Not all margarines have the same amount of hydrogenated oil and some clue to the amount does appear on the label. The law requires that all the fats in margarine be listed in order of decreasing amounts and that the term *hydrogenated*, or alternately *hardened*, be included for any oils treated in this way. Therefore:

- If the only fat listed is "partially hydrogenated or hardened oil," this margarine will be highest in both saturated and unnatural fatty acids.
- If the label states "partially hardened or hydrogenated oil, liquid oil," less of the oil has been processed, but you can still anticipate a high level of the unnatural fatty acids and less of the essential polyunsaturates found in untreated oil.
- If the order is reversed and "liquid oil" precedes the "partially hydrogenated oil," you will receive more of the important fatty acids, but the problem of the unnatural form will not be eradicated.

"No Cholesterol" Claims

As with vegetable oils discussed in the previous chapter, some margarines prominently display the words "no cholesterol" on the package. We cannot understand how others in the food industry have missed this opportunity: Why limit this motto to vegetable oil margarine? After all, beans, beer, wine, coffee, tea, fruit, vegetables, honey, grains, and in fact all products that are free of animal fat are free of cholesterol as well. So why don't we see similar claims on these items? (Perhaps we shouldn't suggest this, even in jest.)

The Little-Known Phytosterols

There is an additional concern regarding the hydrogenation of oils in relationship to cholesterol. Results of extensive studies demonstrate that substances called *phytosterols* that are naturally present in vegetable oils help reduce blood cholesterol. However, when vegetable oils are hydrogenated, much of this phytosterol is converted to a form that no longer exhibits this ability. Thus, the transformation of oil to margarine destroys any part it may have played in a cholesterol-lowering, modified fat diet.

The Nonfat Portion of Margarine

About 18 percent of the contents of margarine is liquid. This liquid can come in the form of milk or any milk product, which may just as likely be isolated whey or casein as well as any drinkable form of milk as we know it. Or, water may be combined with other protein derivatives like albumin (from eggs) or soy protein isolates. Less often, just plain water accounts for this portion.

Bacterial starters may be added to initiate a "natural" butter flavor from the dairy components. The remainder of the product is composed of salt (averaging 44 milligrams of sodium per teaspoon) or potassium chloride in special diet brands, plus a slew of food additives.

Reduced-Fat Margarine

The latest trend in margarine is the "light spread," which contains about 60 percent oil and 25 percent fewer calories. This is a middle ground between regular margarine, with 80 percent fat, and the product called diet margarine, which has 40 percent fat and half the calories. Both these reduced-fat margarine substitutes use water to replace the missing oil and, to keep them suitably "plastic" and "tasty," have a greater dependency on chemical additives.

Note that the term "imitation" is not required on reduced-fat products as long as they are fortified with 15,000 international units of vitamin A per pound as required for "real" margarine.

If we were giving out awards (or demerits) for misleading product labels, one would surely go to the "Light and Natural Spread" that declares "natural goodness," and "no artificial colors or flavors" on the front of its package. Turn it over though and you'll learn that it is made of "partially hydrogenated soybean and cottonseed oils, water, salt, vegetable mono- and diglycerides, lecithin, natural flavor, potassium sorbate, calcium disodium EDTA added as preservatives, sweet dairy whey, natural vegetable color (carrot oil/annatto), natural vitamins A and D." Just about the only ingredient it contains that hasn't been refined in some way is the water.

Liquid Margarine

It is mind-boggling to think that after all the technology that has gone into converting a liquid oil into a solid shortening, someone would develop and market a squeeze margarine for "more convenient" frying, basting, or coating of baking pans. Maybe the people who make it never heard of oil.

Selecting Margarine

Your only consolation is that it's all there on the label for you to see. Personally, we wouldn't bring any margarine into our kitchen, but if you are still not convinced, you may be lucky enough to find one of the few brands on the market that contain a minimum of additives relying on lecithin alone to help maintain texture, using natural colorants like carotene, annatto, or turmeric, and free of acids, alkalis, and preservatives. Of course the oil will still be hydrogenated to some degree.

BUTTER

Admittedly most of the fat in butter is the saturated kind, but we believe if you're going to eat saturated fats you might as well stick to those that are saturated naturally by the cow. Interestingly, several of the fatty acids that are characteristic of butter reportedly do not elevate blood cholesterol.

For most cooking purposes, a properly chosen oil will do. Used sparingly as a spread, butter will be less detrimental to your health than margarine, for at least the unnatural fats and additives are eliminated.

Selecting Butter

The best butter you can buy is *sweet, unsalted butter* and bears the statement "made from sweet cream" on the label. Other butters may be made by reworking stale or soured milk or cream, with salt added to inhibit mold growth and mask its inferior quality. Salt also helps preserve butter, so salted butter can be more easily mishandled. The amount of sodium in a teaspoon of salted butter comes to about 40 milligrams.

Greater care is taken with unsalted butter to ensure its safe arrival at the market. Very often it is found in the freezer, rather than in the dairy case.

At present, butter made from raw cream is available commercially only in California.

Approximately 70 percent of the butter made for consumer use carries an official USDA grade mark. Grades of butter are determined first by flavor, then aroma, body, and color. The top graded product is U.S. Grade AA or U.S. 93 Score. Grades A and B may exhibit a variety of off-flavors.

COLORED BUTTER

According to the Standard of Identity butter may have added coloring, which may be natural (carotene or annatto) or a synthetic dye. This use of color can be concealed from the consumer by the graces of the law. It is commonly "added seasonally" to make up for the diminished natural yellow hue in winter milk. If people would get accustomed to the fact that the color of milk and milk products is variable as a normal result of the decreased vitamin A in winter feed, this additive could be eliminated.

Storing Butter

Producers generally mark butter with a two- to three-month refrigerator shelf-life, although the American Dairy Association does not recommend keeping it for more than four weeks. Salted butter has the advantage of being less perishable than unsalted when it is stored in the refrigerator; however, it is more susceptible to flavor changes in the freezer. Unsalted butter may be successfully frozen for up to nine months. Unfortunately, the dating on butter is not always easily comprehended and, despite all your care, butter may have been held by the store in cold storage for an undetermined period. Make sure you select a package that is well wrapped, and if you detect any off-flavor or odor, return it to the store.

KEEPING BUTTER SOFT AND SPREADABLE

People repeatedly inform us that the real reason they like margarine is its spreadability. Unlike butter, margarine retains its plasticity at refrigerator temperatures. This is both convenient and has a nutritional advantage in that the easier a substance is to apply, the thinner it can be spread—meaning less fat and fewer calories.

To keep butter similarly soft and pliable you can use a "butter keeper." This receptacle has a well to hold the butter, which is inserted into a water bath that seals the butter from the air, allowing you to store it at room temperature up to two weeks without it spoiling. The butter stays fresh and suitably spreadable.

BUTTER BLENDS

Blends made of 40 percent butter and 60 percent oil are a fairly new introduction to the dairy case. To keep consistency, color, and a flavor resembling that of butter, partially hydrogenated oils and the emulsifiers, coloring agents, flavorings, and preservatives found in margarine show up here as well. The manufacturer of a product called "I Can't Believe It's Not Butter" may not be able to tell the difference, but your body undoubtedly can.

SPRAY-DRIED BUTTER

Butter Buds™ are described by the manufacturer as "the concentrated natural flavor of butter, extracted from cream, spray-dried into granules." This "natural flavor" is created using enzymes to release the fatty acids that mimic the butter taste. The result is highly reactive and unstable "free fatty acids" with questionable health effects; little is known about how this form of isolated fat reacts in the digestive system or the blood stream.

In addition to this so-called natural flavor, these "100% Natural Butter Flavored Granules" are comprised of such other "all-natural ingredients" (manufacturer's description) as malto dextrin, corn syrup solids, salt, guar gum, baking soda, and annatto and turmeric for color. We obviously differ with their definition of *natural* and do not find this a commendable option.

OTHER SOLID SHORTENINGS

Lard

The most traditional solid shortening is lard, rendered from "the sound edible tissues of swine." Because lard may be derived from cured as well as fresh or frozen pork, the possible presence of nitrates and nitrites causes some concern. Since the label does not specify its source, this is a chance you take when using lard or products made with it. The label will, however, inform you when BHT, BHA, or propyl gallate are added as preservatives. You may also want to consider the fact that feed additives and pesticides concentrate in fat tissues and thus any accumulated toxins in meat-producing animals would be at their highest level in the rendered fat.

Fat in the Can

People have become so used to semisolid ("plastic") vegetable shortenings for use in baking that we tend to forget they were first synthesized only at the beginning of this century and have had a relatively short history of use. They are all essentially hydrogenated oils with other fatty acid derivatives, and their considerable processing creates yet another fat form unknown to nature.

This type of shortening is extremely popular in the food industry and all this alchemy is merely distinguished on the label by the one word *hydrogenated*. There is no such thing in our book as an Exemplary Brand.

A Nonhydrogenated Spread

There are some all-vegetable spreads that are free of hydrogenated oil but these products are not widely available.

Canasoy Soya Lecithin Spread is composed of soybean oil, lecithin, and milk solids, flavored lightly with salt and colored with the vegetable extract carotene. Edward and Sons Trading Soya Butter is made from roasted soybeans, soy oil, peanut oil, barley malt, and vitamin C. We have not been able to obtain any sodium figures for these spreads, but the soya butter claims that a typical 2-tablespoon serving furnishes 189 calories, 14.5 grams of fat, about 135 percent of the U.S. Recommended Daily Allowance, for vitamin C, 7.5 percent of the U.S. RDA for iron, small amounts of calcium and B vitamins, and a whopping 9.6 grams of protein. By contrast, 2 tablespoons of butter or margarine add up to 200 calories, 23 grams of fat, 23.5 percent of the U.S. RDA for vitamin A, and virtually nothing else.

RECOMMENDATIONS

BUTTER

General Rule of Purchase: Look for U.S. Grade AA or Score 93, sweet cream, unsalted butter. Color (usually vegetable) may be added seasonally and if labeled, it is done voluntarily.

Exemplary Brands

Pasteurized Sweet Cream, Unsalted Butter: all brands similar   Steuve's Natural Raw Unsalted Butter

MARGARINE

General Rule of Purchase: The contents of margarine are on the label. All margarine contains hydrogenated oil and therefore can never be considered an exemplary food.

OTHER SHORTENINGS AND SPREADS

General Rule of Purchase: All ingredients will be on the label of any fat-based spread. Most shortenings, whether described as "blends" or semi-solid vegetable shortening, are comprised of hydrogenated oils, emulsifiers, preservatives, and possibly artificial coloring and flavoring. Look for a product containing only butter or nonhydrogenated oils; milk solids, lecithin, or soybeans may contribute to texture, salt and perhaps barley malt, honey, or other seasonings will enhance its taste, a vegetable color may be added for appearance, and any natural antioxidants like vitamins C or E are acceptable.

*Exemplary Brands*_____

Canasoy Soya Lecithin Spread
Emes Vegetarian Golden Fat Onion Spread

Edward and Son Trading Soya Butter
Gallos Whipped Garlic Butter

Chapter 22

Who Made
the Salad Dressing?

As the headline on an ad for one natural food-oriented dressing declared, "Maybe it's your dressing that should be tossed." We have yet to understand what makes bottled dressings so attractive. It certainly can't be the ingredients, since most oil and vinegar types contain a host of undesirables, including questionable flavoring agents, stabilizers, thickeners, crystal inhibitors, and preservatives. Some even contain artificial color.

What makes the success of bottled dressings so remarkable is that a basic dressing is so simple to make: All you need is oil, vinegar or lemon juice, and a few simple herbs. The reason for all the commercial chemistry is purely cosmetic; most of the extraneous ingredients are there to keep the oil, vinegar, and seasonings evenly distributed and to give the dressing a thick consistency. Without them, you are forced to shake salad dressing before you pour it, hardly a lot to ask.

Apparently, for many people the convenience of prepared dressings supersedes concern about the quality of the ingredients (or the price). Even the proliferation of natural foods has done little to improve the situation—there are still very few products on the shelf we would bring home. Many of those that are free of the most obvious deterrents, like preservatives and coloring, still rely heavily on salt, sweetening, MSG, hydrolyzed vegetable protein, and gum thickeners. The term "natural" or the fact that they may be sold in a natural foods store does not seem to matter much here. Furthermore, those brands marketed in the produce case, seemingly purer and fresher, are often no better than those sold on the dry goods shelf.

THE JARRING FACTS ABOUT THE
CALORIES, SALT, AND SUGAR
IN BOTTLED DRESSING

Salad dressings are mostly fat, since their principal component is oil. This means calories accumulate quickly. Most typical dressings furnish 70 to 80 calories per tablespoon. By adding a conservative 2 tablespoons of dressing to a salad, what is often considered a "diet" dish can reach the caloric proportions of a scoop of ice cream or the average iced cupcake.

The amount of sodium in a tablespoon of a typical bottled dressing ranges from a low of 115 milligrams up to 400 milligrams.

It is one thing when sweeteners are used in moderation in a traditionally sweet dressing, but ¼ teaspoon of sugar per tablespoon in Italian dressing, and better than twice this amount in French and Thousand Island dressings, is another story.

THE BEST OF THE BOTTLES

We feel very strongly about dressing salad properly. After all, why should anyone degrade the vegetables they have selected so carefully? Therefore, our Exemplary Brands reflect the absence of additives and highly refined ingredients and tolerate sweeteners only when necessary to create a special effect. You must pay particular attention to the labels of all products, for invariably within one company's line you will find some varieties that merit consideration and others that you may not welcome at your table.

Dressings that gain creaminess from buttermilk, yogurt, or tofu can add valuable protein as well as interest to a salad. Here, the addition of a vegetable gum is more acceptable since it serves a useful function in binding the ingredients together.

SALAD DRESSING IN A BAG

Dry salad dressing mixes require the addition of oil and an acidifier; this reduces them to little more than a bag of seasonings. Sometimes these are quite innocuous, but you may end up paying close to a dollar for less than an ounce of seasoned salt.

Even in bags of "naturally flavored" salad dressing mixes you are likely to find hydrolyzed vegetable protein, carrageenan, egg albumin, algin, and guar gum. The prominent use of honey powder makes some offerings look more like a table-top sweetener than something that belongs on a salad.

Common supermarket salad dressing mixes are even more objectionable. For example, the following ingredients appear in a typical "reduced calorie" mix:

> salt, modified food starch, malto-dextrin, buttermilk solids, whey solids, garlic powder, lactic acid, onion powder, MSG, calcium lactate, natural and artificial flavors, hydropropyl methylcellulose, spices, casein, citric acid, partially hydrogenated vegetable oil (soy, palm, coconut), whole milk solids, xanthan gum, calcium stearate, dextrose, disodium inosinate and guanylate, sugar, egg solids, mono- and diglycerides, sodium caseinate, turmeric, glycerol lacto esters of fatty acids, artificial color.

You could have prepared a homemade dressing from scratch in the time it takes you just to read this label.

YOUR OWN HOUSE DRESSINGS

If our list of Exemplary Brands seems limited, do not despair. It is amazing how simple it is to prepare your own salad dressing and, since most store well in the refrigerator, you can always have some on hand. The economic advantage of homemade versus prepared dressing can add up to anywhere from 10 cents to $1 for 12 ounces.

FORMULAS FOR "HOUSE" DRESSINGS

Oil and Vinegar Type = 1 part acid ingredient (vinegar, lemon juice, or lime juice) : 2 parts oil (polyunsaturated, olive, or a combination) + seasonings to taste

Russian or Thousand Island = 2 parts plain yogurt : 1 part mayonnaise : 1 part catsup or tomato juice + seasonings (minced sweet pepper, olives, soy sauce, hot pepper sauce) to taste

Creamy, Dairy-Based (Green Goddess, Blue Cheese, Creamy Herb, etc.) = 1 part yogurt : 1 part sour cream or mayonnaise + seasonings to taste

Creamy, Nondairy = ½ pound (1 cup) pureed tofu + 2 tablespoons acid ingredient + 3 tablespoons oil + seasonings to taste + water as needed to achieve desired consistency

---

MAYONNAISE AND EMULSIFIED SALAD DRESSING

Buying mayonnaise is straightforward since its ingredients are regulated by a federal Standard of Identity and fairly well labeled. While the market has long been dominated by the formula of one leading manufacturer (whose recipe we do not recommend), several brands now have improved the selection by using higher quality oils and leaving out the refined sugar, the few permissible additives, and sometimes even the salt.

The Standard of Identity for mayonnaise calls for a minimum of 65 percent oil, plus vinegar and/or lemon juice, with either whole eggs or egg yolks added to form an emulsion. No artificial color or flavor is allowed, but the additive EDTA may be used to preserve color or flavor, the acidity may be adjusted with citric or malic acid, and crystal inhibitors like oxystearin, lecithin, and diglycerides may be included. All ingredients must be declared;

however the form of the eggs (fresh, frozen, or dried) need not be specified, and seasonings other than salt, sweetening, and MSG may be listed merely as "natural flavoring" or "spices." Each individual oil should be revealed, including any hydrogenation. If the ingredients state simply "oil" or "vegetable oil," the product is in violation of the law.

The mayonnaise look-alike known as *salad dressing* (technically, *emulsified salad dressing*) is merely mayonnaise diluted to a minimum of 30 percent oil with a starch-and-water paste.

Sweet and Salty

There is no limit to the amount of salt, but generally you can figure on 70 to 80 milligrams of sodium per tablespoon in mayonnaise and about 85 to 105 milligrams of sodium per tablespoon in salad dressing. Where there is "no salt added," this will fall to about 5 milligrams.

Although very few brands forgo the sweetening, it only accounts for a fraction of a teaspoon per tablespoon of the mayonnaise. Salad dressing is slightly higher, and coupled with the use of starch to maintain its texture, the total refined carbohydrate content comes to about 1 teaspoon per tablespoon.

Reduced-Calorie Mayonnaise and Salad Dressing

A tablespoon of mayonnaise contains 100 to 110 calories; salad dressing measures in at 50 to 65 calories per tablespoon. When the calories are reduced, some descriptive qualifier must be added to the name.

The reduced-calorie mayonnaise we have encountered has half the fat of regular mayonnaise and about 45 calories per tablespoon. A reduced-calorie salad dressing also contains about 45 calories. To achieve this, these dressings substitute water for some of the oil and ensure texture by using modified starches. Note that these products are likely to contain sorbate and benzoate preservatives not permitted in the "real" thing.

YOUR OWN LOW-CALORIE MAYO

Diluting mayonnaise with an equal volume of yogurt will bring it down to about 53 calories per tablespoon. This not only lowers the fat and calorie content, but adds nutrients. It is best to do this mixing just prior to use, as both ingredients will remain fresh longer if they are stored separately.

Selecting Mayonnaise

Due to the presence of refined starch, neither salad dressing nor reduced-calorie mayonnaise is ever on our shopping list.

When it comes to buying "real mayonnaise," we select only those made with nonhydrogenated oils and pass by any with EDTA, crystal inhibitors, and MSG. Our preference is for those brands that use fresh eggs (when expressed on the label) and honey rather than sugar or corn syrup (although refined sweetener does not rule them out). The most popular oil employed is soybean and the fact that it contains substantial amounts of the essential linolenic acid is in its favor. Safflower oil, the choice of some natural food manufacturers, is somewhat lower in linolenic acid, but is higher overall in polyunsaturates. Both are suitable.

Imitation Mayonnaise

When any ingredient required by the Standard of Identity is omitted, and the manufacturer still wants to maintain product identity, the term *imitation* may be applied. This does not necessarily mean inferior. In the case of mayonnaise it may indicate, for example, the absence of eggs and their replacement with a seaweed derivative (algin). For those who do not wish to eat eggs, we find this an appropriate use of a vegetable gum.

Another alternative now available in natural food stores is "soyonaise," a blend of tofu, oil, water, and seasonings which, like the egg-free mayonnaise, relies on vegetable gum to keep it together. This product is commendable in that it contains only 40 calories and 50 milligrams of sodium per tablespoon, which are about half the figures for standard emulsified dressings.

RECOMMENDATIONS

BOTTLED DRESSINGS

General Rule of Purchase: All ingredients are on the label with the exception of the specific herbs and spices. Look for products made with nonhydrogenated oil and natural acidifiers like lemon or lime juice or vinegar. Avoid dressings that use hydrogenated oils, thickeners such as modified food starch, propylene glycol alginate, and cellulose compounds like hydroxymethlycellulose, as well as artificial color and preservatives. Accept gums and seaweed derivatives (algin, carrageenan) only in creamy dairy or tofu dressings where it serves a functional, rather than cosmetic purpose. Avoid those with unnecessary amounts of sodium or inappropriate sweeteners.

Aware Inn French Dressing
Big Deal Lemon Dill, Lime Dill, Thousand Island, Vinaigrette, New Orleans Bisque Dressings
Blanchard and Blanchard Sesame Seed Dressing[3]
Captain Jaap's Lite House Dressing and Marinade
Cardini's Lemon Herb, Lime Dill, Great American Salad Dressings
Casa Ramos Monterey, Mexican Ranch, Sun Goddess, Lemon and Lime Dressings
Cook's Classics Pleasantly Piquant, Tarchon, Honey-Apple-Mustard, Garlic Lover's, Curry Almond, Caesar Dressings
Cuisine Perel Garlic Dill Sauterne, Champagne Mustard Dressings
Hain Natural Herb Salad Dressing
Health Valley Salad Life Italian, Real French, Cheese and Herb Dressings

Life Garlic, Avocado Dressings with Tofu
Lisa Jardine's Vinaigrette Salad Dressing
Maggie Gins Peanut and Sesame, Bean Curd and Chives, Hunan Style Chili and Garlic[3] Dressings
Nasoya Sesame Garlic, Italian, Fine Herb Dressings[2]
Newman's Own Olive Oil and Garlic Dressing
Norganic Herb, Italian Dressings
Pure and Simple Romano Salad Dressings
Sahara Tahini Dressing
Simply Natural Miso Dressings
The Source Regular, Unsalted Herb French Dressings
Walnut Acres Creamy Chive, Creamy Italian, 1000 Islands, Creamy Watercress Dressings
Whole Earth Salad Dream Dressings

MAYONNAISE

General Rule of Purchase: All ingredients appear on the label with the exception of the specific herbs and spices and a declaration of whether the eggs are fresh, frozen, or dried. Look for mayonnaise with nonhydrogenated oil and free of EDTA, diglycerides, oxystearin, and MSG. When salt and sweetening are omitted it is optimal; where honey is used instead of sugar or corn syrup it is preferred.

Acme[3]
Albertson's[3]
Bama[3]
Blue Plate[3]
Coop[3]
Duke's Home Style
Econobuy[3]
Eden
Foodtown[3]
Grand Union[3]
Hain Natural Safflower, Cold Pressed
Health Valley
Hollywood
JFG[3]

Mrs. Clark's
Mrs. Gooch's
My-Te-Fine[3]
Norganic Golden Soya
Parade[3]
Pathmark[3]
Pure and Simple
Rich Harvest
Saffola Polyunsaturated[3]
Shoprite[3]
Staff[3]
Walnut Acres Regular, Unsweetened
Westbrae Natural

SALAD DRESSING

General Rule of Purchase: Salad dressing, as defined in the Standard of Identity, must contain some form of refined starch and thus it is never an exemplary choice.

IMITATION MAYONNAISE

General Rule of Purchase: All ingredients appear on the label. Products made in the image of mayonnaise but without eggs, or perhaps based on yogurt or tofu in order to reduce the fat and calories, are commendable when they are free of refined starch, hydrogenated oil, preservatives, and the other additives you want to avoid in mayonnaise. Vegetable gums such as algin and carrageenan are the norm here and serve a real purpose—that is to keep the dressing emulsified.

*Exemplary Brands*_____

Hain Natural Eggless Imitation Mayonnaise   Nasoya Nasoyonaise[2]

[2]Some organic ingredients
[3]Contains refined sweeteners

Chapter 23

Overview: A Fresh Outlook on Produce

No people have ever had the diversity of produce that is available in the United States. Our melting pot of nationalities has extended into the kitchen and "ethnic" produce now appears far from its native population centers. Eggplants, plantains, okra, avocados, fresh artichokes, escarole, endive, spaghetti squash, celeriac, kumquats, casaba melon, mangoes, and such are found side by side in many parts of the country. Once exotic fruits are now standard garnish for everything nouvelle, from fish with papaya to kiwi-topped pies. In fact, with the exception of the potato, all fruit and vegetable sales have enjoyed a steady growth during the last few years. Some specialty items that were virtually unknown on the American table just a decade ago are now commonplace. All the same, there is still more to discover. When the cashier at the local supermarket no longer looks at us quizzically when we buy jicama, bok choy, quince, persimmon, or pomegranate, we will know for sure that America's fresh produce habits have really changed.

FIBER, THE "NEW" NUTRIENT

The bran in grains is now widely recognized as a source of essential fiber; however, the type of fiber found in fruits and vegetables may be even more vital. The fiber pectin, for example, is credited with helping to lower serum cholesterol levels and regulate blood sugar. Cellulose and hemicellulose fibers are an aid to bowel function and create a feeling of fullness that can assist weight control. A woody fiber called lignin acts both to speed the transport of foods through the digestive tract and to lower blood cholesterol. It is also believed that pectin and lignin may serve to bind some of the agricultural and environmental pollutants our bodies are exposed to, which the bulk-promoting cellulose then helps sweep out. The bacterial fermentation of some fibers may also promote the growth of friendly bacteria that attack these chemical poisons.

Food preparation affects fiber levels. Raw is best. Quick stir-frying and steaming help spare fiber, as well as other nutrients, while boiling and canning have the opposite effect. "An apple a day" is still good advice, since

313

whole plants provide more fiber than products made from them; hence, the apple has more to offer than the juice extracted from it.

PROTECTING THE HARVEST

Protecting the quality of produce after harvest is a subject of great concern to both industry and consumer. It is estimated that as much as 40 percent of all fruits and vegetables grown in the United States never make it to the table. Field disease and decay, plus spillage and waste during transport, storage, and processing, have an enormous impact on supplies and prices. As you can imagine, food purveyors are interested in doing almost anything they can to reduce their losses. Unfortunately for the consumer, quality, purity, and richness of taste may be sacrificed in the process.

Chemical Control

The first step takes place on the farm with the use of pre-harvest spraying to control post-harvest decay. Following harvest, fumigation is likely to occur once or even several times during storage and transport. One fumigant, the cancer-causing pesticide EDB (ethylene dibromide), was used commonly for more than forty years before it was banned. Though use of EDB has been phased out in the United States, it has not been abandoned in other parts of the world and it certainly is not the only product of its kind available.

Atmosphere Control

One important approach to quality maintenance is temperature control. Nutrients dissipate quickly in some items if a cool, humid environment is not maintained. Unfortunately, some produce is actually injured by chilling; other items that are picked immature may never ripen normally after exposure to cold temperatures. This has had a somewhat detrimental effect on the quality of bananas, avocados, pineapples, melons, tomatoes, potatoes, mangoes, nectarines, papayas, peaches, and pears.

Sometimes, too, mature but unripened produce is stored in atmosphere-controlled rooms until later in the season. By the time the produce is called into demand there often has not been much progress towards ripening and it must be initiated artificially by placing the fruit in rooms filled with ethylene gas (which is normally given off in the natural ripening process). Bananas and tomatoes are routinely handled this way; similar treatment for avocados is becoming more common, and other fruits are expected to go this route soon. We would love to see some data comparing the nutrition of sun-ripened varieties with those that depend on a sealed room to initiate their texture and color. The flavor of synthetically ripened tomatoes certainly illustrates one defect of this system to anyone who has had the pleasure of tasting a vine-ripened specimen.

Cleaning

To protect produce from surface contamination, the food may have been washed several times before it reaches you. Prewash soaking often takes place in vats of water that are changed infrequently. This practice necessitates the addition of fungicides and bactericides to moderate the build-up of microorganisms. The washing itself is assisted by an assortment of chemical wetting and sanitizing agents.

Chemical Dips

Where environmental or mechanical controls are deemed insufficient, chemicals may be applied to inhibit decay and rot after harvest. Many of these compounds are highly controversial and have been shown to penetrate the flesh.

Several fresh fruits and vegetables are also routinely waxed to slow moisture loss. The waxes may be applied alone or maybe mixed with fungicides, bactericides, ripening inhibitors, and coloring agents.

```
THIS PRODUCE
HAS BEEN
WAXED
```

All ingredients applied directly to raw agricultural products after harvesting, including waxes, preservatives, and colors, are supposed to be declared either on the item itself or on a nearby sign. Violation of this law is obviously tolerated since we have *never* seen a notice revealing any such information in our extremely wide travels, despite the fact that the following fruits and vegetables may be treated in this manner: apples, lemons, limes, muskmelons, coconuts, bananas, plantains, grapefruits, tangerines, mangoes, papayas, watermelons, pineapples, avocados, sweet peppers, cucumbers, eggplants, sweet potatoes, winter squash, pumpkins, tomatoes, and rutabagas.

Although the FDA assures us that they take into account the possibility of consuming the peel or rind, we are not pleased with the prospect of consuming resins derived from coal tar, petroleum-based waxes and paraffins, mineral oil, polyethylene-derived finishes, or shellac, or the chemical additives that may be embodied in them. Because these waxes are insoluble in water, scrubbing is not likely to remove them. If you are sufficiently concerned, peeling is the only option.

Irradiation

Irradiation is a processing technique that exposes food to low levels of radiation in order to kill insects and some spoilage organisms and to inhibit ripening and sprouting. It was approved in 1986 for fresh fruits and vegetables and when this process is used, it is supposed to be indicated to the consumer (see Chapter 2). Current consumer attitudes toward this treatment are generally negative, and for good reason. (So much so that a test marketing of irradiated papayas in California brought on protest demonstrations outside the supermarket—a practice we hope will be repeated wherever irradiated foods are sold.) It is likely, however, that the government and industry will attempt to turn the public around on this issue.

Irradiation is not infallible. In some cases it has been found to actually increase a food's susceptibility to fungal attack (including the carcinogen aflatoxin) and also to cause undesirable physical changes. Irradiated oranges, for one, develop blemishes four to six weeks after harvest, and in only two to four weeks the irradiation can be detected in texture, taste, and odor. Irradiated lemons have been even more problematic, exhibiting a spongy texture and as much as a 50 percent decline in vitamin C content.

Irradiation is destructive to other nutrients in addition to vitamin C, including vitamin A and certain of the B vitamins (especially thiamin and folic acid), for which fresh fruits and vegetables are deemed valuable. It also breaks down complex carbohydrates like cellulose and pectin, thereby reducing the important function of produce in furnishing dietary fiber. Arguments have been made that other methods of processing such as canning and freezing are similarly destructive to vitamins and also break down fiber. However, irradiation is not being considered as an alternative to these; it is being proposed for marketing fresh produce where we do not expect such losses to occur, as well as for treating produce prior to processing.

Irradiation will not even reduce pesticide use since it will not alter farming techniques, nor will it stop reinfestation of produce that has been irradiated.

Animal feeding studies involving irradiated foodstuffs have raised a number of concerns including the creation of mutagens and "unique radiolytic particles" in food, but perhaps the most frightening aspect of irradiation is the potential danger involved in transporting, storing, and disposing of the radioactive materials involved in the process. Thus, we stand firm in our decision to boycott any foods subjected to irradiation, particularly since there are other safer methods to accomplish the same purpose. (For groups involved in this issue, see page 542, "Private Organizations Working in the Area of Food and Agriculture.")

DESIGNER BEANS AND OTHER MARKETING TECHNIQUES

Most of the sales tactics currently being introduced to attract consumer attention, including appealing display techniques such as outdoor pallets of produce, farmstand-like enclosures, and mini setups of fruit and vegetables throughout the store reflect only a change in merchandizing, not in the merchandise.

Brand name produce is another up-and-coming selling technique and those companies entering the brand name competition see the produce department as the "last frontier" of marketing in the supermarket. In almost all cases, again it is only the packaging, not the produce, that is different.

Biotechnology

If brand name produce is successful, it will lead to more fruits and vegetables that are genetically engineered to emphasize certain physical traits in order to create a product identity. In the past this was done through plant breeding techniques; in the future it may be through biotechnology in which plant genes are manipulated in a laboratory. Biotechnology is a frightening prospect. Inevitably it will mean greater expense for the grower, so that small farms will be even less capable of competing in the commercial market; many genetically engineered crops will have less natural ability to cope with the environment and thus will require more pesticides. Biotechnology may also accelerate the loss of many plant species that make up our traditional food supply, a matter that already concerns many environmentalists. What we need is not more technology, but simpler, less manipulated produce. (For groups working to control this technology, see page 542, "Private Organizations Working in the Area of Food and Agriculture.)

Salad Bars

The salad bar, with its array of fresh produce and prepared salads, is another marketing technique that has mushroomed in the last few years. We have seen some exquisite examples as well as some dismal ones. Here the mode of display and handling can make an important difference to the actual wholesomeness of the foods being offered. Since cut fruit and vegetables lose their nutrients more rapidly than whole produce, quick turnover and frequent maintenance of the salad bar are essential. Greens that have been sitting out all day may hardly be worth your attention. Adequate utensils are another must, especially if there are many prepared items on the cart from which both flavors and microorganisms could readily be transferred. This also minimizes the number of hands that have touched your food. Some kind of shield is also preferable, and in fact is required by law in some states; nicknamed "sneeze guards," the contribution of these shields should be obvious.

Prepared salads at the salad bar (as well as the deli counter) are not subject to labeling requirements so it is probably best to avoid the concocted and canned choices and fill up on fresh items. For dressing, use the oil and vinegar or fresh lemon wedges provided; salad bar dressings are laden with fat, salt, unnecessary food additives, and possibly refined sweeteners as well.

An area of concern to many consumers is the use of sulfites or other color and freshness additives on produce to keep it looking crisp and attractive. Some stores employ a simple citric acid and/or ascorbic acid solution, but the use of additional additives, including a sulfite salt, make the produce longer lasting. Because some people have been found to have severe reactions to sulfiting agents, the FDA has ordered a ban on their use in salad bars. Although you may have heard that retail stores dip or soak other produce in sulfites, this charge is denied by most produce departments. Generally they simply spray the stock with plain water.

THE ORGANIC PERSPECTIVE

The increased use of and dependence on agricultural chemicals places a financial burden on the farmer and a physical burden on our bodies. If you are concerned about this and the other chemical approaches just described, you will be glad to know you do have a choice: Organic or "biologically grown" fruits and vegetables, raised without the assistance of fungicides, herbicides, and insecticides, and treated with similar respect after harvest. While still representing only a small percent of our total agricultural output, organic produce is becoming increasingly available thanks to consumer interest.

Organic fruits and vegetables often present a problem for those accustomed to supermarket "perfect produce." In the past, organic oranges tended to be small and dried up, organic apples wormy, organic broccoli yellow, etc. At this time, however, improvements in growing, harvesting, storing, and shipping methods have enhanced the appearance and shelf-life of organic foods so that you should no longer have to settle for poor quality in order to avoid chemical contaminants. But, as one grower put it, "People need to understand that organic food . . . may not be as pretty." This may be difficult, for we are trained to judge by appearances, not content. (For more on organics, including how to identify these products and where to find them, see Chapters 2 and 3.)

CONSUMER RESPONSIBILITY

All the information in this chapter and the two that follow on vegetables and fruits is wasted if consumers do not play their part in keeping produce at its best.

Select with Respect

Although we resent it when we are not allowed to touch the produce or when everything is prepacked in plastic and cardboard, we can sympathize with the store personnel. Each time you apply severe pressure in search of soft spots or the most tender piece, or when accidentally an apple or tomato crashes to the floor, deterioration is accelerated. So, when you shop, treat fresh produce gently out of consideration to other consumers and the management. If you don't, you can only expect quality to go down, prices to go up, and more prepacked produce to appear.

Store with Concern

The same advice applies at home. Since one rotten apple can indeed spoil the barrel, discard any moldy fruit or vegetables as soon as you notice it. Clean the fruit bowl or storage bin often to discourage microorganisms.

Some foods are so tender that water alone can be abrasive enough to increase their susceptibility to infection. This is why you are counseled in Chapter 25 not to wash berries until you are ready to eat them. Since soil does harbor many infectious organisms though, it is a good idea to clean the surface of more firm-textured items before storage if dirt is visible.

Proper temperature, humidity, and air circulation are as important at home as they are between harvest and sale. Most fruit and vegetables do best in a cool environment—that is, below 40°F. Notable exceptions are pointed out in the individual descriptions in the two upcoming chapters.

Because produce does best in relatively high humidity, we recommend you keep it in the crisper bin of the refrigerator. The need for oxygen makes airtight packaging unsuitable.

Nothing is more effective than speedy use. Making more frequent trips to the market to pick up a few fresh items at a time can do much to improve your enjoyment of fruit and vegetables.

Prepare with Care

Produce should be prepared conscientiously. At the very least, washing is in order to remove microorganisms that have come from both the air and hands. However, it will do little to remove waxes, pesticides, and similar surface treatments. If you buy organic produce, these considerations won't be an issue. If not, you may want to try a mildly acidic cleaning solution made by diluting vinegar or citric acid (also called sour salt) in water. There are also commercial preparations based on this concept, but we have little information about their efficacy, and strong concerns about certain sanitizing agents like chlorine (as some publications recommend), or long-term soaking, which tends to leach out water-soluble nutrients.

Peeling is another possibility. When choosing this approach, try to be sparing. We frequently hear people lamenting the decline of food value due to shipping, commercial storage, and lack of turnover at the store, but according to the USDA, the primary culprit is careless handling at home. Since the greatest amount of vitamin C and other nutrients rests near the surface, excessive peeling and trimming diminish potential nutrients.

The more exposed the surface area and the longer it is exposed, the greater the losses. Cutting produce considerably in advance of service is a significant factor in nutritional deterioration. Letting groceries sit on the counter for hours after you arrive home or during lengthy food preparation is another nutritional pitfall.

We have already mentioned the drawbacks of prolonged soaking; excessive cooking, especially in a volume of water, compounds this effect. The best techniques are steaming, baking, stir-frying, and if carefully monitored, pressure cooking.

Finally, we certainly don't want to suggest you disregard leftovers, but wish to point out that storage and reheating also adversely affect nutritional values, especially if the produce has been cut up in small pieces. If it is not too inconvenient, try not to rely heavily on precooking and recooking. If you do, be sure to add something fresh to your diet daily to make up for any deficiencies.

RECOMMENDATIONS

General Rule of Purchase: Specific advice for purchasing individual fruits and vegetables can be found in the two chapters that follow. One of the most important issues facing consumers today is the damage done to soil, water, air, and our personal health by chemically dependent agriculture. You can participate in protecting the environment by supporting certified organic growers at the marketplace.

Chapter 24

Eat Your Vegetables

At one time, the refrain "eat your vegetables" was practically a national joke, but this is no longer so now that the health benefits and culinary pleasures of vegetable eating have finally gotten through to Americans.

One sign of the new status of produce can be seen in the popularity of what were once considered esoteric varieties. The average number of items carried in the produce case of the supermarket rose from 65 in 1972 to 173 in 1983. Sprouts probably head the list of new offerings. When we did our research for *The Supermarket Handbook* in 1972, sprouts were available only in natural food stores and California supermarkets. Today it's rare to find a supermarket without them. Other vegetables that have come into vogue include avocados, eggplant, fresh chiles, and several Oriental staples like snow peas and bok choy. Even Jerusalem artichokes, jicamas, and fresh water chestnuts are making their way into the standard produce case. Probably the most unusual vegetables to enter the market are the various seaweeds, largely a reflection of the interest in Japanese cooking.

The marketing of vegetables is not without its drawbacks. One sad example is the plastic bags of prewashed, precut, formerly fresh vegetables whose flavor may be enhanced with salt and sugar and whose lifespan is protected with preservatives. We have seen limas, black-eyed peas, carrot sticks, mushrooms, and preshredded cabbage offered in this manner. Another demoralizing development is the bagged vegetable snacks dependent on strains of carrots and celery grown by an agricultural biotechnology company that breeds "improved" fruits and vegetables. This specially grown produce will remain "crisp and crunchy" for up to two weeks after purchase, according to its creator. The price of this technology is high, with a 3-ounce packet selling for almost as much as a pound of the ordinary fresh vegetable.

THE NUTRITIVE VALUE OF VEGETABLES

The reason wise parents work so hard to get junior to eat vegetables is that vegetables make a significant contribution to the daily intake of vitamins and minerals. Every vegetable is well endowed with one or more of all the essential vitamins and minerals our bodies need, except vitamin D. No one vegetable, however, is high in all these nutrients, which is why it is necessary to eat a wide variety for a good diet. When a vegetable is especially rich in any nutrient, it will be mentioned in the upcoming buying guide.

Vegetables generally have the richest flavor and the most to offer nutritionally when eaten raw immediately after harvesting. As time passes, the nutritional makeup and taste diminish. This is one reason why so many people have their own gardens or seek out farm outlets. Deterioration is hastened by warmth, including cooking, and slowed down by cold. In the upcoming buying guide, some storage and handling tips appear for items that are less familiar or require special treatment.

THE ORGANIC OPTION

As we pointed out in Chapter 23, the fact that vegetables are purchased in the fresh natural state does not automatically make them untainted food. Of course, there is such a thing as "natural" vegetables. The label "organic" or "biologically grown" is applied to those vegetables grown in naturally enriched soil, without the help of chemical pesticides. In addition, they will not be colored, waxed, preserved, or otherwise treated to make them seem what they are not. For information on organic certification see Chapter 2.

PICKING THE BEST FRESH VEGETABLES (AND KEEPING THEM THAT WAY)

To help you select the vegetables that are freshest, and therefore endowed with the most nutrients and taste, we have assembled the following buying guide. Many vegetables are in constant supply year-round due to a naturally long growing period or to imports, but otherwise the best way to get vegetables that have these qualities is to buy in season when the supply is ripe and plentiful. Therefore, peak seasons are noted for most vegetables. Fortunately, this is the time when the prices are lowest too. If a particular vegetable is not in season, build your menu around another; there is always something that can be used to create a tasty, nutritious dish.

People who have spent time abroad or who make frequent visits to restaurants that feature foreign cuisines may recognize more of the items in the produce aisle than others will. Experimenting with new foods can add an exciting dimension to meal planning. Depending on where you live and where you shop, some, all, or none of the more exotic items described here may be found. If a vegetable sounds intriguing, ask at the produce department if it can be ordered.

Be aware that federal grades, when they appear, are based on physical appearance, not on flavor, nutrition, or the absence of chemical residues.

ARTICHOKES, GLOBE *(peak season March through May)* Artichokes are now a familiar sight at the market, although many people are still hesitant about preparing them. This vegetable has sharp pointed leaves and a bitter fuzzy "choke" positioned internally just above the succulent heart; it must be cooked in order to be edible. While these may not seem like very welcoming traits, when properly handled, the artichoke is delicious enough to warrant the effort.

Look For: Compact, tightly closed heads that are heavy in relation to size, with olive-green fresh-looking leaves. Streaks of brown, caused by frostbite, do not detract from their quality; in fact, some people say these are sweeter. However, an overall brownish color and scaly-looking leaves mean the artichoke is overdeveloped and will be tough and stringy. Size has nothing to do with quality or flavor; enormous specimens may look spectacular but are actually more tricky to cook. Since the stems are as tasty as the heart, look for artichokes that still have some stalk left.

Avoid: Leaves that are excessively brown or that show dark soft spots, and artichokes that have dried-out cracked stems. Spreading leaves indicate age (except in baby artichokes, which are comparatively loose looking). Old artichokes will be tough, dry, and bitter.

Storage and Handling: Artichokes can be stored successfully in the refrigerator for just a few days and keep best when air is allowed to circulate around them. After trimming they are likely to discolor; a water bath with lemon juice will keep this to a minimum. Except for baby artichokes which can be consumed in their entirety, the choke should be scraped off the base (or heart) before it is eaten.

ARTICHOKES, JERUSALEM *(available year-round; peak October through May)* The Jerusalem artichoke, or *sunchoke* as it is often called, is the tuber of a native American plant that grows wild (a weed, some might say). Above ground the plant closely resembles a sunflower. The edible root is small, gnarled, and beige-skinned on the outside; beneath the skin is a crisp white flesh with a pronounced sweet, nutty flavor.

Look For: Firm specimens with no soft, dark brown, or wet spots.

Avoid: Tubers with a pink cast.

Storage and Handling: Sunchokes keep best in a cool dry spot, although they can be refrigerated for about five days. They should be scrubbed well with a brush before use to remove the dirt from their uneven surface. They needn't be peeled, but if you choose to, you might want to wait until after they are cooked; it's a little easier to scrape the skin off then.

Tips: Jerusalem artichokes are delicious raw or just lightly cooked. They taste much like water chestnuts when added to a vegetable stir-fry. Steamed or baked they are similar to potatoes, but with a subtle, yet distinctive earthy taste.

ARUGULA *(peak season May through October)* Arugula, a well-known salad green in European Mediterranean countries, is gaining popularity in the United States. It is an excellent source of vitamins A and C and the minerals calcium and iron. With a distinct peppery taste similar to watercress, and a slightly bitter aftertaste, it is best used as part of a mixed salad with other, more mildly flavored greens. Some people know arugula by the names *roquette, rocket, rugula, roka,* or *Italian cress.*

Look For: Young leaves that are narrow and pointed; these have the mildest flavor. As the leaves grow larger, their bitterness intensifies.

Avoid: Greens with wilted or discolored leaves.

ASPARAGUS *(peak season March through June)* Asparagus are very expensive out of season.

Look For: Firm, well-rounded spears with compact tips. If you plan to cook them, match their size so they will all be done at the same time.

Avoid: Flat stalks or stalks that are limp or flabby, and tips that are open or decayed. Such asparagus will be tough and stringy.

Handling: To trim the ends of asparagus, break the stalk as far down as it snaps easily rather than trimming with a knife. This prevents stringiness and conserves nutrients.

Tip: Although few people take advantage of this, asparagus can be eaten raw as well as cooked.

AVOCADOS *(available year-round from California; Florida avocados available August to January with a peak in October and November)* Actually a fruit but treated by most people as a vegetable, a good, ripe avocado has a flesh that is tender and creamy but not soft like baby food. The avocado is one of the few fruits that contain protein, and although the amount is small, the quality is reputed to be high. Its fat content (largely monounsaturated) accounts for most of the calories, with California varieties containing almost twice as much fat per cup (and 150 more calories) than their competitors from Florida. Avocados also contain large amounts of potassium and vitamin A as well as substantial amounts of several B vitamins.

Look For: Avocados that yield to gentle pressure are ready for immediate eating. For use in a few days, buy firm fruit and let it ripen at room temperature. The skin should be uniform in color and free of cracks. Irregular brown markings on the skin have no effect on the inside flesh. California varieties have a rough skin and range from dark green to black in color. (The black, or Haas, avocados are touted as the best.) Florida avocados are usually larger, with a smooth, bright green skin.

Avoid: Avocados with dark, sunken spots in irregular patches and a cracked surface, indicative of decay. The stem cavity should be neither excessively deep nor torn. An avocado has passed its prime when it is quite soft, the skin seems to be parting from the flesh, or the pit rattles about when you shake it.

Storage and Handling: Avocados will not ripen in the refrigerator, and chilling may prevent ripening in the future. They do not like temperatures below 40°F. and refrigerator storage causes discoloration and off flavors. Thus, a ripe avocado should be used immediately or stored just briefly in the warmest part of the refrigerator.

Tip: To avoid darkening of the flesh once the avocado has been cut, sprinkle it with lemon juice; if you plan to keep it any length of time, replace the pit and cover.

BEANS, GREEN OR WAX *(available year-round; peak May through August)*
Look For: Young pods that feel velvety. Color should be fresh and bright looking.
Avoid: Beans that are limp, spindly (these were picked prematurely), thick and bulging with seeds (these are overmature and will be tough and woody tasting), or show brown rust spots or serious blemishes.

BEETS *(available year-round; slight peak June through August)*
Look For: Beets should be firm with a smooth surface and lush purple-red color. Beets that are sold in bunches are easiest to judge by the fresh appearance of the tops. Buy beets of fairly uniform size for even cooking.
Avoid: Beets with badly wilted tops, which indicate the beets are less than fresh; however, if the bulbs are still firm they may be satisfactory. Soft, wet areas, scaly areas around the top, and an elongated contour indicate beets that will be tough and strong-tasting.
Tip: The fresh leafy tops of beets, called beet greens, should be removed after purchase; they may be used raw in salad or cooked.

BOK CHOY *(available year-round; peak December through April)* Bok choy, a cabbage of Asian origins, has broad white stalks with dark green leaves projecting from them. It has a mild, sweet flavor, and the succulent stalks and tender leaves can be eaten raw or enjoyed in soups and stir-fries.
Look For: Firm stalks that stand straight up, with crisp, dark leaves.
Avoid: Limp stalks, leaves with many bruises, and excessive moisture or brown areas at the base. Look at the bottom where the stalks are joined; if there is a hole in it the bok choy is old.

BROCCOLI *(available year-round; peak December through March)* Broccoli is a plentiful source of the minerals calcium, potassium, and iron and of vitamins A and C. Although broccoli is available in the summer months, it is not as rich or tasty then as it is in the peak season.
Look For: Firm stalks with dark green or purplish green, compact clusters of buds. Stems should not be too thick or tough.
Avoid: Buds that are spread, yellow, or wilted, all signs of overmaturity or lack of freshness. This broccoli will be tough and stringy. Soft, slippery spots on the buds are signs of decay.

BROCCOLI DE RABE *(available in winter)* Also known as *rape*, this sharp-flavored green of Italian origin is a relative of cabbage and similar in taste to turnip greens. It comes in thin, stalklike bunches with tiny broccoli-like flower buds. The leaves and flowers are all edible and can be steamed and seasoned with a lemon-vinaigrette dressing for cold service or sautéed with garlic as a hot vegetable.
Look For: Fresh looking leaves and tiny yellow buds.

BRUSSELS SPROUTS *(peak season October through February)* Brussels sprouts, which look much like miniature cabbages, are often rendered unpalatable by overcooking.

Look For: Tight, firm leaves with a bright green color, free of worm holes and blemishes.

Avoid: Those that have burst or that have yellow or yellow-green leaves which are soft, loose, or wilted.

BURDOCK *(available year-round)* This long thin root with white flesh and an edible brown covering is popular in Japanese cooking, where it imparts its distinctive earthy flavor to soups and stews. Usually it is grated or chopped and acts more like a seasoning than a vegetable; however, it can be prepared as you would carrots. Sometimes burdock is referred to as *gobo*.

Look For: Young tender roots that are just an inch or less in diameter.

Storage and Handling: Store in the refrigerator layered in paper rather than in plastic. Do not wash until just before using.

Tips: Burdock roots should be carefully scrubbed before use, but the thin brown peel need not be removed. Contact with air causes discoloration, so any cut pieces should be kept in acidulated (lemon) water if they are not be used immediately.

CABBAGE *(available year-round)* Cabbage, especially green varieties, is a good source of vitamin C. Particularly useful in the winter when other fresh vegetables are less abundant.

Look For: Heads that are compact and heavy, with outer leaves that are deep green or purple (depending on the type) and free of blemishes. A few outer "wrapper" leaves may be loose; a head with many layers of wrapper leaves may prove wasteful since these are usually tough and stronger tasting and often end up having to be discarded. Savoy cabbage, with its curly leaves, is the exception, being characteristically loosely formed and rather light in weight.

If the head is already trimmed so that there are no outer leaves and it is pale in color, you can be fairly certain it is not really fresh. As long as it is not wilted or discolored it can still be satisfactory, though not as rich in vitamins.

Avoid: Heads that are puffy or very lightweight in comparison to size, those that have burst and show deep splits or scars, or those with outer leaves that are wilted, decayed, or yellow. Worm holes on the outside usually mean worms on the inside.

CABBAGE, CHINESE *(available year-round)* Chinese or *Napa* cabbage comes as an elongated head of pale green, almost white, crinkled leaves with pronounced veins emanating from a crisp, broad center stalk. It is much more delicate than American green cabbage and may be used as the main ingredient in a salad or combined with other vegetables in a stir-fry.

Look For: A head that is heavy for its size with leaves that hug each other tightly.

CACTUS LEAVES *(available mid-spring through mid-fall)*   If you are looking for something unusual to serve, perhaps the leaves of the nopal cactus will appeal to you. The cooked sections can be served as a warm vegetable or chilled as an appetizer or side dish. Marinated in an oil and vinegar dressing, cactus is said to taste like Italian green beans.

Look For: The smallest and thinnest pieces you can find, as these will be the most delicate.

Avoid: Thick leaves and those that are darkly colored, which will be old and tough.

Tips: Nopales, as the Mexicans call them, need to be carefully handled. Remove the sharp thorns using a paring knife or potato peeler, but leave the peel on. All the recipes we have seen recommend that they be cut in strips or cubes, simmered 15 to 20 minutes until tender, and then rinsed under cold running water to wash away the slippery substance they exude.

CARDOONS *(available in winter)*   A thistle-like plant related to the globe artichoke, the cardoon has large celery-like branches and a taste that vaguely resembles both these vegetables. Although not very common in this country, cardoons are popular in South America and Italy where they may be served raw or cooked in stews. They are especially compatible with tomatoes.

Look For: Cardoons with the smallest shafts as this indicates a young, tender plant. The leaves should be very dark.

Tips: The leafy stalks and the tender inner stalks, or heart, are the parts to use. They discolor quickly and cut surfaces should be rubbed immediately with lemon. If they are cooked alone, the water should be acidulated with lemon or vinegar.

CARROTS *(available year-round)*

Look For: Firm, smooth, well-colored carrots that are fairly regular in shape. Crooked carrots may be just as delicious but lead to greater waste. We find thinner carrots are usually younger and sweeter. If you come across carrots with the green tops still on, choose those with foliage that is fresh-looking.

Avoid: Carrots that have large green areas, those that are flabby or show soft spots, and those with deep growth cracks. Carrots covered with secondary rootlets or forming new shoots at the top are apt to be old, bland, and woody.

Tips: Remove the tops before storage as they are a drain on the vegetable's moisture supply. The skin and surface just beneath the skin are particularly rich in vitamins. Unless the vegetable is old and the skin noticeably thick, do not peel; a good scrubbing is all that is necessary.

CAULIFLOWER *(available year-round; peak October through January)*

Look For: Compact, solid heads with white to creamy white clusters (unless it is a purple variety) and fresh leaves, if they have not been removed.

Avoid: Heads that show many discolorations or soft wet areas—signs of mold and insect injury; check both the buds and the stem. Avoid clusters that appear fuzzy or are spread, indicating age, and heads with the tops trimmed off.

Tips: Before using, soak briefly in cold, salted water to drive out any resident insects.

CELERIAC *(available August through May)* Celery root or *knob* are other names by which this rugged-looking bulb is known. It is most famous for its use in the French classic céleri rémoulade, in which the cooked, julienned root is dressed with a spicy mayonnaise.

Look For: Firm crisp root stocks. The smaller ones are best; when they become too big they have a tendency to be woody.

Tips: Celeriac should be pared before use. While more commonly eaten cooked, the raw slivers can give a definitive celery flavor and crunchy texture to mixed salads.

CELERY *(available year-round)*

Look For: Crisp, thick stalks that snap easily and are tightly nested and bound at the stem end. Choose stalks with many green leaves, which are useful for flavoring soups, stews, and egg dishes.

Avoid: Limp, lifeless celery or stalks that show growth cracks or brown discoloration and rust marks where the branches are attached to the base. A bunch of celery with a distinctly open texture and air spaces in the central portion is described as "pithy" and is likely to be spongy, rather than crunchy. Exceedingly hard stalks may be stringy or woody.

CHAYOTE *(available November through April)* Pronounced "shy OH-tay," this squash, or "vegetable pear," is a specialty item brought in from Mexico and the Caribbean. The variety of chayote that is generally imported is pear-shaped, about 6 inches long, and has a ribbed, pale green rind and one soft edible seed. It is very bland, with a taste that faintly resembles cucumber, and holds its shape well, even when overcooked.

Look For: Hard, firm chayotes that are evenly colored.

Avoid: Specimens with soft, wet, brown spots, scars or bruises on the rind.

Storage: Store at 50° to 55°F. Refrigerator temperature is too cold.

Tips: Chayotes may be eaten raw or steamed, whole or in pieces. The peel is edible so there is no need to remove it.

CHICKORY *(available year-round)* Sometimes labeled *curly endive*, chickory grows in a "bunchy" cluster with narrow, ragged-edged leaves that curl at the ends. The center of the head is yellowish white and has a milder flavor than the dark green outer leaves, which are slightly bitter. It is used both cooked and as a salad green. For more information see Greens.

CHILES *(available year-round)* There are many varieties of chile pepper ranging from tiny to large, mild to fiery hot. The various fresh hot chilies that are used mainly for seasoning and garnish are described in Chapter 38. Those that are used as a vegetable, for stuffing or in cooked dishes, include:

The *California green chile,* or *Anaheim pepper,* which is bright green, 6 to 8 inches long, and just about 1½ inches around, usually with a rounded tip. This chile is quite bland.

The *New Mexico Green Chile,* also called the *New Mexico Anaheim, chile verde,* or *Big Jim,* or a variety of other regional names, which is similar in appearance to the California variety but more often has a pointed tip and also has a distinct bite.

The *poblano,* which is less widely seen in this country and is distinguished from the green chile by its dark green hue. It is also larger and ranges from mild to medium-hot.

Look For: Chiles that are firm, with good color and smooth, unbruised skin.

Avoid: Chiles that have soft or sunken spots. Very misshapen specimens are harder to work with.

Storage: Chiles keep best in the refrigerator if they are layered on paper toweling. Do not store in plastic bags, which hold in moisture and cause them to become limp and eventually moldy.

COLLARD GREENS *(peak season December through March)* A green with large, broad, smooth-textured, medium to dark green leaves. In the South they may simply be known as "greens." For more information see Greens.

CORN *(peak season May through September)* Although you will find it in the market most of the year, do not buy fresh corn out of season, for to call this "sweet corn" is just a courtesy. Corn begins to lose its delicate flavor immediately after harvesting, and unless it is in the prime of its life, it will have less tasty starchy kernels rather than ones that are filled with sugar-sweet milk.

Look For: If possible, corn should be bought and consumed the day it is picked. Ears of corn should still have their husks. Once this casing has been removed, the flavor and nutritional value of corn rapidly dissipates. The husk should be a good green color, with silk ends that are free from decay and stems that are neither discolored nor dried out. The silk should be dark amber or golden brown, smooth to the touch, and just a little damp. If the proprietor will allow you to pull back the husk, look for rows that are well filled with plump, milky kernels. Color is not a reliable indication of quality; some varieties are characteristically pale. Depending on how it has been handled, white, yellow, or bicolor corn can either be intensely sweet or best given to the cow.

Buy corn that is kept chilled. A day at room temperature will diminish its sweetness 50 percent, while refrigeration at 32°F. saves almost 95 percent of the natural sugars.

Avoid: Ears that have already been husked, husks that are yellow or wilted, and silk that is dry or very dark. Pass up corn with kernels that are extremely pale, underdeveloped or shriveled, or ears with oversized kernels. Corn should not be purchased from a bin exposed to the hot sun.

CUCUMBERS *(available year-round, with a slight peak in summer)* In most places it's hard to find cucumbers that have not been waxed. Sometimes kirby or pickling cucumbers are available with skins that are natural. If waxed, be sure to peel before using.

Look For: Unwaxed cucumbers with a trim, even shape and a good green color. Small whitish lumps on the surface are characteristic.

Avoid: The diameter of a cucumber should not be too large; this is the sign of an overgrown vegetable. Overgrown cucumbers will also have a dull color, turning to yellow. Avoid those that are puffy, have withered ends, or reveal a mushy texture under slight pressure. If you make a poor selection, you'll know when you cut into it by the tough seeds, the watery or jelly-like flesh in the seed cavity, and the bitter flavor.

DAIKONS—See Radishes.

EGGPLANTS *(available year-round, with a slight peak in late summer)* This lush purple vegetable is extremely versatile. It may be transformed into a dip, a cutlet, or a stew. It can be stuffed, rolled, layered, fried, grilled, baked, steamed, marinated, and much, much more.

Look For: Firm eggplants that are heavy for their size with a uniform, rich purple-black color. If you want an eggplant with a minimal amount of seeds, look for the males by checking the small scar opposite the stem end. If it is round, you've got a masculine one; an oval scar means it's a female and likely to be more seedy. (Be prepared for some strange looks as you go about your search.)

Baby eggplants are usually harvested from a specially developed variety. They tend to be sweeter and have fewer seeds. *Oriental eggplants* are similarly small and sweet and may be distinguished by a white skin streaked with purple and green.

Avoid: Those that are soft or flabby, or with dark brown spots, poor color, or cracked and shriveled skin.

Storage: Store eggplants in a cool, dry place, rather than in the refrigerator. Kept below 45°F. they will suffer skin damage.

Tips: Although the skin is edible, it may sometimes be preferable to remove it to rid the plant of chemical residues or a waxed surface. Cookbooks often suggest soaking eggplant or dredging it with salt and allowing the "bitter juices" to drain off before using, but this draws out the water-soluble nutrients, too. A good quality eggplant should not be bitter in the first place.

ENDIVE *(available year-round; peak December through June)* Endive is a small, 6-to-8-inch-long, missile-shaped head of tightly furled, pale leaves whose slightly bitter taste is highly prized and highly priced. The reason it is so expensive is not just that the world's entire supply comes from Belgium.

The planting process, which has been the same for more than a hundred years, is very intricate, and done almost entirely by hand. Preparation for market is also labor-intensive as the leaves are much too delicate to be trimmed and cleaned by machines.

Look For: Crisp, fresh looking, tender leaves.

Avoid: Limp heads or those with brown or damaged tips.

ESCAROLE *(available year-round)* This somewhat coarse green has broad, wavy, dark green leaves with irregular edges. The head is somewhat flattened and has the appearance of a flower in bloom. For more information see Greens.

FAVA BEANS *(available late March through early May)* Fresh fava beans, sometimes called *broad beans,* make a brief appearance on the market in the spring. As they are a rare find, you should take advantage of any you come across. If the bean is very young, the entire pod can be eaten, but unfortunately this is seldom found outside of home gardens. You are more likely to encounter large pods filled with a green, kidney-shaped bean that must be shelled, a tedious job that is easier to do after, rather than before cooking.

Look For: Glossy, bright green pods.

Avoid: Those with fat, overly developed beans inside and pods that have soft spots or a good deal of brown discoloration.

Tip: Favas contain an antinutrition factor that is destroyed by heat and thus must be cooked until tender before they can be eaten.

FENNEL *(available during the summer)* Sometimes labeled *finochio,* this vegetable has a bulbous base with blanched stalks and long feathery tops. Its mild licorice flavor goes well in salads and cooked vegetable dishes. Use the bulb and shoots either raw or cooked, as you would celery, and the tops as a seasoning herb.

Look For: A crisp firm bulb with fresh looking greenery at the top.

Avoid: Fennel that seems flabby, or shows "rust" streaks on the bulb end, growth cracks in the stalks, or has limp or dried-out greenery. If the tops have been removed it is a sign of age.

FIDDLEHEADS *(available in summer)* The delicate green shoot of a fern that looks like the tuning-peg of a violin. Many people gather it in the wild, but some stores make it available in season for those who are not interested in foraging.

Look For: Small, green shoots that are tightly furled.

Avoid: Wilt, rot (brown soft spots), and fiddleheads larger than 8 inches. Open shoots are said to be poisonous.

Storage: Fiddleheads do not keep well and should be refrigerated for no more than a day or two.

GARLIC *(available year-round)* The fresh clove is best for giving food a garlicky flavor; any other form is not even a close second.

Look For: Heads (as the cluster of cloves is called) that are compact and well enclosed in their casing. This outer sheath should be crisp and papery. Individual cloves should be plump and firm.

Avoid: Heads that are spreading and individual cloves that are shriveled or have soft, brown spots.

Storage: Heads of garlic should be stored in a cool, dark, dry place—not in the refrigerator.

Green Onions—See Scallions.

Greens *(available year-round)* This loose term encompasses *spinach, kale, collard greens, turnip greens, beet greens, Swiss chard, mustard greens, chicory, escarole, dandelion greens, spinach,* and *sorrel.* Most greens have a slightly bitter but pleasant flavor. Collards and Swiss chard are more delicate, kale is slightly sharp, and mustard and turnip greens can be quite pungent. All can be used raw in salads, and they are extremely tasty cooked. Dark leafy greens are among the best sources of vitamin A and also supply vitamin C, calcium, and iron. Although some contain a substance that inhibits the absorption of this calcium, kale and turnip greens do not.

Look For: Greens that look fresh, with a healthy green color and no apparent blemishes. Tender young leaves are the least bitter.

Avoid: Wilted leaves and those with coarse stems, yellow coloring, and soft, wet decay spots. Leaves with protruding stalks and seeds will be unappealingly bitter.

Jicama *(available year-round; peak November through June)* Pronounced "hee-kah-mah," this Mexican root vegetable is shaped like a giant beet, and has a tan skin and crisp white flesh. Raw, it is sweet and succulent, and peeled slices can be enjoyed by themselves as a snack, used as a dipper, or cut up into salads. Cooked jicama resembles water chestnuts and is a tasty addition to stir-fries.

Look For: Firm jicama, free of soft brown spots or any damp, slippery areas on the surface.

Storage and Handling: Store uncut jicama in a cool, dry place; once cut, it should be refrigerated. Never wrap it in a plastic bag as this accelerates the growth of mold. The cut root does not keep very well, even with refrigeration, so try to use it within a day or two.

Tips: The rough skin must be removed before eating. If a conventional peeler proves too difficult, try a sharp paring knife. If all else fails, cut it into wedges or rounds and peel away the fibrous outer layer with your fingers.

Kale *(most plentiful in winter)* A nonheading form of cabbage that may have curly or flat leaves ranging from green to a bluish purple. Kale can be rather tough and is most palatable when chopped. It is exceedingly high in vitamins A and C and the minerals calcium and iron. For more information, see Greens.

KOHLRABI *(available May through November; peak June and July)*   Kohl-abi, meaning "cabbage turnip," has the rather unusual appearance of a round sea-green globe that, before trimming, has leaves sprouting out of the top. Young kohlrabi can be eaten raw and makes an excellent dipper. Cooked in stir-fries it is similar to bamboo shoots. In Europe, where it is quite popular, it is more commonly cut into thin slices or sticks and steamed and buttered.

Look For: Small solid heads, attractively colored, with a rind that can be pierced with a fingernail.

Avoid: Kohlrabi with skin blemishes or growth cracks. Large heads tend to be fibrous.

Tips: The stem and bulb should be peeled thinly, either before or after cooking, to remove the most fibrous layer. The leaves can be cooked like any greens.

LEEKS *(available year-round; peak winter and early spring)*   Leeks look like giant scallions. They are particularly good steamed or pan-fried in butter and served with a bread crumb topping, for flavoring soups, and in vegetable stews. The taste is similar to that of onion, only milder and sweeter.

Look For: Crisp, firm leeks with medium-sized necks and 2 to 3 inches of white shoots extending from the base.

Avoid: Leeks with wilted yellow tops, brown outer layers, and soggy roots.

Handling: Be sure to wash leeks carefully before use as dirt often becomes lodged between the thin layers that make up each leek. Use both the white and the green parts.

LETTUCE *(available year-round)*   The main commercial varieties are *iceberg, butterhead, romaine,* and *green and red loose-leaf.*

Iceberg accounts for almost three-fourths of U.S. lettuce sales, but do not take this as a sign that it is the best. Iceberg has a nice crisp texture, but lacks both taste and nutrients. All other varieties have far more calcium, iron, and vitamins C and A as the table "Comparing Raw Greens" shows.

Butterhead varieties include *Boston,* with soft cup-shaped leaves that are often oily (a natural property of the plant) and quite succulent; *bibb,* which is similar but smaller, with dark, flat leaves; and, *limestone,* which is more upright in appearance.

Romaine, or *cos,* has elongated, loosely folded leaves that are large and dark on the outside, and paler and more tender toward the center.

Lime green and red-tipped or all-reddish loose-leaf varieties are characterized by broad, tender, softly curling leaves attached loosely by a central base rather than in a head.

Also to be found (usually in a plastic bag with roots intact) is *hydroponic* lettuce, which is not a special variety but lettuce grown without soil in a greenhouse setting. We have seen hydroponic forms of both Boston and limestone lettuce. Rather than actually displaying the word "hydroponic,"

COMPARING RAW GREENS

Type 3.5 ounces	Vitamin A IU	Vitamin C mgs	Calcium mgs	Iron mgs
Iceberg	330	4	19	0.5
Butterhead, Boston, bibb, or limestone	970	8	35	2.0
Romaine or cos	2600	24	68	1.4
Loose-leaf	1900	18	68	1.4

such lettuce often carries a brief explanation alluding to a "controlled" environment. While some people contend that hydroponic gardening will permit cultivation of more food worldwide as it is not dependent on fertile land, it is a costly process in terms of energy and technology.

Look For: The leaves of romaine should be crisp; for other varieties, they should be tender without being wilted. In most lettuce the color will range from medium to light green, and it should always be bright. Except for the loose-leaf varieties, leaves should be nestled fairly tightly against each other and well secured at the stem end.

Avoid: Avoid iceberg lettuce altogether. For all varieties, reject wilted leaves that are brown at the edges and the stem end. Ribs should not have brown streaks or a pink cast. Heads that appear to have been trimmed of several layers of outer leaves or whose tips have been cut away suggest previous defects.

Storage and Handling: Lettuce should be washed carefully to remove clinging sand or soil before it is used, but it should never be subject to lengthy soaking in either plain or acidulated water since this will only extract the vitamins. Do not store lettuce with tomatoes, apples, pears, or other produce that emits ethylene gas as this causes brown spotting on the leaves. Actually, lettuce keeps best in its own sealed container; we generally wash enough to last several days, spin it dry, and then line the storage container with paper toweling to absorb any extra moisture.

LIMA BEANS *(peak season June to September)* Fresh green lima beans, still in the pod, make a brief appearance in specialty markets during the summer. They are a chore to shell, but if you are a lima bean lover, the fresh cooked bean is worth it.

Look For: Bright green pods that are firm and well filled.

Avoid: Pods that are flabby or show many brown areas, especially if damp or mushy. Steer clear of small underdeveloped beans (not worth the time to shell) and overdeveloped pods that are pale colored or yellowish with beans that are hard, starchy, and no longer green.

Tips: Limas, like fava beans, contain an anti-nutrition factor that is destroyed by heat, so be sure to cook them before eating.

MUSHROOMS *(available year-round, with a dip in August)* Mushrooms are naturally high in glutamic acid (found in MSG), which is probably why they intensify the flavor of so many dishes. In addition to the common cultivated mushroom, a few exotic strains are being raised for market. *Oyster* mushrooms, named for their flat, oyster-shell shape and gray-beige color; *shiitake* mushrooms, with a dark brown color and irregular contour; tender, meaty *porcinis*; and cream-colored *enoki* mushrooms, with tiny round caps and long stringlike stalks are popping up in many stores. You will find they all have a more pronounced and definitive taste than the standard variety but can be used in the same manner.

Look For: Young mushrooms, which will be small to medium in size. The caps (the white portion on top) should be closed around the stem or just slightly open to reveal light tan "gills" (the rows of paper-thin tissue under the cap). The cap surface should be cream-colored or white, although a light brown color is acceptable.

Avoid: Those with wide-open caps and dark gills, those seriously pitted or discolored, and those with a spongy texture. Check to avoid preservatives in prewrapped boxes.

Storage and Handling: Mushrooms continue to breathe actively even after they are harvested and, if not consumed soon, develop a woody texture. To keep them, cover with a damp paper towel and refrigerate. Clean by running briefly under water or wiping with a damp cloth or soft brush; do not soak or they will become soft and spongy. Mushrooms do not require peeling.

OKRA *(peak season May through September)* Okra is grown and marketed primarily in the South. It is an essential ingredient in gumbo and in Creole cooking. When cooked, it oozes a thick, gooey liquid.

Look For: Pods free from blemishes with tips that bend with very slight pressure. They should be under 4½ inches long.

Avoid: Pods that are tough, indicated by ends that are stiff and won't bend or by a very hard body, and pods that are pale or shriveled.

Storage and Handling: Use soon after purchase. Long exposure to temperatures below 45°F. spurs decay.

Tip: If cooked in iron or copper, okra turns black, so you may want to stick with glass, stainless steel, or enameled utensils.

ONIONS *(available year-round)* The most popular varieties are the ordinary *globe* onions used for all-purpose cooking and seasoning, the larger and sweeter *Spanish* onions (yellow- or white-skinned), and the somewhat elongated *Bermuda* onions (purplish red), which are also sweeter and ideal for salads. In addition, there are small white boiling onions and long green bunching onions, called *scallions* by many and described under that name in this section.

Onion connoisseurs eagerly await the young Vidalia onions from Georgia, which appear in May and June, the Walla Walla from the state of Washington available from late June through August, and the Maui onion, which is sold only in Hawaii and is so sweet and mild it can be eaten out of hand like an apple.

Look For: Hard, firm onions that have dry skins and small necks. The outer scales should be papery and free of soft spots.

Avoid: Onions that are wet or mushy anywhere, have unhealed wounds, show excessive green on the surface, or are beginning to sprout.

Storage: Store in a cool, dry environment.

Parsley *(available year-round)* Parsley is a delicate herb that usually is used as a garnish, gets shoved to the side of the plate, and is ultimately discarded—a big mistake, as parsley is rich in vitamins C and A, iron, and vegetable protein. It comes in two varieties: *curly-leaf* and *flat-leaf Italian.*

Look For: Crisp, bright leaves. Slightly wilted leaves can be freshened by standing the stems in cold water, but this causes some loss of vitamin C.

Avoid: Leaves that are yellow, brown, or dark and slippery, or those that are wilted.

Parsnips *(peak season October through April)* Parsnips look like bleached-out carrots. Although on the market pretty much year-round, they are really a winter vegetable.

Look For: Small or medium-sized parsnips that are smooth and even-shaped, firm and free of surface blemishes.

Avoid: Large parsnips (which usually have thick woody centers), and those that are flabby (they will be tough even when cooked). The end should not be damp, brown, or mushy.

Tips: Parsnips need cooking. To ensure a sweet, nutty flavor, they should be steamed, not boiled. Scrape away the peel after cooking.

Peas, Green *(peak season March through June)* Peas should be eaten soon after harvesting or they will lose their sweet flavor. Leave them in the pod until you are ready to use them. Raw peas eaten out of the shell make a wonderful snack.

Look For: Pods that are bright green and velvety to the touch. They should be well filled without being swollen.

Avoid: Underdeveloped pods that are swollen with air, flecked with gray, or have poor color. Overdeveloped pods are often wrinkled and faded, with a white or yellow cast. Overripe peas have a flat, starchy taste, similar to raw peanuts. Oversized peas that are starting to sprout taste beany.

Peppers, Sweet *(available year-round, mostly from Mexico January through April)* Although most of the sweet peppers on the market are green, those that are fully mature (and even sweeter) have a bright red color. Purple and yellow varieties have elevated price tags and the return on your money will be largely their decorative effect. Peppers are an excellent source of vitamin C.

Look For: Firm, bright peppers with strong color. Shininess may be misleading since peppers are frequently waxed. They should be relatively heavy for their size. A crooked shape is fine for flavor and nutrition, but may have greater waste.

Avoid: Peppers with very thin walls, apparent by their light weight and flimsy sides, and those that are soft, show water spots, or have a cracked surface.

Storage: Peppers do better at 50°F. than in refrigerator temperatures, so if you have a cool storage area, keep them there.

PLANTAINS *(available year-round)*   Although technically a fruit, plantains are generally served as a vegetable. In appearance, they resemble bananas, but are larger, taste starchier, and are always cooked before eating. Plantains are an excellent source of vitamin A and potassium.

Look For: Plaintains that are yellow or speckled with brown are ripe and ready for cooking. If you're buying for the future, get green ones and let them ripen at room temperature.

POTATOES *(available year-round; new crop appears May through November)*
The potato is almost nutritionally perfect. An average-sized potato (100 to 150 grams) has from 95 to 110 calories, offers seven of the eight essential amino acids, is virtually fat-free, and contains good supplies of vitamin C, B vitamins, iron, potassium, and magnesium.

Although the lines of demarcation are not quite clear, potatoes fall into three general categories: *new* potatoes, *all-purpose* potatoes, and *baking* potatoes.

"New" usually signifies those freshly harvested. The outer skin is very thin and may be tan or red. These do not keep well.

All-purpose potatoes are used for just that—boiling, mashing, frying, baking, and in salads. Those that are "waxy" are less dense and best for frying, salads, and stews.

The dense baking varieties are considered the most desirable for a baked potato that is not soggy or dry. Western-grown varieties, and especially russets, are considered better for baking than eastern potatoes.

Look For: Reasonably smooth well-shaped potatoes that are firm and free of eyes or sprouts. There is less waste in uniformly shaped specimens.

Avoid: Potatoes with large cuts or bruises, a scaly skin, soft spots, areas of green, or lots of sprouts. Potatoes with a greenish color, which is generated by light, should be avoided because they contain a carcinogen called solanine.

Storage and Handling: While cool temperaures inhibit sprouting, cold has a negative effect on flavor and texture, so store potatoes in a cool, dark, well-aerated place—not in the refrigerator. To minimize greening, store potatoes away from light. If potatoes become green in storage, remove the skin and cut away the layer just under the green portion, as well as the eyes and sprouts.

Tips: The method of cooking has a considerable effect on nutritional value. Baked potatoes contain more protein and minerals than fried ones. To conserve vitamin C, cook potatoes with the peel on and, if you must remove it at all, do so after cooking when it is easier anyway and you will not lose much more than the thin outer covering. As much as a third of the nutrients are concentrated near the surface. A word of warning on fried potato skins: studies have revealed that when potato skins are fried the concentration of solanine doubles and may actually exceed recommended levels of safety.

PUMPKINS *(available October to November)* Because pumpkins are used mainly for baking, many people are surprised when pumpkin turns up prior to dessert. We are particularly fond of pumpkin soup and have found that this vegetable can be cooked and served in any way you would use winter squash.

Look For: Firm, heavy pumpkins with bright orange skin.

Storage and Handling: Fresh whole pumpkin will keep for several weeks in a cool, dry place. Cut and wrapped, it can be refrigerated for about five days. It is easier to remove the skin after cooking, although it is rather tedious any way you choose to do it.

Tips: Toast the seeds in the oven for snacking.

RADICCHIO Pronounced "rah-DEE-kyoh," this specialty lettuce is prized by Italians and trendy restaurants. The most common variety in U.S. markets is red-leafed with white ribs and has a slightly bitter, nutlike flavor.

RADISHES *(available year-round; slight peak March through May)* Radishes are a root vegetable with a crisp, clean "bite." Red radishes are most commonly found, but there are also white or *icicle, black,* and the large white Oriental *daikon* variety.

Look For: Medium-size radishes that are firm, evenly shaped, and of good color. Fresh red radishes with tops intact have more zip than cold-storage packaged ones.

Avoid: Large flabby radishes, cracked radishes, radishes with brown, black or soft spots, and those with yellow or decayed tops. Slight pressure will reveal undesirable sponginess.

Handling: Daikons and black radishes must be scrubbed and peeled before use. Icicle radishes often need a thin scraping too. The red varieties can be eaten in their entirety (except for the green leafy tops which should be removed before storage).

RUTABAGAS *(peak season July through April)* A rutabaga is a large yellow root vegetable with a sweet flavor and rather rugged reputation. It makes a hearty addition to winter stews, although it can be served alone, mashed or steamed like potatoes.

Look For: Firm ones that are round to slightly elongated and heavy for their size.

Avoid: Rutabagas that have skin punctures or deep surface cuts.

Storage and Handling: Store in a dry, well-ventilated area. Rutabagas are likely to be coated with paraffin, so be sure to peel them before cooking.

SCALLIONS *(available year-round)* Scallions, a.k.a. *green onions,* possess small white bulb at their base extending to form a tall green shoot. They are quite mild compared to their onion relatives.

Look For: A crisp, tender base with no signs of rot, or discoloration, two o three inches of white extending up from the bottom, and tops that are fresh and of good green color. Slight scarring at the tip is not objectionable.

Avoid: Scallions with dry or excessively damaged green tops, tops that are pale or yellowish, and those with damp, brown, or soft root ends. Slippery outer skins are a warning sign of poor handling and impending spoilage.

SHALLOTS *(available October to May)* Shallots grow in clove form, with several segments joined at the base and covered by a thin, reddish papery skin. They are a mild-tasting member of the onion family, with a very subtle flavor.

Look For: Shallots should have firm, plump cloves that are neither shrunken nor shriveled looking.

Storage: Store in a cool, dry environment.

SNOW PEAS *(available January through June)* These flat pea pods are not underdeveloped green peas, but a vegetable unto themselves and one that you've probably sampled in mixed vegetables at a Chinese restaurant. *Sugar* or *snap peas,* also called *edible pod,* are closely related. As the name implies, the entire pod is edible and may be consumed raw or quickly stir-fried.

Look For: Medium-green pods with no real peas inside are the most tender and sweet. According to the experts, pods that are coated with a whitish film are fresh and have not been handled too much.

Handling: Use as soon as possible and do not wash until ready to use.

SPINACH *(available year-round; peak season spring and fall)* Loose spinach of either the flat-leaf or curly varieties is apt to be fresher and grown closer to home than prepacked spinach. However, spinach in packages has the advantage of being trimmed and washed.

Look For: Loose spinach leaves should be dark green and crisp, with an earthy smell. Sealed bags should feel full and springy.

Avoid: Limp greens with yellow discoloration or bags that are soft or show dark wet spots through their transparent wrapper. Take a whiff; spinach should not have a sour or cabbage-like odor.

Handling: Spinach must be thoroughly soaked and washed in cold water to rid it of sand and dirt. Several changes of water are recommended. It will hold up best if washing is reserved until preparation time.

SPROUTS *(available year-round)* Several varieties of sprouts now appear in the market. *Alfalfa, radish, clover,* and *mung bean* are the most popular commercial ones. Just about any whole bean or seed can be turned into a fresh vegetable in your kitchen, and packets of sprouting seeds may also be found in the produce section of the market.

Look For: Lively looking sprouts with a bright color (even if they are a translucent milky tone). There should be no more than the tiniest green leaf growth.

Avoid: Packaged sprouts that are too tightly packed, excessively wet, or brown (check the bottom of the box); or sprouts that appear dull, grayish, or tired.

Storage: Sprouts need good air circulation to keep them from becoming moldy, but too much air dries them out. Refrigerator storage in a loosely covered container with plenty of room in it is best, but even so they should be eaten as soon as possible.

Tips: Most sprouts are best eaten raw. Exceptions are mung bean sprouts, which can be cooked successfully if you are quick about it, and soybean sprouts, which should always be heated to deactivate anti-nutritional factors.

SQUASH, SUMMER *(some form available year-round)* Although it may be called summer squash, some form of this vegetable is available year-round. The most common varieties are the green *zucchini* and the yellow *crookneck* and *straight-neck*. All parts, including the skin, are edible. Less widely available are the *cozelle* (similar to zucchini but with a slightly ribbed skin with alternate stripes of yellow and dark green), *cymling* or *patty pan* (disk-shaped with a scalloped edge and a pale green skin; peel this before use and prepare as you would other summer varieties), and *spaghetti* squash (something like a honeydew melon in appearance with an inedible rind and flesh that separates into strands after baking or steaming).

Look For: Those with good color that are heavy for their size, with a rind soft enough to puncture with a fingernail.

Avoid: Squash with a dull surface that has soft spots or a rough, tough skin. Such squash will have enlarged seeds and a dry, stringy texture. Also avoid soft, flabby squash.

SQUASH, WINTER *(some form available year-round; peak August through December)* There are several varieties of winter squash, which all have a tough, inedible skin surrounding the flesh and a cavity filled with edible seeds. The most common varieties are: *acorn*, which is dark, green-ribbed, oval with a pointed end and weighs 1 to 3 pounds; *butternut*, which is tan and somewhat elongated with a thick neck and a bell-shaped end; *buttercup*, 3 to 5 pounds with a green turban-like cap on the end; *turban*, a 4-to-8-pound squash that is reddish-orange with a turban-like cap; *Hubbard*, a large, 10-to-15-pound squash with a green, ribbed, rough skin; *delicious*, another large 5-to-10-pound variety that may be either green or golden and shaped like a top; *banana*, which is long and oval, with a pinkish skin and can weigh as much as 30 pounds for a single specimen.

Look For: Squash that is heavy in relation to size, with a tough hard rind. Those with some stem still attached will keep the longest. Some larger varieties may be precut into more convenient sizes; check that the surface is neither dry nor slimy.

Avoid: Squash with soft spots or rot at the stem end.

Storage and Handling: Winter squash will keep for several months if tored in a cool, well-ventilated area and placed so they do not touch one another.

Tip: The seeds can be separated and toasted in the oven.

SWEET POTATOES AND YAMS *(available year-round; dip May through August)* Sweet potatoes are a terrific source of vitamin A and have more minerals and calories, but less protein than white potatoes. True yams are not very common in the United States and what is sold as a yam is usually just a moist-fleshed variety of sweet potato.

Look For: Firm, well-shaped potatoes with a smooth, bright, and evenly colored skin. Skin color may range from tan to brown to coppery and the true quality may sometimes be obscured by waxing.

Avoid: Potatoes with worm holes, cuts, or any surface injury; they lead to waste and rapid spoilage and the potato will have a sour taste. Decay, common in sweet potatoes, is evidenced by shriveled, discolored ends, sunken, discolored areas at the sides, and wet, soft spots on the skin.

Storage: Sweet potatoes deteriorate more rapidly than other potatoes and should be bought for use in the near future. Store them in a cool (55° to 60°F.), dry environment, not the refrigerator.

SWISS CHARD *(available in summer and fall)* Swiss chard has large green or red leaves with white, celery-like ribs. It is an extremely versatile green. Its leaves can substitute for spinach or can be stuffed and rolled like cabbage. Young raw leaves are a tasty addition to salads. The ribs can be used like celery. For more information see Greens.

TARO ROOT *(available year-round)* Taro root is an irregularly shaped tuber with a dark brown skin covering a light white to pinkish flesh. It is rather bland, with a trace of nuttiness and a creamy texture. Taro is the basis for the Polynesian staple called *poi* and a specialty item in every state but Hawaii where it is a staple.

Look For: Tubers that are plump and firm. If there are any buds, they should be small and bright pink in color.

Avoid: Worm holes, which can be found under the strands of "hair" on the surface.

Tips: Taro must be cooked prior to eating; it can be boiled or baked like a potato and served in the same manner.

TOMATILLOS Also known as *ground tomatoes* and *green tomatoes,* this nugget-like vegetable in a brown papery husk may be as small as a walnut or the size of a big lemon. Its flavor is very distinctive, somewhat like a tart, underripe plum when raw, developing an apple-like quality as it cooks. It is quite popular in Mexican sauces but is a specialty item in the United States. Unlike common tomatoes, the tomatillo is never eaten raw.

Look For: Specimens with a dry husk and a green to yellow-green fruit beneath it.

Avoid: Shriveled or bruised tomatillos.

Storage and Handling: Stored in the husks in the refrigerator, preferably between layers of paper toweling, they will keep for several weeks. Remove husks and wash just prior to use.

TOMATOES *(peak season May through August)* The deterioration of the tomato really started with its success. As the demand grew, geneticists set about developing strains of firm, tough-skinned tomatoes that would mature simultaneously so they could all be harvested by machine at the same time. They obviously succeeded, for in his book *Human Scale*, Kirkpatrick Sale contends that the resilience of the MH-1 tomato under impact exceeds by 250 percent the minimum federal safety standards for automobile bumpers. The reporter who discovered this remarkable fact, noted ironically: "This undoubtedly represents a great step forward in tomato safety."

The best-flavored tomatoes are generally locally grown varieties. They can offer as much as twice the amount of vitamin C as those tomatoes picked and shipped green or those raised in hothouses. The poorest quality tomatoes are picked green and artificially ripened by ethylene gas in the truck on the way to the market. These would be better bought green and ripened in a warm place, out of direct sunlight, in your own home, but truthfully, when poor-quality hothouse varieties are all that can be found, it's better to do without.

TomAHtoes™ refers to a new packaging process which supposedly keeps the fruit from spoiling without refrigeration and controls ripening en route to the market so that just the right stage can be maintained. Since it is refrigeration that contributes to the mealy texture and insipid flavor of out-of-season tomatoes, TomAHtoes supposedly taste like real tomatoes even in the dead of winter. If they are displayed in the cooler, however, this alleged advantage will be lost.

Look For: Firm, plump tomatoes that have good color and no serious blemishes. Heavier ones have more meaty solids and less liquid run-off (which carries nutrients with it). One important clue to detecting vine-ripened tomatoes seems to be the smell. Vine-ripened specimens have a fresh tomato odor; gassed tomatoes are odorless.

Avoid: Overripe and bruised tomatoes that are soft and watery, or have growth cracks at the stem, and those with water-soaked spots, depressed areas, and surface mold.

Storage and Handling: Even ripe tomatoes do not like cold and should be kept at 50° to 60°F. to preserve flavor and texture.

TURNIPS *(available year-round; peak October through March)* The most common turnip has white flesh and, in some varieties, purple shading at the top. The leaves can be eaten as greens.

Look For: Turnips that are small to medium in size, firm, smooth, and fairly round.

Avoid: Large turnips with obvious fibrous roots. Yellow or wilted tops are a sign of aging.

Storage: Store in a cool dry place if possible; if none is available, use the refrigerator.

WATER CHESTNUTS *(available year-round)* Fresh water chestnuts are a new and somewhat rare addition to produce cases. They are about the size of a large walnut and are covered with a scaly, dark brown shell, usually encrusted with dirt, that can be peeled away with a paring knife. Washed, peeled, sliced or diced, raw or cooked, they remain crisp and sweet (much more so than canned ones).
Look For: Water chestnuts that are hard and plump.
Avoid: Those that are bruised or sprouting.
Storage and Handling: Unpeeled water chestnuts can be stored for about a month in the refrigerator. Once shelled they decay rapidly and should be used within two days. Any dark spots should be cut away.

WILD EDIBLES *(available in spring and summer)* Foraging for vegetables is too broad a subject to teach in these pages, but we do want you to keep this possibility in mind. Whether you live in an urban, suburban, or rural neighborhood, there will probably be quite a variety of free edibles available to you if you are knowledgeable. *Dandelion greens, sorrel, onion grass, common plaintain, pepper grass, purslane, violets, day lilies, dock, lambs quarters,* and *red clover* are just some of the bounty waiting to be discovered in city parks, vacant lots, and country fields. In some areas there are people who conduct walks that can acquaint you with the local pick, and there are many guidebooks available.

DRIED VEGETABLES

Dehydration of vegetables is probably the oldest form of preservation, dating back to the Incas.

Potatoes

The drying of potatoes began with the Incas. Of course the technique has been modernized, so today the skins are first removed by steam or chemicals, and sulfite whiteners, sequestrants, stabilizers, and preservatives may be added. Such potatoes may appear in the store as hash browns, scalloped potatoes, au gratins, or instant mashed potatoes, or may provide the basis for potato pancake mixes. Not all are so unfortunately mistreated, but be aware that when potato flakes are an ingredient in another food these "incidental additives" may be hidden from view.

Mushrooms

You may come across several kinds of dried mushrooms. Least expensive are the small containers with pieces of dried common mushrooms found on most supermarket shelves. These mushrooms can be added to soups, sauces, stews, or grain dishes to recreate the woodsy flavor of the fresh-cooked vegetable.

Dried whole mushrooms are more expensive. *Shiitake* mushrooms, *straw* mushrooms, *oyster* mushrooms, *forest* mushrooms, and *black* mushrooms are likely to be found where Oriental staples are sold. These should be soaked in warm water to soften before use, and if the stems are very tough they should be trimmed off. You may also find other exotic Oriental vegetables in their dried state such as *lotus root, tree ears,* and *tiger lily buds.*

Seaweeds

Seaweeds have been harvested from the ocean for centuries in Japan. They are now becoming more available in American markets. These sea vegetables are especially rich in minerals including calcium, iron, magnesium, phosphorus, zinc, sodium, potassium, fluoride, and iodine. Some varieties are also rich in vitamins C and A and the B vitamins; even vitamin B_{12}, which is usually associated with animal foods, appears to be present in seaweeds. The Orientals claim seaweeds are good for arthritis, cardiac problems, high and low blood pressure, goiter, nervous disorders, and endocrine system malfunction, possibly due to the presence of omega-3 fatty acids. They also say seaweeds help eliminate the radioactive and chemical wastes we pick up from the environment.

Seaweeds are used in a variety of ways, enumerated in the descriptions that follow. One form, *nori,* is becoming increasingly familiar to Americans as the wrapper for sushi, the Japanese raw fish roll. Others are useful as thickeners and flavoring agents, or are served as salads or vegetable accompaniments.

Some seaweeds must be reconstituted before use by soaking in a small amount of water for five to fifteen minutes. Rinsing before soaking can help remove any sediment and some of the salt. Be sure to use a container large enough to allow the vegetable to expand after it absorbs the liquid. If you've prepared more than you need, keep the leftovers in the refrigerator and use within a week. The soaking liquid should be reused for cooking or at least for feeding houseplants. Because it is apt to be salty, remember not to season foods that contain seaweed or seaweed water without sampling first.

Agar: Agar is a clear, flavorless seaweed sold in flakes or bars that is used like gelatin (see Chapter 35).

Alaria: Alaria has been described as the most beautiful of seaweeds, with slender midribs, golden brown fronds, and spore-bearing leaves at its base.

Its taste is described as "wild." Alaria is especially rich in calcium, magnesium, iodine, chromium, and vitamin A.

Arame: A dark black seaweed that is mild in flavor and aroma. Arame is usually sold cut in thin strands. The reconstituted vegetable can be added to soups, grains, or stews, or served as a cold salad.

Dulse: Dulse, a native American plant, is considered to be one of the most palatable seaweeds for Western tastebuds, with a salty, nutlike flavor. It does not require soaking and can be added to cooked dishes or even eaten dry as a snack. Dulse is reportedly very high in iron.

Hijiki: Hijiki is noted for its high calcium and iron content and a somewhat lower sodium content than other seaweeds. This stringy black seaweed is sold in strands that are a little thicker and stronger flavored than arame, but can be used in the same manner.

Kombu: Kombu is the principal seaweed used in dashi, the traditional Japanese soup stock. Kombu is sold in long strips (or fronds) and as the greenish black powder marketed as kelp (see Chapter 38). Its nutritional strong points are its calcium, potassium, magnesium, and iodine content. Its main drawback is its high concentration of sodium. Try adding a 6-inch piece when cooking up a pot of soup or beans and see if you don't detect a richer taste.

Nori: Nori, also called *laver*, is sold in very thin sheets that look like delicate black or dark brown paper. It is most frequently used for wrapping sushi or rice balls, but it can be crumbled into soups, salads, and stews, or used to garnish just about any savory dish. Nori should be lightly toasted before use, either over a flame or in a 300°F. oven for two to three minutes. Of all the seaweeds, nori is highest in manganese, copper, fluoride, zinc, and vitamins C, E, B_6, and B_{12}. It is also lowest in sodium. In addition, although nori like all seaweeds is low in fat, the fat portion of this seaweed is rich in one of the sought-after omega-3 fatty acids found in fish.

Wakame: Wakame is a long thin green leaf with a sweetish flavor that is considered essential to a proper miso soup. Its sodium content exceeds most other seaweeds.

FROZEN VEGETABLES

Frozen vegetables must go to a packaging plant from the fields; depending on the efficiency of the manufacturer, they may be frozen just at their peak, or some days later. Theoretically, those vegetables frozen almost immediately should be as nourishing or possibly even richer than those that are fresh in your store, but several factors keep this a theory rather than a reality.

For example, vegetables are often kept several days before processing and in the meantime may be treated with chemicals to prevent spoilage and discourage insects; then, before freezing they are blanched, which destroys essential nutrients. Furthermore, cold temperatures cannot preserve vegetables indefinitely and there is no accurate way of knowing how long a package of frozen vegetables has been in the freezer case; continued freezing at home only increases the chance of further losses. What's more, the buyer has little chance of discovering if a package of frozen vegetables has indeed remained frozen the entire time.

Selecting Frozen Vegetables

Plain, unseasoned frozen vegetables are the ones you want for your table when good-quality fresh vegetables cannot be obtained. Unsalted varieties are relatively easy to find with the exception of peas, lima beans, and the combinations in which they appear; according to the label, these all have a "trace of salt."

The most important point we can make when it comes to purchasing frozen vegetables is never to buy if you suspect the package has been totally or even partially defrosted. Packages that give when you apply pressure, or are limp, wet, or sweating are not properly frozen. Packages covered with frost do not let the cold in, so their contents may not be sufficiently frozen. Packages stained by the contents have at one point been defrosted and refrozen. Avoid all of these.

For maximum nutrition, choose vegetables that have been frozen whole over those that are sliced or diced. Vegetables that require peeling—winter squash, potatoes, carrots—are generally treated with lye to make the job easier. This is destructive to vitamins and minerals. Potatoes, which darken on exposure to light and air, are usually "whitened" to their natural color and since the chemicals used to accomplish this are "processing aids" rather than additives, they do not necessarily appear in the list of ingredients.

Packages labeled "quick cooking" or "5-minute vegetables" have the chemical sodium phosphate added to make them that way. The label copy on some pre-sauced vegetables might create the impression of wholeness by proclaiming "made with real cheese," when in reality the recipe may contain many unwholesome additives.

Cooking Frozen Vegetables

To minimize vitamin loss, frozen vegetables should go directly from freezer to pot.

CANNED VEGETABLES

Canned vegetables are widely consumed in this country and are probably responsible for the great number of vegetable haters. Canning (and bottling) is dependent on heat, which is highly destructive to texture, taste, and nutrients, particularly vitamin A and the B vitamins. Many of the remaining nutrients leach into the liquid, which is the portion that usually goes down the drain. The loss of fiber and the increase in sodium are additional drawbacks to contend with.

And this is not the end of the canned vegetable story. To prevent color and textural changes, canning is more dependent on chemical additives, sugar, and salt than most other methods of vegetable preserving. With few exceptions, canned vegetables are not an exemplary buy. For us they will never be first choice, but the recommendations that follow may serve as occasional fill-ins when fresh produce is in short supply.

Selecting Canned Vegetables

If you purchase canned vegetables, do not pick cans that are leaking, swollen, or bulged at the end. Bulging and swelling indicate spoilage. Bad dents are harmful to the contents; avoid these cans, even if they are sold at a reduced price.

Another consideration is the acidity of vegetables and their possible interaction with the lead solder in the seam of the can. Therefore, vegetables packed in either lead-free or enamel-lined cans are preferred (see "Pay Attention to Packaging" in Chapter 1).

No Salt or Sugar Added

We are pleased to see that several companies are marketing "no salt added" and "no sugar added" canned vegetables, even though not all combine these two assets. (That is, some peas and corn may have no salt, but still include sugar, and while cream-style corn may be salt-free, sugar and modified food starch are universally present.)

Most regular canned vegetables contain a minimum of 250 to 300 milligrams of sodium per half cup. Low-salt alternatives average less than 10 to 60 milligrams of sodium per half cup. (The higher values represent inherent sodium, which is naturally higher for some vegetables, such as carrots and beets.)

Green beans, sweet peas, and whole-kernel corn with no salt or sugar are not difficult to find; carrots, spinach, beets, limas, and mixed vegetables are less readily available. When it comes to yams, white potatoes, succotash, mushrooms, asparagus, and poke greens, most shoppers still have very few options.

Canning Updates

There have been some recent innovations in the canning process in an attempt to provide more appealing colors and textures. These include Continental Can Company's Ultra Natural and Veri-Green processes. While we have not uncovered anything that makes these techniques suspect in themselves, we do find fault with the alliances between the manufacturer and certain major seed companies to develop "specific varieties that work optimally with the process. . . ." This is an example of how food processing dictates the kind of crops farmers must grow to compete successfully in a system that promotes processed rather than fresh foods, and eventually leads to a diminished diversity of plant species.

Canned Tomatoes

Canned tomatoes are often the best possibility because they have no frozen counterpart and, except for the brief summer season, not much competition from fresh tomatoes on the market either. The quest for salt-free vegetables has extended to tomatoes and now several companies provide this option. With about 15 milligrams of sodium per half cup, this is a substantial cutback. (Regular canned tomatoes contain about 150 to 220 milligrams of sodium per half cup.)

Stewed canned tomatoes with no salt added have three times this amount (45 milligrams per half cup) and are likely to contain sugar, but the typical salted versions average 355 milligrams.

Many brands of canned tomatoes have calcium chloride added to maintain some degree of firmness; this will be mentioned on the label. Citric acid may be included to help counterbalance the alkali used in peeling and to lower the acidity sufficiently to meet the legal requirements for thermal processing. Citric acid will also be declared on the label and while relatively benign, it does affect the flavor and also suggests lye peeling, so you may prefer a product without it.

A new form of "canned" tomatoes comes in soft cardboard cartons processed just like aseptic-pack juices. The use of brief ultrahigh temperatures in this process holds the promise of improved flavor, more like fresh, but in order for this to be realized the use of salt will have to come way down. Right now these tomatoes pack 680 milligrams of sodium per half cup, far exceeding other processed varieties.

More Canned Choices

Following are a few other canned vegetables that have no convenient counterpart in other forms and for this reason may appear from time to time on your shopping list.

Sauerkraut: Salt is unavoidable in sauerkraut, as salting the cabbage is an integral part of the bacterial souring process. Sodium bisulfite and sodium benzoate, however, are not essential and can generally be avoided by purchasing this product in cans rather than jars. The exceptions to this rule are noted in the Exemplary Brands.

Chiles: The main distinction of canned chiles is that the peppers are generally peeled by flame roasting, not by the use of lye as with other vegetables, and this makes all the difference in the flavor. All brands contain citric acid and salt.

Pimientos: See Chapter 37.

Oriental Vegetables: Canned baby corn, straw mushrooms, ginkos, water chestnuts, bamboo shoots, and such are convenient additions to Oriental and other dishes. Since for the most part they are used sparingly and along with other (fresh) vegetables, the fact that they may be salted can be balanced by reducing the salt or soy sauce used in seasoning the dish. We do not include canned bean sprouts in this list; the fresh sprouts are too nutritious a food to be replaced by such an inferior item in terms of taste, texture, and food value.

RECOMMENDATIONS

FRESH VEGETABLES

General Rule of Purchase: Look for fresh vegetables in season. Select organic vegetables whenever possible. For purchasing guidelines, refer to the individual descriptions in this chapter.

DRIED VEGETABLES

General Rule of Purchase: Dried mushrooms, dried Oriental vegetables, and seaweed contain only the vegetable minus its water. Avoid dried potatoes and the mixes that depend on them if the ingredient list includes sulfites, mono- and diglycerides, and preservatives.

Exemplary Brands

Bonaparte Genuine Mushrooms
Bonavita Dried Mushrooms
California Valley Mushrooms
China Bowl Chinese Vegetables
Eden Seaweeds, Dried Mushrooms
Hime Seaweeds
KA.ME Chinese Vegetables
Kirsch Mushrooms
Lima Seaweeds
Marine Coast Sea Vegetables
Maruka Seaweeds
McCormick's Freeze Dried Mushroom
  Slices
Mum's Seaweeds
Premier Japan Seaweeds
Shirakiku Shitake Mushrooms, Seaweeds
Shushi Chef Nori
Tree of Life Seaweeds
Wel Pac Mushrooms, Chinese Vegetables,
  Seaweeds
Westbrae Natural Seaweeds
Whites Mushrooms

FROZEN VEGETABLES

General Rule of Purchase: Look for those as close to the whole state as possible and without added sauce or seasoning. Make sure the package is frozen solid and shows no signs of prior mishandling (sweat or frost on the outside, staining, etc.). Many frozen varieties have no salt, but when peas or limas are in the package, a trace of salt is generally added. Avoid "quick cooking" varieties treated with sodium phosphate (on the label).

Exemplary Brands

All unseasoned, unsalted brands are basically the same. Many stores offer their own house line.

CANNED VEGETABLES

General Rule of Purchase: Canned vegetables are aesthetically and nutritionally inferior to other forms, especially if you discard the liquid. If you do use them, look for those that are packed in lead-free cans and are unsalted. When unavoidable, citric acid and calcium chloride are acceptable. Many processing aids are hidden, but all ingredients added directly will be revealed on the label. In addition to those listed here, many other stores have their own house brand of unsalted vegetables. All canned sauerkraut is similar (and additive free). We list here jarred varieties that are also acceptable.

Exemplary Brands

Bertolli Strained Tomatoes, Crushed Tomatoes, Whole Peeled Plum Tomatoes

Big Star No Salt Added Sliced Beets, Cut Green Beans, French Style Green Beans, Whole Kernel Corn, Sweet Peas, Sliced Carrots, Mixed Vegetables

Bruce's Mashed Yams, Light Yams

Coop Unsalted, Unsweetened Sweet Peas, Whole Kernel Corn, Cut Green Beans

Country Pure No Salt Added Sweet Peas, Whole Kernel Corn, Cut Green Beans

Dawn Fresh No Salt Added Mushrooms

Del Monte No Salt Added Peas and Carrots, Cut Green Beans, Mixed Vegetables

Diet Delight Tomatoes

Edward's Finast No Salt Added Sweet Peas, Cut Green Beans, Sliced Beets, Mixed Vegetables

Featherweight Natural Pack Cut Stringless Green Beans, Cut Stringless Wax Beans, Sliced Beets, Spinach, Sweet Peas, Whole Kernel Corn, Sliced Carrots, Limas, Mixed Vegetables, Tomatoes

Finast No Salt Added French Style Green Beans, Whole Kernel Corn, Sliced Carrots

Food Club No Salt Added Peas, Whole Kernel Golden Corn, French Style Green Beans, Cut Green Beans, Sliced Carrots, Spinach

Geisha Bamboo Shoots, Water Chestnuts

Giant Foods No Salt Added Cut Green Beans, French Style Green Beans, Whole Kernel Corn, Sweet Peas

Green Giant Unsalted Niblets

Grand Union No Salt Added Cut Green Beans, French Style Green Beans, Whole Kernel Sweet Corn, Sliced Carrots, Sliced Beets, Mixed Vegetables

Hunt's No Salt Added Whole Ripe Tomatoes

Jewel No Salt Added Sweet Peas, Peas and Carrots, Sliced Carrots, Mixed Vegetables

John Wood Farms Sauerkraut

Kozmic Kraut

Krakus Sauerkraut

Kroger No Salt Added Sweet Peas, Cut Green Beans, Golden Corn, Mixed Vegetables

Libby's Natural Pack Peas and Carrots, Succotash, Sweet Peas, Sliced Beets, Whole Kernel Sweet Corn, Mushroom Stems and Pieces

Maypride Bamboo Shoots

National No Salt Added Cut Green Beans, Sliced French Style Green Beans, Whole Kernel Golden Corn, Sweet Peas, Mixed Vegetables

Exemplary Brands (continued)

Nutradiet No Salt Added Cut Green Beans, Whole Kernel Corn, Cream Style Corn, Sliced Carrots, Sweet Peas, Peas and Carrots, Asparagus Points, Sliced Beets, Whole Tomatoes, Stewed Tomatoes

Parade No Salt, No Sugar Whole Kernel Corn

Pathmark No Salt Added Cut Green Beans, French Style Green Beans, Whole Kernel Corn, Sliced Carrots, Sweet Peas, Mixed Vegetables, Sliced Beets, Sliced White Potatoes, Whole Potatoes, Spinach

Pickle Eater's Low Sodium Sauerkraut

Ralph's No Salt Added Cut Green Beans, Whole Kernel Corn, Tomatoes

Reese Water Chestnuts

Springfield No Salt Added Sweet Peas, Sweet Corn

Staff No Salt Added French Style Green Beans, Sliced Beets, Mixed Vegetables

Stater Brothers No Salt Added Cut Green Beans

Sun Luck Bamboo Shoots, Water Chestnuts

Super Natural Crunchy Kraut[1]

Taylor Sweet Potatoes

Thank You Brand Sliced Carrots Packed in Water

The Allens Poke Greens[1]

Veg.All Freshlike Cut Green Beans, Sliced Carrots, Golden Corn, Sweet Peas, Sliced Beets

Von's No Salt Added Peas, Green Beans, Beets, Spinach, Stewed Tomatoes

[1]organic

Chapter 25

Picking Fruit

Fruit that is harvested once it has matured can be as satisfying to your sweet tooth as the richest of desserts. Winning family and friends over to fresh fruit should not be very hard if you select what is ripe and at the peak of its natural sweetness and juiciness. After a thirty-year sales slump, produce stalls are now well stocked with America's favorite fruits and some brand-new offerings from foreign shores as well.

Trivia buffs might be interested to learn that the banana is America's best-selling fruit. Even more surprising is that the world's largest fruit crop is the mango, an item whose appearance on the American table is still relatively novel. If you have yet to experience it or have shied away from equally strange-looking specimens like carambolas, pomelos, persimmons, quince, kiwis, Asian pears and the like, uncertain of what to expect or even how to judge some of them, you are not alone. However, we hope to offer enough assistance and encouragement in this chapter so that you can learn to pick good specimens of these as well as the more familiar fruits.

YOU CAN'T FOOL MOTHER NATURE

In an attempt to maintain "visual quality" after shipping, or to overextend the season to meet what is termed "consumer demand," much of the fruit that is sold has been picked considerably before it has developed enough to ever reach good eating quality. A peach isn't likely to be flavorful in the middle of January if local conditions don't favor its ripening until the beginning of June. Obviously, then, the key is to buy in season, giving preference to fruit that is locally grown.

An additional problem with much fruit on the market today is that it is chilled while still unripe. Consequently, while it may become soft, it will never develop to its full sweet potential.

Commercial fruit is bred for easy harvest, longevity, and appearance, sometimes at the cost of flavor. What's more, chemical pampering is often required. The majority of fruit is grown in soil that is fed chemicals to increase productivity and is routinely sprayed with chemical pesticides. Although the thick rind of some fruits helps protect the underlying flesh from chemical penetration, many of these same fruits, such as pineapples, melons, bananas, and mangoes, are grown on foreign soil where agricultural

352

poisons not allowed here are commonly used. For other fruit there is not much that can be done except to give them a thorough washing or peel them when possible. Grapes and cherries are among those that are heavily sprayed and have no peel that can be conveniently removed; in such cases, moderating consumption may be the only solution if the fruit is conventionally grown (i.e., not organically grown).

A Case in Point

From Eve to Snow White, the apple has been seen as a deadly symbol. Now, ironically, the symbolism may have a basis in reality. What we present in the following discussion exemplifies the state of agriculture today, and is not limited just to apples.

Daminozide, a chemical widely used by apple growers, was identified as a suspected carcinogen in the 1980s. Better known by its trade name Alar, it has been used on apples since the 1960s for cosmetic reasons, i.e., to intensify their color, make them firmer, promote fruit of uniform size, control ripening so that all the fruits can be harvested at one time, and also extend shelf-life. In 1984, tests indicated that daminozide is carcinogenic and, furthermore, that when mixed with water, it forms yet another cancer-causing agent.

Residues of both these chemicals *penetrate to the core* of the apple and cannot be removed by washing or peeling. They also appear in processed apple products including apple juice and applesauce and their "baby food" versions. An EPA notice in August of 1985 suggested that "people who are concerned, especially about their young children's consumption of apples and apple products, may make the personal choice to limit their consumption. . . ."

At the same time that this warning appeared, a ban was proposed for the 1986 growing season, but the manufacturer of the chemical urged the agency to hold off any action until 1988, when its animal studies would be completed.

A VICTORY FOR CONSUMERS

Although the government failed to protect the people, concerned consumers were able to enact a partial ban against Alar on their own. Responding to a request initiated by Ralph Nader, in the summer of 1986 Safeway, the country's largest supermarket chain, refused to purchase apples grown with Alar. Soon other food chains followed Safeway's example, and major food processors, fearful of losing customer confidence, also said they would not buy Alar-treated apples. Knowing there would now be a big market for Alar-free apples, many commercial growers voluntarily stopped using the chemical.

THE ORGANIC OPTION

The story of Alar is meant to encourage you to have an open attitude toward apples and other fruits that are not picture-perfect. An apple can be big, shiny, and spectacularly red and still taste like damp cardboard; it can be small, lopsided, mottled, and russeted and yet be crisp and juicy with a perfectly balanced sweet-tart taste. (Nothing matches the taste of the "ugly" apples on our own apple trees.) Agribusiness may make them look better from the outside, but left alone, nature does a better job in terms of what's inside.

The purchase of organic fruit is discussed in Chapter 23.

JUICE IS NOT FRUIT

Fresh pressed fruit (and vegetable) juices are increasingly popular, but their contribution to your diet may have some unexpected results. Disrupting fruit's fiber by turning it into a juice or puree reduces its appetite-satisfying value and can result in overindulgence and lots of calories. Consuming the juice instead of the whole fruit can also upset blood sugar levels in sensitive individuals. So next time you're looking for a healthy, ready-to-eat low-calorie snack, you may want to grab a piece of fruit, not a glass.

PICKING THE BEST FRESH FRUIT
(AND KEEPING IT THAT WAY)

The following buying guidelines include for most fruits the months in which they are most plentiful, nutrition information where it is noteworthy, and some additional advice on care where it can significantly influence eating enjoyment.

APPLES *(year-round; peak late summer through March)* Judging from most markets, growers' favorites appear to be Red Delicious, Golden Delicious, and Rome, but these are by no means the most flavorful or versatile apples.

It is estimated that at one time there were almost 7,000 apple varieties. While most have been abandoned by growers for a few highly marketable ones, McIntosh, Baldwin, Cortland, Macoun, York Imperial, Staymen, Ida Red, Jonathan, Northern Spy, Newton Pippin, Winesap, Gravenstein, Greening, and Granny Smiths are still available and can be rewarding choices.

Look For: Firm, crisp apples without soft spots, bruises or wrinkles. High color is an indication of maturity and only apples picked when mature will have good flavor and texture. Although the peel is rich in fiber, you may want to remove it to eliminate any waxed coating and pesticide residue.

Avoid: Apples that yield to pressure on the skin. These will have soft, mealy flesh. Bruised areas are a sign of exposure to frost or improper handling.

Storage and Handling: To maintain their quality, store apples at refrigerator temperature. They like a relatively high humidity.

A COLOR GUIDE TO APPLES

All apples are not characterized by a bright red skin.

Variety	Color
Baldwin	Mottled red or streaked red and yellow
Cortland	Red with green and a slight "blush"
Delicious	Bright red or streaked green and red
Empire	Plain red to brilliant red
Golden Delicious	Pale yellow to yellow-green
Granny Smith	Green, may have freckling
Gravenstein	Streaked green and red
Greening	Green to yellow-green, often russeted
Ida Red	Red to bright red
Jonathan	Red with yellow "blush"
Lodi	Greenish yellow
McIntosh	Red with green and a slight "blush"
Macoun	Wine-red with a gray "blush"
Newton Pippin	Pale green to yellow, often russeted
Northern Spy	Pale green or yellow and red streaked
Opalescent	Red with yellow highlights
Rome	Deep red
Staymen	Red shaded with green
Winesap	Deep red
York Imperial	Deep red, sometimes yellow streaked

APRICOTS *(late May through early August; peak June and July)* Persian poets romanticized apricots as "the seeds of the sun." Apricots have a very short season and a very short shelf life; if not picked at maturity they will be tasteless and they can be kept only three or four days before they become mealy. Apricots are a superb source of vitamin A and are also rich in potassium.

Look For: Plump juicy-looking apricots with a uniform golden-orange hue. They will yield to gentle pressure when ripe.

Avoid: Soft, mushy fruit (overripe) and hard, pale yellow or greenish yellow fruit (underriped).

Storage: Ideal storage temperature is in the coldest part of the refrigerator.

ASIAN PEARS   The Asian pear may also be called an *apple-pear, Japanese pear, Oriental pear, chalea* or *shalea*. This exotic fruit is a far-from-routine item on anyone's shopping list, but it is available sporadically, even in our small town supermarket. It looks vaguely like a misshapen green apple, but has a thin rough skin more like that of a pear. Its taste has been compared to both, described as "juicy as a pear, crunchy as an apple." We find it to be more like a sweet water chestnut. It should be eaten raw, and in selecting them, use the same criteria you would for apples.

BANANAS *(available year-round)*   Bananas, we are told, develop their best eating quality after harvesting. Since virtually all bananas are shipped green, it is hard to determine if this is so or not. Bananas are an excellent source of potassium. According to the United Fruit Company, the bananas grown on their plantations in Costa Rica, Honduras, and Panama are not sprayed with pesticides. They do, however, use synthetic fertilizer on the land and fungicides to control leaf disease (as do all other banana growers). Chiquita is their brand name banana.

Look For: Bananas free from surface bruises, with skin intact at both tips. If you buy them green, or partially green, you will know they haven't been gassed into accelerated ripeness.

Avoid: Bananas that are bruised, discolored, or dull and grayish, which means they have been kept in cold storage and will never ripen properly.

Storage and Handling: The stage of ripeness is indicated by color. Ripen at room temperature; when the yellow jacket is speckled with brown, the starch has been changed to fruit sugar and the flesh will be tender, creamy, sweet, and easy to digest. Once they are ripe, bananas can be stored successfully in the refrigerator if necessary. Do not place them in cold storage, however, until they are as ripe as you want them. Although the skin will blacken from the cold, the fruit itself will remain unchanged.

BLACKBERRIES   See Raspberries.

BLUEBERRIES *(peak season July through August)*   As so often happens with produce, the earliest arrivals on the market have a high price tag that the taste rarely justifies. Cultivated blueberries may be harvested as soon as they have turned blue enough to qualify, but the more desirable berries are left on the plant for another week to sweeten. Once picked, they only become softer, not sweeter.

Look For: Berries that are plump and firm, with an attractive blue-gray "bloom." Those that lack good color also lack flavor. The cellophane covering should have little or no moisture on its underside.

Avoid: Containers that are leaking or stained with juice or that have any visible mushy, moldy, shriveled, or "mummified" berries. Don't expect berries that show green to ripen in your kitchen.

Storage and Handling: Cull for moldy or soft fruit, then store unwashed in a well-aerated container in the refrigerator. Use as soon as possible; they do not last long.

Tips: Berry picking is an activity with delectable rewards. Cultivated varieties at pick-your-own farms are at their best when they are tight-skinned but yield to gentle pressure. The perfect blueberry will part easily from the plant.

CARAMBOLAS This somewhat exotic fruit may be more recognizable as starfruit, a name based on the pattern of a cross-sectioned slice. It has four to six prominent ribs that run longitudinally and a thin, waxy yellow-green skin. The fruit can either be eaten raw or lightly cooked as a garnish for fish or in stir-fries.

Look For: Firm, shiny carambolas. Those that are still green are best for cooking; the ripe yellow specimens are ideal for eating raw.

Avoid: Mushy and bruised fruit.

Storage and Handling: Let ripen at room temperature to a golden yellow. The ripe fruit can be stored in the refrigerator for about one week.

CHERRIES *(peak season June to July)* Although sweet cherries appear on the market in May, wait until June before buying them if you want the flavor and price to be right. Sour cherries are rarely sold retail; most go to the processing plant, so unless you have your own tree they'll be hard to come by.

Look For: The most important sign of maturity and sweetness in cherries is a very dark color. The surface should be bright and glossy (although waxing may cloud your judgment). Look for fruit that is plump; the stems should have a fresh look.

Avoid: Cherries that are shriveled, with dried stems and a dull look about them, and those with excessive scarring. Cherries should not be sticky. Decay is common but is sometimes hard to see because of the deep color. Unhealed skin breaks, soft, sunken, or leaking spots, brown discoloration, and surface mold are signs of damage.

CLEMENTINES See Tangerines.

COCONUTS *(peak season September through March)* Coconut meat is most flavorful when it comes right from the fresh coconut. The packaged, flaked variety is treated with chemicals to improve its keeping qualities, and none-theless always has a flat, stale taste. Unlike most fruit, which is practically fat-free, coconuts contain a considerable amount of saturated fat.

Look For: Coconuts heavy for their size that sound full of liquid when you shake them.

Avoid: Those with wet or moldy eyes (those three small circles at one end).

Storage and Handling: An uncracked coconut can be kept at room temperature (60°F. is preferred) for about two months. Once opened, store in a covered container in the refrigerator; it will stay fresh about one week. For longer storage, fresh-grated coconut can be submerged in its own milk and frozen in containers.

CRANBERRIES *(peak season October through December)* No canned cranberry sauce can match the taste of the freshly prepared relish.
Look For: Plump berries with good luster. Even the dull varieties should have a good red color.
Handling: Sort out any shriveled, soft or leaky berries before you use them because they impart an off-flavor.

FIGS *(peak season July to August)* The season for fresh figs is very fleeting. When they are available, buy them for same-day eating; they do not keep very well.
Look For: Figs that are fairly soft, but not mushy. Minor bruises can be ignored; however, breaks in the skin result in rapid deterioration.
Avoid: Figs with a sour odor.

GRAPEFRUIT *(available year-round; peak November through May)* Although the supply may be low and the price high out of peak season, grapefruit will still be of good eating quality even in summer.
Look For: Firm fruits heavy for their size. Thin-skinned fruits are juicier. A coarse skin and pointed end are signs of a thick-skinned, less juicy fruit, but it may be tasty nonetheless. Skin defects are usually no indication of the interior, except for large soft wet spots. Internal color is more a matter of personal preference than any indication of sweetness.
Avoid: Grapefruit with large, water-soaked patches or soft discolored areas at the stem end. The fruit should not be puffy or flabby. Wrinkled and rough skin indicates tough, dry fruit inside. If the skin breaks easily with pressure, assume there is some decay. Fumigation injury may appear as small, thinly scattered spots or as solid or depressed scarring.
Storage: Grapefruit stores best in a cold room rather than the refrigerator, and will keep a minimum of two weeks. Do not store in a closed bag; this inhibits respiration and encourages brown spots.

GRAPES *(available just about year-round; peak season mid-June through November)* Long-standing varieties like Thompson seedless (pale green), Tokay and Cardinal (red with a gray overtone), and Emperor (bright red) have recently been joined by Flame Seedless (red with no seeds), Perlettes (small, white), Ribiers (jet black), and Calmeria (pale green and among the latest to appear). Other varieties are more regional, including the Concord (blue-black) grown in the eastern part of the United States and well suited to juice- and jelly-making.
Look For: Well-colored plump grapes in compact clusters, but not "excessively tight," still attached to the stem. Green grapes are sweetest when the color has a yellowish cast. Red varieties are best when their color is fully developed. Grapes do not get any sweeter after picking; do not expect them to ripen further in your kitchen.
Avoid: Soft wrinkled grapes, sticky grapes, cracked grapes, brown sunken areas, and those that leak or show mildew or mold on their surface.

GUAVAS The guava is popular in Hispanic kitchens where it is often stewed or transformed into a gelatin-like paste. Round in shape, with a 2-to-3-inch diameter, the fruit resembles a small yellow peach. Inside, the flesh ranges from pale to deep pink, with a sweet flavor but somewhat musky odor.
Storage and Handling: Guavas can be kept at room temperature to ripen. Once they begin to soften, they should be refrigerated or eaten.

KIWIFRUIT *(available April through December; peak June through October)* These small, mud-green, fuzzy, egg-shaped fruits are almost animal-like in appearance and certainly offer no clue as to what awaits you inside. Cut a wedge or a round and you will discover descending hues of brilliant sea-green with tiny black seeds implanted at intervals in the central portions of the flesh. The skin is not edible, but is easier to remove after cutting. The entire interior can be consumed.

The taste of a kiwi varies from intensely sweet to bland to tart, with some fruits combining this sweetness and astringency in a most remarkable manner. Kiwi fanciers adore them; many others find them boring. Pound for pound this fruit is said to contain more vitamin C than oranges.
Look For: From the outside, kiwis appear to be identical and the only thing you must judge is when they are ready to be eaten. Hard kiwis should be left at room temperature until they just yield to gentle, even pressure. Soft kiwis are disappointing.

KUMQUATS *(available November through February)* This somewhat bitter fruit, which looks like tiny elongated oranges, is usually preserved whole (skin included) in sugar syrup. If they are used raw, they must be very ripe to be palatable. The rind of the kumquat is edible and actually much sweeter than the pulp. Only the seeds are not meant for eating.
Look For: Fruit that is firm and heavy for its size. Don't be disappointed if the flesh seems dry; that's how nature made them.

LEMONS *(available year-round)* Lemons keep well in the refrigerator for at least two weeks. You should have some on hand at all times for making salad dressings and seasoning your food, so that you never have to resort to bottled lemon juice (see Chapter 38).
Look For: Lemons with rich yellow color and reasonably smooth skin. For the most juice, choose lemons that are thick-skinned and heavy for their size. Paler fruit will be more acidic.
Avoid: Lemons with a dark or dull color, hard or shriveled skin, and soft spots, mold, or punctures. As with grapefruits, fumigation injury may show up as scars on the skin.
Tip: To get the most juice, bring lemons to room temperature or roll them before cutting.

LIMES *(available year-round; peak June through September)*
Look For: Glossy skin and heavy weight in relation to size. Yellow

coloration is normal for some varieties and does not affect quality.

Avoid: Dull dry skin and irregularities on the surface. In all citrus fruit, decay begins at the nipple as a grayish-tan water-soaked spot that spreads to a brownish discoloration on the rind. Limes are not supposed to be bitter.

Storage: Limes are best stored between 45° and 50°F.

MANGOES (*peak season April through August*) Mangoes provide excellent vitamin C, vitamin A, and potassium along with a truly exotic taste—like an unusually sweet and fragrant effervescent peach. Only a small portion of the mangoes in American markets are home-grown. Their import into this country from the Caribbean has frequently been restricted as a result of mango-seed weevils. To increase the supply, the U.S. State Department has permitted importation of mangoes sprayed with EDB (which is banned in the United States). Mangoes are also the first irradiated fruit to be sold in the United States. Since these seem to be the only two means of irradication that are being used, we suggest you buy domestic mangoes, or none at all.

Look For: When ready to eat, a mango will have an orange-yellow to red skin and flesh that yields to pressure. It can be bought green and allowed to ripen at room temperature.

Avoid: Mangoes that have grayish skin discoloration, pitting or black spots, or mushy feel.

Tips: To prepare for eating, mark a band down the side with a sharp paring knife and peel back the skin as necessary. The pulp can be eaten right out of this opening with a spoon, or sliced on the diagonal off the large center pit.

MUSKMELONS As a group, melons are the most nutritious of the world's fruits. All varieties have substantial levels of potassium and vitamin C, with very few calories. In addition, cantaloupe contains impressive amounts of folacin and vitamin A.

Beyond the fact that they are often picked prematurely, many melons tend to be disappointing because they are kept in warehouses at low temperatures where they are subjected to chilling injuries. Another factor that is often ignored is their perishability. Muskmelons should be consumed within two weeks of picking. Allowing for transit plus three to four days at room temperature to ripen adequately doesn't leave much time before their sweet flavor, juiciness, and delicate texture begin to diminish. Since melons have no starch reserves, they do not sweeten after picking; they only soften.

A fully grown melon that is still hard will have excellent eating quality if kept at room temperature for a few days. It can then be stored briefly in the refrigerator.

CANTALOUPES (*peak season June through August*)

Look For: A mature melon will be free of the stem with a smooth, shallow basin where it was attached. If all or part of the stem base remains, or if the stem scar is jagged, the melon was not fully developed at picking time. The netting on the surface should be thick and coarse, and stand out like relief work. The skin between the netting should be yellowish in tone. A pleasant odor and a slight yield to pressure at the blossom end (opposite the stem end) signify cantaloupe that is ready to be eaten.

Avoid: Overripe cantaloupes may have a bright yellow color, sponginess, or softening over the entire surface. Small bruises will not affect eating quality; large ones will. Discolored or bleached sunken areas are due to sun-scald; the flesh of these melons will be tough and exhibit poor color. If the stem scar is wet and slippery, large areas on the surface are flat or indented, or if on cutting the flesh is mushy or noticeably discolored, bacteria or fungi have been at work.

Storage: It is best to keep cut cantaloupe covered to prevent its odor from penetrating other foods.

CASABAS *(peak season July to November)* The casaba is shaped like a pumpkin with a somewhat pointed stem end. The surface is covered with shallow but pronounced irregular furrows. The rind is hard and light green to yellow in color. These melons have no aroma.

Look For: A golden yellow color and a softening at the blossom end signal ripeness.

Avoid: Dark, sunken water spots.

CRANSHAWS *(available July through October, peak season August to September)* The cranshaw tends to be smaller than the casaba, more oval in shape, and have a blunt point at the blossom end. It has shallow, barely detectable furrows.

Look For: A deep golden-yellow rind with a surface that yields to slight pressure and a pleasant aroma.

Avoid: Sunken, water-soaked areas on the rind.

HONEYDEWS *(peak season June through October)* Ripe honeydew has a lovely sweet flavor, much more delicate than cantaloupe. The melon itself is quite large and may be oval to round in shape. The rind is smooth and firm and ranges from creamy white to creamy yellow. The smaller round honeyball melon has much the same characteristics, except for its size.

Look For: A soft velvety surface (the sign of maturity). Slight softening at the blossom end, a faint pleasant aroma, a yellow-white to creamy color, and loose seeds when shaken are signs of readiness.

Avoid: Melons with a dull white or greenish white color and a hard, smooth feel (signs of immaturity), large water-soaked areas (signs of injury), or punctures in the rind (which lead to decay). Small damaged areas will not lead to further deterioration if you plan to use the melon immediately.

PERSIAN MELONS *(peak season August to September)* Persian melons are larger and rounder than cantaloupes, with a finer brown netting imposed on a green background. Choose them as you do cantaloupes.

Nectarines *(peak season July to August)* Nectarines combine the flavor characteristics of peaches and plums. Color ranges from a red blush to a completely red or yellow surface.

Look For: Good color and plumpness and a slight softening along the "seam." Some varieties have a characteristic speckling. As long as the color is rich and bright, you can expect the flavor to be sweet.

Avoid: Very hard, dull-colored or green-tinged nectarines or those that are even slightly shriveled. Also, check for surface decay (soft spots or mold).

Handling: If the fruit is too firm, allow it to ripen a few days at room temperature.

Oranges *(peak season October through June)* Oranges are divided into two types, juice and eating. Florida juice varieties appear on the market in October and include Parson Browns, Hamlins, and Pineapple oranges. Temple oranges, which follow a little later in the season, are considered both an eating and a juice orange. Florida Valencias, which pick up the slack around February, are promoted as "the finest juice oranges available." California contributes the navel orange, named for the cluster of buds at its end, which at its best is a fine eating orange with a firm, meaty flesh and no seeds. This is just about the only orange not suitable for juicing; it has a tendency to turn bitter when exposed to the air. As navels wane in early spring, California Valencias take over and remain on the market even through the summer months. These are suited to both eating and juice. Other states and imports add to the selection and occasionally more exotic varieties appear, such as mandarins and blood oranges (which have somewhat alarming crimson streaks in their flesh and a flavor that is sweet and tart at the same time).

Look For: Firm, heavy oranges. Color is no real indication of quality. Restrictions require oranges to be fully mature before they can be shipped out of state, but their color at this time may still be green, for the orange hue comes with a drop in temperature that usually occurs around the harvest. If temperatures remain unseasonably warm at night or, as in the case of late-season California oranges, the fruit undergoes "regreening" when warm weather returns, streaks of green will be present.

Avoid: Lightweight fruit (which will not be juicy) and a very rough surface (which is a sign of thick skin and little inside). Eliminate those that are puffy or spongy or have soft spots on the skin and weak areas at the ends.

Papayas *(available year-round)* The papaya, whose natural enzymes are reputed to enhance digestion, is one of the best sources of vitamin A. Half of an average fruit (about 7 ounces) also furnishes almost twice the potassium and vitamin C of the average orange.

For those of you who have not yet made its acquaintaince, the papaya is shaped somewhat like a pear, only larger, measuring 5 to 6 inches long and weighing about a pound. When ripe, the smooth, gently ribbed green peel turns a golden yellow-orange. Cut it open and you will find a fragrant golden, rose, or reddish-orange colored flesh (depending on the variety) and a cavity filled with small black seeds. Neither the skin nor the seeds are meant for eating. Its flavor has been described as "reminiscent of a melon and a little like a peach, with rich tropical sweetness." Unless you get a choice specimen, you may not agree.

Early picking has damaged the papaya's image outside its native home of Hawaii, as has the need to fumigate the fruit or otherwise guarantee it to be free of insects before it can be brought to the mainland. Since EDB has been banned, a hot/cold dip has been applied, but in private, Hawaiians admit that this ruins the texture. The only other alternative at the moment is irradiation—not an acceptable one in our book.

Look For: Papayas with smooth, unblemished skin. If the fruit is mostly green, but exhibits a yellow tinge at the larger end, it is only one-fourth ripe and will take five to seven days at room temperature to reach its peak. One-third yellow to two-thirds green means it's half ripe; give it two to four days at room temperature. Equal amounts of yellow and green will turn to mostly yellow-orange in a day or two; this is the fruit that is ripe for eating.

Avoid: Papayas that are all green. Those with shriveled skin or dark spots which penetrate the flesh and spoil its flavor.

Storage: Once ripe, papaya should keep for up to a week in the refrigerator.

PEACHES *(peak season June through September)*
Look For: Peaches that are fairly firm or just beginning to soften. The background color should be red with areas of yellow or at least cream color.

Avoid: Very hard peaches with green tones. These were picked too early and will never ripen properly. Don't buy very soft peaches either, unless you want them to have a watered-down taste. Large flattened bruises are surface signs of inner decay.

PEARS *(some variety available year-round; peak season August through March)*
Since pears become mushy if they are allowed to ripen on the tree, they are always picked hard. Their season has been extended by keeping them in cold storage. Thus, Anjou (light to yellow-green), Bosc (golden to brown with a long neck), and Comice (greenish yellow with a red blush) will be available in the store often as late as May; Bartlett pears (yellow with a red blush) do not keep and will fade from view around December. Small seckel pears are a short-lived, fall variety. In some parts of the country, other specialty types like Winter Nellis (brown russeting on a light green skin), Forelle (golden with a bright red blush), and red varieties of Bartlett, Anjou, and Comice may be seen.

Look For: Color should conform to the variety as described above. They should be firm, but not rock-hard.

Avoid: Wilted or shriveled pears that are weak near the stem; these are immature and will never ripen. Also, avoid those with spots on the sides or blossom end—which indicate a mealy flesh beneath.

Storage and Handling: Pears usually require additional ripening at home.

This is best accomplished by holding them at room temperature under a damp cloth, as the optimum ripening environment is 64° to 72°F. with a 90 to 95 percent relative humidity. When temperatures are too high, they turn yellow and dry.

PERSIMMONS *(available October through December)* These squat, almost heart-shaped, bright orange fruits are still somewhat of a specialty item, with a very limited season and an equally small clientele. The taste is fairly astringent, but this quality can be tempered by ripening them in a closed container with an apple. Eat the flesh while it still holds its shape (as opposed to when it is soft and mushy), and you will be rewarded with one of nature's sweetest tastes.

Look For: Fruit that is evenly shaped, plump, smooth, and highly colored, with the stem cap still attached to the unbroken skin.

Handling: When ready to eat, the persimmon will just yield to pressure. Peel it in sections from the pointed end down to the stem cap, discard any seeds, and dig in.

PINEAPPLES *(available year-round; peak March through July)* Pineapples are picked while still hard and must be allowed to ripen at room temperature. However, unless they are fully matured at picking time, this ripening will never come about.

Look For: As pineapples ripen, the green color fades and orange and yellow take its place. When fully ripe, the pineapple is gold, orange-yellow, or reddish brown, depending on the variety. It should have a fragrant odor and a slight separation of the eyes, and the leaves, or spikes, should pull out without too much tugging. The fruit should be plump and heavy for its size.

Avoid: Pineapples with pointed or sunken eyes, a dull yellow-green color, and a dried-out appearance; all are signs of immature fruit. If the eyes are dark and watery, the odor unpleasant, and the surface has many soft spots, you can be fairly certain the fruit has internal damage.

PLUMS *(available June through September; peak July and August)* Varieties of plums (of which there are nearly 150) differ in flavor and appearance and include a rainbow of colors ranging from red to yellow to blue to green to purple.

Look For: Good color for the particular variety you are choosing, a slight glow to the skin, and fruit that yields to gentle pressure at the tip.

Avoid: Fruit with skin breaks or brown discoloration, immature fruit (which is hard, poorly colored, and very tart), and overmature fruit (which is soft, leaking, and decayed).

POMEGRANATES *(available September through November)* Pomegranates are composed of tiny edible red seeds housed inside an irregular ball about the size of an orange that has a dull red leathery skin. This fruit has no flesh but the seeds can be pressed in a citrus juicer to release their striking crimson juice or used as a garnish.

Look For: Large fruits that are firm and heavy for their size.
Avoid: Shrunken fruits, those with a dried appearance, and any showing surface decay or a cracked rind.
Storage and Handling: Keep in the refrigerator as long as two weeks. Once cut, a pomegranate should be wrapped tightly and used as soon as possible.

POMELOS The pomelo is a relative of the grapefruit; most of what you find on the market is imported from Israel. When you remove the thick skin the segments will have a dry appearance, and when you bite into them the taste is an unusual combination of sweet and tart.

QUINCE *(available October through December)* A quince is a gnarled, round to pear-shaped fruit with a hard flesh, distinctive odor, and tart, astringent taste. In fact, they are so hard and tart that they cannot be eaten raw. One of their main attractions is the high pectin content, which makes them especially suited for fruit butter and preserves.
Look For: Hard fruit with a greenish yellow or pale yellow skin. The fruit is ready to use when the yellow color predominates.
Avoid: Fruit with large spots or bruises. Punctures are a sign of worms.

RASPBERRIES, BLACKBERRIES, AND GOOSEBERRIES *(peak season June through August)* Although they differ in shape and color, these berries are similar in general structure, and the buying and handling considerations are the same.
Look For: Good bright color for the species. The individual bumps on the berries should be plump and tender, but not mushy.
Avoid: Berries that are leaky or show mold. This is fairly easy to spot. Although the berries at the bottom of the basket are hard to see, if the container is stained or wet, you can be pretty sure there are too many spoiled berries in the batch.
Storage and Handling: These berries should not be washed until you are ready to use them since their surface is so fragile that water alone can cause enough damage to start the decaying process. Try to purchase them for immediate consumption; they do not last long.

RHUBARB *(peak season February through June)* Rhubarb cannot be eaten raw, and even cooked it requires a lot of sweetening to make it palatable. Use honey and you'll be able to turn out some delicious sauces and pies. Only the stalks are edible. Don't experiment with the leaves; they contain a substance that can be poisonous.
Look For: For the field variety, select firm, crisp, straight stalks with a deep red or cherry color. Hothouse rhubarb is lighter in color with yellow-green leaves.
Avoid: Wilted, oversized, or extremely thin stalks.

STRAWBERRIES *(peak season April through June)* Most strawberries on the market during peak season are shipped from California. In eastern berry-growing country, principally New York, New Jersey, and Michigan, the season is a little later, about midsummer.

Look For: Full red color, bright luster, and firm flesh. The stem should still be attached and the berries dry. Medium to small berries are generally sweeter than large ones. Don't expect to find a basket with uniformly perfect berries. Look into the container to determine if most of the lower berries are of reasonable quality; if they are, just accept the fact that there may be a few misfits.

Avoid: Berries with large, uncolored areas and lots of surface seeds, a dull, shrunken appearance, extreme softness, and mold.

Storage and Handling: Be sure to sort out any decaying berries right away, before the mold has a chance to spread. Refrigerate to preserve quality, but try to use them quickly. Do not rinse until just before serving.

Tangelos *(available October through January)* Tangelos were created by cross-breeding tangerines and grapefruit. They have retained the better qualities of each and are excellent for eating and juicing.

Look For: Firm, thin-skinned fruits, heavy for their size.

Tangerines *(peak season November through January)* The best variety is the clementine, which is juicy and seedless.

Look For: Bright yellow-orange to deep orange tangerines. The skin is characteristically loose fitting, therefore the fruit will never feel firm.

Avoid: Very pale fruit (although small areas of green don't mean poor flavor) and skin punctures.

Ugli Fruit *(available October through February)* The ugli fruit is another grapefruit and tangerine hybrid, having the size of the former, the loose skin of the latter, and a light green color. Its name comes from its bumpy appearance. The taste is more appealing than its looks might suggest, similar to an orange, and it should be served in the same manner.

Look For: When ripe the skin has tinges of orange; green blemishes are normal.

Storage: Ugli fruit can be held in the refrigerator for about a week.

Watermelons *(peak season May through August)*

Look For: In whole melons, a smooth surface with a slight dullness (not bright, but not washed-out looking either), filled-out rounded ends, a smooth, dish-shaped depression where the stem was attached, and a somewhat yellow underside where the melon lay on the soil are clues to a sweet, crisp flesh. When thumped with a finger, mature melons give a dead or muffled "ping"; immature ones produce a higher pitched sound.

In cut melons, you want firm, juicy flesh with a good red color and no white streaks. Seeds should be dark brown or black.

Avoid: If the melon is very hard, and white or pale green on its underside, it is probably immature. Don't attempt to ripen it, for it will never be any weeter than it was the day it left the vine. Pale-colored flesh, white streaks, nd white seeds are also signs of immaturity. Overmaturity is revealed by dry and mealy, or watery and stringy flesh.

Storage: Watermelons are not well suited to storage. They are best kept at temperatures between 55° and 70°F. Below 50°F. they lose color and pitting of the flesh may occur.

CANNED AND FROZEN FRUIT

Canning and freezing are somewhat less harmful to fruit than to vegetables, perhaps due to the fact that the natural acids in fruit protect the vitamins. Although lye peeling, cutting, and the heat of canning do destroy some of the nutrients, those that leach into the liquid are at least usually consumed along with the fruit, rather than thrown away as is the case with vegetable liquid. As much as 50 percent of the vitamin C may be in the liquid portion.

The main problem with processed fruit is the sugar that is conventionally added. Fruits are inherently sweet and do not need enhancing, but manufacturers add this sweetening to maintain texture and preserve the fruit. One thing we do not need in our diets is more sugar.

Unsweetened Frozen Fruit

Unsweetened frozen fruit is one available option, including whole strawberries, blueberries, and raspberries, sweet and tart cherries, rhubarb, melon balls, and sliced peaches. The greatest loss of nutrients in these comes from pretreatment (peeling, trimming, blanching), improper storage, and home thawing. Since the water lost during defrosting contains nutrients, it should be reserved for fruit salads, drinks, etc. Unthawed frozen fruits make a very refreshing snack and minimize the nutrients lost in the transition to a thawed state.

Be sure to read the label to determine if anything other than fruit is included, as the listing will be complete. In peaches, melons, or mixed fruit, an acid (citric, malic, ascorbic) is often used to preserve color, which is not too objectionable. However, when a baking mix containing salt and modified food starch is included in the box, as it is in at least one brand, along with a name like "Naturally Good" and a boast of "no sugar, nothing artificial," give the product the cold shoulder. Modified cellulose gum is another additive common in melon chunks; we prefer not to ingest highly processed fiber from an unknown source.

Water- and Juice-Packed Canned Fruit

Most canned fruits are packed in a sugary syrup. During the last decade, however, concerns about weight control and sugar consumption have provided sufficient impetus for canners to expand their lines of water- and juice-packed fruits. Where formerly citrus fruit and pineapple in its own juice were the only common unsweetened offerings, today several companies put up peaches, apricots, pears, mandarin oranges, and mixed fruit in water or juice from concentrate. As a result, these items will have from 40 to 70 percent fewer calories than fruit canned in heavy syrup. When sugar is added, fruit packed in *extra light syrup* has less than *light, heavy,* and *extra-heavy pack.* Do not make the mistake of confusing "lite" fruit (as some companies describe the juice-packed product) with fruit canned in light syrup (which is a 14 to 21 percent sugar solution).

All the ingredients added directly to canned fruits must be stated on the label. In addition to sweeteners the possibilities include spice, natural and artificial flavorings, vinegar, lemon juice or other acids, and calcium salts (to maintain texture in canned berries). Chemical preservatives are not permitted and artificial coloring is allowed only in canned pears and plums, in which it is rarely used, and the cherries in fruit cocktail, in which its use is routine. (Actually this coloring is only one small event in the drastic treatment given to cherries to make them maraschino. First they are brined in a mixture of acids and chemical salts, including sulfites, to bleach the fruit to a white or creamy yellow color. Then they are dyed red, using some of the most suspect artificial colors, and boiled in an acid solution to keep them from bleeding.)

Applesauce

You should have no trouble finding unsweetened applesauce, often described by the manufacturer as "natural." It should contain apple puree alone or with water. Some brands also have added ascorbic acid either to act as a preservative, or, in greater amounts, so that a 4-ounce serving furnishes 60 milligrams of vitamin C. Anything else is unnecessary, especially salt, sweetening, color additives, and artificial flavoring, all of which will be revealed in the list of ingredients.

Generally, there is a difference of 65 calories (the equivalent of 1½ tablespoons of sugar) between sweetened and unsweetened applesauce. Although some brands of unsweetened applesauce narrow the gap to 30 calories, this still adds up to 2 teaspoons of added sweetening.

Pumpkin

Pumpkin is a vegetable that is often used as a fruit, as, for example, in pumpkin pies. When it is canned, the words *solid pack* or *natural pack* indicate that the product is all pumpkin with nothing added. Pumpkin pie filling, on the other hand, is presweetened with refined sugars and is also likely to contain a chemical salt that inhibits weeping.

RECOMMENDATIONS

FRESH FRUIT

General Rule of Purchase: Look for fresh fruit following the guidelines in this chapter. Give organically grown fruit priority.

FROZEN FRUIT

General Rule of Purchase: All ingredients are on the label. Look for those that are unsweetened, with nothing else added. Be sure the package is solidly frozen.

Exemplary Brands

Bel Air Unsweetened Strawberries, Blueberries

Big Valley Unsweetened Boysenberries, Blueberries, Strawberries, Red Raspberries, Dark Sweet Cherries, Apricots, Blackberries, Northern Spy Apples, Peaches, Rhubarb, Cup of Fruit

Brady's Unsweetened Blueberries, Dark Sweet Cherries, Whole Blackberries, Peaches

C&W Unsweetened Red Flame Seedless Grapes, Whole Strawberries, Sliced Peaches, Blueberries, Mixed Melon Balls

Cascadian Farms Unsweetened Blueberries,[1] Strawberries,[1] Raspberries[1]

Cleugh's Rhubarb

Flavorland Unsweetened Whole Strawberries, Blueberries, Black Raspberries, Marian Blackberries, Boysenberries, Pitted Red Sour Cherries, Pitted Dark Sweet Cherries, Sliced Peaches, Rhubarb, Melon Balls, Fruit Medley, Plantation Fruit

Kerns Unsweetened Strawberries

Kroger No Sugar Added Strawberries

Overlake Unsweetened Blueberries

Seabrook No Sugar Added Blueberries

Snow Kist No Sugar Added Whole Strawberries

Stillwell No Sugar Added Strawberries, Peaches, Blackberries, Cherries, Rhubarb, Melon Balls, Mixed Fruit

Vons Unsweetened Whole Strawberries

Wilderness Blueberries, Mixed Fruit

CANNED FRUIT

General Rule of Purchase: All ingredients are on the label. Look for those packed in water or unsweetened juice, and be sure to consume the liquid. Avoid products with added sweetening, artificial flavor, or artificial color (which may appear in pears and plums, and is universal in the cherries in fruit cocktail). Berries may contain a calcium salt to maintain texture; this is not especially objectionable.

Exemplary Brands

Pineapple in Unsweetened Juice—all brands similar

Applesauce

Alpha Beta Natural
Appletime Unsweetened
Coop Unsweetened
Country Pure Unsweetened
Del Monte Lite
Eden
Featherweight Unsweetened
Finast Unsweetened Natural
Food Club Natural Style
Gathering Winds All Natural
Golden Harvest
Janet Lee Natural
Lucky Leaf No Sugar Added
Mott's Natural
Mrs. Gooch's Natural

Musselman's Natural
New England Organic
Pathmark Unsweetened
Ralph's Unsweetened
S&W Unsweetened
Seneca 100% Natural
Shiloh Farms[1]
Stater Brothers Natural Unsweetened
The Cherry Tree Unsweetened
Thrifty Maid Natural
Tree Top Natural
Very Fine Unsweetened
Waldbaum's Natural Unsweetened
White House Natural Plus

Pumpkin

Ideal Golden
Libby's Solid Pack

One Pie
Stokely's 100% Natural

Other Fruit

Big Star Peaches in Juice from Concentrate
Coop Pitted Red Sour Cherries
Country Pure Lite Unpeeled Apricots, Pears, Peaches
Del Monte No Sugar Added Peaches
Diamond A Red Sour Pitted Cherries in Water
Diet Delight Bartlett Pears, Mandarin Orange Sections, Apricots in Fruit Juice from Concentrate
F&T Lite Peaches, Pears in Real Fruit Juices
Featherweight Mandarin Sections, Pears, Apricots in Juice
Finast Lite Pears, Chunky Mixed Fruit in Juice from Concentrate
Food Club Unsweetened Grapefruit in Juice from Concentrate
Giant Peaches, Pears, Apricots, Grapefruit Sections, Mandarin Orange Segments in Juice from Concentrate
Golden Harvest Peach Halves, Natural Fruit Mix in Water
Heritage House Lite Peaches, Pears in Fruit Juice
Janet Lee Lite Sliced Peaches, Bartlett Pears
Jewel Peaches, Pears in Juice

Kroger Lite Pears in Pear Juice from Concentrate
Lady Lee Peaches, Pears in Pear Juice from Concentrate
Lucky Leaf Sliced Apples for Pies and Desserts
Mrs. Adler's Fruit Compote
My-Te-Fine Peaches, Bartlett Pears in Juice from Concentrate
National Lite Pears in Unsweetened Pear Juice
Natural Sun Grapefruit Sections in Unsweetened Juice
Nature Maid Peaches in Water
Nutradiet Pears, Peaches, Apricots, Mandarin Oranges in Water, Grapefruit in Unsweetened Juice
Parade Light Pears, Peaches in Juice from Concentrate
Ralph's Lite Bartlett Pears in Pear Juice from Concentrate
Rokeach Compote
S&W Grapefruit in Grapefruit Juice, Natural Lite Pears, Peaches in Unsweetened Juice
Stater Brothers Pears, Peaches in Pear Juice from Concentrate

Other Fruit (continued)

Thank You Brand Sliced Apples
Tillie Lewis Grapefruit in Grapefruit Juice

Town House Red Sour Pitted Cherries in Water, Unsweetened Grapefruit Sections
Waldbaum's Peaches, No Sugar Added

[1]Organic

Chapter 26

Dried Fruit:
Ancient Sweets

In both the Near and Far East, dating back to very early times, dates, figs, and grapes were preserved by drying them in the hot desert sand. While some dried fruit still relies on the sun, today mechanical dehydrators are more apt to do the job of removing 50 percent or more of the moisture, thereby concentrating the inherent sugars and extending the lifespan. Almost any fruit can be preserved in this way.

Dried fruit makes an excellent snack and is an ideal substitute for candy. It is a concentrated source of fruit sugars, providing the quick energy that people often look for in highly sugared foods while in addition supplying most of the vitamins and minerals available in fresh fruit. Many dried fruits are an excellent source of iron, a mineral lacking in most diets and vital for healthy blood; potassium, folic acid, and vitamin A are also generally in good supply.

Because of its density, dried fruit can be deceiving; calories can add up rather quickly since it lacks the water content of fresh fruit. A pound of dried fruit may be prepared from as little as 3 pounds and as much as 10 pounds of its fresh counterpart. Eating just a half pound of dried apricots at a single sitting is not hard to imagine, yet few people would be likely to eat at once the 3 pounds of fresh fruit it took to make it.

ONLY YOUR DENTIST
WILL TELL YOU

One real drawback to dried fruit is the cavity-causing nature of the concentrated sugars that they contain. Many dentists claim that soft, sticky dried fruit may be more harmful than refined white sugar. To offset this problem, try to rinse your mouth with water after eating dried fruit. Another way to help reduce this problem is to combine dried fruits with nuts, especially peanuts, which are said to have cavity-fighting properties.

ALL DRIED FRUIT
IS NOT TREATED EQUALLY

Sun-Dried and Dehydrated

The two major means of removing the moisture from fresh fruit are sun-drying and dehydration indoors by heat evaporation. In the latter process the fruit is commonly bathed or smoked with sulfur dioxide to keep it from darkening. Sulfur dioxide also produces a softer texture and has a somewhat protective effect on vitamins C and A.

The term "sun-dried" implies that no sulfuring has been done, but as you will see in the upcoming section on selecting dried fruit, this doesn't always hold true. With some fruit sulfuring is difficult, but not impossible, to avoid. Golden raisins are universally treated with sulfur dioxide, as is cut dried fruit that exhibits a vibrant color, such as cream-colored apples, bright orange peaches, mangoes, papayas, and apricots, and light, almost translucent pears and pineapple. In general, nonsulfured fruits are darker in color and drier than their sulfured counterparts.

Declaration of the use of sulfur dioxide (and other sulfites) is required on the label. The many violations of this law by packers are finally being rectified now that the role of sulfites in inducing adverse reactions in sensitive individuals has been brought to light and publicized.

Many dried fruits are also fumigated, either during storage or for importation, and the consumer is given no indication of this.

Another practice that many people are unaware of is the use of oils or other protective coatings to retain moisture, provide a sheen, and keep dried fruits from sticking together. Highly processed vegetable oils and vegetable oil derivatives like acetylated monoglycerides are employed in this country; mineral oil (which is not an approved food ingredient in the United States) is a common coating agent overseas. This should be on the label. However, when dried fruits are used in other foods such as cereals, candy, and baking mixes, these additives may be ignored in labeling.

The addition of preservatives is not necessary since the principle behind drying is that the fruits are preserved by their high sugar content. For those fruits that are still somewhat moist, however, like soft prunes, apricots, and dates, fear of mold and fermentation lead some manufacturers to protect their investment with chemical insurance in the form of sodium benzoate, potassium sorbate, or sorbic acid. This will show up on the label.

To avoid spoilage, many people store dried fruit in the refrigerator during warm weather. This accelerates "sugaring," the migration of the natural sugars within the fruit to the surface. Some say this actually improves the taste. Do not mistake the tiny white crystals for mold and discard what is perfectly edible, delicious food.

Organic and Unsulfured

Many natural food stores stock organically grown, untreated dried fruit. If you cannot get this locally, you may want to try to do so via mail order (see Chapter 3). Since dried fruit stores well, this can be a feasible as well as a convenient way of shopping.

Low-Moisture Dried Fruit

"Low-moisture" dried fruit, in which up to 97 percent of the moisture has been removed, represents an innovation in food processing. The low-moisture product is often desirable for industrial use in cereals, baked goods, and candy bars, and for manufacturing special "instantized" fruits that can be rehydrated in minutes. They are also appearing now as crispy fruit snacks, usually packed in small foil bags.

Most low-moisture fruits are treated with sulfur dioxide to prevent browning and some have calcium stearate added to keep the fruit free-flowing. Both these additives should appear on the label.

THE BLUEBERRY YOU'RE EATING MAY BE AN APPLE

A fascinating item made for food processors is "colored and flavored apple nuggets and dice." You can find them in ready-to-eat cereals. In the words of the manufacturer: "The purpose of coloring and flavoring low-moisture apple nuggets and dice was to create inexpensive, high quality, flavored fruits which closely resemble expensive natural fruits such as blueberries, raspberries, strawberries, pineapple, cherries and peaches." They go on to claim that "after rehydration [the fruits] have many of the qualities and characteristics of the natural fruit they resemble." What they have failed to mention is that there are also important differences; the real thing does not depend on synthetic colors and flavors for its appeal. Watch out for purple apples masquerading as blueberries!

SELECTING DRIED FRUIT

The labeling of dried fruit is supposed to reveal all added ingredients. The law is often ignored, however, when the product is sold directly to consumers from bulk bins, or purchased in bulk by stores and repacked into plastic bags.

Apples

Most packaged dried apples owe their creamy white color to sulfur dioxide. An unsulfured product, still moist with only a light tan coloration, is less widely available. The crispy apple snacks on the market come both ways, so be sure to read the package.

Apricots

Most apricots are dried by dehydration and sulfuring usually keeps them moist and bright. In the natural food store, soft but darker unsulfured apricots are often available alongside the sulfured ones. There you may also find sun-dried varieties which tend to be hard and leathery; they are best savored by sucking, rather than chewing.

Compared with all other dried fruit, apricots head the list in iron, potassium, and vitamin A. Grades are based solely on size and in descending size order are Jumbo, Extra Fancy, Fancy, Extra Choice, Choice, and Standard.

Bananas

Soft chewy brown strips of dried banana are considered by some to be a real delicacy. Dehydrated banana flakes, often recommended for babies, are another form in which this fruit may be presented. Do not confuse these with the crisp banana chips that are prepared by deep frying, not drying (see Chapter 30).

Cherries

Small, dark, sun-dried cherries are not standard merchandise, but are an example of a snack food that truly comes alive in your mouth. The more contact they have with your saliva, the tastier they become. Take care in offering them to children, though, for the pits are easily swallowed.

Dates

Some dates are dry and crunchy; others are softened by a process of hydration. Be sure to scrutinize the label for corn syrup or sugar, sometimes added to keep them from drying out. Dates are already very high in natural sugar and the idea of making them even sweeter is ridiculous.

Dates are quite susceptible to injury. While some of this is merely superficial, conditions that cause the skin to separate from the flesh in a balloon-like fashion or to become dark, dry, crusty, and cracked affect their eating quality. Blackening of the flesh will leave the date bitter; souring or fermentation will impart a yeasty or alcoholic taste; mold, dirt, and insect fragments or residues are unattractive and unsanitary. Try to make a visual check of the package to avoid this. Domestic dates are often pasteurized to prevent mold. Note that grading is based solely on aesthetics (size, color, condition, water content).

Among the more popular varieties are deglet noor, kadrawi, bread, halawi, and the large, succulent medjool. Whether to buy them with pits or without, whole or in pieces is a matter of personal taste and intended use.

Soft and semisoft dates keep best in the refrigerator. At warm temperatures they are apt to ferment.

Figs

The two most popular domestic varieties of dried figs are calimyrna, which is tan in color (but may be bleached to accentuate this lightness), and mission, which is purplish black and less likely to be treated with sulfur. Calamata string figs, imported from Greece, are also unsulfured.

Dried figs contain rather impressive amounts of calcium for a fruit. A half cup serving of calimyrna figs offers about as much calcium as an equal volume of milk (but also more than three times the calories). Figs balance this calcium well with phosphorus. They are also rich in potassium and low in sodium.

Mangoes

To prepare dried mango, the fruit is first dipped into boiling concentrated mango juice, causing the natural sugars from the juice to infiltrate the flesh. After drying, the surface resembles glacéed fruit. Here is a real food that can stand up to any jelly bean. (Note, however, that sulfuring is common.)

Papayas

Papaya spears and chunks can be manufactured in the same manner as mango, or they may be dipped in sugar or honey. Because most stores do their own packaging, the label may not reveal which form is being offered or whether sulfuring has occurred.

Peaches

Dried peaches are generally prepared in a similar manner to apricots. Be wary of the foil packets of "naturally good" sun-dried peaches (and other dried fruits). They may be "good" by virtue of "nature," as some labels claim, but they are sulfured courtesy of the manufacturer.

Pears

Dried pears, like peaches and apricots, may be sulfured or not. Generally they are softer, chewier and a lot sweeter than peaches.

Pineapple

Both rings and spears of pineapple may be prepared by drying. The "unsweetened" type is likely to be simmered in concentrated pineapple juice prior to drying, which gives the appearance of a sugar coating. The sweetened variety is soaked in sugar water or a honey solution that may include refined sugar as well. An entirely untreated product is rare and said to be quite sour; even the presweetened varieties possess a rather unusual tart, tangy taste.

Prunes

Prunes are famous (or infamous) for their laxative effect, but in truth many other dried fruits cause a similar reaction. Prunes are usually prepared by dehydration rather than sun-drying to better control the amount of moisture. They may also be steam-treated to keep them soft. It is hard to find prunes that do not have a sorbate preservative, perhaps because the sugar tends to rise to the surface, making the fruit look as if it is moldy. Labeling the product with an explanation of this phenomenon might eliminate this adulteration.

Raisins

Raisins, it should not be forgotten, are dried grapes, and since grapes are among the most commonly sprayed crops, organic raisins are a rare and revered commodity. Zante currants (resembling miniature raisins), seedless Thompsons, sultanas (mostly imported), muscats (which do list the addition of the oil coating we mentioned on the label), and large plump monukkas (which may still contain some edible seeds) are all available sun-dried, with no chemicals applied. As in prunes, with age natural sugars may rise to the surface of raisins and appear as harmless white crystals.

Golden raisins are always sulfured or bleached to preserve their color and are never an exemplary purchase.

FRUIT LEATHER

Fruit that has been pureed, spread to dry until pliable, and then rolled, is popularly nicknamed fruit leather but marketed also as fruit "stix," "bars," "rolls," or "chewy fruit." We limit our exemplary choices to those few that contain only fruit and perhaps an acidifier (lemon juice, citric acid). If you are willing to have fruit enhanced with sweeteners or vegetable gums, you may add several other brands to your list.

If fruit is all you want, be sure to read the label (including the fine print). Despite such declarations, as "no sugar," "no preservatives," "made with real fruit" and "all natural," sugar, corn syrup, honey, pectin, partially hydrogenated oil, mono- and diglycerides, and gums, as well as artificial flavor and color, are not uncommon. One company labels some of their "pocket fruit" as being "all natural," but the ingredient list reveals dextrose, sugar, citric acid, and carob bean gum. Other flavors from the same company in identical-looking packages, labeled "no preservatives," contain artificial flavor as well.

SOME FUN!

Sunkist advertises its Fun Fruits as "chewy real fruit snacks" that are "made with real cherries" (or other fruit). The presence of real fruit is not enough to overlook the remainder of the ingredients: corn syrup, sugar, modified food starch, partially hydrogenated vegetable oil (cottonseed and soybean), natural flavors, malic acid, lecithin, confectioner's glaze, petrolatum, artificial coloring and flavor.

STORING DRIED FRUIT

Dried fruit should be stored in an airtight container at cool room temperature to prevent it from drying out. It will keep this way for six months to a year or more. If your kitchen shelf is especially warm, you might do better to store the dried fruit in the refrigerator.

RECOMMENDATIONS

DRIED FRUIT

General Rule of Purchase: Give preference to organically grown dried fruit available in stores and from mail-order suppliers (see Chapter 3). All ingredients should be on the label; however, with bulk containers, or when the store weighs and packages the fruit on the premises, you may find this regulation has not been followed. Avoid sulfur dioxide and sorbic acid, potassium sorbate, and sodium benzoate preservatives. Dark fruits are less likely to be sulfured. Also avoid added sweetening, and that includes honey.

Exemplary Brands——————————————————————————

Dark Raisins—most brands are similar

Barbara's Dried Apples
Calavo Dates
Carmel Dates
Goodbody Snacks 100% Fruit Crisps
Hawaiian Solar Dried Pineapple, Papaya, Banana
Nabisco Dromedary Dates

Sonoma Dry Fruit[1]
Sun Giant Dates
Timber Crest Dried Fruit[1]
Town House Dates
Tree of Life Organic California Seedless Raisins[1]

[1]Organic

FRUIT LEATHER

General Rule of Purchase: All ingredients are on the label. Look for fruit leather that is nothing more than pure fruit and perhaps an added acid like lemon juice or citric acid. Avoid any with sweetening, partially hydrogenated oil, mono- and diglycerides, and gums, as well as artificial color, flavor, and preservatives.

Exemplary Brands——————————————————————————

Fruit Stix

Stretch Island Fruit Leather

Chapter 27

The State
of Soups and Sauces

The poet Lewis Carroll, who wrote the line "soup, beautiful soup," obviously hadn't visited an American supermarket. There's nothing beautiful about soups (or sauces) that have a multitude of artificial ingredients to keep them fresh-tasting and fresh-looking, to make them just the right consistency, and to keep the manufacturer's costs down by disguising the absence of real substance. Flavor enhancers and intensifiers are particularly popular with commercial soup- and sauce-makers, as are heavy doses of salt, because they mask the lack of rich, natural flavor.

AMERICA'S SOUP KITCHEN

Historically, soup has been a way to get the most from the least; small amounts of meat, vegetables, and grains were made to go a long way. In the prepared soup business this concept has been stretched beyond imagining and, in evaluating a prepared product, not only *what* is in it but *how much* must be taken into account.

Selecting Canned Soup

The fact that the ingredients are listed in descending order of predominance by weight is of real value here; salt, flour, fat, or sugar, when present, should be near the end of the line-up. Consider, for example, this ingredient list for a canned minestrone:

> water, potatoes, tomato paste, white beans, cabbage, green peas, macaroni, green beans, spinach, salt, celery, red kidney beans, rendered pork fat, olive oil, dehydrated onion, flavor, spices, garlic

Certainly these are all ingredients you might find in the kitchen, but can you imagine making a soup from scratch and using more salt than kidney beans!

Nor can the words "all natural" or "home style" be construed to mean that the soup is comparable to a homemade soup, for hydrolyzed vegetable

380

protein, MSG, modified food starch, sugar, dextrose, and even disodium guanylate and inosinate all show up in canned soups described in this manner. Following is a brief description of some of the common questionable ingredients in soups and our thoughts on them:

Sweeteners: Whether in the form of sugar, corn syrup, or dextrose, refined sweeteners rarely belong in the soup bowl. Of course, some varieties like borscht and cabbage soup get their characteristic flavors, in part, from added sweetening. Whether you select these soups is a matter of how you feel about refined sugar. But in all other varieties when you make your evaluations you should consider: (1) whether sweetening is appropriate to the recipe and, (2) how much is used.

Certainly a line of soup that bills itself as "low sodium" and then includes corn syrup as the third ingredient is not doing any great service by leaving out the salt.

Salt: Salt is a valuable traditional seasoning, but just reading the sodium levels in some prepared soups is enough to give anyone high blood pressure. If you want to know more about salt (sodium) and health, turn to Chapter 38. For most people, 1,100 to 3,300 milligrams of sodium daily is considered within safe limits. You can figure on getting from 700 to 1,200 milligrams of sodium when you consume an 8-ounce bowl of the average store-bought soup.

While there are some significant differences from variety to variety and brand to brand, there does not appear to be any consistency. For example, Progresso Minestrone has less sodium than Campbell's Minestrone, but for the two companies' tomato soups the pattern is reversed. Notable exceptions are the soups prepared by Hain and Health Valley, which leave the option of adding salt up to the individual diner and thus have sodium levels ranging from a mere 45 to 140 milligrams per cup. You may find other low-sodium soups where you shop, but in our travels the brands we have encountered are not exemplary in other respects.

Flavor Enhancers: With the variety of herbs and spices available, it is a shame to find so-called flavor intensifiers and enhancers in so many processed soups. Our dispute with such "natural food extracts" as MSG and hydrolyzed plant and vegetable proteins is that they are neither wholefoods nor the most valuable portions of the natural foods they are derived from. These additives are 40 to 60 percent sodium, no more acceptable than their synthesized counterparts disodium inosinate and guanylate.

Moreover, the addition of the amino acid glutamate, which is a component of these "natural" flavor enhancers, is cause for concern. Amino acids play important roles in blood chemistry, particularly affecting neurological functioning of the brain and nervous system. According to John Olney of the Department of Psychiatry at Washington University in St. Louis, Missouri, "human ingestion of these substances in aqueous solution (for example, soup containing glutamate and beverages containing aspartate) might represent optimal conditions for sustaining 'self-inflicted' brain damage.''

Cured Meats: The use of bacon as a flavoring agent is also reason for disqualifying a soup from our list of Exemplary Brands. We do not condone added nitrites in any amount.

Smoke Flavoring: Smoke flavoring is available today in a bottle just like vanilla extract. The safety of both smoke and smoke flavoring in food is uncertain.

Caramel Coloring: Caramel coloring is used in some soup bases. The caramelized sugar from which the coloring is derived is tentatively linked to cancer. There is no compelling reason to add caramel color to food.

Thickeners: On occasion a soup recipe will call for flour to impart body or hold certain ingredients in suspension, as in a "creamed" soup. In most manufacturers' kitchens, however, the addition of a thickener merely creates the illusion of the bulk that one would ordinarily get by cooking down vegetables, grains, and beans. Once again, in judging ingredients consider the appropriateness of using a thickener in the soup you are evaluating. If you feel it is justified, you can go on to decide if the particular thickener in question meets with your approval. The choice will generally include wheat flour, cornstarch, potato starch, and modified food starch. Although we prefer to see none of these, we categorically reject only the modified starch. If a soup is otherwise praiseworthy the other forms of thickening may be tolerated.

One soup line makes use of vegetable gums. While this brand has the distinction of being salt-free, there is no reason to include xanthan or locust bean gum in soup; they may be called "natural" since they are extracts of living plants, but they are neither natural to soups nor to human diets, especially at the rate they are being added to products these days.

Fat: Most soups are low in overall fat content, but we are still concerned with the fats some manufacturers choose. Once again, hydrogenated fat rears its head. Because the process of chemically saturating an oil changes the basic nature of the fat (see Chapters 20 and 21), hydrogenated oil and its offspring margarine are banned from our soup bowl.

Packaging: One final consideration is the packaging itself. Canned soups can pick up lead from the seams in the container in minuscule but detectable amounts. If you rely heavily on canned food, this may be of some concern. Certainly Health Valley and Hain again deserve citations for using lead-free solder and enamel-coated interiors in their soup cans. (See Chapter 1 to help find other lead-free cans.)

Packaged Dry Soup

In general, dry soup mixes are even less commendable than their canned counterparts. When you are considering a purchase, be sure to look out for the unnecessary thickeners and flavoring additives discussed above. Most instant broth and bouillon, you will find too, are devoid of nourishing ingredients, often amounting to nothing more than salt, hydrolyzed vegetable protein, sugar, flavor enhancers, and fat, with a few herbs and spices.

Several dry soups that are free of additives and offer the convenience of premixed dried beans, grains, and dehydrated vegetables still require lengthy cooking. The more "instant" exemplary options often tend to emphasize sodium in their formulation. For example, a packet of miso soup fixings built on freezer-dried miso powder, dehydrated vegetables, and assorted seasonings can range from about 532 milligrams on up to 720 milligrams per 8-ounce serving.

Ramen: Instant Soup from the Orient

An Oriental soup concept that has flooded the market in the last few years is ramen, a thin, quick-cooking, squiggly noodle that comes with a packet of broth fixings. The run-of-the mill supermarket varieties should be ignored. The noodles are made from refined wheat and may also contain partially hydrogenated oil, MSG, and phosphate additives so they soften instantaneously; the broth is likely to include sugar, dextrose, MSG, hydrolyzed plant protein, caramel color, and the flavor enhancers disodium guanylate and inosinate.

The noodles packaged by several of the natural food companies, however, are simply a combination of whole wheat, buckwheat, or brown rice flour with some sifted whole or unbleached wheat flour; the packet of broth seasonings is a flavorful blend of powdered soy sauce, miso, herbs, and dried vegetables.

Ramen provides the basis for excellent one-pot soup dinners. When you add some protein (whether cubes of tempeh or tofu or bits of meat) and some fresh or dried vegetables to a single package of ramen, a nourishing meal for two quickly emerges.

Note: The broth packet included in the exemplary ramens (based on their additive-free formulation) may unfortunately be diminished by a high sodium content (from 1,060 to 1,730 milligrams per 3.1-ounce package). Until lower sodium versions appear, you can use less than the full packet if you wish to cut back on sodium and supplement this with fresh or dried seasonings for added flavor.

PREPARED SAUCES AND GRAVIES

Sauces are a highly cherished convenience food in many homes. A covering of sauce can enhance or disguise almost anything, so naturally you want it to be as flavorful and as wholesome as possible.

Sauce Mixes

We're sad to report that there is not a single dry sauce mix worthy of the wholefoods kitchen. Even the packets marketed as "natural" rely on salt, hydrolyzed plant protein, textured vegetable protein, whey, honey powder, and vegetable gums. They may rate better than those mixes that dominate the shelf which are an amalgamation of sugars, salt, refined starches, saturated fats, flavor enhancers, artificial flavor and color, and antioxidants, but this still does not warrant their purchase.

Tomato Concentrates

Concentrated tomato products like tomato puree and paste are common ingredients in prepared sauces and the foundation of many homemade ones too. The major difference between the two is in the percentage of tomato solids: the paste is much more dense. By reading the label you will be able to see when salt, sodium bicarbonate (baking soda), spices, or flavorings have been added. No other modifications are allowed. While most brands are similar, a few are superior in that they are salt-free.

These cooked-down tomato products are well endowed with the vitamins and minerals for which tomatoes are known, notably vitamins C and A, but they are also highly acidic and over time can react with the metal in the can. Since this action is accelerated in the presence of oxygen, do not store tomato concentrate in the can after it has been opened. For future convenience, extra tomato paste can be spooned into ice cube trays or frozen in dollops on a baking sheet, then transferred to plastic bags for long-term freezer storage. This way you have easy access to the tablespoon or two, which is all that is generally needed at a time.

Another handy way to purchase tomato paste is in a tube. This Italian import allows you to squeeze out just what you need and store the rest for the future. Such convenience does come at a fairly high premium, however, since a comparable volume in a tube costs four times what you pay for a can and, at this time, unsalted options do not exist.

Tomato Sauces

Tomato sauce has become a mainstay of American cooking. Although fresh tomato sauce is much more tasty and takes only twenty minutes to prepare, many people still depend on the premade version for a quick and simple meal.

There is no federal recipe regarding tomato sauce, spaghetti sauce, marinara sauce, etc., except that "meat sauce" must contain 6 percent meat. Other than that it is a manufacturer's free-for-all. Fortunately, some brands are close to homemade recipes.

CANNED TOMATO SAUCE

Most canned tomato sauces consist of tomatoes plus a few basic seasonings, including salt. A few salt-free alternatives are also available. The majority have no added fat, and while a few are sweetened with dextrose or corn sweeteners and thus do not receive our endorsement, most are also unsweetened. These sauces can easily be enriched at home with oil, fresh herbs, mushrooms, peppers, cheese, or meat to taste. Some have already been enhanced with chili peppers and are dubbed "Mexican style."

One universal problem with those sauces packed in soldered cans is the traces of lead which can leach into the acidic contents. For this reason, select products packed in glass unless you are able to identify lead-free cans (see Chapter 1).

BOTTLED TOMATO SAUCE

More complicated tomato sauces, marketed as *spaghetti, marinara, pizza sauce,* and such are commonly packaged in glass, or on occasion in plastic tubs in the freezer. The trend today is to promote these as "all natural" and make a big deal about the fact that they are without preservatives. As you are probably aware by now, the mere absence of preservatives does not make a product exemplary. In any case, after reading the labels on numerous jars we realized that preservatives, which must be indicated on the label, are absent from virtually every "Italian-style" sauce.

The definition of "all natural" varies widely. It is important to decide if the claims of food manufacturers meet your criteria. Sauces calling themselves natural frequently contain the following ingredients: corn sweeteners, dextrose, sugar, molasses and honey, arrowroot, cornstarch, modified starch, guar gum, xanthan gum, and carrageenan. But if sweet ripe tomatoes are used, there is no need to sweeten tomato sauce; and with long, slow simmering, there is no need to thicken it either.

Once again we find great disparities within a single manufacturer's line, with some sauces that include unnecessary ingredients and others that meet our standards for wholefoods. For example, Ragu's "Homestyle 100% Natural Spaghetti Sauces" really are natural, while their "Chunky Garden Style 100% Natural Spaghetti Sauce" is prepared with both sugar and corn syrup, and their "Pizza Sauce" is compromised by the use of modified starch. The Homestyle sauce also contains less sodium than the others. The lesson here is, "Read every label carefully." In the final analysis, the onslaught of new, natural spaghetti sauces was reduced to a mere few that were acceptable.

FROZEN TOMATO SAUCE

You may be able to find an exemplary tomato sauce in the freezer. Most are locally made.

SALSA

Another ethnic variation of tomato sauce is canned, or more often bottled, Mexican-style "salsas," containing acid components such as vinegar or citric acid, hot peppers, and seasonings like cumin and coriander or cilantro. Modified starch and sodium benzoate (a preservative) may also appear, but the selection of good Mexican sauces without these additives does seem to be expanding.

You may also be able to find some Mexican table sauces freshly prepared or in the freezer case.

Other Meal-Enhancing Sauces

From the preponderance of tomato sauces on the market you might wonder if there were any other way to dress foods. Although the choices are limited, we have come across other varieties of prepared sauces—fresh, frozen, and canned—that can assist the cook in preparing an elegant but quick wholefoods meal. These sauces are named at the end of the chapter and embody such familiar types as aromatic garlic-laced pesto, creamy Alfredo, white clam, and curry. For the international gourmet in need of a last-minute meal there are a few more exotic offerings like a sorrel sauce, black bean sauce, bordelaise, and rouille (a thick garlic-herb blend popular in southern France). One of the most intriguing sauces we have come across is a canned "No Cheese Cheddar Like Sauce" made from water, tahini, pimientos, nutritional yeast, lemon juice, tomato paste, sea salt, and seasonings.

Unfortunately, none of these items are in broad distribution. We mention them more as a word of encouragement to those who are manufacturing or seeking high-quality prepared sauces. It can be done, and there is a market!

RECOMMENDATIONS

SOUPS

General Rule of Purchase: All ingredients are on the label. In both canned soup and packaged dry mixes, look for products made only with beans, preferably whole grains and whole grain pasta, vegetables, and common seasonings in the proportions you would use in cooking (which can be determined somewhat by the order in which they are listed). Salt is almost universal, but should appear near the end of the ingredients. Fat, too, should be minimal.

Avoid partially hydrogenated oils and margarine. Sweetening should only be accepted where it is characteristic of the soup. Other ingredients to avoid are MSG, hydrolyzed vegetable protein, disodium guanylate and inosinate, modified food starch, vegetable gums, caramel coloring, and cured meat. Smoke flavoring is also a concern.

Exemplary Brands

Canned

Asti Minestrone[4]
Campbell's Creamy Natural Potato[4]
Hain Regular, No Salt Added Vegetable Chicken, Tomato, Lentil, Minestrone, Vegetarian Vegetable, Chicken Noodle
Health Valley Regular, No Salt Added Chunky Vegetable Beef, Potato, Clam Chowder, Tomato, Mushroom, Chunky Garden Vegetable, Vegetable, Split Pea, Chunky Split Pea, Minestrone, Chunky Minestrone, Vegetable Chicken, Lentil, Bean
Lima Lentil,[1] Pumpkin[1]

Manischewitz Shav[3]
Walnut Acres Chicken Rice, Beef Gumbo, Beef Noodle, Lentil with Hot Dogs, Scotch Broth, Chicken Gumbo, Vegetable Beef, Chicken Corn, Chicken Curry, Tomato Beef Consomme, Seafood Chowders, Cream of Chives, Cream of Pea, Cream of Celery, Corn Chowder, Canadian Pea, French Onion, Lentil, Tomato, Tomato Rice, Vegetarian Vegetable, Cream of Watercress and Potato Soups[1]; Black Bean, Navy Bean Soups[2]

Frozen

Capeway All Natural Chowder
Fresca Gusta Frozen Bouillabaisse
Gourmaid French Onion[4]
Miss Sally's Gumbo
Natural and Kosher Lentil, Barley Mushroom, Vegetable, Split Pea, Minestrone

Ratner's Restaurant Vegetable, Mushroom and Barley, Split Pea[4], Cabbage[3]
Saucier Concentrate of Beef, Chicken, Fish and Lobster

Dry Mixes

Edward and Son Natural Instant Miso Cup
Fearn Split Pea, Lentil Minestrone
Gourmet Farms Almond Cheddar, Gazpacho[3], Vegetable with Country Cheddar, Corn Chowder, Creamed Corn and Mushroom

Lundberg Soup 'r Mixes
Reese's Dried Minestrone
Rokeach Pure Soup Greens
Westbrae Natural Instant Miso

Ramen

Eden Whole Wheat, Whole Wheat and Buckwheat, Whole Wheat and Brown Rice
Erewhon[4]
Premier Japan Brown Rice, Buckwheat, Pearl Barley, Wakame[4]
So'

Soken Brown Rice[4], Jinenjo with Spinach[4], Whole Wheat
Westbrae Natural Whole Wheat, Buckwheat, Brown Rice, Mushroom, Seaweed, Miso, 5-Spice, Curry, Carrot, Spinach, Tofu, Onion

SAUCES

General Rule of Purchase: All ingredients are on the label. Look for sauces containing only vegetables, dairy products, meat, herbs, spices, and other recognizable flavoring ingredients. Once again, salt is almost universal.

"100% natural," "no preservatives," and "home style" may not mean what you think they do and can include ingredients to avoid such as refined sweeteners, cornstarch, modified starch, vegetable gums, partially hydrogenated oil or margarine, MSG, and hydrolyzed vegetable protein. Avoid also disodium guanylate and inosinate, artificial color and flavor, and preservatives.

Note: When choosing canned tomato products, including those listed below, check to see if they are packed in lead-free cans.

*Exemplary Brands*_____

Tomato Paste and Puree—All brands similar except the following, which are salt-free

Contadina No Salt Added Tomato Paste
Coop Unsalted Tomato Paste
Featherweight Tomato Paste
Food Club No Salt Added Tomato Paste

Canned Tomato Sauce

Cento Capri Italiano
Como
Contadina Italian Style, Extra Thick & Zesty
Coop Unsalted
Edward's Finast
Faraon Spanish Style
Food Town
Health Valley Regular, No Salt
Hyde Park
Janet Lee
Las Palmas Mexican Style
My-Te-Fine
Nutradiet
P&Q
Pathmark
Progresso Tomato, Pizza
Ralphs
Rienzi with Onions and Basil
S&W Thick and Chunky
Skaggs Alpha Beta
Springfield
Staff

Bottled Tomato Sauce

Aunt Millies
Ci'Bella Pasta
Classico Tomato and Basil, Beef and Pork
De Boles Meatless Spaghetti, Mushroom Spaghetti
Diate Spaghetti
Eden Spaghetti, No Salt Spaghetti
Enrico's All Natural Home Style No Salt Spaghetti, Meat Flavored, Traditional Recipe
Erewhon All Natural Spaghetti, with Mushrooms and Onions
Francesco Rinaldi No Salt Added All Natural Spaghetti
Gathering Winds Spaghetti
Golden Harvest Spaghetti with Mushrooms, Marinara
Health Valley Bellissimo Regular, No Salt
Johnson's Spaghetti, No Salt Tomato
L.E. Rosellis Spaghetti
Legume Light and Natural
Mamma Seller's Pizza
Nature's Cuisine Spaghetti
Palmieri Marinara, Spaghetti, Spaghetti and Macaroni, Pizza
Prego No Salt Added Spaghetti
Pubix All Natural Spaghetti
Ragu Homestyle 100% Natural Spaghetti, Traditional Style Italian Cooking
Ronzoni Lite 'N Natural Spaghetti
Timber Crest Farms Pasta
Westbrae Spaghetti

Frozen Tomato Sauce

Putney Pasta Tomato

Salsa

Anna Lisa Home Style
Ashley's of Texas Tomatoes and Green Chilies, Jalapeno Taco
Casa Fiesta Green Chili Salsa, Jalapeno Relish
D.L. Jardine's Mild Texacante Piquant, Texas Chili
Desert Rose
El Patio Mexican Style
Embasa Red Mexican, Home Style
Enrico's Hot, Mild, No Salt
Herdez Mexican Green, Home Style
Hot Cha Cha
La Preferida Diced Tomatoes and Jalapeno Chilies

Las Palmas Green Chili
Los Amigos
Mamma Sita's
Mazatlan Suprema
Nature's Cuisine Picante
Ortega Hot Taco, Hot Ranchero, Medium Picante, Tomatoes and Jalapenos
Pace Picante
Pure and Simple Picante, Mild Green Chili, No Salt Added
Ro-Tel Tomatoes and Green Chilies
Rosarita Mild, Hot, Chunky, Picante
Sonoma
Sunburst Farms

Other Sauces

Aranino Farms Frozen Pesto for Pasta
Captain Jaap's Galley Sauce
Casa Di Lisio Pesto, Walnut Pesto, White Clam
Cento Capri White Clam
Country Life No Cheese Cheddar Like
Crabtree and Evelyn Sorrell
Fresca Gusta Frozen Rouille Base[4], Sorrel Sauce Base, Black Bean, Pesto, White Clam

Gathering Winds Curry
Just So Sate Peanut Sauce[2]
Palmieri Frozen Fresh Cream
Putney Mornay with Wine and Mushrooms, Pesto
Saucier Frozen Bordelaise
Tiguellio Pesto Genovese

[1]Organic
[2]Some organic ingredients
[3]Contains refined sweeteners
[4]Contains refined grains

Chapter 28

Prepared Foods:
The Instant Chef

Food markets today look more and more like restaurants, with salad bars, gourmet and deli take-out sections, and frozen dinners not too different from those defrosted in many eating establishments.

When TV dinners first appeared, their popularity was due, in part, to the novelty of having someone else do the cooking. But by the late 1960s and 70s, health-conscious Americans became disenchanted with these premade meals. Nonetheless, as we entered the 80s, frozen entrées and prepared foods in general, geared toward dieters and more affluent consumers, were once again hot news, even finding their way into the natural food market. The question we pose is: What is the buyer getting with the fancy marketing?

Despite our interest in cooking, we have always appreciated prepared dishes made according to wholefoods standards, what were traditionally referred to as "kitchen quality" foods. But you may have to dig through a large (and probably cold) display of unacceptable entries and manufacturers' puffery to find those that are up to this standard.

FROZEN MEALS

Aware of the sophistication of its new clientele, the prepared foods industry has replaced the humble TV dinner with nomenclature that conveys a sense of tradition, using words like "classic"; or they lend a foreign note by turning mundane food into "Le Food." One manufacturer identifies its line with "living well," and product images have also been directed to those who relate to food that is "lite."

"Nouvelle" Frozen Cuisine

Meals from the freezer no longer remind us of school cafeteria fare, for the ordinary mashed potatoes may now be wild rice, the squishy peas are likely to be delicate edible pea pods, and the meat loaf has turned into teriyaki steak. Indeed, the variety and appearance are definitely upgraded, but the taste and nutrition are not always so far advanced. Many foods

390

suffer aesthetically during the freezing and reheating phases. Pasta tends to turn soft, sauces become pasty, fish turns rubbery, chicken gets soggy, and vegetables that must endure the time and temperature needed for the rest of the tray to cook disintegrate at the touch of a fork. Admittedly, these are matters of taste, and taste is a judgment of the individual palate. The concern for nutrients and additives is quite another thing though.

There is nothing "nouvelle" about the salt levels, with many frozen dinners or entrées alone furnishing from 1,000 to 2,000 milligrams of sodium per serving. A majority of these foods also get a substantial portion of their calories from fat, especially those encased in pastry; such innocent sounding vegetables as Spinach Amandine, Zucchini Provençale, and Mushrooms Dijon may actually get as much as 65 percent of their calories from fat when encased in dough.

The most common food additives in these offerings, even those promoted as having "no preservatives or artificial flavors," include MSG, disodium inosinate, hydrolyzed vegetable protein, autolyzed yeast (all added to exaggerate flavors); mono- and diglycerides, modified food starch, and xanthan gum (all added for "mouthfeel"). Sugar and margarine are also prevalent.

Natural Entrées

Some companies have managed to overcome the negative aspects of typical prepared frozen entrées. You can find the results of their creativity at most natural food stores, as well as many supermarkets. The common thread that runs through our Exemplary Brands is not that they proclaim themselves "all natural," but that they are truly kitchen-quality foods, made with the same ingredients that a wholefoods cook would use in preparing a fresh version of these dishes. This means gum thickeners, sugar, flavor enhancers, hydrogenated oils, refined grains, and isolated soy protein are not part of the recipe.

You may still want to pay attention to the amount of sodium and fat you are buying. While sodium may be in the range of only 310 to 410 milligrams per serving and fat a reasonable 20 percent of calories, this does not always hold true. When eggs, cheese, and meat are included, or the vegetables are bedded down in a whole wheat croissant, you can expect a substantial portion of the calories to come from fat. This does not necessarily mean you have to reject these products, but you should try to balance them intelligently with other components of the meal.

Frozen Entrées for Weight Control

The appeal of the calories count can be enormous. One company tells how their seafood-and-sauce frozen dinners drew a nominal audience until, after two years on the market, an advertising agency suggested adding a graphic of a tapemeasure with the words "under 300 (calories)." According to the public relations representative, sales increased 55 percent with this small change in the label.

Frozen meals with a "light" or "lean" slant tend to be more sparing with fat, which generally accounts for their lower calorie content. Unfortunately, sodium and additives do not necessarily follow suit.

Calling a Calorie Recount

Those who rely on nutrition labels for precise information were somewhat shocked to learn, in 1985, that there is a 20 percent government-sanctioned leeway when it comes to listing calories per serving. This makes it permissible to state that a particular food has 1,000 calories, when in fact it could have as few as 800 or as many as 1,200. When the New York State Consumer Protection Board analyzed twenty-one products marketed as "diet foods," they found fifteen of them exceeded the calorie count on the label and four were actually above even the 20 percent limit. Only one had the exact caloric level specified on the package. Six of the mislabeled products were frozen diet dinners or main dish items.

This is no small matter to many. If you think you are on a 2,000 calorie-a-day diet, but are really consuming 2,400 calories, within one year you will be getting an extra 146,000 calories—the equivalent of 40 pounds! As of this writing the calorie leeway remains in place; however, it is hoped that a petition to the FDA by the New York State Consumer Protection Board will change this.

Ethnic Fare

Interest in foreign cuisine has grown to such a degree that enchiladas, ravioli, lasagna, chow mein, egg rolls, and blintzes hardly seem unusual to most children whose parents may remember their first adventurous trip to the exotic restaurants where these foods were once exclusively found.

In the frozen food case these one-dish items, combining meat, cheese or beans, vegetables, and pasta or some other starch, frequently come off better than industry efforts to create a prepared three-course "dinner." Although some of these enjoy additive-free status, their acceptability may be compromised by their use of white flour. However, when you compare a ravioli made with semolina flour, eggs, ricotta cheese, bread crumbs, spinach, Parmesan, salt, and seasonings to a competitor that also includes whey, modified food starch, sodium calcium caseinate, malto dextrin, tapioca flour, and fucelleran, the improvement is worth some acknowledgment.

PIZZA

Pizza is America's favorite take-out food and the opportunity to have some on hand at all times via the freezer has great appeal. In addition to frozen pies, many stores offer "fresh," ready-to-bake pizzas. A well-made product is worth praising, but a perfect, or even almost perfect pizza is not so easy to come by.

Defining Pizza

Cheese is the characterizing ingredient in pizza, but with the exception of meat pizza, which must follow very specific USDA labeling guidelines, it may take some detective work to determine if the cheese is real mozzarella or a cheese substitute. If a mozzarella cheese substitute has been used, the ingredient listing could say:

> water, casein, hydrogenated soybean oil, salt, sodium aluminum phosphate, lactic acid, natural flavor, modified cornstarch, sodium citrate, sorbic acid, sodium phosphate, artificial color, guar gum, and the added nutrients magnesium oxide, ferric orthophosphate, zinc acid, riboflavin, vitamin B_{12}, folic acid, vitamin B_6 hydrochloride, niacinamide, thiamine mononitrate, and vitamin A palmitate

Would you have deduced the presence of a cheese product from this? Would you have guessed that it could contain as much as 200 percent more sodium than a real cheese pizza?

Selecting Pizza

For an exemplary pizza you will probably want to go to a natural food store. There are several brands that have a whole wheat crust, real cheese, a sauce devoid of refined sugars and starchy thickeners, and exotic toppings including tofu or vegetarian pepperoni based on tempeh. If none of this appeals to you, you may even find the whole wheat shell alone for a pizza of your own creation.

At the supermarket the selection will be larger, but the choices less attractive. It is possible to find quality sauce and toppings reposing on a white flour crust that is at least devoid of modified food starch, dough conditioners, and partially hydrogenated shortening. Note, however, that some of these objectionable ingredients may be included in pizzas that bear "100% natural" on the label.

FAT COUNTERS DON'T EAT QUICHE

The eggy custard pie known as quiche is a popular entrée in gourmet and vegetarian circles where elegance and rich taste prevail. Given the fact that all pastry is relatively high in fat, and the traditional quiche filling is dependent on eggs, cream, and cheese, one would hardly expect this to be a calorie- or fat-sparing dish.

Although we don't recommend quiche as everyday fare, for an occasional indulgence it is possible to find one made of quality wholefoods. If you aren't careful, however, your quiche can be adulterated with modified starch, sodium phosphate, mono- and diglycerides, artificial color, partially hydrogenated vegetable shortening or lard, and preservatives.

All quiche is custard-filled, but the flavoring ingredients may vary widely. Make sure the cheese is natural and when meat is included that it is not cured (as are bacon, ham, and some sausage). If the name is Quiche Lorraine, it contains either bacon or ham.

MEATLESS "BURGERS" AND OTHER LOOK-ALIKES

Several of the prepared vegetable, tofu, and tempeh burgers at the natural food store qualify as excellent wholefoods. You will find these items either in the freezer or refrigerator case.

Tofu and tempeh may also be formed more fancifully into mock hot dogs, bologna, bacon, and such. In this case, gums may have been used to create the proper consistency, but at least these products, designed to replace processed meats, are commendably free of nitrites and saturated fat, often have more protein per calorie, tend to have half the sodium or less, and at times are lower in fat than their high-fat, over-salted meat models. Some, however, do get as much as 60 to 80 percent of their calories from fat, just like processed meat.

Sausages fashioned from okara, the pulp that remains after tofu production, are another example of creative new prepared foods. Marketed as soy sausage or "soysage," they are spiced in the manner of sausage and shaped similarly into rolls or patties. Unlike their meat counterparts, these okara-grain combinations contain a moderate amount of sodium and are rich in fiber, not fat. Look for them in the freezer or refrigerator case at the natural food store.

Note that not all of these items are either additive-free or qualify as wholefoods. While vegetable gums may be accepted for want of any alternative at this time, we avoid those based on soy isolates and concentrates because they are too highly processed.

DINNER IN A CAN

Perhaps the worst examples of prepared meals are found on the canned goods shelf: Soggy pasta in starchy sauce; limp chow mein vegetables in a gravy redolent with MSG, salt, and sugar; and meat and vegetable combinations in which it is almost impossible to distinguish one from the other.

Some of the preseasoned canned beans meet wholefoods standards, including chili beans, burrito filling, refried beans, and a few "baked" bean varieties (all presweetened, although some rely on honey and molasses). Those that are acceptable are free of MSG, modified food starch, and other unseemly ingredients. Many of these are supermarket items; a few are solely natural food store commodities.

On occasion you will also find an acceptable canned grain and vegetable combination.

DINNER IN A BAG

Another intriguing item in the natural food line are boil-in-bag brown rice dinners. Most of them are imported from Japan and consist of a mixture of vegetables, seasonings, and precooked brown rice sealed in a retort pouch that can be stored at room temperature. These convenience meals are ready to eat in only ten minutes.

STARTER MIXES

Mixes to help you get started with meal preparation are also popular. Ideally, a mix can save you time by providing premeasured dry ingredients, but when the cost of convenience is high not only in terms of dollars but also in sodium levels, processed flour, and other constituents of questionable value as well, it is not worth it. Full ingredient disclosure is mandatory on all these items.

One such "stew starter," which the manufacturer praises as "homemade," includes in its long list of ingredients: dehydrated vegetables, modified food starch, salt, sugar, bleached bromated flour, MSG, color, calcium chloride, dextrose, sodium sulfite and sodium bisulfite, disodium inosinate, disodium guanylate, plus a variety of seasonings and natural flavor. Perhaps they have done all the "shopping, chopping, slicing, and dicing" for you, but it will still take ninety minutes for the stew to be ready, and unless the family cook is a chemical engineer, you can hardly expect "homemade" stew to contain these ingredients.

Bean and Grain Mixes

Many people have already discovered the wonderful dishes that can be made from ground beans. The most widely known is falafel—deep-fried, crispy, succulent croquettes traditionally packed into pita bread pockets and topped with a garlic-laden sesame sauce. Several companies make a commendable dried mix that can be used to fashion falafel, composed of ground chick-peas, seasonings, and possibly one or more of the following: whole wheat flour, wheat germ, soy flour or textured soy protein, and baking soda.

Similar "burger" mixes are built around other beans, grains, and sometimes nuts. The combination of these vegetable protein foods can make a dish of excellent quality in terms of nutrition as well as taste. While most mixes are free of unwanted additives, many do compromise their otherwise excellent assets by incorporating processed soy in the form of concentrates and isolates.

You may also encounter several mixes intended to turn tofu into burgers or eggless "scrambles." These may be nothing more than a mixture of seasonings, or a composite of seasonings, grains, nut meals, and bean flour to which you are instructed to add tofu. They provide a means of preparing a tasty tofu entrée with a minimum of physical or creative input, but expect to pay for this service.

Another "helper" that some people welcome is a dry mix for preparing tabouli, the cracked wheat-parsley salad that is a staple of Middle Eastern meals.

Dip Mixes

While the standard dip mixes are a frightful blend of salt, flavor enhancers, hydrolyzed vegetable protein, refined thickening agents, and artificial flavoring and coloring, a few natural food companies have managed to come up with viable alternatives. For example, hummus, the garlicky chick-pea dip of Arabic origin, can be prepared from a boxed mix that contains only the precooked bean in dried, powdered form along with the essential flavoring elements. Dried seasoned miso is the basis for another acceptable dip mix that comes in spicy jalapeno style or with chive seasoning.

Macaroni Dinners

Up until recently you had to be pretty crafty to come up with a macaroni and cheese mix not based on process cheese and white flour noodles. However, there are now a few brands on the market that are additive-free and include either whole wheat macaroni, or wheat and soy, or artichoke pasta.

DELI DELIGHTS

Those who want food fast, but not necessarily fast foods, find the deli counter filled with temptations. Unlike packaged foods, however, there is no federally required ingredient labeling for deli foods. Moreover, despite its "homemade" appearance, the creamy coleslaw, pasta salad, or delicate quiche you have your eye on most likely was not made on the premises and may even have a chemically induced shelf-life of more than forty days.

If you shop at a store that emphasizes wholefoods, chances are the selection of prepared foods will reflect what you would like to see going on in your own kitchen. Even so, do not hesitate to question their procedures, for not everyone agrees on the parameters of wholefoods and while fructose, margarine, unbleached white flour, and gum stabilizers might satisfy some natural food purveyors, they do not satisfy us.

Fresh-Packed Wholefoods Salads and Spreads

We have found some exemplary premade salads, often packaged by local businesses, marketed in both supermarkets and natural food stores. Guacamole, hummus, and tofu salads, dips, and sandwich spreads in ready-to-eat form, with all their ingredients listed for you to make an informed decision, are still restricted to the most receptive neighborhoods. We hope this is the first sign of a mass movement.

Seller's Responsibility

The growing numbers of salad bars and deli counters and prepared items to take home increases the potential for food-borne illness. No matter where you purchase premade foods, there are certain handling procedures that should be met to ensure their wholesomeness.

All displayed food should be protected by a shield, and separate utensils should be used for each item. Cooked foods should be either hot (above 140°F.) or cold (below 40°F.), especially when they contain eggs, dairy, or animal products. None of these items should be allowed to remain at room temperature for more than two hours. Only fresh fruits and vegetables, breadstuffs, plain cheese, and pickled foods can be considered risk-free.

When meats or cheese are cut to order, watch how it is done. The slicing of cheese on the same cutting board, with the same knife, or on the same machine used for meat or poultry is a sign of improper sanitary procedures. The possibility of cross contamination from the animal flesh, which is considered the leading causative agent for food poisoning, is considerable when utensils are shared.

RECOMMENDATIONS

PREPARED PACKAGED FOODS

General Rule of Purchase: All ingredients are on the label. Look for prepared entrées and accompaniments, whether refrigerated, canned, or frozen, that meet wholefoods standards. Vegetable gums may be acceptable in soy-based products where they are used to help create a meat or cheese look-alike. Common additives to avoid include MSG, disodium inosinate and guanylate, hydrolyzed vegetable protein, mono- and diglycerides, modified food starch, bleached flour, partially hydrogenated vegetable shortening or margarine, phosphates, artificial color and flavor, and preservatives.

Since high sodium levels are common in prepared foods, if you are concerned, look for this nutrition information or other clues (sodium-containing additives) on the label.

Products listed as Acceptable with Reservation are free of additives but contain refined grains.

Exemplary Brands

Refrigerator/Freezer

Angie's Quiche
California Brand Meatless Chili, Refried Beans
Empress Chili
Graindance Pizza[2]
Health Valley Cheese Eggplant, Spinach Lasagna, Cheese Enchiladas, Stuffed Peppers, Cheddar Chicken, Lean Living Chicken Crepes Marco Polo, Chicken à la King, Spinach Mushroom Casserole
Laughing Moon Incredible Vegetable Turnovers
Leandro's Meatless Lasagna
Legume Frozen Tofu and Kofu Entrees
Love and Quiches Frozen Spinach, Mushroom, Broccoli, Zucchini and Onion Quiches

Natural Touch Lentil Rice Loaf
Old Chicago Deep Dish Pizza
Pizza Naturally Wholewheat Triple Cheese, Deluxe Vegetarian Tofu, Delux Tempeh, French Bread Pizzas, Pizza Shell
Shelton's Chicken, Turkey Pies[2]
Simply Natural Tofu Cheese Ravioli,[2] Tofu Cheese Stuffed Shells,[2] Tofu Linguini,[2] Tofu Spinach Fettucine,[2] Tofu Vegetable Cavatelli[2]
Tree Tavern Whole Wheat Pizza, Original Pizsoy[2]
Tumaro's Enchiladas,[2] Chinese Style Entrees,[2] Croissant Cuisine,[2] Sprout and Tofu Pie[2], Stew Pot Pies,[2] Pizzas,[2] Burritos,[2] Empanadas,[2] Ranch Barbecue,[2] Tamales,[2] Corn Souffle,[2] Spinach Souffle[2]

Canned

B&M Brick Oven Baked Beans[3]
Blue Runner Creole Cream Style White Navy Beans
Casa Fiesta Bean and Green Chili Burrito Filling, Refried Beans
Cedar Lake Meatless Chops, Hostess Cutlets, Grain Burger
Coop Refried Beans
Country Life Brazilian Black Beans[2]
Del Monte Burrito Filling Mix, Refried Beans
Dennison's Chili Beans in Chili Gravy
El Bohio Cuban Black Beans
Fiesta Mexican Style Refried Beans
Fontova Refried Beans with Green Mole Sauce
Friends Brick Oven Baked Beans[3]
Garcia's Black Beans
Gebhardt Refried, Jalapeno Refried Beans
Grandma Brown's Home Baked Beans[3]
Hain Bean Dips, Spicy Tempeh Homestyle Chili; Chili Sauce with Beans and Chicken

Health Valley Boston Style Baked Beans (Regular and No Salt), Honey Baked Style Vegetarian Beans with Miso, Spicy Chili Con Carne with Beans, Vegetarian Chili with Beans, with Lentils, Vegetarian Amaranth Minute Meal
La Preferida Refried Beans
La Victoria Refried Beans
Lady Lee Refried Beans
Lima Hummus, Limapast, Seitanpast, Vegetale, Lentil Spreads[1]
My-Te-Fine Refried Beans
Old El Paso Pinto, Mexe, Refried Beans
Ralph's Refried Beans
Richard's Kitchen Wheat Roast
Rosarita Refried Beans, with Green Chiles, Vegetarian
S&M Vegetarian Baked Beans[3]
Whole Earth Chili Beans, Brown Rice and Vegetables[2]

Boil-in-Bag

Premier Japan Quick Brown Rice with Vegetables, with Azuki Bean
Eden Brown Rice Dinners
Mitoku 3 Grain Cereal, Mixed Vegetable, Hokkaido Azuki Brown Rice Dinners

Soken Brown Rice with Azuki Beans, with Soy Beans

Meatless Burgers and Look-Alikes

Bhakti Burgers
Bud's Veggieburger,[2] Tofuburger[2]
Garden of Eatin' Bible Burgers, Vegie Yaki, Jerky Soy
Golden Soy Soysage[2]
Harvest Earthfoods Tempeh Delights[1]
Jaxon Corn Meal Mush
Lifestream Vegi Patties
Light Foods Tofu Loney, Light Links, Tofu Browners, Light and Spicy Tofu Breakfast Link, Meatless Franks, Bagel Link[4]
Lightlife Fakin' Bacon,[2] New York Style 'Strami,[2] Meatless Deli Slices,[2] Tempeh Burger[2]
Maple Meadows Smoked Vegetable Jerky
Mudpie Vegie Burgers
Nasoya Foods Tempeh Burgers,[1] Marinated Broiled Tofu[1]
New Leaf All Natural Tofu Burgers[2]
Pacific Foods Soysage, Tempeh Burger, Marinated Tempeh Burger, Earthlings Tofu Vegetable Burger

San Diego Soy Dairy Baked Tofu in Teriaki Sauce[2]
Soy Boy Tofu Not Dogs
Soy Power Fried Tofu,[1] Tempeh Burger,[1] Marinated Burger,[1] Savory Baked Tofu,[1] Tempeh-Tofu Burger[2]
Soyfoods Unlimited Tempeh Burger,[1] Cutlets[1]
Spring Creek Soysage[2]
Sunburger All Natural Vegetable Patties
Swan Garden Tempeh Burger,[1] Cutlet[1]
The Soy Shop Baked Savory, 5 Spice Tofus; Soysage[1]
Tomsun Spice, Herb Tofus
Tree of Life Yeast Baked Tofu[1]
21st Century Foods Tofu Burger,[2] Sesame Wheat Tempeh Burger,[2] Soylanie[2]
Wholesome & Hearty Gradenburger, Garden Sausage

Acceptable with Reservation[4]

Aronson's Chicken Breast Parmesan
Caesar's Cheese Ravioli
Cafferata Panzotti di Ricotta
California Brand Lasagna
Celantano Broccoli Stuffed Shells, Eggplant Parmesan, Lasagna Primavera, Ravioli, Spinach Cannelini, Cavatelli, Stuffed Shells, Pizza
Chicago Brothers Cheese Pizza
Cohen's Kasha Varnishkas
Colavita Tortellini
D'Orazio Gnocci
DeVinci Tortellini
Ferrara's Cheese, Meat Raviolis
Genova Delicatessan Ravioli
Gino's Natural Cheese, Vegetarian, Sausage Pizzas for One[3]

Health Valley Egg Rolls
Lucky Spring Rolls
Mamma Lena Frozen Cheese, Beef Ravioli
Mont Rose Ravioli with Cheese
Northern Soy Ravioli
Primo's Cheese Ravioli, Stuffed Shells
Queen Ann Manicotti
Rizzo's Gnocci
Silver Star Cheese Ravioli, Manicotti
Star Cheese Ravioli
Tabashnik Potato Pudding
Tombstone Cheese Pizza
Walker and Wilks Bar-B-Q Tofu, Sweet and Sour Tofu, Tofu Teriyaki

MIXES

General Rule of Purchase: Packages of fixings for meatless burgers, macaroni and cheese, stew, salad, etc., will have all ingredients on the label. Look for whole grains, beans, nuts, seeds, vegetables, real cheese, and so on. Even in "natural products" take care to avoid flavor enhancers, highly processed soy concentrates and isolates, vegetable gums, and excess sodium and fat (where nutritional information is provided).

Exemplary Brands

Ali's Bazaar Falafil, Tabouleh, Hummos
Banzo Falafel Middle Eastern Vegetable Delight
Casbah Falafel, Hummus
Cedar Lane Tabouli
Country Life Natural Foods Sesame Oatburger
De Boles Whole Wheat Macaroni and Cheese Dinner[2]
Edward and Sons Miso Plus Dip Mixes
Fantastic Foods Tabouli, Falafil, Vegetarian Chili, Nature's Burger Tofu Burger, Tri-Bean Casserole, Bean Barley Stew, Blackbean Creole, Frijoles Mix, Tempura Batter
Fearn Brazil Nut Burger, Breakfast Patty, Sesame Burger, Sunflower Burger, Falafel

Fritini Vegetable Patties
Harrington's Hodgson Mills Whole Wheat Macaroni and Cheese Dinner[2,4]
Lite Chef Tofu Mixers
Little Bear Grain Burger Mix[2]
Loveburger
Lundberg Pilaf Dinner
Natural Way Mills Vegetarian Steak[1]
Near East Taboule Wheat Salad, Lentil Pilaf
Norganic Old Country Style Tabouly
Telma Fallafel
The First Great Tofu Burger
Westbrae Natural Tabouly, Falafel Vegetable Croquette, Hummus, Cheese and Herbs Pasta Dinner,[2] Whole Wheat Mac and Cheese[2]

FRESH PREPARED FOODS

General Rule of Purchase: Fresh foods at the deli counter do not have to list their contents and, in fact, the word *fresh* may be used loosely. Many such premade salads often contain preservatives, particularly sodium benzoate or sorbate compounds.

Several small companies market high-quality packaged fresh salads. Most offer complete labeling, although depending on the state, this may not be required.

Exemplary Brands

Brightsong Tofu Cottage Salad,[2] Missing-Egg Salad,[2] Skinny Dip[2]
Cedar Lane Tofu Egg-Free Salad,[2] Hummos
Garden of Eatin Hummus, Super Tofu, Cottage Tofu, Tofu No Egg Salad
Golden Soy Tofu Sandwich Spread[2]
Home Style Natural Tofu Cottage Cheese, Tofu No Egg Salads[2]
Just So Eggplant à la Russe

Nasoya Foods Tofu Eggless Salad,[2] Tofu Vegi Dips[2]
Shakti Tofu Chickenless Salad, Mexi-Tofu Spread
Simply Natural Foods Soft Tofu Cheese[1]
Soy Power Whatta Salad,[2] Tofu Fiesta Salad[2]
Spring Creek Missing Egg Salad,[2] Onion Spread[2]
The Original Tofu Salad, Hot Dip

Exemplary Brands (continued)

The Soy Shop Dill Delight,[2] Terrific Tofu Dip,[2] Totahs Garbanzo Dip

21st Century Food Cream Cheese,[2] Vegetarian Pâté,[2] Tempeh Fiesta,[2] Tempeh Tabouli[2]

Watkin's Hommus Tahini, Baba Ghanouj, Taboule Salad

[1]Organic
[2]Some organic ingredients
[3]Contains refined sweeteners
[4]Contains refined grains

Chapter 29

Building a Better Baby

If you do not have firm convictions about how you intend to nourish a new baby, you will find the baby food industry most eager to help you make your decisions. When a baby is born the hospital often provides a gift pack of bottles, formula, and vitamins, compliments of an infant formula manufacturer. Soon after, new parents begin to receive promotional brochures in the mail from baby food companies offering money-saving coupons and a "step-by-step" feeding guide to "make sure your baby gets the right food at the right age." None of this builds confidence in your ability to feed a child adequately from the repertoire of family foods.

While on the surface convenience seems to be a prime selling point for prepared baby foods, this too may be a myth. Think about the time it takes you to traverse the baby food aisle and choose between powdered, concentrated, and ready-to-feed infant formulas based on soy protein or dairy ingredients with or without iron enrichment, analyze a dozen or more special cereals, decide if your child needs "strained," "textured," or "chunky" foods or is now at "Stage 1, 2, 3, or 4," and once you've figured this out, find the appropriate color-coded jars. But you're not done yet. Not only must you contemplate which brand you prefer, but you will be faced with over 100 different tiny jars of vegetables, fruit, cereals, meat, vegetable-meat-macaroni combinations, and desserts, and more recently about two dozen flavors of dried food you can reconstitute. Few adults receive this much variety in their meals in the course of a year!

On the other hand, many parents have found that real convenience is more easily achieved by offering appropriate foods from the family table as children reach different stages of readiness.

BABY'S FIRST FOOD

Some formulation of milk constitutes the sole source of food in early infancy and actually provides most of the child's nutrition during the entire first year.

Where breast feeding is possible, there is no question that it is the most efficient and healthful form of nourishment. For those seeking advice or assistance on breast feeding, the La Leche League, a wonderful international organization of parents, will give you all the help you need. Your obstetrician, midwife, or childbirth educator can give you the name of the local representative. Otherwise, write to La Leche League International, Dept. GGF, 9616 Minneapolis Avenue, Franklin Park, IL 60131.

Unmodified animal milk is unsuitable for infants, as is soy milk. If a baby is not breast-fed, these milks must be altered to meet the child's nutritional needs.

Although commercial infant formulas have been in use for over half a century, federal requirements have only recently been implemented. It is hoped these new standards will eliminate hazardous and nutritionally inadequate formulas from the market, a problem that has resulted in infant deaths, illness, and product recall in past years.

While current regulations may inspire greater confidence that certain minimal levels of nutrition are now being met, that dating codes promise increased freshness, and that guidelines for preparation minimize mishandling, it is still impossible to guarantee that a manufactured product will meet infant needs.

Most infant formulas are comprised of water, nonfat milk, soy and coconut oils, milk sugar (lactose), and an assortment of vitamin and mineral supplements. Soy-based formulas differ in that milk protein is replaced with soy protein isolate and refined sucrose and/or corn syrup substitute for the milk sugar. You will also find carrageenan in virtually all premixed milk-based products, modified cornstarch in soy formulas, and mono- and diglycerides across the board.

Notable is the fact that while the developing brain requires cholesterol, and mother's milk is its richest known source, it is left out of these products. The polyunsaturated omega-3 fatty acids (discussed in Chapter 19) are also lacking, although they too are present in breast milk and are believed to enhance brain development and vision. Also missing from formula are the natural antibodies contained in breast milk which cannot be reproduced in a laboratory. Another interesting difference is the change in the nutrient composition of breast milk that is believed to occur during each feeding and that adjusts as the months pass to meet the current needs of the growing child. Bottled formulas, on the other hand, remain consistent.

Administering a Bottle

Bottle feeding has been criticized on several grounds—among them that the development of the facial muscles is greater with breast feeding and that the shape of the artificial nipple requires an infant to pucker the mouth and lips in a somewhat unnatural manner. However an issue of greater import is the composition of the artificial nipple itself. Nitrosamines, the same family of carcinogens that have caused such a stir in the processed meat industry, are used to give strength and resilience to rubber nipples and pacifiers. Residues show up in the finished product.

As a result of consumer protests led by the Federation of Homemakers, action levels (the maximum allowed before a product can be removed from the market) have been set, resulting in a significant reduction of nitrosamines in rubber nipples and pacifiers. Nonetheless, some people are still concerned enough about the lingering residue to recommend selecting silicone nipples, which have tested nitrosamine-free, or soft vinyl or latex nipples advertised as 100 percent nitrosamine-free. Whether the plastic bottles and disposable liners will also someday become suspect due to chemical migration remains to be seen.

INTRODUCING COW'S MILK

The American Academy of Pediatrics contends that you can comfortably introduce undiluted cow's (or goat's) milk as early as six months, although other authorities feel that a year is more appropriate.

Avoiding Skim and Low Fat Milk

One thing *is* certain—low fat and skim milks are not suitable; the balance of nutrients in reduced-fat milks will not nourish infants properly and is taxing to their kidneys. This recommendation holds for at least the first two years of life.

SPECIAL JUICE FOR BABY

The juices bottled for babies are made from juice concentrates that are watered down and then enhanced with vitamin C. They are also strained or filtered so that the liquid can flow easily through the tiny hole in the nipple. You will pay about twice as much for the juice to have this questionable convenience. (If the flow of any juice is impeded, you can always enlarge the nipple hole.)

INTRODUCING SOLIDS

Just twenty years ago it was popular to supplement babies' milk-based diets with solids as early as six weeks of age. While some people have not abandoned this practice, pediatric experts today recommend waiting a minimum of four to six months. Before this age, a baby's nervous system is not mature enough to coordinate swallowing or to signal fullness. Thus, feeding solids too soon may result in frustration and overfeeding, and also contribute to food allergies.

Cereal

The first solid food that is introduced into a baby's diet is usually cereal. Unfortunately, refined starches are fed to most babies rather than whole grain varieties.

Today, creamy brown rice (kokoh) and a barley mix especially for infants are available at natural food stores. A combination of ground whole grains and dried banana in convenient ready-to-serve form is another commercial option in which no cooking is required. Muesli, the cold breakfast cereal imported from Switzerland, was originally developed for feeding babies and a special version offers a nutritious cold breakfast cereal to infants over one year. It contains no additives, salt, sweeteners, or refined products.

Other suitable cereals that can be made at home from your pantry supplies include cream of cornmeal (a thin gruel of cornmeal which can be further smoothed, if need be, in the blender) and oatmeal (made smooth for baby by grinding the raw oats in the blender, then cooking as usual). Leftover cooked grains (brown rice, barley, millet) can also be processed in the blender to a creamy consistency. Of course, any of these hot cereals can be enjoyed by other members of the family too, so cook up one big pot for everyone.

Who Needs Baby Food?

Parents who delay introducing food until their child has several teeth may find it is easy to start right out with finger foods and simple family favorites, but until children have enough teeth to do some chewing, their food has to be strained or mashed. This is the appeal of prepared baby food; before most homes were equipped with blenders, food processors, or the simple baby food grinders available today, the mushy ready-made food they provided was widely appreciated. But today it is just as convenient to take fresh-cooked *unseasoned* carrots, potatoes, peas, squash, beans, meat, soft fruits, and similar items being prepared for the family and reduce them to a puree in one of these machines. Other suitable "adult" foods like unsweetened applesauce, plain yogurt, avocado, mashed potatoes, and tofu require no additional effort.

Once children understand the swallowing process, more textured foods like baked potatoes, tiny boneless fish flakes, small pieces of pasta, scrambled eggs, and cottage cheese can be enjoyed. It will be no time before they can handle rice crackers, carrot sticks, peeled fruit wedges, natural cheese, bread spread with smooth nut butters, whole grain unsalted pretzels or bread sticks, ready-to-eat unsweetened cereal, and more. With this approach there will be no need to wean them from baby foods to table foods since they will be one and the same.

What's in a Jar of Baby Food?

We are pleased to report that the picture is less bleak for prepared baby food than it was in 1972 when we wrote *The Supermarket Handbook*. Since that time, baby food manufacturers have removed salt, sugar, and MSG from most of their products, making some untainted choices available (a prime example of what consumer input can do). This does not mean you do not have to read the label, though, for within a single category and brand you may still find some objectionable components like modified starch, refined grains, partially hydrogenated oils, and sugar or corn syrup.

While many vegetables only have added water, others contain starchy fillers. Similarly, while most fruits are combined with just water, citric acid, and vitamin C, for no obvious reason sugar may suddenly show up in a jar of junior peaches, but not in pears. As you move away from the single-food products, ingredients become less attractive, with a variety of refined grains, soy protein concentrates, and salt becoming widespread. Gerber's ads say they offer "chunky foods that are mildly seasoned," yet many of the products for older infants are quite high in sodium, furnishing from 600 to 800 milligrams in a 6.25-ounce jar that is intended as one serving. A 2.5-ounce portion of meat or turkey sticks contains over 365 milligrams of sodium. The "estimated safe and adequate daily dietary intake" of sodium established by the National Academy of Sciences for children one to three years of age is 325 to 975 milligrams.

The most common cause of death by suffocation in young children is not plastic bags but a chunk of a hot dog getting stuck in the throat. To add injury to insult, a piece of a "meat stick," with a diameter of about ½ inch, can form a similar plug. As a precaution the USDA now requires a warning on the label of toddler meat sticks.

While prepared infant desserts may boast that they have no more than 9 percent added sugar, in a 4.5-ounce jar this is close to one tablespoon. No one who put this much sugar into a similarly sized cup of coffee would consider it a modest amount!

Baby Food in a Box

The newest entry into the baby food market is dried instant baby food to which you merely add water. Since water is the first and therefore foremost ingredient in almost every jar of baby food, this product seems to offer an excellent way to avoid paying for something most people get free from the tap.

Freshness has been used as a selling point for these dried baby foods. If you limit the meaning of "fresh" to "newly made" this may be true, but *Webster's* says fresh means "not preserved by pickling, salting, drying, etc." How "fresh" could a food be that has been previously cooked, dehydrated, and stored in a cardboard canister?

Safety is touted as another benefit. While it is true that infants are susceptible to gastrointestinal illness caused by bacteria in foods that have been stored improperly or served with dirty spoons, the problem of unclean utensils exists no matter what your baby eats. Moreover, dried baby foods may be promoted as being less wasteful since you prepare only what you need at a time, but this presupposes you can predict how much your child is going to eat before the meal. If not, unless you throw out any extras, the potential for contamination during storage is equal to that with other foods.

As always, label reading is important before you make a selection. When you do this, you will discover that while instant carrots may contain only carrots and added vitamin E, instant squash contains partially hydrogenated oil as well, as do many other dehydrated products.

Pesticides in Baby Food

Growing concern about pesticide residues in food may actually be motivating some major food processors to change the quality of their product and consequently how food is grown in the United States. In 1986, Heinz Babyfood was reported to have notified growers that the company would no longer buy fruits and vegetables that were grown with pesticides under review by the EPA. According to a company spokesperson, "Baby food is the extreme case, the one that is most sensitive in the marketplace."

This is just one baby step in the right direction, but as any parent can attest, the first step is the hardest. We hope this policy will succeed in the market and will be extended to include all pesticides and other food products too.

TODDLER TREATS

It is a good policy to hold off on sweets and furnish babies with other hard foods like carrots or whole grain pretzels or crackers that can satisfy their teething needs. When it is time for cookies, most of the brands named in Chapter 33 will be fine. You may want to steer clear of any with nuts or other tidbits that a child might choke on, but at the age cookies become appropriate, children should be well past this stage.

If you do not serve refined flour, sugar, and hydrogenated oil to the older members of the family, it is unlikely you'll find them fit for a baby. Yet most of the cookies made specifically for toddlers feature these ingredients. Healthy Times markets a cookie through natural food stores that is especially formulated for young children and is considerably more respectable, containing whole wheat pastry flour, molasses, raw wheat germ, whey, water, and vanilla; another version made with equally commendable ingredients is wheat- and dairy-free.

Because of concerns about choking, the FDA requires a warning on the label of toddler biscuits similar to the one on meat sticks.

RECOMMENDATIONS

INFANT FORMULA

General Rule of Purchase: The best food for an infant cannot be bought. However, if breast feeding is not possible, all brands of prepared infant formulas are similar and should be selected with the advice of your health-care provider.

PREPARED BABY FOOD

General Rule of Purchase: Think first of those foods already part of your shopping list that are also appropriate to babies. You may want to add whole grain cereals manufactured just for infants, but avoid the standard baby brands that are based on refined grains. (For additional choices, any of the Exemplary Brands in Chapter 10 can be employed, pureed if need be.)

All ingredients are on the label of prepared baby food. Look for single-food products, as they are less likely to contain anything other than water, citric acid to maintain color, and extra vitamins. Avoid those with added salt, sweeteners, hydrogenated oil, modified starch, or other refined grains.

When babies begin teething, select one of the whole grain varieties of crackers and cookies listed in Chapter 8 and Chapter 33. Look for those cookies with the least amount of sweetening, and if your baby has trouble chewing, steer clear of nuts, raisins, and other nuggets that might get caught on the way down.

Exemplary Brands

Baby Food—Since manufacturers' lines are so extensive and variable, we suggest you read each label and select accordingly.

Cereal

Eden Kokoh Baby Cereal
Familia Swiss Baby Cereal

Health Valley 100% Whole Grain Rice with Bananas, Sprouted Cereal with Bananas (for Babies)

Teething Biscuits

Healthy Times Original, Allergic Biscuits for Toddlers

Chapter 30

Snacks: Those Frivolous Foods

Snacking does not have to be synonymous with eating junk food, but often it is. In a survey of the most popular snack foods, beverages (mostly soft drinks) led the list, followed by sweets; then, after a wide gap, fruits and vegetables and salty snacks entered the scene on about an equal footing.

Although everyone cannot be expected to forgo foods that are eaten purely for pleasure, the educated consumer may want to have certain guidelines and priorities in selecting "frivolous foods." "With better than one in five U.S. families eating together less than once a week," an executive at General Mills sees "wholesome snacks as filling the breach." At the very least, what you choose for snacking should not add potentially harmful substances to your body. Without much effort it can add some good things as well. Particularly promising new commercial snack products include baked or extruded chips (rather than fried), dry roasted nuts, whole grain pretzels, and flavored popcorn, all of which now come with low-sodium options. On the sweet side, there are toasted brown rice confections, compressed dried fruit bars, nut crunch, and honey-sweetened halvah.

Although in this chapter we will analyze commercial snack foods, the best favor you can do for yourself is to stock your kitchen with nuts, dried fruit, fresh fruit, whole grain crackers and similar high quality foods that lend themselves to eating out of hand. We like to display an assortment of these in jars on open shelves in our kitchen as an invitation to family and friends.

With few exceptions there is nothing worth your attention in the typical candy and snack aisle. Besides the numerous chemical additives that are used in commercial snack foods, there are the possibly more damaging high levels of refined sugar and fat. Those that are free of sweetening often contain reprehensible amounts of salt.

THE CANDY MAN

The candy industry is trying to dispel its bad image with such fantastic claims as "when [candy is] broken into component parts, ingredients like chocolate, milk and nuts are good additions to the diet, providing protein, thiamine, niacin and other essential foodstuffs and minerals. Eating a chocolate bar is not much more fattening than having an apple." Clever statements like this obscure the fact that the nutritious milk and nuts are only

409

minimal components of a typical candy bar and that a mere ounce of milk chocolate is the caloric equivalent of an apple weighing better than half a pound! Moreover, 60 percent of those chocolate calories come from fat, of which the fruit contains only trace amounts.

"The combination of things in Snickers makes it complete," one prominent ad stated. The implication of the visuals was that the peanuts imparted real nutritional worth. In fact, a 2-ounce Snickers bar contains the equivalent of 7.3 teaspoons of sugar, which accounts for 42 percent of its calories and ranks it just one percent below pure chocolate with the highest sugar content.

If you feel proud of your efforts to shop and eat well, don't think the confection industry is ignorant of your intent. Candy and gum manufactured and marketed specifically for the nutrition-conscious consumer has won many converts. Often their image as "healthy candy" is not justified.

Carob Versus Chocolate

Many of the "natural" candy bars get their reputation from the use of carob instead of chocolate. Is chocolate such a villain and is carob such a virtuous alternative?

Migraines, acne, heartburn, and fibrocystic breast disease may all be aggravated by compounds contained in chocolate. Chocolate also contains stimulants, including caffeine. Its inherent fat component accounts for a whopping 57 to 90 percent of its calories, depending on the final formulation, and sugar is added to all but unsweetened baker's chocolate. (On the bright side, chocolate contains a chemical that is supposed to generate feelings of love.)

Carob, a powder ground from the seed pods of a Mediterranean evergreen tree, has a color and consistency much like cocoa and a taste, though different from chocolate, some find equally enjoyable. Carob contains no stimulants and very little fat. Being naturally sweet, carob does not need added sugars. Of course, these qualities are undermined when manufacturers add sweetening—whether honey, fructose, corn syrup, or turbinado sugar—and fats, especially hydrogenated oils or the highly saturated palm oil popular in carob confections. When these ingredients appear on the label, carob can hardly be considered much more healthful than chocolate.

Junk in Bulk

Carob- and yogurt-coated nuts and dried fruits are promoted as natural snacks in many supermarkets and natural food stores. All of these items contain more partially hydrogenated oil and sugar than they do carob powder or yogurt solids and only ruin the potential of the fruit and/or nuts as a wholesome snack. In fact, one ounce of sugar-coated almonds contains somewhat fewer calories, half the fat, and no fewer nutrients than an ounce of yogurt-coated almonds. (Plain almonds have less than half as many calories.) If you eat these candies because you like them, that's your privilege. If you eat them because you think they are more healthful than Goobers or Raisinettes, that's your mistake.

Body Builder's Bars

High-protein candy bars are popular with the athletic crowd. Most candy bars furnish 2 to 3 grams of protein, while these boast from 5 to 8 grams and are actually competitive with cheese, milk, meat, and other accepted sources of protein on a per-calorie basis. When nuts and seeds and their butters, milk, and grains are responsible for this nutrition it is more commendable than when soy protein isolates do the job. In any event, for most Americans, who have more than an ample protein intake, the nutritional significance of these candies is counterbalanced by the potentially harmful role played by the fat and sugar used to create them.

As for those that promise vitamins, minerals, fiber, and other health benefits, you should keep in mind that these confections are rarely the most expedient way to get nutrients; this, however, may be outweighed by the pleasure factor. If refined sugars, partially hydrogenated fat, and food additives are absent, you may wish to ignore some of these other realities.

Something to Chew On

Chewing gum ranks second to candy bars in terms of confectionary revenue, with sugarless gum, which was practically nonexistent in 1970, accounting for a third of sales. Why people feel comfortable putting "sorbitol, gum base, glycerin, mannitol, natural and artificial flavors, softeners, sodium saccharine and artificial color" in their mouths (and their children's) just because it is believed to be less cavity-producing, is a (synthetic) mystery of life.

Others find "natural" gum, with a base drived from blended tree saps, combined sweetening from honey, maple syrup and lactose, guar gum, and flavor oils more appealing. Although we applaud the absence of chemicals, it is hard to recommend any concentrated sweet that is stuck in your mouth for an hour or so.

A Sucker in Every Crowd

What do you suppose is in a hard candy or lollipop with "no sugar, no saccharin, no salt, no artificial flavor or colorings"? Nothing good, we can assure you. While "natural fruit flavor" is what is promoted, "natural" lollipops are made primarily from sorbitol, a refined sweetener which some people erroneously think does not have any ill effects (see Chapter 31).

There are several commendable hard and taffylike sucking candies marketed in natural food stores, however. These are devoid of refined sugars, dependent only on malted rice, barley, or wheat syrup for their sweet taste, and natural oils and herbs for flavor; they contain none of the artificial flavor, color, sugar, corn syrup, or preservatives commonly found in sucking candy. Although they're definitely not the typical "sour ball," many adults and children find them very satisfying.

Brown Rice Meets the Candy Man

Puffed brown rice, marketed as cereal and rice cakes, is now moving into the snack food department dressed in a cloak of carob. Whether plain or flavored with peppermint oil, these treats universally contain the partially hydrogenated palm or soy oil common to all carob coatings. Some are sweetened with fructose, while others rely on date sugar and malt.

Oven-toated brown rice is also making its appearance in candies, adding its crisp and chewy texture to granola bars and chocolate and carob confections. When selecting these, make sure the rice nuggets you get are from whole grain, not milled rice or "fabricated crisp rice" composed of the milled grain plus sugar, calcium stearate, salt, malt, and caramel color. Glenny's, one well-conceived line of brown rice treats available at the natural food store, contains no salt, fat, or sugar—only whole grains (rice, oats, wheat flakes), barley malt as sweetener, and real flavoring ingredients (raisins, nuts, cinnamon, pure vanilla).

SALTY SNACKS

Those aware of the hazards of sweets often get their pleasures from more savory and salty snacks. Analysis of some of these popular items reveals sodium levels that nutritionists have called "alarmingly high," in view of the fact that the recommended ceiling on sodium intake for an adult is 3,300 milligrams daily.

SODIUM CONTENT PER 100 GRAMS (3.5 OUNCES) OF SALTED SNACKS

Snack	Mgs.
Corn chips	665–875
Corn nuts	1,400–1,450
Pretzels	680–2,700*
Popped Corn	1,750
Potato chips	665–875
Salted nuts	400–600

*This varies considerably with the type; thin pretzels may have twice the salt of thicker ones.

Potato and Other Vegetable Chips

According to the FDA, if you were to lay all the potato chips consumed in one year in this country "curled end, to curled end, the chips would extend 8 million miles, enough to go around the world 336 times." To make a single pound of chips, it takes 4 pounds of fresh potatoes. At this ratio you might expect a one-ounce serving of chips to contain close to the same number of calories as a quarter pound of potatoes. In fact, though, an ounce of chips furnishes twice this, or about 150 calories; 90 of these come from the fat absorbed during frying—better than ¾ tablespoon!

When you realize how much oil you end up ingesting, you might want to consider the source of fat used. A look at labels reveals a broad choice, from polyunsaturated varieties like corn, cottonseed, sunflower, safflower, and soy, to partially hydrogenated soy, cottonseed, palm, and peanut oils. This leaves you with the twentieth-century dilemma of choosing between the hazards associated with partially hydrogenated oils and the potential problems created when polyunsaturated oils are subjected to high cooking temperatures for long periods of time. Both choices seem unfavorable. (For more on this, see "Fear of Frying" in Chapter 20.)

While your chips may have "no preservatives," it appears that some brands use this claim deceptively. What they mean is that no preservatives have been *added* to the finished product. This is not to say that prior to frying the potato slices have not been dippped in an antioxidant or whitening solution that may have metabisulfites, hydrogen peroxide, ascorbic acid, or BHT/BHA in it. Also, the frying medium may have contained a preservative. This doesn't appear on the label, but laboratory analysis of several brands has shown the presence of these additives anyway.

Another chemical that escapes the label is the lye that may have been used to remove the peel in some brands. This could be avoided since a steam and an abrasive roller removal process are also available, but no distinction is made on the package. One way to get around this problem is to select a brand that is unpeeled.

"Reduced" and "no salt" chips are now an option. Note that the proclamation "50 percent less salt" only refers to that company's salted product and may not be useful for comparisons with other brands. Actual sodium content per measure is the only truly useful guide.

In seasoned varieties, make sure you read the label to determine if the flavorings are in line with your wholefoods objectives; dextrin, MSG, and hydrolyzed vegetable protein, for example, may not be.

Plantain chips and *carrot chips* should also be selected by the same criteria. Concerned shoppers should be aware that *banana chips* are fried in coconut oil (naturally high in saturated fatty acids) and that the sweetened versions are coated with honey and refined turbinado sugar.

Corn and Other Grain Chips

The main difference between vegetable chips and grain chips is that the corn, rice, wheat, or other grains of choice are formed into a dough before frying.

The distinction between corn chips, tortilla chips, and nachos appears to be whim (the corn chips are usually thinner) rather than content, since all contain corn, oil, lime, and, with a few exceptions, salt. Only some rely on partially hydrogenated oils and there are many brands that are preservative-free, so read the label. As with all chips, those that are seasoned may be tainted with questionable ingredients like MSG, hydrolyzed vegetable protein (HVP), disodium guanylate and inosinate, disodium phosphate, caramel color, and artificial coloring, even in brands that boast "no preservatives."

Other fried grain-based chips are marketed largely through natural food displays and may be formulated with brown rice, chick-pea flour, whole wheat, or a mixture of as many as seven grains.

Typical chinese noodles are prepared from a fried refined wheat dough which usually has hydrogenated oil, salt and often coloring added. As you will see in the Exemplary Brands, however, at least one manufacturer has brought this product up to wholefoods standards with a combination of organic whole and unbleached wheat flours, fresh eggs, and high quality oil.

Baked Chips and Extruded Snacks

When a thin dough is baked rather than fried, it is generally called a cracker, but several new lines of "chips" that are prepared in this manner are now being marketed for their appeal as snacks. Call them what you will, when only whole grains, unsaturated, non-hydrogenated oils, and recognizable seasonings go into the recipe they are a fine alternative to greasy, deep-fried chips. Even those that are salted contain, on average, only half the sodium of an equal weight of chips.

Several clever bakeries have begun to make tasty chips from bread. Flavored pita chips, sourdough chips, bagel chips, and such are as wholesome as the breadstuffs they are built on. If the bread contains only wheat flour (not whole wheat) and the seasonings have modified starch, hydrolyzed vegetable protein, and similar flavor enhancers, select something else.

Puffed snacks can also be made with wholefoods, as several companies who market through natural food outlets have demonstrated. Whether wheat-, buckwheat-, or corn-based, the extruded dough containing grain, unsaturated oil, and seasonings is baked into an airy form that is as much fun to eat as a chip, without the high fat content.

Popped Grains

Old-fashioned popping corn, while not to be counted on for real nourishment, is at least low in calories. Packages of dried corn kernels for home preparation are sold everywhere, and in some natural food stores you can find a brand that has been organically grown.

Save your money and skip the kind that comes in its own pan, ready to pop. These contain hydrogenated oils; in those that are "butter flavored," artificial flavoring creates the illusion. Be wary of microwave popping corn as well, which is presalted and also has fat added to the special oven-designed package. Stay clear of brands marketed as "hot-air popping corn" with gelatin and salt added. So-called gourmet popping corns are derived from special hybrid kernels which explode to many times their size—but at up to three dollars for 8 ounces, your food bill may do the same.

Prepopped packaged corn, prepared in saturated coconut oil or a partially hydrogenated oil, then salted and possibly artificially colored, tastes like encapsulated stale air. One common way manufacturers mask the poor taste is to give it a flavored coating dependent on chemical coloring and flavoring agents. In the natural food store you can opt for cheese-flavored popcorn made with cheese powder, buttermilk solids, spices, coconut oil, plus salt and soy sauce, or popcorn coated in unrefined sweeteners (maple syrup and/or honey), salt, and butter and/or coconut oil. With the classic Cracker Jacks, your prepopped popcorn will be encased in sugar, corn syrup, molasses, corn oil, salt, and lecithin. Anyway you buy it, the added sweeteners, excess salt, and saturated fats detract from what began as a low-calorie, fiber-filled snack.

Corn Nuts

The snack called "corn nuts" is made from corn kernels that are deep-fried rather than popped. Euphemistically described as "toasted sweet corn," the effect is what counts and in this case it is the incorporation of coconut, palm, or partially hydrogenated soy oil into the kernel. If you're looking for a chemical-free treat and don't mind the fat, this may fill the bill. Unless you get an unsalted version, count on plenty of sodium as well. Once you move into the arena of flavored corn nuts, you really begin to compromise with MSG, disodium guanylate and inosinate, and dextrose.

Pretzels

Pretzels do not have to be made with refined flour, partially hydrogenated oil, corn syrup, and loads of salt. Several whole-grain unsalted and moderately salted pretzels are made that are not quite comparable in flavor and texture to common candy store pretzels, but offer a satisfying experience nonetheless. In wholefoods households, the unsalted varieties are popular teething biscuits for infants.

DIPS FOR CHIPS

The preparation of dips is a subject suitable for a cookbook, not a shopping guide, because by and large the dips offered by food companies are of chemical design. A select few, marketed in natural food sections, do provide an option for the busy cook or the noncook, but be cautious here. Even some "natural" products contain hydrolyzed vegetable protein and vegetable gums which strict wholefoods shoppers will want to avoid.

Check Chapters 22 and 28 for Exemplary Brands of premade dips and dried dip mixes.

NUTS AND STUFF

Nuts and dried fruit have been described in their own chapters. The same rules of selection apply when they are sold in snack packs and as "trail mixes." There are so many packaging companies that prepack these items for stores that brand names are almost irrelevant. Just take care to look out for sulfur dioxide in those containing fruit, sugar when banana chips or carob bits are present, partially hydrogenated oils in nutted mixes, refined flour and soy isolates in those with formulated "wheat nuts" or "sesame sticks," and preservatives in all.

Nut Crunch and Chews

When nuts and seeds are combined into boardlike confections called "crunch" or fashioned into chewy "caramels" that stick to your teeth, they become not just fatty but sugary as well. If this is your preference, try to find a brand that omits the preservatives and relies solely on honey and/or malt syrup (no corn syrup or brown sugar) and oils that have not been hydrogenated.

Fruit-Nut Bars

Compressed bars of dried fruit enhanced with nuts, grains, and flavorings come in a variety of shapes (logs, squares, rounds, etc.). While they tend to be sweet from the raisins, dates, and unrefined sweeteners like malt syrup, honey, or molasses that are often added, they are low in fat and sodium and offer both fruit and grain fiber. These are primarily natural food store items.

Crackerballs

Tiny peanut crackerballs can be pleasing snacks. Chico-San Brown Rice 'N Peanut Treats present the nut encased in a brown rice batter that has no added fat or sweeteners. Edward and Sons Crunchy Peanut Crackerballs feature a honey-sweetened cracker shell around a peanut filling.

Halvah

This final entry in the nut section overlaps into the candy bar category. Halvah, a traditional Middle Eastern sesame paste and sugar syrup confection, has always been available without additives. Now, a few brands have been upgraded with honey replacing the sugar. Unfortunately, you will have to pay dearly for this improvement.

RECOMMENDATIONS

General Rule of Purchase: All ingredients are on the label. Look for treats that incorporate nutritious ingredients like dried fruit, nuts, and whole grains. Avoid hydrogenated oils and refined or artificial sweeteners. Give preference to unsalted and reduced-salt chips, as well as those that are baked rather than fried. Check the natural food store for some new and unusual confections made with carob instead of chocolate, and date sugar or malted grain syrups instead of refined sweeteners.

Exemplary Brands

Sucking Candy

Eden Ginger Bonbons, Lotus Root Candy
Edward and Sons Natural Temptations
Soken Plum Candy
Sweet Life Candy
Westbrae Natural Sour Plum Drops

Candy Bars

Aladdin Delight Pure Honey Halvah
Barbara's Peanut Butter, Sesame Crunch; Peanut, Sesame Brittles; Granola Bars
Chico-San Brown Rice 'N Peanut Treats
Christopher's Chewies
Edward and Sons Crunchy Peanut Crackerballs
Fantastic Foods Halvah
Glenny's Spirulina, Bee Pollen, Ginseng, Moist & Chewy Snack Bars; Nookies; Rice Treats
Mega Herb Snack Bars
Nellie's Peanut Butter, Malty Crunch, Fruit and Nut Bars; Carob Coated Fruit and Nut Sticks; All Natural Easter Egg
Sahara Pure Honey Halvah
Shepherdboy Fruit and Nut Bars
Sweet Life Crunch
Westbrae Natural Taffy, Domes
Yinnies Taffy, Caramels
Wha Guru Chews

Popped Corn—Purchase the plain kernels for home popping; all brands are similar unless organically grown.

Country Grown Popcorn[1]
Eden Popcorn[1]
Little Bear Popcorn[1]

New Earth Organically Grown Cheese, Maple Flavor with Almonds Popcorn[2]
Pleasant Grove Popcorn[1]

Pretzels

Barbara's Regular, No Salt Pretzels
DeBoles 100% Whole Wheat Sesame Snack Sticks

Health Valley 100% Whole Wheat Sesame Pretzels

Baked Chips and Extruded Snacks

Amsnack Brown Rice Chips
Barbara's Bagel Chips, Sourdough Crisps, Natural Cheese Puffs
Cedarlane Pita Chips
Charan Crisp Chick Pea Snacks
Eden Brown Rice, Sea Vegetable, Vegetable Chips
Edward and Son Soya, Sea Vegie, Vegie Chips; Corn, Buckwheat Crispy Curls; Teriyaki Nuggets; Mini Snaps; Brown Rice Shells; Ginger Flowers; Sabi Snacks
Estee Wheat Snax
Health Valley Regular, Low Sodium Cheddar Lites

Knudsen 100% Whole Wheat Sourdough Bread Crisps
San-J Sesame, Tamari Chips
Skinny Munchies Nacho Cheese, Crispy Onion, Smokey Barbecue Chips
Soken Brown Rice Wheels, Cheese Snacks, Seaweed Crunch, Mushroom Chips, Vegetable Chips, Vega-Soy with Onion Chips, Regular and No Salt Brown Rice Petals, Gentle Petals, Wasabi Chips
Spicers Wheat Twists
Westbrae Samurai Puffs

Fried Chips

Banana—All brands similar; unsweetened chips are preferable, as sweetened varieties contain both honey and sugar; all are fried in coconut oil
Bananitas Plantain Chips
Barbara's Regular, No Salt, Varietal Corn Chips; Regular, No Salt, Varietal Potato Chips; Sweet Potato Chips
Barrel O' Fun Unsalted Natural Potato Chips
Bien Padres Tostaditas
Caroff's Carrot Chips
Casa Sanchez Tortilla Chips
Corn Cheaps
Diane's Tortilla Chips
El Galindo Natural Tortilla Quarters
Garcia Natural Tortilla Chips
Garden of Eatin' Lightly Salted, No Salt, Barbecue, Blue Corn Chips
Golden Harvest 100% Natural Corn, Potato Chips
Grande Tortilla Strips
Granditos Homestyle, Low Salt Tortilla Strips
Granny Goose Less Salt, Unsalted Potato Chips
Hain Natural Yogurt Sesame, 7 Grain, Whole Grain Carrot, Onion Chips

Havea Corn Chips
Health Valley Regular, Unsalted, Varietal Corn Chips; Tortilla Chips; Tortilla Strips; Potato Chips
Herr's No Salt Potato Chips
Jay's No Salt Added Potato Chip
Knudsen Regular, Unsalted Hawaiian Style Potato Chips; Carrot Chips
La Cocina Nacho Chips
Little Bear Bearitos Regular, Blue Corn, No Salt Tortilla Chips[2]
Little Bear Chow Mein Noodles[2]
Manns Natural Potato Chips
Mexi Snax Regular, Unsalted, Varietal Tortilla Chips
Mission Brand Tortilla Chips
Nalley Golden Light Potato Chips
Poco's Tortilla Strips
Ruiz Natural Tortilla Chips
Seasons Natural No Salt, Lightly Salted Potato Chips
Skaggs Alpha Beta Mexican Style Tortilla Strips
State Line 100% Natural Regular, No Salt Dip Chips
Taco Works Natural Tortilla Chips

Nuts and Stuff—Mixed nuts and dried snacks are too numerous to list by brand. Avoid any with added refined sweetening, refined flour, sulfured fruits, partially hydrogenated oils, and soy isolates

[1]Organic
[2]Some organic ingredients

Chapter 31

Sweet Things:
Concentrated Sweeteners

It was probably nature's plan to use sweetness as the bait to attract us to the vitamin, mineral, and fiber-rich foods in which it is naturally found. But extracting the sugar, refining it, and adding it to other foods in large amounts has had broad repercussions on people's health, and on a good portion of our food system as well. Our national sweet tooth is being catered to not just in obvious ways like candy, ice cream, pastries, jams, and other sweets, but in a variety of more subtle forms including coffee whiteners, salad dressings, soups, sauces, pickles, peanut butter, processed meats, canned beans, and even vegetables. When you add this all up, you find that about 70 percent of the average sweet intake comes from the food industry's sugar bowl, not your own.

The technique for refining beets into sugar was not developed until the nineteenth century, and high fructose corn syrup, which is rapidly replacing sugar in processed foods, was virtually unheard of in this country until the late 1960s. While at the turn of the century the average per-capita world consumption of sugars was estimated to be 12 pounds, today in the United States the yearly consumption of these nutritive (or calorie containing) sweeteners is 127 pounds per person, or approximately 600 sweet calories daily! Moreover, the use of sugar substitutes has multiplied dramatically from what has been described by the FDA as "almost negligible" in the 1950s, to the equivalent of 16 pounds of sugar per person in 1984. When viewed from this historic perspective, not only is the *amount* of sweetening in our diet out of traditional proportion, but the *kind* of sweeteners we rely on are relatively new foods to the human body.

SUGAR BLUES

The nutritional consequences of our overuse and indulgences are unclear. Tooth decay and periodontal disease are the only uncontested direct side effects of consuming concentrated sweeteners, but sugar may influence many other areas of health, including obesity, predisposition to diabetes and heart disease, behavioral problems and, as sweets crowd out more nutritious foods, dietary imbalances.

SWEET DECEPTIONS

In the world of sweeteners the term "natural" may be used to describe any nutritive sweetener, i.e., those that contain calories. This includes all the forms of sugar listed below. Many people misinterpret this to mean "unrefined" or even "nutritious." In fact, many so-called natural sweeteners are highly processed and none really makes any significant contribution to the diet other than calories.

While some people do not much care what form their sweetening takes, others are willing to pay an exorbitant premium for what they believe to be less processed, more natural products. Sometimes they are deceived by the promise of "no sugar," since food labels are permitted to make this claim as long as the common sugar extracted from cane or beets is absent. But this is a vary narrow interpretation of the word "sugar." In terms of chemistry, there are many different kinds of sugar. (They are glucose, fructose, sucrose, maltose, dextrose, lactose, galactose, and levulose.) All nutritive sweeteners, no matter what the name, contain one or more of these sugars. Do not fool yourself—pastries dripping with honey and frozen confections dependent on powdered fructose will not enhance your physical well-being any more than those that are dependent on granulated white table sugar.

THE VARIOUS WAYS SUGARS SHOW UP ON A LABEL

sugar	glucose syrup	lactose	honey
invert sugar	corn syrup	maltose	maple syrup
brown sugar	corn sweetener	levulose	date sugar
raw sugar	dextrose	sucrose	xylitol
demerara sugar	fruit sugar	rice syrup	sorbitol
turbinado sugar	fructose	molasses	manitol
malted grain syrups	high fructose corn syrup	barley malt	

Adding Up Sugars: Less May Be More

When you are trying to assess the total sugar content of a food, keep in mind this popular industry ploy: food processors who wish their sweetening to be less obvious often add several different sugars to their product; in this way, instead of showing up in one lump near the top of the ingredient list, the sweeteners are sprinkled throughout, giving a more innocent impression.

NUTRITIVE SWEETENERS

As we said, "nutritive sweeteners" refers to all concentrated sweetening agents that make a caloric contribution to the diet.

Cane and Beet Sugar

The term *sugar* is usually used to refer to the pure white crystals that remain when sugarcane or sugar beets are refined. (The chemical name for this sugar is sucrose.) Through a series of washings, filterings, and bleaching, cane or beet sugar becomes the common *table sugar* or *white sugar* with which everyone is familiar. While the original sugarcane is rich in such trace minerals as chromium, manganese, cobalt, copper, zinc, and molybdenum, these are all virtually stripped away during sugar refining.

Real *raw sugar* is the product that exists before the cleaning stage. It may contain insect parts, soil, molds, bacteria, lint, and waxes, and is not considered a very healthful, or even a safe food. In fact, it is not even legal to sell it in the United States. *Turbinado* or *Demerara sugar* is often called raw sugar, but is actually a steam-cleaned version of it which retains a fraction of the dark, sticky molasses syrup produced in sugar refining. Any suggestion that this is an unrefined sugar is misleading. It is, however, not subject to the chemical whitening that common table sugar is.

Brown sugar is mostly white sugar flavored with molasses. Its brown coloration comes from a charcoal treatment that may introduce traces of carcinogenic impurities, resulting in a product that is actually more refined and possibly more harmful than white sugar.

Invert sugar is a liquid and even sweeter form of white sugar. It is not commonly available on a consumer level, but is sometimes used by manufacturers of baked goods and confections.

Molasses

Molasses is the heavy-bodied liquid produced from sugarcane juice when white sugar is being extracted. It comes in different types and grades and may contain some of the minerals native to sugarcane, depending on the extraction and refining process.

Blackstrap molasses is the liquid that remains after all the sucrose crystals are removed from the cane. It has a bitter, burnt flavor and actually contains significant levels of the minerals found in the original cane. It may or may not contain sulfur residues from the processing.

New Orleans molasses, made with Louisiana-grown cane, is produced from the whole juice of young sugarcanes. This molasses is clarified using sulfur dioxide and so is classified as sulfured.

Unsulfured or *Barbados molasses* is the mildest, sweetest variety. It is manufactured directly from the whole juice of mature East Indian cane and is free from sulfur. This molasses has only a fraction of the minerals found in blackstrap.

Dried molasses has become increasingly popular in the processed food industry because of its convenience. Note that this product is not usually pure molasses, but a blend of molasses with either corn syrup solids or wheat starch, soy flour, and an anticaking agent.

Fructose

Fructose is the chemical name for one kind of sugar that occurs naturally in honey and ripe fruit. Any connection between commercial fructose and natural fruit sugars, however, is in name only, for while fructose may be found in fruit, the product you buy in the store is not *from* fruit. Powdered fructose is often extracted from refined cane or beet sugar by breaking down the sucrose molecule into its two component simple sugars: fructose and glucose. This makes fructose more processed than regular white sugar.

While calorically equivalent to white sugar, fructose is sweeter, so using less may produce the same effect. Another supposed advantage lies in the fact that fructose reaches the bloodstream more slowly than other kinds of sugar and so does not affect insulin secretion and blood sugar levels as severely. However, some scientists believe that as a component of a meal this biochemical difference is insignificant. Moreover, animal studies have implicated fructose in elevated blood triglyceride and cholesterol levels and, like common cane and beet sugars, fructose promotes cavities. Despite all of this, many "health" and "natural" products promote their use of fructose.

Corn Sweeteners

There are three popular sweeteners produced from corn: dextrose, corn syrup, and high-fructose corn syrup (HFCS). All are highly refined products.

Dextrose is a refined powdered form of corn sweetener used widely by food processors. It is structurally similar and biologically identical to the sugar known as glucose.

Corn syrup, which is composed of dextrose and small amounts of fructose, comes in both solid and liquid form. It is considerably cheaper than sugar, which accounts for its popularity in processed foods.

High-fructose corn syrup (HFCS) is made by converting some of the dextrose in corn syrup to fructose. It is the only variety of corn sweetener that is as sweet as cane and beet sugars and, depending on its fructose content (42, 55 and 90 percent), it may be as much as one and a half times sweeter, giving it a slight edge in reduced-calorie foods. The current consumer infatuation with fructose has made HFCS popular with food manufacturers; however since cane and beet sugars are 50 percent fructose and 50 percent glucose, some HFCS may actually have less fructose than ordinary table sugar. Presently, HFCS is not available to consumers.

Honey

Honey is the oldest known concentrated sweetener. Put simply, it is the natural nectar of flowers converted to a rich golden syrup by hordes of hard-working bees. (At the same time, they are also pollinating the plants, an activity essential to the fruition of orchard crops, nuts, and berries.)

Since there are no laws to define "natural," "old-fashioned," "organic," or "raw" when dealing with honey, they have all become meaningless and often misleading qualifiers. Even the description of flower type may be inaccurate since only a few states regulate how much nectar from a given plant is necessary in order to use an identifying term. This identification is important mainly in that the flavor of honey does vary with the plant the bees feed on. The most common sources are alfalfa and clover, which are mild in flavor and light in color; buckwheat, which is dark and robust; and wildflower, which lies somewhere in between. Tupelo, orange blossom, spearmint, eucalyptus, safflower, sage, heather, and thyme are other popular sources. Blended honeys, however, need not be of any lesser quality than those given a particular identity.

Some commercially raised bees are fed on sugar water or corn syrup. This can adversely affect the balance of trace elements and sugars in the final product and is considered a form of adulteration. The bee keeper is not likely to inform you of this practice.

HONEY VERSUS CANE AND BEET SUGARS

Honey has eighteen more calories per tablespoon than common table sugar, but depending on the variety may have 25 to 40 percent more sweetening power, which means you can use less. Honey does contain scant amounts of nutrients, but you would have to eat an enormous volume to contribute significantly to your daily requirement for B vitamins, potassium, calcium, or phosphorus. In our opinion its real advantage over cane and beet sugar is that honey is a wholefood and no chemicals are used in its production.

SELECTING HONEY

True **comb honey** is the least processed variety. But, unless you can verify that the comb has come straight from the hive, what appears to be comb honey may really be cooked and filtered honey poured back into a clean comb.

Unfiltered or **strained honey** has the impurities screened out, but some enzymes, vitamins, and pollen remain.

The name **raw** or **uncooked honey** is somewhat of a misnomer since all honey is heated to some degree, but the more conscientious producer will keep the heat to a minimum. Raw honey may contain spores of botulism which under certain conditions can produce a toxin to which infants under twenty-six weeks of age may be susceptible; warnings suggest that raw honey should be excluded from the diet of children up to one year. Since parents shouldn't even consider feeding young children any sweetened foods if they wish to lay the foundation of good food habits, this recommendation should present no problem. However, if your infant does get a taste of a food cooked with raw honey you needn't be alarmed, as ordinary cooking and baking destroy the spores.

Common liquid honey is usually heated to higher temperatures and then filtered to remove all minute particles. This makes packaging easier, gives honey a lighter appearance, reduces its tendency to granulate, and also removes most of the inherent beneficial enzymes and nutrients.

Crystallized or *granulated honey*, labeled "granulated," "creamed," "spun," or "spread," makes a smooth, creamy spread. Although the appearance may suggest that this honey has not been cooked or filtered, it is more likely that it was produced from a liquid honey that has been seeded with honey crystals to produce this effect.

Dry honey, designed to overcome the inconvenience of liquid honey, is popular in the baking industry where it creates an opportunity for "natural" labeling. Although some bakers apparently use it and simply call it honey on the label, the product may also contain high-fructose corn syrup, corn syrup, wheat starch, soy flour, calcium stearate, and hydroxylated lecithin. Some of these additives may show up on the final product label, but more likely they are dismissed as nonfunctional ingredients and not divulged.

GRADING

Honey grading is voluntary and based on appearance, so that the highest rating, U.S. Grade A, really reflects greater heating and filtration. Thus, from a wholefoods standpoint, the honey the government extolls may be less "whole."

STORAGE

Honey does not support the growth of any infectious bacteria and requires neither pasteurization nor refrigeration. If it is properly handled, mold and yeast will not grow either. The sugar in honey may crystallize, but this does not affect its quality; crystallization can be reversed by placing the container in a pan of warm water.

Maple Syrup

The concentrated sweetener maple syrup can be characterized as a wholefood in that it is the boiled concentrate of maple sap, rather than a refined extract. It takes thirty-five to fifty gallons of sap to make one gallon of pure maple syrup, which helps explain its cost and its sometimes limited availability. Trees are tapped from late February to early April and many people who live in maple country take a drive to get the freshest syrup of the season from small, local "tappers" who still follow traditional sugaring practices.

You will be able to find maple syrup in the store with less effort. However, while it is labeled "pure," there are some modern innovations that are questionable. For example, formaldehyde pellets may be used to keep the tap holes open, yet there is no labeling requirement or data measuring its presence in the finished product, even though formaldehyde is a known carcinogen. Use of these pellets is prohibited in Canada.

The law permits salt, chemical preservatives, and defoaming agents to be added. You should be able to detect their presence from the label.

Maple sugar products, from soft spreads to granulated crystals, are made by driving off the liquid portion with heat and evaporation.

GRADING

Grading of maple syrup is not uniform from state to state and is voluntary. Federal grades range from U.S. AA, to A, B, and Unclassified; Vermont considers its highest grade Fancy or "light amber." As with honey, grade is based on appearance; often maple syrup fanciers prefer the lower or B grade, which is darker and more flavorful.

STORAGE

To prevent fermentation or mold growth, store maple syrup in a cool dry pantry or the refrigerator. If mold develops it can be skimmed off and the syrup boiled to destroy any remaining microorganisms, but you should probably use it as soon as possible to prevent a recurrence.

Other "Syrups"

Sugar cane syrup (which may be purchased by itself or appear as an ingredient in the popular table syrups described in the next paragraph) may contain salt, defoaming agents, and preservatives. *Sorghum syrup*, derived from sorghum cane, may contain similar ingredients plus anticrystallizing and antisolidifying agents. If sugarcane or sorghum syrups are purchased directly, these optional ingredients will appear on the label; however, if they are an ingredient in another product, these additives will not necessarily show up. Sulfiting agents used during production of sugarcane syrups are also hidden, although if the law is strictly monitored in the future, there should be some indication of this if residues exceed 10 ppm (parts per million).

Maple-flavored syrup, pancake syrup, waffle syrup, table syrup and just plain *syrup* (or sirup) are often confused with pure maple syrup, but are actually only concocted look-alikes made from a blend of any nutritive sweetener, plus emulsifiers, stabilizers, salt, viscosity adjusting agents, acidifiers, alkalizers or buffers, defoaming agents, artificial flavors, color additives, chemical preservatives, and edible fats and oils, as desired by the manufacturer. The inclusion of any of these ingredients should appear on the label.

Maple- or honey-flavored syrup must contain at least 10 percent of these characterizing sweeteners and the actual amount must be declared on the label if they are promoted anywhere other than the list of ingredients. Despite this, consumers still frequently assume that these products are the real thing. Interestingly, when Log Cabin Syrup first appeared in the 1880s it was intended to be an economical substitute and actually did contain 45 percent maple syrup. Over the years this has diminished to 3 percent. Some similar products contain no maple syrup at all.

Blended syrups which are labeled "natural" add to the confusion. They may contain corn syrup, sugar, honey, molasses, fruit juice, caramel color, and natural flavors. Although free of chemicals, their reliance on highly refined sweeteners and use of caramel color, which may be carcinogenic, disqualifies them as wholefoods in our book. This does not mean that all blends are unacceptable. We are very much in favor of the clever use of less refined products, as in one maple-honey mixture that describes itself as "100% made by trees and bees." (We don't agree, however, with this same manufacturer's claim that this is the "good-for-you combination," implying that it is health-giving and can be used indiscriminately.)

Malted Grain Sweeteners

Malt is a grain, usually barley, that has been sprouted to convert its starches into sugars, then dried and cured. Liquid and powdered malt have been popular for years as sweetening agents in commercial baked goods. Recently, in their quest for unrefined sweeteners and "no sugar" labeling, "naturally oriented" food manufacturers have become enamored of malted barley and other malted cereal grain syrups.

The principal sugar in malted grains, known chemically as maltose, does not stimulate insulin production and thus is better tolerated by people who have blood sugar disorders. The absence of chemicals is another plus. Individuals with food sensitivities should note, however, that what appears simply as "malt" on the label of a prepared food could contain corn, wheat, or vinegar.

Malted barley syrup and **rice syrup**, produced by using malt enzymes to convert the starch in barley and rice respectively, are now also available directly to consumers in natural food outlets.

Real Fruit Sugar

Fruit juices and dried fruit offer a source of sweetening with fruit nutrients still intact. Commercial food processors are beginning to employ these inherently sweet foods with greater frequency. *Fruit juice concentrates, date sugar* (ground dehydrated dates), and *natural fruit mixes* (based on ground fruit heated with fruit juice and/or honey) are all showing up now in "no sugar added" products and by themselves in food stores.

The benefits of using these concentrated fruit sugars for sweetening include a good taste, high fiber (pectin) content, slower more uniform digestibility, and added vitamins and minerals. Some of them also act as preservatives due to their acidity; their natural bulk often replaces some of the flour to give a lower calorie content in the finished baked goods. Their moisture-retaining properties can also mean less dependence on emulsifiers and added fats. However, use of these products does not mean that the end result will be less sweet or have fewer total "sugars" or calories.

GUIDELINES FOR THE COOK

For uncooked and stove-top dishes, unrefined liquid sweeteners like honey, maple syrup, molasses, and malted grain syrups, and ground dried fruit can substitute for cane or beet sugar without any change. When more than a quarter cup of sweetening is called for, however, you can reduce the honey, maple syrup, or molasses, using only one half to three-fourths the amount specified, without sacrificing flavor.

For baking, there are a number of cookbooks available as guides in the use of these more natural sweeteners. Those who object to the strong taste of honey, maple syrup, and molasses will find that their distinctive flavors can be mellowed for more delicate baked goods by combining two or more of them in a recipe. This principle is used frequently in our cookbook, *American Wholefoods Cuisine*, where everything is free of refined sugars.

Malted rice and malted barley syrups are very delicately flavored, but are only about half as sweet as honey and therefore require more adjustments in a recipe. If you cannot find recipes written specifically for these sweeteners and are willing to experiment, here are some guidelines. If the recipe can tolerate less sweetness, use the syrup to substitute for an equal measure of honey, maple syrup, white sugar, or brown sugar. For equal sweetness, use 25 percent more syrup than the sugar called for. If the recipe calls for liquid, reduce the amount by two tablespoons per cup of malted grain syrup. When honey or maple syrup is being replaced, do not use extra syrup; instead, boost the sweetness if need be by retaining a little honey or maple syrup. No other changes are required.

SUGAR ALCOHOLS

Sorbitol, mannitol, malitol, and *xylitol* are known as sugar alcohols and are derived commercially from dextrose and glucose, or in the case of xylitol, from birch trees. The terms "sugarless" and "sugar-free" applied to gum, candy, and other products made with these sweeteners is somewhat deceptive since, once broken down by the digestive system, sugar alcohols can act similarly to all other forms of sugar. Moreover, they are not, as many assume, free of calories. Xylitol, in fact, is identical to cane sugar in energy value, and while mannitol and sorbitol furnish half the calories, they are also only half as sweet.

Only xylitol doesn't promote cavities, but this may be a minor asset since inconclusive studies in animals have linked it to bladder stones, tumors, and liver anomalies. Consequently, xylitol is now being reviewed by the FDA.

Sugar alcohols tend to ferment in the digestive tract, causing cramping and diarrhea in much the same way that undigested lactose affects those people who have lactose intolerance. This is not only uncomfortable and embarrassing, but may deplete the body of fluids and nutrients. The problem appears to be more pronounced in children so that offering them "sugarless" candy and gums made with sorbitol, mannitol, malitol, and xylitol may not be a wise alternative.

ARTIFICIAL OR SYNTHETIC SWEETENERS

The popular sweeteners that fall into the "artificial" or "synthetic" category are cyclamates, saccharin, and aspartame. The main distinguishing feature of these sweeteners is that they have no molecular counterpart in nature. While the manufacturer has been promoting aspartame as "natural" since it is composed solely of two amino acids (phenylalanine and aspartic acid), such a combination does not occur except by virtue of scientific technology. In fact, this description has been criticized by the National Advertising Division of the Better Business Bureau as "inaccurate as a scientific statement in [its] magazine advertisement."

The main reason most people give for using these sugar substitutes is weight control. Cyclamates and saccharin have no real caloric value, and although aspartame has the same number of calories as an equal weight of cane sugar, its sweetening power is almost 200 times more intense, so that it takes a mere tenth of a calorie's worth of aspartame to achieve the sweetness of one teaspoon (or sixteen calories) of table sugar. Aside from safety considerations, which we discuss below, we have two objections to these sweeteners. First, instead of introducing our palates to alternative but equally attractive tastes, they foster a love for sweets and this makes them counter-productive in building good food practices. Second, they do not satisfy the real physical craving that some people have for sweets; while the tongue perceives them as food, the rest of the body is not as easily fooled, which may lead consumers to seek those carbohydrates elsewhere.

Perhaps if these sweetening agents were used in otherwise nutritious foods there could be some justification, but generally they are components of candy, soft drinks, and other refined and fabricated foods that don't provide real nourishment. However, given the fact that in 1977, when the FDA first announced its intention to ban saccharin, legislators received an estimated one million letters of protest (more mail than any issue other than the Vietnam War generated in the last decade), many people may need extra evidence of their potentially harmful effects.

A Message from a President

In 1985, United Press International reported that President Reagan had recently stopped putting sugar or artificial sweeteners in his coffee, stating, "I decided there was no reason I should be putting artificial sweeteners in it because we don't know what is in them." If the people who run the country aren't satisfied about their safety, you shouldn't be either.

Cyclamates

Cyclamates were banned from use in this country in 1969 on the basis of still controversial evidence citing the chemical as a carcinogen in animals. However, they are still on the market in forty countries.

Those who oppose the sweetener say that carcinogenicity is not even the major question. They are more concerned about whether cyclamates cause birth defects and alter chromosomes. Noted health experts acknowledge an adverse effect on the reproductive systems of male animals.

Saccharin

Saccharin is the oldest available artificial sweetener. Although studies have implicated it as a weak carcinogen, due to politics and delayed studies it has been granted a reprieve (ten years as of this writing) from the proposed FDA ban.

"Use of this product may be hazardous to your health. This product contains saccharin, which has been determined to cause cancer in laboratory animals."

SIGN OF OUR TIMES

Despite this warning, which has appeared on the label of all foods containing saccharin since 1977, the yearly consumption continues to grow. It would seem that a substance eaten by so many people should command a very high degree of safety, especially in view of the fact that there is no evidence that it is of any benefit to the majority of consumers. As a matter of fact, despite all the artificial sweeteners, Americans in the 1980s are fatter than ever.

SACCHARIN IN DISGUISE

The most common form of saccharin used by consumers is Sweet and Low. There are several other sweeteners on the market available for table-top use that contain saccharin, although at first glance this may not be obvious. One of these is "light sugar" with "the natural taste of sugar" yet only 50 percent of the calories—no great savings when you realize that a teaspoon of cane sugar has sixteen calories and this stuff has eight. Another is a "low sodium, salt-free sugar substitute" with one-tenth the calories of cane sugar and 500 times less sodium than sodium saccharin sweeteners. In promotional materials the manufacturer of this last product emphasizes that it contains "CALCIUM which is an essential nutrient for the human body," but glosses over the fact that this mineral comes in the form of *calcium saccharin*.

Aspartame

Aspartame, marketed under the tradenames Equal and Nutrasweet, has been promoted as a natural sweetener that is "not artificial like saccharin." In the few years it has been on the market the controversy about this sweetener has not ceased.

Questions have been raised concerning the dangers of certain compounds that can form in aspartame-containing soft drinks stored at high temperatures. Concern has also been voiced that pregnant women who use aspartame may transfer excess stores of the amino acid phenylanine across the placenta and, depending on the developmental stage of the fetus, injure the baby's brain. Harvey Levy, a physician at Boston Children's Hospital, estimated that this could mean a drop of as much as ten to fifteen I.Q. points, and Dr. William M. Partridge at the University of California, Los Angeles School of Medicine says five servings per day of food containing aspartame may cause "a subtle yet distinct impairment in brain function in fetus, children, and adults."

A particularly interesting aspect of the debate is the evidence that aspartame reduces levels of the brain chemical that acts as a natural appetite control mechanism. Thus, in fact, it may actually increase the craving for sugars!

Consumer complaints have included seizures, dizziness, severe headaches, slurred speech, blurred or decreased vision, depression, loss of memory, menstrual problems, nausea, skin lesions, mood swings, and hyperactivity and aggressive behavior in children.

To add to all these problems, as aspartame becomes more widely available, consumption may turn out to be a good deal higher than anyone anticipated, including those who originally approved it. According to USDA estimates, in 1982 per capita disappearance for aspartame was 1 pound, in 1983 the figure was 3.5 pounds, in 1984 it was up to 5.8 pounds, and by 1985 it about doubled the previous year at 11 pounds per person. Unless you have some idea of how much aspartame there is in the foods you or your children eat, you have no guarantee you are within the acceptable limits.

The Sweet Smell of (Synthetic) Success

You should be aware that aspartame may soon be followed by other similar sweeteners composed of individual amino acids. The Pfizer Company has already petitioned the FDA for approval of its version called alitame (from the amino acids D-alanine and L-aspartic acid). The FDA has acknowledged that it does not have adequate scientific information concerning the neurological consequences of products containing free-form amino acids. Until it does, we advise you to avoid them.

RECOMMENDATIONS

NUTRITIVE SWEETENERS

General Rule of Purchase: Use concentrated sweeteners in conjunction with nutritionally sound foods. Look for the least processed product. *Fruit juice concentrates* and *ground dried fruit* provide sweetening with the most nutrition. Honey, unsulfured molasses, maple syrup, and malted grain syrups may also be appropriate. Demerara and turbinado sugars, sometimes called "raw sugar," are just slightly less processed than regular crystalline sugar. Avoid brown sugar, fructose, corn sweeteners, and sugar alcohols which are even more refined products.

Honey labeled "raw and unfiltered" will have more of the original trace nutrients present. Otherwise, all honey is similar except for flavor, which is determined by the flowers the bees feed on. Terms such as "organic," "natural," "old-fashioned," and even "raw" have no standard meaning when applied to honey.

Molasses described as unsulfured or Barbados is preferred to New Orleans or blackstrap molasses, which are prepared using sulfur dioxide. All brands of unsulfured molasses are similar.

Maple syrup should be 100 percent pure and contain no added salt, chemical preservatives, or defoaming agents (which, if present, should show up on the label). Beyond this it is difficult to judge one brand against another due to the possible presence of chemical residues from processing. Be aware that U.S. producers can use formaldehyde pellets during tapping, while in Canada this is prohibited. However, this does not necessarily make all Canadian maple syrup untainted, nor does it mean all domestic brands have chemical residues. (You can write to companies to learn their practices.) Grading is not uniform and does not reflect purity. Note that many people prefer the richer taste and color of the "lower" grades.

Malted barley syrups and *rice syrups*, found almost exclusively in natural food stores, are all similar and contain no added ingredients.

A Genuine Note About Artificial Sweeteners

Right now there is no low-calorie sugar substitute available that is not the subject of considerable misgivings. Since there is no evidence that the use of these products in any way helps people control their weight, and in fact one of them, aspartame, may actually enhance the appetite for sweets, there does not seem to be much point in their use. Even diabetics would do better to satisfy their desire for sweets by using high-fiber fruits.

Chapter 32

Jams, Jellies, and Sweet Spreads

For years the jelly aisle has been dominated by products designed to appeal to children. At one time, cartoon characters and give-away glasses were as much a companion to jam and jelly as peanut butter is. Today, however, things are different. Fancy and imported brands selling for as much as four times the cost of standard supermarket varieties share the shelves with the familiar standbys. Sometimes, to give the impression that they are special, these "gourmet" preserves are positioned in a chilled bin in the produce department. In reality, most of these differ only in their marketing approach.

Manufacturers also try to influence your purchase by advertising "no artificial coloring, flavoring, or preservatives," but the presence of any of these additives must be revealed in the list of ingredients and a review of labels shows they are rarely used in any jams and jellies. Thus, this claim is just a diversionary tactic, for it's not what *isn't* there, but what *is*, that you should be concerned about.

We are delighted to see a growing trend toward the manufacture of unsweetened fruit spreads. Until recently, sweet spreads uniformly followed the standard for jam and jelly, with the result that most of them were at least half added sweetener. The new products, often described as "spreadable fruits," "unsweetened fruit spreads" or "conserves" (although this name is also used on products that are sweetened), are well suited to an everyday peanut butter and jelly sandwich, and also worthy of elegant service with "tea and crumpets."

JAM AND JELLY

Although one typical sugar-laden jam promotes itself as "naturally good because it's naturally made," large-scale jam- and jelly-making is not quite that straightforward. This could very well be the formula for your favorite jam:

Jam = 55% Sugar + 45% Frozen or Canned Fruit + Pectin + Acid + Antifoaming Agents + Buffering Agents + Preservatives

More Than Half Sugar

The recipe for jelly and jam (which may also be called a preserve) is dictated by the Code of Federal Regulations. Most commercial jams and jellies comply with the minimum standards requiring only 45 to 47 percent fruit or fruit juice, with the balance sweetener. Thus, by their very definition, jam and jelly are sweet and the fancy, high-priced imported kinds are no exception.

Any nutritive sweetener can be employed. Usually cane or beet sugar is the manufacturer's choice, often in combination with corn syrup. Some companies with a more natural orientation prefer honey and malt syrup. Whatever is used, it will be revealed in the list of ingredients.

The Fruit Ingredient

Fruit juice is used in making jelly and mature fruit in jams or preserves. The fruit component may be fresh, concentrated, frozen, or canned. In this instance the particulars need not be specified on the label.

The Optional Ingredients

Pectin: Pectin is the natural component in fruit that gives preserves their smooth, jellied consistency. In the preparation of fruits for jams and jellies the pectin normally present is often diminished since much of it is concentrated near the skin. To make up for the resulting deficiencies, commercial pectin is added to most brands.

Thickeners: To enhance their consistency, low-sugar and artificially sweetened jams and jellies may also contain thickening agents like agar, algin, carob bean gum, carrageenan, cellulose gum, guar gum or similar vegetable gums.

Acidifiers and Buffers: As anyone who has ever tried to make preserves knows, the balance between pectin, fruit acid, and sugar is a tricky one. Large-scale producers ensure success by adding acids and chemical salts that assist the gelling action.

Antifoaming Agents: The formation of foam during processing is a problem common to highly acidic foods like fruit. Antifoaming agents are consequently the next thing to be included in the formula.

Preservatives: The concentration of sugar should be sufficient to prevent the growth of microorganisms. Nevertheless, the manufacturer does have the option of adding a preservative, and often low-sugar and artificially sweetened jams and jellies take advantage of this by introducing methyl and propyl parabens and/or some form of sorbate, propionate, or benzoate mold inhibitor.

Artificial Flavoring and Coloring: According to the Code of Federal Regulations, no product labeled as jelly, jam, preserves, or fruit butter can contain artificial flavor or coloring except apple, pineapple, and crabapple jellies to which artificial mint flavor and red or green color may be added.

LABELING

The use of any of the optional ingredients will be included on the label for both regular and low-sugar jams and jellies. Artificially sweetened varieties are exempt from certain of these labeling requirements, but given the fact that we have no confidence in any of the nonnutritive sugar substitutes on the market, we cannot recommend any artificially sweetened jams and jellies in any case.

MARMALADE

Which do you suspect has more added sugar, jam or marmalade?

The composition of marmalade is not controlled by a Standard of Identity, and while all the ingredients will be found on the label, there is no indication of their relative proportions. Orange marmalade, the most common variety, may be made from either sweet or bitter oranges and even though the latter are prized for their astringent flavor, marmalades made from both varieties are likely to have as much as seventy to seventy-five parts sweetening to twenty-five to thirty parts fruit, peel, and juice.

FRUIT BUTTER

Fruit butters are another popular sweet spread, apple butter being the most common. Fruit butter, as defined in the government standards, is a smooth blend of fruit and sweetening, this time in a ratio of not less than five parts fruit to two parts sweetener. Exemplary fruit butters omit the sweetener entirely.

The fruit ingredient may be fresh, frozen, canned, or dried, although only if the fruit is dried will this be indicated on the label. Other permissible ingredients are natural flavorings and spices, salt, fruit juice, acidifying agents, antifoaming agents, pectin, and preservatives. Once again, the label should tell all.

THE NATURAL CHOICE

The list of exemplary offerings has improved in recent years, most noticeably, as we mentioned, with the introduction of unsweetened fruit spreads.

Unsweetened Fruit Spreads

We prefer unsweetened fruit spreads which take maximum advantage of the ripe fruit flavor and do not mar it with chemical acidifiers, buffers, antifoaming agents, preservatives, or any nonfruit sweetening ingredients. It is the concentration of inherent fruit sugars that keeps them from spoiling. The natural sweetness of the principal fruit may be enhanced with other fruit juices and concentrates. Some products rely on the pectin inherent in fruit; others boost it from an outside source. Lemon juice or citric acid may be added to elevate the natural acidity.

Fruit Spreads with Unrefined Sweeteners Added

Second choice is given to the fruit butters, spreads, jams, and jellies that gain additional sweetness from honey and/or malt syrup. Be on the alert for brands that try to attract attention by boldly declaring "made with honey" on the label, when in reality sugar shows up in the ingredients as well.

A CALORIC CAVEAT

The absence of added sweeteners does not make unsweetened spreads less caloric than common jams. The type of fruit is really the determining factor, and all fall within the range of 11 to 18 calories per teaspoon. The advantage of unsweetened varieties lies in the slightly higher concentration of vitamins and minerals, and the absence of refined sugars. Note, however, that total sugar content (which includes the sugar inherent in the fruit) is similar.

RECOMMENDATIONS

General Rule of Purchase: All ingredients are on the label, with the exception of artificially sweetened varieties, which should be automatically disqualified by the wholefoods shopper. Look for those products that capitalize on the natural sweetness of fruit alone; spread, butter, and conserve are names commonly used to describe them. Second in preference are the ones that add honey or malt syrup to assist the fruit.

Exemplary Brands

Unsweetened

Arrowhead Mills Fruit Butters, Naturally Sweet Fruit Spreads
Baugher Apple Butter
Eden Apple Butter
Filsinger's Apple Butter
Gathering Winds Apple Butter
Göbber Conserves
Hain Pure Natural Fruit Butters
Judy and Toby's Totally Fruit Preserves
Knudsen Fancy Fruit Spreads
Kozlowski Farms No Sugar Jams, Apple Butter
L & A Fruit Juice Sweetened Preserves
Legend Hills Old Fashioned Apple Butter
LIHN Natural Fruit Spreads
Poiret Spreads
Polaner All Fruit Spreadable Fruit
Somerset Farms Fruit Preserves
Sorrel Ridge Unsweetened Conserves
Tap 'n Apple Apple Butter
Timber Crest Farms Fruit Butters
Tree of Life Unsweetened Fruit Spreads
Westbrae Natural Fruit Conserves, Unsweetened Fruit Spreads
Whole Earth Fruit Spreads
Woodstock Farms Conserves

Sweetened with Honey, Malt Syrup, and/or Natural Fruit Sweeteners

1852 Brand Honey Apricot
Arrowhead Mills Jams
Cascadian Farms Conserves[1]
De Sousas Jams
Eden Jams
Emma's Jambrosias
Everything Natural Jams, Jellies
Halgren Pure Jams, Jellies, Marmalade
Hawaiian Honey Jams
New England Organic Honey Apple Butter
Norganic Preserves
Pure and Simple Fruit Butters
Sorrell Ridge Honey Sweetened Conserves
Tree of Life Preserves
Wax Orchard Conserves, Fruit Butters
Wm. Escott's Honey Packed Preserves

[1]Organic

Chapter 33

A Nation of Cookie
(and Cake) Monsters

There is no nutritional need for desserts, but there certainly seems to be a cultural one. And why not? Baked goods are one of civilization's most highly developed culinary arts and while traditionally these offerings have little food value, this need not be the case.

We've said it before, but it bears repeating: "Wholefoods fans can have their cake and eat it too." By this we mean that it is possible to prepare delectable cakes, pies, and cookies that contain no overprocessed or chemicalized ingredients—baked treats that are satisfying *and* sustaining. Our own experiences in the kitchen confirm this, but unfortunately, with the exception of some natural food selections, most notably fruit-juice-sweetened cookies, there are few similar mass-produced products available.

Furthermore, commercial bakeries are responsible for many misleading practices, from rendering the name "granola" virtually meaningless, to deceptive and dishonest advertising. To give you an example, the company that popularized frozen cakes, and is a household word in this country, was forced to discontinue advertising its products as "all natural" when it was disclosed that a number of rather unnatural ingredients such as chemically modified food starch, mono- and diglycerides, and gums were included (plus, of course, refined flour and sweetening). Another common ploy in cookie marketing is to conjure up the fond image of Mom in the kitchen mixing a batch of cookies by adding a tag line like "home style," or employing adjectives like "old-fashioned" and "homemade goodness," (or perhaps using a trade name like "Almost Home"). But even when they do forgo chemical additives, these cookies are essentially refined carbohydrates and hydrogenated fats. Mother may have baked cookies this way, but she wasn't always right.

SATISFYING YOUR SWEET
TOOTH SANELY

In order for a baked dessert to make a positive contribution to your table, it should contain some nutritious ingredients in the form of whole grains,

439

nuts, seeds, or fruit; it should use fat and sweetening judiciously and preferably in an unrefined form; and it should be devoid of synthetics. There are a few national natural food companies and many local bakers who produce such exemplary products, so there should be something available at the natural food store to satisfy your sweet tooth and your standards for wholefoods. Unfortunately, supermarket shoppers may not be so successful.

In the Recommendations we consider those baked goods that contain some refined flour or sweetener but otherwise use quality ingredients Acceptable with Reservation. We make this allowance because these foods are meant to be consumed in moderation and are not considered an essential part of the menu.

FILLING THE COOKIE JAR

The Coopted Granola Bar

The best hope the public had a few years ago for a generally available healthful cookie has been effectively destroyed, along with its name, *granola,* due to unprincipled marketing by America's food giants. Ironically, granola was developed by John Harvey Kellogg, the brother of the founder of the cereal empire. The story of how W. K. Kellogg took John's ideas and turned them into a sugar-coated fortune has been told many times. With the commercialization of granola and the granola bar, the last vestige of John's work has virtually been neutralized.

When granola bars first appeared, bakers copied the wholesome combination of oats, dried fruit, nuts, oil, and moderate amounts of sweetener that was the basis of the cereal that once symbolized the health food movement. Today, granola bars are not only heavily sweetened, but chipped, and dipped in chocolate, and even stuffed with nougat.

Companies that cater to the natural food market use unrefined sweeteners exclusively in their granola bars. Most other brands get their sweetness from a combination of honey and brown sugar; the latter is judged to be more attractive to health-minded shoppers than plain sugar, although the informed consumer knows there is little difference.

The label may still boast "naturally sweetened with brown sugar and honey," but in the move toward chewy granola bars and granola clusters this list has been extended to include sugar, corn syrup, corn syrup solids, and dextrose in sufficient quantity to just about double the previous level of sweetening. Consumers would do well to leave these phony health foods in the supermarket.

Most granola bars are shortened with coconut oil; a few contain palm kernel oil. Although these oils are naturally high in saturated fat, they are better than the hydrogenated oils which are the common alternative.

Granola bars are often rather salty and the more candy-like adaptations are doubly so. About the biggest thing in their favor is that they usually depend on oats as their principal grain, offering the consumer a break from the ubiquitous wheat.

An "exemplary" label should look something like this:

> rolled oats, honey, whole grain brown rice, palm kernel oil, coconut, malted cereal grains (barley, corn), nonfat dry milk, natural flavors, lecithin.

A label that is Acceptable with Reservation might read:

> oats, brown sugar, coconut oil, salt, sesame seeds, soy lecithin, natural flavoring

Any other refined sweetener or a hydrogenated oil removes them from even this secondary status, as of course do glycerine, sorbitol, artificial flavor, and BHA and BHT, all common granola-bar spin-offs.

Graham Crackers

One of the earliest popular "healthy" cookies was the graham cracker. Since *graham* signifies whole wheat, a cookie with a name like "honey grahams" would appear to provide a nourishing, satisfying combination of whole wheat flour and unrefined sweetener. However, today's mass bakery operations have gone on to incorporate refined wheat flour, partially hydrogenated oil, caramel color, corn syrup, artificial flavoring, and artificial coloring into the recipe, so that the typical supermarket offering is no longer exemplary.

Happily, some of the naturally oriented cookie producers have managed to revive the old-time character of the cookie. Sylvester Graham, the grandfather of the food reform movement after whom the cookie was named, would probably be pleased to find one of the more wholesome brands featuring only whole wheat flour, honey, molasses, soy oil, sodium bicarbonate (baking soda), salt, lecithin, and natural flavors in his local natural food store. Somewhat less attractive are those that contain some unbleached flour.

Traditional graham crackers are only lightly sweetened and contain a minimum of fat. When they are coated with chocolate or carob this advantage is lost. Note that the carob-covered graham crackers now appearing in many natural food stores often incorporate partially hydrogenated oil.

Fig Bars

Another popular cookie that has tried to improve its image is the fig bar (popularized as the Fig Newton) and its other fruit-filled relations. Whole wheat versions now abound, but for some reason these creations do not take full advantage of the sweetness of the dried fruit in the filling and instead add sugar, corn syrup, and dextrose to it. Caramel color is common and hydrogenated shortening is universal, even in "natural food" versions. Remember, just because it's whole wheat, it isn't necessarily a wholefood, and even if the manufacturer boasts that "the heart of the cookie is real fruit," keep in mind that it may be supporting a body constructed of artificial parts.

Fruit-Juice-Sweetened Cookies

In the 1980s a new concept took hold in the cookie industry. Fruit-juice-sweetened cookies with "no added sugar" became popular in the natural food store. These cookies boast a commendable list of whole grains (some are even wheat-free), nuts and pure nut butters, fruits, natural flavors, unrefined oils (in most cases), and no artificial anything. Their considerable sweetness is derived from a combination of fruit juice concentrates.

In sampling these cookies, we were suprised to find no taste of fruit juice. This is because some of these juice sweeteners are processed to remove their flavor. The manufacturers of these sweeteners and the commercial cookie bakers who employ fruit juice concentrates in place of sugar have been very difficult to pin down as to the specifics of this ingredient. Thus, we cannot guarantee that fruit-juice-sweetened cookies are all made with what we usually think of as a juice concentrate. Nor does "no added sugar" necessarily make these cookies low-calorie; their calorie content depends more on how much fat and how much fruit juice concentrate go into the recipe.

CAKES

As one can see from the label of most packaged cakes, the story here is even more discouraging. Hydrogenated shortening and emulsifiers are particularly popular because they help to create cakes of unprecedented lightness. The cost of milk is frequently reduced by using a milk replacer composed of dairy derivatives. Even natural flavors become questionable when you read trade magazine ads promoting highly processed ingredients that impart "rich butter flavor to a variety of bakery products as Danish, cakes, rolls, cookies, icings and split top breads." Preservatives, while generally excluded from cookies, are frequently found in packaged cakes.

The baking industry is very aware of the consumer's perceptions. In trade publications we also learn how "trendy new products like carrot cake are drawing from that portion of the population that are 'health conscious.'" A "healthful connotation," not the actual integrity of the cake, is often its best selling point.

Selecting Cakes

If you would like to experience a homey cake that is at the opposite end of the spectrum from the typical supersweet store-bought offerings, there are some choices. Holland Honey Loaves, found in many supermarkets, are sweetened with honey only and, based on rye flour, are wheat-free. Sprouted fruit cakes, available at many natural food stores, are made entirely of sprouted grains, dried fruit, and nuts. Both are fat- and salt-free. They are unusual and perhaps will not appeal to everyone, but if you can appreciate their coarser grain and earthy sweetness, you will have a truly virtuous dessert to enjoy.

If you have something more traditional in mind, the natural food store may be able to help you out with a whole wheat banana, carrot, or date-nut cake made by a commercial natural food bakery. Most likely the cake will be frozen or refrigerated, since there are only a few sources for these items (most of them based in California) and, unlike cookies, cakes have a short shelf-life.

Another option that may be found in your natural food store, but will not appear in our Exemplary Brands, are cakes made by local bakers.

Boxed Cake Mixes

Many people find reassurance in a packaged mix to which they need add only familiar staples like water, eggs, sweetening, and shortening, although baking from scratch requires few additional steps. There are a few cake mixes, mostly available through natural food merchandisers, that offer a commendable recipe. The best example we have seen to date comes from Fearn, whose Spice Cake Mix is composed of:

whole wheat pastry flour, peanut flour, natural soy powder, yogurt solids, whey powder, cinnamon, nutmeg, baking soda, salt, natural flavor, lecithin, and clove

There are other similar mixes with a combination of flours, including some unbleached white, which is as much of a compromise as you should have to make.

The Icing on the Cake

If you plan to ice a cake, don't mask it with synthetics like those in this typical packaged frosting:

sugar, partially hydrogenated vegetable oil (soybean and/or palm and/or cottonseed oil), water, corn syrup, food starch (provides body), modified food starch, salt (a flavor enhancer), nonfat milk, soy lecithin, potassium sorbate (to preserve freshness), mono- and diglycerides (provides smoothness), pectin (from citrus), polysorbate 60 (for smoothness), citric acid (aids in preserving freshness), yellow #5, artificial color, and flavor.

If you don't want to take the trouble to make a frosting from scratch, just top the cake with fresh fruit and real whipped cream, or yogurt enhanced with fruit puree or honey.

Cellulose-Filled Cake?

The U.S. Department of Agriculture has developed what some people might consider the perfect substance for the consumer who wants to maximize fiber and minimize calories, and is now trying to license it to food manufacturers. It is called fluffy cellulose; it feels like flour, and it has no taste, odor, nutrients, or calories. It is pure fiber, manufactured from wheat bran, corn bran, or citrus pulp that has been processed, bleached, and ground for use as a flour substitute in low-calorie cakes and baked goods.

We are already concerned about the use of plain bran in so many products and certainly a highly refined version of what is already a fractionated food is nutritionally distasteful and questionable as to its health effects. If cakes made with fluffy cellulose do eventually make it to the store, don't let them make it into your shopping basket.

PIES AND PIE CRUSTS

Most premade crusts, whether frozen empty or sold with a filling, are not representative of fine pastry. For the conscientious wholefoods shopper the options are limited. A trip to the natural food store in a few select neighborhoods may turn up a frozen whole wheat crust, but it is likely to be marred by the inclusion of hydrogenated shortening. Crusts made with refined flour and hydrogenated shortening or lard can be found at the supermarket. Not much to praise, but they begin to look good when compared to others with:

> flour, shortening (hydrogenated oil with BHT, BHA propyl gallate, citric acid to preserve freshness), water, corn syrup, whey solids, salt, baking soda, sodium benzoate, artificial color with FD & C yellow #5

As for finished pies, the freezer at the natural food store may hold something you want; the one at the supermarket definitely will not.

RECOMMENDATIONS

General Rule of Purchase: All ingredients are on the label. Look for baked goods made with whole grain flours, nuts, fresh and dried fruit, real dairy ingredients, and unrefined sweeteners. Take advantage of offerings that employ grains other than wheat to broaden your diet. Avoid artificial coloring, artificial flavoring, modified starch, hydrogenated fats, preservatives, vegetable gums, cellulose, mono- and diglycerides, polysorbates, and glycerol derivatives.

Exemplary Brands

Cookies

Barbara's 3 Fiber Bran, Butter and Nut, Fruit Juice Sweetened Cookies, Macaroons, Russian Tea Pastry
Betsy's Wild Animal Cookies
Chef Thanos Cookies
Cookie Heaven Ready to Bake Cookies
Farm Verified Organic Barley, Maple Wafers[1]
Good Stuff Honey Oatmeal Raisin, Honey Carob Chip Cookies
Grain Land Chewy Granola Bars
Harvest Farms Cookies
Health Valley Graham Crackers; Animal Snaps; Fruit Bakes; Fruit, Honey Jumbos; Amaranth, Date Pecan, Wheat Germ and Molasses, Peanut Butter, Raisin Bran, Oatmeal Cookies
Healthy Times Cookies
Jennies Macaroons
Little Bear Oatmeal Raisin, Almond Rice, Carob Butter, Fortune Cookies[2]
Lotus Bakery Cookies

Mi-Del 100% Whole Wheat Honey Grahams
Natural Food Mills Cookies
Nature's Cuisine Fruit, Coconut, Carob Pumpkin, Granola, Oatmeal, Sunflower Seed, Carob Chip, Molasses Cookies
Nature's Warehouse Fruit Sweetened Cookies
New Morning Honey Grahams
Pride O the Farm Date Oatmeal, Fruit Sweetened Cookies
Robbie's Butter Sesame Cookies
Sovex Granola Cookies
Spanky's Almond Butter Cookies
Spruce Tree Sweet Rice Cookies[2]
Survival Surviva Cookies
The Best Cookie Around[2]
21st Century Foods Cookies[2]
Uprisings Bakery Cookies[2]
Westbrae Snaps[2]
Women's Community Bakery Cookies[2]
Your Black Muslim Bakery Cookies

Cakes

Back to Nature Banana, Carrot, Date Cakes
Barbara's Chocolate, Carob Brownies; Carrot Cakes; Fruit and Nut Muffins
Big Deal All Natural Carrot Cake
Cedarlane Whole Wheat Baklava
Donut Lite Wholly Natural Donuts
Food for Life Banana, Carrot, Pound Cakes
Holland Date Honey Loaf; Honey, Honey Fruit Cakes
Lifestream Natural Foods Essene Fruitcake[2]

Natural Food Mills Carob Brownies
Nature's Cuisine Carob Brownies
Nature's Path Little Honey Cakes
Nature's Warehouse Brownies
Spruce Tree Sticky Buns
Women's Community Bakery Cinnamon Swirl[2]
Your Black Muslim Bakery Natural Honey Carrot Cake, Whole Wheat Bread Pudding, Natural Sweet Roll

Pies

Justice Bakery Miniature Pies

Natural Nectar Frozen Apple Pie

Mixes

Country Life Oatmeal Raisin Cookie
Fearn Spice, Carob, Banana Cake

Nature's Choice Cookie,[2] Cake[2]

Acceptable with Reservation

Sweet bakery foods were never meant to become a dietary staple. If you think of them as an occasional treat or indulgence, then some of the items recommended with reservation below containing refined flour and sugar may be acceptable to you. They are certainly less troubling than some of the more concocted commercial products.

Cookies

Acme Granola Bars[3]
Back to Nature Fruit Filled Cookies,[3] Fruit Squares[3]
Big Deal Chocolate Chip, Oatmeal Raisin Cookies[3]
Butternut Granola Bars[3]
Food for Life Fruit Delites[3]
Giant Foods Granola Bars[3]
Good Stuff Chocolate Chip Cookies[3]
Health Valley Carob Peanut Butter Sandwich Cookies[4]; Ginger, Coconut, Lemon, Yogurt, Carob Snaps[4]

Kroger Granola Bars[3]
Matt's Oatmeal Raisin, Peanut Butter, Chocolate Chip Cookies[3,4]
Nature Valley Granola Bars[3]
Nature's Cuisine Chocolate Chip Cookies,[3] Fruit Squares[3]
Sunrise Carob Chip Cookies[4]
Survival Coconut Oatmeal Chews[3]
Susan's Cookies[3]

Cakes

Big Deal Fudge Brownies[3,4]
Dutch Mill Whole Wheat Donuts[3]
Food for Life Date-Nut Cake[4]

Mother Earth Health Food Cakes[3,4]
Natural Foods Milk Creek Bakery Cakeletts[4]

Mixes

Arrowhead Mills Cakes[4]
Fearn Carrot Cake[4]

Harrington's Hodgson Mills Old Fashioned Whole Wheat Buttermilk Coffee Cake,[3] Whole Wheat Gingerbread[3,4]

[1] Organic
[2] Some organic ingredients
[3] Contains refined sweeteners
[4] Contains refined grains

Chapter 34

Frozen Desserts:
The Cold, Hard Facts

Frozen desserts are certainly "hot" today, with more "natural" and premium brands in the stores and ice cream boutiques and gelaterias offering exotic new flavors proliferating in almost every neighborhood. Even those people who are making some attempt to modify their diets have been lured into the market by such temptations as frozen yogurt, soy ice creams, and "100% Natural Juice Bars." The success of frozen desserts is evidence that people are willing to make certain concessions when it comes to pleasure, but even so, there should be limits as to what to tolerate.

ICE CREAM

All ice cream exacts a toll, with one half to two thirds of the calories coming from saturated fat, and concentrated sweeteners contributing a good deal of the rest. It is difficult to determine precisely how much sweetening is contained in any one brand since this is not disclosed on the label; however, in a typical quart of vanilla ice cream there is about ½ cup of sugar, or 1 tablespoon in each 4-fluid-ounce (½ cup) serving.

If you've ever had real old-fashioned ice cream, churned from rich cream, ripe fruit, and salt-packed ice, you know something different is being done these days. That "something" is about sixty different additives which simulate real food flavors and colors, enhance the creaminess and texture, prevent crystal formation during storage, slow down the melting process, and do whatever else can be done to cut the cost of simply using fresh, whole ingredients to begin with.

The FDA's Ice Cream

The dairy ingredients in ice cream can be as pure as cream or as refined as modified whey, and while these ingredients are on the label, their precise form may not be revealed. Thus, what appears as "cream" or "milk" may actually be dried, evaporated, condensed, or similarly modified unless it is preceded by the word "fresh."

447

The final milk-fat content must be at least 10 percent. Premium ice creams often go as high as 16 percent and this accounts for an additional 4.5 grams of fat and forty more calories per half cup. If eggs are added, they account for less than 1.4 percent; otherwise, the product becomes known as "frozen custard" or "French ice cream."

NATURAL AND ARTIFICIAL FLAVOR

For your amusement we have included the details of the law as to how ice cream flavor is labeled. It is not constructed to make life easy. To be able to translate labels at the store you'll have to memorize the following:

■ If no artificial flavor is added, the specific flavor only will be written in letters at least one half the height of the words *ice cream,* as in "strawberry ICE CREAM," on the principal display panel.

■ If both natural and artificial flavor are present, with a greater percent of the natural, the label will have the word *flavored* in letters at least half the height of the words *ice cream,* as in "STRAWBERRY flavored ICE CREAM."

■ If there is more artificial flavor than natural flavor, or artificial flavor is used exclusively, the words *artificially flavored* or *artificial* must precede the characterizing flavor in letters not less than one half the height of the flavor, as in "artificial STRAWBERRY ICE CREAM."

■ If an artificial flavor other than the main flavor is used, somewhere on the label it will say *artificial flavor added,* but it might not tell you what flavor.

Since we *do* want to make things easy for you, all you need to know is that any time you see the word *flavored* on a container of ice cream, you can assume that some amount of artificial flavoring has been added.

ARTIFICIAL COLOR

Ice cream is one of the three food products that are not required to reveal the use of artificial color—except for Yellow #5, which must always be listed. Interestingly, in the Standard of Identity, although the FDA recommends voluntary disclosure of all colors in ice cream, Congress has the final authority over this particular food and to date has done nothing to force coloring to be revealed. This is particularly unfortunate since as a group, artificial colors have been banned more than any other additive (see "Additives That Have Been Banned," page 534).

Overrun

Some might say that the labeling of ice cream is full of hot air; equally as disturbing is that ice cream itself is full of cold air. One of the requirements for making ice cream is that it be stirred during freezing. This incorporates air (called "overrun"), which in turn influences the texture. Ice cream that is "cold" and wet and melts slowly is likely to have a high percentage of fresh, real ingredients. The fluffier and "warmer" the ice cream seems, and the more foam on the surface when it melts, the more air it is likely to contain. Because the air displaces some of the food components, its presence does result in fewer calories and less fat per volume, but it also usually necessitates a greater dependence on additives to increase whipping capacity, slow down the melting process, decrease the crystal size, and otherwise improve the "mouthfeel."

The limit on how much air is allowed comes to a 100 percent overrun (or 50 percent air). Most premium brands are below this and their high price may be justified somewhat by the fact that there is almost as much substance in a pint as there is in a quart of cheap aerated brands.

GUMMED-UP ICE CREAM

The most common ice cream additives are the stabilizers, emulsifiers, or "viscosity modifying agents," as they are known in the trade. Several vegetable gums, cellulose compounds, mono- and diglycerides, polysorbates, and chemical salts may be employed to prevent the formation of large sugar crystals which make the ice cream "chewy."

One trend we have observed since the publication of *The Supermarket Handbook* is the tremendous growth in the use of gums in foods, particularly frozen desserts. Where we used to find one gum, now there are two, three, or four. We are alarmed by this, as gums decrease the food value of the product and introduce more nontraditional ingredients to the food supply. Even the federal government has shown some concern about the proliferation of gums in food products and feels they should be reviewed in terms of possible limits on how much may be used and the implications of prolonged intake.

Natural Ice Cream: The Cream of the Crop

Many of the additives that can be used to enhance the texture of ice cream are considered natural since they are derived from plants. Thus, despite the objections we have just posed, locust bean gum, karaya bean gum, carrageenan, the alginates, micro crystalline cellulose, and mono- and diglycerides may all be incorporated into brands calling themselves "all natural." What manufacturers base their definition on is that these ice creams are devoid of artificial color and flavor.

We limit our selection of ice cream to those made the old-fashioned way, containing only dairy products that have been minimally processed, and fruit, nuts, natural flavors, and fresh eggs where applicable. Sweetners are obviously essential to the recipe and thus sugar, corn syrup, fructose, etc., do not disqualify a brand, although we prefer honey and maple syrup. Because of these guidelines you may find that very few of the so-called all-natural ice creams are included in our Exemplary Brands.

ICE MILK

Many weight-conscious people replace ice cream with ice milk because of its lower fat content (2 to 7 percent). Although ice milk may have "half the fat of regular ice cream," as one brand advertises, it does not have half the calories. Extra sweetening is added to compensate for the reduced butterfat and this creates a product that has more refined carbohydrates than ice cream, with only about forty to fifty fewer calories per half-cup serving.

In an attempt to bring the taste and texture up to par, stabilizers, emulsifiers, and a host of artificial ingredients seem to be universally included. One noticeable difference between ice milk and ice cream is the mandatory listing of artificial coloring on the label. To date, we have not been able to find a single brand we can recommend.

SHERBET

Fruit sherbert may contain the same basic ingredients as ice cream, but it has a milk fat content of only 1 to 2 percent. Even with low fat content to its credit, however, sherbet may be equal in calories to many ice creams since as in ice milk, the slack may be taken up by sugar.

Any fruit flavoring that characterizes the sherbet must be real fruit or its juice; however, imitations may be used to enhance or replace nonfruit flavoring ingredients such as spices, coffee, chocolate, cocoa, and alcohols. When artificial flavor or color is used, it will say so on the label.

WATER ICES

Water ices are sherbet without any milk or milk-derived ingredients. If any egg is added, it will be only the white.

ICE JUICE

Frozen juice bars provide a cold, refreshing confection. Except for the presence of vegetable gums "to improve texture" in almost every commercial bar, some are quite commendable, remaining low in fat and free of added sugars. Others are shocking in their caloric content; a figure of 79 to 195 calories for a 2½-fluid-ounce bar makes them more fattening than most ice cream.

Keep in mind that even though the label may advertise "100% natural" or "pure fruit juice," the inevitable vegetable gums may not be the only detraction; sugar, fructose, corn sweeteners, malic and citric acid, as well as "fruit punch" and "natural lemonade" (which both contain added sweeteners) are all possibilities. While we are willing to tolerate a small amount of vegetable gum in order to obtain popsicles made of frozen unsweetened juice, that allowance does not extend to a product that is sugar-water on a stick.

FROZEN YOGURT

Frozen yogurt, a product that barely existed in the 1970s, is accepted today even by those who would never give its predecessor, yogurt, the slightest attention. Sad to say, the reason for its easy favor is simple—sugar, and plenty of it. Frozen yogurt may garner only 8 to 20 percent of its calories from fat (considerably less than ice cream, with 50 to 60+ percent), but often the gap is reduced by sugar, fructose, honey, corn sweetener, etc., with the result that a 4-ounce (½-cup) serving of frozen yogurt contains about 135 calories and approximates many ice creams. When you add chocolate and granola coatings to yogurt bars, the fat soars to ice cream levels and the calories match those of comparable amounts of premium brands.

Frozen yogurt does have the potential for more protein, calcium, and riboflavin than all other frozen dairy desserts, but unfortunately if a significant amount of air is incorporated, even these nutrients may be in short supply. If you see soy protein or vegetable protein on the label, you could get the idea that the manufacturer is trying to boost the nutritional content, but this is not so. These are additives especially geared to hard-frozen yogurt that help increase product overrun to as much as 129 percent. Since it appears that sugar-air may be in greater abundance than any actual yogurt, perhaps the amount of air should also be revealed in the list of ingredients.

Some frozen yogurts are made with gelatin to help maintain texture. Gelatin, as you will discover in the next chapter, is extracted from animal bones and is a more traditional part of the human diet than the other commonly used stabilizers like microcrystalline cellulose, gum stabilizers, mono- and diglycerides, and polysorbate 80. Other common additives include salt and artificial color and flavor. It's all right there for you to read on the label, so there is no point in pretending that commercial frozen yogurt is the "health alternative."

There is also considerable debate as to whether the healthful bacteria which proliferate in yogurt remain viable in the freezer. Time is one influential factor and it is speculated that the bacteria in home-frozen yogurt and soft-frozen yogurt from a machine, which is usually made on a daily basis, have a better chance of survival than in commercial hard-frozen yogurt, which is more likely to undergo long-term freezing.

ICE CREAM IMITATORS

If lactose intolerance crosses ice cream and other frozen dairy desserts off your shopping list, one of the dairy-free frozen desserts based on soy or rice may attract your attention. However, if you are trying to cut out calories, fat, sugar, or additives, you may want to look more closely at some of these products before you get too excited. Note, though, that vegetable stabilizers like guar gum, carob bean gum, pectin, carrageenan, and lecithin are somewhat more acceptable here than in ice cream because a product of this sort would be very difficult to keep smooth and free of ice crystals without such assistance.

Iced Beans

Although Tofutti was responsible for the surge of interest in nondairy frozen desserts, and like Jello-O it may become the term by which all frozen soy-based desserts are characterized, it was not the first. Long before ice cream parlors and retail stores (and probably most consumers as well) were willing to embrace this concept, The Farm in Tennessee and a few smaller health food entrepreneurs had their own brands of soy-based frozen concoctions. It's a pity their products didn't win the praise they deserved earlier, for with soybeans (or soy milk), honey, unsaturated oil, and only natural flavors and vegetable stabilizers, they are truly a no-cholesterol, milk-free, moderately sweetened dessert. While these soy-based desserts still derive a significant percentage of their calories from fat, there is less of it per portion compared to ice cream and it is largely unsaturated. They are also more welcome to the calorie-conscious because they contain from 100 to 120 calories per half cup (4 fluid ounces).

Unfortunately, Tofutti caught the public's eye and became the trendsetter. Made primarily of water, corn oil, and high fructose corn sweetener, it is more like frozen sweetened mayonnaise (that is, an oil emulsion) than ice cream in our opinion. Most of the frozen soy bean desserts on the market today mimic this formula. Although in most people's minds these desserts are associated with the virtuous bean curd, in reality the presence of tofu may be minimal, and furthermore the tofu may be made from the highly processed soybean isolate without divulging this on the label.

With a whopping 40 to 60 percent of calories coming from fat, and with 200 to 275 calories in a 4-ounce scoop, this is far from the "guilt-free, nondairy frozen dessert" it is often billed as. When it comes to designer desserts, read the label; you may want to consider selecting one of the less fashionable brands.

Ice Rice

Another entry into the frozen dessert arena is in a category all its own. Based not on soy but on cultured rice, Rice Dream, too, is free of cholesterol, lactose, and all dairy ingredients. Its sweetening comes from the culturing of the rice and in some varieties "a touch" of pear concentrate. Its flavors and colors are all natural. Once again, it does have added vegetable stabilizers in the form of Irish sea moss (i.e., carrageenan) and guar and carob bean gums. The original formula had very little fat, but in the new rendition with safflower oil about 40 percent of the calories come from fat. Even so, Rice Dream is comparable to the leaner ice creams, with 130 to 150 calories per half cup.

THE ICE CREAM CONE

If it is unpatriotic to criticize ice cream, to malign the cone may amount to treason. But consider the ingredients—refined flour, sugar, partially hydrogenated oils, salt, leavening, lecithin, and often artificial color and flavor—and perhaps you will agree with us that there must be a better way to ensconce the frozen dessert you've gone to so much care to select.

Most so-called natural ice cream cones are still not the perfect container but at least they are headed in the right direction, with unbleached flour, honey, partially hydrogenated oils, soy flour, wheat germ, raisin syrup, salt, leavening, and lecithin. A less refined grain and a better choice of oils could result in near perfection. To the best our knowledge only one company has this integrity.

RECOMMENDATIONS

ICE CREAM

General Rule of Purchase: All ingredients except color are on the label, but the precise form of the dairy ingredients (fresh, dried, concentrated, etc.) may not be revealed. The word "flavored" accompanying the name is a quick clue to the presence of artificial flavor.

Look for real milk or cream, fruit, natural flavoring ingredients, and if the information is volunteered, *fresh* dairy ingredients and *fresh* eggs. Some form of sweetening is inevitable; honey and maple syrup are preferred. Although vegetable gums may appear in many brands labeled "natural," these do not get our endorsement.

Breyer's[3]
Café Glacé
Erivan Old World
Frusen Gladje[3]

Haagen Daz[3]
Meadow Gold Old-Fashioned Recipe[3]
Sara Lee[3]

ICE MILK, SHERBET WATER ICES

General Rule of Purchase: All ingredients including artificial color will be on the label. Follow the same buying guidelines as for ice cream.

Exemplary Brands

Angelo Brocato Lemon, Strawberry Italian Ices[3]

Le Sorbet French Ice[3]
Nouvelle Sorbet

ICE JUICE BARS

General Rule of Purchase: All ingredients are on the label. Look for a product containing only fruit and/or unsweetened juice. More likely you will encounter a vegetable gum stabilizer. If combined only with juice, this can be acceptable. Avoid if sweeteners are added.

Exemplary Brands

Fruit Tops Frozen Pops
Garden of Eatin' Frozen Joy

Nezra's Natural Foods Fresh Frozen Juice Pops
Tree Top All Natural Juice Bars

FROZEN YOGURT

General Rule of Purchase: All ingredients are on the label. You may want to accept a refined sweetener, nonfat dry milk, and gelatin. Avoid other stabilizers and artificial color and flavor.

Exemplary Brands

Dannon Frozen Low Fat Yogurt[3]

NONTRADITIONAL FROZEN DESSERTS

General Rule of Purchase: All ingredients are on the label. All soy- and rice-based products in this category contain added gums, but you can avoid refined sweeteners (including fructose), and sorbitol, as well as isolated soy protein, polysorbate 80, microcrystalline cellulose, and mono- and diglycer-ides. Look for a brand sweetened with honey or maple syrup only, with the added vegetable stabilizers confined to carob bean gum, guar gum, and/or carrageenan (Irish sea moss).

Exemplary Brands

Farm Foods Ice Bean
Garden of Eatin' Ice Dreem, Nuclear Freeze[2]

Macremes Mauka Freeze
Rice Dream

ICE CREAM CONES

General Rule of Purchase: All ingredients are on the label. Look for a brand made with whole grains and unrefined sweeteners. Avoid hydrogen-ated oil and artificial color and flavor.

Exemplary Brands

Tree of Life Honey Wheat Cones

[2]Some organic ingredients
[3]Contains refined sweeteners

Chapter 35

Set Ups: Puddings
and Gelatin Desserts

One of Nikki's first jobs included developing recipes for unflavored gelatin, a product she had never even heard of, having grown up in this age of Jello-O. To her surprise she discovered that the amount of time and work involved in preparing genuine food-containing desserts using unflavored gelatin was almost identical to what it took to reconstitute the packaged ersatz mix.

What did people do before dessert mixes came in a box? Why they made their own puddings and gelatin desserts from real fruit juices, fresh dairy products, and cornstarch, arrowroot, tapioca, and pure, unflavored gelatin.

G–E–L–L–O

The popularity of gelatin desserts needs no documentation; rarely has a food product been able to enter our language as effectively as Jell-O. Today, the word "jello" is invariably used to mean gelatin desserts, no matter what the brand. It is a pity that such a successful advertising campaign has been in support of such a barren food item—colored sugar-water you can eat.

That is not an exaggeration. Gelatin mixes are made of about 85 percent sugar, 10 percent gelatin, plus factory-made flavorings, colors, and acids.

Natural Gel Dessert Mixes

Sometimes the natural food version of a supermarket product isn't much of an improvement. If you prepare one of Jello-O's "natural" copycats containing dried honey or turbinado sugar, a vegetable powder extract, and natural fruit flavor, you still have only edible sugar-water. It has none of fruit's assets.

Unflavored Gelatin

Unflavored gelatin is a protein extracted from bones, but it is of extremely low quality and therefore doesn't help satisfy your protein requirement. What it has is the ability to stiffen or gel liquids, so it can be used in combination with juice to obtain real fruit value.

Every supermarket carries unflavored gelatin and all brands are similar. Most are packaged in individual envelopes premeasured to gel up to one pint of liquid. If not premeasured, one tablespoon is the equivalent of one envelope.

Vegetable Gels

In the Orient, where seaweed is abundant, a gelling medium known as agar is made from various species of red algae. Much of this agar is still produced by an age-old, completely natural technique. It is formed into bars known as *kanten* or *agar flakes,* and is used in much the same manner as gelatin for a strictly vegetarian gel. You can find kanten and agar flakes in natural food stores and Oriental groceries.

PUDDING

Pudding Mixes

Instant pudding mixes woo consumers with convenience, but the hitch is it comes with lots of sugar, plus modified starch, sodium phosphate (to aid setting), salt, hydrogenated vegetable oil (with BHA added as a preservative), mono- and digylcerides (to prevent foaming), nonfat dry milk powder, artificial color, and artificial and natural flavors. Noninstant varieties replace the sodium phosphate and mono- and diglycerides with polysorbate 60 and carrageenan.

"Natural" pudding mixes are a definite improvement, but they are still overly reliant on highly processed ingredients such as whey, carob bean gum, and carrageenan, include salt for no good reason, and are not a great time-saver since you have to add milk and sweetening when you prepare them.

Prepared Puddings

Since most of the mass-produced premade puddings start out with ingredients similar to those in the mixes, they are generally just as unappealing. When preservatives are added, they look even worse.

One interesting natural food store item that dispenses with all the additives and is dairy-free as well is made by a company that specializes in soy products. Brightsong Light Foods manufactures a line of "Lite & Creamy" and "Diet DeLite" desserts with a pudding texture that comes from tofu, sweetness from honey, and flavor contributed by fruit, cocoa, nuts, vanilla, and similar natural sources. The only other ingredient is lecithin. While this is all commendable, don't construe the "Lite" or "Diet" to mean low-calorie. According to their own figures, 3 ounces of the strawberry product furnish 90 calories, escalating to 170 for the almond variety. What makes the prospect of obtaining even more calories than this per sitting likely is that these "puddings" come in 6-ounce plastic yogurt-like containers that look like an individual serving. The company may recommend a 3-ounce serving, but how many people will quit when the carton is half gone? On the bright side, a 3-ounce serving will give you 5 to 9 grams of protein.

Homemade Puddings

There is no mystique to pudding-making. You can easily make some pretty nutritious desserts without the additives included in the mixes by using cornstarch, arrowroot, kuzu, or pearls of tapioca.

All four of these starch products have the capacity to swell in hot liquids and thicken them on cooling to produce a spoonable dessert. As we have discussed previously, *cornstarch* is a tasteless powder extracted from maize, and *arrowroot* is the refined starch of a West Indian tuber. *Kuzu,* a similar product described as "wild arrowroot powder," is imported from Japan. *Tapioca* is derived from the root of the tropical plant known as manioc or cassava. Because this starchy powder tends to become stringy in liquids, tapioca is made into pregelatinized "pearls" which react more compatibly with liquid.

Cornstarch and tapioca pearls are common supermarket items. Arrowroot may also be found there, or you may be able to locate in it a natural food store. Kuzu is sold in more specialized outlets such as Oriental markets or natural food stores. There is no significant difference between brands, so choose whatever is most available.

RECOMMENDATIONS

GELATIN AND PUDDING MIXES

General Rule of Purchase: Gelatin and pudding mixes reveal all ingredients on the label. Since none are without drawbacks, we suggest you purchase the raw materials and prepare fresh gels and puddings from unflavored gelatin, agar flakes or kanten bars, cornstarch, arrowroot, kuzu, and tapioca pearls. All brands are similar.

GELATIN AND PREPARED PUDDING

General Rule of Purchase: All ingredients are on the label. Most prepared products are full of the same additives as the mixes, including refined sugar, artificial coloring and flavor, a variety of vegetable gums or modified starch, phosphates and mono- and diglycerides to assist the thickening agents, salt, and possibly preservatives as well. To be acceptable, only fresh dairy products, unsweetened juice, a nutritive sweetener (preferably unrefined), the thickeners recommended under Mixes, and real flavoring agents should be present. We have not found any commercial items that fit this description, but we do recommend the following tofu and amazake dessert lines.

Exemplary Brands_____

Brightsong Lite & Creamy, Diet Delite   Infinite Foods Amazake Puddings

Chapter 36

Drink Up!

In the last few decades, America's drinking passions have shifted significantly. The traditional favorites, coffee and milk, are no longer secure in first and second place; they have been displaced by soft drinks, which have doubled their market in the last decade and are now the No. 1 choice. Pure fruit juice consumption is also on the rise, and bottled water sales have grown astronomically. Moreover, in 1985 *Forbes* magazine reported that alcohol consumption suffered its first overall decline in a generation.

The drop in coffee consumption which began in the mid 1950s was reinforced in the 1970s by the rising cost of coffee. Now more people are having tea, particularly herb teas, both hot and cold. The success of soft drinks, on the other hand, is largely the result of relentless advertising and public relations campaigns aimed at youngsters, culminating in promotions by rock and roll stars at fees in the multimillion-dollar range.

An awareness of the relationship between diet and health is credited with the growth of low-calorie soft drinks, decaffeinated coffees, and "lite" beers. To our way of thinking, this reflects a somewhat perverted view of nutrition, since removing unwanted calories and caffeine from soda, coffee, and alcoholic beverages still does not make these drinks commendable.

WATER WATER EVERYWHERE . . .

But is it safe to drink?

The safety of the water that comes from your tap depends on where you reside. Most of us tend to deny that a problem exists, telling ourselves that we feel all right so why question one of the most fundamental aspects of our lives—the purity of the water we drink. On the other hand, concern over water quality has resulted in a growing market for bottled water, often without much regard for what is actually in the bottle or without even justifying the need for such a purchase. If you are concerned about the water in your area, have it tested. If your water report is not satisfactory, you can then proceed to explore the options. You may want to invest in a home purification system. Or, you may choose to buy your drinking water. But even buying water is no simple matter.

Many of the potentially dangerous substances that can get into the water supply are environmental—pesticides, herbicides, asbestos, petroleum, industrial wastes, arsenic, lead, mercury, other heavy metals—and even acid rain. There are few places so remote that the water can be guaranteed to be free of pollutants, and thus bottled mineral or spring waters may not give you total protection. In fact, as of 1987 the Safe Drinking Water Act only requires bottlers to test for six pesticides and a few other chemical contaminants. Moreover, this regulation just covers bottled water marketed in interstate not local commerce and completely excludes mineral water. No standards exist for many of the most common pollutants, some known to be carcinogens, and although many large bottlers do use carbon filters to help remove chemical contaminants, this is not required by federal law. The actual level of minerals (some of which can be toxic in large amounts) and bacteria are also not monitored. In addition, an estimated 75 percent of bottled water is simply processed water from the tap and may even contain the same defects as your own water.

All of this leaves us quite insecure about recommending any one brand. If you cannot manage to make the water from your faucet drinkable, or find a brand you can trust, perhaps the best approach to buying bottled water would be to vary the brand so that at least the accumulation of minerals, chemicals, and bacterial contamination from a single source will be offset.

Taking the Waters

Water is the ultimate "lite" beverage, but to make a suitable purchase you should be familiar with the various available forms.

Still water has no bubbles. The water from your faucet is still water. So is the water sold in bulk containers as "drinking water," which is often nothing more than someone else's tap water.

Sparkling water is charged with carbon dioxide gas which makes it effervescent; this "carbonation" can occur naturally in the ground or may be added later. To maintain the carbonation in naturally carbonated water, the gas may be siphoned off after the water is removed from the ground, then reinjected during bottling. While there are no restrictions as to whether the bubbles are in the water naturally or added by the bottler, it probably makes no significant difference. Mineral and spring waters (see below) may or may not be effervescent.

Seltzer, man-made sparkling water, is generally tap water that has been filtered and carbonated. No mineral or sodium salts are added, which distinguishes seltzer from its cousin, club soda.

Spring water rises to the surface due to its own pressure, unlike well water, which is pumped up. "Natural spring water" undergoes no processing from the source to the container. When only the words *spring water* are used, the water may have been modified in some way. The word *spring* is no indication as to purity of content.

Mineral water is water which contains dissolved minerals. Actually, all water other than distilled water fits this definition. The use of the word *natural* means the minerals were there when the water was removed from the ground; the word does not imply purity per se. The description "mineral water" without the word *natural* means some minerals have been removed or introduced. Not all mineral waters are the same. Their calcium, iron, magnesium, fluoride and sodium contents vary widely depending on the source. While some contain a minimum of sodium, others may have as much as 400 milligrams per cup. The label rarely furnishes any relevant information.

Distilled water has had all the minerals removed, but any chemical pollutants and heavy metals that may have been present before processing, for the most part, remain. The use of distilled or soft water for drinking, whether purchased or as the product of a home-softening system, is not advised. The hardness of water (a measure of the mineral content) has been inversely correlated with atherosclerosis; that is, the harder the water, the lower the incidence of coronary and hypertensive heart disease. The precise reason for this apparently protective effect is not known. Water rich in natural minerals is also beneficial to teeth and bones.

JUICES

100 Percent Fruit Juice

Even though they label their products "100% pure" or "natural," manufacturers can manipulate the proportion of the fruit and vegetable components. Processing and packaging techniques can result in a product that is all juice, but is not necessarily the same drink you get when you extract juice from fruits or vegetables yourself.

One subject of concern is the effects on food value of concentrating juice by removing some of the liquid portion and then later adding water back to reconstitute it. Is something important lost in the evaporation stage? What water source is used in reconstituting the juice when it is prepared commercially? And, how can you tell when a juice is actually made from concentrate?

Orange, grapefruit, tomato, and pineapple juices are governed by a Standard of Identity and are required to reveal the use of concentrates. Although general labeling laws state that this practice should also be indicated for other juices, a friend in the business tells us "there is widespread noncompliance in the industry and little or no enforcement by government agencies."

"Filtration," "depectinization," "stabilization," and manipulation of the "brix/acid ratio" are some of the processes that alter the composition of the juice. Many fruit mashes used in juice-making are treated with heat, sulfites, and sorbate preservatives to inhibit enzymatic and microbial deterioration. These steps may be taken in the manufacture of any juice (bottled, canned, boxed, or frozen) without being indicated on the label.

ORANGE AND GRAPEFRUIT JUICE

Fresh It's a lucky customer who can shop at a store offering freshly squeezed citrus juice. Although the numbers are still small, many markets have installed mechanical juicers in the produce section.

Fresh juice should be purchased as soon as possible after it is squeezed so you can enjoy it before the natural enzymes in the fruit go to work to alter both the vitamin C value and the flavor. Be sure to buy from a chilled display since warmth accelerates deterioration.

Frozen Concentrate Frozen concentrate, if properly handled, is considered by some to be the best nutritional buy. According to the Florida Citrus Commission, the preparation and freezing of the concentrate takes place within a day of harvest and if cold storage is well maintained, the food value is preserved. (To retain high-level nutrients, however, you should not thaw the frozen concentrate at room temperature and juice should be refrigerated immediately following preparation and consumed soon after.)

In manufacturing frozen concentrate, after the initial extraction of the water, it may be modified with orange oil, pulp, juice, "essence," sweetening, and water so that when it is diluted by the consumer the percentage of solids conforms to the legal minimum. Some companies add extra pulp to create the sensation of drinking fresh juice. Only the addition of sweetener must be specified on the label.

For consumers who are sensitive to the acidity in orange juice, there is a reduced-acid concentrate devoid of added sweetening and manufactured by an intricate ion-exchange process. It is purported to have the same nutritional content as regular frozen concentrate.

Chilled Juice Does the promotional phrasing "the fresh squeezed taste of Tropicana" mean that this chilled orange juice in a container is no different from fresh-squeezed oranges? Not quite, for fresh juice is not promised, only fresh-squeezed "taste." Even this expectation is not likely to be realized since, as noted on the label (in letters at least one-half the height of the words "orange juice"), the juice is *pasteurized,* a process which extends the shelf-life at the expense of nutrients and, by all accounts, flavor.

In the preparation of pasteurized orange or grapefruit juice, the pulp and citrus oil may be adjusted by adding up to 25 percent frozen concentrate. In order to maintain a favorable "brix"—the standard measure of sugar, citric acid, and fruit solids relative to water—a variety of sweeteners may be added. If either juice concentrate or sweetening is used, the law requires they be indicated on the label wherever the name appears, as in the following illustrations.

Prepared juice from concentrate may be sold in a container identical to the one with pasteurized juice, except that the words "from concentrate" in letters at least half the height of the words "orange" or "grapefruit juice" must appear. This can get confusing since the same company may offer both products.

**Required Descriptive Labeling for Containers of
Pasteurized Orange and Grapefruit Juices**

**Required Descriptive Labeling for Containers of
Pasteurized Orange and Grapefruit Juices from Concentrate**

While prediluted juice from concentrate is a convenience, it is not as "fresh" as frozen concentrate diluted at home because of the delay between the time it was reconstituted and the time you buy it. Moreover, by allowing someone else to add the water for you, you may be getting a good deal more than you anticipated. Routine testing of prediluted orange juice by the Florida Citrus Commission in 1981 found that of 250 samples, nearly 60 percent had added sugar that was not indicated on the label, as well as orange pulp wash (the spent pulp of the fruit which is permitted in other beverages but not in orange juice). There is no way for the consumer to detect such fraudulent practices, but they might be noticed (and certainly not appreciated) by those sensitive to sugar or to the preservative sodium benzoate which is added to the pulp-wash solids.

Bottled and Boxed Pasteurized juice or juice from concentrate may also provide the basis for shelf-stable orange juice packaged in bottles or aseptic boxes. To guarantee a long life, these juices must be heat-processed more extensively than either of the products marketed in the chilled form. Therefore, in terms of processing, they are more like canned juice.

Canned Most people consider canning a rotten way to treat an orange. This may be true in terms of enjoyment since canned citrus juice has a somewhat tart taste and thinner consistency than other forms of the juice. Surprisingly, though, USDA figures actually indicate that canned juice has slightly higher vitamin C levels and significantly more vitamin A than chilled pasteurized juice or chilled juice from concentrate. As with other orange and grapefruit juice products, if sweetening is added to canned juice it will be stated on the label.

One other consideration here is the possible interaction between the can and the acidic juice. If you buy canned juice, avoid soldered cans (see "Wrapping It Up" in Chapter 1). Once the can is opened you should transfer any juice you wish to store to another container.

APPLE JUICE

The only apple juice that truly possesses all the virtues of the apple is the fresh-pressed juice that appears on the market shortly after harvest time. This chilled juice, generally referred to as *cider*, contains native enzymes, pectin, and other fibrous components of the fruit that are missing in shelf-stable juices.

Unfortunately, even local fresh cider is not always additive-free. Before the apples are pressed, the cut fruit can be treated with chemicals to inhibit oxidation and microbial spoilage and you will never know. In addition, sorbate preservatives are often added; this will be stated on the label or the cap.

While we are very pleased that the number of apple juice drinkers is on the increase, we advise you to seek out fresh juice from unsprayed apples if you can. This will help protect against residues of daminozide, a dangerous chemical spray popular with apple growers which penetrates to the core and remains in processed apple products (see Chapter 25). Another problem common to apples that we hope industry and the government will soon address is a carcinogenic mold that is, unfortunately, relatively stable in the juice.

Although cider is technically the fresh-pressed juice from ground apple pulp, this is not a legal definition and you may find filtered, clarified, pasteurized bottled juice claiming this distinction.

Bottled, Boxed, or Canned   There are no federal standards to regulate apple juice. While the words "pure" or "natural," popular on labels, are usually construed by consumers to mean whole or intact, actually the juice may be filtered and/or reconstituted. In addition, the label may not say "pasteurized," but every nonrefrigerated juice is treated in this way.

Apple juice is not especially rich in the most popular nutrients, but it is a decent source of some less appreciated ones like potassium and silicon. Its most important component, though, is natural fruit pectin, one of the more highly touted complex carbohydrates. Pectin, however, is only present if the juice is unfiltered. Therefore, our recommendation is to buy not only unsweetened but also unfiltered apple juice. This is generally (voluntarily) revealed on the label, and unfiltered juice often can be detected visually by its somewhat thick, cloudy appearance and the fruit sediment at the bottom. Shake the container before drinking to redistribute all the particles. If you buy the juice in an opaque container and there is no such descriptive adjective, assume that filtering has occurred.

Addition of sweeteners, coloring, flavoring, and preservatives must appear in the list of ingredients. If water is added in excess of natural proportions, the juice loses its "pure juice" title. Laboratory tests commissioned by *The New York Times* in 1979 found "non apple" sugars and excess dilution in many brands. These practices are not illegal, but failure to mention them on the label is.

Ascorbic acid (shown on the list of ingredients) is sometimes added to apple juice to protect the color and flavor. Amber glass bottles are also utilized to shield against deterioration by light.

Frozen Concentrate   Sugar and ascorbic acid (vitamin C) are commonly added to frozen apple juice concentrate and their presence is acknowledged on the label.

GRAPE JUICE

Full-strength purple grape juice (as opposed to diluted grape "drinks"), is generally juice and nothing else. Most brands prominently state "unsweetened." Some are enriched with ascorbic acid (vitamin C). This is one of the few varieties of juice that a natural food store may carry made from organic fruit.

White grape juice and rose-colored varieties are less pristine, containing potassium metabisulfite to preserve color.

Frozen Concentrate Until a few years ago, frozen grape juice concentrate was always sweetened. Now most brands offer an option. While the sweetened version is usually fortified with vitamin C, the unenhanced concentrate is not.

PINEAPPLE JUICE

Pineapple juice and frozen pineapple juice concentrate may have sweetening added; however, this is not usually the case and, should it be, it will be stated on the label. Vitamin C (ascorbic acid) is generally added to protect color and flavor; this too is revealed. If the juice is made from concentrate, the label will say so.

In the processing of pineapple juice, dimethylpolysiloxane may be employed as a defoaming agent. For once, this practice is shown on the label and, if manufacturers are to be believed, it is not very widespread.

PRUNE JUICE

Prune juice is not only a natural laxative but also a good source of potassium as well as iron, an element lacking in many diets, particularly those of young women. It is, however, missing the vitamin A which abounds in the dried prune from which the juice is made.

If the manufacturer wishes, the flavor can be adjusted with lemon or lime juice or citric acid for slight tartness, or with honey for added sweetness, but neither is common practice. The addition of vitamin C is widespread and while there is not enough to make the juice a good source of this nutrient, the amount added probably does enhance the absorption of the iron. The use of any of these ingredients must be revealed on the label.

There is little difference among brands with the exception of prune juice prepared from certified organically grown fruit, which we have encountered in a few natural food stores.

MIXED FRUIT JUICES

The wide selection of 100 percent fruit juice blends today compared to ten years ago when there were only three canned options, demonstrates how the market can be responsive to consumer demands. You can now find choices ranging from apple-grape and apple-berry to multijuice mixes in frozen concentrates, bottles, and aseptic cardboard boxes. Most of these blends are prepared at least in part from concentrates. Sometimes they become quite exotic, incorporating, for example, passion fruit, mango, papaya, banana, guava, and kiwi. When coconut is added, so is a "gum stabilizer." It may be as innocent as citrus fruit pectin or as high-tech as polysorbate 60; you will not know these details unless the company wants you to. While most mixed juices are sweetened with pear and white grape juice concentrates, some do contain honey or fructose, so it is important to read the label.

"CALIFORNIA" FRESH-PRESSED JUICES

Chilled juices from fresh fruit or a combination of fresh fruit, concentrates, and purees, and "smoothies" incorporating banana or yogurt into the fresh juice, are featured in select parts of the country. California seems to be the home of these juices, but they do show up with less visibility in natural food stores, produce markets, and occasionally even supermarkets in other locales. Labeling is often inadequate, but a properly labeled container should alert you to the presence of any added sweeteners, emulsifiers, or preservatives.

Juice Too Sweet

You may find, as we do, that many juices, particularly the bottled varieties, are too sweet (probably due to the use of concentrates). To make them more palatable and economical, dilute to taste with water or seltzer.

Diluted Fruit Juices: What's in a Name

Juice drinks, drinks, nectars, punches, and *ades*—even those that call themselves "100% natural" and contain "no artificial color, flavor, or preservatives"—are never 100 percent juice. Many could be more accurately described as "juice-flavored sweetened water."

The original government standards specified how much juice had to be used in order for these beverages to bear the above titles, but did not require any statement of juice content on the label. The consumer had to learn what the terms meant, and most of us had no idea what the difference was, for example, between a "juice drink" and a "drink." Since 1974, several proposals have been made for revealing this information. In 1984, federal guidelines were established requiring that containers of diluted beverages divulge how much total juice they contain and, when more than one juice is present, how much of each is included as well. However, before this could go into effect (and after a third extension), the order was rescinded. This was a big setback for consumers, although fortunately many companies now voluntarily offer this information. (If the percentage of juice is revealed, be sure to look closely. We were reminded how important this is when a friend's daughter read the tiny "with 10 percent juice" on a label as "with 100 percent juice.")

The law does mandate that fruit nectars, depending on the kind, contain at least 25 to 40 percent single-strength fruit derived from puree, pulp, juice, or concentrates. When composed of more than one fruit, the name must make reference to all the principal types in descending order of predominance; any fruit that is less than one-tenth of the total gets tagged onto the name as "added," for example "Apricot and Pear Nectar, passion fruit added."

Optional sweeteners, acidifers, and ascorbic acid must be labeled in all diluted juice beverages, but the source of sweetening can be kept secret. For additional flavor, citric acid (or sodium/potassium citrate), malic acid, fumaric acid, ethyl malitol, as well as artificial flavor, may be included. The "mouthfeel" may be improved with cellulose or xanthan gum, which keeps the pulp in suspension, and the life span may be extended with sodium benzoate or potassium sorbate preservatives.

Unless you are determined to pay for sugar-water, all this hardly matters. Bear in mind that even though these diluted drinks might be cheaper on a per-volume basis, if you watered down pure juice an equal amount at home, you would end up paying less.

VITAMIN SUPPLEMENTS DISGUISED AS SOFT DRINKS

Even when diluted beverages contain "natural flavors" exclusively, they do not offer much natural nutrition. In order to impress the consumer, many of these beverages are "vitamin C enriched," supplying as much as 100 percent of the U.S. RDA per serving. But vitamin C is only one of the nutritional benefits derived from drinking full-strength fruit juice and thus this is only a minimal improvement.

Furthermore, as we explained in "Food Is More Than a List of Nutrients," in Chapter 2, fortification of foods with unnatural levels of individual nutrients may have undesirable consequences. We find it disturbing to see that there is even a full-strength juice that is fortified with 100 percent of the U.S. RDA for vitamins A, C, D, E, B_6, B_{12}, thiamin, riboflavin, niacin, biotin, and pantothenic acid in a single cup. Perhaps this is useful for people who wish to take supplements and have trouble swallowing pills, but to think of this as food is misguided. You wouldn't down a handful of vitamin tablets indiscriminately, and any beverage that is equally as potent must be viewed with the same respect.

COLORED FLAVORED WATER DISGUISED AS JUICE

With a more enlightened public these days, artificial coloring is likely to occur only in those beverages that contain no juice at all. No juice at all? Yes, this is possible, even when the image of a fruit appears on the container.

The label on one "breakfast beverage," for example, boasts "a full day's supply of vitamin C," and also informs us on the principal display panel that it "contains no orange juice." Turn the carton around and you will find it is made from

> water, high fructose corn syrup, sugar, citric acid, potassium citrate, modified cornstarch, potassium phosphate, pectin, partially hydrogenated soy oil, vitamin C, natural and artificial flavors, soy protein, and artificial color

What a way to start the day!

LEMONADE

Lemonade is never a full-strength juice, but many consumers are justified in wondering whether there is any real lemon juice in beverages sporting this name. Although the dictionary and the FDA define lemonade as containing some real lemon, just how much may not be clear. Moreover, no lemon juice need be present in order to describe a beverage as "lemon flavored" or to use the phrase "with real lemonade flavor" on the label. You can determine the manufacturer's standards from the ingredients.

ATHLETIC SUPPORTS

Thirst-quenchers intended to replace the fluids and electrolytes lost in perspiration were first promulgated in the form of Gatorade, and more recently have been copied in a more natural juice format. The American College of Sports Medicine contends that these drinks may contain "too many electrolytes."

With heavy perspiration, the body's sodium-fluid ratio is already increased. The athlete's goal, therefore, should be to dilute the extra sodium. This is best accomplished by water—one to three cups prior to heavy exercise and a cup or two every twenty to thirty minutes during prolonged, intense activity. Since sugar slows water absorption into the gut, plain water is best. After exercise, you can replace lost carbohydrates and minerals with a large glass of potassium-rich orange juice or a banana.

Vegetable Juices

Fruit juice may be more popular, but vegetable juices are generally lower in calories and offer a good supply of potassium and vitamin A, along with some iron and other assorted minerals. In the last few years, permission has been granted to fortify tomato juice with vitamin C so that it can compete with other breakfast beverages.

While sodium content may not concern everyone, you might be interested to learn that regular canned or bottled tomato juice and tomato-vegetable blends average 485 milligrams of sodium per 8 ounces, while salt-free counterparts usually contain less than 50 milligrams in an equal volume. A single cup of sauerkraut juice may contribute as much as 1900 milligrams of sodium. Canned carrot juice appears to be unsalted.

Within the last decade, more companies have turned to preparing tomato juice from concentrate where formerly almost all were fresh-packed. The law requires that the phrase "from concentrate" accompany the name if this is the case.

Aseptic Juice Packaging

Probably the most successful new item in the juice department is the aseptic container, exemplified by the soft-sided boxes now being used for beverages. These paperboard cartons, often referred to by one company's tradename "Brik-Pak," are flushed with hydrogen peroxide prior to filling, a process that has been a controversial issue due to Japanese studies that cast this sterilant in an unfavorable light. Some people also worry about the polyethylene plastic coating that lines the box.

Aseptic packaging is still a fairly new concept, and while it has the advantage of being lightweight and easily packed into lunch boxes, we are unsure about its health consequences (see "Wrapping It Up," in Chapter 1).

CARBONATED BEVERAGES

To someone born and raised in the "Pepsi Generation," it is hard to imagine a time when no one drank soda. Of course, it isn't news that soft drinks aren't great for our health. In every 8 ounces of regular soda you get from 5 to 8 teaspoons of sugar, plus acidifying agents ranging from natural fruit acids to phosphoric acid. This combination of acid and sugar is a major contributor to enamel erosion of teeth—this holds true, by the way, for all sweet fruit beverages, including juices (although the problem there is much less severe). Other well-known concerns center on the caffeine, artificial sweeteners, and artificial coloring soda contains.

The Nonfood with the Nonlabel

Today, you can get your soda any way you want it—with caffeine or without, with an abundance of calories or practically none at all, and even with and without sodium. While some soda manufacturers are paring down the calories and adding nutrients and fruit juice to lure the nutrition-conscious, one company actually touts its cola as offering "all the sugar and twice the caffeine" of traditional colas.

Another soda says on its label, "no calories, no sodium and no caffeine." Never has a product declared so boldly what it *didn't* have.

No matter how their formula is manipulated, soft drinks add up to a big nutritional minus and still remain largely a chemical brew: flavors, whether artificial or natural, conveyed in a carrier of ethyl alcohol, glycerin, or propylene glycol, artificial colors, and a long list of acidifiers, buffers, emulsifers, viscosity-producing agents, foaming and antifoaming ingredients, chemical preservatives, and such. Very little of this appears on the label, but what does is disturbing enough.

Diet Soda

Since aspartame, marketed under the name Nutrasweet, is the current sweetener of choice for diet sodas, you should know that despite assurances of safety, serious questions regarding aspartame have arisen. As mentioned in Chapter 31, some of the compounds formed when this synthetic sweetener decomposes are of particular concern. Studies indicate that aspartame is relatively unstable in carbonated soft drinks and storage in a warm environment can accelerate this decomposition. Since most soda is stored before it is consumed, you must worry not only about the effects of aspartame itself, but about its breakdown products as well.

"Natural" Soda

A new kind of soda, presenting itself as a "healthy alternative," is made with only natural coloring and flavoring, no preservatives, and no caffeine. These "natural" sodas do not contain added sodium salts, sugar, or corn syrup, preferring to obtain their sweet taste from fructose and honey. Although an improvement over traditional soda, this does not change the fact that 100 percent of their calories come from some form of concentrated sweetener.

There is also a new category of carbonated drinks made with juice. Manufacturers may promote the fact that their beverages contain 10 to 15 percent natural juice, but we still fault the remaining 85 to 90 percent of the product. We do not think any drink containing added sweetening and acidifers, and possibly caramel coloring, is exemplary.

On the other hand, we do consider the few natural sodas that are devoid of chemical additives and composed solely of sparkling water, fruit juice (or concentrate), and fruit flavors exemplary, as they actually provide real food value along with the bubbles.

Sparkling Supplements

If one soft drink manufacturer manages to make a good show of it, a sugar-free soda that's vitamin-enriched is in store for us. The first of the lot has fifty percent of the recommended daily allowance of vitamin C and 10 percent of the recommendation for several B vitamins. While beverage analysts do not expect this drink to sweep the market initially, they do see a bright future five or ten years down the road. An informed public could prove them wrong (see "Food Is More Than a List of Nutrients," in Chapter 1).

Despite America's current emphasis on calcium, milk has not fared well lately in the marketplace. Now, to reverse the declining trend, milk producers are thinking about taking a tip from the soft drink people and are researching a process for turning skimmed milk into carbonated, flavored dairy drinks. Your bones and teeth may need calcium to grow strong, but they probably will not welcome the opposing effects of the sweetening and phosphates that will undoubtedly be present in these dairy drinks, as they are in other carbonated soft drinks.

Seltzer

Unlike club soda, which may have added sodium salts and sometimes even artificial flavor, seltzer is nothing more than carbonated tap water. For decades it was quite popular in many cities, where it was delivered to people's homes bottled in special glass siphons. Although seltzer in that form has practically disappeared, it resurfaced in the 1970s in conventional soda bottles. We were delighted to see more and more seltzer appear in supermarkets after we demonstrated its usefulness on national television but were amazed when a buyer for a large supermarket chain told us that it had become the fastest moving item in his company's warehouse!

What is so wonderful about seltzer? It allows you to enjoy a carbonated beverage with no drawbacks. By mixing seltzer with juice you can have the pleasure of bubbles combined with the benefits of fruit. It works especially well with the multifruit juices that, in their full-strength form, are often too sweet for many palates. Seltzer can also be a calorie-free beverage, plain or with a piece of fresh lemon, lime, or orange squeezed into it.

Sparkling Water Plus

A new twist are carbonated waters with added fruit essence. Made up of either seltzer or more costly sparkling mineral water and the oil from the fruit skin (called essence), these flavored drink are wonderful alternatives to diet sodas.

Watch out that you are not deceived by brands like Zeltzer Seltzer, Anheuser Busch's look-alike which actually contains refined sweeteners in addition to the flavoring oil.

Sparkling Water Minus

Unfortunately, success has its price and most seltzers and many sparkling mineral waters, which were originally bottled in glass, are now being packaged in plastic. Since all plastics migrate to some degree into the contents, we urge you to avoid plastic containers if you can. Independent beverage distributors often carry these items in glass bottles.

ALCOHOL ANONYMOUS

The techniques employed in creating alcoholic beverages are so complex, and the number of brands on the market so numerous, it is virtually impossible for us to offer any general rule of purchase or specific recommendations. The repeated requests for complete labeling of alcoholic beverages, which is under the auspices of the Treasury Department's Bureau of Alcohol, Tobacco and Firearms (BATF), may one day soon be fulfilled. In 1986, a federal court declared that beer, wine, and alcohol labels must begin to list all ingredients; however, this order has been issued and rescinded before. When we see it, we'll believe it, but even then we're not sure it will be of great value.

After working long, hard hours on this section of the book, we have some understanding of why the BATF maintains that trying to make an informed choice from an ingredient listing "would baffle the average consumer unless they are chemists, physicians, pharmacologists, or toxicologists." There are currently an estimated fifty-two different chemicals approved for beer and seventy additives for wine. We agree consumers may not be able to comprehend the technical terms, but they certainly will be able to contrast a label that says "water, hops, rice, and barley malt" with one that lists dozens of unfamiliar ingredients. Even ingredient labeling, though, will not inform of the vast number of compounds that may be used as "processing aids."

If you wish to drink alcohol that is relatively chemical-free, write to the brewer, vintner, or distiller of your favorite brand and ask what ingredients and processing aids are used. If you don't get a satisfactory answer, try another brand.

Wine

Sodium bisulfite and sulfur dioxide are two additives commonly employed by the wine industry that may cause adverse reactions in some people, especially asthmatics. They are found in almost all domestic and imported wines, although alternative measures do exist. By January, 1988, all wines that contain sulfite residues in excess of 10 parts per million (ppm) will have to warn consumers of the fact on the label. Since normal sulfite levels in wine run between 150 and 200 ppm, you should be seeing some mention of this.

Of course, sulfites are not the only additives in wine. Other less well-known chemicals are used to decolorize the juice, smooth the wine, improve its "bouquet," and preserve it. These are still hidden from the buyer.

While the use of insecticides is not unique to grape-growing, vineyards are heavily and repeatedly sprayed, and residues on the grapes are measurably present and permissible. In 1985, seven American wines were taken off the shelf in Canada because their pesticides levels exceeded Canadian standards of acceptability—not pleasant to contemplate as you relax over dinner sipping your favorite wine.

"Coolers" May Not Be So Cool

To bridge the gap between the soda set and the wine drinkers, coolers were introduced in 1980 and have since been described as "one of the hottest new consumer items in years." Seagrams advertises their cooler as "a splash of cool clear white wine with crisp natural citrus flavor." Made up of wine, fruit juice, sweeteners, and carbonation, most coolers have an alcohol content that ranges from 3 to 7 percent, making them more potent than most beers.

Note, too, that the purpose of coolers is not to reduce alcohol consumption. They are marketed to portray wine as a recreational beverage and attract the attention of the nondrinker with the promise of the taste of juice.

De-Alcoholized Wine

While some of the nonalcoholic beverages bottled to look like wine or sparkling hard cider are really just grape or apple juice in a different package, others are produced in the traditional manner but are de-alcoholized by heat or pressure prior to bottling; these look, feel, and taste like their former alcoholic selves. In fact, most still retain a faint trace of alcohol, or up to 0.5 percent, plus all the additives including the sulfites and the sorbic acid preservatives.

Note: On one front, de-alcoholized products may help reduce alcohol abuse, but on another they may have the negative effect of gradually getting those who do not normally enjoy alcohol to accept its taste in a veiled form. Former nondrinkers may actually begin to add alcohol back into their diets. Moreover, many of these beverages are aimed at a young market and reinforce the image that it's cool to have a drink in your hand. This sets up a milieu which makes it easy for teens to see drinking as socially acceptable when they reach some magic legal age. This is yet another reason to be selective about how you use these beverages, if indeed you are not already deterred by their chemical content.

A Hundred Bottles of Beer . . .

For the beer drinker, who may be feeling a bit smug right now, we hasten to inform you that water, malt, rice, barley, corn, hops, and yeast may not be all that are in your favorite brew. We received an inkling of this in 1978, when nitrosamines, the carcinogens associated with bacon and hot dogs, started showing up in beer. The FDA acted swiftly (for once) in setting maximum levels and most brewers were just as quick to comply. (One method of reducing nitrosamine levels, which fortunately does not appear to be widely used, is adding sulfur to the malt during the drying stage—bad news for those sensitive to sulfites.)

Popular additives and processing aids used in beer are geared toward "water correction," "stabilizing the foam," "chill proofing" and filtering the brew so it does not appear cloudy in the glass, protecting the color and flavor against deterioration by oxygen, trapping the charged ions that can cause the beer to gush violently when the container is opened, and preservation (although pasteurization is more common for this purpose than chemicals).

ALCOHOL CONTENT

Since April, 1986, malt beverages labeled "nonalcoholic" or "alcohol-free" must show either on the label or in their advertising that the product contains less than 0.5 percent alcohol. This is helpful to those trying to avoid alcohol. Unfortunately such information is not yet available to the regular beer drinker trying to monitor alcohol intake since, unless the law changes, the actual alcohol content is not permitted to be given on beer labels.

To qualify as *beer,* federal law requires a minimum of 0.5 percent alcohol and no maximum. Some states have higher minimums and upper limits of 5 to 8 percent. *Low-alcohol* beer contains less than 2 percent. Most domestic beer is about 3.5 to 4.5 percent. *Malt liquor* and *ale,* including *porter* and *stout,* approach 5 or 6 percent. It is unlikely that you will find any of these figures on the label.

The terms *malt beverage, cereal beverage,* or *near beer* are used to designate an alcohol content below 0.5 percent. In addition, these beverages must be labeled "nonalcoholic" when there is some but less than 0.5 percent alcohol, and "alcohol-free" if there is no measurable alcohol content.

With no standard definition, *light* beers are not necessarily lower in calories or alcohol than other beers. The BATF has been petitioned to set an upper calorie limit for light beers, but under the present prevailing laws one can only assume they have fewer calories than regular beer of the same brand. Although most light beers also have a reduced alcohol content (2.75 to 3.2 percent), some brands only have fewer calories. At least light beers now reveal their calorie content, but since regular beers do not, comparisons are difficult to make. As a general rule, a light beer will contain about one-third fewer calories than the regular version produced by the same brewer. But with a range of 70 to 135 calories per 12-ounce serving, some are still higher than their "unlightened" competition.

COFFEE

The coffee industry reports it is engaged in a "generic advertising campaign designed to change the image of coffee . . . so that it will appeal to more young people and appear better suited to modern life-styles." Promotion will be geared "to encourage consumption out of the home, especially in the workplace and on university campuses."

In one popular commercial the scene opens with two lovers on a romantic moonlit balcony. They look longingly into each other's eyes. Finally he/she speaks: "Let's have a cup of coffee." While it seems absurd to associate coffee with such quiet, intimate moments, we recognize that caffeine's transient hyperactive effects are not felt by everyone. Of course, coffee isn't the only culprit either, but as you can see from the table below, it measures well above most other sources of caffeine. Furthermore, the great variation in caffeine content among coffees leads us to conclude that caffeine labeling would be very useful.

THE CAFFEINE IN YOUR CUP*

Beverage (5 ounces)	Caffeine (milligrams)
Drip coffee	60 to 180
Perked coffee	40 to 170
Instant coffee	30 to 120
Leaf Tea, imported brands	25 to 110
Leaf Tea, domestic brands	20 to 90
Sodas	12 to 25
Cocoa	2 to 20

*Sources: The FDA's Food Additive Chemistry Evaluation Branch and the Institute of Food Technology (based on data from the National Soft Drink Association).

Heavy caffeine consumers may also be courting some long-term risks. Recent studies show coffee consumption elevates total serum cholesterol and triglyceride levels and may reduce high density lipoproteins (HDLs), the cholesterol factor thought to have a heart-protecting effect. Since caffeine stimulates stomach acid secretions, some feel it may cause or aggravate peptic ulcers. There is a suspicion, too, that caffeine may promote fibrocystic (painful, noncancerous) lumps in the breast. Studies linking caffeine to birth defects have been highly controversial but have caused enough concern among FDA scientists that they have issued a warning to pregnant women. If this weren't enough, coffee is included in a list of foods (along with tea) that interfere with iron absorption.

Coffee With Less Kick

Coffee may be marketed to the connoisseur by country of origin and by type of roast, but botanically there are only two species marketed commercially: arabica and robusta. Robusta is faster fruiting, grows at lower elevations, is more tolerant of heat and cold, is resistant to disease, and gives higher yields. As a result, it is usually less expensive. Arabica is considered to be of finer flavor, body, and aroma, and contains only half as much caffeine. Thus, if you are searching for a coffee naturally low in caffeine, arabica may be the answer.

Another way to get less caffeine in your coffee cup is to buy a commercial coffee-chickory blend. In the southern United States, they are quite common for both brewed and instant preparation; elsewhere, you may find only the one instant brand, Sunrise, that is distributed nationwide. Unfortunately, the ratio of chickory to coffee is rarely revealed, so it is impossible to estimate how much you've reduced the caffeine load, but it is certainly not true that you can "enjoy as many cups as you want all day," as this national brand advertises on its label. More likely, only about a third of the coffee will be replaced with roasted chickory and you can expect to get just under 40 milligrams of caffeine per serving.

Decaffeination

For coffee with just about no caffeine there is "decaf." Today, virtually every major coffee manufacturer offers a brand of decaffeinated coffee.

A promising development in decaffeination are the new techniques for removing caffeine without contaminating the coffee. At present, the most common method of caffeine extraction uses a chemical solvent, and the story of these solvents is enough to make you jittery. In the mid-1970s, after years of use in decaffeination, the solvent tricholoroethylene (TCE) was discovered to cause liver cancer in mice. TCE was never officially banned, but most processors voluntarily replaced it with methylene chloride, the active ingredient in paint remover. Despite early reassurances as to its safety, after widespread use for about six years, methylene chloride was also declared to be carcinogenic. It, too, has not been banned and continues to be used by several companies.

But the industry has now discovered another alternative: ethyl acetate. This substance, found in some fruits as well as in the coffee bean itself, breaks down to form supposedly harmless alcohol and acetic acid. There is no way of telling which solvent is being used unless the manufacturer chooses to inform you. If some allusion to a natural solvent is made, it is probably ethyl acetate.

Coffee drinkers who are skeptical about all these substances do have another option: water-process decaffeination. With so much secrecy about this technique both here and abroad, it is difficult to determine if you are getting anything more (or perhaps in this case we should say less) for your money, since two types of water process exist. One, more accurately described as "steam process," still utilizes chemicals to extract the caffeine in consort with steaming. In the other, known as the "Swiss water process," the beans are said to never come in contact with any chemicals.

Acid Indigestion

Removing caffeine may not solve all your coffee complaints. There still appears to be an unidentified compound in coffee that causes stomach acid secretion. Paradoxically, the lighter the roast, the more acidic the coffee; thus, French roast and espresso, which most people regard as strong coffees, actually cause less discomfort than what is known as "city" or American roast coffee.

The Circle of Poison Around Your Coffee Cup

All the concern about the dangers of caffeine and the chemical residues in decaffeinated coffee has obscured what may be an even greater health hazard—that is, the pesticide residues. Coffee is raised almost exclusively outside the United States in countries where agricultural chemicals that are banned here are still widely used. (Many are actually purchased from American firms.) What kind of protection does our system provide if we are allowed to import what we prohibit domestically? And what kind of people sell to others what they deem dangerous to themselves?

In the Exemplary Brands section we list those brands of coffee that we know to be organically grown.

Storage

All coffee keeps best in a moisture-proof container in a cool environment such as the refrigerator or freezer.

COFFEE SUBSTITUTES

Coffee substitutes are beverages that are reminiscent of coffee, with a rich brown color and more full-bodied taste and aroma than tea. They vary in their makeup, but most are composed of some blend of chickory root, figs, barley, wheat, carob, beet root, rye, dahlia tubers, acorns, molasses, and similar innocuous ingredients. Since some are more successful than others in meeting expectations, if you are disappointed by one, it is worth your while to sample another.

Most coffee substitutes are of the instant variety, but there are a few brands ground for drip filters that can be brewed alone or blended in your pot with coffee. Plain roasted chickory can be similarly employed.

Note: We have encountered at least one product that may not be so benign. It contains the herb cascara sagrada, a potent laxative. If you come across a product with an ingredient you do not recognize, be sure to ask about it and obtain an answer that satisfies you before you buy.

TEA

Leaf Tea

There is some good news and some bad news about tea. For centuries, tea has been prescribed as an antidote for everything from depression (according to the British) to the plague (Japanese lab tests have shown green tea inhibits the growth of cholera, typhoid, and dysentery bacteria). Closer to home, tea has been said to fight tooth decay, and since it is one of the few plants that absorbs fluoride from the soil it grows in, it may also help strengthen bones against osteoporosis. Tea is a fair source of other minerals as well, but one of its major drawbacks may be its binding effect on iron, reducing absorption of this essential nutrient.

Dried, rolled, untreated tea leaves are marketed as *green tea*. When the leaves are partially aged they are known as *oolong,* while longer aging turns out common *black tea.* During the aging process caffeine develops, so that while green tea is nearly caffeine-free, black tea can contain significant amounts. While oolong and black tea are widely found in food stores, green tea is more of a specialty item, but available wherever Oriental products are sold.

Most of the descriptive phrases that accompany tea are a reference to size, not, as in former days, quality. *Suchong* refers to any large-leaf black tea. *Orange pekoe* no longer bears any trace of scented orange blossoms; the term simply means that the leaf is larger than plain pekoe or broken orange pekoe. Other names like Earl Grey, Russian, Caravan, English, or Irish Breakfast are more or less fanciful, although some have become associated with the addition of flowers, scents, and smoky overtones. Many tea afficionados judge quality by country of origin, but by and large, choice is a matter of personal taste.

DECAFFEINATED TEA

For tea drinkers troubled by caffeine, a decaffeinated product has been developed. While the method is more complicated than that used with coffee, right now the only approved chemical solvent for removing the caffeine from tea is ethyl acetate (see "Decaffeination," page 478). No standards have been set for the amount of chemical residue permitted. One company claims that the small amount of solvent in the tea will vaporize when the leaves come in contact with boiling water, but interestingly, in the case of methylene chloride the tests that produced cancer in animals used inhalation as the principal mode of exposure.

Herb Tea

Ten years ago, herb teas were a rarity outside the natural food store. Today, there is hardly a food store in the country that doesn't offer a choice of several herbal blends that sport such aromatics as orange blossoms, peppermint leaves, hibiscus, lemon grass, lemon verbena, apples, alfalfa, comfrey, cinnamon bark, licorice root, ginseng, fennel, orange peel, cardamom, and more. Many people are now making iced herbal teas their summer beverage.

Herb teas, with the exception of those containing the herb maté, are caffeine-free. While it has been against the law to make medical claims for food, many herbs are potent medicinals and many herb teas certainly convey the idea that they are designed with a specific purpose in mind (e.g., Lively Daytime, Tranquil Evening, Fasting Tea, Smooth Move, Tummy Mint, Herbal Long Life). Despite media attention to the toxicity of some herbs, all the commonly marketed herbal teas are considered perfectly safe. People with ragweed allergy, however, may find certain floral components like chamomile or linden flowers can precipitate allergic reactions. At least once you are aware of this, the label, which reveals all ingredients, enables you to avoid them.

In reviewing an herbal beverage, also check the label for the following unnecessary ingredients: cornstarch, artificial flavor (found in some fruit-flavored blends), and sugar (the first ingredient in one popular Swiss herb beverage found in almost every natural food store).

Bulk Tea Versus Tea Bags

One other point to consider in reference to both leaf and herb teas is how they are packaged. To most people, tea means tea bags but, of course, tea can be purchased loose like coffee. Loose tea generally has a better flavor because it is in the leaf form, as opposed to the fine particles known as "dust" that go into the tea bag to facilitate brewing.

Although there is not enough information available to render an adverse judgment, another consideration in choosing loose tea over tea bags is the avoidance of materials used in tea bag construction, including the bleaches and dyes in the paper, the heat sealant, and the metal used to attach the string. Some more ecologically minded companies like Traditional Medicinals use only natural hemp fiber bags, no chemical sealants, and 100 percent cotton strings, but most simply ignore the issue. If you have any reservations, pick up a stainless steel, ceramic, glass, or bamboo tea strainer (we don't recommend any other metals or plastic mesh) and stick with bulk tea.

Storage

While the typical tea bag dunker may not notice it, tea does get stale, a process that is accelerated by heat, light, air, and humidity. To preserve its flavor, store tea in an airtight container at room temperature, away from the stove or other heat source. With proper care, black tea will maintain its quality as long as two years, green and oolong for about half that time. Scented teas will begin to go stale after about six months.

Herbal teas, too, can become musty and their fragrance will diminish if not consumed within a reasonable time. To ensure optimum flavor, try to purchase only as much as you can drink in a six-month period.

Instant Tea

Instant tea, often intended for making iced tea, comes in regular and herbal blends. In addition to the finely ground tea leaves that are the basis of the beverage, the flavored brands contain malto dextrin to protect the flavor, and they may derive additional impact from citric acid, malic acid, artificial color and flavor, caramel color, vegetable oil, an anticaking agent, and the preservative BHA. Don't be seduced by the proud claim of "natural flavor" that instant tea manufacturers accentuate on the label. The flavor may be natural, but not everything else is.

HOT COCOA

If you plan to serve a hot beverage of this type, you have agreed to accept some form of concentrated sweetener. Even those that are promoted as sugar-free are sweetened in some manner, while those that are unsweetened call for sweetening to be added by the cook. At least in the latter case, you can maintain control over how sweet the beverage will be.

Cocoa (and chocolate) contain theobromine, a caffeine-related chemical found in the cocoa bean. Keep this in mind when you serve hot cocoa to kids.

When you buy cocoa, select plain rather than "Dutched" or Dutch process cocoa. This cocoa isn't made, as you might think, from special chocolate imported from Holland; Dutch is a euphemism for "treated with alkali."

Another chemical that can compromise the quality of cocoa is dioctyl sodium sulfosuccinate, added to make the dry powder blend more readily when added to a liquid. This compound is used medically as a stool softener, and results of the few tests conducted in animals show it can cause gastrointenstinal irritation and suppress weight gain. When cocoa is treated with this agent, it is supposed to be indicated on the label.

After plain unsweetened cocoa, the simplest cocoa mixes contain sweetening (usually sugar and dextrose), cocoa, lecithin (an emulsifier extracted from a natural food source, generally soybeans), and vanillin (an artificial vanilla flavor). Some also contain salt. While we do not particularly recommend such products, when compared with more contrived mixes containing whey, partially hydrogenated coconut oil, artificial flavor, carboxymethyl cellulose, sodium silico aluminate, mono- and digylcerides, bipotassium phosphate, guar gum, cellulose gum, and such, they seem almost innocent.

CAROB DRINKS

Those who wish to avoid chocolate may find carob a suitable alternative to cocoa, for it is free of stimulants. Note that most of the prepared beverage powders and syrups based on carob are also sweetened, although some take advantage of less processed sweeteners like malted barley.

Just because it is made with carob doesn't mean a product is above criticism. We do not recommend any drink mixes that contain soy protein isolates, xanthan gum, or carrageenan because all these highly refined ingredients have already been overly imposed on our diets by food processors and they are not as "natural" as they are often represented to be.

RECOMMENDATIONS

STILL WATER

General Rule of Purchase: Look for mineral and spring waters in glass bottles. Since there are no standards of purity or regulations as to mineral content, all brands must be considered similar. Do not buy distilled water for drinking.

CARBONATED WATER

General Rule of Purchase: Look for sparkling mineral waters or seltzer bottled in glass (listed below), either plain or flavored with fruit oils or essence. Avoid beverages that appear to be flavored seltzers but have sweeteners added.

Exemplary Brands

A Santé Flavored Mineral Waters
Arrowhead Sparkling Mountain Spring Water
Calistoga Sparkling Mineral Water
Cap Ten Pure Artesian Mineral Waters with Natural Flavor
Costa Seltzer
Crystal Geyser Sparkling Mineral Water, with Flavor
Evian
Good Health Seltzer
Hawaiian Plain, Flavored Pure Sparkling Artesian Waters
Kentucky Bubbling Water

Perrier, with a Twist
Syfo Seltzer Water, with Flavor
Mendocino Brand Flavored Sparkling Waters
Montclair Sparkling Natural Spring Water
Mountain Valley Water
Nehi Plain, Flavored Seltzers
Poland Spring Natural Carbonated Spring Water, with Essence
Ramlösa Sparkling Mineral Water
San Pellegrino Sparkling Natural Spring Water
Saratoga Mineral Water
Val's Naturally Sparkling Mineral Water

JUICE

General Rule of Purchase: Look for unsweetened juices. All ingredients are on the label, although the use of juice concentrates may not be specified. Look for a full-strength juice over prediluted juice from concentrate when noted. Orange, grapefruit, pineapple, and tomato juices will always inform you when concentrate is employed. Look for unsweetened frozen concentrate for home dilution. Avoid diluted juice-drinks, drinks, ades, punches, and nectars.

In selecting a juice you may also want to take its packaging into consideration. Glass is preferred, as there is no chance of chemical migration.

Exemplary Brands _____

Fresh-Pressed Juice

Adwalla
Cascadian Farm Carrot[1]
Ferraro's

Govinda's
Shiloh Farms Carrot
Sunny Days Carrot, Celery

Orange/Grapefruit Juice

Choose fresh-squeezed juice if you have the opportunity. Second choice is unsweetened frozen concentrate. Unsweetened canned citrus juice and chilled pasteurized juice (unsweetened) are better choices than prediluted juice from concentrate. All brands are similar.

Apple Juice

Look for unsweetened, unfiltered juice. Buy cider when in season, but be sure to avoid any with preservatives.

Alpha Beta Unfiltered
Apple and Eve
Balanced Natural Old Fashioned
Bonnie Hubbard Unfiltered
Coop Unfiltered
Country Pure Coarse Unfiltered
Eden
Food Club Natural Style
Giant Food Country Style
Golden Acres Biologically Grown[1]
Heinke's Organic[1]
Hi Country Naturally Pressed
Knudsen Organic[1]
Kroger Natural Unfiltered
Lakewood

Lincoln 100% Natural Unfiltered
Lucky Leaf Unfiltered
Martinelli Old Fashioned Unfiltered
McCutcheon's Unfiltered
Mr. Natural[1]
My–Te–Fine Unfiltered
NEOPC Natural
Red Cheek
Seneca Natural Style
The Cherry Tree Unfiltered
Tree Top Old Fashioned
Tree of Life East Coast
Westbrae Natural, Organic[1]
White House Natural Plus
Whole Foods Pure Unfiltered

Grape Juice

Look for those that are unsweetened; except for organic juices (listed below), which may be available at the natural food store, all brands are similar.

Cappelluti Organic[1]
Chater's[1]
Four Chimneys[1]

Jory Farms Zinfindel[1]
Knudsen Organic[1]

Pineapple Juice

Look for unsweetened frozen concentrate or unsweetened juice labeled "pineapple juice" as opposed to "pineapple juice from concentrate." Most are enriched with ascorbic acid (vitamin C) and all brands are similar.

Prune Juice

Most brands are unsweetened and contain added vitamin C. There is no difference between brands, unless you can buy an organic version (listed below).

Morning Glory[1]

Mixed Fruit Juice and Other Fruit Beverages

Look for unsweetened varieties. Note that mixed fruit juices will probably contain some concentrate. Check the label of those with coconut if you wish to avoid added stabilizers.

After the Fall
Apple and Eve Apple Cranberry, Apple Grape, Apple Cherry, Raspberry Cranberry, Cranberry Grape
Campbell's Juice Works
Cherefresh Unsweetened Cherry
Coop Cranberry, Apple Raspberry, Grape Cranberry Cocktail
Country Pure Apple Cranberry, Apple Strawberry, Apple Boysenberry, Banana Bonanza, Orange Strawberry, Pineapple Orange
Eden Apple Blends, Cherry
Fred Meyer Cherry Cider, Apple Cranberry, Northwest Cherry Blend, Papaya Nectar, Strawberry Colada
Hansen's
Health Aid
Health Mate
Health Valley Apple Strawberry
Healthway
Heinke
Heinke's Organic Pear[1]

Indian Summer Apple Blends
Knudsen
L&A
Lakewood
Mission San Juan
Mott's Apple Blends
Mrs. Gooch's Cranberry Crush
New Life Black Cherry, Plum and Prune
Nice and Natural
Norganic Cranberry, Creamed Papaya
Purity
Red Cheek Apple Grape
Snapple
Speas Farm 100% Fruit Punch, Apple Blends
The Cherry Tree Apple Blends
Tree Top Fruit and Berry, Fruit and Apple, Fruit and Grape, Fruit and Citrus
Tree of Life Apple Blends
Welch's Orchard Blends
Westbrae
White House Apple Cherry
Winter Hill

Tomato Juice and Tomato Blends

Look for fresh-packed (preferred) or from concentrate, with or without added vitamin C. Most often salt is added. We list only those that are salt-free.

Coop Unsalted Vegetable
Diet Delight No Salt Added Tomato
Featherweight No Salt Added Tomato
Hunt's No Salt Added All Natural Tomato
Jewel No Salt Added Tomato

Knudsen Low Sodium Very Veggie
My–Te–Fine No Salt Tomato
Nutridiet Tomato, Vegetable Juice Cocktail
V–8 Salt Free

Other Vegetable Juices

Biocarrotin,[1] Biorandin[1]
Biotta Juices with Cultured Whey[1]
Bush's Kraut Juice
Diamond A Carrot

Eveready Carrot
Hain Pure California Carrot
Jack and the Beanstalk Carrot
Steinfeld's Sauerkraut

SODAS

General Rule of Purchase: For soda, mix an exemplary juice with seltzer or sparkling mineral water, or look for one of the rare bottled sodas made with just juice and sparkling water. Avoid all added concentrated sweeteners, artificial sweeteners, acidifiers, phosphate buffers, artificial coloring and flavoring, preservatives, and other sundry additives.

Exemplary Brands

Apenglow Virginia Sparkling Cider
Bel Normande Sparkling Cider
Bertolino's Sparkling Cider
Chamay Sparkling Cider, Red Grape Juice
Franche
Fruitzer Sparkling Fruit Juices
Hansen's Natural Cidre
Hawaiian Sodas

Health Valley Coolers
Il Hwa Ginseng Up Natural Juice Sodas
Indian Valley Sparkling Juices
Knudsen Spritzers, Sparkling Juices
Lake Wood Soda, Sparkling Juices
Martinelli's Sparkling Cider
Napa Natural Soda
Summer Song Sparkling Juices

COFFEE

General Rule of Purchase: Look for coffees made with arabica beans as they contain less caffeine than those with robusta; French roast and espresso are the least acidic. With the exception of those that are organically grown (listed below) all brands are similar.

Decaffeinated coffee may contain chemical residues. Give preference to "Swiss water processing." Coffee decaffeinated with ethyl acetate is not suspect at present, but avoid brands using methyl chloride. Note that any reference to the method employed is voluntary.

Exemplary Brands

Organic

Cafe Altura[1]

Cafe Tierra[1]

Decaffeinated

Bow Mills Decaffeinated
Nescafe Decaf
Rombouts

Sanka Brand
Taster's Choice Decaffeinated
White House Decaffeinated

COFFEE SUBSTITUTES

General Rule of Purchase: Look for those composed of a blend of different roasted cereal grains, roots, and perhaps molasses and herbs.

Exemplary Brands

Bambu Instant, Brewable
Cafe Lub
Cafix
Coffee Partner Chickory
Dacopa
Fini Reform Swiss Instant Beverage
Golden Harvest Instant Mountain Roast
Inka

Kafree Roma
Lima Yannah-Instant[1]
Pero
Pioneer Instant Swiss Coffee Substitute
Postum
Sipp
Wilson's Heritage Non Coffee Beverage

LEAF TEA

General Rule of Purchase: Green tea is almost caffeine-free, oolong contains some caffeine, and black tea has the most, though still less than most coffees. Green tea is usually not available in supermarkets, so look for it in a natural food store or Oriental market. All brands of unflavored tea are similar.

For quality, loose tea is preferable to tea bags (and also does not introduce the non-tea elements found in the tea-bag packaging). Avoid presweetened teas, aromatic teas containing artificial flavoring, and decaffeinated tea which may contain chemical residues.

HERB TEA

General Rule of Purchase: All ingredients are on the label. Avoid blends that contain sweetening, cornstarch, and artificial flavor. Note that maté contains caffeine and that people with allergies may have problems with certain floral ingredients. Again, loose tea may be preferable to tea bags.

COCOA/CAROB

General Rule of Purchase: Look for unsweetened brands or those sweetened with barley malt. Look for cocoa that is not processed with alkali ("dutched"). Avoid gum thickeners, caramel color, artificial flavor, partially hydrogenated oils, mono- and diglycerides, soy protein isolates and similar additives; their presence will be stated on the label.

Exemplary Brands

CaraCoa Carob Powder
Chatfield's Carob and Compliments Carob
   Powder

Hershey's Cocoa
Martin's Carob Powder

[1]Organic

Chapter 37

Condiments and Other Accessories

Sometimes it's not the main dish but the garnish that you add to the plate that really makes a meal appetizing. Today, a great variety of prepared relishes, pickled salads, peppers, olives, chutneys, and such, packed with fine fresh vegetables and spices and made the way you would at home, adorn the market shelves. An assortment of these condiments in your pantry will help make a salad more interesting, fill out a meal, or come in handy for spur-of-the-moment entertaining. They can remain unopened for months; once opened though, they must be stored in the refrigerator, where they will keep beautifully without the chemical preservatives the food industry is so fond of adding.

In these items, you will almost always have to put up with salt or sugar, and generally in large amounts, but at least these ingredients serve an understandable purpose—preservation.

PICKLES

The pickle, America's famous delicatessen specialty, is found more often today in a jar than in the old-fashioned pickle barrel. If you do select your pickles from the barrel, the addition of alum, a relatively nontoxic aluminum-based salt used as a firming agent, will be the only unfortunate processing it has been subjected to.

Selecting jarred pickles is a different story. It can take a lot of digging to ferret out a brand that does not make use of a polysorbate emulsifier to keep the flavoring oils evenly distributed, calcium chloride to maintain texture, xantham gum to impart body to the liquid, yellow dye, and a benzoate preservative (all of which will be listed). Not on the label are chemical "processing aids" to retard foam formation.

Many of the "no salt added" pickles compensate for the loss of flavor by adding a sweetener such as corn syrup, a practice we do not condone. Of course, all sweet pickles will have a concentrated sweetener of some sort.

PICKLED VEGETABLES

Pickled vegetables and relishes liven up antipasto platters, sandwiches, cold meats, cheese, bean burgers, and the like. Many companies are inconsistent in their offerings—some are exemplary and others dismal—so rely on the list of ingredients, not the brand name, as guarantee of purity. Products made by small-scale manufacturers and distributed within a limited locale may provide additional choices.

In sweet relishes, honey is the sweetener we prefer, but if sugar or corn syrup is the only processed ingredient in a store-bought variety, you will still have a better product than most.

PEPPERS

Pickled Peppers

Pickled peppers, both sweet and hot (sometimes called pepperoncini), frequently come packed in jars with vinegar and seasonings only. The ingredient list will inform you when unnecessary stabilizers (polysorbates are particularly widespread offenders here), sulfites, and preservatives are added.

Pimientos

The sweet roasted pimiento, another form of pepper, is available in every market. Acceptable brands contain nothing more than red peppers (preferably described as "flame roasted"), water, salt, and citric acid. Most conform to this formula, but every so often a brand with sweetening shows up, so be sure to check the ingredients to avoid this unnecessary addition.

OLIVES

In the Mediterranean countries, where olives are practically a dietary staple, the fresh olive is immersed in a saltwater bath that is changed daily until the olive is soft, dark, and ready to be savored. This is the procedure that is followed for the olives marketed fresh as Greek or salt-cured. Sometimes these olives are packed into jars with brine for long-term storage. Benzoate preservatives are not necessary, but some companies add them anyway. Remember, the word "brine" describes a saltwater solution, so even though salt may not be stated on the label, it is in the jar. Next to the fresh, these brine-packed olives are the most authentic and flavorful.

Canned Olives

To prepare canned olives, a short-cut is employed that relies on the use of lye, rather than time, to destroy the inherent bitter taste of the olive and turn it into a desirable food. Since it is considered a processing step, this lye treatment is kept a secret from the label reader.

Olives prepared in this manner are relatively mild tasting. Since they have not been allowed to ferment naturally, they must be preserved to prevent spoilage. While canning solves this problem, it further diminishes the flavor. Indeed, the ubiquitous inclusion of salt accounts for practically the only distinguishable taste.

Three types of canned olives are available: green-ripe olives, ripe black olives, and tree-ripened or home-cured olives (which are bronze in color). The black olives are dipped in ferrous gluconate to fix their color. This harmless iron salt is indicated on the label.

Processed Green Olives

Green "cocktail" olives are prepared by the direct addition of lactic acid rather than traditional fermentation. These olives, which come packed in jars, have a somewhat more developed flavor than the canned variety.

Green olives that are pitted and stuffed usually have more than just bright red pimientos inside. To reduce the laborious task of hand stuffing, a puree of pimento thickened with alginates and gums allows machines to do the job. The result is a more uniform, albeit bland product, with less waste. Sorbate preservatives are often added. All these additives show up on the label.

Olive Salad

Olives may be premixed with peppers, capers, and such and marinated in an oil and vinegar dressing for an appetizer salad. There are several high-quality examples on the market devoid of gums, processed sweeteners, coloring agents, sulfites, and preservatives.

SUN-DRIED TOMATOES

This imported delicacy comes packed in oil with seasonings. Due to its high price, this is a condiment you will probably want to use sparingly, and it's just as well because it is usually highly salted. Small amounts will add flavor and interest to pasta sauces and fillings, pizza toppings, sandwiches, and marinated antipasto salads.

We have found that many of the imported varieties do not contain an English-language version of their ingredients. This is in violation of the law and if you do not read Italian, you may have trouble deciphering the kind of oil or seasonings used. At least we have not yet come across any which appear to have chemical additives.

ARTICHOKES

Canned artichoke hearts are a common supermarket item and all brands are similar, containing the vegetable plus water, salt, and citric acid.

Artichoke hearts in jars and marinated artichoke salads are not all alike, however; some add only vinegar, oil, and seasonings to the above, while others demean their product with dextrose. Another common ingredient is erythorbic acid, a laboratory-synthesized form of ascorbic acid which has no vitamin C value for humans.

CAPERS

This delicate little vegetable, which is actually an unopened flower bud from a Mediterranean shrub, comes packed in a jar with vinegar and/or water and salt. Just a few go a long way to glamorize salads and vegetable platters.

SWEET ACCOUTREMENTS

Chutney, the sweet and spicy relish that traditionally accompanies Indian food, and duck sauce, used to round out a Chinese meal, can often be purchased ready-made and additive-free if you are willing to accept refined sugars. A trip to the natural food store might yield a honey- or fruit-sweetened option.

Cranberry sauce sweetened with honey, maple syrup, or fruit juice concentrate rather than sugar and corn sweeteners is also a possibility in some natural food markets.

MISCELLANEOUS CONDIMENTS

This catch-all category includes a variety of prepared condiments: caponata, an eggplant-tomato mélange that is delicious in salade Niçoise and antipastos, and on hero sandwiches; tiny eggplants and grape leaves ready for stuffing or already stuffed with seasoned rice; antipasto salads in which tuna, eggplant, cauliflower, artichoke, pepper, and similar vegetables are dressed and enhanced with anchovies and olives.

A more unusual offering which may intrigue some adventurous shoppers is *natto*. This is a fermented soybean preparation of Japanese origin with a strong, cheeselike flavor and sticky, threadlike consistency. It is traditionally used to garnish soba dishes and is widely available in Oriental markets and natural food stores. Natto may not be appreciated by the uninitiated because of its unfamiliar taste and texture.

See also Chapter 37 for other accessories not covered in this chapter.

CATSUP

Catsup (also ketchup or catchup) starts with a tomato base to which vinegar, a nutritive sweetener, salt, spices, flavorings, onion, and garlic are added. No artificial color or flavor or preservatives are permitted. Most brands are similar, with the exception of those that are salt-free, replace the usual sugar and corn syrup with honey, or leave out the sweetening entirely. (Unsweetened varieties usually have 2½ to 3 tablespoons less sugar per half cup.)

We have been using unsalted catsup for years and to our knowledge no one notices any difference. There is a definite distinction, though, when you compute the sodium levels. Standard catsup has approximately 160 milligrams of sodium per tablespoon; "no salt added" catsup has only half this amount, or on average 70 milligrams of sodium per tablespoon.

CHILI SAUCE

Chili sauce is catsup to which chopped onions, peppers, green tomatoes, celery, and pickle relish have been added. It can be judged by the same standards as catsup.

MUSTARD

These days the sales of mustard are as hot as its taste and the choices are so vast we have barely been able to scratch the surface in our travels. No longer is the yellow ballpark mustard, or even the once-sophisticated Dijon sufficient. With more than 300 mustards currently being manufactured, there certainly seems to be no reason to settle for one burdened with such misguided ingredients as wheat flour, vegetable oil, sugar, propylene glycol alginate, preservatives, or cheap synthetic acidifiers like tartaric and citric acids. All ingredients are on the label and they need not be more than mustard seeds, vinegar, salt, and spices. Specialty mustards may have additional natural flavorings like wine, miso, sherry, peppercorns, hot pepper, garlic, shallots, horseradish, and such.

One perhaps unfamiliar ingredient that often appears on the label is turmeric; this is not a chemical, but a perfectly acceptable spice added to highlight the yellow hue.

HORSERADISH

Horseradish, a plant grown for its pungent root, can be purchased fresh for grating into sauces for flavoring (see Chapter 38 for buying guidelines). The most common form, however, comes in a jar, grated, salted, and mixed with vinegar and occasionally beet juice for color. Nothing else need be added to retain its characteristic sharp flavor; nonetheless a few manufacturers add sodium benzoate and sodium bisulfite preservatives (indicated on the label).

SPICY AND SWEET GARNISHING AND DIPPING SAUCES

Several garnishing sauces such as mustard sauce, plum sauce, barbecue sauce, cocktail sauce, tartar sauce, sweet dessert toppings, and a few more exotic offerings come in configurations worthy of both praise and scorn. Added sweetening should be the only concession you need make.

RECOMMENDATIONS

General Rule of Purchase: All ingredients appear on the label. Many of these items are highly salted. Sweeteners are extraneous in some, essential to others. Where sweetness is the predominant flavor, an unrefined sweetener is preferred. However, if a product is otherwise well conceived, you may be willing to accept one.

Avoid products with EDTA, sodium bisulfite, sodium benzoate or benzoic acid and potassium sorbate preservatives, polysorbates, modified starch, vegetable gums, MSG, hydrolyzed vegetable protein, disodium guanylate and inosinate, and caramel or artificial color.

Note: Since our research began, labeling laws regarding sulfites became more stringent. Be sure to verify in the ingredient list that the Exemplary Brands are still devoid of sulfites, especially the pickled vegetables and peppers.

Exemplary Brands

Pickles

Au Vinaigre Cornichons
Cascadian Farms Kosher Dills,[1] Less Salt[1]
Cosmic Cukes
Felix Dill
Granite Falls Dill
Howard's Sweet Mustard[3]
John Wood
Krakus Polish Dill[3]

Kuhne Gerkins[3]
Manz Fresh Cucumber[3]
Nalley Fresh Kosher, Banquet Dills
Pickle Eater's Pookie Size, Spears, Barrel Cured, Whole Dills, No Salt Kosher Dills, Chips with Honey
Pure and Simple
Westbrae Home Style Dill, Lo Salt

Pickled Vegetables

Bell's Pickled Cauliflower
Braswell's Artichoke Pickles[3]
Cento Capri Olive Appetizer
Cisa Porcini Mushrooms
Dell' Alpe Marinated Mushrooms, Sliced Eggplant in Vinegar, Giardiniera in Oil
Gourmet France Baby Corn[3]
Marin Brand Piccola Eggplant
Mexican Kitchen Mexi Mix, Nopalitos Tiernos
Miss Scarlett Miniature Eggplant
Muradomo Farms Portuguese Style, Sweet,[3] Spiced[3] Pickled Maui Onions
Nick's Il Primo Brand Hot, Mild Mix Giardiniera

Poppa Lolo Hot Pickled Salad
Progresso Petite Marinated Asparagus, Giardiniera, Eggplant, Marinated Mushrooms
Reese Giardiniera, Fiesta Hot Mix, Miniature Corn
Sechler's Mixed Vegetables, Garlic Dill Tomatoes, Sour Cocktail Onions
Snak Pak Italian Mix Giardiniera
Star Holland Cocktail Onions, Hors d'Oeuvres Onions
Talk O Texas Crisp Okra Pickles
Town House Mixed Vegetable Giardiniera, Pickled Cauliflower
Zorba Giardiniera

Relish

Hain Kosher Dill
Howard's Pepper,[3] Hot Pepper,[3] Piccalilli[3]
Pickle Eater's Sweet Pickle, Piccalilli, Corn

Progresso Pepper Piccallili
Pure and Simple Sweet Pickle

Peppers

Alma Golden Peppers
B & G Hot Red and Green Cherry Peppers
Bruno's Waxed Peppers
Capella's Italian Style Marinated Pepperoncini
Cristo's Greek Salad Peppers
D.L. Jardine's Texas Popcorn
Dell' Alpe Sweet Cherry Peppers, Sport Peppers in Olive Oil
Faraon Chilies Gueritos, Faro Pickled Jalapeno Peppers
Golden Gate Pepperoncini
Goya Hot Pickled Peppers

Mexican Kitchen Jalapenos en Escabeche
Napoleon Pepperoncini
Pellegrino Hot Peppers with Tomato Sauce
Polli Red and Yellow Peppers in Wine Vinegar
Progresso Pepper Salad, Tuscan, Cherry Peppers
Reese Pepperoncini, Jalapeno Peppers
Rosina Pepperoncini
S&T High Sierra Chileno Peppers
Star Peppers in Wine Vinegar
Town House Hot Cherry Peppers
Zorba Pepperoncini

Pimientos—All contain citric acid and salt. Avoid any with added sweetening.

Olives

Big Alpha Calamata
Bocquet
Dell' Alpe Oil Cured Olives, Olive Condite
Goya Olives with Pimientos, Salad Olives Condito
Graber
Marin Brand Primavera
Mezzetta Greek
Minasso Serafino
Miss Scarlett
Moquet
Old Ranchers Brand California Tree Ripened[1]
Pastene Condite
Peloponnese
Progresso Salad, Oil Cured, Olive Appetizer
Santa Barbara Olive Company Olives
Scarla
Syrian Bakery and Grocery Company Olives
Torino Green Ripe
Westbrae Natural
Zorba Olives

Canned Olives—All brands similar, with black olives all containing ferrous gluconate.

Sun-Dried Tomatoes—All brands similar, packed in oil with seasonings and salt.

Canned Artichokes—All brands similar and contain citric acid and salt.

Marinated Artichokes

Reese Quartered Marinated Artichoke Hearts

Capers—All brands similar, with either vinegar alone or with salt and water.

Sweet Accoutrements

Bombay Brand Major Grey's Mango Chutney[3]
Cuisine Perel Chutneys
Reese Maharaja Pineapple Chutney[3]
Stowe Hollow Kitchens Chutneys[3]
Wax Orchards Fruit Mincement, Chutneys

Miscellaneous Condiments

Carpi Italian Antipasto
Chico-San Natto
Coral Stuffed Vine Leaves[4]
Dell' Alpe Grape Leaves
Embasa Tender Cactus
Fancifood Grape Leaves
Hime Brand Natto
Hinoichi Natto
Kanai Natto
Kendell Food Company Natto
Krinos Stuffed Eggplant
Lima Ratatouille[1]
Napoleon Green Almonds
Peloponnese Stuffed Baby Eggplant
Premier Japan Takuan Radish, Pickled Ginger
Progresso Eggplant Caponata[3]
Reese Hearts of Palm
Zanae Melitzanes Imam
Zante Grape Leaves in Brine

Catsup—Most brands similar, containing salt and sugar and/or corn syrup. Give preference to those that deviate from this pattern and are salt-free and/or honey-sweetened or unsweetened as listed below.

Del Monte No Salt[3]
Enrico's Honey Sweetened, No Salt
Hain Imitation
Health Valley Regular, No Salt Catch-Up Tomato Table Sauces
Life Tomato Ketchup
Nature's Cuisine Unsweetened, No Salt
Westbrae Unsweetened Un-Ketchup, Thick Honey, Hot and Spicy

Mustard—There are numerous choices without sugar, flour, vegetable oil, propylene glycol alginate, preservatives, or acidifiers like tartaric acid and citric acid. Those that are listed here are salt-free.

Ducros Salt Free Dijon
Hain No Salt
Maitre Jacques No Salt Added Dijon

Mother's Mountain Original
Reese No Salt Added
Reine de Dijon

Prepared Horseradish—Most brands come packed in vinegar and salt only, or if red, with added beet juice.

Brede Pure Beet
Chadalee Farms
Farmers
Gold's
Jim and Lottie's Country Style

Kraft Regular, Cream Style
Manichewitz Prepared, Beet
Silvers Springs Regular, Cream Style
Sittlers

Spicy and Sweet Garnishing and Dipping Sauces

Barbara's Chocolate, Barbecue Sauces
Captain Jaap's Mariner's Sauce
Carob Dream Dessert Toppings
D.L. Jardine's Hot Barbecue, No Salt Vaquero, Steak Sauces[3]
Escoffier Roberts Sauce[3]
Garden Island Sauce
Henry Robert's Barbecue Sauce[3]
Jackie's Oklahoma Style Barbecue Sauce[3]
Jake's Carob Fudge Topping, Almond Syrup
KA.ME Plum, Hoisin Sauces[3]
Maggie Gin's Chinese Mustard Sauce[3]
Marie's Piquant Tartar Sauce

McMurphy's Magical Mustard Sauce[3]
Meadowsweet Maple Almond Topping
Mitoku Carob, Ginger, Lotus, Vanilla Syrups
Mother's Mountain New England Chili Sauce
Robbie's Barbecue, Cocktail, Sweet and Sour Sauces
Sam Dillard's Barbecue Sauce
San-J Natural Tamari Teriyaki Sauce
Shady Maple Farms Pecan, Walnut Sundae Toppings
Teva Carob Syrup[1]
Wax Orchards Fudge Sweet, Ginger Sweet Toppings

[1]Organic
[3]Contains refined sweeteners
[4]Contains refined grains

Chapter 38

Seasonings: Natural Flavor Enhancers

Flavor enhancers in the form of herbs, spices, and extracts are the key to rich-tasting, aromatic dishes and one of the most important allies of any cook. These seasonings, mostly derived from fresh or dried plants, lend a characteristic flavor and add excitement to what might otherwise be bland food. This is accomplished without any of the drawbacks associated with salt, sugar, MSG, hydrolyzed vegetable protein, disodium guanylate and inosinate, and other masking techniques employed by the food industry.

SALT TALKS

Common table salt (sodium chloride) is probably the most frequently used seasoning world wide, and this country is no exception. In fact, its over-abundance in the American diet has been a matter of great concern. This is due particularly to salt's sodium component (40 percent by weight), which medical authorities believe plays some role in precipitating hypertension. A direct cause and effect relationship has not been firmly established, though, and some researchers contend that it is not sodium alone, but a complex interaction between sodium, potassium, and calcium that deserves more consideration. More recently, the role of chloride in salt (60 percent by weight) has been suggested as perhaps being a significant factor. Consequently, recommendations regarding salt consumption are still somewhat speculative.

In addition to its possible adverse health effects, there is the further offense that salt is commonly used in foods to cover up overprocessing—something you can see for yourself in the table on page 499, which compares the sodium content of over forty popular food items.

Getting Back Our Balance

Sodium is an essential nutrient and although no minimum need has been established, anything less than 200 milligrams daily could prove dangerous. The best evidence we currently have indicates that a sodium intake of 1,100 to 3,300 milligrams per day provides a "safe and adequate" amount for the average adult. One teaspoon of salt equals about 2,100 milligrams of sodium. While daily intake estimates of 4,000 to 6,000 milligrams have been made for most Americans, for some it is as high as 10,000 to 12,000 milligrams.

Throughout our *Guide to Good Food* we have pinpointed potential sodium pitfalls in various foods and given praise to products with reduced-sodium formulations. Before we go on to discuss other seasonings, we want to emphasize that just because a food doesn't taste salty, you shouldn't assume it is low in sodium. Sometimes foods that are obviously flavored with salt are actually lower in sodium than less suspect foods that use salt as one of several seasonings (see table below). When salt must compete with strong-flavored herbs and spices, a considerable amount may be required to make any impression on your palate; on the other hand, when salt alone is sprinkled on the surface of pretzels, nuts, or chips, its flavor is immediately apparent. It also may surprise you that salt is used in highly sugared foods where it acts on taste receptors to enhance the perception of sweetness. This is why McDonald's apple pie averages 390 milligrams of sodium per piece and ½ cup of prepared instant chocolate pudding contains 515 milligrams of sodium. Furthermore, because there are more than seventy sodium-based compounds used by food processors, salt itself is not the only culprit.

AVERAGE SODIUM CONTENT OF TYPICAL PROCESSED FOODS*

Food	Amount	Milligrams of sodium
Corn Flakes (Kellogg's)	1 oz	280
Wheat flakes (Wheaties)	1 oz	370
Shredded wheat (Nabisco)	1 oz	<10
Instant oatmeal (Quaker)	1 oz packet	400
Oatmeal, regular	1 cup prepared	1
Salted cocktail peanuts (Planters)	1 oz	160
Salted dry roasted peanuts (Planters)	1 oz	250
Potato chips (Wise)	1 oz	190
Potato chips (Health Valley Unsalted)	1 oz	1
Salted popcorn	1 cup	175
Ritz crackers	1 oz (8 crackers)	240
Saltine crackers	1 oz	460
Whole wheat matzoh (Manischewitz)	1 oz	<10
White bread (Pepperidge Farm)	1 oz slice	135
Bagel (Lender's)	2 oz.	352
Pancakes, from mix (Aunt Jemima)	3	643
Instant chocolate pudding (Jell-O)	½ cup prepared	515
Bologna (Armour)	1 oz slice	285
Bacon (Swift)	1 oz or 4 strips	464
Caviar	1 tablespoon	352
Tomato juice	6 oz	243
V–8 (Campbell's)	6 oz	620

AVERAGE SODIUM CONTENT
OF TYPICAL PROCESSED FOODS* (continued)

Food	Amount	Milligrams of sodium
Canned carrots (Del Monte)	½ cup	265
Fresh carrots	½ cup cooked	25
Canned green beans (Del Monte)	½ cup	355
Frozen green beans	½ cup	<1
Cottage cheese (Breakstone)	½ cup	550
Cottage cheese, no salt (Friendship)	½ cup	31
American cheese (Kraft)	1 oz	390
Cheddar cheese (Kraft)	1 oz	180
Fruit yogurt (Breyer's)	1 cup	125
Buttermilk (Crowley)	1 cup	390
Hot chocolate (Carnation, from mix)	6 oz	120
Italian dressing (Wishbone)	1 Tbs	240
Pickle	1 average	928
Peanut butter (Skippy)	2 Tbs	150
Peanut butter (Arrowhead Mills)	2 Tbs	2
Tuna (Chicken of the Sea)	2 oz	310
Ketchup	1 Tbs	156
Mayonnaise (Hellman's)	1 Tbs	80
Yellow mustard	1 Tbs	190
Dijon mustard (Grey Poupon)	1 Tbs	445
Chicken noodle soup (Campbell's)	8 oz prepared	840
Chicken pot pie (Morton)	8 oz	1246
Long grain and wild rice (Minute)	½ cup	530

*Source: Manufacturer's figures and *Nutritive Value of American Foods,* Agriculture Handbook No. 456, USDA, 1975.
< = less than

Sodium Strategy

It has been estimated that 70 percent of our average sodium intake is from processed foods. Therefore, the best way to keep sodium in proper proportion is to minimize your intake of salt and other sodium-based ingredients in prepared and processed foods and rely on common sense to guide your hand with the salt shaker when eating and cooking. Since the desire for salt is to a large extent addictive, those who are currently drawn to salty foods may have to retrain their taste buds, but there is substantial evidence that taste preferences can be lowered. Reducing salt intake and replacing it with other seasonings is a painless approach.

Although label reading is one way you can help reduce your sodium intake from processed foods, it is not infallible. Salt may be hidden in some of the product's ingredients such as soy sauce, catsup, mustard, pickles, anchovies, bouillon, etc. Also the word "sodium" may not be included in the names of many additives that actually contain sodium. For example:

- *Sodium saccharin* may appear as saccharin;
- *Sodium carrageenan* may be listed simply as carrageenan;
- *Disodium ethylene diaminetetracetate* is otherwise known as EDTA;
- *Sodium ferrocyanide* is the chemical name for yellow prussiate of soda;
- *Hydrolyzed vegetable* or *plant protein* (HVP or HPP) has an inherent sodium component.

Be on the lookout for blatant forms of sodium such as:

Monosodium glutamate	Sodium guanylate	Disodium guanylate
Sodium inosinate	Disodium inosinate	Sodium benzoate
Sodium propionate	Sodium citrate	Sodium nitrate
Sodium bisulfite	Sodium silicoaluminate	Sodium phosphate
Sodium carboxymethylcellulose		

Selecting Salt

Salt is obtained either from mining rock salt deposits of ancient sea beds or from evaporating sea water. Differences between so-called land salt and sea salt are minor. In nature, salt contains over seventy elemental substances. To quote a Japanese salt researcher, common "salt is not sodium chloride; it's dehydrated ocean." The fact that sodium chloride is the most abundant component of salt does not make it the most important.

One reason why common table salt may adversely affect us is that in the refinement process it is reduced to almost pure sodium chloride. Salt processed by solar dehydration is said to retain a higher level of other minerals, but unless the processing method is voluntarily mentioned on the package, there is no sure way to find out how a particular brand of table salt has been handled.

Most common brands of table salt are *iodized* (treated with potassium iodide), and packaged salt enriched in this manner will state on the label: "This salt supplies iodine, a necessary nutrient." Otherwise, the name will be followed by the statement: "This salt does not supply iodine, a necessary nutrient." Iodine enrichment was designed to help counteract goiter (a dangerous enlargement of the thyroid gland) and, indeed, today this ailment has nearly disappeared in America. Now concern about iodine has shifted from too little to too much (excess iodine can suppress thyroid function). As you would suspect, as salt consumption has grown, iodine intake has increased dramatically.

Dextrose, sodium silico aluminate, sodium bicarbonate, magnesium carbonate, and yellow prussiate of soda are often added to table salt to maintain its pure white color and prevent moisture absorption. This information will appear on the label. *Kosher salt* is coarser ground than other common table salts, and although no less refined, it does not contain any of these additives.

Seasoned Salt

On a per-measure basis, seasoned salts may contain less sodium than pure salt, but they certainly cannot be considered effective salt alternatives. Garlic salt, onion salt, and celery salt are examples of salt-based seasonings as are many seasoning blends. When selecting a premixed seasoning, do not be taken in by a product that creates the illusion of being a natural or gourmet item by adding a few dried herbs and spices to common salt and putting a pretty label and high price on the package.

INSTEAD OF SALT

Gomasio

Gomasio is a traditional Japanese seasoning that combines ground toasted sesame seeds with salt in a ratio of about 9:1. The sesame seeds act as an extender (kind of a "salt helper") and improve the balance of minerals by contributing calcium and potassium. The oils that surface when the sesame seeds are crushed also act as a carrier for the salty flavor and thereby transfer an adequate amount of seasoning with a substantially reduced volume of salt. Gomasio can be purchased in many natural food stores.

Kelp

Kelp is dried seaweed ground into a fine green-brown powder. It has a delicate salty flavor, yet less than 8 percent of the sodium of table salt. This is nicely complemented by twice as much potassium, a good supply of iodine, and a range of other minerals in small amounts including calcium, phosphorus, iron, and magnesium. Kelp is sold in Oriental markets and natural food stores.

Nutritional Yeast

Nutritional yeast, also known as *brewer's yeast* and *torula yeast,* is another nutritious flavor enhancer (rich in B vitamins) useful in cutting back on sodium consumption. It imparts a savory, somewhat meaty flavor that works especially well in casseroles, soups, and stews. Nutritional yeast is sold in natural food stores.

Commercial Salt Substitutes

The best way to reduce salt consumption is to tempt the palate with other tastes, not mimic sodium chloride's sensations through the use of contrived chemical salts. Despite this, the food industry is intent on discovering an alternative that offers the same "flavor profile" as salt, and to date, potassium-based substitutes are the most common choice. There is no guarantee, however, that a concentrated source of potassium is any more sound than a concentrated source of sodium. Several no-salt alternatives make use of potassium chloride in concert with lactose, corn syrup, 1-glutamic acid, calcium silicate, adipic acid, fumaric acid, polyethylene glycol 400—all of which begin to make salt seem a lot more appealing than its touted "substitute."

There are some commendable salt-free seasonings offering nothing more elaborate than a blend of dried herbs and spices. Note however that hydrolyzed plant protein (HPP) is found in several "natural" seasoning mixes. As we have mentioned elsewhere in this book, HPP (a.k.a. hydrolyzed vegetable protein or HVP) is a highly refined substance and not at all sodium-free, despite the fact that its name bears no trace of sodium. We cannot accept it as an ingredient in an exemplary seasoning compound. Nor do we support the use of corn syrup solids and other sugars in products intended to reduce salt.

FRESH SEASONINGS

Fresh seasonings offer both gustatory and nutritional rewards. Because they are derived from plant sources, many of them are rich in vitamins and minerals.

Aromatic Fruits and Vegetables

GARLIC AND ONION

The two most widely used flavoring agents in home cooking are garlic and onion. Not only are they valuable seasonings, they are among the oldest folk remedies. Both are sold fresh, dehydrated, and as a ground dried powder (with and without salt). Stick with the fresh. Nothing approaches the taste of these vegetables in their original form. (See Chapter 24 for buying guidelines.)

CELERY LEAVES

The fresh leafy tops of celery are excellent for seasoning soups and are an essential ingredient in homemade stock. To obtain them, buy untrimmed celery with fresh looking greenery; discard leaves that are brown at the tips or wet and slippery. If you have more leaves than you can use, freeze them.

CHIVES

Chives are a member of the onion family, although much milder, and can be used uncooked to flavor salads, dips, sauces, and spreads. They are sold as a growing plant that is usually jammed into a tiny pot and soon dies because the roots are too plentiful for the container. To have a long-lasting source of this herb in your kitchen, repot the plant in a larger container and continually cut the tops so the shoots remain upright.

GINGER

Fresh ginger is available in most markets and can add its punch to many dishes. Since ginger can get quite nippy, use it cautiously until you have learned to judge its strength.

Select a piece that is rock-hard and heavy. Ginger that is no longer fresh feels light and has a wrinkled appearance. The less fibrous the better; you can sometimes get a clue if fibers stick out from the freshly broken knob. Occasionally mold grows where the ginger has been severed; if it is still firm, this ginger is usable, but be sure to scrape off the damaged portion. Hawaiian ginger is the finest.

Storage and Handling: To store, wrap in paper towel or a brown paper bag, then in a plastic bag, and refrigerate. Change the paper when it becomes moist (generally a week or so). Stored in this manner, ginger will keep several weeks.

If ginger is well washed it does not really need to be peeled, but if the surface is especially grimy, tough, or shows signs of age, it is best to peel it before slicing, mincing, or grating.

HOT PEPPERS

There are many varieties of fresh chilies suitable for seasoning and often they are not identified by type in the store. The fact that the names, when provided, are not always consistent, coupled with an element of uncertainty stemming from differences in soil, climate, and growing conditions, means you cannot always predict the potency of an individual specimen.

Cayenne chilies are the most widely available. They may be red and/or green, are long and thin (about 3 inches by ⅜ inch), and tend to be "picante," although to a lesser degree than the serrano and jalapeno. *Jalapenos* are small (about 2 inches long by 1 inch wide), green, and plump, with a smooth, shiny surface and a hot to very hot impact. *Serrano chilies* look like a small version (1 to 1½ inches) of jalapenos and are considered "muy picante."

As a general reference, chilies with pointed tips are said to be hotter than those that are round tipped and, within a single variety, the smaller chilies usually have the most bite.

Handling: First a warning—Be careful when you use chilies. Not only are they hot to taste, but fresh chili pulp will burn the skin. Sensitive people may want to wear rubber gloves when handling them. Avoid fumes when toasting them over an open flame.

Use all of the pulp, but take it easy when it comes to the seeds and veins, which are the hottest parts.

LEMON

In many parts of the world a wedge of lemon is routinely served along with meats, fried foods, and salads for flavor enhancement. Lemon works equally well in many sauces, soups, and fruit and vegetable dishes to enliven their flavor and is a special favorite of ours.

Fresh lemon will serve you far better than bottled lemon juice, which is rather flat tasting and may be prepared from concentrate and/or preserved with chemicals. (See Chapter 25 for buying guidelines.)

HORSERADISH

Prepared horseradish is discussed in Chapter 37, but a small amount of the fresh root can be grated into sauces, dips, and salad dressings as a seasoning.

Select firm roots with a fairly smooth surface that is not barklike or pitted. Avoid specimens that are flabby or have an exceedingly rough skin.

Handling: Do not grate the root in advance of use as it will blacken and turn bitter. Once it is mixed with other foods it is protected against further deterioration. For longer keeping, the grated root can be preserved in vinegar.

Fresh Herbs

Herbs are the aromatic leaves, stems, and sometimes flowers of soft, succulent plants that are both edible and flavorful. To preserve their essence they are frequently dried (see page 507), but many of them are just as popular in the fresh form and have a far more pleasing flavor.

Fresh herbs will last about a week in the refrigerator. We have found that wrapping fresh herbs in paper toweling to absorb moisture, then placing them in plastic bags prevents excessive wilting and also keeps the herbs from drying out or becoming slimy from wet mold. For longer storage, herbs can be frozen.

BASIL

Enthusiasm for fresh herbs has brought fresh basil to the produce department, although it is available only seasonally (warm weather). The soft, silky leaves, which have a faint licorice-like flavor and aroma, should still have some life in them and retain their green color when you buy them. A few fresh leaves are sufficient to season a tomato sauce or salad dressing, while a good-sized bunch is essential to the preparation of a proper pesto, the green garlic sauce served on pasta.

Handling: Fresh-cut basil turns black with prolonged exposure to air, especially if it is washed and left out to dry. It is best to prepare the leaves just prior to use. Fresh basil can be wrapped in foil and stuck in the freezer for use out of season, but only the fresh leaf can be pulverized for pesto. Since the flavor diminishes in the freezer you may need to double the amount you normally use.

CILANTRO

Sometimes called Mexican or Chinese parsley, this herb is actually the leaf of the coriander plant and has a far more distinctive taste than the common parsley often used in its stead. David says it tastes like soap, others swear that it is essential to authentic Indian and Mexican cooking. Since hardly anyone is neutral on the subject, if you have never used the fresh leaf, which looks like flat parsley, we suggest you proceed with a light hand.

DILL

You probably are acquainted with dill through the flavor of dill pickles. Its use extends to soup (particularly potato, tomato, vegetable, and bean), salads, and all manner of fish as well.

Select sprightly looking stalks, free of seed heads, with lots of soft, green spikes; reject any that are black or excessively damp or slimy.

FENNEL

All parts of this plant, from the bulbous base to the tall stems and narrow feathery leaves, can be used. The leaves resemble dill in appearance and are well suited to many of the same foods, imparting a sweet anise-like flavor.

Look for fennel with fresh green tops and firm, unscarred bulbs. (See also Chapter 24.)

MINT

Fresh mint may be found in the wild or in your market. The leaves should be attractively colored, although slight browning at the tips is all right.

Add mint to yogurt for a refreshing salad; mince it with parsley and you have the foundation for tabouli. Mint is also good in fruit salad, and can be steeped in boiling water for a Mideastern tea. For an instant breath refresher, chew a few leaves.

Handling: Mint should be washed just prior to use for, as with basil, exposing the wet green leaves to air turns them an unappealing black.

WATERCRESS

This spicy herb may be found in the produce department of your market or, if you are fortunate, in the bed of a nearby shallow, moving stream. Either way, the peppery leaves are cherished for their ability to enhance a bowl of mixed greens or a dressing. It is pungent herbs like this one that make salt-free salads enticing.

Watercress does not keep well. Avoid damp, dark, slippery leaves and stems when you buy it or it will deteriorate rapidly. It should never have a sour or unpleasant odor.

PARSLEY

Fresh parsley, often used as a garnish only to be pushed to the side of the plate, is actually a fine source of vitamins A and C, and of vegetable protein. It is also rich in chlorophyll; eating your garnish sweetens the breath.

Use fresh parsley to season soups, salads, stuffings, bread crumb coatings, and thousands of meat, grain, and vegetable dishes. The dried form doesn't compare in flavor or nutrition. (See Chapter 24 for buying guidelines.)

Handling: For long-term keeping, wash, dry, and chop the parsley and store it in a plastic bag in the freezer. When you need a spoonful, take some from your freezer stock; it thaws almost instantaneously.

DRIED HERBS AND SPICES

The promise of herbs and spices has lured men halfway around the globe. Columbus risked his life in search of spices, not the New World, and Marco Polo excited all of Italy with tales of ginger in China, cinnamon in Ceylon, cloves and nutmeg in Molucca, and pepper on the coast of India. Surely we can find enough inspiration from these adventurers to journey through our local markets in search of herbs and spices to complement quality wholefoods.

Herbs, as we have said, are the leaves, stems, and sometimes flowers of soft, succulent plants. Those herbs not readily available fresh may be dried and packaged for your convenience. While some are not as distinctive in this form, if properly handled the flavor and aroma can be satisfactorily retained. As a general guide for interchanging fresh and dried herbs: ⅓ to ½ teaspoon of dried herbs = 1 Tablespoon of fresh.

Spices are dried flavoring elements produced from the buds, flowers, fruit, bark, and roots of certain plants. Among the popular spices are also the dried fruit (or seeds) of plants including caraway, poppy, sesame, celery, mustard, cumin, and dill. If you are trying to cut back on sweeteners, some of the "sweet" spices like allspice, anise, cardamom, cinnamon, fennel, ginger, licorice, and nutmeg can help. They aren't actually sweet, but they enhance the natural sugars in foods and their aroma adds to this perception.

Since dried seasonings are susceptible to insect infestation, they are often fumigated, although this fact is not revealed to the purchaser. Several major companies have also been granted permission to use irradiation to control insect and microbial contamination. The consumer is not privy to this information either. The fact that these herbs and spices are generally used in small amounts does lessen the concern about these practices somewhat, but people still have the right to be informed.

Selecting Dried Herbs and Spices

Always buy the form of dried herb closest to the whole-leaf state; avoid finely pulverized leaves whenever possible. Crumbling releases the essential-flavoring oils, so it is best to crush the leaves between your fingers just before adding them to food.

Similarly, spices that are whole retain their flavor better than those that are preground, but convenience sometimes dictates use of the latter. Nutmeg is easily converted from the whole to the ground state at home using a special nutmeg grinder or the fine side of a metal grater. The taste of peppercorns freshly ground in a mill is far more distinguished than that of pepper purchased ready-ground. A mortar and pestle serve well to reduce other spices like cumin seeds, cardamom pods, spikes of clove, and even cinnamon quills to a finer, more usable consistency.

Many seasonings, such as curry powder, chili powder, pumpkin pie, and pickling spice are sold already blended. Be careful that in your selection you do not inadvertently buy salt as well, an easy oversight with poultry seasoning especially, which may also be compromised by tricalcium phosphate and partially hydrogenated oil. Note that chili seasoning and taco mixes are really an expensive way to buy chili powder, plus salt and cornmeal thickeners. If you select such a seasoning, look for one that is not presweetened or diminished by modified starch, dried potato prepared with sodium sulfite, MSG, trisodium or tricalcium phosphate, calcium stearate, and artificial color and flavor.

Unless you use a particular herb or spice in huge quantities, buy the smallest packet available; the flavor diminishes with age and exposure to air. When the characteristic odor is no longer pungent, it is time to replace it. Old herbs and spices add little more than the flavor of dust to a dish.

Dried Chilies

The best dried chilies are sun-dried. Commercial varieties that are oven-dried may have a bitter-tasting skin. Properly dried and free of mold and insects, chilies will keep indefinitely, but the fresher and crisper they are, the easier it will be to remove the peel. Good quality pods have a uniform reddish color, free of black or yellow spots. Use care when you work with them, washing your hands immediately so you don't accidently rub your eyes or other sensitive areas with the stingy pepper residue.

SOME VERY BRIEF ADVICE ON SEASONING

The best way to judge the right amount of seasoning is by taste. Adding too much can be worse than not adding enough. Adjust as you go along. A dish that has not been sampled during cooking usually reflects this neglect.

Storing Dried Herbs and Spices

Dried herbs and spices should be stored in airtight containers (jars and tins rather than cardboard boxes) away from heat and direct light. Many cooks make the mistake of keeping their herb and spice rack over the stove; while it's a handy place, the heat dissipates the flavor and quality of the seasonings. Try to have a permanent storage place in a cooler part of your kitchen.

MONOSODIUM GLUTAMATE

Monosodium glutamate is a flavor enhancer of natural origin which has no taste of its own, but has a remarkable ability to bring out the flavor in other foods and help them to blend into one another. Many foods have an inherent amount of glutamate in them.

The extracted MSG that is added in unnatural amounts to foods is believed to produce undesirable physical manifestations including headaches, sweating, tingling, chills, hot flashes, and even temporary paralysis. We suggest you ignore MSG when it is called for in a recipe and don't buy any seasoned salt or prepared foods that count on MSG for flavor.

PREPARED LIQUID SEASONINGS

The following prepared flavoring products are worthy of a wholefoods shopping list.

Vinegar

All varieties of vinegar—whether white, wine, cider, rice, malt, or a fancy balsamic or berry are made by diluting the acid derived from fermented grains or fruit with water. A dash of vinegar, like a squirt of lemon juice, can perk up soups, stews, vegetable dishes, meats, and more. It can help cut the oiliness of fish, French fries, and pizza. Of course, vinegar is also an important flavoring ingredient in salad dressing.

Plain *white vinegar,* the most pungent variety, is best reserved for pickling. *Wine vinegars* are a good all-around choice, with the white preferred for light colored foods that turn an unattractive bluish pink when red wine vinegar is added. *Cider vinegar* is a bit sweet and can be used for pickles, relishes, and dressings where a hint of sweetness is welcome. *Malt vinegar* is also good for pickling; the British prefer it to catsup on French fries. (Note that this particular vinegar is sometimes tainted by the addition of caramel color.) *Rice vinegar,* used in Japanese and Chinese cooking, is another sweet-tasting vinegar that suits Oriental salads and enhances plain rice. *Fruit vinegars* like raspberry, strawberry, and blueberry make delightful salad dressings and a perfect accent for lightly steamed vegetables and delicate sauces. Probably the most exotic vinegar of all is *balsamic.* Made in northern Italy, it goes through a ten-year aging process in wood kegs. The red-brown vinegar that results has a very mellow, sweet-sour flavor that highlights vegetables or salads beautifully.

While *herb vinegars* can offer additional flavor possibilities, these preseasoned vinegars are less versatile.

Liquid Pepper

Liquid pepper, also known as *pepper sauce* and *hot sauce,* is a liquid mash of blended tiny red-hot peppers. Since vinegar and salt, both natural preservatives, are invariably present, the addition of chemical preservatives by some manufacturers is absurd. The use of vegetable gums or other thickeners is equally unnecessary. The ingredient list on the label tells all.

Soy Sauce

Almost everyone recognizes this dark brown salty liquid produced from fermented soybeans, but few people are aware that there are different types of soy sauce. In addition to plain soy sauce, *shoyu* and *tamari* are common names. While technically there are differences between them, these are often ignored in labeling. The proliferation of brands doesn't make selection any easier.

Shoyu, Japanese for soy sauce, is traditionally made in the age-old manner, in which soybeans and wheat are fermented together from one to three years. The liquid shoyu is then pressed out and heated, without boiling, to stop the fermentation and prevent the growth of mold

Tamari, strictly speaking, is a soy liquid drained off after miso production (see Miso, page 511). In actuality, very little tamari of this type is available; however, a product called tamari is specially brewed in a manner similar to shoyu, but without using wheat. Be aware, however, that many companies use the term "tamari" improperly, so if you wish to detect the presence of wheat, be sure to read the ingredient list. (Although one of the main attractions of authentic tamari for some people is the fact that it is wheat-free, according to one American distributor, the wheat in shoyu is not an allergen because after twenty-four months or more of fermentation the components that bother those sensitive to wheat are completely broken down.)

Soy sauce may be used to describe shoyu or tamari or it may refer to the product of a more modern technique in which defatted soybean meal (which has been exposed to chemical solvents to remove the fat) is heated with hydrochloric acid, neutralized with sodium carbonate, and filtered. To compensate for its deficiencies, caramel color and corn syrup are added for color and flavor; sodium benzoate is frequently used as a preservative. This soy sauce is produced in a matter of days rather than the months or even years called for in the traditional fermentation process.

The qualities that Orientals prize in their soy sauce appear to be entirely absent in this modern processed soy sauce, since it is the by-products of fermentation to which they attribute soy sauce's unique effect on human metabolism. For example, during fermentation the nutrients released are "predigested" to a degree that makes them readily absorbed. Moreover, the Japanese believe that the enzymes present can make other foods more digestible. Shoyu is said to foster the growth of healthy bacteria in the intestinal tract and to stimulate the flow of digestive juices in the stomach. Manufactured soy sauce is believed to have just the opposite effect, inhibiting stomach secretions and diluting the strength of the digestive juices already present.

LOW-SODIUM SOY SAUCE

Low-sodium or "lite" soy sauces are a welcome innovation to some people since traditionally soy sauce contains from 300 to 500 milligrams of sodium per teaspoon. Without knowing the sodium content of a particular brand (and this is rarely on the label), it is hard to determine whether buying low-sodium soy sauce has any advantage. However low-sodium versions average around 40 percent less sodium than the company's regular line, and the figure can go as low as 50 milligrams per teaspoon. Some brands add vinegar and/or alcohol to act as preservatives. This will be noted on the label.

Miso

Miso is a fermented soybean paste (not a liquid) that has been a staple in the Japanese diet for centuries and is now becoming known in the United States. Interest in macrobiotics was responsible for its introduction to the West and several different varieties are available in natural food outlets.

Miso is thick and spreadable and ranges from light yellow to orange to dark brown in color. The lighter varieties have a subtle, sweet quality; all are intensely salty, with a wide range of 200 to 450 milligrams of sodium per teaspoon. Since miso is meant to be used as a seasoning, not as a condiment to be eaten by the spoonful, its strong flavor is ultimately diluted.

Miso is an excellent seasoning for salad dressings, stews, soups, bean dishes, nut butters and tahini spreads, and almost anything that benefits from a robust, salty overlay. Miso soup is one of its most popular uses; if you eat in a Japanese restaurant you can sample miso in the clear broth offered with every meal. An old Japanese proverb is said to state: "A bowl of miso soup a day keeps the doctor away," and some Japanese reports even claim that miso can counter the effects of nicotine, radiation, and other environmental pollutants and thereby provide a safeguard against cancer. It is also reputed to be one of the few nonanimal sources of vitamin B_{12}.

The basic ingredients in miso are soybeans, salt, and usually a cereal grain. You may find miso labeled as *hacho* or *hatcho* (no grain added); *mugi* (made with a barley starter), the most versatile; *soba* (with 50 percent buckwheat); *genmai* (using a whole brown rice starter); and *kome* (with a polished rice starter), the sweetest and least salty, with the version of kome known as *shiro* or white miso the lightest, sweetest, and quickest to spoil.

Kept in the refrigerator, all misos are long lasting and there is no need to add preservatives as some manufacturers do. Moreover, pasteurization, as practiced by some companies, is said to reduce the level of the very organisms that make miso so beneficial. Since heat is believed to destroy some of its attributes, miso is best added to cooked foods just before serving.

Cooking Wines

While any alcoholic spirits can be used in food preparation, certain wines are prepared exclusively for this purpose. **Cooking sherry** is the most commonly available cooking wine, sold in every supermarket. It is a potent 17 percent alcohol by volume, but so you aren't tempted to drink it, cooking sherry is preseasoned with salt, usually the equivalent of one teaspoon per cup. Be sure to take this into account and adjust the salt when you add cooking sherry to a recipe.

Mirin is a sweet Japanese rice wine also meant only as a seasoning. It is pale golden in color, slightly thick and sticky. It is designed to balance the saltiness of other popular Oriental seasonings like soy sauce and miso. Mirin is sold in natural food stores and Oriental markets.

Cooking wines can be stored indefinitely at room temperature. Note, too, that with a few minutes' cooking the alcohol content burns off and only the rich taste remains. However, if you use cooking wines in salad dressings or other uncooked foods, or add them to cooked dishes at the last minute, the alcohol will remain.

Worcestershire Sauce

Worcestershire sauce is a blend of some or all of the following: vinegar, molasses, honey, sugar, corn syrup, salt, sherry, shallots, anchovies, tamarinds, raisins, walnuts, chili peppers, cloves, garlic powder, onion powder, and lemon oil. Its very nature dictates the presence of salt and sweeteners, but what can be avoided are hydrolyzed vegetable protein or vegetable protein extract, caramel, artificial flavoring, and stabilizers in the form of vegetable gums.

Liquid Smoke

Bottled liquid smoke has recently made its appearance in retail outlets. Although it may be called "100% natural liquid smoke," its application to foods is questionable.

Chemical analysis of liquid smoke and smoked foods reveals the presence of a class of compounds known as phenols. Phenol or carbolic acid is also one of the main components of dyes derived from coal tar. The carcinogenicity of many coal tar dyes is well established; smoked foods are similarly suspect. While no smoke compound has been singled out as the villain, to bottle one common element that runs between these two potential carcinogens and then add it to foods does seem to be an invitation to trouble.

Some studies done with smoked meats also show a form of carcinogenic nitrosamines that can be traced directly to the use of liquid smoke in their formulation. Until more is known, we suggest you minimize using liquid smoke and buying foods with added smoke flavor, even if it is "natural."

Seasoning Oils

Sesame oil, an unrefined oil pressed from sesame seeds, and **chili oil,** the same product to which hot chili pepper has been added, are two of the most popular Chinese seasoning aids. Used sparingly, they can lend authenticity to Chinese soups, stir-frys, and salads. The flavor is highly concentrated, so do not use more than a scant teaspoon in a potful of food, and sample the dish first to determine if more is warranted.

FLAVOR EXTRACTS

Flavoring extracts are generally sold in two forms: the pure extract and an imitation flavoring. The pure offers real flavor (from vanilla beans, almonds, lemon, etc.) diluted with ethyl alcohol. Imitation flavoring, on the other hand, is based on a chemical compound which simulates a real flavor; some are even "color enhanced" to match the flavor they represent.

Most varieties of "pure" flavor extracts provide full ingredient disclosure on the label. *Pure vanilla extract,* however, may not be quite as "pure" as its name implies. It may be doctored with glycerin, propylene glycol, sugar, dextrose, and corn syrup, without revealing any of this. The product called *vanilla flavoring* is not an imitation, but the same as the extract only with less than 35 percent (and possibly no) alcohol.

RECOMMENDATIONS

SALT, SEASONED SALT, AND SALT SUBSTITUTES

General Rule of Purchase: Look for unsalted powders and salt-free herb and spice blends; avoid seasoned salts.

In buying *table salt* look for a brand that is solar dehydrated and not laden with additives like dextrose, sodium silico aluminate, sodium bicarbonate, yellow prussiate of soda, and magnesium carbonate (this last one being the least objectionable). All ingredients are on the label.

Gomasio or sesame salt, and *kelp,* while not sodium-free, do help to reduce sodium intake. *Nutritional yeast* has no sodium. All brands of these seasonings are similar.

Don't accept potassium chloride or glutamates as a substitute for salt.

Look for *premixed seasoning blends* containing only pure herbs and spices. They are the only sensible sodium-free salt substitutes on the market. All ingredients are on the label. Avoid brands with salt, hydrolyzed vegetable protein, MSG, and sugars like corn syrup, lactose, and dextrose, all of which may be found in products that are promoted as natural.

Exemplary Brands

Bakon Seasoning
Bell's Seasoning
Capello's Italian, Steak and Salad, Herb and Cheese Seasonings
Chico San Sesame Salt
Diamond Crystal Kosher Salt
Eden Shake
Galster's All Natural Salt Free Seasonings
Grandma's Spanish Seasoning
Health Valley Instead of Salt
Judith's Natural Deli Gomasio
Lima Gomasio
Maine Coast Sea Seasoning
Nature's Gourmet Salt Free Seasonings
Parsley Patch Salt Free Blended Spices
Peter's Garlic Mix
Sea-zun
Slim Fixings Salt Free Seasonings
Spice Medley Low Sodium Beef, Vegetable, All Purpose Seasonings
Westbrae Gomashio

HERBS AND SPICES

General Rule of Purchase: Give fresh seasonings priority, then look to dried herbs and spices. Make sure you do not accidently select the "salt" version. It is best to buy those closest to the whole form. All brands are similar.

In blends, particularly poultry and chili seasonings, avoid added tricalcium or trisodium phosphate, MSG, modified starch, calcium stearate, partially hydrogenated oil, artificial color, and artificial flavor.

PREPARED LIQUID SEASONINGS

General Rule of Purchase: All ingredients are on the label.

Vinegars are derived from a variety of sources, but within each type all brands are similar. The sole exception may be an occasional variety distilled from an organically grown foodstuff. Avoid malt vinegars with caramel color.

Look for *liquid pepper sauce* that is simply peppers, vinegar, and salt. Avoid any with vegetable gums, modified starch, and preservatives.

Look for *soy sauce* containing soybeans, water, salt, and possibly wheat. Alcohol or vinegar may be accepted in low-sodium varieties as a preservative, but avoid anything else, including caramel color, corn syrup, and sodium benzoate.

Miso will contain soybeans, water, salt and, depending on the type, a grain. Avoid brands that have been pasteurized or have added preservatives.

Cooking sherry and *mirin* are wines for cooking and salt is added to the former to make it undrinkable. All brands are similar.

Sesame and *chili oils* are both unrefined oils, with chili peppers in the latter. All brands are similar.

Exemplary Brands

Alpamare Seasoning Sauce
Arrowhead Mills Tamari Soy Sauce
Bodhi Soy Sauce
Chico San Lima Tamari Soy Sauce, Miso
Cold Mountain Miso
Cross and Blackwell Worcestershire Sauce[3]
Crystal Louisiana Hot Sauce
D.L. Jardine's Texas Champagne Brand Hot Sauce
Durkee Frank's Louisiana Red Hot Sauce
Eden Miso, Wheat-Free Tamari, Shoyu, Low Sodium Shoyu, Organic Shoyu[1]
Ellegro Marinade
Erewhon Shoyu Tamari Soy Sauce
Gathering Winds Worcestershire Sauce
Golden Harvest Tamari Soy Sauce
Hawaiian Miso and Soy Company Miso
Health Valley Tamari-Ya Soy Sauce
KA.ME Tamari Soybean Sauce
Kikkoman Milder Soy Sauce
Lima Mugi Miso
Louisiana Hot Sauce
Marmite Concentrated Yeast Extract

Marufuku Miso
Minute Maid Frozen 100% Pure Lemon Juice from Concentrate
Mitoku Mirin
Pickapeppa Sauce[3]
Premier Japan Shoyu, Miso, Marinade, Ponzi
Pure and Simple Tamari Shoyu
Robbie's Worcestershire Sauce
San-J Real Tamari
So' Tamari Soy Sauce
Soken Natural Tamari, Wheat Free Tamari, Gentle (Low Sodium) Soy Sauces
South River Miso
Tennessee Sunshine Hot Pepper Sauce
Tree of Life Tamari, Miso
Uncle Steve's Louisana Hot Sauce, Green Hot Sauce, Pepper Sauce
Westbrae Natural Traditional Tamari, Organic Tamari,[1] Mild Soy Sauce, Organic Shoyu,[1] Shoyu Johsen, Miso
Yamasa Reduced Sodium Soy Sauce

FLAVOR EXTRACTS

General Rule of Purchase: Look for pure, not imitation flavoring extracts. *Pure extracts* other than vanilla reveal all ingredients on the label and most are similar. Most vanillas, unlike the brands listed below, are likely to hide glycerin, propylene glycol, sugar, dextrose, and corn syrup. All contain ethyl alcohol.

Vanilla flavoring (or *flavor*) is vanilla extract with a reduced alcohol content, or no alcohol, as in the Exemplary Brand below.

Exemplary Brands

The Grocery Shoppe Vanilla Flavor
Walnut Acres Real Vanilla Extract

Westbrae Natural Vanilla Extract

[1]Organic
[3]Contains refined sweeteners

Chapter 39

Leavening Agents:
Rising to the Occasion

When you do any home baking, chances are you follow the directions given in the recipe for leavening without giving much thought to the nature of this ingredient. A little knowledge about leavening, however, can help improve both the physical and nutritional quality of your baked goods.

CHEMICAL LEAVENING AGENTS

Chemical leavening agents include baking soda and baking powders. Their leavening action is based on the principle that an acid and a base, in contact with a liquid, release carbon dioxide gas, causing batters to rise. When placed in the oven, heat solidifies the structure, trapping the gas inside. (Thus, for maximum volume products containing baking soda and baking powder should be baked soon after the liquid and dry ingredients are combined.)

In most commercial baking soda and baking powder the base, or alkaline component, is sodium carbonate or bicarbonate. When the reaction is over, the sodium remains; thus, by their very nature, chemically leavened baked goods contain sodium. A potassium salt may be substituted in special diet products; however, potassium reacts more quickly and may lose its power before the dough has a chance to bake and entrap the leavening gas. Moreover, the potassium residue has a slight bitter aftertaste and so is not as popular with bakers or consumers.

Baking Soda

Baking soda is nothing more than sodium or potassium bicarbonate, a long used and accepted food ingredient. When the baking soda comes in contact with an acid ingredient in the recipe, like buttermilk, sour cream, yogurt, vinegar, molasses, or fruit juices, the leavening gas carbon dioxide is produced.

In addition to its role as a leavening agent, baking soda is a fantastic nonpolluting cleanser.

517

Baking Powder

The ingredients in baking powder are a bit more complex. The leavening comes from the interaction of the basic salt (baking soda) and an acid furnished not by a food ingredient but by another chemical salt in the mixture. This carefully balanced combination produces a more controlled reaction than baking soda alone does. Some form of starch, usually cornstarch, keeps the powder from caking or absorbing moisture and reacting in the can.

There are three types of baking powder available, each named after the acid salt it contains.

Tartrate depends on cream of tartar and tartaric acid, a by-product of wine-making. This type of baking powder releases most of its leavening gas at room temperature on contact with liquid, so when it is used the batter must be baked immediately or the gas will escape before it can be trapped inside.

Phosphate contains monocalcium phosphate, which may be combined with sodium acid pyrophosphate. Two thirds of the gas is released at room temperature on contact with liquid. The rest will not be released until heat is applied, making it a little slower acting than the tartrate variety.

SAS-Phosphate, or double-acting baking powder, only releases a small portion of its carbon dioxide at room temperature; most of it is not activated until heat is applied. Because of this the prepared batter can be kept for baking later in the day. However, the acid salts here are calcium acid phosphate and sodium aluminum sulfate; many people question the safety of the aluminum residues that remain. We prefer to play it safe by using tartrate or phosphate baking powders and cope with the fast action by adding the liquid at the end and getting the batter into the oven right away.

BIOLOGICAL LEAVENING AGENTS

Biological leaveners are actually microscopic fungi that feed on the carbohydrates in flour and sugars, generating carbon dioxide gas and alcohol (which vaporizes during baking).

Yeast

The most common of the biological leavening agents is bakers' yeast. It is used primarily for bread, pizza, and crackers, although certain cakes and pancakes may also rely on yeast for leavening.

Two forms of bakers' yeast are commonly available: compressed yeast and active dry yeast. *Compressed yeast* is a partially dried product containing some 100 billion yeast cells compressed into a small solid cake. It has a limited life span and must be preserved by refrigeration or freezing. In order for it to work, there must be some form of fermentable sugar in the dough.

Active dry yeast is shelf-stable (although it will retain its viability better in a cool place). This yeast must have a warm moist environment in order to begin its job. Active dry yeast can feed on starch alone, but a little sweetening added to the dissolving yeast will speed up its activity. *Rapid-rise yeast,* fairly new on the market, is a type of active dry yeast made from a stronger strain, previously available only to commercial bakers. It works faster because the yeast is more active, and is as acceptable as traditional yeast.

There is no need to have anything but yeast cells in your purchase. The BHA and sorbitan monostearate sometimes included in the packet serve no essential purpose. Be sure to note the expiration date on any yeast you buy and use it before then, or chances are your bread will be as flat as matzoh.

Sourdough

Sourdough fermentation is another biological leavening process which also employs yeast, but of a different strain. The preparation of sourdough bread depends on a "mother" or "starter," which traditionally is a piece of leftover dough that is carried over to start a new fermentation. By picking up bacteria from the environment, the starter derives its own unique characteristics. The passion for San Francisco sourdough bread is attributed to the microorganisms that flourish in the damp California air.

Today you can purchase dried sourdough starter in packets.

RECOMMENDATIONS

CHEMICAL LEAVENING AGENTS

General Rule of Purchase: All ingredients are on the label. *Baking soda* is all the same, unless it is a special low-sodium variety, in which case the sodium in the bicarbonate salt will be replaced with potassium.

When it comes to *baking powder,* look for a tartrate or phosphate type and avoid the aluminum compound common in most double-acting SAS baking powder. Baking powder will have a high sodium content unless it is manufactured for special diets with potassium salts.

Exemplary Brands

Ener–G Baking Powder
Featherweight Baking Powder
Oetker Baking Powder

Rumford Baking Powder
Walnut Acres Baking Powder

BIOLOGICAL LEAVENING AGENTS

General Rule of Purchase: All ingredients are on the label. Look for *yeast cakes* or *active dry yeast* (regular or fast-rising) with no preservatives (BHT/BHA) or sorbitan monostearate. Be sure to note the expiration date.

Look for dried *sourdough starter* that is preservative-free and contains nothing but the starter culture and flour.

Exemplary Brands

El Molino Active Dry Yeast
Fleischman's Active Dry, New Rapid Rise
  Yeasts

Gold Rush Sourdough Starter
Oetker Instant Dry Yeast
Red Star Quick Rise Yeast

A Glossary
of Food Additives

There are approximately 2,800 additives intentionally added to food to produce a desired effect. The following table lists those most commonly encountered on food labels with a brief description of their function and a statement regarding their safety. This information was included at the request of many readers who wanted to be able to judge additives on their own. It does not alter the basic premise of this book which is that, in general, all additives lessen the integrity of a product and thus should be avoided whenever possible.

Note that when the FDA conducts its review, additives are evaluated in terms of their potential to cause cancer (carcinogenicity) and possible reproductive effects (mutagenicity and teratogenicity). Many other possible adverse outcomes are usually ignored; additives may also act as allergens or influence the central nervous system or other bodily functions.

When judging the following additives keep in mind that all sodium-containing additives add to sodium intake. The problems of excess sodium are discussed in Chapter 38.

ADDITIVE (with alternate names)	USE	EVALUATION
ALGIN Propylene glycol alginate and ammonium, sodium, calcium, potassium, and aluminum alginates	Emulsifier, thickener	No record of adverse effects.
ASCORBIC ACID Sodium ascorbate, isoascorbic acid, erythorbic acid, erythroascorbic acid, sodium erythorbate	Antioxidant	Can enhance absorption of certain minerals and inhibit nitrosamine formation. Ascorbic acid and sodium ascorbate forms have vitamin C value.
BENZOATES Sodium benzoate, benzoic acid	Preservative	May trigger allergic reactions, behavioral changes, or intestinal upsets in sensitive individuals. Benzoic acid occurs naturally in some foods.

ADDITIVE (with alternate names)	USE	EVALUATION
BENZOYL PEROXIDE	Bleaching agent	May damage vitamins C, E, and A in foods.
BHA: BUTYLATED HYDROXYANISOLE	Preservative	A highly controversial additive. Some factions claim no adverse effects and possibly even some benefits in inhibiting tumor formation. Yet numerous animal feeding studies also show signs of stress in the liver and increased vulnerability of tissues to cancer-causing agents and other toxic substances, as well as behavioral changes affecting normal neurological development. May also have an adverse effect on reproduction. Allergic reactions include chronic nasal blockage and polyps, headaches, and asthma-like symptoms. People who are sensitive to aspirin may be similarly affected by BHA.
BHT: BUTYLATED HYDROXYTOLUENE	Preservative	Animal tests indicate adverse effects on the lungs, kidneys, heart, blood clotting factor, and liver metabolism of fats, and a mutagenic effect on sperm. BHT has been shown to both inhibit and enhance tumors and various mutagens. People who are sensitive to aspirin may be similarly affected by BHT.

ADDITIVE (with alternate names)	USE	EVALUATION
CALCIUM CHLORIDE	General-purpose additive, firming agent in canning	No record of adverse effects; however, use in canned fruits and vegetables may diminish levels of the fiber pectin.
CALCIUM DISODIUM EDTA	Sequestrant	Can reduce bioavailablity of some minerals.
CALCIUM PROPIONATE Sodium propionate, propionic acid	Preservative	Considered one of the most benign food additives, but may trigger behavioral changes in sensitive individuals. Although manufactured from chemicals, propionic acid occurs naturally in Swiss cheese.
CALCIUM STEARATE Magnesium stearate	Anticaking agent	The World Health Organization has requested monitoring to determine if an excess of stearate-containing additives (which are derived from saturated fatty acids of animal origin) could have any adverse health effects.
CALCIUM STEARYL LACTYLATE Sodium stearyl lactylate	Emulsifier, stabilizer, dough conditioner	*See* Calcium stearate
CALCIUM SULFATE Gypsum	Coagulant, dough conditioner	Adds to the calcium content of foods.
CARRAGEENAN Irish sea moss	Emulsifier, thickener	A seaweed extract that is generally bleached with sulfur dioxide and exposed to harsh alkalis and alcohol. May be compounded with sodium, although this is rarely indicated on food labels. While effective in lowering cholesterol, carrageenan has been associated with ulcerative colitis and is a promoter of colon cancer.

ADDITIVE (with alternate names)	USE	EVALUATION
CASEIN Sodium caseinate, calcium caseinate	General-purpose additive	Can precipitate an allergic reaction in people sensitive to milk. May contain a substance known to interfere with the body's ability to metabolize certain nutrients.
CELLULOSE Methyl cellulose, sodium carboxymethyl cellulose, sodium hydroxymethyl cellulose, microcrystalline cellulose, cellulose gum	Anticaking agent, thickener/bulking agent	No record of adverse effects. Highly refined fiber from cotton or wood pulp.
CITRIC ACID Sodium citrate, potassium citrate, isopropyl citrate	Antioxidant, seque-strant, acidifier, general-purpose additive	Probably safe; however, high doses, especially in a diet in which a calcium-phosphorus imbalance exists, can alter blood levels of calcium and erode tooth enamel.
DISODIUM GUANYLATE	Flavor enhancer	Belongs to the same family as monosodium glutamate (see). Elevates uric acid content in the body and can aggravate gout.
DISODIUM INOSINATE	Flavor enhancer	Belongs to the same family as monosodium glutamate (see). Elevates uric acid content in the body and can aggravate gout.
GLUCONO DELTA-LACTONE	Acidifier	No record of adverse effects.
HYDROGEN PEROXIDE	Bleaching agent, preservative	A suspected carcinogen.
HYDROGENATED OIL Partially hydrogenated oil	Emulsifier	Hydrogenation of oils converts some of their naturally polyunsaturated fats to saturated fats. Suspected of having many adverse effects on health. (For details see "Hydrogenation: Fatty Acids Molded by Technology" in Chapter 21.)

ADDITIVE (with alternate names)	USE	EVALUATION
HYDROLYZED PLANT PROTEIN HPP, hydrolyzed vegetable protein, HVP	Flavor enhancer	Contains 35 to 50 percent sodium and a high glutamate content (see monosodium glutamate). The protein constituent is of low biological value.
LECITHIN Hydroxylated lecithin	Emulsifier, general-purpose additive	Tests to determine the safety of the hydroxylated version are considered inadequate. Lecithin is food-derived and contains varying amounts of triglycerides, free fatty acids, and other fat constituents, as well as the B vitamin choline.
MAGNESIUM CARBONATE	Anticaking agent	No record of adverse effects.
METHYLENE CHLORIDE	Solvent	Classified as a potent carcinogen by the FDA in 1985; however, no action to prohibit its use in decaffeinated coffee was taken. Need not be revealed on the label.
METHYLPARABEN Propylparaben	Preservative	People who are sensitive to aspirin may be similarly affected by this additive.
MODIFIED FOOD STARCH	Thickener	Additional long-term feeding studies needed before safety can be determined. A highly processed form of grain or root starch that has been altered dramatically by exposure to chemicals. Can be problematic to those sensitive to certain grains. (For more information see "Choosing a Thickening Agent" in Chapter 5.)

ADDITIVE (with alternate names)	USE	EVALUATION
MONO- AND DIGYLCERIDES Glyceryl monostearate, monostearin, acetylated mono- and digylcerides and a variety of related compounds	Emulsifier, stabilizer	Derived from fats and adds both saturated and unsaturated fatty acids to the diet, as well as calories.
MONOSODIUM GLUTAMATE MSG, monopotassium glutamate, MPG	Flavor enhancer	Questions of safety, in addition to possible "allergic" response, center on its effects on the brain in test animals. While infants and young children are more vulnerable than adults, its effects on all humans is believed to be significant.
NITRATES Sodium nitrate, potassium nitrate	Curing agent, color fixative, preservative	Nitrates are converted to nitrites in the digestive tract and can form potent cancer-causing nitrosamines. (For more information see Chapter 17.)
NITRITES Sodium nitrite, potassium nitrite	Curing agent, color fixative, preservative	Nitrites interact with natural food components called amines to form nitrosamines, potent carcinogens. They also react with hemoglobin in the blood of susceptible individuals to produce a form of anemia. When cured meats containing nitrites are fried, another carcinogen, nitrosophyrrolidine, is formed. (For more information see Chapter 17.)
OXYSTEARIN —	Sequestrant, defoaming agent, crystal inhibitor	One long-term study involving rats resulted in testicular tumors. Derived from the partial oxidation of fatty acids, generally of animal origin.

ADDITIVE (with alternate names)	USE	EVALUATION
POLYSORBATES	Emulsifier, dispersing agent	Prepared from a base of sorbitol (see Chapter 31), and fatty acids derived from animal or vegetable sources. May be contaminated with a carcinogen.
POTASSIUM BROMATE	Maturing agent in flour	Probably safe in amounts used in food.
POTASSIUM CHLORIDE	Yeast food, gelling agent, salt substitute	Should be consumed with caution by anyone with kidney, liver, or heart ailments.
PROPYL GALLATE	Antioxidant	Testing is not considered adequate and carcinogenicity is suspected.
SODIUM BICARBONATE Potassium bicarbonate	Leavening agent, general purpose additive	Baking soda. (See Chapter 39.)
SODIUM HYDROXIDE Caustic soda, lye	General-purpose additive	Causes major changes in protein component of foods and probably other food elements as well. May not appear on label.
SORBIC ACID Calcium sorbate, sodium sobate, potassium sorbate	Preservative	Considered one of the least harmful preservatives, although extended feeding studies show some effect on the liver.
SORBITAN MONO-STEARATE ———	Emulsifier, stabilizer, defoaming agent	Related to the polysorbates (see also Calcium stearate).
SOY PROTEIN ISOLATES Isolated soy protein	Filler	A highly processed bean derivative that may interfere with the body's ability to metabolize certain nutrients; frequently contaminated with nitrites. (For more information, see "High-Tech Soy" in Chapter 12.)

ADDITIVE (with alternate names)	USE	EVALUATION
SULFITING AGENTS Sodium or potassium sulfite, sodium or potassium bisulfite, sodium or potassium metabisulfite, sulfur dioxide	Antioxidant, processing aid	Reduces the vitamin B_1 (thiamin) content of foods. Between March of 1983 and December of 1985, thirteen fatalities and hundreds of complaints of severe reactions allegedly associated with sulfited food were reported to the FDA. Allergic reactions include nausea, diarrhea, itching, hives, dizziness, rapid pulse, constriction of bronchial passages, acute asthma attacks, loss of consciousness, and anaphylactic shock. Asthmatics seem most at risk; however, about 30 percent of the reactions that have been reported occurred in healthy people with no previous history of allergies. Moreover, reactions can become progressively worse with increased exposure. Regulations require foods containing residues of 10 parts per million or more to list the use of sulfiting agents, but for those who are sensitive to sulfites, levels as low as 5 parts per million can trigger adverse reactions.
TERT-BUTYL- HYDROQUINONE TBHQ	Antioxidant	Information regarding safety is conflicting.

ADDITIVE (with alternate names)	USE	EVALUATION
VEGETABLE GUMS Gum arabic or acacia, carob or locust bean gum, furcelleran, gum tragacanth, guar gum, karaya, ghatti, zanthan	Emulsifier, thickener	Short-term studies have not shown any damaging effects but research was based on outdated estimates of intake which has accelerated rapidly in the past decade. Adequate long-term feeding studies have not been made for most vegetable gums. All are derived from plants but are highly processed and often represent parts of the plant not traditionally eaten. Note: Gums often contain benzoates or other preservatives which are not reflected on the label of foods containing gums.
YELLOW PRUSSIATE OF SODA Sodium ferrocyanide	Anticaking agent	Long-term safety studies have not been conducted.

COLORING AGENTS

Early scandals concerning poisonous coloring agents prompted many of our food laws, culminating in the Color Additives Amendment in 1960. Under the provisions of the amendment, all commercial color additives in use at that time were placed on a provisional list and their permit was to be continued "for a reasonable period of time" until safety could be reviewed and regulations for use issued. Testing was scheduled to end in January of 1963. This compliance date was extended for fifteen years before the first determination was reached. In 1976 Red No. 2, then the nation's most widely used food dye, was banned based on evidence that it caused malignant tumors in test animals.

The coloring agents currently in use may be totally synthetic (known as *certified FD&C colors* or *artificial colors*) or obtained from vegetable, animal, or mineral sources, technically referred to as *uncertified* and commonly called *natural*. Since 1976 the tests that have been concluded on the remaining synthetic coloring agents have resulted in the removal of several others; those that are still in use are the subject of controversy ranging from their possible role in affecting behavior to their ability to cause cancer. Even some of the so-called natural colorants may have harmful effects, and most have not been subjected to thorough testing. Most authorities, however, feel that in the amounts currently in use in the diet, natural colorings are probably safe.

FD&C (Synthetic or Artificial) Colors

Only Yellow No. 5 (or Tartrazine) must be listed by name on all food labels.

Blue No. 1—inadequately tested; indications of carcinogenicity.

Blue No. 2—tests suggest relationship to brain tumors in male mice.

Green No. 3—possibly carcinogenic, but fortunately infrequently used.

Yellow No. 5 or Tartrazine—high incidence of allergic reactions.

Yellow No. 6—also known to cause allergic reactions, but to a lesser extent than Yellow No. 5.

Red No. 3—short-term studies prove adverse effect on the thyroid; also may affect behavior.

Red No. 40—key tests flawed, with inconsistent results; thus this most widely used dye has never been cleared as harmless.

Uncertified (Natural) Colors

The following may appear by name on a food label.

Annatto—a natural yellow coloring extracted from a plant seed; no record of adverse effects.

Carotene or beta carotene—a yellow plant extract that can be used by the body to manufacture vitamin A.

Canthaxanthin—a pink to red plant or animal extract; data considered inadequate to determine safety.

Cochineal or carmine—a red insect extract; short-term studies indicate possible adverse effects and research on long-term effects is lacking.

Caramel—made from burnt sugar and all burnt foods are suspected carcinogens; also, sulfiting agents are used in its manufacture.

Ferrous gluconate—a source of iron.

Paprika oleoresin—a concentrated red pepper extract; studies indicate possible adverse effects.

Saffron—an orange plant extract; data considered inadequate to determine safety.

Turmeric—a yellow herb; short-term studies indicate safety but long-term studies are lacking.

FLAVORING AGENTS

Flavoring agents make up one of the largest groups of food additives and include some 2,000 natural and synthetic substances that may be used individually or in combinations sometimes of 100 or more. Flavors are usually listed on labels in general terms, i.e., spices, herbs, natural flavor, artificial flavor. Many artificial flavors are suspected of causing hyperactivity in sensitive children.

Natural flavors are no less subject to technology, for in order to isolate these flavors from their natural source, they may be fermented, crystalized, freeze-dried, spray-dried, plated on salt, encapsulated, converted to paste, dispersed in hydrogenated oil or ethyl alcohol, or prepared in an emulsion using vegetable gums or one of a number of emulsifiers. Mannitol, lactose, dextrose, sucrose, modified food starch, magnesium carbonate, and silica are common carriers for these flavors. None of this is likely to appear on the label.

Other natural flavors are achieved by chemically modifying fats, proteins, and carbohydrates, or through the use of enzymes. Their effect on the palate may depend on reactions formed within the food they are used in; according to a technical handbook on flavor ingredients they are "not added to a foodstuff with the intention of being kept unchanged. The exact compositions and amounts of all compounds thus formed are unknown, and consequently the toxological status of the 'reaction product' is uncertain."

NUTRIENTS

The subject of nutrient enrichment is discussed fully in "Food Is More Than Just a List of Nutrients" in Chapter 2. Keep in mind that adding nutrients to an already abundant diet is of questionable benefit and, as described in that chapter, can lead to nutritional imbalances and false confidence in the food supply. Following is a list of the most common supplements to help you recognize them on the label. They will always be revealed; however, along with the added nutrients you may also be ingesting their carriers, dispersing agents, preservatives, and other additives essential to their formulation that do not appear on the label.

Alpha tocopherol or alpha tocopherol acetate—vitamin E

Ascorbic acid—vitamin C

Biotin—a B vitamin

Calcium carbonate, citrate, oxide, phosphate, or sulfate—calcium

Calcium pantothenate—vitamin B_5

Beta carotene—vitamin A

Choline—a B vitamin
Cobalamin or cyanocobalamin—vitamin B_{12}
Ergocalciferol or cholecalciferol—vitamin D
Ferric phosphate or pyrophosphate—iron
Ferrous fumarate, gluconate, lactate, or sulfate—iron
Inositol—a B vitamin
Niacin or niacinamide—vitamin B_3
Potassium chloride—potassium
Potassium iodide—iodine
Pyridoxine or pyridoxine hydrochloride—vitamin B_6
Riboflavin—vitamin B_2
Thiamin hydrochloride or mononitrate—vitamin B_1
Vitamin A acetate or palmitate—vitamin A
Zinc chloride, gluconate, oxide, searate, or sulfate—zinc

MINERAL SALTS

Many additives contain minerals such as calcium, magnesium, and potassium that you may recognize as nutrients, and indeed they do add to the daily intake of these elements. While this can be beneficial, in some cases it can also add up to high levels that are suspected of producing adverse effects on the body.

Aluminum Compounds

Aluminum is frequently present in food additives as aluminum ammonium sulfate, aluminum chloride, aluminum calcium silicate, aluminum potassium or aluminum sodium sulfate (alum), or sodium silicoaluminate. Excessive amounts of aluminum can interfere with phosphorus retention and disturb bone formation. Moreover, aluminum can aggravate kidney conditions. High concentrations of aluminum found in the brain tissue of those suffering from Alzheimer's disease have led some researchers to speculate that there may be a connection, but thus far no direct link with aluminum ingestion has been established.

Phosphate Compounds

Phosphoric acid, calcium phosphate, tricalcium phosphate, ammonium phosphate, disodium phosphate, sodium aluminum phosphate, sodium acid pyrophosphate, sodium tripolyphosphate, sodium hexametaphosphate, and potassium phosphate are just some of the many common phosphate-containing additives. Their widespread use in processed foods may contribute to mineral imbalances that can have a negative impact on calcium absorption, affecting bones and teeth. Phosphate in excess can cause kidney damage.

SUSPENDED AND CANCELED PESTICIDES*

Dinoseb—October 7, 1986; emergency order banning all uses.
EPN—August 31, 1985; all uses as mosquito larvacide.
TOK—January 18, 1984; all uses.
Silvex—October 18, 1983; all uses (currently in dispute).
2,4,5-T—October 18, 1983; all uses, one-year depletion permitted.
EDB—October 11, 1983; treatment of export citrus permitted to 9/1/84.
Heptachlor—July 1, 1983; all uses except termites.
DBCP—March 31, 1981; all uses except pineapples in Hawaii.
Endrin—July 25, 1979; all uses on tobacco, cotton, small grains, apples, sugar cane, ornamentals with some area and label reservations.
Chlorabenzilate—February 13, 1979; all uses on citrus except in Florida, Texas, California, and Arizona.
Benzene hexachloride—July 21, 1978; all products except gamma isomer.
Chlordane—March 28, 1978; all uses except termite control.
Kepone—December 15, 1977; all uses.
Phenarzine chloride—November 21, 1977; all uses.
Safrole—June 10, 1977; all uses.
Copper arsenate—April 7, 1977; all uses.
Chlorinil—January 19, 1977; all uses.
Mirex—December 29, 1976; all uses.
Mercury—August 26, 1976; all uses except fresh-sawn lumber, Dutch Elm disease, preservative in water-based paints, and winter turf disease.
Strobane—June 28, 1976; all uses.
OMPA—May 28, 1976; all uses.
Aldrin—May 27, 1975; all uses except subsurface ground insertion for termite control, dipping of non-food roots and tops, mothproofing by a "closed" system.
Dieldrin—May 27, 1975; all uses with same exceptions as Aldrin.
Vinyl chloride—January 2, 1975; all uses inert or active.
Lindane—December 2, 1974; all uses in vaporizers. June 27, 1984; all uses in smoke fumigation.
DDT—July 7, 1972; all uses except Public Health Service.
Thallium sulfate—March 9, 1972; all uses.
DDD—March 18, 1971; all uses.
PCB—October 29, 1970; all uses inert or active.
Sodium fluoride—June 1, 1970; all formulation over 40 percent.
Bithional—August 14, 1968; all uses.

*A Strategy for Improved Pesticide Management in Michigan, Michigan Department of Agriculture, December 1985.

Additives That Have Been Banned*

Additive	Function	Source	Last used	Reason for ban
Agene (nitrogen trichloride)	Flour bleaching and aging agent	Synthetic	1949	Dogs that ate bread made from treated flour suffered epileptic-like fits; the toxic agent was methionine sulfoxime.
Dyes	Artificial coloring	Synthetic		
butter yellow			1919	Toxic, later found to cause liver cancer
FD&C Green 1			1965	Liver cancer
FD&C Green 2			1965	Insufficient economic importance to be tested
FD&C Orange 1			1956	Organ damage
FD&C Orange 2			1960	Organ damage
FD&C Orange B			1978†	Cancer
FD&C Red 1			1961	Liver cancer
FD&C Red 2			1976	Possible carcinogen
FD&C Red 4			1976	High levels damaged adrenal cortex of dog; after 1965 used only in maraschino cherries and certain pills; it is still allowed in externally applied drugs and cosmetics.
FD&C Red 32			1956	Damages internal organs and may be a weak carcinogen; since 1956 used under the name Citrus Red 2, to color oranges (2 ppm).
Sudan 1			1919	Toxic, later found to be carcinogenic
FD&C Violet 1			1973	Cancer
FD&C Yellow 1 and 2			1959	Intestinal lesions at high dosages

ADDITIVES THAT HAVE BEEN BANNED*

Additive	Function	Source	Last used	Reason for ban
FD&C Yellow 3			1959	Heart damage at high dosages
FD&C Yellow 4			1959	Heart damage at high dosages
Cinnamyl anthranilate	Artificial flavoring	Synthetic	1982†	Liver cancer
Cobalt salts	Stabilize beer foam	Synthetic	1966	Toxic effects on heart
Coumarin	Flavoring	Tonka bean	1954	Liver poison
Cyclamate	Artificial sweetener	Synthetic	1970	Bladder cancer
Diethyl pyrocarbonate (DEPC)	Preservative (beverages)	Synthetic	1972	Combines with ammonia to form urethan, a carcinogen
Dulcin (p-ethoxyphenyl urea)	Artificial sweetener	Synthetic	1950	Liver cancer
Ethylene glycol	Solvent, humectant	Synthetic	—	Kidney damage
Monochloracetic acid	Preservative	Synthetic	1941	Highly toxic
Nordihydroguaiaretic acid (NDGA)	Antioxidant	Desert plant	1971‡	Kidney damage
Oil of calamus	Flavoring	Root of calamus	1968	Intestinal cancer
Polyoxyethylene-8-stearate (Myrj 45)	Emulsifier (used in baked goods)	Synthetic	1952	High levels caused bladder stones and tumors
Safrole	Flavoring (root beer)	Sassafras	1960	Liver cancer
Thiourea	Preservative	Synthetic	c. 1950	Liver cancer

*Ref.: 21 CFR 189; "Food Colors", Nat. Acad. Sci. Committee on Food Protection (1971); other sources.

†Ban not yet finalized.

‡NDGA was banned by the FDA in 1968, but the Department of Agriculture did not ban it until 1971.

A Guide to
Government Agencies

There is no single place or simple way one can get complete information pertaining to our food supply, for several federal agencies share the responsibility and sometimes, depending on where a food is produced and sold, state and local authorities may prevail. If you wish to learn more about any food-related topic or register a specific complaint, it will speed things up if you can find the appropriate office.

WHAT DO YOU WANT TO KNOW?

The following is a list of food-related matters that the federal government is directly involved in, and the agencies responsible. The complete addresses of the federal governing agencies follow in the section "Where to Direct Queries and Complaints."

Ingredients/Additives

General information on GRAS (Generally Recognized As Safe) substances, prior-sanctioned substances, and direct and indirect additives (all discussed in Chapter 1) is the concern of the Director of the Division of Regulatory Guidance at the Food and Drug Administration's (FDA) Center for Food Safety and Applied Nutrition. Its Division of Food and Color Additives is responsible for color additives.

Questions about the use of additives and ingredients in meat and poultry products should be directed to the Food Ingredient Assessment Division at the U.S. Department of Agriculture, Food Safety and Inspection Service (FSIS).

Labeling

Most food labeling is handled by the Food and Drug Administration, and a letter to the main office will be forwarded to the appropriate division.

Nutritional labeling is handled by FDA's Center for Science and Applied Nutrition (CFSAN), Division of Regulatory Guidance.

Labeling of meat and poultry is the concern of the Director of the Standards and Labeling Division at the U.S. Department of Agriculture, FSIS.

Packaging

Information about packaging material and chemicals that come in contact with food via packaging are handled by a number of offices at the Center for Science and Applied Nutrition within the FDA. First try CFSAN's Division of Chemistry and Physics.

The migration of packaging material might also fall under the auspices of CFSAN's Division of Food and Color Additives.

For products packaged in U.S. Department of Agriculture inspection plants, the Food Ingredient Assessment Division of the USDA is your target. They handle not only packaging material, but cleaners, sanitizers, and coatings for equipment and contact surfaces.

Standards of Identity

Information about the Standards of Identity can be obtained from the Center for Science and Applied Nutrition at the Food and Drug Administration, Division of Regulatory Guidance. If you need more detailed information about any particular standard, try the Associate Director for Nutrition and Food Sciences at CFSAN.

U.S. Department of Agriculture Composition Standards

The USDA has established some mandatory standards for the composition of processed meat and poultry products. Questions about them can be directed to Directory of Standards and Labeling Division at the Food Safety and Inspection Service.

U.S. Department of Agriculture Grade Standards

Any questions about USDA's voluntary grading system should be directed to the Agricultural Marketing Service.

WHERE TO DIRECT QUERIES
AND COMPLAINTS WITHIN
THE FEDERAL GOVERNMENT

The U.S. Department of Health and Human Services (HHS)

The Department of Health and Human Services is the umbrella organization for several different agencies that oversee the health and welfare of the American people. Although you will not usually need to go directly to the HHS to get your questions answered, if you wish to comment on proposed legislative or regulation actions it is always useful to send a copy of your letter to:

The Secretary of Health and Human Services
U.S. Department of Health and Human Services
Washington, DC 20201

The Food and Drug Administration (FDA)

The Food and Drug Administration is one of the agencies within the Department of Health and Human Services and is responsible for protecting the nation against impure foods, drugs, cosmetics, and related hazards such as medical devices. Its jurisdiction includes production, storage, and labeling of all foods—with the exception of meat and poultry, which are regulated by the U.S. Department of Agriculture, and alcohol, which is handled by the Bureau of Alcohol, Tobacco and Firearms at the Treasury Department. The FDA is also responsible for enforcing tolerances for pesticide residues.

Commissioner
Food and Drug Administration
5600 Fishers Lane
Rockville, MD 20014

Within the FDA, the Office of Regulatory Affairs is responsible for policy and compliance with industry and government regulations and international policy and the Office of Consumer Affairs handles consumer letters and consumer-related activities. Questions or opinions about FDA policy can be directed there.

There are also ten regional offices that may be able to help you deal with specific issues that arise pertaining to local products in terms of labeling, ingredients, safety, or other matters where you feel official intervention might be needed.

Region I: 585 Commercial Street
               Boston, MA 02109
Region II: 830 Third Avenue
               Brooklyn, NY 11232
Region III: 900 U.S. Customhouse
               2nd and Chestnut Streets
               Philadelphia, PA 19106
Region IV: 1182 W. Peachtree Street, NW
               Atlanta, GA 30309
Region V: 175 W. Jackson Boulevard
               Chicago, IL 60604
Region VI: 500 South Ervay
               Suite 470–B
               Dallas, TX 75102
Region VII: 1009 Cherry Street
               Kansas City, MO 64106
Region VIII: 500 U.S. Customhouse
               19th and California Streets
               Denver, CO 80202
Region IX: 50 United Nations Plaza
               Room 254
               San Francisco, CA 94102
Region X: 909 1st Avenue
               Room 5003, Federal Office Building
               Seattle, WA 98174

The Center for Science and Applied Nutrition (CFSAN)

Formerly the Bureau of Foods, the Center for Science and Applied Nutrition handles many regulatory matters for the FDA and may be your best resource for getting action on specific issues.

Center for Science and Applied Nutrition
200 C Street, NW
Federal Building 8
Washington, DC 20204

The two offices at CFSAN of most use to consumers, as well as the food industry, are the Office of Nutrition and Food Sciences and the Office of Compliance. The Office of Compliance includes the Division of Regulatory Guidance and the Division of Food and Color Additives which both deal largely with food additives and related substances. CFSAN also contains an Industry Programs Branch which provides all sorts of brochures and guidelines to industry and can give the consumer great insights into many areas of food processing.

The U.S. Department of Agriculture (USDA)

The Department of Agriculture handles all meat and poultry concerns, including inspection and labeling. The Secretary of Agriculture heads the USDA and its seven units. If you wish to comment on legislation affecting meat and poultry items, be sure to send a letter to:

The Secretary of Agriculture
U.S. Department of Agriculture
Washington, DC 20250

THE FOOD SAFETY AND INSPECTION SERVICE (FSIS)

The Food Safety and Inspection Service of the USDA is responsible for meat and poultry inspection and ingredient standards, and labeling for all processed meat and poultry products. The address is the same as above.

THE AGRICULTURE MARKETING SERVICE

The Agriculture Marketing Service of the USDA handles grading of eggs, poultry, meat, dairy products, and produce. The address is the same as above.

The Environmental Protection Agency (EPA)

The Environmental Protection Agency was established in 1970 to coordinate all the government's environmental control programs including problems of air and water pollution, solid waste management, toxic substances, pesticides, noise, and radiation. It is responsible for establishment, enforcement, and monitoring of environmental standards enacted by Congress.
Of particular interest is the:

Office of Pesticide and Toxic Substances
Environmental Protection Agency
Washington, DC 20460

National Marine Fisheries Service (NMFS)

This office within the Commerce Department oversees voluntary inspection and grading of fish, allowing participants to use a "Packed Under Federal Inspection" (PUFI) mark on their products and in advertising.

National Marine Fisheries Service
U.S. Department of Commerce
Washington, DC 20236

The Federal Trade Commission (FTC)

The Federal Trade Commission deals with unfair and deceptive business practices and anticompetitive behavior. Most advertising concerns fall within the FTC's duties and inquiries can be directed to its Bureau of Consumer Protection.

Federal Trade Commission
Washington, DC 20580

The Bureau of Alcohol, Tobacco and Firearms (BATF)

The Bureau of Alcohol, Tobacco and Firearms, a part of the Treasury Department, regulates the alcohol industry, making and enforcing ingredient labeling and advertising policy.

Bureau of Alcohol, Tobacco and Firearms
Treasury Department
Washington, DC 20226

Congress

Congress is responsible for making laws, including those that pertain to food. When you want to have input into any food issue before Congress, you should write your state representatives and also:

The Chairman of the Committee on Agriculture, Nutrition and Forestry
U.S. Senate
Washington, DC 20510

The Chairman of the Committee on Agriculture
U.S. House of Representatives
Washington, DC 20515

STATE GOVERNMENT MATTERS

Federal laws cover only foods in interstate commerce (that is, foods shipped out of state). Local products sold only within state lines (that is, intrastate) come under the jurisdiction of state and/or local authorities. State agencies can be located by contacting the office of your governor, state legislative representative, district attorney, mayor, or consumer protection agency.

A Guide to Private
Organizations Working
in the Area of
Food and Agriculture

Food-Related Issues

Center for Science in the Public Interest
1501 16th Street, N.W., Dept. GGF
Washington, DC 20036

Area of Interest: A public-interest group working for pure foods and labeling.

Foundation of Economic Trends
9200 Edmonston Road, Suite 117, Dept. GGF
Greenbelt, MD 20770

Area of Interest: Preventing misuse of biotechnology.

Natural Resources Defense Council
25 Kearney, Dept. GGF
San Francisco, CA 94108

Area of Interest: A public-interest group involved in food safety, pesticides, and the environment.

Health and Energy Institute
236 Massachusetts Avenue, N.E., Room 506, Dept. GGF
Washington, DC 20002

Area of Interest: Food irradiation.

National Coalition to Stop Food Irradiation
Box 59–0488, Dept. GGF
San Francisco, CA 94159

Area of Interest: Food irradiation.

Public Citizen
2000 P Street NW
Suite 700, Dept. GGF
Washington, DC 20036

Area of Interest: Public-interest group working for pure foods.

Soyfoods Center
P.O. Box 234, Dept. GGF
Lafayette, CA 94549

Area of Interest: Promotes use of soyfoods.

Federation of Homemakers
P.O. Box 5571, Dept. GGF
Arlington, VA 22205

Area of Interest: A grassroots organization which has been effective in fighting for pure foods since 1959.

Community Nutrition Institute
2001 S Street, N.W., Dept. GGF
Washington, DC 20009

Area of Interest: Food safety and hunger.

Advertising

National Advertising Division
Better Business Bureau
845 Third Avenue
New York, NY 10022

Area of Interest: Deceptive advertising.

Farm and Agricultural Issues

Institute for Alternative Agriculture
9200 Edmonston Road, Suite 117, Dept. GGF
Greenbelt, MD 20770

Area of interest: Works to develop small and organic farms.

California Agrarian Action Project
433 Russel Boulevard, Dept. GGF
Davis, CA 95616

Area of Interest: Small-farm issues and pesticides.

National Coalition Against the Misuse of Pesticides
530 7th Street, S.E., Dept. GGF
Washington, DC 20003

Area of Interest: Pesticides.

Environmental Policy Institute
218 D Street, S.E., Dept. GGF
Washington, DC 20003

Area of Interest: Biotechnology.

Cornucopia Project
Regional Agricultural Association
222 Main Street, Dept. GGF
Emmaus, PA 18049

Area of Interest: Promotes small and regional farming.

Trade Associations

Organic Food Production Association of North America
P.O. Box 937, Dept. GGF
Belchertown, MA 01007

Support organization for organic food certification programs.

National Nutritional Foods Association
125 East Baker Avenue, Dept. GGF
Costa Mesa, CA 92626

Natural foods trade organization.

Food Marketing Institute
1750 K Street, N.W., Dept. GGF
Washington, DC 20009

Educational and trade association.

Grocery Manufacturers of America
1010 Wisconsin Avenue, N.W., Dept. GGF
Washington, DC 20007

Food processors' trade organization.

Cooking Education

International Association of Cooking Professionals
1001 Connecticut Avenue, N.W.
Washington, DC 20036

To locate wholefoods-oriented cooking schools.

Index

545